MANAGERIAL AND SUPERVISORY PRACTICE
cases and principles

MANAGERIAL AND SUPERVISORY PRACTICE

cases and principles

WILLIAM M. BERLINER

Professor of Management
Graduate School of Business Administration
and College of Business and Public Administration,
New York University

SEVENTH EDITION • 1979

RICHARD D. IRWIN, INC. Homewood, Illinois 60430
Irwin-Dorsey Limited Georgetown, Ontario L7G 4B3

The previous edition of this text was published under the title of
Management Practice and Training: Cases and Principles.

ISBN 0-256-02040-X
Library of Congress Catalog Card No. 78–70944

Printed in the United States of America

1 2 3 4 5 6 7 8 9 0 MP 6 5 4 3 2 1 0 9

To the potential supervisor and the
practicing manager: Maybe this will help you do a
better job — and to my wife Bertha who has always
helped me do a better job

PREFACE

In the last edition of this book management practice was compared to the practice of medicine. This comparison is still valid since both are dynamic subjects grounded in theory; they both prepare people to deal with risk and ambiguity; and practitioners in both fields are frequently confronted with unique situations. Perhaps the most conclusive factor in both fields is the measurement of performance. Effective practice is the yardstick, not the understanding of theory, and results are the reward for both the manager and the physician.

This edition, which represents a continuation of an effort started over a quarter of a century ago by the late William J. McLarney, is still very much practice-oriented. The study of management has gone through many and varied theoretical approaches in this period. As a result of reading about process, industrial engineering, traditional theory, management science, behavioral science, and contingency theory, users of management texts have been informed, confused, and perhaps exasperated.

Hoping not to add to this variety of interpretations, this text attempts to describe management in the manner it is practiced by people who perform the job in all types of organizations. Many people who are promoted to a supervisory position are technicians who are chosen for promotion because they are very good at what they do. This text attempts to show what is necessary to assist in the transition from effective technician to effective manager. The material is designed to give supervisors and middle managers an understanding of managerial practice which, if effectively used, should assist in their growth and development. After careful reflection and consideration of the text's central theme, the title of this edition has been changed to *Managerial and Supervisory Practice* with the hope that the new title more clearly reflects what can be learned from this book.

Because all students of management think they know something about the subject, management is difficult to teach either in college classes or in organizational training programs. This text is for college level courses and company training programs. It covers material pertinent to effective managerial practice in first-level and middle-management positions in complex organizations. Since practicing managers are usually responsible for many of the process areas such as control, organization, planning, decision making, and policy implementation, and for many of the behavioral-personnel administration areas such as conflict resolution, training, appraisal, and change, these areas are covered along with others. The practicing manager doesn't make a distinction between process, behavior, or quantitative methods. He or she simply uses a combination of knowledge, skills, and experience to solve problems and get the job done. That essentially is the focus of this text.

The text has been reorganized so that material is in better sequence. Every chapter has been tightened with new material added to reflect the dynamism of the subject. Attention has been given to the growing importance of women in management and the material presented is described in both female and male dimensions. Every attempt has been made to diminish the usual use of masculine terminology in both position descriptions and pronouns. A new chapter has been added to emphasize the importance and increasing impact of government and society in general on managerial practice. The chapter on change has been thoroughly revised and made separate from the handling of employee problems. Three chapters from the previous edition have been eliminated although some of the more pertinent material has been included elsewhere. Each chapter has been given four learning objectives which should help focus attention on what can be grasped from each chapter. Cases have been reorganized to reflect chapter material more carefully and there are approximately 30 new cases. There are ten cases for each chapter, allowing the teacher or conference leader considerable latitude to develop discussion.

I am indebted to many practicing managers for ideas and case material. Any human being is the product of knowledge and experience and education, and I am no exception. My understanding of managerial practice is the product of many years of teaching and serving as a consultant and as a practicing manager. Over these years both admiration for the sound managers and disdain for the inept ones have inspired the concepts and ideas in these pages. The hope is to produce better practitioners.

A long association with the Manufacturers Hanover Trust Company as a consultant has allowed me a laboratory for testing and using many of my ideas. Particular thanks is due to Robert W. Keith, senior vice president and personnel director of this organization, for the cooperative climate created for me.

Acknowledgment and thanks are due to all of the companies, associations and publishing firms credited in the footnotes throughout the book. Many of these firms have furnished examples and forms which were used to enrich the text material. Special thanks goes to E. E. Holman of Essex Community College in Baltimore County, Maryland; Gary W. Falkenberg of Oakland Community College in Auburn Heights, Michigan; and S. Kyle Reed of the University of Tennessee, all of whom carefully reviewed the prior edition, offering many helpful suggestions, most of which were followed. The author is also in debt to John Dory, a colleague at New York University, who offered much help.

February 1979   **William M. Berliner**

INTRODUCTION TO THE UTILIZATION OF THE CASE APPROACH

To the teacher and the training director

This text offers a college course in management theory and applications as a preparation for effective performance of a management position. It can be used in a college classroom for students interested in managerial careers or in company training programs for first-level and middle-manager development. The text materials and actual case problems present a combination of management fundamentals and practical operating experience—a linking of theory to relevant job problems.

There is more than enough material for a one-semester course meeting three hours a week, or a two-semester course if all of the case material is utilized. For supervisory or management training programs, the text could be assigned for reading at home while the cases could be used to develop discussion using the conference method. The book is unique in the sense that it combines personnel administration and industrial management to reflect the performance characteristics of the supervisor's job. The selected materials are integrated and presented from the point of view of the manager rather than from the separate, and often conflicting, points of view of the various specialists such as the personnel manager or the production manager.

The text deals primarily with management on the first and middle-management levels—the activities that the college graduate will be undertaking in the management of a section, unit, or department. For students preparing for a career in management or for potential managers in business, this is the area in which they must prove their worth early in a managerial career.

From management training a student should get a method and a habit of applying management principles to the solution of job problems. The text provides the method in the seven-step problem-solving technique, and provides the job problems in the form of case studies. Thus it sets up the means and the materials for practicing a systematic approach to analyzing problems, working out solutions, and making decisions.

Working as a group member on case problems helps students to see interpretations and solutions other than their own. The cases give them a fund of job information covering an area more diversified than would be found within the personal experience of a teacher. Cases show the environment in which principles have to operate, show how things are done in a number of companies, and show what will be expected of managers or management trainees. Many of the cases present situations that they will be in soon after starting a job—problems of trainees, of new supervisors, and of conflicts between line and staff. New cases in this edition reflect changes and trends in the industrial environment, particularly the trend toward a more highly educated work force.

The case material is based on actual events, all of which have happened. In this sense they are objective in nature and do not demonstrate a right or wrong way. Some of the cases show men and women in effective situations while others indicate failures in the behavior of women and men. Essentially this is reality and there is no intent on the part of the author to discriminate in any way.

Since the basic purpose of case material is to give students of management a vicarious experience in attempting solutions to real problems, there obviously are cases which present real problems. The fact that human beings may be portrayed in situations which can be interpreted as undesirable or discriminatory simply indicates that such situations exist. If the students and the trainees are to become aware of how to cope with these problems in the real world, cases in the classroom or conference room are an effective way to start.

This book supplies cases and principles to be used in a conference program of management training. It is for first-level supervisors and their bosses and the area of management up to and including the middle-management level. It is designed to improve the performance of people on these jobs and to prepare them to advance to these jobs.

The conference case-study method of training is used because it requires and gets active participation of the people being trained in group discussion of cases and the principles involved. Managers profit by the exchange of ideas with other supervisors having like problems. They evaluate solutions not only in terms of their own jobs but in terms of their jobs and the organization as a whole. They develop skill in analyzing problems and applying principles and techniques within the framework of the policies of their own organizations. They get practice in achieving realistic, workable, and effective solutions. They carry back to their jobs an understanding of principles and techniques of good management and a method and habit of applying them to problems.

By coordinating cases and principles and keying them to supervisors and middle management, the book saves the time of many people. It relieves the conference leader of having to spend time gathering materials beforehand and then having to spend the time of conferees while he or she develops cases and principles during the conference. When the conferees have the textbook before them, then the whole time of the conferences can be devoted to the solution of cases and the application of principles.

The arrangement of 16 chapters in four parts permits a rational development of the subject matter. Starting with "Management's Job" and going through "Job Management," "Developing Employee Potential," and "Managing Human Behavior," the book covers the range of the manager's efforts and concerns. Completion of a course using text and cases should give the participant a good understanding of managerial responsibility in complex organizations.

Normally a chapter can be handled in two conferences—one for lecture and discussion of principles, techniques, and practices, and the other for discussing, analyzing, and solving cases. The plan of the text permits picking and choosing the chapters to be used. The integration of human and technical factors in each chapter enables the teacher or training director to select chapters most relevant to the training needs of the group and to get a complete and integrated treatment of the topics chosen. These particular chapters can be combined into a training course to fit the time available for handling the most urgent needs of the group. Subsequent programs and refresher courses can cover other chapters that are next in the order of need.

The text is flexible also in the levels of training it offers. The case studies cover a wide range of subject matter, depth, and difficulty—permitting the discussion to be pitched at the level appropriate to the group. The 150 cases came from a wide range of authority levels in a wide variety of enterprises in which the author conducted training programs. Over a period of 30 years these cases were collected from and used in aircraft companies; hospitals; manufacturers of electronic equipment, machine tools, hand tools, and furniture; railroads, public utilities, banks, insurance companies, retailers, other service organizations; college courses; and government installations.

Most of the cases have been stripped of the nonessentials of their backgrounds and are presented in a form that makes them applicable to businesses other than the ones from which they came. The wording is such that details can be added and assumptions made to fit the conditions existing in a specific company. A bare case can be slipped into the background of a big company or a small one, and this is important because problems will be solved one way in a large company and another way in a small one; one way in a company that has a union contract and another way in a company that hasn't; one way in a company that is owner managed, and another way in a company that has professional management.

The cases are workable ones on which conferees can show how principles should be applied or modified to fit the situation and how company policies need to be interpreted or modified in terms of basic principles. Most of the cases involve more than one principle. Their inclusion in one chapter rather than another is not for the purpose of limiting discussion; they should not be warped to fit some particular principle. In looking for cases to fit the training needs of a group, it is advisable to consult the index. Each case is indexed under as many topics as it applies to. There is a close tieup between cases and text, with a case applying to almost every topic that is listed in the Contents.

The principles of good management presented in the text are not new or revolutionary; they are in accord with the best in the literature of management. The presentation of them is interspersed with techniques and practices based upon them—techniques and practices that have been used and tested by supervisors in a variety of enterprises.

The contents of the text represent a selection of topics on which there is the greatest need of supervisory training and which for the time required yield the greatest results. They were chosen from successful training programs conducted by the author, and they are selected and arranged to meet the needs of conference training programs for first-level supervisors and managerial people up to and including the middle-management level. Topics are presented to be discussed and interpreted in the framework of company policies and conditions and to be applied in the solution of problems and thus made a part of an individual's thinking.

To the supervisor and the student

The cases are for group discussion. A person solving a problem sees it only from a personal angle and decides on a solution that is based on individual knowledge and experience. But one person's solution is seldom as comprehensive as a solution that is the product of group thinking and group experience. When a group is trying to arrive at the most practical solution—the one that will work in this instance—each person contributes experiences of success and failure, the techniques used, and the cautions found necessary to observe. It is from the pooling of this knowledge and experience that a solution is arrived at and agreed upon; and it is this fund of knowledge and experience that a group member should draw upon for personal use.

Preparing for case discussion.   A person approaching case discussion naturally asks: What good will it do me? What can I expect to learn from it?

Active participation in group solving of case-study problems makes a person more expert in handling problems on the job. Members of a case-study group are not trying to accumulate a bagful of ready-made solutions to apply to whatever problems come along. They are getting practice in methods of analyzing and clarifying problems, in looking for causes, and working out a number of possible solutions. They are getting practice in making good decisions, in choosing the solution that is best suited to the time, place, and conditions—the solution that is in line with good management principles and practices, that is practicable, acceptable, and most likely to accomplish the results desired.

Working members in a conference problem-solving group can clarify, interpret, and evaluate their own study and research on the problem. They can integrate knowledge of separate specialties by applying it to the solution of problems. Furthermore, they can acquire a stock of ideas and techniques suggested by other conferees and evaluated by the group. In solving case problems, people contribute suggestions and pool their ideas. They evaluate other people's suggestions, improve upon them, consider alternatives, integrate various points of view, and take the best of the thinking and combine it into solutions. The decisions made should embody the thinking and experience of all the members.

Conferees should not be looking for one "right" answer to a case problem. They should be looking for all possible solutions from which to select the one—or ones—most likely to succeed under existing conditions. A solution that will work in one time and place may not work in another; a solution that will take care of this problem may create other problems. It is well to develop several solutions to be evaluated. Becoming wedded early to a single solution (or a single reason for everything) limits thinking and stands in the way of using the ideas of others.

The questions following a case are not intended to direct the discussion. They are there to help the conferee analyze the case in advance and prepare for the discussion of it. In the first few sessions of case study, people are inclined to jump to conclusions without digging deeply enough beneath the surface, without weighing the circumstances, or thinking through the results of proposed actions. The problem-solving technique described in the text should deter people from prescribing the cure before they've diagnosed the ailment. It should keep them from wasting time redesigning the mousetrap when they should be looking for better ways to eliminate mice.

The management principles involved in a case are not limited to the chapter in which the case appears. Job problems—and the cases describing them—are seldom limited to a single issue. The cases came from a wide variety of businesses. They are problems on which someone had to make a decision. "Facts" of a case include opinions and inferences; they must be lined up and evaluated in a thorough and orderly manner. If the group wants more data in the framework of a case, the thing to do is to make assumptions and evaluate their reasonableness.

A side value of case study is that supervisors and students often recognize some personalities very like the people they deal with daily, or very like themselves and they begin to see problems, motives, and relationships from the other person's point of view. Some of the case problems are difficult to solve—some have been going on for a long time and still have no ideal solution. But it should be encouraging to remember that a group of people working together on a problem bring to it a combination of many years of experience and individual interpretations of management theory which can lead to some remarkably effective conclusions.

W. M. B.

CONTENTS

tion. Words are tricky. Learning to listen. Jargon. Symbols and symbolism. Behavioral factors in communication. Distractions muddle orders. Putting across a new idea. Difficulties in discussion. Unfavorable attitudes build up listener resistance. Good attitudes facilitate understanding. How to give orders. Getting orders from the middle manager. Keeping the middle manager informed. Lack of understanding between subordinate and superior. How managers can promote more effective communicating. Communications systems, networks, and the flow of management information. Summary. CASE STUDIES, 515.

Supervisors, managers, and value systems. Environmental considerations. Legal considerations. The supervisor's and the manager's role. Unions and employee problems. Disciplinary policy. Rules. Penalties. Incompetence and negligence. Gripes and grievances. Handling grievances. The handling of gripes. The managerial impact of OSHA. Absenteeism and tardiness. Effects of tardiness and absenteeism. Finding and treating the causes. Counseling the absentee. Problems with alcoholics. Drug use and abuse problems. Preventing disciplinary problems. Dealing with offenders. Discharge. Summary. CASE STUDIES, 552.

The nature of change. Change in perspective. Employee problems and change. Managing change. The supervisor and change. Higher management and change. Resistance to change. Organizational development. Summary. CASE STUDIES, 579.

PART I

MANAGEMENT'S JOB

○ What managers do: The job of managing

○ Organizations and organization structure

○ Organization dynamics

○ Organizations and individuals

○ Decision making and problem solving

○ Policies and procedures

Chapter 1

Learning objectives

○ *To gain an understanding of the role of the first-level supervisor and the middle manager in an organization*

○ *To appreciate the types of knowledge, skills, and attitudes necessary for supervisory and managerial performance*

○ *To create an awareness of the several tools of management and their application to the manager's job*

○ *To indicate the difficulties and methods involved in learning to be a manager*

What managers do: The job of managing

Major topics

The job of internal management.

The manager's resources.

Knowledge, skills, and attitudes the supervisor needs.

The tools of management.

Planning.

Organizing.

Directing.

Coordinating.

Controlling.

Decision making.

Problem-solving techniques.

Management theory versus management practice.

Learning to be a manager.

Starting a book on managerial practice and the development of managers would seem to be a relatively simple task. After all, the number of books and articles written about management is probably countless. One could say this indicates that there is a tremendous amount of knowledge about management and managers. To a certain extent this is true; but when a student about to enter a basic course in management or an employee about to take over first-level supervisory responsibilities asks, "What does a manager do?" it gives one pause. When the student follows up this question with, "If I major in management, what will I be when I graduate?" the teacher of management cannot shrug it off with a simple reply.

For college students the tangibilities of studying accounting, engineering, physics, finance, marketing, psychology, or computer science, among other subjects, will give them direction and career goal expectations that are easily visualized. Getting a degree in accounting will enable the student to apply for a job in a public accounting firm, the accounting department of a business organization, a hospital, a university, or a government agency; and in most instances the starting job will have a direct relationship with the material studied as an accounting student. This is true for most other subjects they might study. Management majors do not usually have such clear goals in the job market.

Whether you are a management major in college or a newly appointed first-level supervisor in an organization, the following scenario will give you some insights into the complexities, confusion, and lack of clear direction inherent in the responsibilities of the job of first-level supervisor. Some of the same uncertainty exists for all levels of management practice, but it is the first management level that presents the greatest difficulty to most people. In the first place, you were probably promoted because you were an outstanding performer in some kind of nonmanagerial work. On top of this, you were probably told you would be a working supervisor with a personal responsibility for continuing to produce a given amount of work. It is quite natural for you to continue working as you had before and give little attention to being a supervisor. The excellence of your work got you promoted, and it is from this work that you receive satisfaction and recognition.

Even though you worked for a boss before being promoted, you most likely did not give any great amount of attention to what that boss did other than how some actions affected you personally. You joined in with fellow employees in the normal "gripe about the boss" sessions and were part of the easy camaraderie of these discussions. Perhaps your first recognition of the managerial role is that you are no longer a part of these sessions. You are now the boss, and there seems to be some distance between you and your former peers. They treat you differently and you find that they come to you for advice, to ask for favors, to complain about the work load, and to settle arguments. A host of other problems not of your making crop up, and you have to solve them or go the next level of management for help.

Slowly but surely you begin to see that being a supervisor means responsibility for other people. No longer can you depend on your own ability to turn out work. You have to use other skills to get subordinates to meet deadlines. You have to learn more about these subordinates, even though you thought you knew them well when you were one of them. You have to learn more about company policies, procedures, rules, and practices, because your employees and your superiors keep questioning you. You have to plan work not only for yourself but for all your employees. You become involved in evaluating performance, raises, promotions, transfers, discipline, resource allocation, budgets, and meetings with other supervisors on your level and higher levels in the organization. In short, you are becoming a manager.

Even though both the student and the new supervisor have observed managers in practice, understanding what the manager really does is difficult until one is confronted with that role. One of the interesting problems is that most people have performed some of the things a manager does at one time or another in their daily lives. Being a patrol leader in the Girl Scouts, a fraternity president, a church fund-raising chairperson, or heading a charity organization all have managerial implications. The trouble is that individuals consider such effort normal and do not look upon it with any special significance. None of those personal or extracurricular activities seem to have the importance of something called a management job in some organization that pays a salary. One thing is certain, however. If individuals prefer to do things alone without having responsibility for the efforts of others, they will most likely not be very effective as managers.

The president of General Electric and a first-level supervisor in the same company have similar responsibilities. Neither operates in a vacuum regardless of the autonomy of the position. Both have superiors and both supervise and are responsible for the work of others. Their titles differ as do such things as salary, status, job complexity, breadth of responsibility, and fringe benefits. But they both have relationships with peers and subordinates on various levels of the organization, and it is these relationships and how they are carried out among the levels of management that create the managerial climate for a particular company.

Some confusion arises about the terms *supervisor* and *manager*. Even though the nature of their responsibilities have similarities, there are differences. The essential difference is that supervisors generally are at the first level of management and they are responsible for nonmanagerial employees while managers are at higher organizational levels and are usually responsible for other managerial and supervisory employees. Another rather important factor is that the term *supervisor* is the traditional designation for the first level of management in most organizations.

This designation has several implications for the people who become supervisors. They are part of the management team of the organization, starting an activity that is professional in nature. The new supervisors enter a world where they will have to obtain knowledge about a variety of things that were given little attention by them before. Much of the material covered in this text will be a part of their daily lives. The need for greater attention to the efforts of others is perhaps the most important part of the new position. In fact the first full recognition of the responsibilities of supervision comes about when the new supervisor realizes the ambiguities of the new position.

The challenges facing new supervisors vary in each organization, but the importance of the position becomes evident when the job is described. Supervisors are usually responsible for orienting and training employees, wage and salary recommendations, job safety, equal opportunity compliance, discipline, promotion and transfer recommendations, relations with higher management levels, union contract compliance in unionized organizations, and a large number of other tasks. The complexity of the job is considerable, and one of the most difficult aspects is the balance that must be maintained among the fulfillment of employee expectations, the requirements of the position, and the demands of middle management. It soon becomes apparent to supervisors who want to succeed and grow and be promoted to greater managerial responsibility that they must acquire more knowledge about managerial practice and become truly professional in that practice.

This text is written to show the supervisor his or her management position in its many and varied dimensions; to point out what it demands in knowledge, skills, and attitudes; and to help meet these demands. The su-

"This is J. Harley Wainwright, and I want to
speak with whomever the buck stops at."
Reprinted by permission The Wall Street Journal

**The manager has ultimate responsibility for the
work of all subordinates.**

pervisor's job has been complicated by a multitude of scientific discoveries and technical developments that have brought about new systems, new processes, and new methods—all of which are changing the nature of jobs and the skills needed to perform them and to supervise them. Technological advances and the rapid growth of industry combine to create a demand for supervisors who have the high level of skill and knowledge to handle technical problems. Additionally, they must have the managerial knowledge, skills, and attitudes which will allow them to work successfully with people on all levels of the organization. The complexities developing in our society make the human relations aspects of the supervisor's job particularly difficult and challenging. Perhaps the most essential contribution the supervisor can make is determined by the ability to perceive and present ideas in a way that will enlist the cooperation of others.

The job of internal management

All types of organized activity require management. While there is some difference of opinion regarding a definition of the process of management, there is little doubt that the process exists in every type of organization our society has produced. Churches, hospitals, labor unions, universities, schools, foundations, and government, along with the business firm, are just some of the areas of our society where the function of management is carried out. It can be readily assumed that there is considerable universality to the practice of management. This does not imply, however, that it is practiced in a similar fashion in all organizations. In fact it is practiced differently on the various managerial levels of one organization. Even individual managers contribute differences in practice by their perceptions of the manager's role and their development of a particular management style. The process of management is practiced when the manager engages in the many activities—such as decision making, planning, coordination, control, and general leadership—which are parts of the process.

While the manager's efforts must be applied on all levels of the organization from the chairman of the board to the first-level supervisor, there are differences in perception, emphasis, responsibility, and focus on each level. The complexity of the organization determines the number of managerial levels, but for explanatory purposes most books on the subject usually describe three; top management, middle management, and first-line or supervisory management. Top management usually concerns itself with the establishment of objectives, overall planning of the long- and medium-range variety, external relationships, and the achievement of the goals established for the major components of the enterprise. The principal emphasis of this text is on the middle manager and the first-line supervisor. Their contributions to the welfare of the organization and how they go about managing will be explored rather thoroughly.

Trying to define the role of manager has proved to be somewhat elusive, as the many studies of this role seem to indicate. Perhaps one of the more well known is the philosophical one mentioned by Peter Drucker:

> Who is a manager can be defined only by a man's function and the contribution he is expected to make. And the function which distinguishes the manager above all others is his *educational* one. The one contribution he is uniquely expected to make is to give others vision and ability to perform. It is vision and moral responsibility that, in the last analysis, define the manager.[1]

The concern for establishing an understandable definition of the manager's role is a valid one. Both students and practitioners would benefit from such an understanding, along with the multitude of people in our society whose work is nonmanagerial but who are supervised by managers. The simple statement found in many books that "managing is getting work done through other people" does not seem to be reflected in practice. All of us know managers on various levels of organization who perform clerical, technical, and other tasks that could be considered nonmanagerial by any test. In fact a great many of these people are quite proud of their abilities to perform these tasks better than the people they supervise.

One can understand the desire of the first-level supervisor who was promoted because of his productivity to continue nonsupervisory tasks. After all, he knows he can do the work and managing is something new and perhaps frustrating. But when higher level managers type their own letters and take home mountains of clerical work and refuse to or do not want to delegate the more routine tasks to subordinates, the student of management begins to wonder if the management texts are at all correct. This is particularly true of the manager performing these nonmanagerial tasks has achieved some of the accepted success status factors such as title, salary, private office, and secretary.

Perhaps we must accept the evidence that managers continue to do a variety of work in addition to their managerial responsibilities even though it may be desirable for them to give up nonmanagerial work. Job pressures, satisfaction of accomplishment, lack of trained help, poor planning, misplaced emphasis, and inadequate knowledge of management, among other factors, may contribute to the manager's desire to remain partly a worker. In any event this text will try to define the role of the manager in all of its chapters. To a certain extent it is desirable to recognize the role of the manager as it is practiced generally, with all of the limitations imposed on or possessed by individual managers. This may lead to better understanding of management as it should be, and the blending of theory and practice will become a reality for the reader.

---

[1] Peter Drucker, *The Practice of Management* (New York: Harper & Row, Publishers, 1954), p. 350.

The manager's resources

Probably the principal effort of all managers is devoted to effective allocation of the resources available to the tasks at hand. The resources that managers have to work with are people, money, machines, materials, time, and methods. People are the most valuable of the resources and the most difficult to utilize to maximum effectiveness.

The performance of any group of people depends on the effectiveness

Figure 1-1
Levels of management

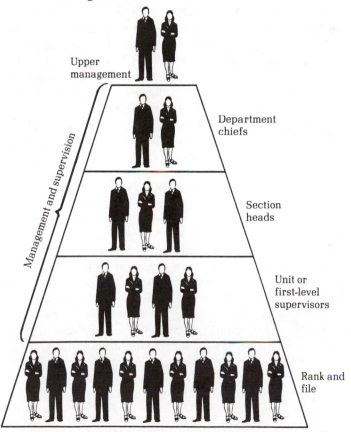

The supervisory hierarchy has at the top that part of management concerned with overall company policies and external relationships. Between the company officers at the top and the rank-and-file employees at the bottom is the part of management primarily concerned with the internal running of the business: middle management and the supervisors—the management group treated in this text. It includes department chiefs, section heads, and the first-level or unit supervisors.

of its manager, and it is to an individual manager that this book is directed—the first-level supervisor and his or her superior,[2] the area of management up to and including middle management. The picture of the first-level supervisor's job would be incomplete without including the next level in it, because the boss is the one who sets the pattern for the behavior that is expected and rewarded. The middle manager's attitudes and ways of operating have a profound influence upon subordinates in shaping their jobs, molding their attitudes, and determining the way they will operate and how successful they will be.

Responsibilities of the first-level supervisor.   The first-level supervisor is the member of management who directs the work of nonmanagerial employees, supervising both work and worker.[3] This person is the management representative at the bottom of the management pyramid—the manager who is in direct contact with the rank and file. In this respect the supervisor's job differs from that of higher level managers. He or she must relate to two quite different groups, worker subordinates and managerial superiors. Other levels of management normally relate only to managers who report to them and managers to whom they report. This characteristic of the first-level supervisor's job causes several complications involving status, self-confidence, and the extent to which there is an assumption of the manager's role. In this role the person may be called supervisor, foreman, section manager, unit manager, chief clerk, department head, group chief, project manager, head nurse, sales manager, or some other similar title.

The first-line supervisor has in most cases advanced from a job characterized by individual production to a job that now requires obtaining production through others. The supervisor may now have the authority to make decisions and manage or be an overseer who carries out orders and sees to it that rank-and-file workers carry out orders. If the job falls in this second category, the reason may lie in the design of the job, in the nature of the work being done, in the managerial philosophy of the company, or in the attitude and ability of his or her boss. Or the fault may lie with the supervisor who may not know how to handle a managerial job and may not even consider himself a member of management. Supervisors who picture themselves as people squeezed (but unloved) between the line of

---

[2] In discussing the supervisor and his or her boss, the text uses the title "supervisor" to refer to both jobs in those cases where no distinction need be made between them.

Jobs vary in title and content from one type of business to another. In many companies there are levels of supervision between first-level and middle management. Figure 1–1 shows such an organization structure.

[3] Below the first-level supervisor there are a number of positions which have some supervisory duties along with operative duties. For example, there are assistants who instruct or assist fellow employees or who examine and coordinate their work. Titles of some of these jobs are assistant supervisor, assistant foreman, production assistant, lead worker, group chief, setup person, layout person, assistant unit head, project assistant, and so forth.

workers below them and the line of managers above them need help in developing themselves to assume a managerial role. All too frequently they are promoted on short notice, and little or nothing is done to orient them and help them understand new responsibilities. They are expected to learn on the job; and this is very costly and frequently disastrous.

In many organizations the supervisor's job is really not thoroughly analyzed. Individual expectations and interpretation of the job may differ markedly from those of higher management; yet the two viewpoints are not communicated and each party goes on its way adding confusion. Most supervisory training programs and many books on supervision place a good deal of emphasis on the desirability of good human relations skills for the first-level supervisor. They are told to keep morale high and labor turnover low and to develop a work force free from conflict and disagreement. Yet, they are promoted if productivity is high, the work gets out on time, and deadlines are met. They are expected to be management's representatives to the worker; yet management does not really welcome them, and they frequently are the last to know things that affect their area of responsibility. In many instances they cannot hire, fire, transfer, or promote, and they may have very little to do with salary changes for employees. They may be expected to turn out a significant amount of work, leaving little time for supervision and the training and development of subordinates. In short, while they may be called managers, many of the things managers do have been taken away from them.

The supervisor's job has been undergoing considerable change in recent years for a variety of reasons. There is no doubt that in many organizations the first-level supervisor has very limited authority. This is particularly true where a union contract carefully spells out the rights of the bargaining unit thus limiting supervisory discretion and judgment. Likewise, supervisors in many public and semipublic agencies are limited by a myriad of written rules and procedures. The same limiting characteristics hold true in those organizations where tradition and the lethargy of higher management do not allow the supervisor to function as a manager. Even though descriptions of the job include lists of virtues, qualities, and abilities possessed only by saints, the supervisor in reality rarely has the attributes necessary to be "management's representative to the worker."

Probably the outstanding change that has taken place is the increasing shortage of people to fill supervisory jobs. Two factors contribute to this shortage. Business firms as well as other organizations have increased in size quite rapidly, thus creating the need for more first-line supervisors. Secondly, young people now enter the work force with more education and higher levels of aspiration. These two factors, coupled with the increased complexity of organized activity, have caused organizations to seek managerial personnel from sources other than the apprentice route. It is not unusual for a college graduate to become a first-line supervisor after a relatively short training period and a minimum of experience in the type of work supervised. Manufacturing, service, and other types of industries have all started to choose some supervisors in this manner.

In those organizations that have been choosing supervisors who do not have seniority but who are well educated and ambitious, the supervisor's job has become a more responsible one. The very factor of size and long lines of communication has necessitated greater flexibility in the position. While there is still a need for technical knowledge in many supervisory jobs, a number of companies (particularly in service industries such as banking, insurance, and retailing) have promoted people to supervisory positions because they demonstrated managerial attitudes and capability rather than excellent technical competence. As this trend continues, the supervisor will of necessity become more of a manager rather than a lead worker. Shortages will also increase the span of control of the individual supervisor; and the rising educational level of our society, with its emphasis on the desirability of managerial positions, will force even the organizations with strong traditions of limited authority for supervisors to evaluate carefully their view of the supervisor's role.

Responsibilities of the middle manager. The distinction between the responsibilities of the middle manager and the first-level supervisor is a matter of degree and emphasis. Both jobs are concerned with the direct operations of the firm, but the middle management responsibilities are heavier and the results harder to measure. The middle manager supervises supervisors, while the first-level supervisor supervises work and workers, telling workers what to do and training and instructing them so that they can do it. A middle manager tells subordinate supervisors what *is to be accomplished* and tells them in fairly specific terms, then counsels them to the extent necessary for them to accomplish the objectives. Higher management sets up the overall objectives which the middle manager translates into specific projects for the subordinates. The manager develops plans and directs and reviews progress toward them but does not supervise the details of their accomplishment.

While the first-level supervisor spends a larger proportion of time in directing and controlling, the middle manager does more planning (medium range rather than long range), more organizing, more integrating and coordinating of the work performed by the subordinate supervisors within the department. He or she also coordinates the department's special function with the functions of the other departments. The middle manager designs departmental procedures, formulates departmental policies, draws up budgets, and analyzes costs, along with the responsibility of gathering information, sifting it, and transmitting it to upper management in the form of progress reports and explanations of unusual circumstances.

The same factors in our society that have produced changes in the first-line supervisor's job have naturally affected the middle manager. There is pressure from below for competence from those supervisors who know their jobs and expect their bosses to have similar ability. Pressure from higher management for more effective decisions, increased productivity, and expense control truly make the word "middle" stand out in the middle manager's job.

Knowledge, skills, and attitudes the supervisor needs

Effectively utilizing human resources, getting the product or the service completed on time, keeping costs down, and maintaining established quality standards are the supervisor's primary responsibilities. Accomplishing these results calls for knowledge and skills in dealing with people, in managing, and in the particular processes and methods of the work being done. The managerial, technical, and human elements are inseparable on the job, and they are combined in the discussion presented in each chapter of this text.

The basic managerial skills to be mastered are those of planning, organizing, directing, coordinating and controlling, solving problems, and making effective decisions. The groundwork for studying the supervisor's managerial job is presented in the first six chapters:

1. *The job of managing.*   An overall look at the supervisor's job and a charting of the course designed to improve performance on it.
2. *Organizations and organization structure.*   The shape and size and authority relationships which affect the supervisor's way of operating.
3. *Organization dynamics.*   The employee-manager relationships; Principles and techniques of delegating responsibility and authority.
4. *Organizations and individuals.*   Characteristics of relationships important to managers on all organizational levels; responsibilities of individuals to their organizations as well as the organization's responsibilities to its employees, considered as a fundamental part of the establishment of a mutually beneficial relationship. The building of an effective work team is absolutely necessary for organizational and managerial success.
5. *Decision making and problem solving.*   Decision-making processes which are fundamental to management practice. Actions determined by a manager's decisions are usually carried out by other people, whose effectiveness may in large measure depend on how well the manager makes decisions.
6. *Policies and procedures.*   Policies as guides to decision making, and procedures as ways to move work through the department; both are necessary as ways to measure managerial performance and adherence to organizational goals.

In handling the technical side of the job, the supervisors may have the help of technical staff specialists in methods and standards, procedure analysts, and job analysts, or they may apply the techniques themselves. In either case they need technical knowledge of, and skill in, the work that is being performed. If they lack skill in it, they should have the analytical ability and competence necessary to direct it, make good decisions concerning it, compare and improve methods, instruct workers, and evaluate their work. Moreover they must keep up to date on technical developments, because skills and techniques become obsolete as technological advances make possible new ways of doing things.

Innovations in product or service and in process, equipment, and method are essential to the continued profitability of a business. Therefore a supervisor's attitude toward change and his or her skill in introducing it are matters of concern to the whole organization. Efficiency of operation calls for knowledge and skill in the application of the principles and techniques for improving methods, designing jobs, developing standards of work performance, designed procedures, and controlling costs. The supervisor's multiple problems and lack of time call for a look at the design of the job and a careful study of the way the supervisor uses time.

It is the purpose of the text to present understandable and usable information about staff techniques for improving efficiency and productivity. There are examples and reports of how things are being done in a variety of companies. There are samples of forms that are used and examples of ways to use them. Problem solutions that other managers have found to be effective are also included.

Knowledge, skill, and attitudes in dealing with people.   Human relations practices are aimed at motivating people to work for management objectives. The supervisor's effectiveness in dealing with people depends upon an understanding of their abilities, wants, and behavior, upon skill in communicating with them, and upon the attitude displayed toward them. Attitudes are of prime importance in the job of supervising. Most misunderstandings and mishandlings of job problems occur because people's attitudes prevent them from understanding why others are behaving as they do. Figure 1–2 presents this idea graphically. Robert Katz says, for example:

> An employee may seem to be stupid, stubborn, or lazy, but his behavior may be the result of some managerial action which to his way of thinking has taken the dignity, skill, or responsibility out of his job, has reduced him to a position of less importance, has damaged his estimation of his own worth, or has shut off his hopes of advancement. As he sees the situation, the job isn't worth putting in the effort.[4]

If surveys of what people want from their jobs are translated into attitudes they want their bosses to have toward them, the list includes:

1. Respect for their personal dignity and worth.
2. Concern for their success on the job, their safety, and health.
3. Acceptance of their limitations and appreciation of their abilities.
4. Understanding of their needs for security, fair play, approval, belonging, importance, and recognition.

---

[4] R. L. Katz, "Human Relations Skills Can Be Sharpened," *Harvard Business Review*, July–August 1956.

Figure 1–2
Factors affecting a person's interpretation of a situation

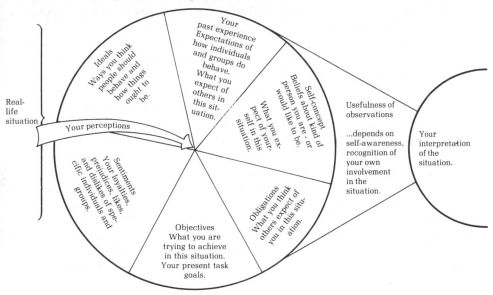

Source: Robert L. Katz, "Human Relations Skills Can Be Sharpened," *Harvard Business Review*, July–August 1956.

Each person's perception of a situation is distorted by his or her values: expectations, loyalties, prejudices, likes, dislikes, ideals, and objectives. These factors may prevent the person from seeing the real situation and understanding why others are behaving as they are.

5. Willingness to listen to them, to try to understand them, to spare them from unnecessary unpleasantness and worry.

Knowledge, skill, and attitudes and the environment. While the basic managerial skills and attitudes are similar for all managerial jobs, there are differences in approach and emphasis depending on the nature of the organization and the level of management. Generally speaking, it is more difficult for a first-level supervisor to develop a management attitude. In a sense the organizational environment at this level is different than that of the middle manager. With the constant pressure placed on the first-level supervisor by higher authority to get the work out, he or she may find it easier to sympathize and identify with subordinates than with superiors. This is particularly true if the manager is a so-called working supervisor with a quota of work to produce along with supervisory activities.

Middle managers are usually more concerned with the coordination and control, planning and development of people. As a result they will more likely develop a managerial attitude. It is very important to the manager's own growth that subordinates are allowed to function as managers. By doing so their supervisory abilities and their identification with management in the organization are developed. The middle manager can make a considerable contribution to the health of the organization by developing subordinates' managerial skills and attitudes.

Supervisory attitudes vary in relation to the nature of the work as well. Where the work pattern is relatively stable and there is no undue pressure, the supervisor may be more relaxed and less autocratic. Supervisors may also feel that they can communicate more effectively with their superiors when time pressure is not as strong as it would be in a high-production, dynamic work environment. In organizations where change is rapidly taking place due to technology, methods, and procedures, as well as equipment, the supervisor frequently meets resistance from subordinates. To be an effective change agent may require human relations skills that are extraordinary as well as the time necessary to train employees properly. Since this combination of time and outstanding human relations skills is not too common, the supervisor has more difficulty in the dynamic environment. This type of environment requires a high order of cooperation between the middle manager and the first-level supervisor. If both apply their collective skills and knowledge to the needed change, then there is greater chance for smoother transition.

The tools of management

The five tools or main activities of management mentioned earlier are supervisory skills to be learned and practiced.[5] The discussion of them in this chapter is a preliminary one to introduce the student to the management process. Since decision making is also vital to the management process, it will also be briefly discussed, with more detailed analysis left to a later chapter.

Planning

A business is dependent for its very existence on the abilities of its top planners. Failure to forecast the demand for a product and to plan how to meet a rising or shrinking demand spells the difference between success and failure of an enterprise. Top-level plans may be projected 20 years or more into the future. A paper manufacturer, for instance, forecasts the sales of its products and then plans a reforestation program to supply the wood pulp it will need.

---

[5] This division into five activities comes from Henri Fayol, *General and Industrial Management*, Constance Storrs, trans. (New York: Pitman Publishing Corp., 1949).

Other authors divide the activities differently—for instance, into planning, organizing, analyzing, and commanding; or into planning, organizing, and controlling. In this latter division, "controlling" would be defined to include both commanding and checking up. The difference between authors is not in essential material covered but in the way the activities are defined.

Since top-level plans are implemented and carried out at lower levels of the organization, the first requisite in supervisory planning is to know the objectives to be attained, the policies to be followed, the organizational and procedural structures to be used, the people who will be involved, and the environmental factors that have to be taken into account. In order to operate effectively toward the objectives, the supervisor must have a long-range plan, a plan for each day's work, and a plan for the apportioning of personal time. Since time is so scarce, so essential, and so easily lost, he needs to allocate it wisely. The supervisor who uses time to good advantage reserves a sizable portion of it to be spent in planning. All the work that comes into the department must be planned; it must fit into the overall plans of the department and into the plans of other departments.

Organizing

Organizing is defined as the formal arranging and balancing of activities, the determination of who is to do what, the assigning of authority and responsibility in order that the plan can be accomplished. Organizing an enterprise is the process of setting up the formal framework of activity groupings and authority relationships that make up the organization structure. The various kinds of structures, the authority responsibility relationships of the people within the structure, and the accommodations that must be made to enable people and departments to work together effectively within the confines of the structure are analyzed and discussed in later chapters.

Directing

Directing includes assigning tasks and ordering, telling, and instructing subordinates what to do and perhaps how to do it. Since the supervisor's job is to get things done through people, effectiveness is closely tied to getting ideas across to them clearly and in a way that will get the action desired. It is essential that subordinates understand the orders or they won't be able to carry them out. In directing people, it is important to know how much information and what kind of information to give them. Orders should be fitted to the receiver: the new person needs to be instructed in detail, but the experienced one may need only the objectives and can choose the means to attain them.

When supervisors get together in management training conferences and discuss order giving and receiving, many of them complain that the orders they receive contain too much emphasis on how to do it and too little on why it needs to be done. People by nature are curious; when they are doing a job they want to know what it is all about. One of the things that a person asks of a job is that it have meaning and purpose. The employee also likes to be helpful and to contribute individual ideas to the project.

Good communication between employees and their bosses is essential for intelligent performance of a job. Workers have no way of knowing the significance of what they are doing unless the superior tells them. People can't make good decisions if they lack essential information. The person carrying out an order always has to do some planning of details because an order can never be absolutely complete or cover all possibilities. Often unanticipated conditions arise that call for interpretation of the instructions. The person understanding *why* the order was given is in a better position to adapt actions and interpretation to the overall purpose than the person who is given only the detailed *how*.

Coordinating

Coordinating refers to that element of precision which makes sure the right thing will be at the right place at the right time. Anyone who has visited an automobile assembly plant and watched the right subassemblies arrive at the main assembly line at just the right time has seen a job of coordinating. Getting out the payroll is another good example of coordinating. Lack of coordination can bring about some chaotic conditions, as, for example, when a sales promotion plan breaks down because the advertising isn't ready or the samples aren't there, or the mailings haven't gone out, or there has been no provision for taking care of the extra load of office work or production work.

Middle-management people do a great deal of coordinating in fitting together the work of their subordinate managers and integrating it into the work of other departments. The basis of this fitting together is good planning. When a supervisor subdivides a department job and hands out the parts for various people to do, the activities of those people must fit together so that the whole job is done in the proper manner and on time. In order to meet deadlines, the supervisor must know how long it takes to do the jobs and when they must be started. It is a sure sign that coordination is breaking down if a piece of work is held up because some part is not finished on schedule. Coordination becomes even worse if the needed part is cannibalized from another job.

Certain parts of jobs have to be completed before other parts can be begun. Therefore, the supervisor must coordinate the activities of the department with those of other departments. To do this, he or she must know where the department fits into the whole picture and how it affects the operation of other departments. This knowledge of how the various parts of a job fit together enables a supervisor to plan the work so that there is no duplication of effort and no parts are left undone—no gaps.

Controlling

Controlling involves the checking of performance against standards or goals to find out what people are doing and comparing it to what they should be doing. It is a type of inspection activity. A superior must know how well subordinates are performing to determine whether the job is being done in the desired manner, whether people are putting out work of a satisfactory quality and in a satisfactory quantity.

In order for a supervisor to perform this inspection aspect of the job, there must be standards by which to measure. How much work can a qualified employee put out in a unit of time? What should be the accuracy or quality requirements of the job?

These standards of quantity and quality should be determined as accurately as possible. Until they are determined and established, a job is going to be judged by three standards—workers have ideas of a fair day's work and also what they think might be expected of them; supervisors have ideas of what they would like to have done and what they think can be done; and top management has its criteria and expectations. Whether or not quantity and quality standards are recognized, they exist, and each level in the organization—the workers, the supervisor, and the big boss—may be judging jobs by different standards. Until uniformity is achieved, there will be misunderstandings. Good standards set up and recognized let the department head know what can be expected and let the first-level supervisor and each worker know just what and how much is expected of each of them.

Measuring supervisory performance.   Cost and performing records give supervisors a measure of their own performance against a common standard. A standard against which the middle manager can measure individual performance is the budget: Are actual expenses of the department staying within the amount that was budgeted? If cost figures are higher than the amount budgeted, then the manager must investigate the causes *while the work is still in process.* The governing philosophy of this type of control—as with all controls—should be to prevent poor performance rather than just to assess the blame after the job is done.

The ideal form of control is management by objectives and self-control. Supervisors are able to operate that way when (1) they have reached an understanding with their bosses about objectives of the company and what contributions the department is expected to make toward attaining those objectives; (2) they know not only what kind of performance is expected but by what kind of statistics or records it is measured; and (3) they are kept supplied with information in a form that enables them to check up on their own performance, and they get this information soon enough to enable them to take corrective action. Management by objectives and self-control motivates managers to set high goals for themselves because their performance is measured by the actual contribution they make to the company rather than by the showing they make on certain reports.

Decision making

Managers are paid to make good decisions. The very existence of a business can depend upon decisions made by its top-level administrators. The importance of management's decision-making function is indicated by the growing number of training programs and training devices designed to improve it.

The supervisor's area of decision making is in managing work and worker. The supervisor's superior makes decisions about managing the department, supervising the supervisors, and coordinating their work. Making good decisions about the work to be done calls for knowledge and skill in the technical side of the job and an understanding of the managerial techniques of planning, directing, and controlling the work of others. And since decisions must be made in terms of the whole organization, a supervisor must know the organization's policies and procedures, the union contract, the extent of his own authority, the way the boss wants things done, and the way the decision will affect other areas in the organization.

Decisions, in order to be workable, must not only be technically sound but must take into account the attitudes of the people who will be affected by them. How will this decision be interpreted by subordinates? Is there anything in it that will upset them unnecessarily and have a bad effect on their will to work? No decision is going to be very successful if it arouses fears or hostility in the people who are expected to give their best efforts to carrying it out.

Almost every decision the supervisor makes involves people in some way, and the problems arising from decisions stem from the fact that the situation doesn't look the same to the other person as it does to the decision maker. Figure 1-2 shows how a person's perception of a situation and its interpretation are conditioned by personal involvement and by individual background. Of all the people viewing a situation, no two see it in the same way. Each person sees things through a lens shaped and colored by personal experiences, beliefs, and sentiments; perceptions are distorted by values, expectations, loyalties, prejudices, likes, dislikes, ideals, and objectives.

If supervisors are aware of their own attitudes and how they affect judgment, they are better able to evaluate the information on which to base decisions.

Problem-solving techniques

Most of the supervisor's daily problems are fairly routine in nature and can be handled by the commonsense method—a quick evaluation of the situation against experience and logic. Some problems require deeper and wider consideration, however, particularly problems relating to planning, improving methods, disciplining, and handling grievances. There are various methods of handling difficult problems: the more complicated the problem, the more elaborate the technique. Six problem-solving techniques are presented here. Each has merit and is particularly adaptable to certain types of problems.

   Technique A.   What is the problem? Why did it arise? What can be done about it? Who should do it? When should it be done? How should it be done?

Technique B.   What is wrong? Evidences? Causes? What can be done?

Technique C.   The problem. Effects of the present method or policy. Suggestions for improvement. Evaluation of suggested methods. Conclusions as to method to be adopted.

Technique D.   The problem. Facts. Analysis. Evaluation. Conclusions.

Technique E.   The JMT formula. This formula (job methods training) has been used with success in getting workers to study their own jobs and discover better ways to perform them. JMT can be found in Chapter 9 in the discussion of methods improvement.

Technique F.   The seven-step problem-solving technique which will be described and explained in subsequent chapters contains all the essentials of the other five techniques and has the advantage of being more precise.

Management theory versus management practice

Formalized learning of any subject which has practical applications confronts the student with an age-old dilemma. Will the theory he or she reads in books and discusses in the classroom or training conference work out in the world of reality? The subject of management theory is no exception to this dilemma. It is burdened even further because much of its vocabulary is made up of words that are not mysterious or technical and many relatively naïve people characterize the practice of management as nothing but common sense—neglecting to mention that common sense isn't very common.

The fact is that the practice of management is a complex process that is both functional and behavioral. It is functional in the sense that such tools as planning, organizing, directing, and controlling are available to all managers. They are used by managers in varying ways, with wide degrees of competence, and with differing perceptions and abilities to apply them. In many respects the functions of management are like oil paints, brushes, and canvas to the artist. Each artist has this equipment available, yet the same scene will have as many interpretations and levels of quality on canvas as there are artists painting it.

In the practice of management, the manager's degree of success is dependent to a great extent on how well he or she applies theory along with other managers in the same organization. Each manager, and for that matter each organization, brings some uniqueness to the practice of management in much the same way that each artist's painting is unique.

Every organization has a particular climate, certain traditions and policies and procedures that bring differences to the ways the managerial functions are carried out. The individuals concerned have varying degrees of talent, different levels of aspirations, and many kinds of knowledge. In addition the manager must at least partially rely on the work of others for personal success and these other people are not wholly controllable by the individual manager. This reliance on others is the essential difficulty of managerial work and is its sharpest difference from working as an individual. Loners or individual technicians can control their own performance and presumably know their capabilities.

Frequently the issue of whether management is an art or a science is raised. Obviously a definition of what is meant by science is necessary. If one views science as describing traditional subject areas such as physics, chemistry, biology, and mathematics, then management is not a science. But if it is compared to economics, psychology, sociology, anthropology, and other social sciences, then management can be called a science. However, this argument has little importance in the practice of management. If one is looking for a set of rules for each potential management problem, there simply aren't any which can be universally applied.

Managers deal principally with resource allocation and the dynamic nature of human relations. Because of constant and frequently unpredictable changes in human behavior, the manager will find it difficult to solve problems using one or two approaches. What is needed is an understanding of widely accepted management theory blended with knowledge gained from experience in the practice of management.

Managing is not a suitable career for those who prefer to depend on their own performance rather than the work of others for achievement. But there are rewards for the capable manager who can successfully inspire his subordinates to achieve the goals of the organization. The rewards are both material and psychological, encompassing higher pay as well as recognition and prestige.

Learning to be a manager

A reasonable question the student might ask is, "Can I learn management in a course on the subject?" Like many questions of this kind it is not so simple to answer. Many things about management can be learned from books, articles, and courses. An exposure to the skills, attitudes, and practices of management can be very useful to a person interested in becoming a manager. But in the final analysis an individual must be a manager to determine effectively how well the knowledge acquired about the subject can be applied on the job.

The fact that there are so many management development programs offered by companies, universities, colleges, and other organizations gives some credibility to the idea that exposure to managerial subject matter can be helpful. Probably the most important lesson to be learned is that there is a body of knowledge about management practice and the application of this knowledge is quite different than nonmanagerial job performance. In short, no one automatically becomes a manager by being promoted to a management job. No course instructor can make a person into a manager, but you can be prepared for management responsibility by studying the subject.

One of the ways you can gain experience is through the use of cases such as those in this book. They give the potential manager or supervisor a laboratory in which to analyze attitudes of people in the case and the people discussing the case. Your analytical skills are developed by being exposed to a slice of reality. Each of the cases in this text have actually happened. By carefully involving yourself in the ideas, values, facts, and circumstances presented in each case, you will gain experience in identifying problems, causes, and alternative approaches to solutions.

Cases represent one type of simulation useful in the development of managers and supervisors. Others include role playing, computer assisted business games, and a variety of group exercises. All of these are called experiential learning. Of course they do not substitute for actual management experience, but they do enable the novice manager to gain some knowledge of the types of things that do happen to practicing managers. The principal benefit is the time saved by these methods when compared to gaining the same variety of experience on the job.

It is important to remember that cases or other types of simulations provide no easy or correct answers. In most situations there is rarely a completely clear right or wrong answer. What is gained are useful insights into managerial behavior where there are no simple answers. Case discussions in particular allow students to test their ideas and theories in a public situation. This can give the student recognition of the fact that he or she may be wrong or at least incomplete in the analysis of the case. Such experience can be very valuable to the budding manager.

Summary

This chapter was designed to give both the supervisor and the student an idea of the broad responsibilities of management. To function effectively, the manager must develop the knowledge, skills, and attitudes necessary for the practice of management. The fact that these can be developed is demonstrated by the thousands of people who each year go through management development programs of various kinds. The practice of management can be learned, although each practitioner will bring to such efforts a particular individualism in much the same way an artist will interpret a scene in his or her own unique way on the canvas.

Of particular importance is the development of a managerial attitude and a problem-solving approach. It is desirable for the supervisor to identify with other members of management in the workplace and to try to establish personal goals which closely resemble the goals of the organization. Because the manager is largely concerned with solving a variety of problems, the cases which follow this chapter and all other chapters in this book present typical managerial problems. Group discussion of these cases will help the aspiring manager sharpen his problem-solving ability. It will be helpful to read the Foreword of this text for a further explanation of the use of cases and their value as a development tool for the supervisor.

CASE 1-1

Mary Roberts had been with the company three years when she was promoted to manager of the tax department which was part of the controller's division. Roberts started with the company when she graduated from college as an accounting major. She entered the organization as a management trainee, and during the one-year program she demonstrated considerable leadership ability as an informal leader of her peers. Mary also impressed many senior managers in the company with her sense of responsibility and her willingness to work hard. All of her training assignments were completed on time with considerable skill for an inexperienced person. Since she was very interested in tax accounting, Roberts was assigned to the tax department to be developed further as a staff accountant. Within four months she became a supervisor of ten staff tax accountants to fill a vacancy created by an unexpected early retirement. Her superior believed her to be the most qualified individual to fill the position even though others in the department had more experience in tax accounting. None, however, demonstrated leadership ability or the commitment to work that Mary possessed.

The tax department manager was promoted to fill a vacancy in the financial planning department eight months later, and he recommended to the controller that Mary Roberts be promoted to fill the position he was leaving. He mentioned that her work was excellent and that she was a very effective supervisor.

The tax department had 45 employees including 3 supervisors, 10 clerical employees, and 3 typists. Several people in the department were senior personnel with 10 to 30 years of experience in tax work. Some of these were more technically knowledgeable in taxation than Mary. There was some resentment in this group that so young a person was made a department head, and three of these people were particularly upset because they desired the promotion and felt they deserved it. What made them even more upset was the fact that the tax manager did not discuss the promotion with them.

1. *What can Mary Roberts do about the resentful senior employees?*
2. *Can higher management do anything to help Roberts make the transition to greater responsibility?*
3. *Will her lack of technical knowledge hinder Mary's managerial effectiveness?*
4. *Should Mary's superior have discussed the promotion with the senior employees before announcing it?*
5. *Could some of the resentment be based on the fact that Mary Roberts was a young woman?*
6. *Should she have turned down the promotion to gain more technical experience?*
7. *Can a person turn down such a promotion without hindering her career in the company?*

CASE 1–2

Leo Harris, one of your assistants in a fire insurance company, is in charge of a group of clerical workers who review changed policies, endorsements, and riders, calculate commissions, and maintain records. He is very meticulous, and everything coming out of his group is perfect. He does not delegate authority and responsibility but rechecks in detail all the work turned out by his group. He keeps turning back to them careless and inaccurate work until it is perfect. As a result he is busy from early morning until late at night doing detail work and neglecting his role as supervisor.

His workers have figured him out and are taking it easy. They do slapdash work and correct it as often as he returns it.

You are afraid that Harris is overworking and heading for a nervous breakdown. You have told him in general terms to delegate authority and responsibility and to discipline his group. He says that you just can't find people any more who have pride in their work or concern for the company and that if he fires any of his people or they quit the replacements would probably be worse.

1. *What are some of the reasons why people do not delegate authority and responsibility?*
2. *What are Harris' responsibilities as a supervisor?*
3. *Which can he delegate?*
4. *How should he go about delegating them?*
5. *What are some of the leadership characteristics that Harris lacks?*
6. *How can you go about developing them in him?*

CASE 1–3

Helen Flagg was an outstanding sales person in the Ajax Discount Store. She knew the products well, kept up to date with her recordkeeping and was willing to work overtime whenever necessary. None of her co-workers came near her level of overall sales performance. Because of this effective record Helen was promoted to manager of the children's-wear department. Almost from her first day in the new position trouble began to occur. Flagg complained about her subordinates' lack of motivation and dedication, feeling that they were overpaid and that many should be fired.

Naturally this caused difficulty in the department, and two of the better sales people quit abruptly. Flagg's superior discussed these problems with her, but after several such discussions Helen still couldn't understand why she should approach her job differently. Finally her superior offered Helen her old job back as a salesperson with no cut in pay. At first Helen was happy about this switch back to her old job. No more problems with those lazy employees. But then she became worried about her lack of success as a manager, and this caused her sales to fall. Even though her boss reinforced her on several occasions, telling her that not everyone can succeed as a manager and that excellent sales people are very valuable to the store, nothing seemed to give assurance to Helen Flagg.

1. *What can Flagg's boss do now?*
2. *Should she have been demoted back to her old position? Why? Why not?*
3. *Why was she promoted in the first place?*
4. *What might her superior have done to help Helen in the managerial assignment?*
5. *What kinds of problems might Helen have with co-workers when she was back in her old job?*

CASE 1-4

You were working as a first-level supervisor in a branch store of a large retail chain when your boss told you that you were being promoted to a better position at the company's headquarters within two weeks and you should pick one of your rank-and-file employees to take over your job.

You chose Harry Wilson because his sales efforts were good, he was well liked by the other employees, and he had seniority. (It was not necessary, however, that the promotion be based on seniority.) You explained your choice to everyone involved and started Harry off handling the paper work to be sure he would be well acquainted with the system and the forms and reports he would be responsible for. This took up a whole week, since you couldn't devote all your time to Harry. You expected to crowd a lot into the second week, but you didn't have the opportunity because your boss told you that you were needed at once on the new job. You told him that Harry wasn't too well acquainted with his new job, but he said for you to keep in touch with Harry by phone.

Your new position occupied all of your time, and you did not phone Wilson. Since he did not call you, you assumed he was not getting into trouble. After you had been on your new job for a month, your new boss called you into his office one morning and wanted to know what was the matter with Wilson—the sales of his group were far below normal. He then told you to go back to the branch and stay there until you had the situation straightened out.

1. *List and define the duties of a first-level supervisor.*
2. *What kind of supervisory skills might Wilson be lacking to cause "sales far below normal"?*
3. *How should Wilson have been prepared for his new job? Be specific.*

CASE 1-5

John Matthews, a new sales representative for the company, had just returned from a trip to the company's headquarters where he had undergone a six-week training program. Before John left the regional office where he was hired, he drew $500 for expenses, which was normal practice. His travel and hotel expense had been paid for by the home office. Upon his return he carefully prepared his expense account, itemizing all expenditures. His total expenses for the trip came to $350, and he was prepared to return the surplus to the cashier. He turned in his expense account for the sales manager's approval, which was required of all sales representatives.

The sales manager called John to his office and told him he was a fool for returning the surplus. John replied that he only spent the amount stated and naturally thought the surplus must be returned. The sales manager smiled and then proceeded to show John how to pad his expense account. He remarked that John's honesty would make the other sales people and the sales manager look bad when the expense accounts were checked by the company's internal auditing staff.

1. What should John do in view of the sales manager's objection to his honest expense account?
2. Can John refuse to comply with the sales manager's request for expense account padding and still stay with the company?
3. Should John go to the sales manager's superior with his problem?
4. What would cause the sales manager to encourage expense account padding when it increases the cost of doing business and this would tend to reflect on his managerial competence?

CASE 1–6

You have recently been promoted to the position of branch manager. In the six weeks since you were transferred to this branch as its manager, you have been able to assess the various capabilities of your subordinates.

The operations manager who is in charge of all clerical work at the branch has been with the company for 18 years and has held most of the clerical positions in a branch. He has been at the branch for four years as its operations manager. His knowledge of operations is excellent, but he is very excitable and tends to speak very loudly when under pressure.

The assistant branch manager has 25 years of service with the company, the last 14 years in this branch. He has also held most branch positions and is one of the best when it comes to technical knowledge. He was first assigned to the branch as chief clerk, and he subsequently served as operations manager until he was promoted to his present post and was replaced by the present operations manager. The assistant manager has, with the consent of two former branch managers, retained most of the responsibilities he held as chief clerk and operations manager. As a result there is a weak chief clerk, a staff with a feeling of dependency on one man, and an operations manager who is frustrated since he cannot do his job.

You want to realign duties and responsibilities and accomplish more delegation to strengthen the staff. You have found, however, that your assistant manager resists change, and he has worked himself into a position where he can make change very difficult. He is a man who is set in his ways, and once he has taken a position on a subject he is almost impossible to change on a friendly basis.

1. *What can you do to assign managerial responsibilities properly and to utilize your staff more effectively?*
2. *Why does the old operations manager refuse to relinquish his past responsibilities?*
3. *Can such a man be utilized effectively under the circumstances?*
4. *Should you maintain the status quo as your predecessors have done?*

CASE 1–7

Janet Larson, the office manager, had always used her secretary to handle various personal things for her. These tasks included addressing Christmas, birthday, and other cards; keeping records and handling mailings for her church finance committee; and doing similar jobs for her husband.

Over the years this had become established routine, and each time Larson employed a new secretary she was assigned these tasks and accepted them. Her most recent secretary had resigned to go with her husband to another city, and Mary Bennett was hired as her replacement. Mary was a community college graduate with three years' experience and excellent references. After three weeks on the job, Larson showed her the church records and explained a mailing that was to go out for a fund drive. Mary asked her if she wanted this done on company time and expense. She was surprised at her question but responded in the affirmative. She then told her that she would be willing to do the work after hours and for extra pay, which should be paid for by her and not the company. She went on to say that personal work was not part of her job, and she flatly refused to do it on company time.

1. *How would you handle Mary Bennett's response?*
2. *Should an executive use employees for personal work?*
3. *If the behavior has been traditional, how will Mary be able to cope with her job?*
4. *Should a company have a written policy covering such situations?*

CASE 1–8

Recently you were promoted from the job of first-level supervisor to middle management, and you now have under your supervision several of your former equals. You get along well with them, and there is no resentment about your advancement because they recognize that you are the best person available for the job.

You know from past associations that you will have to straighten out three of these subordinates; the rest are all right. The three are Black, Blue, and White. Black has always been against the organization, Blue has always been snowed under by work, and White has always been a weak individual.

Black, the anticompany man, always sides with his people against the organization and sympathizes with them when things go wrong. He wants conditions to be perfect and is always pointing out to his people the defects in the company and finding fault with the way the organization is run. (Conditions, while not perfect, are above average.) He does his job grudgingly and does not get along well with other people in the organization. The morale of his people is low, and they, too, are always grumbling.

Blue, on the other hand, is snowed under by her work; she carries the whole load of the department on her shoulders. Her people take no initiative, and she is continually correcting their mistakes. She sees that whatever little work comes out of her section is letter-perfect, even if she has to have her people do their jobs over and over again and she has to put on the finishing touches. Often her people are standing around waiting for her to get around to checking their work. They know their jobs but wait for Blue to make all the decisions.

Finally, there is White, the weak person. Instead of running his employees, he is letting them run him. The people do their jobs in any manner they wish. They do not respect his authority, and they question all his decisions. They argue with him when he gives orders, and they raise so many objections that he lets them do whatever they want. Often they boast of how they tell him off.

All the other supervisors under your jurisdiction are doing a good job. You would like to take the easy way out and fire Black, Blue, and White, but they have been with the company for quite a while. Besides, you feel that if you can lick these problems you will receive quite a bit of recognition from upper management.

1. *How would you go about straightening out Black?*
2. *How would you go about straightening out Blue?*
3. *How would you go about straightening out White?*

CASE 1-9

The management training program at Andrews Electric involved a series of rotational assignments among the several administrative activities, each for a specified period. The manager of the particular activity was responsible for the trainee during the period he was assigned to that activity. The manager was supposed to see to it that each trainee was exposed to a variety of experiences and to give such formal instruction as might be necessary.

At the end of the assignment the manager prepared an evaluation of the trainee's performance and attested to the nature and duration of the instruction and experience the trainee received.

Carl Patrick had just completed his assignment in the accounting department. He wasn't too pleased with the six-month exposure. In the first place he wasn't really interested in accounting, and in the second place all he seemed to have done were routine clerical tasks. The accounting manager kept telling him he would get around to the more interesting work, but it never happened. The one exception was the two days in cost accounting at the end of the six-month period. That seemed to have possibilities, but two days wasn't much on which to base an opinion.

Now Carl was with the accounting manager, who was completing the evaluation form on Carl's tenure in the department. The manager was supposed to discuss the evaluation with the trainee and have him sign the form to indicate that he had been made aware of the evaluation and that it had been discussed.

While looking over the evaluation form, Carl noticed that it was not accurate. It did not reflect what Carl had actually done during his stay in accounting. Rather, it seemed to indicate what he probably was supposed to have accomplished. The accounting manager had him down for two months in cost accounting, and he had only spent two days on that assignment. It appeared to Carl that the accounting manager had used him as cheap labor, since his salary was charged to a training payroll and he hadn't received the training he was supposed to receive.

1. *What should Carl Patrick do?*
2. *What are the ethical implications of the accounting manager's behavior?*
3. *What impact might this experience have on Carl Patrick's tenure with the company?*
4. *How can senior management determine if a trainee is being handled effectively on a rotational assignment?*

CASE 1–10

Charlie Lyons, the president of Varsity Tool and Die Company, had just returned from a visit to the plant of one of his big customers. The plant was a new one in a modern building in an industrial park. Charlie was particularly impressed with the employee lounge and cafeteria the company had installed.

Varsity Tool and Die was in an old building and there were 75 employees. Lyons didn't feel he could afford a cafeteria, but the unused storeroom would make a great lounge for the employees. The company had just completed a profitable year and Charlie decided to give his employees a lounge.

The next week he had the storeroom painted and new lighting installed, and his wife bought several easy chairs, couches, and three bridge table and chair sets. In addition, Charlie bought a pool table and a Ping-Pong table from a local sporting goods store.

On the following Monday Charlie announced the establishment of the employee lounge and, with a grand gesture, opened the door. He told the employees that it was a symbol of his appreciation for their efforts. He was quite surprised by the silence that greeted his announcement. One employee remarked, "If he made so much money, why didn't he give us a bonus?" This was followed by a few murmurs of "yes," "yeah," and "damn right." Then the employees went back to work.

No one used the lounge. Two weeks later the furniture was removed and it reverted to storeroom status.

1. *What went wrong here?*
2. *Should a manager make a unilateral decision of this kind?*
3. *How could Charlie Lyons have reaped the benefit he desired from the employee lounge?*

Chapter 2

Learning objectives

○ *To gain an understanding of traditional organization structure and theory*

○ *To develop a knowledge of organizational relationships and types of structure*

○ *To develop an understanding of the considerations necessary for organizational design*

○ *To become aware of evolving practices in organization design and structure*

Organizations and organization structure

Major topics

Development of the structure—The traditional viewpoint.

The bases upon which organizations are built.

Line and staff in organization.

The tall organization.

The flat organization.

Decentralization versus centralized organization.

Contingency theories of organization design.

Organizations are one of the complexities of modern life, but few of us realize the impact they have on our daily lives. Perhaps in a desire to simplify our daily activity we refuse to recognize the role organization has in our existence. If we pause to reflect for a moment, we can think of some of the many organizations, large and small, informal and formal, that affect us. The family, church, schools, hospitals, fire and police, other governmental agencies, businesses, social clubs, charities, work groups, and informal leisure groups such as card players and gardeners are among the many and varied organizations we are affected by and of which we are members. One could say that civilization and organization have gone hand in hand throughout history. Philosophers, statesmen, militarists, clergymen, and educators (among others) have devoted considerable time and energy to the analysis of organization and organized effort. The patriarchal family group, the tribe, the army, the church, the government, and, in our society, the business organization have all been carefully studied and evaluated to try to discover effective ways of organizing effort.

Chris Argyris presents a clear rationale for the creation of organizations:

> Organizations are usually created to achieve objectives that can best be met collectively. This means that the sequences of activity necessary to achieve objectives are too much for one individual and they must be cut up into "sequential units" that are manageable by human beings. At the individual level the units are roles; at the group level the units are depart ments. These units are integrated or organized in a particular sequence or pattern designed to achieve the objectives, and the resulting pattern constitutes the organization structure.[1]

The discussion in this chapter is concerned with organization structure—that framework of activity groupings and authority relationships within which people work together to achieve objectives. For supervisors to understand where they fit into an organization and how they should operate within it, they need to understand the design of the structure and how it will influence relationships and regulate behavior.

Development of the structure—The traditional viewpoint

The most prevalent approach to the study of organization structure is the one that looks upon the individual enterprise as a unit with a hierarchical arrangement. Few companies start out with the idea of building a particular type of structure. In most cases a new business is just put together by the founder, who divides the work up among a few subordinates on the basis of their talents and abilities—or maybe on the basis of which one has the least to do at the moment and can take on a few more responsibilities. New functions are placed into this or that department or

---

[1] Chris Argyris, *Integrating the Individual and the Organization* (New York: John Wiley & Sons, Inc., 1964), p. 35.

split between departments in a hit-or-miss fashion. Little consideration is given to whether the activities belong together or whether having them together promotes a logical work flow and harmonious working relationships.

Eventually lack of sound organizational relationships shows up in delays and disagreements in decision making, overlaps and gaps in responsibility, duplication and waste motion, jealousies, frictions, and buckpassing between managers. No one is sure who is responsible to do what or who has the authority to do it.

Traditional principles. The chaos that usually evolves as a new organization grows generally leads to a more orderly approach if the enterprise is to survive. In order to operate smoothly and efficiently, a company needs a structure built according to sound organizational principles. The subject is a complex one, but the following guides are offered here because they apply to organizing on any level. The supervisor can use them in studying the structure of the company or in organizing his or her own department.

1. The organization structure must be designed to provide for the activities necessary to accomplish the objectives of the business. What work has to be performed? What kinds of work belong together? What amount of emphasis should be given to each activity?
2. The structure should be as simple as possible and have the fewest possible levels of management necessary to accomplish its purpose.
3. Decisions should be made as close to the scene of action as practicable. That is, they should be made at the lowest level at which can be taken into account all the areas that will be affected by the decision.
4. No one in the organization should report to more than one line supervisor. (The principle of unity of command.)
5. The organization should be set up primarily in terms of the jobs to be done rather than around the personal characteristics of individuals.
6. Employees reporting to a manager should not be more in number than can be effectively directed and whose work can be coordinated. This is the span of control principle (also called span of supervision or span of management). The number of subordinates a manager can handle effectively depends on knowledge, ability, energy, and personality. It depends also on his or her level in management, the design of the job, the type of business, the complexity and variety of the work subordinates perform, the ability and geographical dispersion of subordinates, the interrelationship and interdependence of the work of subordinates.
7. Responsibility should be coupled with corresponding authority and should be published and understood. *Authority* is the power and the right necessary to make possible the performance of the assigned work. *Responsibility* is the work assigned to a position and the obligation to do it in a suitable manner or see that it is done. Responsibil-

ity = performance of work + accountability. *Accountability* is the obligation of a subordinate to report to his or her superior on the way the authority is being used and the work being done—to report in terms of standards and goals.

The bases upon which organizations are built

The organization structure is simply a means of achieving the purpose of the enterprise. It is successful if it is operating at the lowest overhead cost and utilizing its human and material resources at their highest capacities. There is no one perfect organizational plan. Each structure must be tailored and adjusted to meet the specific requirements of the business. The usual bases for dividing the work of a company are according to function, product, operation, customer, and region, or a combination of these.

Reprinted by permission The Wall Street Journal

Even a complex organization has to start someplace.

Charting.   There are many organizations in all types of activity that do not have charts; yet sound organizational planning can be increased by the drawing of organization charts. At least a chart gives some evidence that planning did take place. At best the chart gives one the ability to see organizational relationships graphically, and this can lead to more effective planning and a better structure.

It is important to remember that a chart is a picture of the organization at a moment in time. Like a picture it is in two dimensions. Just as a picture does not allow seeing the many fine distinctions of a scene or in the portrait of an individual, neither does a chart depict all the complex relationships existing in an organization. Yet the chart is a useful device for the manager since it identifies existing positions, the chain of command, and formal authority relationships. This aspect of the organization chart is desirable when a manager must explain reporting relationships and possible promotion opportunities to employees. The chart's usefulness is particularly evident when planning organizational changes. A variety of structures can be easily drawn to generate discussion and develop understanding of the change possibilities.

Function as a basis of organizing.   Most businesses in their beginnings are organized on the basis of their main functions. These primary functions or responsibilities in a manufacturing business would be manufacturing, sales, and finance. Organization on this basis puts people together according to their specialties—all the sales people together, all the accountants, all the engineers, and so on. This type of organization is economical and flexible to start with, but it tends to grow "tall." A further disadvantage is the clannishness that develops and interferes with teamwork between departments. Each department thinks its work is more important than that of other departments and tends to promote its own specialty at the expense of the total enterprise. Since this cleavage runs from top to bottom of the organization, an elaborate system is required to coordinate and control the specialties.

Product as a basis of organizing—Mass production.   Where several standard products are made in large quantities, organization according to product sets up separate divisions so that each type of product is produced in its own division or department and not mixed with the other types of products. A company making office machines would have a separate line of equipment for manufacturing adding machines, another line for manufacturing typewriters, and a third line for manufacturing cash registers (see Figure 2–1). A company might have separate plants to manufacture its separate products.

Mass production fits into organization according to product. The economies of mass production are achieved by turning out a great quantity of good-quality product on special-purpose machines. In a typical mass-production industry, the tasks which make up a worker's job may be so few and so simple that they fit into a time cycle of less than a half minute.

Figure 2–1
A line organization with functional
departments and manufacturing department
divided on a product basis

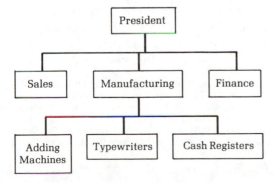

In some companies job enlargement has resulted in a better grouping of tasks so that the individual worker performs more operations and has responsibility for the quality and quantity of an identifiable stage of the work. Job design is discussed in Chapter 10.

From the supervisor's standpoint, each unit or department tends to be immediately dependent on other units for its work. Any changes in one department affect other departments. Interlocking operations call for close supervision because if one machine stops others may have to stop also. Planning is done on a high level. Control is centralized at a high level. A number of responsibilities have been removed from the line mangers' jobs and are handled by staff departments. The supervisor must maintain a schedule set by the product control department. Conditions are highly standardized, and there is little opportunity to develop individual ways of doing things.[2]

Operations, processes, or equipment as a basis of organizing—The jobbing shop.   At the opposite extreme from mass production is the business that is organized according to the operations or processes that are performed on the products—or according to the equipment needed to perform these operations. Such an organization is charted in Figure 2–2. The departments shown in this chart might be further divided according to operations. The machine shop might have within it a milling machine section, a drill press section, a grinding section, and so on. An order for 50 pumps to be made according to the customer's specifications would be routed from one section to another according to the type of operations that need to be performed in the fabrication of the parts.

A jobbing shop is a type of organization set up according to operations. It may be a distinct business by itself or it may be a department within a manufacturing business. Its distinguishing characteristic is variety of work: It is set up to manufacture orders to customers' specifications. (The customers may be other divisions of the same company.)

Each order as it comes in for the first time must be analyzed to determine the types of operations required, the proper machines on which to perform them, the proper order or sequence in which to schedule them, and the operators who should perform them. Job shop machines are a general-purpose type which can be adapted to a variety of operations by the attachment of auxiliary tooling and equipment and by the application of operator skills. Work is put through the shop in batches (intermittent manufacture) rather than in a continuous flow through fixed production lines (as in mass production). The flexibility of the machines and the

---

[2] For a study of the foreman's job on an automobile assembly line, see Charles R. Walker, Robert H. Guest, and Arthur N. Turner, *The Foreman on the Assembly Line* (Cambridge, Mass.: Harvard University Press, 1956). For worker reaction to assembly line jobs, see Charles R. Walker and Robert H. Guest, *The Man on the Assembly Line* (Cambridge, Mass.: Harvard University Press, 1952), or *Harvard Business Review,* May–June 1952. The studies were made by the Institute of Human Relations of Yale University.

Figure 2–2
A line organization with manufacturing divided on an operational basis

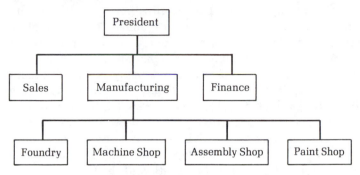

adaptability of worker skills enables the job shop to accept one-of-a-kind orders and experimental work. The control of manufacturing operations is decentralized, and the line supervisor has greater managerial responsibilities than in mass production.

As compared to mass production, job shop workers have higher skills, a wider variety of skills, and more flexibility. Their work has in it more variety; more decision making; and more responsibility for using proper methods, taking care of equipment, saving material, and turning out work of the required quality and quantity without close and continuous supervision. The jobs in a jobbing shop are more apt to belong to a family of jobs, graded according to skill, and the machine operator can see a pathway to advancement through acquiring higher skills.

Customers as a basis of organizing. A company may be divided according to the types of customers it serves; a supplier of furniture might be organized into divisions to serve wholesale, retail, and institutional customers. An advantage of this type of division is that the company can adapt its products, prices, terms, and selling approach to fit the three kinds of customers. This basis of organizing allows for more accurate measures of cost and the profitability of doing business with different types of customers. More attention can also be given to the particular desires and problems of each type of customer.

Region as a basis of organizing. Region (territory or geographical location) is the basis for dividing many companies—oil companies, railroads, chain stores, insurance companies, manufacturing organizations, and sales organizations. A company that does business nationally might divide the country into a number of zones and operate from a headquarters in each zone. Or a company might have headquarters in one part of the country and branches or plants throughout the country. Plants and offices set up to serve various parts of the country may be run from headquarters with an elaborate system for directing and controlling activities. Or regional divisions may be almost as independent as if they were in business for themselves and simply contributing their profit to the company.

From the standpoint of supervisors, decentralization of authority and responsibility puts fewer layers of management above them and gives them more opportunity to use initiative, make decisions, and prepare for advancement into jobs that exist throughout the company.

Organization according to several bases. A company is seldom organized completely on any one base. At the top it may be divided according to the product; then the product divisions may be split into manufacturing, sales, and finance. The sales department may be divided according to customer or region. The manufacturing division of a company mass-producing several standard products can be departmentalized according to product or according to operations, or a combination of the two.

New engineering companies are apt to be organized according to project. As they take on additional projects of a similar nature, several divisions may be manufacturing the same components and performing other duplications of activities. Then new departments are set up on a functional basis to take care of the overlap. Such hybrids are common in aircraft and in some electronics companies.

Organizing the service company. The years since World War II have seen a tremendous growth of various service companies such as banks, insurance companies, finance companies, real estate firms, retail stores, and advertising agencies. Most of these types of business follow the same evolutionary pattern of organization structure that the manufacturing company does. Usually starting with the basic functions characteristic of the particular business, the structure evolves into regional, project, and divisional structures similar to the complex manufacturing enterprise. For instance, a large commercial bank will have a metropolitan division to administer branches in the city in which it is located, an international division to manage its overseas operations and branches, a national division to supervise its correspondent banking relationships with banks all over the country, a personnel department, a treasurer's department, a controller's department, an auditing department, a security department, a data processing department, and an internal operations department. Marketing and advertising departments, along with business development, personal and corporate trust, personal loan, credit card, and other departments, indicate that banks organize around product lines as well as functions.

Similar structures have evolved for retailing, finance companies, and other service companies in our economy. A word might be said for the multitude of nonbusiness organizations in our society. Schools, colleges, universities, hospitals, government agencies, and religious and charitable organizations all evolve into complex structures as they grow. They do, however, follow the same pathways that other organizations do. Starting with functional areas, they break up into specialized divisions as the need for additional management becomes evident. All of the structure problems experienced by complex business firms are shared by public, quasi-public, and nonprofit organizations as well.

Departmentation. As one becomes familiar with the organizing process, it becomes apparent that the grouping of various activities is basic. An analysis of any organization, even a very small one, shows that many and varied activities are being carried out. In the small organization several of these activities may be done by one person. Hence, the president of a small company may also be its principal sales representative and handle finances as well. Another individual in the same company could be responsible for production, quality control, purchasing, and employee relations.

As the company grows, each of the activities becomes more complex and requires more attention. The process by which these specialized activities are grouped is called departmentation. For example, sales may grow to the extent that the president can no longer give this activity the attention required. A sales department is created, and a manager is hired to supervise and coordinate all selling activity. Similarly, each major functional area such as finance and production can be departmentalized as the need arises. Departments also result from the way a company is organized. Thus, as manufacturing becomes more complex, it can be departmentalized on a product or a function basis or both. A separate quality control operation for each product manufactured would be an example. As a matter of fact each of the ways of organizing discussed earlier can result in departmentation of the activity when it is sufficiently large or important to require the specialized attention of an individual manager.

Effective grouping of activities into departments contributes to more efficient coordination and enhances organizational growth. While the quality of managerial performance is critical to organizational effectiveness, Peter Drucker indicates the importance of structure by indicating that while correct structure does not guarantee results, the wrong structure aborts results and smothers even the best directed efforts. He goes on to say that the structure has to highlight results that are truly meaningful and are relevant to the idea of the business, its excellence, its priorities, and its opportunities.[3]

Line and staff in organization

Line organization and the authority it implies is an easy concept to understand. It represents the simplest form of organization structure with direct vertical links between the various levels of the hierarchy. There is a clear authority relationship between a supervisor and a subordinate.

---

[3] Peter F. Drucker, *Managing for Results* (New York: Harper & Row, Publishers, 1964), p. 216.

Most companies start out with an organization that is predominantly line; that is, a boss runs a department with a minimum of outside interference or help—performing such activities as hiring, firing, purchasing, maintenance, and inspection. When the number of employees becomes too large to manage, some subordinate managers are appointed. Vertical expansion of this type reaches a point of diminishing returns, because each manager is handling a great variety of tasks calling for a variety of talents and duplicating the tasks that the next person is handling. As these tasks increase in volume and complexity, it becomes advisable to start taking some of them away from the line managers and giving them to specialists.

When specialists are added to the line organization, it becomes line and staff. These staff activities are usually advisory and supportive to the entire line organization. They might include maintenance, personnel administration, quality control, work measurement, and public relations. Figure 2–3 is an organization chart showing line and staff departments. Figure 2–4 illustrates industrial engineering services that are available to the line organization of a large corporation.

It is well to remember that what is line in one company may be staff in another. If a company's business is manufacturing and selling, purchasing is a staff activity. If the business is buying and selling, purchasing is a line activity. Research and development is a staff activity in a manufacturing company but a line activity in a design and development firm. Generally speaking, office functions are staff activities in a manufacturing company and line in an insurance company. Theoretically the distinctions between line and staff are easy to understand. In practice, however, the distinctions are not so clear and are likely to cause confusion between line and staff executives.

This view of the distinction between line and staff lies in the activities they perform. Those functions which directly contribute to the attainment of organization goals are called line functions. Staff people contribute indirectly and in a supportive manner by performing services for line people that aid in goal achievement and by providing advice and counsel based on their specialized knowledge.

The notion that certain activities contribute more to organizational objectives than others is one of the principal reasons line and staff organization is difficult to understand. It is also a primary cause of individual and organizational conflict which is discussed in Chapter 4. How one makes a clear distinction between the organizational importance of the sales function which is considered "line" in most companies and personnel administration which is a staff activity is rather difficult to explain. It is useful to look at an organization as a whole entity. This makes it easier to see the nature of relationships in that organization. Some departments such as personnel support the entire organization, while sales or manufacturing are distinct self-contained activities. The specialists in personnel advise

Figure 2–3
A line and staff organization

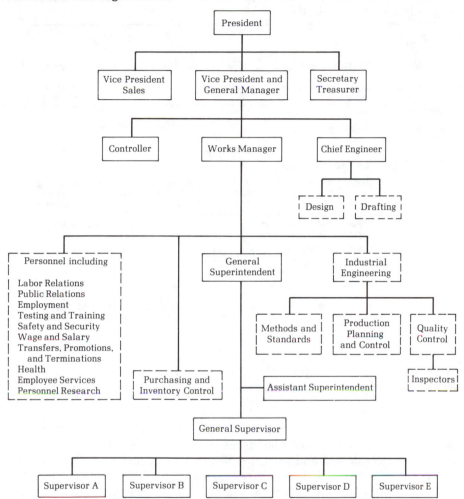

The staff departments are those enclosed by dotted lines.

The personnel department might be placed higher in the structure; it might be called employee relations, industrial relations, or labor relations. Among the variations in the organization of personnel departments are: (1) labor relations and personnel administration may be combined under one head as shown here. (2) labor relations and personnel administration may be separate departments. (3) public relations may be included in the personnel department or be a department by itself. The activities handled by the personnel department might be set up as sections of a large department or, in a small company, combined as duties.

Figure 2–4
Management directive outlining services that the industrial engineering department renders to the line organization

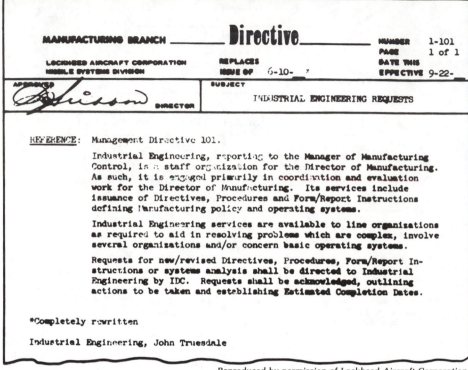

MANUFACTURING BRANCH _____ **Directive**_____ NUMBER 1-101

LOCKHEED AIRCRAFT CORPORATION   REPLACES   PAGE   1 of 1
MISSILE SYSTEMS DIVISION   ISSUE OF   6-10- *   DATE THIS
                                                                   EFFECTIVE 9-22-

APPROVED   SUBJECT
                                            INDUSTRIAL ENGINEERING REQUESTS
               DIRECTOR

REFERENCE: Management Directive 101.

             Industrial Engineering, reporting to the Manager of Manufacturing
             Control, is a staff organization for the Director of Manufacturing.
             As such, it is engaged primarily in coordination and evaluation
             work for the Director of Manufacturing. Its services include
             issuance of Directives, Procedures and Form/Report Instructions
             defining Manufacturing policy and operating systems.

             Industrial Engineering services are available to line organizations
             as required to aid in resolving problems which are complex, involve
             several organizations and/or concern basic operating systems.

             Requests for new/revised Directives, Procedures, Form/Report In-
             structions or systems analysis shall be directed to Industrial
             Engineering by IDC. Requests shall be acknowledged, outlining
             actions to be taken and establishing Estimated Completion Dates.

*Completely rewritten

Industrial Engineering, John Truesdale

managers in sales and manufacturing on such things as salary ranges, wage rates, job design and analysis, hiring, and promotion. This type of advising activity is called a staff relationship. To try and determine the relative importance of personnel's contribution as against sales or manufacturing is somewhat futile. What is important is that all parts of the organization are working together as effectively as possible to achieve departmental and organizational objectives.

The tall organization

The supervisor's job is shaped by the organization structure, the bases upon which the organization is set up and the type and amount of staff development. Another factor—a related and important one—is the tallness or flatness of the organization.

The "tall" organization is one that has added so many levels of supervision between top and bottom that the people at the top have lost contact with the ones at the bottom and have to depend upon elaborate procedures, reports, and other devices for keeping informed. Tallness is not limited to huge companies; some medium-sized ones have as many as ten layers of management through which information must find its way to the top for a decision to be made.

If a sales representative phones in a change on a customer's order that is already in production, and the change requires overtime to meet delivery dates, how far up the line must the supervisor go for approval? How many levels must be consulted before reaching the one that can authorize the extra expense of overtime? Or suppose the customer phoned the order change to the president of the company, how long would it take for the information to trickle down to the bottom and how accurate would it be when it finally got there?

The piling of layer upon layer of management is apt to take place in the types of business in which each unit and department is immediately dependent on others for its work. Mass production is an example of the interlocking and interdependent operations which must be closely coordinated in order to keep the whole company working as a unit. Layering of management is less common in a retail store because there is little interaction between departments: The men's clothing department is not affected by inefficiencies in housewares.

In a tall organization, decision making is done at the upper levels, and upper management has a tight system of controls to see that orders are carried out in the proper manner. These controls call for additional staff people to operate them, which in turn piles a greater burden on the system for communicating, controlling, and coordinating.

When an organization grows too tall, people are apt to lose sight of its objectives. Just keeping the system running becomes an objective in itself. When the opportunity to get ahead depends upon conforming to the system, then people up and down the line conform to the utmost; they do just what they are told, they won't take any chances, they protect themselves at all times, they take every problem to the boss; and this is repeated at each level of management.

Whenever the number of employees in an organization is increasing at a faster rate than business, top management should suspect that some of these people are there just to keep the system going and that the system is becoming more important than the business.

The flat organization

The "flat" organization, with its three or four levels of management, escapes the disadvantage of impersonal leadership; but personal leadership can be good or bad, depending on the leader. In the flat organization the lines of communication are short. Decisions can be made quickly, mistakes can be discovered quickly, and the consequences of mistakes are not usually as serious as they are in a tall organization. Where the levels of management are few, the coordination problem is not so great, and controls can often be exercised by spot checks by department heads as they pass through their departments. There is less turning of wheels within wheels.

Just having fewer levels of management does not guarantee that authority and responsibility will be decentralized, however; some companies have flat organizations and still have a highly centralized management.

A flat organization in a big company is an indication that managers have a fairly wide span of control (span of supervision) and therefore don't have the time to supervise their subordinates closely. Sears Roebuck Retail is an example of flat organization: president, vice president, store manager, section manager. A vice president may have responsibility for a hundred stores, each one an autonomous unit. A store manager may be responsible for 30 section managers, each responsible for the marketing and profit in his or her own section.

Decentralization versus centralized organization

As an enterprise grows in size and complexity, it becomes apparent that managers cannot do everything by themselves. Human factors have to be taken into consideration. Many companies have grown and geographically decentralized their operations so that they could be nearer their markets or raw materials or both. The growth pattern of an individual company may result in its expansion into other industries. Oil and rubber companies have moved into chemicals, companies in basic industries have moved into consumer products, and consumer products companies have moved into wholesaling and retailing. Such diversification has caused organizational structure problems. Questions arose as to the efficiency of the old structure, since control with a high degree of centralization became very difficult. There were the attendant problems of doing business in a new or different sphere. A decentralized organization structure with decision-making authority on the lowest possible managerial level was the result. Of course, managerial decentralization cannot be achieved overnight. It requires the retraining of people all the way up and down the line; it requires a change of attitude toward the job—a willingness to risk having subordinates make more managerial decisions. Bittel contrasts centralized and decentralized control, indicating both problems and rewards:

> One of the key decisions to be made when establishing policy is the extent to which control will be centralized or decentralized. Centralized control tends to provide greater assurance that top management goals will be achieved. Decentralized controls—especially when they apply broadly to profit responsibility—present four difficult problems. First, they are costly to administer. Second, they require a tighter, more complex information system. Third, they depend upon a more highly qualified middle management staff.

Finally, there is always the danger that the lower echelon managers will not be motivated, or act, in the best interests of the company.

Weighed against these disadvantages are the greater resilience, balance, and diversity that a decentralized system can develop and maintain.[4]

Decentralization of management involves:

1. Giving subordinates more authority to make decisions and holding them responsible for these decisions.
2. Providing guidance in the form of realistic policies.
3. Using procedures to save time and labor but not to stifle initiative and judgment.
4. Telling subordinates more of the *what* and *why* and less of the *how to.*
5. Retraining the people in management so that they can handle authority and make better decisions and do it on a greater variety of problems.
6. Instilling in the personnel a feeling that they don't always have to be 100 percent correct.
7. Having people feel that they will have time to gather and prepare information—that having a lot of precise data on tap at all times is not a measure of their managerial ability.
8. Simplifying the system and placing more dependence on people.
9. Enlarging and enriching jobs.
10. Making more use of staff activities.
11. Making more use of the "rule of the exception" at each level in order to prevent authority and responsibility from climbing upward.

Perspective on the two extremes. In general, organizations start out highly centralized since management usually believes that this is a better way to control the organization. As the organization grows in size, complexity, and diversification, it moves toward a decentralized structure. As is the case with most managerial practices, there is no absolute in organization design. The amount of decentralization in any organization depends upon individual conditions and circumstances. Management attitudes, capability, and style along with the nature of the enterprise are the usual determinants. Technological developments in recent years have caused several changes. The high cost of automation has resulted in centralized manufacturing of many parts and assemblies that were produced in separate decentralized plants. Computer technology has developed centralized information processing for such paperwork as payrolls, accounting data, and inventory among many others. Interestingly, the recent development of small computers and desk-side terminals has started to reverse the centralization of information processing.

Perhaps there is no contest between the two extremes of centralization and decentralization. Probably no pure form of either structure exists in

---

[4] Lester R. Bittel, *Management by Exception* (New York: McGraw-Hill Book Co., 1964), p. 106.

practice. It is just another example of the dynamic nature of management practice and in particular the process of organization design and structure. Most well managed organizations are constantly seeking better ways to organize their work so that goals can be achieved effectively.

Contingency theories of organization design

The purpose of organization is to coordinate the many diverse elements of the enterprise and to optimize the goal achievement of the total structure. The traditional viewpoint, with its many principles of organization, has attempted to achieve this. To a certain extent, the success of American business is a tribute to the success of its managers in their application of traditional organization theory. Nevertheless the search for more effective ways of organizing goes on. As our organizations grow both in size and complexity there is an increasing recognition that traditional approaches are found wanting. As a result management theorists have been paying greater attention to both human and environmental factors in their search for more effective ways of organizing. Traditional theory emphasizes formal structure, principles applicable to all organizations, policies, rules, and procedures, thus leading to the view that an individual organization is a closed system operating with little or no relationship to its environment. Additionally, people are viewed as being governed by the structure, principles, and rules, with little or no attention given to their individual aspirations, needs, goals, and behavior patterns.

Any recognition of reality will demonstrate that traditional organization theory does not give us a broad enough framework for understanding the modern complex organization. William G. Scott and Terence R. Mitchell have developed the following viewpoint:

> The distinctive qualities of modern organization theory are its conceptual-analytical base, its reliance on empirical research data, and, above all, its synthesizing, integrating nature. These qualities are framed in a philosophy which accepts the premise that the only meaningful way to study organization is as a system.
>
> System analysis has its own peculiar point of view. Modern organization theory accepts system analysis as a starting point. It asks a range of interrelated questions which are not seriously considered by the classical and neoclassical theories of organization. Key among these questions are:
>
> 1. What are the strategic parts of the system?
> 2. What is the nature of their mutual interdependency?
> 3. What are the main processes in the system which link the parts and facilitate their adjustment to each other?
> 4. What are the goals sought by the system?

Modern organization theory is in no way a homogeneous body of thought. Each writer and researcher has his special emphasis when he considers the system. Perhaps the most evident unifying strand in modern organization theory is the effort made to look at human systems in their totality.[5]

The systems viewpoint.   A study of the recent literature[6] of management theory indicates a ferment as part of the evolutionary process to develop more effective ideas about organization. Essentially the manager is concerned with the allocation of the resources available to him and the rationale for organization is to optimize this allocation. By approaching the organization from a systems point of view, the manager becomes aware that it is made up of many interdependent but individual managers working on problems and processes requiring a variety of techniques, knowledge, and capabilities. The systems approach makes an attempt to analyze and integrate the human beings, processes, technology, information needs, communication networks, and goals of the total organization.

The basic difference between the systems approach and the traditional approach to organization seems to be the recognition that process is more important than structure. The traditional approach, with its fixed hierarchical authority and responsibility relationships, is changing into the recognition of the organization as a group of interrelationships of people, materials, money, and information, with behavior, time, and change as critical factors. The rapidly growing and widely accepted activity of organization planning and development, taking the total system into account, seems to be the wave of the immediate future.

The systems approach.   Perhaps the outstanding contribution of the systems approach to organization theory is that it gives us a way to visualize the complexities of organizations and their relationships in our society. In systems theory, every organization is viewed as a part of a larger whole. The whole is the total system and each part is a subsystem. Traditional organization theory considers the business firm to be a separate and independent entity, while the systems approach looks upon the firm as one subsystem of the total system. This subsystem (the firm) must relate to many other subsystems, all of which make up the total system.

One firm may relate to many subsystems, such as suppliers, customers, competitors, and governments (and even further subsystems within each subsystem mentioned). There is constant interaction among all of these subsystems, and each must respond and possibly change or adapt to these interactions. For instance, new antipollution legislation in a town where one

---

[5] William G. Scott and Terence R. Mitchell, *Organization Theory: A Structural and Behavioral Analysis*, rev. ed. (Homewood, Ill.: Richard D. Irwin, 1972), p. 55. © 1972 by Richard D. Irwin, Inc.

[6] For example, see ibid., chap. 4; R. A. Johnson, F. E. Kast, and J. E. Rosenzweig, *The Theory and Management of Systems*, 3d ed. (New York: McGraw-Hill Book Co., 1973); Stanford L. Optner, *Systems Analysis for Business Management*, 2d ed. (Englewood Cliffs, N.J.: Prentice-Hall, Inc., 1968); John A. Seiler, *Systems Analysis in Organizational Behavior* (Homewood, Ill.: Richard D. Irwin, 1967); Joseph A. Litterer, *The Analysis of Organizations*, 2d ed. (New York: John Wiley & Sons, Inc., 1973).

of a company's plants is located may increase costs and reduce profits. A reduction in profits may mean the company will pay less taxes to that community, thus affecting that government subsystem. The closing of such a plant could have an even more drastic effect. A profit reduction would also have a less drastic effect on the state government subsystem and the federal government subsystem.

Traditional organization theory views the individual business organization as being made up of independent units or departments such as engineering, manufacturing, sales, and finance. The efficiency of the particular firm rests on the effectiveness of the management in each unit. Systems theory, on the other hand, views the firm as the total system and each department as a subsystem. The lines of authority are blurred, because the purpose of each subsystem is to optimize results of the total system, even if one or more of the subsystems is underoptimized.

Another way of explaining the term "system" is as a set of interrelated and interacting variables, with each system being part of a larger system. In a particular company, a department is one system, encompassing such variables as equipment, people, structure, location, size, and procedures. The introduction of some major new equipment resulting from technological progress may necessitate retraining of employees, new procedures, and even a change in attitude among those employees unhappy with the new equipment. In other words, changing one variable (equipment) has an effect in varying degrees on all other variables.

Because the department is a part of the total system or company, some of the variables in other departments are bound to be affected. For instance, the new equipment requires financing, thus affecting the finance department; and it may produce the product at lower unit cost, affecting the marketing, manufacturing, and finance departments among others. Lower unit costs may mean lower prices, thus affecting wholesalers, retailers, consumers, and competitors. A little further thought will lead to additional chain effects on such other parts of the total economic system as governments, suppliers, unions, and the like.

Organization restrictions.   In every organization, every person is delegated some degree of authority and responsibility; at the very least one is accountable for a job or assignment. In management, each person is accountable to someone for something and also for somebody (for the actions of subordinates). One must function within the organizational constraints of the firm as well as the external and internal environmental limitations. The amount of freedom one has in doing a job depends on the boss, on the stage of growth and profitability of the company, on the health of the economy in general and the individual industry in particular, and on the complexity and level of sophistication of the entire firm. It will also depend on the philosophy of top management as evidence by policies, objectives, and strategic planning.

If supervisors are aware of the ways in which the organization restricts them, they can determine what can be changed around them and strive to bring about these changes. Also they can determine what changes must be made within themselves—what adjustments they have to make to fit the organization. People who are knowledgeable about themselves and the situation are generally better adjusted to it than those who are ignorant of or do not understand the pressures and what must be done to accommodate to them.

No person fits a job perfectly; each individual has several strong and weak points, interests, goals, drives, and attitudes which determine somewhat the parts of the job that will be done well and the parts that will not. Also, personality causes one to work better with some people than with others; it influences the amount of authority and responsibility the person will delegate to subordinates and the amount of delegation expected from the individual's superior.

Because people do not fit their own jobs perfectly, their strong and weak points affect the jobs around them. Collectively, each activity in the firm has a similar relationship. These interdependencies and their degree of effectiveness determine the level of success of the firm. The departmental and hierarchical compartments of traditional organization structure do not fully allow for the recognition of the mutual dependency of all parts of the company. If the enterprise is to take full advantage of emerging managerial techniques—quantitative methods, the computer, information systems, and the behavioral sciences—it seems that it must move away from the traditional approach to organization structure. As innovation continues and control and measurement of operations improves, traditional departments and lines of authority will tend to blur. By approaching the organization as a total system operating in an external environment, management will be able to more effectively allocate resources and optimize results.

The matrix organization. One of the outgrowths of the application of systems theory to organization structure has been the design of different types of organizations. Many of these are characterized by less well-defined lines of authority than in traditional hierarchical organizations and by the expressed purpose of better utilization of employee knowledge, technology, and available funds.

The most frequently mentioned of this type is called matrix organization. Its development is based on project management, where the work of the organization is carried out by a group or groups who are responsible for the production of a given product or the completion of a particular program. The organization has a typical functional structure and then the matrix or project structure is added to this. Individuals from the traditional functional departments are assigned to the project based on the need for their expertise. They have a dual reporting relationship, to the functional department head and to the project manager. Project managers usually report to a project coordinator. An example of this type of structure is depicted in Figure 2–5.

Figure 2–5
A matrix organization

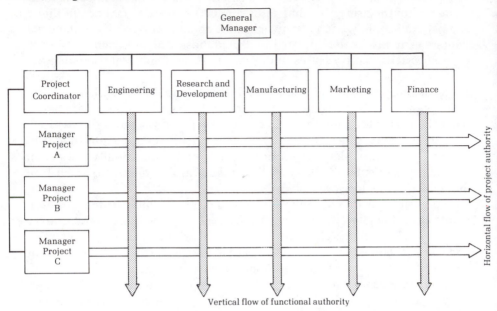

Vertical flow of functional authority

As the chart demonstrates, both functional and project authority are imposed on the individuals working on a project. The impact of matrix structure is analyzed as follows by George R. Terry:

> Care should be exercised in adopting matrix departmentation. The "one man, one boss" honored management practice is severely modified into a one-man, one-boss relationship plus other relationships. The line and staff may be primarily for one aspect of a man's job, then eventually several superiors may be coequal for other aspects of his job. The matrix arrangement requires extensive communication, and preferably it should meet internal company needs and not simply be grafted onto the existing organization in hope of demonstrating progressive management thinking. Decision making may be slowed down by following matrix departmentation and the amount and type of authority of each manager must be clearly delineated. In addition, all managers must understand the rules of the game, and this usually necessitates an educational effort so that none feel their authority is threatened and nonmanagement members learn how to function with two managers.[7]

An example of project management should aid in understanding this type of structure. The organizational unit is called a project. Usually complex projects are difficult to accomplish in the traditional functional organiza-

---

[7] George R. Terry, *Principles of Management,* 7th ed. (Homewood, Ill.: Richard D. Irwin, 1977), p. 274. © 1977 by Richard D. Irwin, Inc.

tion. They may be bounced around among several departments, none of which are capable of doing the entire job plus the fact that ongoing work may seem more important to the functional department head. Too many conferences are held among the several department heads, and none of them has any real commitment to the completion of the project. This is the type of situation where project management is most useful. It has been successfully implemented in high technology organizations and in the space program. But even service organizations have complex projects to accomplish. An advertising agency may have a client who has a new product to introduce to the public, and the client wants a special marketing and advertising program developed for this product. The agency could staff a project group made up of a copywriter, a media specialist, an artist, an audiovisual expert, and a member of the agency's financial staff along with an account liaison person as the project manager. The specific goal is to develop and prepare the program for the client's new product. A time deadline is established, and when the project is completed to the client's satisfaction, each of the individuals return to their specific functional departments for new assignments or to continue ongoing work.

It can be seen that matrix structure and project management is not a complete answer to organizing, though it may be useful in some organizations for particular types of work. It has been successfully used where a particular project could be identified requiring people with varied backgrounds from different functional areas and where a time deadline was necessary. It obviously requires strong top management support and effective cooperation from functional department heads.

Other structures.   The project team is a temporary structure designed to accomplish a specific goal. Other types of temporary structures may be used such as a product development group which could be disbanded when the product is ready for production. A task force to develop a corporate ethics policy is another example of a temporary structure.

Organizational design has become increasingly dependent upon environment and technology. As these two variables change, structural change must occur. (See Figure 2–6.)

Environment and technology are usually characterized in three ways: stability, predictable change, and turbulence. Each of these results in differing organization structures.

1. Stability.   In relatively stable industries with mass production such as automobiles and television sets or service companies such as banks and insurance companies with large routine clerical operations and big full function retailers, there will be formal traditional structures with clearly defined lines of authority. These are usually the tall structures mentioned earlier with several levels of management. Environmental factors are also stable with longer term union contracts, limited competition, and a good labor supply. Technology is also relatively stable with few radical innovations and controlled progress.

Figure 2–6
Common relationships among environment, structure, and task

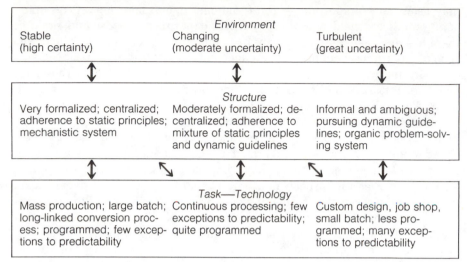

Source: Ross Webber, *Management* (Homewood, Ill.: Richard D. Irwin, 1975), p. 439. © 1975 by Richard D. Irwin, Inc.

2. Predictable change. As the environment changes with introduction of new technology, more government control, and a less stable labor supply, organization structures change as well. Increased competition and product or service innovation may prompt companies to try different structures. This is the type of environment which has developed in recent years. Automobiles have become smaller, energy consciousness has risen, government has intervened in more areas of the private sector, and service companies have introduced more innovations. For example, banks have introduced automatic teller machines, insurance companies are experimenting with different types of policies, and retailers are seeking more effective ways of controlling inventories and merchandising products. Most of these changes have been evolutionary, and they have resulted in structures which are flatter with fewer levels of management and less formal authority relationships.

3. Turbulence. Some experts believe we are entering a period of turbulence where environmental and technological changes will be more radical and less predictable. Products and services may change rapidly, government regulation can increase as energy needs become more critical, and rapid technology changes can cause disruption in labor relations. Such an environment can result in more informal structures with less defined authority relationships and more decentralization. Organizational structure would be more fluid and characterized by constant experimentation to achieve goals with some degree of effectiveness.

What must be clear to the student is that no one type of structure is universal. Organizing is one of the tools the manager has to create an effective structure to accomplish the goals of the organization. The process of organizing is dynamic, and structure should be changed to meet changing organizational needs.

Summary

Whenever the services of more than one person are necessary to carry out a project, an organization must be formed to divide up the work and delegate to others the authority to perform it. The organization structure is the framework within which people work together to carry out company objectives. There is no one best structure. The best organization is the one that operates at lowest overhead cost and makes the best use of people and material resources. The work of a company may be divided up and assigned according to function, product, operation, customer, or region, or some combination of these bases.

Increase in size and technical complexity cause a business to make a further division in its work—this time along the basis of line and staff. Line departments are those carrying out the main responsibilities for which the company was organized (buying and selling, for example). Staff performs specialized functions which provide advice, service, or control.

The shape and size and authority relationships of an organization determine the amount of freedom supervisors will have in doing their jobs. A tall organization with tight controls and big staff departments to operate them will restrict decision making. Managerial decentralization, on the other hand, results in more freedom but makes greater demands upon managers for a high level of performance.

If supervisors understand the organization they are a part of, they are better able to make the adjustments necessary to get along in it. They are also better able to organize the work of their own departments.

Recent developments in organization theory indicate that there are changes in thinking regarding the traditional structure with its lines of authority and departmentalization. To take advantage of rapidly developing managerial techniques utilizing quantitative methods, the computer, information systems, and the behavioral sciences, many firms are approaching the organization as a total system. This concept allows for the more effective utilization of the available resources and helps the firm to optimize results.

There is increasing evidence that the changes caused by environment and technology have considerable impact on organization structure. All types of organizations in our society are experimenting with different structures to attain greater effectiveness, and there is no one type of structure designed to meet all needs.

CASE 2–1

The general manager has hired the services of a personnel administrator but has purposely not defined the newcomer's role in the organization.

You, a line supervisor, have become involved in several arguments with this personnel administrator when he attempted to relieve you and other supervisors of the authority for transferring and promoting employees, changing pay rates, and other matters on which he should only be advising line management. You feel that he does not have the proper perspective for his job and that he is trying to take over more and more power in order to create a good job for himself.

You have mentioned this usurping of authority to your boss, the general manager, and have asked him to define the personnel job. The boss has answered that he is allowing the personnel administrator to find his own niche in the organization. You feel that the morale of the people in your department will suffer unless the personnel administrator's position is made clear.

1. *Discuss the above situation from a line point of view.*
2. *Discuss the situation from a personnel administrator's point of view.*
3. *Develop a practical working relationship based on the principles of good organization.*
4. *Is it desirable to allow the personnel administrator to find his own niche in the organization?*

CASE 2–2

Bill Corwin was employed by a large bank for several years. He started as a messenger, then was assigned to a branch. He progressed in this branch from a bookkeeping clerk to a platform assistant. In this position he had a variety of duties largely centering on administrative assistance to the officers of the branch.

The bank's many branches were divided regionally, each region having a group of officers responsible for the branches in that region. Bill was transferred from the branch in which he had worked for 12 years to a branch in another region. At the time of his transfer he was told that the branch was completely "run down" as to operational procedures and systems. The branch had a normal complement of 4 officers and 35 staff members. One month prior to Bill's transfer, one of the four officers had retired, and two weeks after this retirement the branch manager was hospitalized with a serious illness.

When Bill arrived at his new assignment, he found a rather demoralized situation. Complete lack of interest was shown by the two remaining officers and the rest of the staff was not properly trained or disciplined. The two officers did not know Bill, and they were informed by the regional office that he was being assigned to the branch as a platform replacement for only two weeks.

During his first week at the branch Bill discovered that the senior clerks were not qualified to train other staff members, customer complaints were rampant, there was both a record of excessive absenteeism and excessive overtime, and the branch had received very poor audit reports by the bank's internal auditors with the same major exceptions reported on the previous four audits.

After two weeks Bill was called to the regional office and offered the job of operations officer. He was told that he would receive the official title in two months. He was also told that the present operations officer, who had held the job at this branch for seven years, was to be relieved of all operational responsibilities and that he would be instructed to work with Bill until the branch was functioning effectively.

Bill returned to the branch and started on his assignment. He found the former operations officer cooperative for about one week. Bill then decided to go ahead without the help of the former operations officer. Over the next three months he worked almost every night until 8:00 or 9:00 P.M. He tried to correct the problems that had developed over several years. The training of employees involved considerable time, and he found it necessary to release 12 clerks who were causing trouble in various ways. The remaining staff and replacements started to function smoothly. He received his title as promised. Then the branch manager returned to work after his prolonged illness. A week after his return he called Bill to his office and questioned his efforts in the branch. He told Bill that the former operations officer had mentioned that he was an upsetting influence in the branch, had fired several good people, did not know his job, and that he left his job early several days a week.

1. *If you were Bill, how would you answer the branch manager?*
2. *Did the regional office handle Bill's transfer properly?*
3. *What should be done by the regional office now?*
4. *Do you believe that Bill can function effectively in this branch?*

CASE 2–3

The L. J. Thomson Company, a large chain store operation, recently reorganized their structure after a six-month study by an outside management consulting firm. Prior to the reorganization each branch outlet sold company and other products at both retail and wholesale. Retail sales were made to customers who came to the branch while wholesale sales were made by sales representatives who called on customers in the branch marketing area. These sales representatives handled large sales to other retailers and industrial firms who bought in large quantities.

The consulting firm suggested separation of the wholesale and retail business into profit centers so sales could be more carefully measured and costs more accurately determined. Wholesale sales representatives were moved out of the branches and combined with the sales force from adjacent marketing areas into regional wholesale sales offices. Because the retail branches maintained the stock of merchandise, they performed the warehousing and shipping functions for the wholesale selling force. In addition returns and adjustments were handled by the retail branch since it retained the clerical force in existence before the reorganization.

Ben Dixon was the manager of one of the new retail branches. He had been in charge before the reorganization, and he resented his assignment to the retail branch, believing that wholesale sales were easier and more profitable. He was particularly angry to be saddled with the responsibility for warehousing, shipping, returns, and adjustments. Clerical work was costly and he simply didn't believe that the transfer credits to cover costs which the branch received for handling all but the sales function for wholesale selling would really fully compensate the retail branch. He felt he was in a "no-win" situation, believing it virtually impossible to show a profit. He was telling anyone who would listen that the new organization would not work.

1. *Was the new organization structure a sound one?*
2. *Should Dixon give it more time before concluding that he was in a "no-win" situation?*
3. *Could his opinion be based on the fact that he resented the retail assignment?*
4. *Could the organization have been designed differently? Explain.*

CASE 2–4

A project leader in charge of a small engineering group has guided her project through the initial phases of design, and hopes to have all the hardware assembled in a few weeks. During the design phase of the project her supervisor gave her complete responsibility and authority to handle any matters concerning the project. But now, as the hardware stage is beginning, the supervisor has jumped in and is duplicating his subordinate's efforts in the procurement of parts and the supervision of technicians responsible for the fabrication of the engineering prototype.

1. *What should the project leader do about it?*
2. *Why would such a situation arise?*
3. *How can the situation be improved?*

CASE 2–5

The president of a small company that had been growing rapidly engaged a management consultant to conduct an organization survey so that proper organizational development and planning could result. After considerable analysis the consultant developed a proposed organization structure. Before preparing the necessary position descriptions and an organization manual, he discussed the proposal with the president. The recommended structure was thought to be sound by the president, but he believed that all employees should be involved in the discussion so that they could see the reporting relationships and lines of authority and responsibility. The consultant advised against this idea, suggesting that only supervisors be involved. He felt it should be their responsibility to discuss it further with their subordinates. The consultant further believed that many of the employees were unsophisticated about management theory and practice and that such a discussion would be confusing.

The company president was insistent in his desire to communicate the proposed structure to all employees. A meeting was scheduled one evening after the close of the business day. Approximately 100 employees crowded into the company's reception area, where a blackboard had been set up. The president opened the meeting with a brief statement of its purpose and then turned it over to the consultant. The consultant explained the desirability of organization planning and the need for sound structure to allow the company to achieve its objectives. He discussed responsibility and authority and the need for establishing accountability and effective reporting relationships. He then proceeded to draw the proposed structure on the blackboard, indicating the major functional areas, their relationships to each other, and the resultant lines of authority down from the chief executive. In short, he depicted a typical organization chart on the blackboard. Several questions ensued, since the company had never had any chart and this was all new information to the majority of those present. After answering several questions, the consultant closed the discussion by emphasizing the fact that the chart was one aspect of sound organizational development and that it wasn't static but would be changed as the company developed and grew. The president thanked the group for coming to the meeting and concluded the program.

Several employees then came forward to talk to both the president and the consultant. Additional questions were raised and the consultant answered them. The consultant felt that the meeting was successful, since all of the questions were good ones and he thought the discussion created greater understanding of the proposal among the employees. Just as he was mentally congratulating himself on the apparent success of his efforts, one of the clerks from the accounting department grabbed him by the arm and took him to the blackboard. The clerk, an old-timer with the company, then said, "Where is my box on the chart?"

1. *How would you answer the clerk's question?*
2. *Should the president have included all employees in this discussion group?*
3. *What do you think prompted the clerk to raise his question?*

CASE 2-6

The normal arrangement of a credit department would be to have the department head report to the controller. The problem in our company is that the credit manager of the division reports to the credit manager of the parent company, who in turn reports to the controller of the parent company. The division controller is thereby completely bypassed by people whose activities are directly his responsibility.

The way things are set up, the parent credit manager and the division controller are on about the same management level. The division controller has no say in credit matters although he is responsible for the amount of accounts receivable outstanding. This makes for a frustrating situation for him.

No complaints have been made to management, as the various heads do not want to suggest that management may be wrong in using this setup.

1. *In a large corporation having a number of manufacturing divisions, what might be the reason for this form of organization?*
2. *What is the relation of organization structure to responsibility?*
3. *What problems exist in this type of setup?*

CASE 2-7

Ben Williams had just been promoted to the position of department head. Along with the private office, he inherited the previous department head's private secretary, Dottie Staples. Dottie was a departmental fixture, having been there for over 20 years. She was unmarried and her whole life seemed to revolve around her job. She was an excellent typist and stenographer, and she enjoyed her status, which was often referred to as "departmental mother."

During his eight years with the company, Ben had ample opportunity to observe Dottie in action, and he was unimpressed with her gossipy approach to the job. Dottie had several favorites in the department, but Ben Williams wasn't among them. Ben's feelings about Dottie were well known, and several of the employees wondered what would happen now that Ben Williams was the boss.

When Ben was told of his promotion, he asked the personnel vice president about transferring Dottie. He was told that company tradition had long established the practice of leaving secretaries in their jobs when new managers were appointed. With the exception of the company's president, none of the executives dictated the choice of their secretaries. It was felt that an experienced secretary helped make the new manager's transition into his job an easier one by lending continuity. Since Ben had just been promoted, he felt that discretion was necessary and did not press his request.

When Ben moved into his office, Dottie congratulated him and said, "Well, you're the fifth department head I've broken in." Ben simply thanked her for her congratulations and said nothing further. Having decided that he had no choice at present, he thought he would try to work with Dottie. Over the next few months there were several polite clashes between them, particularly when Ben tried to introduce new methods and approaches and Dottie kept reminding him that this was not the way it had been done in the past. Ben then heard through the grapevine that Dottie had been talking about him to her previous boss, who had been transferred to another job when Ben was promoted.

The final straw among many came when Ben discovered that Dottie had countermanded an order he had given earlier to a subordinate to prepare some data for an analytical report Ben was developing on departmental operations. He called Dottie to his office and asked her why she had done this. She replied that she was only trying to save the person from extra work which she thought was unnecessary. She said that in her opinion the report would not be welcomed by Ben's superior and she was just saving him from criticism. Ben exploded and furiously berated Dottie. She rushed out of his office very upset. Ben called the personnel vice president, vowing to tell him that either Dottie would be transferred or the company could look for another department head.

1. *Was the company tradition a wise one?*
2. *Should an executive be allowed to choose his secretary? Why?*
3. *Should Ben have been more forceful in trying to have Dottie transferred when he took over the department head's position?*
4. *Should he now threaten to quit if Dottie is not removed from her job?*
5. *What can a company do about employees like Dottie who seem to overstep their authority because of long seniority on the job?*

CASE 2–8

Fred Josephs supervises the tax department in a large company's finance department. Three first-level supervisors report to him. Fred is quite content with his job and takes life as it comes. He is not particularly ambitious and feels that if a promotion comes he will take it, but if not, that will be okay too.

On the other hand, he has a very ambitious young woman working for him. Mary Blunt is aggressive and well educated; she is a CPA with an MBA degree in accounting as well. Mary and her husband (who works for another company) recently moved to a house next door to the financial vice president of Mary's company. The Blunts have become quite friendly with their neighbors, the financial vice president and his wife.

At various social occasions, business inevitably comes up. Mary has frequently discussed company tax matters with Jack Walker, the financial vice president. She has also mentioned other work problems, and Jack has helped her with solutions.

This has become apparent to Fred Josephs, who finds it increasingly difficult to supervise Mary Blunt. Fred feels quite resentful about being bypassed by Mary, and his animosity is directed at both Mary and his boss, Jack Walker.

Recently Fred has become very nervous and has sought medical advice. His wife called the personnel manager to report Fred's absence and told him about the whole problem. The personnel manager decides to tell Jack Walker so that something can be done about the problem. Walker is surprised, saying, "Easygoing Fred, nervous and upset about Mary talking to me—I can't believe it!"

1.   *What can be done about this type of problem?*
2.   *Should senior managers socialize with lower-level people?*
3.   *Did the personnel manager do the correct thing by informing Walker?*
4.   *What can Fred Josephs do about the problem?*

CASE 2-9

A young engineer slated for rapid advancement in the company was rotated from staff to line jobs in her training program. After six years with the company she was given the post of assistant to the president. She had scarcely started on her new duties when the president left on a business trip of two weeks. The new assistant wanted to have something worthwhile to show for the two weeks and had a great many ideas for improvements that she had never been able to put through in her previous positions. Since several new products were being readied for production, she sent word to the heads of manufacturing, industrial engineering, and industrial relations that she would like a report on the possibilities of using the learning curve for setting up learners' incentive rates.

These three department heads had never been very receptive to her suggestions. Since they were not sure how much attention they had to pay to her in the new position, they sent her a memo that it would take a couple of weeks to assemble the information. Then, when the president returned, they asked for a clarification of the young woman's authority.

What is the authority of the assistant to?

CASE 2-10

As the head of the market research department reporting to the marketing vice president, you weren't at all pleased by his statement that the company was going to begin using a matrix organization for some recent projects being developed. You lost three of your best employees, each a specialist. They were to be project managers for the duration of the experiment.

You simply could not see how they were still supposed to be reporting to you, yet also responsible to the general manager in charge of projects. Well, if they were reporting to you, you certainly would have something to say about how they used their time.

After the projects had been under way for several weeks, you got a rush job and the one person who could really help you was the manager of one of the projects, Al Toner. You went to see him to get his help. "Al, we need you on a rush job for one of our biggest customers." Al laughed and said, "Boss, I'm all tied up on the project, you know that. I can't spare the time; we have deadlines too." "You mean you won't help me out, Al?" "I can't—I have responsibility for 15 people and a very expensive project," Al responded. "I'll remember this when it comes time for your performance evaluation," you replied.

1. *How can this problem be resolved?*
2. *What can Al Toner do about his dilemma?*
3. *Does the above situation indicate a weakness in matrix organizations?*
4. *If so, how can such weakness be overcome?*

Chapter 3

Learning objectives

- ○ To gain an understanding of the concepts of authority and responsibility

- ○ To appreciate the nature of and complexity of delegation and span of control

- ○ To understand informal organization and its relationship to the formal structure

- ○ To become aware of the problems involved in organization relationships

Organization dynamics

Major topics

Authority and responsibility.

Delegation of authority.

Learning to delegate.

Rule of the exception.

Barriers to delegation.

Span of supervision or control.

Extending the span of supervision.

Managerial attitude.

The informal organization.

Unity of command.

Violations of the chain of command.

The supervisor's view of the short circuit.

Analyzing violations of the chain of command.

Preserving the chain of command.

Flexibility in the chain of command.

Although classical organization theory is being critically analyzed in much of the current management literature, it is still a vital factor in organization life. Most large organizations adhere to its concepts of formal structure and prepare charts depicting the various levels of management and the reporting relationships of each level. The formal organization chart is still very much in use as a depictor of career tracks for budding executives, and it also serves as the indicator of authority relationships and scope of responsibility for managers on all levels.

The increasing interest of behavioral scientists in organization theory has given us many useful insights in the application of traditional concepts to the day-to-day activity of the organization. Structure is recognized as one of the variables to be considered by the manager, along with such others as delegation of authority and responsibility, assignment of accountability, span of control, status, and power. What is emerging is a more dynamic, cohesive, and multidimensional view of organization theory.

Given objectives, policies, procedures, and a formal structure, it becomes necessary to take these relatively static concepts and make them dynamic. It is reasonable to assume that if an organization structure evolves from the work to be accomplished, the people in the organization require direction and knowledge as to how they will get their jobs done. The dilemma that modern managers face in trying to get work accomplished in an area of responsibility has plagued managers through the ages. The Bible indicates that Moses had this same managerial problem several thousand years ago:

> On the morrow Moses sat to judge the people, and the people stood about Moses from morning till evening. When Moses' father-in-law saw all that he was doing for the people, he said, "What is this that you are doing for the people? Why do you sit alone, and all the people stand about you from morning till evening?" And Moses said to his father-in-law, "Because the people come to me to inquire of God; when they have a dispute, they come to me and I decide between a man and his neighbors, and I make them know the statutes of God and his decisions." Moses' father-in-law said to him, "What you are doing is not good. You and the people with you will wear yourselves out, for the thing is too heavy for you; you are not able to perform it alone. Listen now to my voice; I will give you counsel, and God be with you! You shall represent the people before God, and bring their cases to God; and you shall teach them the statutes and the decision, and make them know the way in which they must walk and what they must do. Moreover choose able men from all the people, such as fear God, men who are trustworthy and who hate a bribe; and place such men over the people as rulers of thousands, of hundreds, of fifties, and of tens. And let them judge the people at all times; every great matter they shall bring to you, but any small matter they shall decide themselves; so it will be easier for you, and they will bear the burden with you. . . ."

> So Moses gave heed to the voice of his father-in-law and did all that he had said. Moses chose able men out of all Israel, and made them heads

over the people, rulers of thousands, of hundreds, of fifties, and of tens. And they judged the people at all times; hard cases they brought to Moses, but any small matter they decided themselves.[1]

In this short quotation from the Book of Exodus we see the problems of delegation of authority, span of control, and reporting relationships. It is also interesting to note that Moses' father-in-law was playing the role of a management consultant.

Authority and responsibility

In the traditional sense, all authority and responsibility is vested in the chief executive of an organization and is delegated by this individual in varying amounts to immediate subordinates, who in turn delegate to their immediate subordinates, and so on through all the levels of management in the organization. This is called the authority of position. The path along which authority and responsibility go downward and accountability goes upward is known as the chain of command.

The concept of authority of position deserves further explanation. Chester I. Barnard in his classic work describes it as follows:

> Thus men impute authority to communications from superior positions, provided they are reasonably consistent with advantages of scope and perspective that are credited to those positions. This authority is to a considerable extent independent of the personal ability of the incumbent of the position. It is often recognized that though the incumbent may be of limited personal ability his advice may be superior solely by reason of the advantage of position.[2]

It is quite common for subordinates to react to the authority of a superior in an organization without much regard to the person who occupies the position. Simply stated, when a vice president asks a subordinate to do something, compliance usually results because he or she is a vice president. Obviously, there is no qualitative dimension to the authority of position. An individual executive who possesses considerable ability and who has a professional viewpoint along with a positive personal characteristic may have more authority over subordinates than his or her position may indicate in the formal structure. Conversely, the poorly performing executive may find it difficult to exercise authority even with a high position in the formal structure.

Superior-subordinate relationship. It becomes apparent that the key to understanding concepts of authority is a full awareness of the relationships of superiors with their subordinates in the formal organization structure. Positions of delegated authority in the formal organization re-

---

[1] *The Holy Bible,* Exodus 18:13–26, revised standard version (New York: Thomas Nelson & Sons, 1953).

[2] Chester I. Barnard, *The Functions of the Executive* (Cambridge, Mass.: Harvard University Press, 1938), p. 173.

sult from the process of organizing and the subsequent development of the formal structure as depicted by the familiar hierarchical organization chart. These positions have little to do with the occupant of the position at any particular time. In other words, a company needs a sales manager and the position is shown on the formal chart. The chart also indicates reporting relationships and the scope of authority. An accompanying organization manual and position description will give, in great detail, his duties, responsibilities, and accountabilities. Such charts and manuals have relative permanence, usually going beyond the incumbency of any given individual. Changes may take place in the formal structure from time to time as the need arises for such change, but the structure rarely changes when a new person is moved into the particular authority position. It is in this sense, then, that we arrive at the concept of the authority of position.

While the authority vested in the position is a determinant of the exercise of authority by the superior over the subordinate, nevertheless, the ability of the superior along with leadership style, experience, and knowledge enable the manager to control subordinate performance with varying degrees of success. There is no doubt that an authority relationship exists when one individual has the power to exercise control over another individual by using rewards and punishments commonly accepted in the particular organization. Given the authority of position, we find that in practice some managers are better able to exercise their delegated authority than others. For instance, a given manager may train subordinates more effectively, may be better able to secure raises for them, may have better relationships with superiors, and may be considered fair and competent by peers and subordinates. In short he or she may be a better manager; and subordinates react to this by more readily accepting this manager's authority.

Another concept of authority that should be considered is called the acceptance theory of authority. William G. Scott and Terence R. Mitchell describe it as follows:

> Authority is proposed in this theory as emanating from those led rather than from the delegation process in hierarchical systems. This theory, as the name indicates, is based upon the acceptance by followers of the authority exercised by those in superordinate positions. The idea essentially is that authority is meaningless unless consent is secured from subordinates. Action is impossible without the willing cooperation of those who are led to act.[3]

It might be said that subordinates allow their superiors to exercise authority over them in exchange for a certain salary, a given quality of working conditions, and a certain amount of job security. If these things

---

[3] William G. Scott and Terence R. Mitchell, *Organization Theory: A Structural and Behavioral Analysis,* rev. ed. (Homewood, Ill.: Richard D. Irwin, 1972), p. 218. © 1972 by Richard D. Irwin, Inc.

(among others) are present, the subordinate has job satisfaction and willingly accepts the authority of the superior.

The subject of authority is a rather complex one, and it will be considered further in this book. There is no doubt that the style of leadership is an important factor in the exercise of authority. But such things as a fringe benefit program, work hours, job title, and general working conditions loom large in any superior-subordinate relationship.

Delegation of authority

As an organization grows in complexity, it soon becomes apparent that delegation must take place. Organization dynamics requires that authority-responsibility relationships be established so that the hierarchical structure can accomplish its objectives. The process of delegation must take place whenever a supervisor's responsibilities become too heavy. The only way he or she can do the job effectively is to delegate some of the work to others. Delegation frees managers from a multitude of time-consuming tasks and permits them to give proper attention to the important parts of their jobs. Delegation involves authority, responsibility, and accountability.

Authority. Authority involves the right to make decisions, give orders, and expect to be obeyed in relation to work assignments. It is the right to require action of others. It is a permission to make commitments, use resources, and take other necessary action to make possible the performance of the assigned work. Authority is described and defined in job descriptions, policies, procedures, instruction manuals, routines, and special instructions.

Responsibility and accountability. Responsibility is a double obligation: (1) the obligation to perform the assigned work in a suitable manner or to see that someone else does it in a suitable manner, and (2) accountability for its proper performance. Accountability is defined as the obligation of a subordinate to report to the delegating superior upon the exercise of authority and the performance of the assignment. The report may involve a statement of causes and grounds explaining or justifying an act, event, or circumstance. Actually, an employee is responsible for two things: performance of the work assigned, and then feedback to the boss as to the way the authority was exercised and the work performed. Accountability is being answerable for one's conduct in respect to obligations fulfilled or unfulfilled; it is a rendering of stewardship.

Generally, the activities an individual has to do are called *duties*. The word *responsibilities* is used in this text to include duties plus the activities that can be delegated to somebody else. The process of delegation does not relieve the delegator of any responsibility, accountability, or authority. The delegator is still responsible for seeing that the work is done satisfactorily and for reporting on it to his or her own boss. If need be, the

delegator can take back the authority and can keep it or give it to someone else.

Responsibility and authority must be coextensive. If one is responsible
for an activity, one must have sufficient authority to carry it out or to see
that it is carried out. On the other hand, if a person has authority (permission to perform an activity or have it performed), that person should be
responsible for the wise use of that authority.

Delegation.   Delegation is the act of transferring selected responsibilities, with commensurate authority, to one or more subordinates.

Delegation of authority should be from a superior to his or her immediate subordinates. Theoretically the delegation should be to the position
and not to the person, but actually the kind of person determines the kind
of delegation. First of all, the subordinate must be able and willing to receive the authority. To be able, the individual must have sufficient knowledge and experience to make good decisions and must be able to exercise
authority so that the goals will be achieved. And that person must be willing to accept responsibility.

In the second place, the amount and kind of delegation depends on the
delegator; some people can't bring themselves to let go of authority. The
third factor influencing delegation concerns the philosophy and attitude of
the company about the level at which decisions should be made; some
companies believe in holding authority close to the top.

Learning to delegate

The first problem in delegation is *what* to delegate. Each job has certain
residual duties that the jobholder must perform. There may also be tasks
too difficult, confidential, or delicate to be turned over to a subordinate.
But the essential criterion is a matter of how important the responsibility
is. The boss should delegate less important responsibilities in order to be
able to allow more time to devote to the more important ones.

How much authority to delegate depends upon the ability and training
of the subordinate. Starting out small and increasing steadily is much better practice than throwing an unprepared subordinate in to sink or swim.
Whatever the amount of authority, it must be equal to the amount of responsibility, and it should be defined and published. Decisions which the
subordinate is authorized to make can be divided into categories for
clarification:

1.   The area in which subordinates are free to be on their own.
2.   The area in which they report only unsuccessful results.
3.   The area in which they report all results.
4.   The area in which they can make decisions but should report them to
     the boss.
5.   The area in which they should contact staff for information before
     making decisions.

6. The area in which they must consult the boss before taking final action.
7. The area where they present possible approaches to the boss for decision.

Before a boss can delegate, an accepted fact must be that subordinates will make mistakes and that he or she will be responsible for them. Supervisors must be prepared to stand up and protect subordinates against criticism by others. They must not let anyone else punish them for their mistakes. They must also realize that the work isn't going to be done just the way they would do it themselves. A boss who expects perfection is apt to get excuses rather than actions. If they are too meticulous, they may need to remind themselves occasionally that the business would carry on without them if they should quit or die.

Teaching a subordinate to exercise authority is a matter of building up a relationship of mutual trust. Subordinates must be confident that the boss won't sacrifice them in order to escape blame. Bosses must show that they are interested in results rather than details and that they're willing to help the subordinate over bad spots. Bosses must be consistent in their behavior and in their decisions; otherwise the subordinate won't know what to do or what to expect.

Good management practices which supervisors should observe when delegating authority and responsibility to a subordinate can be summarized as follows:

1. Observe the principle of unity of command: Each person should have one and only one boss and should know who that boss is.
2. Assign homogeneous tasks; that is, when making up a job, see that it consists of tasks that call for the same or similar skills.
3. Define the amount and extent of authority and responsibility involved in each job; avoid overlaps and gaps.
4. Set up standards of performance so that people know what is expected of them.
5. Set up policies and procedures—policies to guide subordinates in making decisions, and procedures to take care of routine activities.
6. Train subordinates so that they know how to manage; then rely on them.
7. Develop a control system so that work can be checked during performance.
8. Delegate authority and responsibility as far down the line as possible, so that decisions will be rendered as close as practical to the origin of the problems.
9. Be available to help the subordinates when they get into difficulty.
10. Make use of the rule of the exception, so that a problem outside a person's jurisdiction is passed up the line to the point where there is sufficient authority to solve it.

Rule of the exception

The rule of the exception provides that managers do not have to pass personally on every matter that comes within their jurisdiction. Only the exceptions are called to their attention. Under this system managers should delegate to their subordinates as much of routine operations as possible, leaving the difficult problems and the exceptions to routine for themselves. To delegate successfully, managers must have policies, procedures, and standing plans to guide subordinates; they must have trained and equipped them to handle matters; and they must have established a system of controls in order to get reports telling how well subordinates are carrying out the job.

In line with the rule of the exception (or exception principle, as it is also called), when a problem is outside a person's jurisdiction, it is passed up the line to the point at which there is sufficient authority to solve it. If the solution is not within the authority of the superior, it is passed up to the next level, and so on until it reaches a level at which the requisite authority exists. There it is settled as a routine problem. This concept is an extension of Frederick W. Taylor's principle that a manager should receive only condensed and comparative reports pointing out all the exceptions—both good and bad—to the past averages and standards.[4]

Barriers to delegation

Most managers acknowledge the need to delegate, but some find themselves unable to let go of authority. They are responsible for the proper performance of the work, and they feel that no one can do it as well as they can. Even on relatively unimportant tasks, they are unwilling to settle for a performance that is merely adequate. They insist on giving minute instructions and checking up on details. Such bosses are afraid to take a chance, because they don't want to be blamed for mistakes. They lack confidence in the ability of their subordinates, but they give the subordinates no opportunity to improve by practice.

Sometimes managers can't delegate because they simply do not plan work far enough ahead to be able to line up a project and turn it over to someone else to handle. If they do not have it worked out in their own minds, they are unable to describe the problem to a subordinate or tell them what it is that is to be done.

Some bosses won't delegate because they enjoy the importance of being in on everything that goes on, and they feel they would lose some power or prestige if they turned over a part of the job to a subordinate. Some bosses have had unsuccessful experiences in delegating because they turned over authority without preparing the subordinate to handle it. Or they may have tried to delegate without having any standards by which to measure perfor-

---

[4] F. W. Taylor, *Shop Management* (New York: Harper & Bros., 1911).

mance or any system of controls by which to get reports on how well the work was being done.

A boss may complain that subordinates just don't want responsibilities and won't use the authority given them—that all the problems come home to roost. Perhaps subordinates find the risks are greater than the rewards. If they've been criticized unmercifully for making mistakes, they'll avoid making decisions. Or if there are ironclad procedures and rules to cover every minor matter, subordinates may be afraid to use their own good judgment.

Some subordinates complain that they just don't have enough authority to do their jobs. It's true that many bosses assign responsibilities but hold back on the authority. It's possible also that subordinates aren't using the authority they have. They may be reluctant to face up to unpleasant decisions or afraid to stick their necks out. Some people are unable to handle authority; they can't discipline themselves or they can't stand the uncertainty that goes with decision making. Sometimes the trouble is that they simply don't know what it is the boss wants.

Span of supervision or control

Span of supervision[5] refers to the amount of managing a person is able to do as measured by the number of subordinates reporting directly to that person. The relationship of the span of supervision to delegation and to the chain of command can be seen most easily by looking at the way an organization develops from its beginnings as a shop supervised by one person.

When a company grows to the point that the president cannot personally supervise all the managers, salespersons, and accountants, then a production manager is hired with the authority and responsibility for production. A sales manager is hired with the authority and responsibility for the sales department, and a treasurer the authority and responsibility for finance. The president has put a link in the chain of command between himself and the workers, because he could extend his span of supervision no farther.

As the business continues to expand, the work of purchasing is delegated to a purchasing manager, an engineer is hired and so on until there are ten managers reporting to the president. Then he finds that he does not have the time to plan, organize, direct, coordinate, and control the work of these ten and at the same time take care of his own duties. This time the president appoints a vice president to help, and this person takes over the responsibility for sales, purchasing, and finance. The new vice president is an added link in the chain of command.

It can be seen that the chain of command results from the fact that one

---

[5] Span of supervision is more commonly called span of control. The word *control* is used in this text in its meaning of establishing performance standards and then measuring performance against the standards. Control includes a checking and reporting system for information on performance.

manager can't do everything nor can the manager keep adding indefinitely to the number of people reporting directly to him. As the manager directs more and more people, that manager's span of supervision is exceeded and he or she begins to become less effective. The span is limited by such factors as the nature of the work—its complexity, importance, and amount; the competence of subordinates and the amount of authority that can be delegated to them; the effect of poor decisions (how much damage they can do); the availability of staff assistance; the growth rate or stability of the enterprise; and the existence of policies, objective standards for measuring performance, and a system of controls for checking and reporting information.

A first-level supervisor has a wider span of supervision than a higher level manager. In the higher levels of the organization, problems are more complex, more people are affected by decisions, and a greater variety of interests must be considered; therefore higher level managers usually have fewer people reporting directly to them than do those on the lower levels.

But outside of these factors that are tied to the nature of the job, there is another set of limiting factors that is tied more closely to the person. The number of subordinates directly reporting to one manager is limited by time, distance, attention, knowledge, energy, and personality.

Time. There aren't enough hours in the day to do an unlimited amount of managing. For each person reporting to a manager, assignments must be planned, instructions given, work progress checked, and problems handled. In addition to supervising subordinates, the manager has other managerial duties to perform—such as overall planning, working with staff departments, and attending conferences—activities which also consume time.

Distance. Supervisors have to keep in contact with their people even though they are spread out over large areas, as in maintenance, custodial, and sales work, and in any work done outside the shop or office.

Attention. Some people are able to attend to many activities, while other people become flustered when a number of demands are made upon their attention. Each person reporting to the boss adds to the number and variety of problems the boss has to handle and the number of decisions to be made.

Knowledge. As problems increase in variety and complexity, a boss needs more and more specialized and technical information in order to make good decisions. People vary in their backgrounds of education and experience and in their ability to assimilate information.

Energy. Jobs vary in the amount of energy they consume and people vary in the amount of energy they can generate and expend effectively. The energy involved is both physical and mental. The mental energy or nervous energy provides the drive by which people get things done. Exhausted or half-alive supervisors can't extend themselves as far as the human dynamo.

Personality. The relationship of personality to the span of control is not simply one of how effective a person is at communicating or at motivating and guiding subordinates. There is involved also that facet of personality that enables individuals to see and handle a whole project and not be mired down in the details—to keep their sights on the objective and push steadily toward it, letting others take care of the details. Bosses who fret over trifles are limited in the extent of their span of supervision.

Extending the span of supervision

Each new link added to the chain of command is an additional level of supervision, putting more distance between the people at the bottom and the leaders at the top. The people at the top lose contact with the ones at the bottom and have to depend on elaborate procedures, reports, and devices for keeping informed—a tight system of controls to see that orders are carried out in the proper manner. Authority may be tightly held at the top, and a person may be better off conforming to procedure rather than using his own good judgment.

In order to keep down the number of levels and maintain a short chain of command, managers should try to increase their span of supervision; that is, they should try to do a more effective job with their present subordinates rather than create another level of management below to handle them. Starting with the personal factors that limit one, the manager can get better control of *time* by planning and scheduling and seeing that recurring problems can be handled by procedures.

The drains on the individual's *energy* can be reduced by cutting down on confusion, crises, and anger. Remedies here are better planning, establishing routines, and changing personal attitudes toward people who are troublesome. Conflicts and hostilities become less distressing if a person makes an attempt to understand the other individual's problems and point of view.

The demands on a manager's *attention* can be made fewer if subordinates are taught to use the rule of the exception—that is, to handle the normal routines themselves and bring to the boss's attention only the unusual situations outside their authority. A manager's limits of *knowledge* can be pushed back by study, by use of the problem-solving technique, and by use of staff help. *Personality* factors can't be changed easily, but if a manager becomes aware of the effect of personal behavior upon others, much can be done to improve it.

Managerial attitude

There is general agreement in management literature that executive growth is enhanced when delegation is practiced. Equal emphasis is placed on the desirability of forcing supervisors to supervise by expanding their span of supervision. As is the case with many sound managerial principles, there is considerable difference between theory and practice. In most organizations there are several variables which cause the gap between acceptance of theoretical principles and daily managerial practice.

The formal organization chart depicts a static situation in the dynamic framework of ongoing organizational activity. This does not mean that formal structure should be criticized because it doesn't inform managers how their jobs should be done. Formal structure supports managers by indicating reporting relationships, areas of responsibility, the chain of command, and it identifies peers. What it does not do is indicate how they shall exercise their authority, what relationships they shall have with peers, how they will report to superiors, and how they will discharge responsibilities.

To a very great extent the style of an organization is established by its leaders. If a concerted effort is made by higher management to delegate work downward and constant pressure is exercised to force supervisors on all levels to devote the major portion of their effort to the tasks of supervision by consciously expanding their span of supervision, then the climate is created for decentralized managerial activity. Effective decentralization of authority exists only where top management is convinced of its value and is willing to risk a few mistakes in order to have the flexibility that comes with having decisions made as close as possible to the scene of action.

"You need rest and quiet; maybe your
company could kick you upstairs."
Reprinted by permission The Wall Street Journal

**What impact can a manager who is "kicked
upstairs" have on the formal organization?**

When upper mangement subscribes to and practices decentralization of authority, individual supervisors have the opportunity to exercise general supervision rather than close supervision over their subordinates. General supervision is distinguished from close supervision in the greater amount of authority delegated, in setting goals rather than giving detailed orders, in providing the training and support that enables subordinates to accept responsibility and exercise authority, in supervising by results and meeting standards, and in spending more time on long-range planning and little time doing the same work being done by the subordinates.

General supervision is not laxness; it demands results and sets up definite limits within which people are to work, but it lets the subordinate make individual decisions within those limits and doesn't hover over those subordinates while the decisions are made.

General supervision isn't a magic formula which will take care of all the supervisor's problems. Some people don't want responsibility on the job. A subordinate who has been poorly supervised and has developed attitudes antagonistic to management will not perform well under general supervision. And general supervision won't work well if there are poor relations between union and management or if there are internal conflicts. Supervisors can't very well use general supervision if upper management exercises tight controls or if superiors exercise tight controls.

Supervisors have to take all these factors into account and suit their method of supervision to the company situation, the type of work to be done, the ability and personality of the subordinates, and their own personality, ability, and experience.

The informal organization

As was mentioned earlier in this chapter, ongoing organizational activity is dynamic. Part of this dynamism is the variety of interactions which go on among people in the formal organization. These interactions or relationships frequently lead the involved individuals to become aware of common interests and ideas. The work environment encourages association of people who are concerned with similar or related activities in the formal organization. Quite often these relationships are based on the nature of the work, feelings about the company, attitudes toward higher management, and other attitudes which are job-related. A natural tendency to meet socially develops, and the commonality of work leads to friendship and even similarity of outside interests.

Actually humans join groups because they desire companionship. Lack of social contact on the job frequently leads to poor performance and dissatisfaction with the job. Coffee breaks are frequently taken by noncoffee drinkers simply for the human relationships involved. Individuals tend to need the emotional support of their peers on the job. Informal work groups fill that need. One of the problems of newly appointed woman managers is their lack of affiliation with the usual informal network of male managers in the organization.

Informal work groups can develop a level of group cohesion which allows them to express opinions and gain attention more quickly. This cohesion can also allow the group to be both independent of management and also effectively support it depending on the situation. Group cohesion is also important when unusual stress arises. Everyone has seen an informal group rallying around an individual member when that person is faced with extraordinary problems. In a similar manner, the informal group might work extra hard to achieve a goal under stress just to demonstrate their power as a group or to support a popular manager.

Such is the background of what is known as an informal organization. Status develops within the group, and an undesignated hierarchy can even become apparent. The group itself accepts the leadership of one of its members. Another name for such a group is a clique, and membership is sometimes considered very desirable by employees outside the group. This is particularly true if the clique is thought to have considerable influence within the formal organization.

The manager should be aware of the informal organization; and of course he or she must cope with it, since each informal group tends to establish its own norms regarding work quality and quantity and response or reaction to company policies, procedures, rules, and working relationships with other groups. In this sense the informal organization can influence the effectiveness of goal attainment by the formal organization. The fact that a given manager may have several informal groups within the formal structure under his or her supervision is part of the dynamics of organizational life and one of the challenges of the manager's job.

At times, informal organizations or cliques can cause problems for supervisors. The informal leader may be looked to for advice and assistance by the group, and this leader's influence may be greater than that of the actual supervisor. Significantly, informal leaders do not have formal responsibility for their acts. They do not have to decide who will get raises and promotions or, for that matter, make any critical decisions. However, they can contribute to group cohesiveness and help establish norms of conduct that are acceptable to the formal supervisor. The formal supervisor may also find potential promotables among the informal leaders.

Unity of command

Unity of command means that each person, from the bottom to the top of the organization, has just one boss, and no one but that boss should be giving that person direct orders. In the average business this principle of unity of command—that no person can serve two masters—is violated frequently and flagrantly. Organization structure may be properly designed and policies and procedures carefully set up, and yet the principle on which the whole structure is built—and the principle with which everyone agrees—is violated left and right.

A superior has direct authority and responsibility for his or her subordinates and is responsible for their actions. But if someone else is coming in and giving orders to them, that someone is assuming authority over them, taking the authority away from their boss, and leaving that boss with the responsibility. This is contrary to the principle that authority and responsibility must be coextensive. A person giving orders to someone else's subordinates is violating the chain of command.

Violations of the chain of command make management's job more difficult as well as less effective: The organization structure becomes distorted, authority and responsibility are no longer coextensive, people are taking orders from more than one boss, and there is no accountability for the discharge of duties and responsibilities. The supervisor finds it difficult to plan and organize the work of the department under these conditions. Subordinates can't be directed effectively if someone else is giving them orders or if they can choose to accept one order and reject another. Coordination becomes next to impossible if other people are issuing orders, assigning work, and interfering with the planned flow of work while the supervisor is trying to set up priorities and schedules. Controlling the work of the department becomes impossible when the people who are giving the orders do not have the responsibility for seeing that the orders are carried out.

One of the problems involved in establishing a matrix organization is its violation of the normal chain of command. Any form of organization structure which tends to blur or complicate lines of authority requires considerable education of participants and their acceptance of these changes in familiar authority patterns before it has a chance for effectiveness. There must also be very strong goal orientation on the part of all individuals in the nontraditional type of organization structure.

Violations of the chain of command

The chain of command is violated when one organization member communicates in an official capacity with another who is not an immediate superior, subordinate, or colleague. These violations occur in a number of ways. The big boss comes into a section and tells a worker to do a job. Or someone from a service department tells a worker that a certain job ought to be done. Or a staff specialist gets a line worker to push one of his or her projects. The superintendent may go directly to a trouble spot and instruct the worker to use a different method. The head of another group may come over to see how a job is progressing and start giving the worker orders about it— all this without keeping the person's immediate superior informed. Or a subordinate may go to one or all of these people and ask for directions. Thus numerous people are giving orders to the subordinates of another, and the supervisor is held responsible for work he or she may know nothing about and which may even be contrary to the superior's orders.

In a well-organized business in which authority and responsibility are properly delegated, why are there so many violations of the chain of command? It is because organization merely sets up the framework for unity of command; the business of maintaining unity of command is up to the people concerned and how they perceive their responsibility and do their jobs.

Most of the violations arise from wanting to get things done in a hurry.

The big boss may be in a hurry to get certain things done and be trying to save time by going directly to the worker. Again, the manager may want a particular job done in a certain way, and, to be sure that it will be, thinks that information has to be given to the worker firsthand. Or the big boss, wanting to keep close contact with everyone in the organization, likes to talk things over with the group, and so, before he or she knows it, instead of just discussing jobs and working conditions, orders are being issued on how to do things and what to do next.

Some violations can be charged to ignorance, some to failure to consider the consequences, and some to the ambition of supervisors who are trying to take over the authority for a particular activity in order to enlarge the area of their jobs.

A staff specialist, concentrating on a personal specialty and sometimes forgetting that it is only part of the whole picture, often oversteps bounds and gives orders to the people under the line supervisor.

Finally, a subordinate may short-circuit the superior and seek directions from others. Some of the reasons here could be ignorance, malice, or a desire to promote his or her stock with someone close to the top. Or the reason could lie in the attitude of the boss. This boss may be unapproachable, critical, blustering, or impatient. The subordinate may be afraid to admit ignorance or to insinuate that the boss is not capable of clear expression or might have made a mistake.

The supervisor's view of the short circuit

Supervisors who meet in management training conferences have a great deal to say about violations of the chain of command. They claim that short circuits lower morale in general, reduce the incentive of the person being bypassed, and cause good people to quit. They find that shortcuts across the lines of authority interfere with them in their getting the work out—that a job ordered by an outsider may not be done properly and may actually result in wasted time; that outside interference unbalances the work loads, interferes with scheduling, and defeats the purpose of planning.

When supervisors gathered in training conferences discuss Case 3–1 of this chapter, each person seems to see the case situations existing right in his or her own company. Even though the case has been analyzed by a number of groups and the groups have been made up of supervisors from a variety of organizations, the answers to the questions always fall into the same pattern. To show what experienced supervisors have found to be the causes of violations of the chain of command in their own companies, their analysis of the case is produced here (see the chart which accompanies Case 3–1):

> Situation 1: Why does employee D ask boss A instead of his supervisor U for orders and receive them?
> *Because:*
> Supervisor U is too busy.
> Employee D formerly reported directly to boss A.

U renders poor decisions.

D is seeking recognition.

A and D do not realize the importance of maintaining the chain of command.

U avoids responsibilities.

Situation 2: Why does B, another line supervisor, give orders to employee D?
Because:

B is in a hurry; U is not available.

D is doing an operation in an incorrect or unsafe manner.

Boundaries are not clear-cut between the departments or sections supervised by U and B.

B wants to absorb U's section.

D is wasting materials or time.

D is violating a company rule.

Situation 3: Why does C, a service supervisor, give orders to employee D?
Because:

C sees D abusing equipment.

The distinction isn't clear between the responsibilities of the operating and service departments.

D is using inefficient methods.

U is avoiding his full responsibilities.

C wants to get a special job done in a hurry.

D is doing a job for C in payment for a special favor or job that C has previously done for D.

Situation 4: Why does E, a staff specialist, give orders to employee D?
Because:

E wants to avoid the bother of explaining a project to both U and D.

U does not cooperate with E.

U is permitting staff to usurp his authority.

E forgets that he has no line authority.

E is impatient with going through channels.

E wants to make sure his project is handled promptly and properly.

Situation 5: Why does A, the supervisor's boss, give orders to employee D?
Because:

U is not available.

A likes to keep in close contact with what is going on.

A thinks he is giving advice, while D thinks he is receiving an order.

D and A are old friends.

A does not have confidence in U in relation to a special job.

A does not realize the importance of maintaining the chain of command below him.

Analyzing violations of the chain of command

When supervisors find that the chain of command is being violated or short-circuited, they should study each case of violation and find out the cause—starting with themselves. Are they bottlenecks? Perhaps they are not issuing orders correctly or clearly. Perhaps they are not giving subordinates enough authority and responsibility. Perhaps they have not thought through the job on which they are giving orders. Perhaps they are not explaining the why of each job. Perhaps they are too vague in giving orders or directions, or possibly too precise and detailed.

Are upper level managers short-circuiting them in order to get a true picture of what is going on in the group? Maybe these managers are not being properly informed or are afraid they are not. Perhaps the supervisor is filtering the information that is given to the boss—just relaying the favorable things and suppressing or coloring the unfavorable ones. Perhaps the supervisor needs to find out exactly what the boss wants.

Why are the supervisors running into conflict with the departments that were established to provide service to them? Is there a clear demarcation between the activities of their departments and those of the service departments? Perhaps they are antagonistic. Do they know how to utilize their services in order to do a better job? Do the service departments know supervisory problems? Would an understanding with them clear things up?

As to the staff specialist—does this person realize that he or she is stepping outside established bounds? Because the staff person is close to the top boss, is the subordinate kowtowing and inviting the violation?

Why are the supervisors of other departments interfering with a supervisor's subordinates? Perhaps they are impatient to get things done. Maybe they are after part of that supervisor's job. It may be that the boundaries of the activities of the various departments are not clearly defined.

Why do the supervisor's subordinates accept, allow, or seek directions from someone who is not their boss? Perhaps the supervisor is not giving them the recognition they want and they are seeking it elsewhere. Maybe his or her orders are not clear. Maybe he or she is not approachable or available and is possibly disagreeable. Some of the workers may be out to show the supervisor up and get rid of him or get his job.

Preserving the chain of command

In order to correct and prevent violations of the chain of command, supervisors need to let outsiders know that they run their departments efficiently and that all work must clear through them so that they can route and schedule it. They must be a strong and necessary link in the chain of command and must manage their groups so well that subordinates will not be receptive to orders from outsiders.

Short circuits can often be controlled by good job descriptions and good supervision. The supervisor should examine the job descriptions to see if they:

1. State the purpose of the job and its relationship to other jobs.
2. Carefully define the duties and responsibilities of the job.
3. Define authority in relation *to what, to whom,* and *for whom.*
4. State the standards of work performance.

Supervision can be improved if the supervisor will:

1. Schedule work assignments in advance.
2. Check the progress on work assignments frequently.
3. Distribute work equally.
4. Keep subordinates fully occupied doing the work assigned to them.
5. Train subordinates to report immediately if outsiders assign work to them.
6. Be available for consultation about work assignments.

Flexibility in the chain of command

Maintaining the chain of command does not mean that all information must go all the way to the top of the organization in order to be cleared before it can be acted on. One way that the flow of information on routine matters is sent horizontally is by means of procedures. They follow paths laid out for them at low levels across the organization. But there are other matters, not controlled by procedures, that need to be taken care of by means of informal cross contacts that expedite the exchange of information.

People in separate chains of command need work contacts with one another. They need to get and give advice and information and coordinate their work. It would be impossible for them to take any kind of prompt action on daily problems if each matter had to be carried up the line to a common boss and then back down the other side.

Fayol's bridge. The need for a cross channel was recognized by Henri Fayol in his writings on management in 1916. He was particularly concerned about government agencies and the tendency to send everything up the chain of command for decisions rather than take the responsibility for action. He illustrated his remedy as a plank, "Fayol's bridge," across the lower span of a double ladder representing two chains of command united at the top in a single boss. In the illustration, employee F and employee L are in contact; but the plank is a shortcut to be used at every level in order that people may work together directly and speedily without sacrificing the unit of command.

If F and L were to stick to the channels of the chain of command, the matter of their discussion would have to be sent on a climb up the ladder of authority, stopping at the desks of managers E, D, C, and B on the way to boss A, who would send it down the other side through managers H, I, J, K, and finally to L, who would work on it and send it back up the chain for the return trip. All of this might take months, the time of many people, and the need for great masses of paper work. Fayol emphasized the need for direct contacts at all levels and the necessity for the superior to grant permission for them and to be kept informed of what went on in them.

Channels of communication. In a big organization the channels of the chain of command become overloaded and unable to give expeditious handling to the quantity of information that must be transmitted for the running

Figure 3–1
Fayol's bridge for cross communication

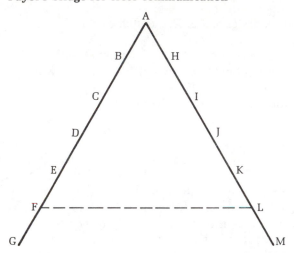

of the business. To improve the situation, upper management establishes channels of communication in which staff specialists perform an active role. Permission to maintain direct contacts with people in other lines of authority is established through policies and executive decisions and through authority and responsibility assignments in the design of procedures. In this way, specialized technical knowledge can be brought to the point of application without being handed down the chain of command from boss to subordinate. And conversely, reports on the performance of the line organization at various levels are sent up the channels of communication in staff reports.

The line mangers' view of these upward reports is colored by the fact that part of the success of staff lies in finding faults in line operations. Staff communications downward may become so heavy that the line supervisor might feel smothered by them. Staff people in direct contact with the supervisor are bringing advice, instructions, and suggestions from personnel, accounting, industrial engineering, production scheduling, quality control, and safety—to name a few.

A policy for cross contacts.   As an example of the way an industry provides the benefits of cross contacts while still protecting the chain of command, the following section is quoted from Jones and Laughlin Steel Corporation's *Organization Planning Guides:*

Channels of Communications

Organization structure defines lines of responsibility and authority, but it should not place restrictions on channels of communication. J&L permits and requires the exercise of common sense and good judgment, at all organizational levels, in determining the best channels of contact necessary for expeditious handling of work. All are urged to follow these simple rules:

1. *In making contacts*
   Be simple, direct, and practicable.
   Use common sense and good judgment.
   Seek rather than demand information.
2. *Keep your superior informed*
   When he will be held accountable.
   When differences of opinion exist.
   When change in policy is involved.
   When coordination with other organization units is required.
   When you need his advice.
   When changes in established policies may result.[6]

Summary

Classical organization theory is still a vital factor in organizational life. Behavioral science concepts have given us many useful insights in the application of traditional concepts to the day-to-day activity of the organization. Among the organization dynamics that are critical to management are delegation, span of control, and the chain of command.

An understanding of various concepts of authority enables the manager to use the formal structure to achieve organizational goals. The authority of position is not enough, for if the manager is to function effectively he or she must earn authority from subordinates by virtue of performance as a manager.

There is little disagreement on the desirability of delegation as a managerial process. Nevertheless many managers are reluctant to use delegation so that they may function as managers in a better manner. Barriers to effective delegation must be overcome if managers are to utilize fully available resources. Increasing the span of supervision to require full-time attention to supervisory duties, plus strong examples of delegation established by higher management, tends to force lower level managers to practice supervision more effectively. One way to widen the span is to delegate more responsibility to subordinates and give them the authority necessary to handle the responsibilities. Delegation does not relieve the delegator of any responsibility, authority, or accountability.

In order to delegate, managers must plan and organize the work, train subordinates to handle it, and set up policies and procedures to guide them and controls to keep track of what is going on. Managers must also overcome a number of barriers that stand in the way of successful delegation and must accept the fact that they are responsible for the subordinate's mistakes and must take the blame for them. If a boss expects perfection and

---

[6] From the *Organization Manual* of Jones and Laughlin Steel Corporation, rev. ed. (1960). Used with permission.

is too harsh about mistakes, too interfering, changeable, or hard to get along with, the subordinate is apt to avoid using the authority.

General, rather than close, supervision is a means of developing capable subordinates and increasing their job satisfaction.

The principle of unity of command is that each person—from the bottom to the top of the organization—should have just one boss, and no one but that boss should be giving the individual direct orders. A person violates (short-circuits) the chain of command when that person gives direct orders to someone else's subordinates.

The manager must contend with the informal organization, usually composed of employees who have a common bond of interest based on the work environment.

The organization provides channels of communication in addition to those of the chain of command. It would be inefficient to send each matter up the line of authority to the top boss, down another line of authority, and then on a return trip to the point of origin. The boss, therefore, gives permission to subordinates to maintain cross contacts with people in other chains of command—just so long as he or she is kept informed and approves of what they are doing.

CASE 3–1

How can you overcome violations of the chain of command?

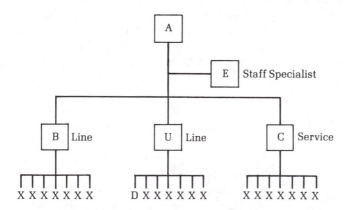

1. *D asks A for orders and gets them.*
    What might be five or six plausible reasons?
    What should U do about each reason?
2. *B gives orders to D.*

What might be five or six reasons?
What should U do about each reason?

3. *C (service) gives orders to D.*
   What might be five or six reasons?
   What should U do about each reason?

4. *E (staff) gives orders to D.*
   What might be five or six reasons?
   What should U do about each reason?

5. *A gives orders to D.*
   What might be five or six reasons?
   What should U do about each reason?

CASE 3–2

The safety engineer has taken upon himself the authority for enforcing the safety rules in your department. He stops in about ten times a day to check up, particularly on the lift truck operators to see if they observe the safety rules. If they are traveling more than five miles an hour in an area where visibility is partially obscured, he stops them and warns them. The people have become antagonistic toward him, and accidents are increasing. Recently he equipped himself with a whistle on which he blew a blast behind a truck that was going faster than the limit allowed. The operator stopped short, and the load fell off and was damaged. To make it worse, one of the cartons came within inches of hitting an employee.

The safety engineer holds you accountable for all of this. He says that the foreman is responsible for the safety of his people.

1. *Is the safety engineer correct in his attitude?*
2. *Is the foreman responsible for the safety of his people? Explain.*
3. *Should the safety engineer take upon himself the authority for enforcing the safety rules? Explain.*

CASE 3–3

Jack Levin has worked for you just three months. He was transferred from another section, and you accepted him since he knew the work and you had an open position. Almost from the beginning you noticed that Jack went out of his way to mingle with upper management. You checked with his previous supervisor and found that Levin had a reputation as a handshaker who sought out middle managers whenever possible.

You felt secure in your position and didn't pay much attention to Levin's antics. One day your boss told you that he was tired of telling Levin that he should discuss any thoughts and problems with you and told you to do something about Levin. Since then, you have admonished Jack Levin on several occasions, and while he doesn't bother your boss any more, he still seeks out other middle managers.

1. *Should you have corrected Jack Levin when you first noticed his behavior?*
2. *What action can you take now?*
3. *Should you discuss it with your superior?*
4. *Can this type of behavior be corrected?*

CASE 3–4

Charlie Stine is one of the brightest young men who has ever worked for you. A graduate of a business school, he came to the company right out of college. After completing the company's training program, he was assigned to your department to work as a senior expediter with responsibility for materials movement through a part of the production process and relationships with the outside suppliers of those materials.

Charlie has great enthusiasm about his work and frequently comes up with excellent ideas. You have used several, giving him full credit for them. Your relationship with him has been excellent, and you consider him a prize catch for your department.

One day at lunch in the plant cafeteria you happen to be seated next to the production manager, and you mention how much Charlie Stine impresses you. In response you get an icy stare from the production manager. "Why don't you find out how he treats people?" he says. You press for more information and find out that Charlie is something of a bull in a china shop when dealing with plant supervisors. He makes arbitrary demands on them and places blame without careful analysis.

Later that same day, one of the typists in your department comes to you to resign. You ask her why and she replies, "Ask Mr. Stine." After you calm her, she tells you that he pressures the typists to get his work out first, with no consideration for other priorities, and that he generally treats the women as servants. She mentions that no one cares for him and that some of the typists have made errors in his work on purpose just to try to trip him up.

Charlie has been with the company just over a year, and you face an annual performance appraisal of his work. What was going to be a pleasant task now takes on problem dimensions.

1. *What should you do about the information from the production manager and the typist?*
2. *How can you handle the appraisal so that Charlie's enthusiasm and ideas will not be lost to the company?*
3. *Why do you think Charlie's relationship with you is apparently so different from his relations with others in the company?*
4. *What might you have contributed to the reasons for Charlie's behavior?*

CASE 3–5

You are the manager of a large clerical department, and seven supervisors report to you. One of these supervisors is causing you a problem because of his lack of appreciation of the responsibilities of supervision. The problem is complicated by the fact that he is an effective supervisor when he chooses to exercise his managerial prerogatives.

The supervisor in question is a senior employee with many years of experience who was promoted to his position as a reward for long service shortly before you came to the department as its manager. He is intent on doing nothing but the routine work and leaving all supervisory matters to wait until he finds it convenient to handle them. Naturally some of them are neglected, and it is this neglect which has caused your problem.

Because this supervisor busies himself so frequently with everyday routine work, he has failed to set disciplinary standards for his subordinates. As a result they are taking longer lunch hours and excessive coffee breaks, making personal telephone calls, and there is frequent tardiness. The other supervisors in your department have complained to you about these infractions, since it is becoming difficult for them to control their employees effectively.

1. *What can you do to motivate this senior employee to assume his supervisory role more effectively?*
2. *Should a senior experienced employee be promoted to a supervisory position as a reward for long service?*
3. *Can this man be returned to a nonsupervisory job in the department?*
4. *How do you handle the complaints of the other supervisors under your jurisdiction?*

CASE 3–6

Frank Benner was the plant manager of a small electronics manufacturing company. He had recently had a heated discussion with the company president about the plant porter. The porter was the lowest paid employee, and it was his job to keep the floors clean in the plant and office, empty trash, keep aisles free from debris, pack shipment, and do general maintenance work. Since the plant was a small one, the porter usually completed his tasks before the workday was over, and when he did, he would occupy himself reading comic books or just do nothing.

In the opinion of the plant manager, the porter performed his tasks efficiently, promptly, and with a good attitude. This was the heart of the discussion Frank had with the company president. After noticing the porter's inactivity on several occasions, the president told Frank Benner that the porter should always be doing something useful, such as learning how to be a wiring technician or a solderer so that he could advance. Mr. Benner told the president that the porter had no interest in learning new or additional duties; he had already tried to teach him other jobs without success. Mr. Benner could not understand the president's desire to push a man who was doing a fine job as a porter and had no ambition. The discussion ended when the president told Frank Benner to fire the porter and hire a more ambitious replacement.

1. *Did the president have an unrealistic level of expectation for the porter?*
2. *What can a supervisor do, if anything, about an employee who is performing his job well but has no ambition?*
3. *Should an employee be criticized because he finishes his work assignment before the end of the workday?*
4. *Was the president justified in forcing the plant manager to fire the employee?*

CASE 3-7

You are in charge of a department employing a large number of men. You have two men working on a project which, when completed, you think will help you expedite production in your department. One day while you are working on this new idea, the superintendent walks by and asks you what they are making. You explain your idea to him. He says it is very good and tells you to go ahead with it.

The next day your immediate supervisor, the general foreman, walks by. He sees the men working on your project, comes to you, and wants to know what they are making and why they are not on some other work directly connected with production. You explain your idea to him. He tells you to discontinue the project and rebukes you for doing that kind of work without first getting his permission. You tell him that you wanted to have it in a more complete form before showing it to him and taking up his time. You also mention to him that the superintendent saw it and told you to go ahead with the job.

The general foreman has always been very obliging as well as considerate and quite friendly toward you. But apparently he is annoyed because you did not tell him of your plans, even though he knows you had good intentions and planned to tell him before anyone else. He says now that *he* is your foreman and you must do as *he* wishes. You comply with his request, and the following afternoon the superintendent pays you a visit to see how you are progressing. He sees that you have stopped the project and asks why.

1. *What would you say to the superintendent?*
2. *If you told him the facts, would you lose your boss's friendship and confidence?*
3. *Is this what we call "short-circuiting"? On whose part?*
4. *What effect would this situation have on the two workmen?*
5. *Explain briefly how this situation could have been avoided.*

CASE 3–8

Recently you were transferred from one branch office of the company to another to relieve Dan Davis, the middle manager, who is being shifted to a recently started branch. He will move within the next couple of weeks, but he is still in charge. He is supposed to be acquainting you with his job but instead is spending his time cleaning up his work. He introduced you as his successor and then left you on your own. You are becoming acquainted with your new subordinates—the first-level supervisors. From what you gather, Davis has delegated a minimum amount of authority and responsibility to these subordinates. There are no job descriptions, but rather complete personnel records are available.

Since you are from another branch of the same company, you are familiar with the overall policies. One of these policies is to delegate authority and responsibility as far down the line as possible. You believe that your predecessor's violation of this policy may be the main reason he is being shifted to the new branch; in a newly formed branch, liberal delegation is not advisable at first.

The company has been turning out a standard product for a long period. This and other conditions indicate that decentralization of authority and responsibility is desirable. You plan to delegate as much authority and responsibility as possible to the first-level supervisors under you.

1. *How would you go about finding out the what, who, where, when, and how of the work of the branch?*
2. *How would you go about delegating authority and responsibility?*

CASE 3–9

Bill Boylan was a college graduate who had successfully completed the company's executive training program. At the time of his completion he was interviewed by the regional manager, who was impressed with Bill's ability and promised him the manager's job in a new branch the company was opening in a suburban city. The branch was going to be both a wholesale distribution center and a retail store for the company's many products. Bill was pleased with the offer and looked forward to the job.

A few weeks before the branch opened, he again met with Joe Flint, the regional manager. At this time he was told that management had decided to give the branch manager's job to Lou Stern, who had been with the company for 17 years and who at present was serving as credit manager in a large branch in the central city. The regional manager went on to say that even though Lou was not a college graduate and had not completed the executive program it was felt that his loyal service for 17 years made him deserving of the promotion. Mr. Flint then mentioned that Bill was young and other opportunities would certainly arise. Bill was offered the assistant manager's post in the new branch and he reluctantly accepted.

It soon became apparent to Bill that Lou was not a very competent manager. He was very autocratic and petty and was constantly creating animosity among the 15 employees in the branch. Because Bill was responsible for the preparation of the weekly branch control report sent to regional headquarters, he found that the branch was running at a loss due to Lou's poor pricing of wholesale sales. He pointed this out to Lou, who replied that these customers were being cultivated and had to be given a price break. Bill became quite unhappy with his job and began thinking about leaving the company for a better opportunity.

One Thursday afternoon Bill was alone in the office he shared with Lou, who was out calling on customers. Joe Flint, the regional manager, came in and started questioning Bill about Lou's performance. Bill felt awkward about talking about his boss, and when Joe pressed him, he merely confined his comments to material known to Mr. Flint, such as the information contained in the branch control reports. He refused to gossip about Lou, telling Flint that he was not responsible for evaluating the performance of his superior. Flint then asked him if he thought he could run the branch. Bill replied in the affirmative, mentioning that he thought he could six months earlier when Joe Flint had first offered the position to him. Flint then replied that Bill should take over effective the next day and that when Lou came back from his customer calls, Bill should fire him. Bill was flabbergasted at this request and protested vigorously, stating that it was Flint's responsibility to fire Lou. Flint replied that he didn't want to see Lou at all because he would only lose his temper.

1. *What would you now do if you were Bill Boylan?*
2. *Why do you think the regional manager did not want personally to fire Lou?*
3. *Should Bill have accepted the assistant manager's job? Having done so, should he now accept the manager's job?*
4. *Do you feel Joe Flint has fallen down on his responsibilities in ways other than his refusal to fire Lou?*
5. *Is an effective superior-subordinate relationship possible between Bill Boylan and Joe Flint?*

CASE 3–10

Until six months ago, you were quite successful in achieving high morale and efficiency in your organization by maintaining close contact with all your employees on the several levels of supervision. Everyone felt that they could drop in on you at any time and discuss their work and personal problems, and many availed themselves of the opportunity. The organization ran smoothly. You were in close contact with the work situations and could render many spot decisions which promoted efficiency.

Six months ago, because your work load and your organization were expanding rapidly, you added another assistant to your staff. You had a choice between Smith and Jones. Smith is a brilliant, aggressive, lone wolf, who often rubs people the wrong way and does not have too much respect for regulations. Jones is well liked by everyone, has average intelligence, follows directions closely, but does not have a great deal of initiative. You chose him for the job instead of the more brilliant Smith.

Since then, owing to the pressure of work, you have been too busy to keep in close touch with the lower supervisors and have been getting more and more of your information from your several assistants. As far as you know, everything is going pretty well in all departments except Jones's. The other supervisors are old-timers and their work is under control.

However, in Jones's department you are getting worried about what might develop. For two months Smith has been dropping into your office quite frequently. You have encouraged the visits because he is a good man and you want to adjust him to his new relationship with Jones. Often you give him a few hints on how to handle a job he is doing for Jones, with the result that he exerts the maximum effort and goes beyond the requirements. However, on any job handled exclusively through Jones, Smith's work is just passable. You ask him about this, and he replies that Jones either does not know how, or does not wish, to lay out a job for him in the best manner. According to Smith, Jones wants his subordinates to do just as they are told and nothing more.

Recently Jones has been complaining to you that Smith is unsatisfactory and that his work, though fundamentally superior, does not coordinate well with the work of the rest of the group, with the result that other jobs often have to be modified to fit Smith's work or Smith's work has to be modified to fit regulations. Smith knows that his work is superior and has been indicating to Jones and others that they had better follow his pattern if they want to keep up the group's efficiency.

1. *What are the issues involved?*
2. *How should you handle Smith?*
3. *How should you handle Jones?*
4. *What are the advantages and disadvantages of the open-door policy?*
5. *What are the advantages and disadvantages of the chain-of-command policy?*
6. *How could the situation have been prevented?*
7. *What are the possible solutions for the problem? Which is the best?*
8. *Can the open-door policy and the chain-of-command policy be integrated? If so, how?*
9. *Formulate a policy to prevent the occurrence of similar situations.*

Chapter 4

Learning objectives

○ *To appreciate the relationships that exist between individuals and organizations*

○ *To understand the sources of conflict, particularly in line and staff relationships*

○ *To appreciate the nature of staff work and its contribution to an organization*

○ *To become more aware of the role of the first-level supervisor and its complexity*

Organizations and individuals

Major topics

Individuals and organizations.

Sources of organizational conflict.

Level of aspiration.

Line and staff relationships.

Expansion of staff.

The service activity of staff.

The advising activity of staff.

The control activity of staff.

The first-level supervisor as a member of management.

Superior-subordinate cooperation.

Cooperating with peer supervisors.

Teamwork, conformity, and conflict.

Relationships between individuals and the organizations they associate themselves with form one of the most popular topics of recent writing and research in management theory. It seems as if a new wheel has been invented. Yet these relationships have been going on for thousands of years, and the organized effort of individuals has given us what we call civilization.

Nevertheless, the characteristics of these relationships are important to every manager on all organizational levels. Each person in management has the task of giving and getting the help that enables people to operate jointly. If managers are to give and get help, they must have a common cause: they must see that they will benefit if the cause is successful and that they will lose if the cause fails. In a business enterprise the "cause" is the attainment of the objectives for which the business exists. In order for the personal aims and ambitions of people to be directed toward achieving the aims of the organization, people must see that they have a stake in its success. Since the objectives of a business can be attained only through group effort, top leadership must organize the team and set up the conditions and rewards for teamwork.

When an organization loses its sense of mission and its ability to direct personal ambitions toward a common goal, the organization is torn apart by strife and contention. The production head who deliberately slows down production on a large order to get even with the sales manager who this manager dislikes, the secretary who breaks the typewriter hoping to get a new one, and the military commander ordering troops to take a useless hill so that he can amass a greater combat record are some examples of individual and organizational goal conflict. A person has only to look at the spontaneous cooperation of people performing wonders in volunteer organizations to realize the amount of waste in business enterprises when frictions and hostilities set people to working against one another. Recognition and analysis of some of the issues involved in teamwork and the nature of cooperation in organizations should be helpful to managers concerned with achieving group goals, reconciling individual differences, and developing their own careers.

Individuals and organizations

It has been said that the person whose personal goals most closely coincide with those of the organization worked for has the greatest chance for achieving success. Formal organizations encourage the individual to accept and perform a job according to methods and desired results chosen by the organization. Ideal employees are those who accept the job description and produce results accordingly.

During the last several years, a number of writers have developed a thesis which places the individual and the organization in conflict. One of these, Chris Argyris, wrote in 1957: "An analysis of the basic properties of

relatively mature human beings and formal organization leads to the conclusion that there is an inherent incongruency between the self-actualization of the two. This basic incongruency creates a situation of conflict,
frustration, and failure for the participants."[1] Obviously the organization
of any group involves common restraints on its members. The very purpose of an organization is to achieve goals collectively which the group
members believe they cannot achieve individually.

To achieve these goals, they accept constraints which they might not if
they were acting as individuals. Individuality and conformity are opposing
forces, and all persons find that certain organizational demands are disagreeable from time to time. Returning from a vacation, getting to work on
time after a late party, and disagreeing with a superior's opinion can all
cause an individual to come in conflict with the organization. It is natural
for people to seek some independence and freedom; but the very fact that
we live in a society implies restraint on some of our actions. Working
with others in an organization, the individual may have to modify or
change some personal goals as he or she seeks the security and greater effectiveness of group achievement.

The emphasis in much recent research seems to be on an organization's
responsibilities to the individuals in that organization. There is no doubt
that such responsibilities exist; yet it must be remembered that individuals
also have responsibilities to organizations. When a person is employed by
a business firm, a mutual relationship is established. The business firm expects the employee to accept reasonable organizational requirements. Presumably the employee is hired to fill a particular opening requiring a
certain amount of knowledge, skill, and experience. The employee filling
this opening is expected to perform adequately. Attendance and punctuality, along with positive response to reasonable orders from superiors, are
also expected. The employee may also be required to exercise some restraint in dealings with outsiders, such as the avoidance of disclosure of
material the company considers confidential. Certain established dress
and behavior patterns are frequently also a part of the conditions of
employment.

In turn, the employer is expected by the employee to pay an adequate
salary or wage and appropriate fringe benefits and to provide a working
environment (including reasonable supervision) which will be conducive
to proper performance of the job. Obviously both parties to this relationship are affected by prevailing economic conditions, the labor market, and
the nature of community cultural values.

Reaching some acceptable relationship between the expectations of individuals and of the company is one of management's critical responsibilities. Compromise solutions to difficulties are frequently the case. For

---

[1] Chris Argyris, *Personality and Organization: The Conflict between the System
and the Individual* (New York: Harper & Row, Publishers, 1957), p. 175

example, in recent years dress requirements have been controversial, and such things as length of hair, beards, sideburns, skirt or dress length, the wearing of pants or slacks by female employees and necktie use by male employees have been causes of conflict. These employers who have tried to maintain a strict conformity to standards which substantially differed from those in existence in the community have had considerable difficulty. Where the employer has been reasonable, the employee has usually responded positively to requests about grooming. If the employer could effectively demonstrate that dress length or hair length was job-related, most employees would go along. Some employers solve the dress problem by furnishing uniforms for certain types of employees. Dress codes have caused the most controversy where they have been determined by higher management without recognition of community realities and implementation was left to first-level supervisors, who found themselves cast in the role of style arbiters with neither qualifications nor desire for such a role.

In some of the literature there is an implication that large organizations are more restrictive of individual initiative than are small enterprises. The "big frog in a small pond" notion is believed to indicate that in smaller organizations the individual has more power. In other words, bigness is the problem. Research, however, seems to indicate that managers believe that large companies provide them with more challenge, satisfaction, and reward than small firms. Apparently large organizations provide much psychological support to go along with the economic support they provide.

In every organization there are malcontents who never seem to be satisfied with their lot. This does not mean that an individual can only succeed if he is a conforming "organization man" who exercises great caution and has traded his birthright for the security of the large enterprise. Robert Dubin, a sociologist, has developed an interesting thesis about man and society. He characterizes man's attachments to the institutions of his society as follows:

> Most men have certain central life interests at any given time focused in one, or at most, several institutional settings. They have to participate in other institutions, but do so in terms of the behaviors required in them, and without reference to the voluntary choices that may be available in them. Thus the areas of voluntary social action are precisely the institutions that are central to a man's life interests and that are therefore at the focus of his attention. . . . Self-realization may, however, be a matter of indifference to people for whom work is not a central life interest. Their self-realization comes in other institutional settings outside the productive institution.
>
> What about those people in industry and commerce for whom work is a central life interest? These are the people who find the fulfillment of their life goals in work itself. They make the work institution central to their lives. The interesting fact is that for such people the work environment is challenging and rewarding. . . . The consequence is that he becomes a real striver in the institutional setting, securing many rewards and often encountering deprivations and frustrations. But this is no different

from the man who experiences his family life as the institutional center of his interests. The point is that there is nothing about the organization of productive work, or the supervision of people doing it, that is so antithetical to human personality needs as to result only in frustration and disappointment.[2]

It becomes apparent that it is difficult to generalize about any particular individual and his or her relationship with an organization. While there are many similarities among the people in a work group, each person perceives work differently and it meets needs shaped very much by a personal value system.

What is significant is the idea that not all people desire autonomy, nor do they want to participate in the activities of management. Many individuals desire direction and prefer to know what is expected of them. The development of an autonomous or participative work climate may stir considerable anxiety and fear in such individuals and destroy the security for which they voluntarily joined the organization.

"My ultimate goal? Retirement."

Reprinted by permission The Wall Street Journal

Individual and organizational goals may differ and cause conflict.

This is not to say that participative managerial techniques are not desirable under certain conditions such as highly creative work in a research laboratory or an advertising agency. It does mean that many individuals can adapt themselves to the needs of the organization, perceive its goals and work productively toward them. In fact the gregarious nature of human beings causes them to associate voluntarily in a variety of groups to achieve group-desired results.

---

[2] Robert Dubin, *Human Relations in Administration*, 4th ed. (Englewood Cliffs, N.J.: Prentice-Hall, Inc., 1974), pp. 126–27.

Herbert Simon adds another dimension to the holistic nature of organizational behavior with what he calls the process of composite decision:

> The central theme around which the analysis has been developed is that organization behavior is a complex network of decisional processes, all pointed toward their influence upon the behaviors of the operatives—those who do the actual "physical" work of the organization. The anatomy of the organization is to be found in the distribution and allocation of decision-making functions. The physiology of the organization is to be found in the processes whereby the organization influences the decisions of each of its members—supplying these decisions with their premises.
>
> It should be perfectly apparent that almost no decision made in an organization is the task of a single individual. Even though the final responsibility for taking a particular action rests with some definite person, we shall always find, in studying the manner in which this decision was reached, that its various components can be traced through the formal and informal channels of communication to many individuals who have participated in forming its premises. When all of these components have been identified, it may appear that the contribution of the individual who made the formal decision was a minor one, indeed.[3]

It can be seen that behavior in an organization is a series of interactions, all accomplishing (with various degrees of success) the purposes of the organization. There are superior-subordinate, peer, line-staff, and many other relationships that make up the daily activity in the organization. That all of these do not always go smoothly is surely an understatement.

Sources of organizational conflict

The very nature of large organizations is apt to discourage spontaneous cooperation. A particularly significant factor is the conflict between teamwork and individualism. One of the primary desires in the business organization is for a smoothly functioning team. A great deal of emphasis is placed on the competitive nature of business and the need for cooperation and loyal teamwork so that the company can succeed in the marketplace. The organization is divided into departments, each concentrating on only one phase of the total operation. This specialization of managerial labor was designed to bring about efficiency, but it also brings about frictions and conflicts between departments. Each department may push its own special interests and resist demands made upon it by other departments. Each feels that its own work is most important, that it knows more about it than anyone else, and that it should protect itself at all costs against encroachments on its territory.

Adding to this conflict is the well-publicized ideal that every employee should be personally ambitious to achieve a good record. Each manager is

---

[3] Herbert Simon, *Administrative Behavior,* 2nd ed. (New York: Macmillan Co., 1957), pp. 220–21.

eager to do a good job as far as his or her own specialty is concerned, because that is how performance is measured. Each may be sincere in thinking that what is good for one's own specialty must be good for the enterprise as a whole. Organizations set up formal devices for coordinating the activities within them; but managerial plans require the efforts of people to carry them out successfully, and people can use their ingenuity either to make the plans successful or to find ways to beat the system.

In a sense individual managers are encouraged to outperform their peers. In fact, they may even be encouraged to outperform their superiors. If they can demonstrate that a person, department, or group is not doing a good job, and they can further point out that they can do a better job themselves, they are usually rewarded by higher management. It becomes apparent that competition and cooperation, individualism and group loyalty, and personal goals and company goals are not necessarily compatible concepts. Conflict within the individual exists also. Very few of our actions and reactions are black and white. All of us have experienced ambivalence quite frequently in our lives. How can a person be honest and not hurt others? When the boss asks for an opinion, should you tell the truth as you perceive it or what you think he or she wants to hear? Can you satisfy a boss who asks you to speed up production, eliminate errors, cut overtime, and keep the workers happy, all in the same breath? Should you tell that boss what you really think or does your desire for personal survival override your desire to be truthful?

In effect, we reach compromise solutions to most of the ambivalent situations we face, and in this manner we resolve personal conflict. The individuals who do not do this generally seek other work where there may be greater compatibility between personal goals and group goals.

Organizations must be concerned with the resolution of conflict in much the same way that individuals are. To keep the parts of an organization working toward company objectives, the structure, policies, procedures, and controls must be designed to make cooperation rewarding. Every manager from top to bottom must be able to see that their personal objectives are closely related to the objectives of the firm. They must understand what is expected of them and their units toward achieving these objectives. They should also know what help they are expected to give to other units and what help they can expect to receive.

When upper management establishes the conditions for teamwork and rewards people for playing their parts on the team, then each person knows what must be learned to give and get the help that it takes to operate as a member of the team.

Level of aspiration

A common bit of American folklore is that anyone can become President of the United States. A moment's reflection will lead to the conclusion that while few of us want to try for that position, the desire to succeed is very much a part of our way of life.

People in all walks of life aspire in varying degrees to better positions and their accompanying higher salaries, status, and other rewards. As was mentioned earlier in this chapter, the very nature of organizational hierarchies encourages some people to seek the next higher job up the ladder. Individuals who aspire to higher positions and express great interest in career advancement are said to have upward mobility. This upward mobility can be both financial and social, involving more income as well as the improved status a better job can give. Certain occupations have higher status than others, and some people may be encouraged to change occupations to achieve a status goal.

In general, supervisory and management positions have both financial and social status, thereby having built-in factors which encourage individual upward mobility. The extent to which any person is prepared to work and undertake a program of self-development is called one's level of aspiration. It is hard to define in concrete terms, since even a given individual may not know what it is while he or she is in the process of achieving higher goals. It is not unusual for a person to change his or her level of aspiration many times during a career, based on achievements to date and what are perceived as needs at a particular time.

Individual levels of aspiration are difficult to measure and most attempts at evaluation are subjective judgments. These are usually based on experience and what the particular individual demonstrates by work performance, willingness to assume greater responsibility, quality of relationships with others in the organization, along with self-development. The individual's personal life in respect to material things as well as social relationships may also be part of the measurement process. Attitude about the job, the company, and the broader aspects of our society may be useful indicators as well. In any event, level of aspiration is closely related to the complexities of personality of the individual. While these may be difficult to completely understand, the outward signals an individual communicates can give some indication of his level of aspiration.

Line and staff relationships

The lack of clear distinction between line and staff activities mentioned in Chapter 2 can cause conflict in an organization. The idea of relative importance to the entire enterprise of each department is certainly a basis for possible differences of opinion, and when this is combined with authority relationships, then conflict can result. In many organizations staff people tend to be younger and have more formal education than many line supervisors and managers. These line managers were most likely promoted from within and learned their jobs through many years of experience. Obviously conflict can occur if a young staff person tries arbitrarily to introduce ideas or methods with which the line supervisor does not agree. Often this staff person may be an "assistant to" a high-level manager. Even though this staff person has no direct authority, an assistant to a major executive can carry implied authority. Some line managers may find it difficult to question this type of authority.

It must be pointed out that staff functions can be performed by line managers. The production manager may give advice to the sales manager on the particular benefits of a new product which the sales manager may or may not use in the development of a sales program for that product. Developing an understanding of the usefulness of many staff activities is one of the line manager's many responsibilities. A recognition that both line and staff people work for the same organization can help resolve conflict.

Expansion of staff

Staff departments tend to grow in size and authority. In times of general expansion, when problems increase in size and complexity, staff tends to take more and more activities from the line. For example, the personnel department might start out primarily as a recordkeeping and recruiting agency for the line organization. Then in a period of rapid expansion complicated by human relations problems, personnel might be authorized to handle all the company's hiring, firing, transfers, raises, and discipline.

Theoretically, staff has no authority over line. Actually, authority relationships develop in a number of ways. Line managers are required to conform to policies and procedures (purchasing procedures, for example) set up and administered by staff agencies. Or line managers may surrender authority to staff by handing over unpleasant duties (discipline, for instance), or by making a habit of accepting staff advice rather than taking the responsibility for decisions contrary to it. On the other hand, staff specialists may be authorized to issue orders in the name of their line superior. Or they may just assume authority and start giving directions to line people. Or management might, wittingly or unwittingly, shift an activity over from line to staff simply by saying, "That's a good idea. Go out in the plant and put it into effect."

Some shifting of the balance between line and staff is necessary to make adjustments to meet changing conditions. An organization should be flexible enough to distribute power in a way that meets the demands of the moment. But shifting must be controlled so that the organization continues to serve the purpose for which it was intended.

Line employees in a training conference set up the following criteria by which to judge whether there is too much or too little staff in an organization.

Indications of too little staff	*Indications of too much staff*
Line people doing a great variety of tasks.	Too much paper work.
Faulty or nonstandard procedures.	Too many conferences.
No innovations.	Too many coordinators.
Lack of planning.	Too many changes.
Lack of progress; stagnation.	Too many opinions.
Poor coordination.	Too many people involved in decisions.
Upper management always asking for reports.	Too many people being hired and no corresponding increase in output.
Going outside the firm for information and assistance.	

The service activity of staff

Activities such as purchasing, maintenance, engineering, and personnel are turned over to staff specialists to get the benefit of their particular skills, the economy of centralized handling, or the uniformity needed in company-wide application. Staff people render services, but conflicts sometimes develop between them and the line people receiving the services. Staff and line people have trouble working together because they have different backgrounds, different bosses, and different outlooks. Each sees the situation from a personal angle and may not understand the problems of the other. One such trouble area concerns relations between the production and the maintenance departments. A machine operator on an incentive wage may abuse the equipment but then expects the maintenance department to deliver immediate and top quality repair service; the operator's earnings depend upon it. The line supervisor has to get the work out on time. If a machine breaks down, rush repairs are demanded. But the maintenance department has to spread its service throughout the plant. Its efficient operation depends on regular scheduling to eliminate or reduce emergency calls. In most cases it can't do a perfect job for each one. Within the limitations of time and budget it has to compromise and give an average service. The shop supervisor complains, "If maintenance kept the machines in good repair, they wouldn't break down so often." The maintenance supervisor answers, "If your people oiled their machines and kept them clean, they wouldn't break down so often." What hasn't been settled is: *Who* should clean and oil the machines?

Conflicts of opinion in an organization are normal and desirable in that they bring trouble spots out into the open and keep people and departments from getting too far out of line. But there must be a plan and a pattern by which people can work out their differences in terms of the good of the organization. Otherwise conflicting interests build up into personal hostilities and set people and departments to opposing one another as a matter of habit.

The advising activity of staff

Technical staff specialists may serve line management in a number of ways. The service function of staff was discussed above. The advice-giving and controlling functions of staff also need line-staff teamwork to make them effective. Since a staff department—personnel, engineering, or quality control, for instance—may operate in all three capacities at one time or another and provide service, advice, and control, misunderstandings arise over the authority staff employees are exercising. Are they performing a service for which the responsibility and authority were delegated to them by upper line management? Or are they exercising a control over some action of line management? That is, have they been given the authority (again by upper management) to check up on, regulate, or ensure compliance with some particular policy or procedure or method? Or are they giving information or advice to the line? If they are giving advice, then the line is free to accept or reject it, because in the advisory capacity staff has no authority over the line but must "sell" its proposals for improvements.

Technical staff specialists are brought into an organization because line management does not have the specialized knowledge or the time or objectivity to carry on extensive investigations into the possibilities or merits of new ideas. Staff people are essentially idea-oriented individuals who concentrate specialized attention on specific areas. They provide line management with information and advice in the form of plans, policies, procedures, techniques, methods, and systems designed to improve the line manager's performance without taking over the job or relieving the manager of the responsibility for getting results. Staff improves methods, establishes standards, and works out plans for reducing costs.

The authority that staff has is delegated to it by the line manager to whom the head of a staff specialty reports. Staff's closeness to higher management carries a certain implied authority that makes lower line managers cautious about refusing staff advice. Even if the staff employees have no direct authority to force the line supervisor to take their advice, they do have a type of informal authority that is accorded to them because they are experts and because they can sell ideas persuasively.

First-line supervisors sometimes complain that they are swamped by staff—that each staff department is promoting its specialty and pushing to get its ideas adopted. Supervisors in training conferences claim that even if they had the time they couldn't possibly adopt all the ideas from staff because some contradict or are incompatible with others—that the several staff departments don't get together to integrate their various proposals and fit them to the line operations.

One explanation for the situation is that the staff person's performance is measured by the *number* of improvements that he or she is able to install for the line. If a staff department must justify its existence (and it is overhead expense), the way to do it is, unfortunately, by exposing problems and difficulties occurring in the line and needing staff's attention. Staff's need to "look good" on reports is a stumbling block to line-staff cooperation.

Line supervisors in some companies complain that the personnel department is making decisions that should be made by the line.[4] Personnel people say that line supervisors shirk their responsibilities and turn over to them the undesirable parts of their jobs. A line supervisor is avoiding responsibilities if he or she turns over to personnel unpleasant disciplinary duties or if the supervisor says to a subordinate, "I'd like to get you a raise, but all that is now handled by the wage and salary administration people." But a study of both sides of the problem can be expected to bring about a better understanding of the job that each is to do and the accommodations each must make in working together.

The staff employee needs to maintain a good working relationship with the line by understanding line problems in order to give the kind of help the supervisor needs. "Helpfulness" is defined by the receiver rather than by the giver. Line supervisors must *see* that they have been helped before they will turn to staff as a source of help. There will be conflicts of interest as staff brings in new ideas and challenges the old. There will be conflicts of viewpoint. Conflicts of ideas are necessary and desirable if present ways of doing things are to be improved and if proposed ways of doing things are to be evaluated. Conflicts should be recognized, analyzed, discussed, and resolved in a way that enables people to work together for the good of the organization.

The control activity of staff

The control activity of staff often produces conflicts, because people don't like to be restrained or checked up on or reported up the line. For example, in inspection, inspectors are the people who pass on the quality of the operator's work. They are sitting in judgment, and their decisions may influence the operator's pay. As far as the operating group goes, the inspector is not one of the gang, and the situation may deteriorate to the point where inspector and operator are pitted against each other—the inspector trying to prevent work from getting through, and the operator trying to slip it by. Under these circumstances, line operators do not feel responsible for

---

[4] See Dalton E. McFarland, *Cooperation and Conflict in Personal Administration* (New York: American Management Assoc., 1962). This study, based on interviews with personnel executives and chief executives, reports on the scope of employee relations functions, the wide varations in the amount of authority exercised by the personnel director, and the processes by which line and staff accommodate to one another. See also Maynard N. Toussaint, "Line-Staff Conflict: Its Cause and Cure," *Personnel*, May–June 1962, and his "Problems of Maintaining Uniform Personnel Practices," *Personnel*, September–October 1962. Both articles are based on a study of the authority exercised by various industrial relations departments. For an excellent chapter on personnel as a staff function, see George Strauss and Leonard R. Sayles, *Personnel: The Human Problems of Management*, 3d ed. (Englewood Cliffs, N.J.: Prentice-Hall, Inc., 1972), pp. 348–70.

maintaining the quality of the product; they will let somebody else worry about the mistakes.

In its control capacity, the industrial relations staff may have the responsibility for obtaining compliance with companywide policies and procedures for dealing with labor matters, but if it issues direct commands to the line supervisor or threatens to discipline them for failure to conform, the result is hostility. This shouldn't be necessary if the line organization agrees with labor policies and procedures. The staff person should work *through* the line rather than *on* it in getting individual compliance. Staff doesn't get into the situation of giving orders to a line supervisor if the line supervisor's boss will do it. Teamwork between line managers and the labor relations staff is improved when supervisors are consulted about provisions in the labor contract—when they get the training and information they need to understand labor policies and to handle their jobs of administering the provisions of the contract.

The first-level supervisor as a member of management

The first-level supervisor's place on the management team is sometimes a disputed one. In some companies supervisors are not treated as members of management but are regarded—and regard themselves—as just an in-between group. In this situation they are very apt to feel that (1) they have no stake in management and no responsibility to support its programs for increasing output, reducing costs, or improving methods; (2) they have no chance of advancing in management; (3) they are powerless to get action in matters affecting their work groups; (4) they had better look out for themselves. The work group may even reject the supervisor if they feel the person is powerless to do anything for them. When supervisors are in this in-between position, they will look first to their own protection and later—if at all—to the good of the organization.

The supervisor who identifies with his or her employees rather than with management may try to win favor with these employees by relaxing discipline or going easy on production goals. Then when the superior pressures the supervisor for production, the employees will most likely resent this change of behavior as the pressure is passed along to them. This supervisor loses their confidence, as he or she already has lost the confidence of upper management. The supervisor has to try to cultivate a dual loyalty, learning how to reconcile the conflicting interests and needs of those above with those he or she supervises.

The management-mindedness asked of first-level supervision is that they orient to the good of the organization—that their personal objectives be in line with those of the organization. The supervisor's objectives must be those of the boss, but the techniques for achieving them will necessarily be different. The boss's techniques are designed for managing managers; the first-level supervisor is managing nonmanagement people.

Subordinates don't have management attitudes or management objectives. The supervisor belongs to two organizational families: one as the leader of a work group and the other as a member of the management group. The job of getting subordinates to work for management objectives makes conflicting demands on personal loyalty—demands that higher level managers don't have to face. The supervisor must be close enough to subordinates to see their point of view and be accepted as their leader. He or she must be loyal to them in order to win their loyalty. He or she is dependent upon their willingness to cooperate. They in turn depend upon the supervisor to help them get what they want from the job. He or she must champion the group and still keep a balance between their personal objectives and the company's objectives.

Middle management must foster those things that build the management stature of first-level supervision. If they are to feel and act like members of management, they must be treated as managers. Their financial success must be tied to management objectives. They must be given the backing they need to reinforce their positions as leaders of work groups. They should be kept informed about management plans and the reasons for them and should have opportunities to participate in management decisions. They should be included in training conferences that bring supervisors and their bosses together. Thre is little point in training supervisors to do things that are against the beliefs or orders of their superiors. Reducing the social distance between supervisors and their bosses helps to build relationships of mutual trust that are essential to teamwork. Supervisors need "influence" with their bosses in order to look after the interests of the work group and get action on the legitimate requests of their subordinates.

The short circuit.   The short-circuit violation of the chain of command described in Chapter 3 is one of the principal trouble areas for first-level supervisors. Where the supervisor has no formal management training and is expected to be a productive worker as well, the difficulty is compounded. In effect, the nature of the job requires the supervisor to continue to function as a technician and give less attention to supervision. When problems arise, the employees concerned seek out the individual who can make decisions and offer solutions. If this is not forthcoming from their immediate superior, they seek out the supervisor's boss.

When this happens with any frequency, the first-level supervisor is effectively short-circuited, and the middle manager is performing the supervisor's role. This frequently leads to an expansion of the middle manager's staff to enable the handling of the increased load. Quite naturally the middle manager takes on such responsibilities as discipline, salary recommendations, performance evaluation, promotions, probation decisions, and terminations. In short the first-level supervisor has become a weak authority symbol and is really only a lead worker.

To overcome this, there must be clear understanding between the first-level supervisor and middle management as to what responsibilities and authority each has. Otherwise the organization is paying individuals for supervision who are simply not functioning as supervisors.

Superior-subordinate cooperation

Supervisors have no way of knowing what their bosses expect from them unless they hear it from the bosses themselves, but in many cases the boss fails to get the information across. Surveys indicate that there is often a serious lack of agreement between superior and subordinate as to the subordinate's job: the extent of supervisory authority,[5] the duties to be performed, their relative importance, the qualifications needed to perform them satisfactorily, the obstacles to contend with, and the changes that can be expected to affect the job (and therefore the planning) in the next few years.[6]

Some conclusions to be drawn from these surveys are: (1) the superiors have been mistaken in assuming that their subordinate supervisors see eye to eye with them, (2) that superiors are making decisions without having sufficient information about what's going on at the work level, (3) that there should be some provisions for discussing job problems, exchanging information, and arriving at a better understanding of what middle managers expect of their subordinates, how well they think they are measuring up, and how they can give them the help they need.

When supervisors in training conferences are asked what kind of help they want from the boss, their lists reveal a need to put the relationship on a personal basis. They want the boss to:

1. Back up the subordinates' decisions.
2. Tell subordinates what is expected of them and how they are doing.
3. Give recognition for work well done.
4. Be interested in subordinates as people—make them feel they belong.
5. Provide good leadership and be competent for the job.
6. Give constructive criticism.
7. Tell the why of jobs.
8. Follow the chain of command.
9. Pass along information—both up and down the line.

---

[5] Lee E. Stern, "The Foreman's Job: What Are the Boundaries?" *Supervisory Management,* vol. 3, no. 7 (July 1958), pp. 15–23. The article is based on a survey of 187 first-line foremen and their bosses reported by Chester E. Evans in *Supervisory Responsibility and Authority* (American Management Assn. Research Report No. 30, 1957). Most of the foreman interviewed considered their authority more limited than their bosses reported it to be.

[6] Norman R. F. Maier, L. Richard Hoffman, John J. Hooven, and William H. Read, *Superior-Subordinate Communication: A Statistical Research Project* (American Management Assn. Research Study No. 52, 1961). The researchers interviewed 58 superiors in high middle management and a subordinate of each, and found only a little more than 50 percent agreement on the subordinate's job duties, and much less agreement than that on job requirements, obstacles to performance, and future changes to be expected.

10. Get raises for deserving subordinates and for the workers they recommend.
11. Have confidence in the ability of subordinates.
12. Recognize the difficulties in getting jobs done.
13. Take the responsibility rather than pass the buck.
14. Make good decisions.
15. Be loyal to the subordinates and to the company.
16. Train subordinates—teach them the tricks of the game.
17. Delegate authority equal to responsibility and make clear the extent of it.
18. Welcome ideas and opinions; let subordinates have a voice in decisions.
19. Don't play favorites; be fair.
20. Help subordinates in problems beyond their depth.
21. Carry up the line problems of subordinates that require higher level solutions.
22. Understand the problems of the subordinates' work groups.

But when these supervisors who want too much from their bosses are asked what they want from their own subordinates, the list is short and it boils down to three main items: performance, loyalty, and information. Since the superior-subordinate relationship is the one through which the organization's work is done, it is important that there be a way to find out what each wants, needs, and expects from the other.

The supervisor's boss can provide for this exchange of information and have vastly improved relationships with subordinates if that boss will include them in problem solving and decision making. The boss who is able to lead a problem-solving conference will find that the techniques of case study learned in a training program can be applied to the solution of departmental problems. Ingenious decisions are worked out in discussions in which supervisors feel free to contribute information and opinions, to thrash out differences, to suggest and evaluate solutions, and to select the most practical solution on the basis of their knowledge of operating problems. There are several important by-products from such get-togethers. The discussion that is a part of problem solving provides an opportunity to exchange information about job duties and impending changes; it serves to remove misunderstandings and fears and hostilities that come from lack of information; it motivates a subordinate to carry out the decision as a personal one rather than one that was thrust upon the supervisor.

Decisions handed down by top management (cost cutting, rules, policies, and so on) become more palatable if the boss gives subordinate supervisors an opportunity to discuss and decide upon the best way to carry them out. Not every problem can or should be hashed out with subordinates. There just isn't time, and some problems are so tied in with unpublished plans that they can't be put out for free discussion. The boss can still make use of coordination meetings to announce decisions, fix responsibilities, set deadlines, and let individuals know what is expected of them, as well as to listen to their problems, ideas, and opinions.

Presumably the common wisdom dictates that the first-level supervisor represents management to the employee and the employee to management. If the supervisor is able to develop a cohesive work group that is meeting production or other goals, higher management is well advised to allow the supervisor to do the job—that is, to devote most of the time to supervision and upward communication as a representative of the group, a task for which the supervisor is uniquely qualified—and then to allow such autonomy as is necessary to handle the group as he or she sees fit.

Cooperating with peer supervisors

Supervisors who are supposed to work together are annoyed with one another a great deal of the time. The very nature of their contacts can easily lead to conflict. When one supervisor contacts another, it is to complain about some failure of the other or to demand something that is going to cause extra work for the other. Supervisory success depends upon the departments that precede a supervisor's department in the order of operations and on the departments that render service to the department. Naturally, the supervisor demands that those departments deliver the work on time and in satisfactory condition. And when those departments see that supervisor coming or hear that person on the phone, they start working up a good offense as the best defense.

Much of the communication between supervisors is by telephone, memo, or a hurried stop-in at the other person's department, interrupting a particular supervisor at a busy time. There is seldom enough personal contact—enough opportunity to find out that the other person is not so bad and might even be likable if met somewhere else.

One of the great benefits of having management training conferences is that they bring supervisors together for something other than complaints and making demands on one another. Conferences give them a chance to become acquainted with each other and to study each other's problems in an atmosphere of comparative calm. A good-natured discussion of a trouble zone between departments may reveal that what looks like a power grab in one case and like a "refer to Jones" in another is actually a matter of overlap and void in the assignment of duties—one duty has been assigned to both of them and the other duty to no one. Perhaps there has never been a clear boundary between the two jobs, and the lack of definition of their duties and authorities has brought about an overlapping and inefficiency that has been a source of continual irritation or conflict.

At the start of a series of conferences for supervisors, there will probably be some sparring, some feeling out of other people, and some caustic remarks made to get a load off the chest. Then, as problems are discussed, the supervisors see that the other person has troubles, too. They begin to have ideas of how to help each other and gradually they begin to work cooperatively on those problems that have been causing conflicts. The relationship built up in problem-solving sessions carries over into other areas. For instance, supervisors can get together to study an accident or injury that happened in one department and, by applying their findings to other departments, prevent such accidents from happening there.

Supervisors say that getting together in supervisory clubs, safety committees, and company social events promotes cooperation. When supervisors get to know one another better, they are willing to go more than halfway to reduce the conflicts on the job. Then they are more apt to be in a frame of mind to understand one another's problems, to help work out solutions for them, and to regulate their own work so that they will be helping their fellow supervisors instead of putting obstacles in their paths.

Supervisors say they would like to have cooperative relationships with their peer supervisors in which all of them would be willing to:

1. Exchange ideas and information.
2. Have work completed on time for the next supervisor.
3. Give and take constructive criticism.
4. Keep one another informed about new procedures, policies, and rules.
5. Respect one another's authority.
6. Achieve uniformity in the interpretation of policies and enforcement of rules.
7. Try to understand one another's problems.
8. Render necessary assistance to one another
9. Straighten out differences in private and among themselves rather than carry them to the boss.
10. Refrain from putting one another on the spot.
11. Practice teamwork and refrain from passing the buck.
12. Show loyalty to the company and respect for its policies.

Teamwork, conformity, and conflict

There are some who confuse genuine teamwork with conformity. Likewise, any emphasis on teamwork could be interpreted as a condemnation of conflict. Neither case is true. Every organization tends to develop some conformity among its members through the development of objectives, policies, and procedures. These are necessary if there is to be a reasonably unified approach toward organizational goals. Similarly, conflict is detrimental to the organization only when it subverts these goals. If it absorbs resources and efforts without any productive result, it obviously has to be eliminated. On the other hand, conflict can be useful in an organization. In fact it can encourage teamwork of the best kind. Assuming that teamwork is a series of interactions among people in the organization, then some conflict is bound to result.

Role conflict. One cause of conflict is based on the expectations individuals have about their supervisor's behavior. For instance, they may expect the supervisor to bend rules for them so that an infrequent lateness is not recorded or to be allowed to leave early for personal reasons. At the same time the supervisor's boss may be expecting costs to be monitored carefully and productivity to increase. There may even be a drive on lateness and absenteeism. The supervisor's peers may expect some assistance in getting work out even to the extent of borrowing some employees.

Supervisors are always facing conflicting expectations from peers, subordinates, and superiors. To remain effective, they must deal with these role conflicts in some way. One possibility is to place organizational goals as indicated by superiors at the forefront and handle peer and subordinate expectations using the organizational goals as the reference point. Another possibility is to identify with subordinates and allow them to break rules occasionally and cover up for them. This approach requires considerable cooperation of all subordinates so that productivity will not decline too noticeably. The supervisor may also try to satisfy all groups by reacting to each as they expect and hoping there won't be any cross checking.

Another type of role conflict is worth mentioning. It arises in informal organizations when group pressures may conflict with an individual's desire to work harder than the group norm. The group taking a longer than usual lunch hour may ridicule the individual who wants to return to work early. There are a variety of possibilities for role conflict in informal groups. That is why it is desirable for the formal supervisor to be fully aware of the existence of the informal organization and to monitor its behavior.

Win-lose conflict. A particularly destructive type of conflict occurs between groups when they believe there is a win-lose situation. Each group believes they can win, and there is grim determination to prove it. Group conflicts usually do not start this way. A series of minor incidents over a period of time among the various group members can deteriorate if nothing is done by either of the supervisors concerned. Finally the inevitable straw that breaks the camel's back occurs, and the two supervisors have a confrontation. The battle lines are drawn and each side wants to win. Even when solutions are proposed, each group tends to exaggerate differences and pay little attention to potential agreement. Pressure is placed on each supervisor by their respective groups to hold out to the bitter end. Little desire exists on either side for a compromise solution, and the conflict frequently has to be resolved by a higher level of management. A close scrutiny of the list of cooperative relationships that supervisors desired, mentioned earlier in this chapter, will surely indicate areas that could give rise to conflict. Successful resolution of this conflict, however, can result in effective and desirable organizational change. Such is the raw material of progress. Rensis Likert points out that effective organizations have extraordinary capacity to handle conflict. He mentions that their success is due to three very important characteristics:

1. They possess the machinery to deal constructively with conflict. They have an organizational structure which facilitates constructive interaction between individuals and between work groups.

2. The personnel of the organization is skilled in the processes of effective interaction and mutual influence. (Skills in group leadership and membership roles and in group building and maintenance functions.)

3. There is high confidence and trust among the members of the organization in each other, high loyalty to the work group and to the organization, and high motivation to achieve the organization's objectives. Confidence, loyalty, and cooperative motivation produce earnest, sincere, and determined efforts to find solutions to conflict. Thre is greater motivation to find a constructive solution than to maintain an irreconcilable conflict. The solutions reached are often highly creative and represent a far better solution than any initially proposed by the conflict interests.[7]

Last, teamwork requires an environment which will support it. This means that all of the managerial actions must make it desirable for the individual to be a team player. If the individual does not fully understand this he will most surely revert to individual survival goals.

A large multiproduct rubber manufacturer expected each of its wholesale salespersons to meet a territorial quota every month. The company also had regional quotas encompassing the territorial quotas of several salespersons. Many regional managers complained that regional quotas for individual products were not met on a monthly basis because of the company's policy of not making the salesperson aware of the regional quota and the contribution of individual sales efforts to that quota. By natural inclination and established practice a salesperson would delay reporting a sale of batteries, for instance, if he or she had already reached the battery quota in the territory for that month. This would allow the individual to start off the next month with a cushion in that product category. Because of this widespread behavior among the sales force, monthly regional quotas in product categories might not be reached and the regional manager was required to file an explanatory report with headquarters. The managers found this distasteful, since they knew the real reason but could do little about it. Despite a regional manager's efforts to encourage teamwork, the company policy in a sense forced the sales representatives to be concerned only with their own performance.

The middle manager is often cast in the role of "person-in-between" in the implementation of a poorly formulated policy. The manager finds it difficult to develop a cohesive work force, yet must satisfy the wishes of superiors by adhering to policy. Teamwork, in this instance, would require a free

---

[7] Rensis Likert, *New Patterns of Management* (New York: McGraw-Hill Book Co., 1961), p. 117

and open exchange of information with evidence given to higher management that company policy is minimizing the development of team spirit.

Summary

Organizations and individuals need each other. Each has a responsibility to the other as a part of the employment contract, and their efforts are not incompatible. Reasonable supervision and an effective working environment are desired by individuals, and most respond positively to this type of treatment. The level of aspiration of an individual, while difficult to measure, is nevertheless an important factor in his or her reaction to organizations.

The aims of an organization can be achieved only through the cooperative efforts of people. In a big organization, people are separated from one another by the particular interests and aims of their specialties, by their levels in the managerial hierarchy, and by divisions into managerial units. If their efforts are not joined together in a common purpose in which each has a stake, they may be working against one another—at the expense of one another and the company.

Even though there are situations where individuals and organizations conflict, this is not necessarily detrimental to either party. Progressive change can result from such conflict if it is handled effectively. While some writers believe the restraints imposed by organizations on individuals are negative, there are many people who prefer and accept the requirements of the organization in exchange for the more orderly existence it affords them.

There are several factors which are widely accepted in organizational life but which are sources of conflict. Among these are competition and cooperation, teamwork and individual ambition, staff advice and line responsibility, and group goals and individual goals.

Top management must set up the kinds of structure, system, policies, and rewards that make it possible and mutually beneficial for people to work together cooperatively. People must see that they can attain their own objectives more fully through working for the objectives of the company, and that they need each other's help to do it. In order for people to help one another, they must be formed into teams, and the teams must be joined in a common effort toward company objectives in which they can see a benefit to themselves.

If individuals realize that each can gain from helping the other, they will establish better ways of working together. Then differences in background, training, interest, and point of view can be made to contribute to the success of the organization rather than be a source of discord. Each person has a position to play on the team, and an individual's success depends upon the help of others. Line managers must learn how to get the kind of staff help they need. Staff people must learn about the line manager's needs and problems in order to be a source of help to the line. Each boss must find out subordinates' needs, problems, and expectations and give help as needed in order to get the help the *boss* needs. Supervisors must find out how to help one another so that they can all profit from team accomplishment.

To be successful, teamwork requires a supportive environment and careful nurturing by all levels of management. There must be a free exchange of ideas and opinions, since teamwork is really a series of interactions. Because individuals are usually rewarded for their own performance, they must be fully informed on how their performance relates to group goals.

CASE 4–1

Several of your fellow supervisors are very closely associated with one another both on and off the job. They belong to the same fraternal organization, and their families visit back and forth a great deal. In fact, they might be considered a clique. They favor one another on the job in relation to maintenance, supplies, and priorities of work. This results in their having better production records than yours.

1. *Are they justified in their action? Explain.*
2. *Should you try to get into the clique? Explain.*
3. *Should you complain to your boss? What arguments could you give?*
4. *How could such a situation have been avoided?*
5. *Who should correct it? How?*

CASE 4–2

Carter Industries is a large corporation engaged in a variety of businesses and is commonly known as a successful conglomerate. Each of the individual businesses is organized as a wholly owned subsidiary with its own officers and board of directors. The individual businesses are organized into groups of similar companies such as the retail group made up of several retail chains owned by Carter. Each president in a group reports to a group executive vice president at Carter headquarters in Los Angeles. This group executive will have several individual company presidents reporting to him or her.

Sally Martin is the president of one company in the retail group. It is a chain of 27 women's apparel stores located in several midwestern states. Six months ago Martin hired a financial vice president for the retail chain. Phil Swanson had an excellent background in finance and several years experience in other retail organizations. He had impressed Sally Martin with his enthusiasm and good ideas about what he would do in his new job. Phil became the financial vice president, and although not a member of the chain's board of directors he attends every director's meeting and is an officer of the company.

Sally Martin is now having second thoughts about her choice of Phil Swanson. Her relationship with him has been deteriorating lately. Martin's negative opinion derives from Swanson's attitudes and behavior. He thinks of the retail chain as a separate entity and can't seem to see the overall picture and the fact that the chain is one of several in the retail group reporting to Carter headquarters. Even Phil's social conversation revolves around something he has done to show how important he is. Comments such as, "They don't know what they are doing," and "You aren't doing your job if you allow them to do that," have been particularly annoying to Sally Martin. Phil Swanson's lack of identification with Carter Industries decreases his effectiveness to the point where he declines to take on assignments under the pretext that they should be done in Los Angeles. Sally Martin has commented on Phil's negative attitudes and the fact that some of his complaints are not even in his area of responsibility. Swanson has taken these comments as a personal insult and responded with periods of childish silence.

Sally Martin knows that Swanson has considerable ability and is an expert in retail finance, but she wonders how long she can tolerate his negative attitudes about the parent company.

1. *How can Sally Martin deal with this problem?*
2. *Why might Swanson feel that some things could be done at Carter headquarters?*
3. *Why would an individual criticize overall company goals when working for a subsidiary?*
4. *Can a person with Swanson's parochial attitudes be successful in a large, complex organization such as Carter?*

CASE 4–3

Fred Smith had been with the company for five years when he was chosen to be a union steward representing his work area in negotiations with management on grievances and other matters relating to the collective bargaining agreement. For three years he served his co-workers well, did a good day's work on his job, and earned the respect of both employees and management.

Recently Fred was asked if he wanted a promotion to the salaried work force out of the bargaining unit. Management offered him the promotion because of his dedication and fairness in his work as union steward and they believed he would make an excellent supervisor. Fred thought it over, and even though it would mean giving up union membership, he decided to accept the promotion to the quality control department. He was ambitious and this was the first rung up the ladder. Besides, he had enjoyed dealing with management and felt he could do well as a supervisor.

Now Fred is finding out that he is not being accepted by some peer supervisors who look upon him as a union spy. Some of his former peers in the bargaining unit feel he is being too harsh on them in his new role as quality control supervisor. Fred believes he is following the same fair and even-handed approach he used when he was a union steward and can't understand why he is now having difficulty with those same people.

1. *Should a person who has been a union steward be made a first-level supervisor?*
2. *Should such a person receive some training and orientation to the new role before being promoted?*
3. *What are some obstacles Fred may have to overcome in relation to management? In relation to former peers?*
4. *What are some advantages and disadvantages to a supervisor who has been a union steward?*

CASE 4–4

Herb Townes had been the division manager for 20 years, and he was now a year from retirement. For the past seven years, Dick Denton had been working as his assistant. Dick was in his early 30s, and during the time he worked for Townes, they had developed what could be called a father-son relationship. Herb was married and had one child, a daughter, now grown and living in a distant city.

Herb was openly grooming Dick to be his successor and had in fact promised Denton the division manager's job. This was not mentioned to anyone at headquarters, but Herb believed that his suggestion would be followed because of his fine record with the company.

Recently the senior management, at the direction of the board of directors, started to develop and install a manpower planning program. A consulting firm was retained to aid in the effort. One of the consulting firm's assignments was to assess the capabilities of middle and first-level managers for promotability to higher positions in the firm. Because of Herb's closeness to retirement, his division got top priority. One member of the consulting firm's staff spent three months in Herb's division. Among the things he discovered was the close relationship that existed between Townes and his young subordinate. Because it was apparent that Denton was looked upon as a crown prince, the consultant gave this special attention.

He discovered that Denton took very little action on his own initiative, even though he was assistant division manager. He checked nearly everything with Herb before making a decision. The consultant discussed this with both Townes and Denton separately. He mentioned to Townes that

Denton did not have enough autonomy and that Townes should delegate more to test Denton's ability to manage on his own. Townes disagreed with the consultant, feeling that he did indeed delegate and that Dick was only checking with him to keep him informed, since he was the division manager.

When the consultant spoke to Denton, he found that Dick realized he wasn't being given any authority; but he said that he didn't want to press Townes, since he had been so good to him. "I'll be able to handle the job when Herb retires—why upset him now?" Dick said.

After careful evaluation of the situation, the consultant's recommendation to senior management was that Denton was not ready for the division manager's job and might be just a good number two man. He felt that Herb Townes had not developed Denton effectively and that the company should consider someone else for the post when Herb retired.

1. *If you were Denton, how would you relate to Townes?*
2. *How can you get a paternalistic boss to delegate?*
3. *As a member of senior management, what would be your reaction to the consultant's suggestion?*
4. *What do you think Denton's reaction will be if the consultant's suggestion is followed?*

CASE 4–5

Jean Gordon has been with the company for about six months. She is a keypunch operator and has developed considerable speed and accuracy. As her supervisor, you have noticed that she generally finishes her work earlier than the other employees. After observing her for several days, you find that after she completes her work, she reads a magazine, writes personal letters, or makes telephone calls.

You call her to your office to compliment her on her efficient performance and to ask her to help some of the slower operators complete their work on time. She accepts the compliment as a matter of fact and proceeds to tell you how unfair your request is. "I finish my work because I don't fool around and gossip, so I'll be darned if I'll help the slowpokes," Jean says emphatically. You go on to tell her that you know she is a very good worker, but you emphasize the need for a team spirit and a cooperative attitude. Jean still protests, saying, "I work as hard as anyone in the department, and I don't get paid for extra work." You tell her that you are not taking advantage of her and that you would appreciate her help in getting the department's work out. You go on to say that you do not expect her to consistently do extra work. Jean leaves your office seemingly accepting your request, but evidencing very little enthusiasm. You thought of promising Jean a raise and a promotion, but you were reluctant to do so because of her negative attitude.

During the next two weeks you notice that Jean finishes her work at quitting time each day. She has no spare time and, while she is no longer using the telephone or reading, she is not available for any extra work. Her past performance definitely indicates she has slowed down her work pace, but she still is efficient and accurate.

1. *What can you do now about Jean Gordon?*
2. *Should an efficient employee be given extra work?*
3. *What can you do to motivate and challenge an employee like Jean?*
4. *Is she justified in her refusal to do extra work?*

CASE 4–6

A department store branch in a suburban shopping center found that it was taking in more money in the four hours that it was open at night than it did in the preceding eight hours of the day. So management decided to keep the store open five nights a week and run the store on a two-shift basis. The second shift would work 24 hours a week—four nights plus an 8-hour day on Saturday—and would get full employee benefits of hospitalization, life insurance, discounts, paid vacations, and paid holidays.

The night and Saturday shift was to be made up of the people who had been working two nights a week and on Saturdays. They were mostly college students and public school teachers. The managers of the night crew were to be those members of the night shift who had been authorized to OK checks and fill in as acting managers after the day managers had delivered their briefings and departed for the night. Management decided, however, that the new night managers should not be left in their old departments but should be shifted to manage other departments, so they would be separated from the people with whom they had been working side by side.

The day managers were going to have to give up their authority over the night crew and were to retain responsibility only for merchandising at night.

The changeover was made, the store was opened five nights a week, and problems arose immediately. The night managers in their new departments didn't know the merchandise, and the day managers stayed on into the evening to supervise them or else left long lists of instructions to be followed. These new pairs of managers hadn't worked together before and didn't get along well together. The night managers complained that the day managers were overbearing. The day managers complained that the night managers were not following procedures or carrying out instructions. Some night managers requested that the day managers be barred from coming in at night to run things.

The night managers had no way of knowing what stock had come in or what had been ordered, and the day people had no way of knowing what the night people had done.

The night people were a lively and adaptable crew, and the revenue from the night hours was so good that top management wanted to build the best possible relations between day and night shifts.

1. *Set up a plan for making a smooth transition to a two-shift management.*
2. *Design some system for handling communications between day and night shifts.*
3. *What are the main causes of conflict between the day and the night managers?*
4. *How can they be made to realize they are all working for the same organization?*

CASE 4–7

Long burdened with a growing amount of detail, Charlie Klinger decided to ask the personnel department for one of the college graduates now completing the company's executive training program. He wanted to make this employee a staff assistant who would assume responsibility for some of the detail and work on various projects which Charlie had been postponing because of lack of help. Charlie's department performed an internal sales function largely concerned with business development and the necessary research to support it.

The personnel director agreed to Charlie's request and assigned Al Davis to the position. Al was a business school graduate who had majored in market research, and he was very interested in the challenges his new assignment presented. In a few months Charlie became convinced that Al Davis was all that he had hoped for. Each assignment given to Al was completed on time and with great effectiveness. Charlie was able to increase the complexity of the assignments and also give Al greater responsibility. Al welcomed all of these assignments and continually told Charlie how grateful he was for the many opportunities he had been given. By turning over many routine chores as well as several projects to Al, Charlie was able to spend more time on planning and the supervision of the department which he had neglected before Al came to the department.

One morning Charlie was having some coffee at his desk and silently congratulating himself on his success with Al Davis, who was functioning so effectively as his staff assistant. His thoughts were interrupted by Bill Franklin, a longtime member of the department and an old friend of Charlie's. Bill asked if he could join Charlie for a cup of coffee because he had something to tell him. Charlie, of course, agreed and Bill proceeded to tell him that Al Davis had been undermining him with other members in the department. Charlie couldn't believe it and mentioned Al's gratitude and cooperativeness as well as his efficiency. Bill agreed but went on to say that while Al was convincing Charlie of his usefulness he had been telling other employees that he was doing Charlie's job and frequently commenting on how lazy Charlie was. Bill frankly stated that he thought Al was trying to get Charlie's job and that it would only be a matter of time before he would start his campaign with people in higher management and the personnel department.

Charlie thanked Bill for the information but he still couldn't believe it. He wondered about what to do next and decided to talk to a few other employees in the department. Even though they were not as frank as Bill was, by using careful questions and allowing them to talk, Charlie was able to substantiate everything Bill had told him. It was apparent that he had created the proverbial monster. He then called Al to his office and confronted him with the information he had gathered. Al first denied any wrongdoing, but when Charlie mentioned dates and circumstances, he admitted his criticisms of Charlie's performance. He went on to say that he felt he was doing the lion's share of Charlie's work and that he was in fact after Charlie's job.

1. *What should Charlie do about Al and his frankly stated ambition?*
2. *Was Bill Franklin correct in telling Charlie about Al's efforts to undermine him?*
3. *Could Charlie have prevented such a problem from arising?*
4. *If you were Charlie's boss, what would you tell him to do?*
5. *Can an employee like Al be retained by the company?*

CASE 4–8

Jane Clark, an employee of over 17 years' tenure, was recently promoted to head a work group of 20 clerks and typists. The promotion was based on her demonstrated initiative, technical knowledge, ability to organize work loads, and her management attitude.

Because of her management attitude and excellent work performance, Clark had developed a reputation for being a "company woman" and was unpopular with some of the people she now supervised. In addition, there had been several personality clashes with her associates over the years, largely caused by Jane's desire to please her superiors.

Perhaps because of her vulnerability now that she is a supervisor, several of her subordinates have complained to higher authority. These complaints are very general in nature, mentioning that it is extremely difficult to work under Clark's supervision.

Her superior reports that she has had several interviews with her, and they reveal that she understands her situation completely and is making an honest effort to be fair and reasonable in the treatment of her work group. She is not using herself as a standard of performance for the group, and she is as pleasant as possible in her employee relations. Her superior feels that the criticism leveled at her is undeserved and a direct result of past grudges on the part of some of her co-workers.

Recently an employee working for Jane Clark went to the personnel department to request a transfer to another department. She was qualified in the type of work done in that department and desired to perform in that area. In the course of conversation with the personnel manager she mentioned that Miss Clark was difficult to work for, but she had no specific complaints.

1. *Was it ill-advised to promote Clark to a supervisory position?*
2. *Should popularity be an important factor in determining promotability?*
3. *Can a superior who has recommended promotion objectively evaluate employee criticism of a supervisor?*
4. *Assuming the superior is correct in her evaluation of the situation, what can she do to help Jane Clark with her supervisory problems?*
5. *Can she assume that the employee animosity existing now will die a natural death in time?*
6. *Should Jane Clark be transferred to another department as a supervisor? As a regular employee?*

CASE 4–9

You are the supervisor of a large production department. Your newest assistant is a young man named Bill Smith. Smith is considerably younger than the other assistants and lacks their experience; however, his rapid rise to the position of assistant supervisor was based on outstanding ability. Smith learns quickly, has shown great initiative, and maintains excellent relations with the employees under his supervision.

The older supervisors under your jurisdiction resent this Johnny-come-lately intruder into their ranks. While not openly hostile, their opposition is reflected in lack of cooperation, a certain reluctance to coordinate fully, and the failure to include Smith as an insider in their group. The acts are not so open as to permit you to make a clear case; yet you are acutely aware of the situation and apprehensive that it might result in a serious lowering of your department's morale and efficiency.

Smith, meanwhile, is making the best of a bad situation. He has managed to keep his subdepartment operating in an acceptable manner and has been wise enough not to force himself upon the other assistants or to reveal his discomfort and resentment. As yet, he has not complained.

1. *What might be some of the reasons for the attitude of the older assistant supervisors?*
2. *Is Smith approaching the problem correctly? What suggestions do you have for him?*
3. *What is your responsibility in such a situation.*
4. *How should you go about increasing cooperation among your assistants?*
5. *How should you go about creating a spirit of management-mindedness among your assistants?*
6. *How are you going to get your assistants to put company interests before their own interests?*

CASE 4–10

Ron Blake is an industrial engineer. He is black and was born, raised, and educated in the South. His first job after graduation from college was as a technician in the Midwest division of a large company where there was a high percentage of black employees. The company gave him additional technical training and after two years gave him management training and promoted him to first-level supervisor. The promotion was based on superior technical ability combined with natural leadership and drive. He performed well as a supervisor for two years, and then the Midwest division was shut down and Blake was transferred to the Northwest division of the company, where there were few black employees.

Within a year he had been relieved of three supervisory assignments, each time with a general unsatisfactory performance rating. The fourth assignment was made with the understanding all around that if he did not work out in this one he would be terminated.

During the first month on this new assignment Blake complained regularly to the manager that he had been discriminated against in the three previous assignments and had not been given a fair opportunity. He claimed that he was being railroaded out of the company. He also objected to certain duties of this new assignment as being degrading to his position as a supervisor and thought he should have more responsibility and authority. He complained that some of the other supervisors did not cooperate with him and that some of the employees did not accept his supervision. Actually none of the other supervisors had complained about him. A few employees had made rather general complaints and asked to be transferred to a different supervisor.

Blake was bright, well groomed, and businesslike. He handled himself well in contacts with individuals and groups. He handled authority well, accepted responsibility, analyzed problems quickly, and made good decisions.

What is the problem here?

Chapter 5

○   *To gain an understanding of the nature of managerial decision making*

○   *To appreciate the several factors that are a part of the decision-making process*

○   *To develop an understanding of the different types of decisions managers and supervisors must make*

○   *To gain insight into the problem-solving process*

Decision making and problem solving

Major topics

The nature of decision making.

Who should make decisions?

Rationality and decision making.

Decision quality.

Individuals, groups, and participation.

Decision-making tools and techniques.

The seven-step problem-solving technique.

Although decision making is a topic which frequently appears in texts about management, it is a process that is not exclusive to managers and supervisors. Everyone makes decisions of one kind or another every day. You choose a college to attend, how to spend a weekend, where to go on vacation, what to eat for dinner, to spend or save money, to invest in a stock, to buy a new car, a particular job, and whom to marry. Obviously some of these decisions are more important than others; and some have a known outcome while others represent greater risk.

How well one makes the decisions that involve greater risk can have considerable effect on that person's future. The interesting thing about decision making, however, is that while everyone does it few of us really know how we make decisions. Supervisors and managers spend a good deal of their time making decisions; yet when asked how they perform this task, the responses range from, "I don't now, it's automatic," to a complicated description of the relationship of thought processes to information and the use of complex mathematical techniques.

The nature of decision making

Any practicing manager knows that decision making is inherent in all of the management functions, such as goal setting, planning, organizing, and controlling. It is a managerial process in the sense that decisions made by managers affect the organization and its people. Yet decisions are frequently made without awareness or understanding of the processes involved. The reason why many managers don't know how they make decisions is that it is difficult to conceptualize a process that includes such relatively vague factors as individual judgment, past experience, tradition, personality, environment, organizational relationships, communication, and uncertainty or risk. It is worthwhile exploring each of these briefly.

Individual judgment. Each of us is a product of many and varied experiences too numerous to measure. We build a fund of these experiences and then tend to frame future actions on the basis of what we consider successful past experiences. If a particular course of action worked out well in the past, we will most likely try it again when a similar circumstance occurs in the present or future. This can be called exercising judgment, and the skill varies among people. Those who seem to be correct with greater frequency are said to have good judgment, and good judgment tends to improve with experience. It has often been said that the effective manager rarely makes the same mistake twice. The extent to which we learn from past experience is the bench mark of good judgment.

Past experience. It can be seen that past experience has a vital role in the decision process. The nature and frequency of the experience contributes significantly to the effectiveness of one's decisions. In some instances an individual's past experience can determine how much risk one will take when faced with a present set of alternatives. How much one has learned from these experiences, both positive and negative, can affect the person's current viewpoint and cause judgments to be made that are too subjective. This can be particularly true in human relations decisions. For instance, judging the performance of an apparently reformed alcoholic can be biased by an individual's past experience with alcoholics.

Tradition. When a person is promoted to a management position, he or she assumes a job which has to some extent been determined by predecessors. There is usually a set of procedures and rules to go by, along with the inertia of the group to be supervised. If the group is effective, the new manager will be quite reluctant to upset the status quo. However, if the situation being entered is not successful, the reaction is also traditional, as evidenced by the old cliche, "A new broom sweeps clean."

The manager's concern is how to get things accomplished through other people. Consequently the experience and patterns followed by older people in the same position are frequently copied. In entering this ready-made world, the manager is often coerced into adopting traditional patterns of thought and action. In some cases traditional behavior should not be followed, but the new manager is often hesitant to be an upsetting influence—particularly when the company is successful and the manager is not a senior member of the team. Hence tradition can impair the judgment of managers, causing them to be overcautious and less innovative.

Personality. Individual personality is a complex subject, but it is easy to recognize that a manager's personality can and often does have an effect on how and why he or she makes certain decisions. In many work situations subordinates discuss how they can please the boss. There is nothing wrong with this if pleasing the boss means performing their jobs efficiently as measured by objective standards. If, on the other hand, pleasing the boss means dealing with his or her idiosyncrasies and catering to whims, difficulties can arise. There are bosses who make unreasonable demands, who have explosive tempers, and who don't like opposition from subordinates. These can be classified as personality problems. Nearly everyone has heard of people who have been fired or transferred because of personality clashes. A boss who dislikes bright young people not only encourages mediocrity but stops innovation, because weak subordinates anxious to please will not rock the boat. By the same token, a boss with a healthy personality can be very effective. Such a person will tend to make decisions on objective information gathered from many sources and not use emotional reactions as the basis for decision.

Another aspect of personality that affects the decision process is an extreme concern about orderliness and a strong desire for arbitrary conclusions. The manager who asks, "Is everything okay?" is usually expecting a positive answer. If that manager wanted specific answers, the question would be more specific. "Which machine caused the bottleneck yesterday?" would get an answer that could enable the manager to evaluate the cause and determine if it was the machine itself, the operator, maintenance, or some combination of all three.

Insecure people frequently do not like problems and their implications so they seek the firm, quick conclusion. They do not want the uncertainty of questions or new ideas. "Don't bother me with facts; my mind is made up!" is the type of response which tends to stop discussion and stifle creativity. Those people who look at everything as being either right or wrong neglect the vast middle ground where most problems occur and most solutions are found.

Environment. Both the internal environment of the particular company and the external environment of which the company is a part impact on individual decision makers. Some companies are more risk-oriented than others. Some are pacesetters and others are followers. The external environment—including such things as all levels of government, labor unions, consumer groups, suppliers, customers, stockholders, and the general public—has an effect on decisions managers make. In recent years the external environment has had an increasingly greater impact, as is indicated by expanded attention to social responsibility, minority employment, and consumer pressure.

Organizational relationships. Relationships can be viewed in two ways in the analysis of the decision process—from the individual supervisor's viewpoint, whose influence with the hierarchy can have an impact not only on personal decisions but on the decisions other people make about the supervisor and his group. Obviously, if one relates well to others in the structure, that individual may personally receive more favorable treatment and his other subordinates may also be treated similarly. The supervisor may be able to get them better raises or promotions or other kinds of advantageous treatment. These relationships can be based on outstanding performance in the positive sense and on company politics in the negative sense.

From an organization structure view, the relationships of one department to another and how well all the divergent elements in the structure are coordinated has considerable impact on the quality of decisions. If the sales department and the production department are frequently at odds, the profit of the company can be negatively affected. If favoritism or an inordinate amount of attention is given to one department at the sacrifice of other departments by senior management of the firm, this will have an effect on the quality and nature of decisions down the line.

Communication. The gathering of information, a part of the communication process, is vitally necessary to sound decision making. If poor or inadequate information is the basis for a decision, it will be less than optimal. If some employees are reluctant to inform their supervisors of pertinent data or if they color that data, the supervisor will be deciding on inaccurate information.

Another dimension of communication and decision making is when, if, and to whom decisions should be communicated. Some companies operate on a need-to-know basis, restricting information only to those directly involved with the decision. Other companies practice a more open type of communications network, informing many people of a decision and soliciting their support and cooperation. More discussion on communication will be included in the chapter on that subject.

Uncertainty or risk. It might be said that each of us has a risk quotient, ranging from extreme caution to foolhardiness. While there are few people at either extreme, individuals tend to lean in one direction or the other. How one perceives a situation in relation to the amount of risk it presents, the alternatives available, and the risk one is willing to take determines the nature of the decision.

Predictability of outcome is another dimension in this category. The amount of uncertainty present in the various courses of action available may also affect the nature of the decision. Trying to fathom the future is difficult at best, even with excellent information. Therefore the amount of uncertainty inherent in the alternatives, coupled with the individual's risk quotient, has a considerable impact on the decision process.

Who should make decisions?

Even though all individuals in an organization make decisions about a variety of things, both personal and organizations, the question as to what level in the organization structure should be responsible for given types of decisions is a matter of some controversy. Ernest Dale comments in his book:

> Classical theory states that decisions should be assigned to the lowest competent level in the organization, which is an excellent rule as far as it goes. The closer a decision maker is to the scene of action, the quicker the decision can be made. And, of course, if too many decisions are passed up the line, higher executives will be overburdened, and those in the lower echelons will have little opportunity to use initiative.
>
> The problem is to determine the lowest competent level. Leaving aside the competence of the people who happen to be holding the various jobs (which, of course, will have a bearing), it may be said that the lowest competent level is the lowest level at which the jobholder has both access to all available information pertinent to the decision and the incentive to weigh the factors impartially.[1]

There is little disagreement that managers on all levels of an organization do make decisions. This is an integral part of management practice. Organization, with its goals, plans, performance standards, policies, procedures, and controls, is designed to both implement and facilitate the decision process. On any workday, events occur which require the manager to decide on one course of action or another. In a sense it is a relatively simple stimulus-response type of activity. The determination of who should make the decision often has to do with the nature and magnitude of that decision. Chester I. Barnard, in his classic work, comments as follows on the nature of decisions as they affect the actions to take place:

---

[1] Ernest Dale, *Management: Theory and Practice,* 4th ed. (New York: McGraw-Hill Book Co., 1978), p. 437.

The limiting (strategic) factor is the one whose control, in the right form, at the right place and time, will establish a new system or set of conditions which meets the purpose. Thus, if we wish to increase the yield of grain in a certain field and on analysis it appears that the soil lacks potash, potash may be said to be the strategic (or limiting) factor. If a tank of water is to be used for cleaning purposes and is found to contain sediment, the sediment is the strategic (limiting) factor in the use of the water for cleaning. If a machine is not operable because a screw is missing, the screw is the strategic (limiting) factor.

. . . The fact that a strategic factor is always involved is overlooked because the personal or organization action required often seems trivial; the necessary effort is less than required to analyze the situation or system. For example, it may require great effort to determine that the land needs potash, but little effort to get the potash. Nevertheless, when the need has been determined, a new situation has arisen because of the fact of knowledge or the assumption that potash is the limiting factor; and instead of potash, the limiting factor *obtaining* potash then becomes the strategic factor; and this will change progressively into *obtaining* the money to *buy* potash, then *finding* John to *go* after potash, then *getting* machines and men to *spread* potash, etc., etc. Thus the determination of the strategic factor is itself the decision which at once reduces purpose to a new level, compelling search for a new strategic factor in the new situation.[2]

Magnitude of decisions.   Magnitude and nature are critical factors in the decision-making process. Magnitude is frequently handled by setting limits on the types of decisions that can be made by managers on a given level in the organization's structure. The first-level supervisor quite naturally has to make many decisions related to his or her area of responsibility. These will have to do with the work flow, discipline, recordkeeping, performance evaluation, compliance with standards, pay recommendations, and other things directly concerned with the group and its work. The supervisor may even make expenditure decisions up to a given figure, such as $100. A superior will handle decisions of greater company importance, including those referred upward by first-level supervisors. Similarly, higher levels of management will be concerned with decisions of still broader significance and longer range impact. It is on this level that goal and policy decisions affecting the entire firm are made.

Perception of decisions.   Obviously a decision made by one manager can affect another area of the company, though the manager making it may not be aware of that fact. For instance, a supervisor who interprets company policy on lateness loosely, by not considering an employee late until 15 minutes after starting time, may make it difficult for a supervisor who strictly observes the policy and penalizes employees accordingly.

Each manager may have a parochial view of problems, and decisions tend to be biased by this. The manager will consider the effect of a deci-

---

[2] Chester I. Barnard, *The Functions of the Executive* (Cambridge, Mass.: Harvard University Press, 1938), pp. 203–4.

sion primarily in relationship to his or her own welfare and that of the work group. Other supervisors may have an entirely different view of the same problem. Bertram M. Gross uses the chart shown as Table 5–1 to demonstrate this phenomenon of organizational life, using the example of machinery breakdowns. An analysis of the chart indicates a number of differences in purpose and accompanying roadblocks. This is the nature of many problems requiring a decision solution in a company.

Table 5–1
Different views of "machine breakdown problems"

People	Purposes	Blockages
Foreman	High output. Operations without breakdowns. Proper machine care by workers.	Machine breakdown. Improper machine care by workers. Disinterest of workers in output.
Workers	High output. Higher wages. Better jobs.	Bad machines. Management wage policies. Few opportunities.
Maintenance man	Proper machine care. Controlling maintenance activities of workers.	Interference from foreman. Insufficient authority.
Accountant	Proper allocation of repair expenses. Lower production costs.	Current or capital account? Machine breakdowns.
Engineer	Better products. Technological advance.	Bad machines. Inadequate capital budgeting.
Salesman	Higher sales. Lower prices.	Lower prices. Higher production costs.

Source: Bertram M. Gross, *Organizations and Their Managing* (New York: Free Press, 1968), p. 560.

Because it is difficult for the various parties to go beyond their perceptions of the problem, they must be led there by the next level of manager, who should perceive the problem more in relation to organizational goals and in a general management way. Of course that manager must have the authority to act, as well, to enforce the solution chosen.

Rationality and decision making

From the discussion thus far it can be seen that decision making is essentially a human mental process. Because of this managers usually are not totally objective when making decisions. The concept of rationality evolves from the economic-man concept of classical economic theory. Simply stated, it is concerned only with the amount of utility the consumer and the producer will receive from a particular product or service.

The individual's objective is supposed to be maximization of the total utility by the use of the limited resources of time, effort, and money.

Translated into the decision process, this concept holds that managers make decisions only on the basis of careful weighing of alternatives after gathering all pertinent data and with organizational goals uppermost in their minds. Unfortunately, rationality must be viewed as a relative concept, if for no other reason than that most organizations have conflicting goals and managers must cope with them. Of course, another outstanding reason is the personal value system that each manager brings to the decision process. The experience and personality factors that contribute to this value system were mentioned earlier in this chapter.

"I know to err is human, Hagstrom, but
I'm not human."
Reprinted by permission The Wall Street Journal

Every manager must face the reality of making a wrong decision.

Rarely can managers obtain maximum solutions to problems that confront them, so they most often settle for an optimum solution at the particular time. Further, their choice of alternatives may be limited not only by their availability but also by their awareness of them and the amount of time they can give to the search for and evaluation of alternatives.

Decision quality

Because many managers do not know or understand how they make decisions, they frequently find it difficult to assess the quality of their decision making. In a sense they go through a trial-and-error process. Managers do not know if a decision is proper or satisfactory until the decision is made and the chosen course of action is carried out. If the end result is satisfactory to the group or groups concerned, the decision is deemed a proper one. Otherwise the analysis must go on over again. Alternate courses of action must be reevaluated and a different one chosen.

Nevertheless, managers are under considerable pressure to be right most of the time. The trouble lies in the differences of opinion on the meaning of "right" in the minds of managers on various organizational levels. Where there is a difference of opinion, the lower level manager may "play it safe" and please the boss even though he or she firmly believes in a different approach to the problem from the one proposed by the superior. This, of course, does little for the quality of decisions, but it does preserve a form of superior-subordinate harmony in the short run.

Everyone has been confronted with a deadline when making a decision. More often than not the deadline is set by others. A good example is a job offer from the viewpoint of a company and an individual. A position is open and quite naturally the manager wants it filled as rapidly as possible. Depending on the labor market, a number of candidates are interviewed, and two or three are presented to the manager as being qualified for the position. After seeing them, the manager chooses one because work is backing up. But there is the nagging thought that if there was more time a better person could be found. The individual chosen also has doubts. This person has been interviewed by three companies and this is the first offer. The job candidate wonders whether waiting for the two other companies to respond will result in a better offer. Meanwhile bills are piling up so the decision is made to accept. Obviously, when time pressures are great decisions may be made that would not be if more time was available to gather additional information.

Another factor that makes it difficult to determine decision quality is the time lag between deciding and fully implementing. This time lag is more evident in complex decisions, since implementation is more complicated and may have long-range implications. Yet the manager must make this kind of decision as well as the more simple ones. Even a decision to promote a person to a higher level of responsibility has the time lag of performance evaluation built in. The person must be given a reasonable period of time to learn the new job and function in it before an evaluation of performance can take place. As a result, probation periods are often defined for a job. Such periods are particularly used with new hires.

As mentioned earlier, all decisions are not equally significant. The president of the United States undoubtedly would give more careful thought and analysis to establishing a foreign base than to proclaiming a national appeal for a recognized charity. Frequently made decisions such as buying a particular brand of toothpaste are certainly less significant than that of buying a house. One is routine, requiring little thought, and the other occurs perhaps no more than two or three times in one's life. In managerial decision making the amount of time necessary to gather information for a reasonable decision, the number of employees and others affected by it, and the amount of money involved are all important factors in determining decision significance. Obviously the effective manager or supervisor should devote more effort to the nonroutine decisions.

In trying to assess decision quality, it may be desirable to attempt to conceptualize the decision process. Even though many managers cannot identify what they go through when making a decision, many writers have attempted to diagram the decision process. By so doing they at least make us aware of most of the ingredients of the process and give us some idea of how it may be carried out in an organization. Figure 5–1 is one such diagram which appeared in a recent book on management decisions.

In the final analysis decisions made by managers represent a balancing of the several factors mentioned earlier. Three dimensions are included, each with several items.

The manager:	Organizational objectives:	Organizational climate:
Experience	Economic considerations	Traditional patterns
Education	Profit goals	Organization structure
Knowledge	Growth pattern	Nature of the job
Personality	Market development	Personality of superior
Values	Product mix	Management style
Perceptions	Product improvement	Communication quality
Expectations	Customer relations	Information quality
Aspirations	Employee development	Reward structure
Time pressure	Stockholder relations	Recognition pattern
People pressure	Social responsibility	Responsibility pattern
Money pressure	Position in industry	Nature of the industry
Goal conflict	Political considerations	Location

The effective manager should weigh all factors and then choose alternatives that represent his or her best judgment at the time of the decision. The balance among personal viewpoints, climate considerations, and organization objectives usually results in a decision that is not totally efficient but is most desirable or optimal for the situation.

Individuals, groups, and participation

In most of the discussion in this chapter, decision making has been described as an individual process. The manager is confronted with a problem and decides how to solve it. It was also described as a part of the practice and process of management. Other approaches to decision making have also been tried and have some use.

Many decisions made in organizations have an effect beyond the area of responsibility of the manager making the decision. One of the problems in the decision process is the effectiveness of implementation and follow-

Figure 5–1
The decision-making process in organizations

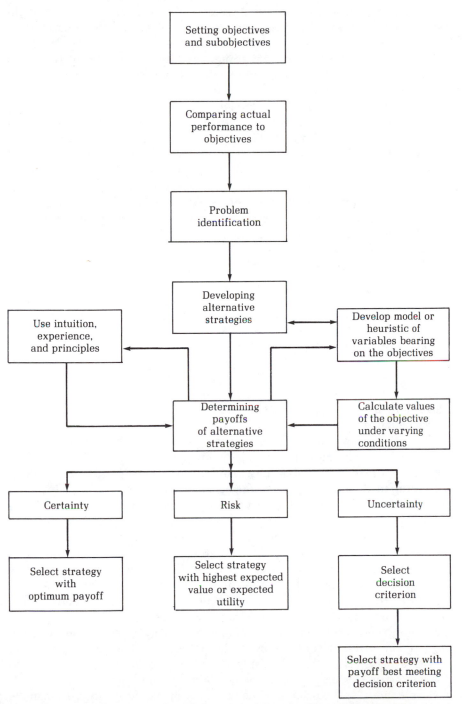

Source: Max D. Richards and Paul S. Greenlaw, *Management Decisions and Behavior*, rev. ed. (Homewood, Ill.: Richard D. Irwin, 1972), p. 87. © 1972 by Richard D. Irwin, Inc.

up. The question arises as to whether or not it is desirable to involve in the decision process all parties who may be affected by that decision before it is made.

Information gathering and the group. A principal argument for group involvement is that better and more information can be brought to bear on the selection of alternatives. If we analyze how many managers gather data for their decisions, this argument can be seen to have some substance. Since most managers are under time pressure, the search for information is necessarily limited. The manager is usually in contact with a relatively few subordinates and one or two superiors. Information comes to the manager in the form of words and figures, written and spoken, obtained from machines and the few people close to him or her. These figures and words are then interpreted on the basis of his or her own fund of experience, which may be narrow. The information may be biased, incomplete, or inaccurate, for frequently subordinates tell or show the manager only what they think he or she wants to see and hear. It takes a broad, astute individual to recognize this limitation and be critical and analytical in the use of information.

Hence, the argument goes, if there is direct involement of all parties, the information is less biased since it goes through the cauldron of group exposure. Discussion and participation in the process before the decision is made will also enhance effective implementation.

The counterargument is that decision making is essentially an individual process and a basic managerial prerogative which should not be shared. At least the manager, who may listen to all parties and take their suggestions under advisement, should reserve the right to choose the alternative believed to be best.

Even if participation is desired by the manager, time frequently is limited, and he or she may not be able to involve all parties. The manager's approach to problem solving may also be a limiting factor. Some managers prefer to depend on a few trusted subordinates for information and then decide. Others want to involve several people to gain the benefits associated with participation. Figure 5–2 shows how George Terry diagrams this characteristic of the decision process in his recent book.

Committee decisions. One form of group participation in the decision process is the use of committees. Particular use of this approach is made by large organizations in which the choices of alternatives and decision implementation are a way of life. Despite an organization chart and manual with position descriptions that define areas of responsibility, many decisions that have to be made can involve several people across departmental lines of authority. Because coordination is necessary in the implementation of a decision of this kind, many managers believe it worthwhile to involve the interested parties at the beginning of the process.

People with specialized knowledge as well as direct interest can be utilized in a committee to bring information to bear on the search for a de-

Figure 5–2
Relative degrees of decision making

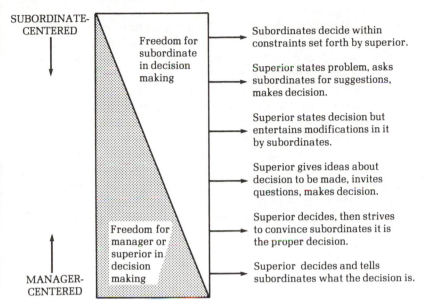

SUBORDINATE-
CENTERED

Freedom for
subordinate
in decision
making

Freedom for
manager or
superior in
decision
making

MANAGER-
CENTERED

Subordinates decide within
constraints set forth by superior.

Superior states problem, asks
subordinates for suggestions,
makes decision.

Superior states decision but
entertains modifications in it
by subordinates.

Superior gives ideas about
decision to be made, invites
questions, makes decision.

Superior decides, then strives
to convince subordinates it is
the proper decision.

Superior decides and tells
subordinates what the decision is.

Source: George R. Terry, *Principles of Management*, 7th ed. (Homewood, Ill.: Richard
D. Irwin, 1977), p. 138. © 1977 by Richard D. Irwin, Inc.

cision that will be pertinent and timely. The hope is that there will be a resolution of differences after thrashing them out in committee meetings. While
this may not happen, at least it can be said that many viewpoints will be
heard. The significant problem with a committee is that a compromise
solution will result which may not satisfy any of the participants.

A popular form of committee in use by several organizations is a task
force. This type of committee is usually formed with a particular problem
to solve and disbanded when a decision is made. Its composition usually
consists of line managers directly involved with the problem at hand. At
times staff experts may be attached to a task force in an advisory capacity
to facilitate the information-gathering process.

Decision-making tools and techniques

While decision making is a human process, there are several techniques
and tools which the manager may use to aid in the decision process. With
the advent of electronic data processing, many of these techniques have a
mathematical base. Some of these—such as operations research, break-
even analysis, and the program evaluation review technique (PERT)—will
be discussed in the chapter on planning and control. Such mathematical
techniques are useful because managers are often faced with decisions that

have quantitative aspects. Quality control, production control, sales and market analysis, labor turnover, and other areas of business have numerical dimensions which can be measured.

Decision tree. One of the decision-making techniques is a decision tree (see Figure 5–3). It is a graphic representation of a number of possible future events that may affect a decision. It enables a more ready visualization of the alternatives available, along with the risks and possible outcomes. This technique is particularly useful when making decisions under conditions of uncertainty, as in the case of the job choice problem. Figure 5–3 is an oversimplified version of the problem; yet the depicted diagram can give one a grasp of the approach and its potential usefulness. Numerical values can be assigned to each alternative, probability, and action, as they are in real situations using the decision-tree technique. Decision trees are most often used in helping to solve such problems as providing more office or plant space, a major equipment purchase, market expansion, product development, and increases or decreases in staff size.

Figure 5–3
A decision tree

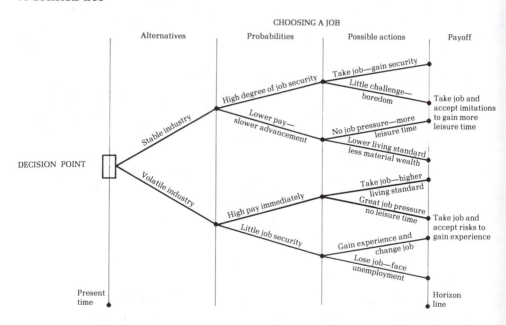

The seven-step problem-solving technique

The seven-step approach to decision making is a most useful and universally applicable technique. It was mentioned briefly in Chapter 1, and a complete explanation follows. Examples of its use are given in other chapters; and it certainly can be applied to many of the cases following each chapter in this book. In fact, such use will demonstrate the variety of problems that the seven-step technique can help solve.

Step 1.   Clearly define the problem or problems.   Supervisory awareness of a problem may be a feeling of concern over a number of undesirable conditions that there hasn't been enough time to do anything about—poor performance by subordinates, schedules not met, work piling up. The supervisor's first statement of the problem may be that more people or more overtime are needed. If this idea is examined critically, the supervisor may discover that conclusions are being drawn too soon and that the situation is not being considered in terms of the objectives of high production at low cost.

If the problem has arisen because of poor management, there may be a need for one solution to take care of the immediate problem and then some long-range improvement to avoid future problems. In other words, a present cure is necessary and then a plan of prevention which might include methods improvements, training, delegating, motivating, and other good supervisory practices. (Chapter 7 prescribes a course of action for the supervisor who goes from one crisis to another and never has the time to take action necessary to prevent the problems from arising.)

In defining a problem, the supervisor should determine the area it covers and ask: Do I have the authority to do anything about this myself? Do I have the knowledge? The time? Could I get somebody else to do it? Suppose I don't do anything, what then? If the total problem is too big for me, what are the parts that are most urgent? How broad should the investigation be? How deep? What benefits can be expected from solving the problem? A list of the expected benefits serves as the criterion by which to evaluate and compare alternative solutions. Also, the list puts a price tag and perhaps a priority number on the investigation. How important are these benefits? How much are they worth? What expense should be gone to to attain them?

Step 2.   Gather the information.   Although information gathering is listed as the second step in the process, it is actually an activity that continues all through it. Information has to be gathered in order to define the problem, in order to work out and evaluate solutions, and in order to check up on the effects of the chosen solution. The information gathered will probably be a combination of facts and feelings, because in any problem that involves people there will be attitudes, prejudices, opinions, inferences, and maybe illusions that must be considered.

Experience is a good source of information—the supervisor's own experience, the experience of other people in management, and the experience of the people involved in the problem. Everybody involved has ideas of what should be done about it, and many of these ideas turn up good information and suggestions. But whether these ideas are fruitful or not, *asking* for them is important because the person who is consulted in the analysis and solution of a problem will have a better attitude toward that solution and any changes it entails than would a person who was not consulted. People are anxious to tell what is wrong with a situation (provided it's not their fault). If they think the company is making it hard for them to do a good job, it is important that they get a chance to air their opinions. Employees want a voice in matters that affect them, and asking their opinions is one way to help satisfy this want.

If the problem being investigated is a personnel problem, something can be learned about the people involved in it by asking their former supervisors. Good information can often be gotten from production, personnel, and office records; time and attendance reports; inspection reports; and histories of transfers, promotions, raises, layoffs, and so on. The information gathered will never be complete; some of it will be useless, some will be inaccurate, some will open up new avenues for investigation.

Step 3.   Interpret the information.   Information should not be judged piece by piece as it is gathered; there is too much danger that the investigator will develop a theory (this employee is a born troublemaker, or accident prone, or insecure) and then ignore or discount any evidence that doesn't fit into the pattern. Conflicting accounts have to be pieced together and evaluated against additional evidence. Information might be sorted into some orderly arrangement, such as one of the following:

1.   Line up the information in the order of its reliability.
2.   Arrange the information in terms of major importance, minor importance, and no importance.
3.   Set the information up in terms of time: What happened first? Next? What came before what? Why did it? What were the surrounding circumstances?
4.   Set the information up in terms of cause and effect: What is the cause of what?
5.   Classify the information into categories: Human factors such as personality, health, age, relationships between people, off-the-job problems. Technical factors such as method, skill, training, tools, machinery, workplace. Time factors such as stage of growth or development of the company, length of service, overtime, night shift, or the question, "How long has this been going on?" Policy factors such as policies, procedures, or rules applying to the problem.

Since the information is never complete, it is necessary to make assumptions, and all assumptions should be supported by evidence and logical thinking. The investigator should be aware of personal prejudices and try to be objective in judgments. In considering circumstances he or she should try to get the point of view of the people who were involved in the incident. For example, was everybody violating the smoking rule, or the chain of command? Or was only one person doing it? Did the sequence of events have something to do with it? If this sort of thing has been going on for a while, what has been the attitude toward it?

As the investigator you might put yourself in the place of the person being investigated and ask: If I were this person how would I see the situation? Would I have acted the same way? Would the "normal" person have acted in this manner or was there something special in the situation or in the person that caused the reaction? Is the individual new on the job? What is his or her physical condition? Age? What difficulties does this person have or think he or she has? Was this behavior a mask for some feeling the person didn't want to show? Is the person afraid of job loss or that he or she won't be able to do the work?

Step 4.   Develop solutions.   As a person interprets information, numerous ideas about possible solutions suggest themselves. The first one might well be: What will happen if I do nothing about it? Some problems clear up by themselves; others call for immediate action. In considering possible solutions, the supervisor must be guided by established policy and the principles and practices of good management. What principles or practices of good management are being violated, thus causing the difficulty or contributing to the undesirable situation? What principles or practices, if applied, would offer solutions to the problem? What obstacles stand in the way of a solution? Sometimes considering obstacles one by one yields ideas for solutions.

After several possible solutions have come to mind and have been put in writing, supervisors should start developing ideas about them. They should not limit themselves to a single solution, because doing so seems to limit thinking and cause too much concentration on detail. Developing several alternative solutions makes it possible to combine the best parts of them into one superior solution. Also, alternatives are valuable to have in case the boss finds something wrong with the first one—a bad flaw in it or incompatibility with broader company plans that the boss has information about.

Step 5.   Select the best practical solution.   In selecting the best solution to a problem, supervisors should consider the short-term and long-term effects of each of the possible solutions. They might compare the solutions in terms of the following questions:

1.   How far has the situation deteriorated? Must drastic steps be taken or can time aid as a cure? Is the problem just arising or has it existed for a long time?
2.   To what extent will the objectives in Step 1 be realized by each of the solutions?
3.   What will be the effect of each possible solution on the quality and quantity of production?
4.   Which solution is most readily applicable and will produce the quickest results?
5.   Have these solutions been used before? What have the results been?
6.   What will be the side effects of each of the possible solutions?
7.   What are the difficulties involved in the application of each of these solutions?
8.   What will be the cost of each solution?
9.   How does the cost of each solution compare with the results that it will give?

Step 6.   Put the solution into effect.   Some solutions have to be put into effect quickly—matters of discipline, for instance, may have to get some kind of immediate treatment. Company policy and union contract must be followed; so supervisors should know in advance what authority they have to act in an emergency and what the penalties are for various offenses.

If the problem is a technical one and the solution to it brings a change in the method of doing work or calls for a new arrangement of facilities or a new type of machine, it may run into resistance. People become disturbed by changes that break up their habit patterns and threaten their security or status. Rather than have a good plan fail because people resist the changes it entails, the supervisor might consider breaking the plan up into a chain of events, each to be introduced when the time is ripe.

Sometimes changes can be tried out in a limited area and the bugs uncovered and corrected before the area of application is widened. Pilot studies and dry runs permit a person to adjust plans to unforeseen circumstances and to make corrections and refinements before final application under full operating conditions. A change may be put in on a temporary basis and then modified in terms of the reactions to it. (A policy might be introduced in this manner.) A change in procedure might be put in step by step and the installing schedule worked out with the people who would be affected by it. If the change is a new program to be launched—for instance, a job evaluation program—people could be prepared for it by a great amount of advance publicity. However a change is introduced, people should be assured that they will get training and assistance for adjusting to the new situation, and they should be helped to see the new situation in a favorable light.

Step 7.   Evaluate the effectiveness of the solution.   Periodically supervisors should review the plan they put into operation and compare the actual practice with the ideal of the solution. People are prone to fall back into old habit patterns. The benefits resulting from the plan should be measured against the objectives set up in Step 1: Are the objectives being realized? If not, why not? If the results are better than expected, what favorable factors cause this to be so?

Periodic checkups on solutions give supervisors valuable experience to use in solving other problems. Supervisors should study the operation of their solutions somewhat as the quarterback studies the films of the football game. Where were mistakes made? How can their repetition be avoided? What decisions were brilliant successes? What were the contributing circumstances? If supervisors will evaluate and build on their experience and deliberately direct their efforts in practice, they can develop skill in solving problems.

Summary

This chapter has explored the decision-making process. It is a human and mental process that is highly complex. Many managers are not aware of the way they make decisions and try to solve problems, yet it is something they do every day. In fact, making decisions is a task practiced by all humans as they go through life.

Decision making is a part of all of the management functions. Managers making decisions use their own judgment, past experience, a personal value system, and the work environment as the frame of reference. Organizational relationships, communication, and risk all have a role in the decision process. While decisions should be made at the lowest competent level in the organization, it is difficult to define that level for all decisions due to both organizational and decision complexities.

In an organization people involved in decision making perceive the problems and alternatives from a parochial viewpoint. To try to enhance decision making, some organizations use committees and task forces. This approach may aid information gathering and involvement, but committee decisions are often compromise solutions which may be difficult to implement.

There are several tools and techniques to aid the manager in the decision process. Many of these are based on mathematical techniques and utilize computers. Among these are operations research, PERT, break-even analysis, and decision trees. A method that is widely used is the seven-step problem-solving technique, which can be applied to relatively complex problems by managers and nonmanagers alike.

CASE 5–1

One of the problems managers face when making decisions is something called tunnel vision. This means that one tends to look at things in a traditional way, from established frames of reference. Try the following exercise on a sheet of paper. Connect all the dots by drawing four continuous straight lines, being sure not to go through any dot more than once. (The answer will be found at the end of the chapter.)

•   •   •

•   •   •

•   •   •

CASE 5–2

The new dean of the graduate business school at Gibson University was anxious to build student morale, which he had found to be rather low due to the autocratic regime of his predecessor.

After a lengthy meeting with the governing board of the student organization, he agreed to their request to allow a student-developed and -administered faculty evaluation program to be instituted. The students wanted to publish the results, so that they could be used in promotion and tenure decisions and also demonstrate to the faculty where they stood in student opinion of their classroom performance. One of the students' central arguments was that many faculty members were poor classroom teachers, though they might be good at research and writing. Another was the student opinion that several faculty members were remote and difficult to see after class.

The dean believed the idea a good one, and one which would help establish his popularity with the student government. He didn't believe the faculty would mind the evaluation, and the results could be used by department chairpersons as a part of the faculty development process. Because the dean thought highly of the idea, he didn't bother to discuss it with any of the department chairpersons or other faculty members.

It was announced in the student newspaper the following week, and the forms were distributed in classes during that week. One of the school's best known full professors, who had a worldwide reputation for incisive writing and provocative research, received a poor rating because of a foreign accent which was sometimes difficult to understand and his impatience with what he considered stupid questions. Many senior faculty members received inadequate ratings. The highest ratings seemed to go to young, nontenured faculty who were close to the students in age, grooming, and behavior.

The uproar among the majority of the faculty was deafening, and the dean was confronted by a committee of department heads who told him the rating system had to go or he would lose significant numbers of his most qualified faculty members and department heads.

1. *Did the dean introduce the program effectively?*
2. *What should the dean do about this ultimatum?*
3. *Discuss the pros and cons of student-run faculty evaluations.*
4. *What implications are there in these programs for the business world?*

CASE 5-3

A company hired Frank Packard as a group vice president. He had an excellent reputation as a manager, and the company was short of talent. His principal responsibility would be to try to turn around the unprofitable divisions in his group. He got a free hand to reorganize structure and release anyone that he believed was not competent.

When Frank arrived, he was pleasantly surprised to find his old college roommate heading up one of the divisions. They had lost touch over the years, but the friendship blossomed again.

After several months, the expected turnaround was not as good as the president expected. He particularly noted that the division headed by Packard's buddy was doing even worse. Packard had fired several people, some of whom were doing a better job than the college friend.

The president called Packard into his office after reaching the conclusion that Packard was protecting his friend. This suspicion was confirmed after 15 minutes of conversation. The president asked for and got Packard's resignation.

1. *Can friendship and business mix?*
2. *Should Packard have protected his friend?*
3. *What are the moral issues here?*
4. *Should Packard have been fired?*

CASE 5–4

Louis Beck, the president of Herald Manufacturing, had been a basketball star in college. Over the years he followed the fortunes of the team and developed a strong friendship with the coach, who had been one of Lou's teammates in college days and started coaching when he graduated.

He had just finished lunch with the coach, who had told him that he was resigning since he didn't like the new athletic director, thought the players were getting too independent, and no longer got much enjoyment from coaching.

Beck told his friend not to worry and offered him a job with Herald. The company was a large producer of electronics for both government and consumer use, employing 15,000 people in 25 plants around the country.

That afternoon Beck called the personnel vice president and told him of the job offer to the ex-coach. The vice president asked what kind of a job, and Beck's response was, "I don't know—you decide. As long as it pays around $20,000 a year—that's what he got for coaching." "Where can we place him if his only experience is coaching college kids?" the vice president asked. "Well, I'm really interested in helping him, so suppose we put him in public relations for the time being and see what develops," said Beck.

1. *Should the president have made the job offer to the coach?*
2. *How might it affect other employees in the company?*
3. *Did the personnel vice president react effectively?*
4. *Is there anything wrong with hiring a good friend who needs a job?*

CASE 5–5

During the last 25 years, the Union Fidelity Trust Company had grown quite rapidly. Technology had caused several job changes and the elimination of others. However, company policy had always dictated that no employee was to be fired because of job changes or eliminations. Normal attrition was believed capable of handling any employee surplus problems that resulted from the job changes.

Two years ago a new chief executive was appointed. He was 39 years old when he assumed the presidency of the bank. At about the same time the cost-price squeeze began to affect the banking industry, and Fidelity Union was no exception. The two largest expense items on the balance sheets of most banks are interest expense and salary and fringe benefit expense. Since interest expense is a function of the money market and no one bank can control it, the obvious category for expense control lies in salaries.

This fact did not escape the new president in his desire to maintain a reasonably high level of earnings for his bank. After discussing expense control with other members of senior management, he decided to introduce two new policies. One of these he thought of as a short-term policy subject to reevaluation if conditions permitted; it involved a hiring freeze of any new employees. The other, which he wanted to be a permanent policy, was an early retirement program designed "to eliminate obsolete older employees."

While the president realized that both of these policies would be controversial when he made the decision to implement them, he was surprised at the depth of the controversy. The early retirement policy was the most controversial. Each major division head was required to submit the names of those individuals who were considered least competent and candidates for suggested early retirement in the next year. The policy also allowed any employee over age 55 to request early retirement. In both cases, benefits would be less than those that would have been received if the employee stayed until the usual retirement age of 65, unless the retirement took place at age 60 or later. In such instances, the benefits would be the same.

The controversy seemed to center on the need for making the hard decision about who was "obsolete." Though the division heads could refer to all past performance appraisals and discussion with the individual's present supervisor, they resented having to make such a decision. Certainly a significant factor was that most of the potential candidates were long-service employees well known throughout the bank. The other part of the controversy related to the possibility of losing very capable employees, who under the policy could opt for early retirement if they so desired.

1. *Why would the division heads be reluctant to make an early retirement decision regarding obsolete employees?*
2. *Could the new president have implemented such a policy differently?*
3. *What is wrong about an early retirement policy? What is right?*
4. *Could the new president's age have anything to do with his decision?*

CASE 5–6

The second controversial policy in Case 5–5 had to do with a hiring freeze. Under it, no hiring of a new employee, even if it was for a replacement of a termination or retirement, could take place without the approval of the manpower planning manager. In effect, the policy was designed to reduce the total number of employees on the payroll.

Before even trying to cope with the implementation of this policy, department managers' complaints began to mount. All kinds of dire predictions about poor service to customers, excessive overtime, and poor morale began to circulate. No one believed that requests would be approved by the personnel planning manager; the managers believed that all departments would be understaffed.

1. *Explain the department managers' reaction to the hiring freeze.*
2. *To what extent did traditional behavior play a role in their reactions?*
3. *Could the new president have handled the implementation of this policy differently?*
4. *Why might managers faced with the need for expense control not want to implement such a policy?*
5. *Is a hiring freeze and early retirement policy better than an arbitrary layoff?*

CASE 5–7

Ben Lowry had just finished reading an article on group participation in decision making. The idea fascinated him, since it promised better morale and group cooperation. He had to admit he had been having trouble with his group lately. Bickering, backbiting, and generally poor relations characterized the 20 people reporting to him.

No one had wanted to work overtime recently, so Ben's boss was going to start a quota system. Although overtime normally would start (at time and a half) after seven hours of work, each employee was to be given a production quota, and as soon as that was reached, he would start on overtime pay. If he finished the quota in four, five, or six hours, he would get time-and-one-half pay for any work over quota.

Ben thought he would try group participation when he mentioned the overtime decision. He was going to offer his group a choice—overtime when the quota was completed or, if the employee chose, he could go home. This choice was not an authorized one, but Ben strongly believed that the group would choose the extra money, since that was his choice (although supervisors were not to participate in the plan). So Lowry felt he had nothing to lose, and he wanted to give participation a whirl.

Ben called his group together and gave them the details of the offer. He then left the room to allow them to discuss it. In about 15 minutes he returned, and they told him they chose the option of going home early as soon as quota was made.

1. *What does Ben do now?*
2. *Did he really allow group participation?*
3. *Why do you think the effort backfired on Ben?*

CASE 5-8

Ray Miller, a middle manager in a large company manufacturing office equipment, needed an assistant, since his area of responsibility had grown in the last two years. This person would report directly to him and would supervise about half the first-level supervisors in the department.

Miller decided to have a meeting of the 8 most senior of the 20 first-line supervisors reporting to him to discuss the choice of his assistant. These eight supervisors all had worked for Ray for a number of years. They were fully familiar with the area and the need for a new assistant. In fact, they believed that one of them would be chosen, and while each of them wanted the job, they didn't know what Ray had in mind when the meeting started.

He opened the meeting by telling them they would help him in the choice of his assistant. He had decided that one of them should fill the job, but he wanted to discuss the choice openly among all. "I want you people to tell me who should get the job," Ray said, throwing the meeting open to discussion. Even though the eight knew each other well, they were nonplussed by this approach. They really weren't prepared to discuss each other's strong and weak points in an open meeting. Neither did any of them want to be too forthright in claiming the job for himself.

Miller firmly pushed the discussion, telling them he wanted the group to pick one of themselves for the job and make the suggestion before the meeting terminated that afternoon. They looked at each other somewhat sheepishly and then started to speak. Each of the group voiced opinions and the discussion became quite lively. After about two hours of hot and heavy conversation, the choice narrowed down to two supervisors.

Ray saw that the group couldn't arrive at choosing one of the two by talking, so he asked them to vote on which one should get the job, with the two candidates not voting. The ballots were written and secret. Ray collected them and told the group he would give them his choice the next day.

The six supervisors voted five to one for one of the two choices, and they fully expected that this person would get the job. They appreciated the secret ballot because they didn't want to make their choice an open one. The next morning Ray called them all to the conference room and announced that he was choosing Tom Johnson. Tom was not one of the two the group had chosen. He was the youngest of the eight, however, and quite popular.

The people were surprised, even shocked, and they asked Ray why he held the elaborate charade the day before if he had chosen Tom Johnson. Miller replied, "It is my responsibility to decide, but I wanted the benefit of your thinking. You had a chance to express opinions, and I listened to them. But I acted on what I believe to be best for the department."

1. How do you feel about Miller's method for choosing an assistant?
2. What effect might it have on group relationships?
3. How will it affect Tom Johnson's ability to serve as Ray's assistant?
4. How will the group react to future discussions of vital departmental issues?

CASE 5–9

Jim McCarthy wanted an administrative assistant, and no one was available from within the company. He received authorization to recruit one from the outside. At about this time one of McCarthy's friends told him of a Roman Catholic priest who was presently serving in an administrative capacity in a local Catholic high school but who wanted to leave the priesthood. All he needed was a job and he would make the move. Jim, being a Catholic himself, had mixed feelings about hiring an ex-priest but thought he would interview him anyway. The priest showed up for the interview, and since he had not left the clergy as yet, he was dressed as a priest. Jim, out of habit, showed deference and the interview was carried out in that manner.

The priest was articulate and handled Jim's questions very well. He had a master's degree in business administration, and Jim thought this was a definite plus. Although the priest's entire working life up to the present had been spent in the Catholic church, he had held some administrative posts in hospitals and schools. Jim was impressed and offered the priest the job, which was promptly accepted.

Jim gave his new assistant instructions about the job and, still maintaining a somewhat awed relationship, started him on several projects. He didn't expect too much at the beginning; but after six months he found no improvement in the ex-priest's ability to accept responsibility for an assignment and see it through. On every project, Jim got questions and then some. It seemed as if the assistant were afraid to make a decision. McCarthy kept making mental excuses and rationalizations, afraid to ask himself the hard question. After all, the man had been a priest and was well educated—he would adjust and learn.

1. *What should McCarthy do about his assistant?*
2. *Why might it be difficult for the ex-priest to adjust to the business world?*
3. *How can one avoid the "halo effect" that faced Jim in this case?*

CASE 5–10

Because you are a recent graduate of a business school, having majored in management, you have been employed as an administrative assistant to the president of a private college. The president not only wants the benefit of your educational background but also your views as a recent college graduate.

The private college, like so many others throughout the country, has been suffering from increased costs of operation and falling enrollments. In addition it is competing with a rather strong state-supported higher education system which charges lower tuition. The private college's tuition is 40 percent higher than that charged by state schools.

The president believes that further tuition increases will only shrink the market for the college. Endowment income covers about 30 percent of operating costs. Ten percent comes from government contract research and the rest from tuition income. The college has a good reputation and offers associate, bachelors', and masters' degrees in liberal arts, education, and business administration.

A committee made up of several trustees, alumni, faculty members, and students has been formed to determine the approach the college should take to alleviate its problems. The president has asked you to serve as his representative on this committee.

Apply the seven-step problem-solving technique to this case.

The answer to the problem in Case 5–1 is:

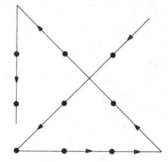

Chapter 6

Learning objectives

- ○ To understand the nature of policies, objectives, and procedures and their relationship to organizations

- ○ To gain awareness of the policy formulation process

- ○ To understand how managers and supervisors use policies and procedures

- ○ To understand different types of policies, objectives, and procedures and why they are necessary

Policies and procedures

Major topics

Formulating and establishing policies.

Policy development.

An example of policy implementation.

Characteristics of a good policy.

The supervisor interprets and applies policies.

Departmental policies.

Objectives.

Transforming policy and objectives into action.

The purpose of procedures.

Why supervisors should be interested in procedures.

How procedures should be developed.

Why procedures should be kept simple.

Procedures depend on people.

The formulation of policies, objectives, and procedures is a natural out-growth of the decision process. When a company desires some uniformity of practice in relation to both long-range and daily activity, policies are developed as guides to action. In a sense, a policy is one kind of decision, designed to encourage managers on all levels to focus on company objectives. The purpose is to have supervisors implement policy uniformly, with equitable treatment of all employees as the goal. Conflicts arise when supervisors interpret the same policy differently.

To understand policy formulation there first must be an understanding of how an organization develops policies. Any company's policies usually reflect the attitudes and values of the present top management on a variety of issues. Some of these issues are of greater importance than others, and some management attitudes are likewise more rigid on what is considered vital to the firm. Organizations differ in their approach to the management of the several functions making up the enterprise. Even companies in the same industry vary in their dynamism and their emphasis on the importance of various activities. All of us know companies that are sales-oriented, research-oriented, production-oriented, and so on. Then there is another classification system with which we are all familiar. In any given industry there are conservative companies, innovative companies, leader companies, follower companies, and those that could be described as ambivalent since they seem to shift from one pattern to another. In essence this is the organization's style and attitude. The result of the application of managerial attitudes and values to the activities of the firm is the development of a management philosophy. Haynes and Massie describe this process:

> A *philosophy of management* covers those general concepts and integrated attitudes fundamental to the cooperation of a social group. Philosophies for firms may differ. One might be good for firm A but not useful for firm B. Often a firm's own members may not be conscious of a philosophy; yet it is effective. To understand the philosophy of a given firm, the *concept of the firm* must be understood. This will provide a picture of the "character" of the firm—how the firm got where it is, the place that it occupies in the industry, its strengths and weaknesses, an idea of the viewpoints of its managers, and its relationship to social and political institutions.
>
> Specifically, this concept can be determined from understanding:
>
> 1. the existing personnel and their relationships,
> 2. the history of the firm,
> 3. the ethical framework of its managers, employees, customers, competitors, and suppliers,
> 4. the industrial setting, which includes its operating processes and economic structure of the industry,
> 5. the institutional setting, including the social forces and framework of government relationships.[1]

---

[1] W. Warren Haynes and Joseph L. Massie, *Management Analysis, Concepts and Cases* (Englewood Cliffs, N.J.: Prentice-Hall, Inc., 1961), pp. 142–43.

Perhaps the term "philosophy" may be ambiguous to some individuals. Essentially one might call it a "life-style." Each of us has developed an approach to doing things and attitudes about their accomplishment. This gives people some idea of what we believe in and how we go about achieving our goals. It may also give some indication as to how we might react to various situations. The combination of beliefs, attitudes, education, and experience becomes a life-style or philosophy. For instance, some students may work and study very hard to achieve high grades while others settle for a "C" grade and still others cheat on examinations.

Organizations react in much the same way. Organizational life-style or philosophy is shaped by a variety of forces, not the least of which is the value system of its top management. So we find some companies that adhere to strict policies in their public dealings and work very hard to establish good reputations while others conduct business using marginal practices and bribery.

Formulating and establishing policies

An organization's philosophy evolves by day-to-day practice, conscious effort on the part of management in the establishment of goals and strategies, or some combination of both. A successful company's philosophy must be developed by taking into consideration several factors beyond the internal needs of the company. Increasing social awareness on the part of business has resulted in policies which affect the company in its relationships not only with employees, customers, and stockholders but with the government on all levels, communities in which the company is located, suppliers, and various national organizations (including political parties).

Policies evolve out of the philosophy of the company as expressed by its management. Determining objectives and the means to accomplish these objectives results in the formulation of policies. These policies should be broad enough to allow employees to exercise creative action, but they should also establish parameters so that the whole company is directed toward optimum achievement of its goals. In short, a policy is a guide for action. It is also a statement of the company's intentions to achieve certain goals. As such it should be clear in language and readily understandable to those who must implement the policy. Above all, policy should not be so restrictive that it eliminates judgment by managers, for one of the most significant developers of managerial ability is decision making in an environment which allows for individual initiative and judgment. With this thought in mind, it becomes apparent that the number of policies formulated by the top management of an organization should be kept to a minimum. Only those that contribute to the attainment of established objectives in a broad sense and those that give direction toward these goals should be considered necessary.

Policy is recognized by most managers as a form of authority imposed on them by the top management. Because of this restrictive interpretation, it becomes necessary to evaluate each existing policy periodically to determine its relevance to current organizational objectives. In fact, some companies build in a review procedure at the time a policy is formulated by indicating a date for its reevaluation. In other companies, this review takes place annually. Certainly some review is necessary if policy is not to become red tape which is bent and skirted by managers down the line. The obvious danger of obsolete policies is that all policies become suspect and implementation by line managers is very difficult.

Significantly, effective policy formulation takes place when the individuals charged with this responsibility are aware of the needs of the organization as well as its goals. This means that line managers should be brought into discussions whenever possible. Feedback on the effect of policy is vital to its proper evaluation and continuance. Such feedback will only take place when managers feel their opinions are listened to. (See Figure 6–1 for a graphic illustration of the policy formulation process).

Policy development

Everyone has been confronted at one time or another with some individual who, in answer to a request, merely states, "It can't be done; it's against our policy." This may happen in a restaurant when you want a menu change or in a retail store when trying to exchange some item previously bought there. These and other similar experiences are frustrating and may cause one to wonder about the usefulness of policies and about how they are developed.

As mentioned earlier, managerial attitudes and philosophy form the backdrop for policy formulation. Out of this, some policies evolve as a deliberate action by top management to support its philosophy. Examples are such policies as those specifying a particular rate of growth, choosing markets for company products and services, and deciding on the location of plants and branches.

Tradition and precedent also form the basis for some policies. The statement "We've always done it that way" is heard in nearly all organizations. Hence past behavior establishes tradition or precedent for present behavior, and policies evolve and are followed even though they may not be written. Examples of this type are purchasing from a particular supply source, doing business with a particular bank, recruiting employees only from certain schools and colleges, and weighing seniority heavily in the promotion of employees.

A third kind of policy could be described as that which is externally generated. This type of policy has become increasingly important in recent years as society's demands on business organizations have increased. Laws passed by government on all levels create the need for developing policies to cover such things as environmental pollution, hiring practices, pricing, consumer information, customer relations, supplier relations, and employee relations.

Figure 6–1
The policy formulation process

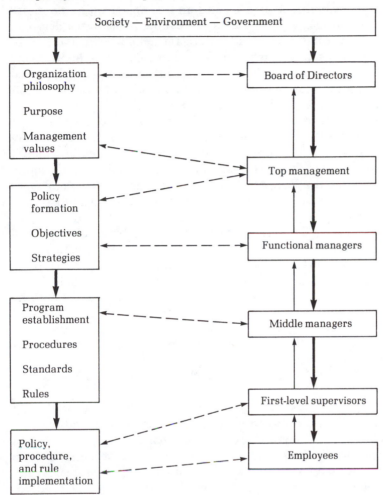

Policies, objectives, and strategies are developed by the board of directors and top management with the assistance of functional managers representing major areas of responsibility such as finance, production, marketing, and personnel. Middle managers and staff people design programs, procedures, standards, and rules to aid in the implementation of the policies. First-level supervisors and employees implement the policies using procedures, standards, and rules. Their performance is communicated upward, and the effectiveness of this performance will determine how well the policies are implemented. Changes in policy can result from this type of feedback.

An example of policy implementation

When an organization increases in size and complexity and there are several levels of management, top managers cannot make every decision. Policy allows them to indicate broad guides for action down the line so that lower level managers will make decisions implementing the thinking of top management when the policy was formulated. If a policy is traced from its formulation by top management to its implementation by a first-line supervisor, this process will be easy to understand.

Personnel policy committee of the board of directors. A committee of the board of directors states that the company intends that its rates of pay be commensurate with compensation practices in the markets in which it competes for people. This may be based on an organizational philosophy which indicates that the company wants to compensate its employees fairly for work performed but that it does not want to engage in extreme competition for employees.

Personnel vice president. The vice president in charge of personnel establishes a job evaluation program to determine the relative value of one job compared to all others in the company in purely objective terms, without regard to the person who holds the job. Then salary ranges are established, taking into account the results of the job evaluation effort and the salaries paid for comparable jobs in other companies. A performance review program is developed. All managers in the company are made aware of the salary ranges for the jobs they supervise as well as the salaries being paid to the incumbents. Additionally they are instructed in the use of the performance review and are given the dates when this is to take place.

Middle manager. Middle managers gather all the first-line supervisors reporting to them for a meeting to discuss the salary ranges and the performance review form. They are prepared to answer any questions and make themselves available for consultation. They instruct supervisors to be objective in evaluating performance, emphasizing the problems that can arise by playing favorites, and makes them aware of the need for thoroughly discussing the results of the performance review with the employee. They go on to mention that they will assist them in their recommendations of specific amounts of increase in rates of pay should the performance review warrant an increase for a particular employee.

First-level supervisor. The first-level supervisor looks at lateness and absentee records of all employees, studies production records and the error ratio, and evaluates employees on the other criteria established by the personnel department, such as ability to work with others, cooperativeness, promotability, and accuracy. The supervisor rates each employee and then discusses the rating with each employee in private, indicating good points and offering suggestions for the improvement of those areas where the employee is lacking. He or she then indicates the recommendation for salary action for the employee and passes both salary recommendations and performance reviews to the superior, remaining available for discussion. The supervisor notes that several employees are being paid below the minimum of the range established for the job they occupy and firmly recommends increases which will bring their pay above the minimum.

Characteristics of a good policy

Supervisors should have some criteria for judging the quality of policies, since they have so much influence on their actions. Some policies are out of date; they haven't been examined and revised to keep up with changes inside and outside the company. Economic conditions and markets may have changed. The company may now be mass producing instead of jobbing; it may be producing a different line of products and in need of a different type of labor skills; it may have expanded into branches far from the home office. It may have changed completely to meet changing conditions, yet never revised its policy manual. Some of the policies may have always been ineffective because they just grew out of a few decisions that set a precedent. Some other decisions might have been better, more timely, more in line with objectives, and more in harmony with other company policies.

There are certain characteristics to look for in evaluating policies. Good policies are stable, flexible, compatible, sincere, realistic, understandable, and written.

A policy should be as *stable* as it is possible to make it. It will be necessary to discard policies when they have outlived their usefulness, and it is necessary to modify them to keep up with the times, but these are changes that should not be made lightly. The stability of a policy can be improved by making it sufficiently *flexible* to take care of problems that vary from the normal, and flexible enough not to have to be adjusted too frequently to allow for changing conditions. If, however, a policy doesn't require reformulation from time to time to take care of inevitable changes, then that policy may be too vague to ever have much meaning or it may be so inflexible that it is actually a rule.

A good policy must be *compatible* with the "body" of policies; that is, it must not contradict or be in conflict with other policies. If it is a department policy, it should be subordinate to and in harmony with broader company policies. If the company has a policy of promotion from within, the department's hiring and training policies must be designed to take people in at the bottom and train them for advancement.

Policies are a way of publicizing the philosophy and ethics of a company—at least they are a commitment by management on how the company will act. Therefore they should be *sincere*. In their intent and in their wording they should express trustworthiness and build goodwill and cooperation, but they still have to be *realistic*. They can't be just high-sounding platitudes which would be followed if things were different.

They must be guides to steer a business and must provide for its survival and profitability in the actual working world.

Finally, a policy must be *understandable* if it is going to have a chance to be uniformly interpreted and applied. The meaning of it must be clear not only to the supervisors who will interpret and apply it but to everyone who will be affected by it. A policy maker will make a policy more understandable, plan it more carefully, and express it more clearly if he or she knows that it is going to appear in writing. For these reasons, and for many other reasons, a policy should be *written* in the policy manual. It should be reviewed periodically—preferably by a committee—and kept up to date and in harmony with changing conditions.

If a policy meets most of these conditions, it stands ready to serve its purpose.

The supervisor interprets and applies policies

When supervisors are confronted with problems requiring a decision—such as a discipline problem or whether to allow overtime or to lay off some workers—they first determine whether they have the authority to render the decision. If they do not have sufficient authority, they pass the problem up to the next management level (the rule of the exception). If on the other hand the decision should be made on a level of management lower than their own, they send the problem back down the line to their subordinates and with it they send guidance to aid in the solution. If such guidance or policy does not already exist, it is formulated and in so doing, they are formulating policy.

Once supervisors know that they have the authority to render a decision, they look to policy for guidance. And policy will mean more if they know why it was adopted in the first place, what changes have been made in it and why, and what trends will influence its application in the future. Being aware of trends is particularly advisable in the field of equipment replacement policies, hiring policies, and policies toward unions. When supervisors have background information on policies, they are better equipped to interpret them and use them for their true purpose—as a guide to decision making rather than as an inflexible formula for action.

Understanding the reason for a policy and knowing its history makes supervisors feel more in accord with the policy. Their attitudes toward policy are sensed by subordinates and influences the subordinates' attitude toward it and toward the decisions made in accordance with it. Supervisors must interpret policy accurately and clearly, in language that employees can understand; they must do it impartially, in the spirit in which the policy was intended; and they must give the reasoning behind it, the why and the wherefore.

Supervisors cannot assume that their subordinates know the policies just because they were explained in the induction program or in a talk a

"Safe!"

Reprinted by permission The Wall Street Journal

A punctuality policy can be implemented in many ways.

year ago. Workers come and go, they forget, and any piece of information becomes garbled in time. When supervisors make a decision on a controversial matter, they will do well to remind their subordinates of the policy under which that decision was made. Then people will know that the supervisor is not being arbitrary, operating by whim, or playing favorites. If an employee wants a raise or a transfer and isn't worth it or shouldn't have it, the supervisor should not blame policy or hide behind policy; it's better to tell the employee where he stands than to say something like, "Company policy says that the average should be close to the middle of the range."

Policies commit management to specific courses of action and specific types of decisions. If the company acts contrary to policy or if decisions down the line are made contrary to policy, the result is consternation and confusion. Policies that are strictly adhered to and well publicized help employees to understand, anticipate, and accept specific managerment decisions. For instance, if a company has a policy of a trial working period before an employee becomes permanent, and during that trial period the company can fire without cause, then people are forewarned. Or if during a recession it is known that the company will first cut out overtime and then shorten the work week before a wholesale layoff, people will be prepared to accept what is coming.

Uniformity of application is essential. Employees lose respect for a policy if they see it being violated with impunity in other departments or units—or, worse still, if they see their own supervisor being inconsistent in decisions that should be based on it.

Departmental policies

Since policies formulated by top management have to be broad enough to cover the whole organization, they are seldom detailed enough to guide the various major departments in their internal operations. Using the broad general management policies as a guide, the major department head must develop policies to guide his or her own department and must also interpret broad policies to determine their relevance to that area of responsibility. The example of a compensation policy given earlier in this chapter indicates how a major department head (the personnel vice president) would develop a policy from the broader policy formulated by higher management.

When the head of a department or section finds subordinates coming *for* decisions rather than *with* decisions, that manager should suspect that he or she has been spending too much time solving their problems for them and too little time formulating policies to help them do the problem solving themselves. In formulating policies for his or her own department, the superior might use the following outline:

1. Ask the questions: Why is this problem recurring? Why isn't it solved automatically without coming across my desk?
2. Find out if the principles and practices of good management are being applied to the situation that has given rise to the problem. If the company has staff specialists in policy and procedure analysis work, consult them and get their assistance.
3. Investigate or have a staff specialist investigate to find the best practices elsewhere in the company and in other companies in handling this type of problem.
4. Determine a tentative course of action for solving the immediate problem.
5. Develop a guide or policy for solving this type of problem in the future.
6. Make sure the proposed policy is not in conflict with company policy.
7. Discuss the proposed policy with the people who will have to enforce, interpret, and abide by it; get the benefit of their ideas and ex-

perience. Find out from them some of the difficulties that may arise when the proposed policy is applied to specific cases or situations.

8. Apply the policy on a temporary basis and modify it if necessary to get greater acceptance.
9. Put the policy in writing and explain it to all concerned.
10. Keep informed on the experiences of those enforcing the policy, the reaction of others to the policy, and any changes going on that are making it difficult to apply the policy.
11. Revise the policy when it no longer serves its purpose—that is, when there have been changes in the labor situation, the product, the skill requirements, or the broad company policies. A policy should be revised when there are an increasing number of exceptions to it, when the interpretations have to be farfetched, and when people start coming for decisions and interpretations. In revising, consider what the effect will be on the commitments and procedures based on the policy.
12. If there is a policy manual, remove the old policy from it and put in the new one. Explain the change to all concerned.

Objectives

Once policies are formulated, objectives can be established within the policy guidelines. The very nature of management practice is to achieve stated objectives within the scope of the organization's purpose and area of operations. Since organizations are hierarchical, it naturally follows that objectives are also hierarchical. The broad objective of increasing productivity established by top management may be translated to the purchase of new machinery which would be an objective of the functional areas of finance and production. Retraining employees to use the new equipment could be objectives of both the personnel department and manufacturing. More effective work performance then becomes the objective of first-level supervisors and employees using the new machines.

Obviously the achievement of objectives is related to several factors. Among these are the financial condition of the firm, management and employee abilities, market conditions, government regulation, size of facilities, economic climate, competition, position of the company in its industry, and social climate.

Time also has an important role in the achievement of objectives. Companies usually establish long-range and short-range objectives. If we return to the productivity improvement objective mentioned earlier, it is easy to see that such an objective might be a long-range one. New machinery may take considerable lead time to finance and acquire. Then the retraining of employees to use it, new work methods, standards, and possible related union negotiations may also consume considerable time.

In Chapter 4 it was mentioned that one of the principal causes of conflict was differences that may exist between individual objectives and those of the organization. A major responsibility of management on all levels is to state objectives clearly and make every attempt to obtain understanding and performance which will achieve the stated objectives. This is very difficult to accomplish bcause of the diversity of people concerned along with their varying attitudes, ambitions, and abilities.

In recent years a technique called management by objectives (MBO) has been developed. It will be discussed in Chapter 8 in detail. However, one of the critical factors in such a program is the establishment of sound objectives on all management levels. The following list is adapted from guidelines for the establishment of management objectives developed by George R. Terry.

1. Objectives should be the result of participation by those responsible for carrying them out.
2. All objectives wihin an enterprise should support the overall enterprise objectives.
3. Objectives should have some "reach" or challenge.
4. Objectives should be realistic.
5. Objectives should be up to date as well as innovative.
6. Objectives established for each management member should be limited in number.
7. Objectives should be ranked according to their relative importance.
8. Objectives should be in balance within a given enterprise.[2]

It is apparent that careful attention to the definition and establishment of objectives increases the chances for successful achievement of the objectives. Any process that involves all of the people concerned with accomplishment increases understanding. Participation in the process also develops pride among managers and can more effectively motivate them to succeed. In fact any methodology that encourages communication among the various levels of management can develop more cohesion and reduce conflict.

Transforming policy and objectives into action

One of the essential responsibilities of all managers is problem solving. The seven-step problem-solving technique already described can be very useful to managers once they have decided that the problem is worth solving. Each day on the job presents several occurrences which managers must confront and do something about. Given the guide of overall company policy, they must translate this policy into action so that the objectives established for their areas of responsibility can be accomplished. To do this effectively, they must identify those situations which recur frequently.

In the previous pages, policies have been defined and discussed as guides

---

[2] George R. Terry, *Principles of Management,* 7th ed. (Homewood, Ill.: Richard D. Irwin, 1977), pp. 101–2. © 1977 by Richard D. Irwin, Inc.

to be used in deciding *what* to do. The following discussion will consider the development of procedures that allow for the implementation of policy and attainment of objectives. Procedures can be defined as standing plans or predetermined courses of action for recurring situations telling *who* should do it, *where* it should be done, and *when* it should be done. The detailed description of *how* it should be done (machine and motions) is defined as method. Procedures form a network that extends throughout a company and ties together its various parts. This network of procedures is part of the total system, which encompasses people, devices, and plans.

Anyone discussing procedures should be prepared for differences of opinion in definitions. Procedures may be defined as the orderly and logical arrangement of functions, acts, or steps that constitute a process. They could be considered as a system for the completion of an operation. They may be given the importance of lifeblood for a cohesive organization structure. Or, at the other extreme, they may be called red tape—the forms, paper work, control reports, and oral and written instructions that prescribe and govern the steps or operations that make up a process.

The activities covered by procedures are the ordinary recurring ones of a business, and the routines are established to make sure that these activities are accomplished in the proper manner, at the proper time, by the proper people, in the proper place, and in the correct sequence.

In the personnel department the employment procedure is the process of putting people on the payroll—a systematic manner of handling the application forms, initial screening of applicants against openings, interviews, tests, physical exams, checking of references, assigning payroll number, and other steps necessary to the process.

The routine for making up the payroll is a procedure of the accounting department. The routine for processing a piece part is a procedure in a manufacturing department. These are departmental procedures.

An example of a procedure that crosses departmental lines and involves several departments is given in Figure 6-2, showing the activities and operations necessary to ship equipment under a government contract. This procedure involves the project engineer, technical liaison people, packing, carpenter shop, purchasing, quality control, and shipping departments. Figure 6-3 shows the first four steps (of the 35 steps in Figure 6-2) in more detail. Reading the steps of this procedure and analyzing them as they appear on the flowchart in Figure 6-2 serves to show how a procedure arranges for things to be done. Each step tells someone to do something: to fill out information on a form and distribute it to the people who must use it, to type up a list and distribute the copies to the people who need them, to order materials, to get approvals, to fabricate parts, to have inspections made.

It can be seen from this example that procedures involve several people, oral or written instructions, a sequence of steps, information to be moved, forms to be filled out, checkings and verifications to be made. The recurring activity governed by a procedure is not just a repetitive task performed at a

Figure 6-2
Flowchart showing 35 steps of a procedure for shipping equipment

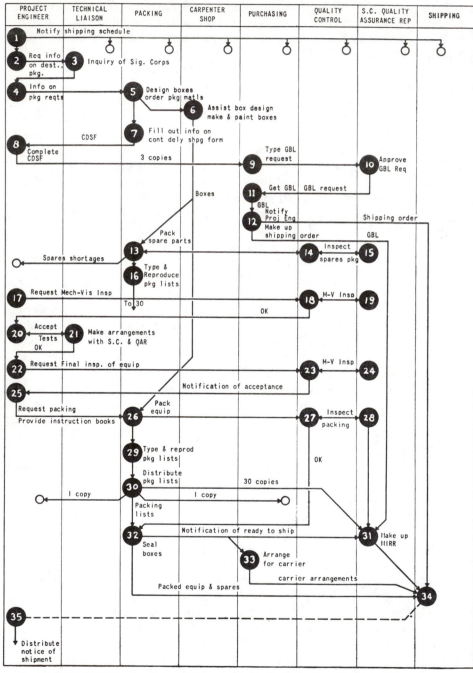

Source: Reproduced by permission of Sylvania Electric Products, Inc., Electronic Defense Laboratory, Mountain View, California.

Figure 6–3
First four steps of the procedure shown in Figure 6–2

| **SYLVANIA** ELECTRIC PRODUCTS INC. | INDEX NO. 70.01 |
| ELECTRONIC DEFENSE LABORATORY | PAGE 1 OF 6 |

POLICY AND STANDARD PRACTICE

SUBJECT: PROCEDURE FOR CONTRACT SHIPMENTS

(Supersedes No. 82.01 of 4/11/77)
DATE ISSUED: April 7, 1978
APPROVED BY: A. Brolly
J. Lien

I   SCOPE

The activities and operations necessary to ship equipment fabricated under an EDL contract.

II   POLICY

The Project Engineer will be responsible for meeting contract requirements. Shipping arrangements may be delegated by him to the Products Control group, technical matters excepted.

III   PROCEDURE

The procedural steps listed below refer by number to steps on the attached flow diagram.

1. At the earliest date on which the Project Engineer can reasonably anticipate when equipment will be shipped on his project, he should notify
   all people concerned with the shipment of the schedule. Two weeks, advance
   notice is desirable and preferably will be given with an internal memorandum. Schedule delay or acceleration deserves the same notifications.

   A tickler file will be maintained by Contracts Administration to provide
   an advance check for all projects in the Laboratory.

2. The Project Engineer will request of Technical Liaison information regarding destination of the equipment, the type of packing required (domestic
   or overseas) and the level of classification.

3. Technical Liaison will inquire of USASERU to obtain the desired information and will transmit it back to the Project Engineer.

4. The Project Engineer will advise the Packing group of his requirements.
   He will provide the following information:

   (a) Itemized list of all units to be shipped, including quantities,
       full description and serial numbers.

   (b) Type of packing (Will some packing boxes also be used as perma-
       nent carrying cases?)

   (c) Security Classification.

   (d) Spare parts list.

Source: Reproduced by permission of Sylvania Electric Products, Inc., Electronic Defense Laboratory, Mountain View, California.

work station—not, for instance, typing a letter or filing one. What the typist and the file clerk are doing is termed an operation. Such an operation would be a step in a procedure. The equipment used and the motions involved in performing an operation are the *method*.

The purpose of procedures

It would be difficult to run a business if upper management had to issue a series of specific orders covering all the details for each transaction. The establishment of standing plans (organization structure, policies, procedures, and methods) makes it possible for subordinates to carry on the actions according to plan. When procedures and methods are set up and standardized, it becomes possible to delegate responsibilities to a low level in the organization. Less time is needed for explanations of what is to be done. Methods can be made more efficient; standards of performance can be established. Coordination and control become easier because consistent actions are taken on similar cases and actions are thus predictable.

Procedures may follow the chain of command or they may flow horizontally across the organization. When an order comes into a business firm, information about it must somehow be carried to all the departments that will work on it—sales, credit, billing, fabricating, shipping, accounting, to name a few—where the proper chain of events will be started for doing all the things that need to be done. The work relationships for this horizontal flow are set up by procedures.

The type of procedure that flows from department to department acts as a horizontal coordinator and controller: It ties the organization together by horizontal lines that are channels for carrying information across the network of vertical lines that separate one department from another. If there were no procedures cutting across departments, theoretically it would be necessary for information between departments to go up the line to a common point and then come down again (see Chapter 3). Theoretically, if there were no procedure to cover the requisitioning of materials, each time a supervisor needed something for a job it would be necessary for the department head and the heads of all the other departments involved to meet with the plant superintendent and work out the details. When procedures exist, it becomes possible for the whole transaction to flow across the organization at a low level, in most cases never going any higher than the first-level supervisor. If procedures did not exist, management would have to develop a whole body of plans for organizing, directing, controlling, and coordinating each piece of work.

A procedure by definition is a routine for processing the ordinary activities of the business; therefore, if a process has become or is going to become repetitive, a procedure should be established for it so that it can be handled automatically and without the waste of managerial time and effort.

Why supervisors should be interested in procedures

Supervisors should be interested in procedures because they can make them work for them, can use them to relieve a load of routine and save time for the more important aspects of the job. Also, if they understand procedures they can do a better job of explaining their purpose and their importance to the subordinates who are expected to carry them out.

If supervisors look critically at some of the procedures in their departments, they may see that they are not being followed—that steps are being skipped—and that some of the failures they have been blaming on subordinates may be caused by weaknesses in the procedures. Procedures usually grow from the bottom of the organization, and they aren't always in line with policies, which start from the top. Procedures develop from custom or habit, or they may be put in as stopgaps. They develop piecemeal; part of an old procedure doesn't work well or people make too many mistakes under it, so a new procedure is tacked on to take care of the weak place. A procedure that has not been carefully planned is probably inefficient.

Some procedures have outlived their usefulness but are still followed because people resist change. The product changes, the organization changes, people change, related procedures change, but still some of the expensive old routines are continued like bad habits. The supervisor who is called upon to cut costs will find a fruitful field in the investigation and redesign of the procedures under his or her control.

Supervisors may find that some of the information being collected in their departments are no longer needed or that it is also being collected elsewhere. Some of the forms being filled out may be useless. Some of the records being kept in the department may be just "protection" in case someone should ask for information that could be gotten elsewhere. One of the benefits of procedural analysis is in getting rid of needless work. There is more saving in abolishing the *need* for the sorting, checking, typing, posting, distributing, or filing than there is in improving the methods of performing these operations.

How procedures should be developed

Procedures that cross department lines should be developed by staff specialists who have experience in systems analysis. These specialists are equipped to make complete investigations crossing department lines, to draw elaborate interrelations and design forms, and to put proposed procedures in writing and help install them. When companies do not have these specialists, supervisors who know the fundamental principles of procedure design can set up efficient procedures for their own departments.

A supervisor should learn the fundamentals of procedure design even though the company procedures are designed by specialists from the system design department. The line person who knows what staff specialists can and cannot do can get full value from their services. This person knows what kinds of information they need in order to do a better job of designing procedures, and knows how to relate the procedures to the abilities and status relationships of the subordinates who will be responsible for carrying them out.

Why procedures should be kept simple

A procedure is effective if it fulfills its purpose and does it at the lowest possible cost. Procedures cost money, because it takes time to handle information—to gather it, record it, transport it, and check if for accuracy. The more complicated the procedure, the more costly it is. Involved procedures arise from trying to make the procedure foolproof—putting in a great number of checkpoints so that nothing can possibly go wrong. Bosses who hate to assume any blame for mistakes made in their departments may build extra steps into procedures just to be sure that there will be no slipups that they can be held responsible for (for example, requiring a signature before any action can be started and then again after it is accomplished). If a mistake cannot be made under a procedure, the procedure is probably too complicated.

A number of things cause procedures to become complicated. They may be designed to cover too wide an area—that is, cover the unusual as well as the routine. For example, if the processing of a special order can follow the same routine as that of a regular order the procedure is probably too complicated. Special cases and cases that occur rarely should be treated as exceptions to the routine. Procedures have a tendency to become elaborate in manufacturing establishments because of the need to meet deadlines and coordinate various activities in preparation for assemblies. As a company becomes larger, there is a tendency for procedures to become more elaborate so that more control can be achieved.

Procedures depend on people

Although procedures are spoken of as being automatic and self-starting, they are not. A form cannot fill itself out and start its several copies on their way to the departments that need the information. Procedures and systems have to be designed for the people who are going to carry them out. The best a form can do is be designed so that people will use it promptly, fill in the information accurately, interpret the information correctly, and take the proper action on it. Procedures must be designed to cut down the possibilities of human error. People forget, have bad days, put things off, make mistakes in copying information, mislay things; so procedures should be designed to catch errors and correct them before they have caused much damage. For instance, forms should have numbering systems to call attention to any that are missing from the series. Copies should be matched at some control point to catch any that have gone astray or been improperly handled.

The various steps of procedures should be assigned to people who are fitted to perform them adequately and economically; highly paid personnel should not be assigned detailed routine work. A procedure will be carried out more effectively if people accept it as logical and necessary and if it is also an easy starter, quick and simple to handle, with all the steps designed to reduce the possibility of any being skipped or of action being stopped before reaching completion. Procedures need built-in attention callers.

Since procedures cannot and should not cover every situation, one of the dangers of management-by-procedure is that people will hesitate to use their own good judgment even when they can see that the application of a procedure is not in the best interests of the company. In some organizations, systems become an end in themselves rather than a means to an end. When getting ahead depends on how well a person follows procedure, then any deviation from procedure is frowned upon, and nobody will risk using initiative or judgment but will follow along, keeping his or her nose clean.

There should be more emphasis on the purpose or *why* of routines; more dependence upon people and less upon the system. The trend in better management today is to build meaning into jobs—to design jobs in such a way as to promote individual responsibility. If people feel that responsibility rests upon them rather than upon a system, they will exercise initiative and judgment. But if they feel that they have to buck the routine in order to protect the company's interests, they may choose to follow routine. As a result they will be of less value to the company and will have less satisfaction in their jobs. Procedures can't operate without people, and the performance of people hinges upon their knowledge, ability, and attitude, the design of their jobs, and the quality of the supervision.

Summary

Policies evolve from an organizational philosophy and effort on the part of management to establish goals and strategies. To give the organization direction toward its objectives, policies must be formulated by top management. Each major department head must also develop policies for his or her area of responsibility that are in the context of broad company policy.

Policies are guides to action to help all levels of management in decision making—to let them know what kind of action is expected of them and to let others know what kind of action to expect. Policies enable all levels of management to make decisions that are in line with the organization's philosophy and goals. They also give management criteria by which to judge the decision-making capability of managers on all levels. Lower level managers usually interpret policy to guide their actions, although they may be involved in policy formulation if consulted by higher management.

After policies are formulated, objectives can be derived from them. Managers and supervisors are concerned with achieving objectives for their areas of responsibility so that overall organizational objectives may be met. In recent years a process called management by objectives (MBO) has been developed to enhance this process.

Procedures are standing plans establishing the manner, step by step, for handling the recurring activities of the organization. They provide for coordination and control of the flow of work through an organization and cut down on the need for carrying routine matters through the chain of command for a decision.

Procedures should be designed to minimize the possibility of human error. They should be sure-starting, uncomplicated, and fitted to the people who will use them. They should not become an end in themselves or be permitted to discourage initiative and judgment. They should be examined periodically and redesigned to bring them up to date and make them more efficient.

CASE 6–1

Stone, Roberts, and Jackson Company, a firm of stockbrokers with several branches in a large city, decided to open a branch in a wealthy suburb about 35 miles from the central office. The branch manager decided to keep the office open two evenings a week so that he could more effectively serve the customers.

At this branch it was necessary for employees to drive to work, since no public transportation was available. Because of the salary ranges for lower level clerical jobs, the manager experienced difficulty in recruiting such help. The employees were aware of this difficulty, and they exhibited considerable independence and were difficult to discipline. The manager was unable to convince most of them to work overtime on the two evenings a week the branch was open.

The manager sought the help of the company's personnel director. In particular he wanted to increase the salaries and the ranges for the clerical positions which were giving him trouble. The personnel director told him that this could not be done, because it would mean changing the ranges for all clerical positions; and, of course, it would mean increases for all clerks, not just those in the suburban branch. He went on to say that this would be too costly and that the company was not having any unusual difficulty with clerks at its metropolitan branches.

1. *Should a company have a flexible salary policy to handle unusual situations such as the one depicted in this case?*
2. *Was the personnel director being realistic in his explanation to the branch manager?*

3. *What can the branch manager do to operate his branch effectively?*
4. *Do you feel the employees' independent behavior was attributable solely to the salaries paid?*

CASE 6–2

You are head of the general services department, made up of five sections—correspondence, stenographic, stationery, files, and reproduction. The supervisor of the filing department has just brought you this problem:

One of her file clerks, Mary Kamp, will be celebrating her 25th anniversary with the company next month—celebrating, that is, if anybody can be found who will celebrate with her. It's a medium-sized company, family-owned, and upper management pays no attention to what goes on with the people at the lower levels. The problem of 25th anniversaries never came up before because the only people who ever stayed that long were a few salesmen and engineers who started with the founder (now dead), and they had their own celebrations.

Mary Kamp is well known all over the office, but her job and her personality haven't endeared her to anybody. In the early days of the company she was the combination mail clerk and file clerk, and she still takes full responsibility for the handling of all the important mail that comes into the house. Her job now is to get customers' folders so that new correspondence can be attached to them and turned over to the people responsible for handling their accounts. She spends her day rummaging through the work on people's desks, urging them to finish with folders right away, or to copy out what they need, or to promise them to her within the hour. She has a memory for customers' names, and she knows everything that is going on in the business and who should be handling it. She is probably the most conscientious worker in the company. She is also pushy and raspy, along with being speedy, efficient, and dependable.

Her supervisor has tried to stir up some enthusiasm for a filing department lunchtime party or a gift collection to give some token of appreciation for 25 years of devotion, but the people she approached don't want to handle it. Their reaction is, "She bugs everybody." Mary Kamp has been on the giving end of office collections for years—baby showers, bridal showers, wedding presents, housewarmings, and hardship cases. But nobody wants to pass the hat for her, and the supervisors never do any collecting.

1. *What are you going to do about the occasion?*
2. *What would be the effect if you do nothing?*
3. *Would this be a good time to shut off on all the collections, gift presentations, and lunchtime festivities that employees seem to spend so much time on?*

CASE 6–3

Over the years the Cambridge Manufacturing Company had relatively loose personnel policies. Much actual policy was made by supervisors and managers as events arose. Reactions to these events became practice, practice became tradition, and this evolved as policy.

One of these so-called policies was the way compensation was handled. In general employees received increases in pay for a variety of reasons not related to job performance. Among these were seniority, cost of living, size of family, sex (males receiving more than females in the same job), and the dominant feeling among many managers to "take care of good employees" with no clear definition of a "good employee."

Six months ago a new personnel director was hired, and one of her first assignments was to bring order out of the chaos that existed in the development and implementation of personnel policies. With the legal requirements of affirmative action compliance and other complexities in personnel practice in mind, the company's top management recognized the need for professionalism in personnel administration, and they were prepared to support the new personnel director completely.

Since the new personnel director believed compensation practice was vital to overall policy change and implementation, she developed an objective performance based appraisal form to be used in evaluating employee job performance and to be the basis for compensation recommendations by supervisors and mangers. All managers and supervisors were informed and given a through explanation of the new form and the procedures for its use. The need for objective judgments of employee performance was particularly emphasized. When the new appraisal forms started to come in to the personnel department, the director noticed that even though the appraisals were well done in general they did not reflect the salary recommendations that accompanied them. People were still being rewarded for seniority. Women with excellent job performance were still recommended for smaller increases than their male counterparts, and even employees who did not perform well were recommended for token increases to reflect increased living costs.

1. *What went wrong here?*
2. *How can the personnel director implement the change?*
3. *Are new policies necessary?*
4. *Why would the supervisors and managers continue their old compensation practices?*

CASE 6–4

The company had no policy regarding supplementary employment. The thought was that what employees did in their spare time was their business.

Vince Adkins was employed as a forklift truck operator, and his work was above average. In his spare time Vince had been working as an upholsterer. He decided to try some jobs at home. He solicited work from his fellow employees and got several jobs.

One morning five angry employees appeared in your office. It seems they had all advanced money to Vince Adkins for upholstery jobs and the work was not finished. They had been waiting for six months and were now tired of his excuses. As the plant manager, they have come to you for help.

1. *Should you do anything about their problems with Vince Adkins?*
2. *Should a company have a policy regarding off-hours employment for its full-time employees?*
3. *How might Adkins's job performance be affected by his problems?*
4. *Should you choose to do nothing, what might occur in the plant when the angry employees spread the word about Vince Adkins?*

CASE 6–5

The Benson Tabulating Company was a large computer service bureau employing several hundred people and was located in a suburb of a large city. The company had a policy of giving 12 paid holidays each year: New Year's Day, Presidents' Day, Good Friday, Memorial Day, Fourth of July, Labor Day, Rosh Hashanah, Yom Kippur, Columbus Day, Veterans' Day, Thanksgiving, and Christmas.

Because of increased costs and declining profits, the company started a cost control program. One of the costs to be reduced was holiday expense. The company decided to eliminate one holiday. They accomplished this by eliminating Good Friday, Rosh Hashanah, and Yom Kippur and replacing these three holidays with two floating holidays. Employees could take them any time and for any reason as long as a department was not forced to close down. It was thought that Jewish employees could choose their holy days, and Christians could pick Good Friday if they so desired, but neither religious group was restricted to this choice.

Another aspect of the floating holiday idea was to allow black employees to take Martin Luther King's birthday off, which many of them had requested. In fact, the two floating holidays were thought to be the solution to all requests for ethnic, racial, and religious holidays that were not celebrated by the general population.

Two Jewish employees filed a discrimination complaint against the company with the state commission on discrimination. They claimed that they had lost two holidays while the Christians lost only one. Although they could use the two floating holidays for the two lost days, they believed the intent was to discriminate against members of the Jewish faith.

1. *Do the two employees have a justifiable complaint?*
2. *If you represented the company, what would you tell the hearing examiner?*
3. *How should a company handle religious, racial, and ethnic holidays?*
4. *To what extent should tradition play a role in a company's holiday policy?*

CASE 6–6

Ross Dixon got his first private office when he was promoted to department head. With it went the standard furnishings for his level of management: a desk, a chair, two side chairs, and a two-drawer file cabinet.

The company had developed procedures for furnishing offices, and these were based on the level of management. Both the size of the office and its furnishings were included in the procedure. Ross Dixon got the furnishings allowed for a department head.

After he was in the office for a week, Ross purchased a painting, a chrome water jug, and an expensive desk set. He wanted to give his office some individuality and thought it all right since he paid for all the things he added. Besides, he felt they gave an air of prestige to his office that was lacking in the other department heads' offices.

Several department heads come to you to complain about the furnishings in Dixon's office.

1. What do you tell them?
2. What do you tell Ross Dixon?
3. Should a person be allowed to upgrade the furnishings in his office at his own expense?
4. Why do companies have procedures such as those described in the case?

CASE 6–7

You are a second-level supervisor in the R&D division of a company. The company policy is that only graduate engineers or those having an equivalent background may be considered for first-level supervisory jobs. You have under your jurisdiction Sid Smith, an engineering designer. He has no college training or equivalent background, but he has such outstanding ability and leadership qualities that you promote him to the job of first-level supervisor. The other first-level supervisors in the department, as well as your boss, believe that Smith is the man for the job. The boss advised you to process the necessary papers. Smith has now been on the job for two weeks, and he looks very promising. In the mail this morning you received from the personnel department a rejection of the promotion because Smith does not have the necessary background. There is a good chance that Smith will quit if he is demoted.

1. Evaulate the company's policy. Justify your answer.
2. What should you do now?
3. How could the situation have been prevented from occurring?
4. Work up a procedure to prevent similar situations from occurring.

CASE 6-8

The reproduction department in a large corporation handles a heavy load of security-classified documents. Lack of sufficient automatic equipment prevents the manager of the department from establishing production line techniques even with the routine blueprint operations. He has a limited budget and believes that his biggest problem is avoiding the "brush fire" type of operation associated with excessive rush requests, so he has established detailed procedures and follows them rigidly. One of these procedures is to require the signatures of section supervisors on all rush jobs.

The department manager feels that he is doing his best within his budget, although there are complaints about having to wait for service. The scheduling and engineering departments constantly complain that they can't get a "few quick copies" of their working papers and sketches. Because of the delays and the inflexible procedures, some engineers have been copying by hand their sketches and material lists. The chief engineer, wanting to put a stop to this waste of time, requested his own departmental copying machine. The request was turned down by management because all reproduction services fall within the responsibility of the reproduction department and all the machines are located in that one area.

The chief engineer believes that the inadequate reproduction service is hampering his department and decreasing output, but he hasn't sufficient records of job and time charges to prove his point.

1. *Should engineering have its own copying machine?*
2. *What can be done to improve the reproduction service?*
3. *How might procedures be improved?*

CASE 6-9

You are the manager of a branch bank in a section of a large city which is now considered a ghetto area. Formerly it was a residential and retail business neighborhood. The complexion of the area has changed in a few years from middle income to a predominance of welfare recipients. There has been a marked increase in crime, causing former residents to relocate. Many of the homes and stores are abandoned and boarded up.

During a normal business day it is not unusual to hear of robberies and muggings taking place, with the branch's customers the victims in several instances. As a result of these conditions, several employees are alarmed about their safety coming to work and going home.

In the past month, two employees have requested transfers; they claim their families do not want them to work in this section. Both are key employees, excellent workers, and have been with the bank over ten years. You have little choice but to grant their requests for transfer, for if you don't they have threatened to resign and thus two superior employees would be lost to the bank. This leaves two vacancies that will be hard to fill. It seems that the

bank's personnel department has been finding it exceedingly difficult to recruit either new or experienced employees for this branch.

Despite the conditions mentioned above, the branch is maintaining high
balances in checking accounts and loans. Although many of the business
accounts have moved, they continue to bank in this branch because of the
years of pleasant relationships they have had with you as manager and financial adviser.

1. *Should you have allowed the two key employees to transfer?*
2. *Could you have done anything to convince them to stay at the branch?*
3. *Can you help the personnel department with its recruiting efforts?*
4. *How will you continue to serve your customers effectively if you lose more
   employees and cannot get replacements?*
5. *Even though business continues to be profitable, should you recommend that
   the bank close your branch?*
6. *Can a large organization such as a bank afford to stop doing business in de-
   pressed areas?*

CASE 6–10

The president of a medium-sized company needed a new secretary, since
his present one was leaving to be married. After screening several applicants sent to him by the personnel department, he chose Mrs. Jane Black.
She had considerable experience as a secretary and her last position was
very similar to the one she was chosen for.

When she started her new job, she was given the usual formal orientation
program that all new employees of the company received. This program
was handled by the personnel department, and it encompassed, among
other things, an explanation of all company personnel policies and how
they affected the employee. These policies included such items as vacations,
holidays, insurance, other fringe benefits, probationary period, and sick
leave.

In relation to sick leave, the company policy clearly stated that an employee was entitled to five days' sick leave after three months of employment, which was the normal probationary period for new employees.

After being employed for one and a half months, Mrs. Black was absent
for two days. When she received her next paycheck, two days' pay had been
deducted. She stormed into the president's office, complaining quite bitterly
about the deduction and the fact that she thought it very unfair. The president waited until she was finished complaining and then told her he did not
have time to discuss it with her. Two more weeks passed, and Jane Black
complained to her boss once again. He called the personnel manager and
asked him to handle the problem. Another week passed and Mrs. Black was
now complaining to anyone who would listen to her.

Finally, the personnel manager called Jane Black to his office and asked her about her problem. She went into a lengthy explanation, particularly emphasizing the unfairness of the salary deduction. He asked her if she had been informed of the company policy on sick leave when she was hired and she replied in the affirmative. He then asked if she fully understood that she was not entitled to any sick leave until she had been with the company for three months. She again replied in the affirmative. He told her that he could not understand why she was complaining so forcefully. Jane then stated, with great emphasis, "But I was really sick!"

1. *Did Jane Black have a legitimate complaint? Explain.*
2. *Did the president handle the problem properly?*
3. *Did the personnel manager handle the problem satisfactorily?*
4. *Why do you think Jane Black complained about her salary deduction?*

SUGGESTED READINGS: PART I

Chapter	**Books**
1,2,3,4,5,6	Albanese, Robert. *Management: Toward Accountability for Performance.* Rev. ed. Homewood, Ill.: Richard D. Irwin, Inc., 1978.
2,4	Argyris, Chris. *Human Behavior in Organization.* New York: Harper & Row, Publishers, 1957.
2,3,4	———. *Integrating the Individual and the Organization.* New York: John Wiley & Sons, Inc., 1964.
2,4	———. *Personality and Organization: The Conflict between the System and the Individual.* New York: Harper & Row, Publishers, 1957.
1,3	Barnard, Chester I. *The Functions of the Executive.* Cambridge, Mass.: Harvard University Press, 1951.
1,2,3,4	Bittel, Lester R. *Management by Exception.* New York: McGraw-Hill Book Co., 1964.
1,2,3,4	Dale, Ernest. *Management: Theory and Practice.* 4th ed. New York: McGraw-Hill Book Co., 1978.
2,4,5	Davis Keith. *Human Relations at Work.* 5th ed. New York: McGraw-Hill Book Co., 1977.
1,2,3,4,5,6	Donnelly, J. H.; Gibson, J. L.; and Ivancevich, J.M. *Fundamentals of Management.* 3d ed. Austin, Tex.: Business Publications, Inc., 1978.
1,2,3,4	Drucker, Peter F. *The Effective Executive.* New York: Harper & Row, Publishers, 1966.
1,2,4	———. *Management: Tasks, Responsibilities, Practices.* New York: Harper & Row, Publishers, 1974.
2,3,4,5	Elbing, Alvar O. *Behavioral Decision in Organizations.* Glenview, Ill.: Scott, Foresman & Co., 1970.
1,2,3	Fayol, Henri. *General and Industrial Management* (trans. Constance Storrs). New York: Pitman Publishing Corp., 1949.
2,3,4,5	Gibson, J. L.; Ivancevich, J. M.; and Donnelly, J. H. *Organizations.* Rev. ed. Austin, Tex.: Business Publications, Inc., 1976.
1,2,3,4	Gross, Bertram M. *The Managing of Organizations.* New York: Macmillan Co., 1964.
6	Higginson, M. V. *Management Policies I.* Research Study No. 76. New York: American Management Ass., Inc., 1966.

Chapter	**Books**
6	———. *Management Policies II.* Research Study No. 78. New York: American Management Assn., 1966.
2,3,5,6	Johnson, R. A.; Kast, F. E.; and Rosenzweig, J. E. *The Theory and Management of Systems.* 3d ed. New York: McGraw-Hill Book Co., 1973.
1,2,3,4,5,6	Kast, Fremont E., and Rosenzweig, James E. *Organization and Management: A Systems Approach.* 2d ed. New York: McGraw-Hill Book Co., 1974.
1,2,3,4,5,6	Koontz, Harold, and O'Donnell, Cyril. *Principles of Management.* 6th ed. New York: McGraw-Hill Book Co., 1976.
1,2,3,6	Learned, Edmund P., and Sproat, Audrey T. *Organization Theory and Policy.* Homewood, Ill.: Richard D. Irwin, Inc., 1966.
1,2,3,4,5,6	Leavitt, H. J.; Dill, W. R.; and Eyring, H. B. *The Organizational World.* New York: Harcourt, Brace, Jovanovich, Inc., 1973.
2,5	Levin, Richard I., and Lamone, Rudolph P. *Quantitative Disciplines in Management Decisions.* Belmont, Calif.: Dickenson Publishing Co., 1969.
2,3,4	Likert, Rensis. *New Patterns of Management.* New York: McGraw-Hill Book Co., 1961.
1,2,3,4,5,6	Litterer, Joseph A. *The Analysis of Organizations.* 2d ed. New York: John Wiley & Sons, Inc., 1973.
1,2,3,4	McGregor, Douglas. *The Professional Manager.* New York: McGraw-Hill Book Co., 1967.
2,3,4	———. *The Human Side of Enterprise.* New York: McGraw-Hill Book Co., 1960.
5	Maier, Norman R. F. *Problem Solving and Creativity.* Belmont, Calif.: Brooks/Cole Publishing Co., 1970.
2,3,4	March, James G., ed. *Handbook of Organizations.* Chicago: Rand McNally & Co., 1960.
1,5	Miller, David W., and Starr, Martin K. *The Structure of Human Decisions.* Englewood Cliffs, N.J.: Prentice-Hall, Inc., 1967.
1,2,3,4,5,6	Newman, William H., and Warren, E. K. *The Process of Management.* 4th ed. Englewood Cliffs, N.J.: Prentice-Hall, Inc., 1977.
1,2,3,4,5	Ready, R. K. *The Administrator's Job: Issues and Dilemmas.* New York: McGraw-Hill Book Co., 1967.
1,2,3,4,5,6	Richards, Max D., and Greenlaw, Paul S. *Management: Decisions and Behavior.* Rev. ed. Homewood, Ill.: Richard D. Irwin, Inc., 1972.
1,2,3,4,5,6	Rue, Leslie W., and Byars, Lloyd L. *Management: Theory and Application.* Homewood, Ill.: Richard D. Irwin, Inc., 1977.
1,3,4	Sayles, Leonard R. *Managerial Behavior.* New York: McGraw-Hill Book Co., 1964.
1,2,3,4	Scott, William E., and Cummings, Larry L. *Readings in Organizational Behavior and Human Performance.* Rev. ed. Homewood, Ill.: Richard D. Irwin, Inc., 1973.
1,2,3,4	Scott, William G., and Mitchell, Terence R. *Organization Theory: A Structural and Behavioral Analysis.* 3d ed. Homewood, Ill.: Richard D. Irwin, Inc., 1976.

Chapter	**Books**
2,3,4,5	Seiler, John A. *Systems Analysis in Organizational Behavior.* Homewood, Ill.: Richard D. Irwin, Inc., 1967.
1,3,4	Simon, Herbert A. *Administrative Behavior.* 2d ed. New York: Macmillan Co., 1957.
3,4,5	Strauss, George, and Sayles, Leonard R. *Managing Human Resources.* Englewood Cliffs, N.J.: Prentice-Hall, Inc., 1977.
2,3,4	Sutermeister, Robert A. *People and Productivity.* 3d ed. New York: McGraw-Hill Book Co., 1976.
2	Taylor, Frederick W. *Scientific Management.* New York: Harper & Row, Publishers, 1947.
1,2,3,4,5,6	Terry, George R. *Principles of Management.* 7th ed. Homewood, Ill.: Richard D. Irwin, Inc., 1977.
1,2,3,4,5,6	Trewatha, Robert L., and Newport, M. Gene. *Management: Functions and Behavior.* Rev. ed. Dallas, Tex.: Business Publications Inc., 1979.

Articles

2,3,4	Aldrich, H., and Herker, D. "Boundary Spanning Roles and Organization Structure," *Academy of Management Review,* April 1977.
1,2,3,4	Anthony, T. F., and Carroll, A. B. "An Overview of the Supervisor's Job," *Personnel Journal,* May 1976.
1,2,3	Benson, Carl A. "New Supervisors: From the Top of the Heap to the Bottom of the Heap," *Personnel Journal,* April 1976.
1,3,5	Boettinger, Henry M. "Is Management Really an Art?" *Harvard Business Review,* January-February 1975.
2,3,4	Browne, P. J., and Cotton, C. C. "The Topdog/Underdog Syndrome in Line-Staff Relations," *Personnel Journal,* August 1975.
2,3,4	Cherns, Albert B. "Can Behavioral Science Help Design Organizations?" *Organizational Dynamics,* Spring 1977.
1,3	Culbert, Samuel A. "The Real World and the Management Classroom," *California Management Review,* Summer 1977.
2,3,4	Cummings, L. L., and Berger, C. J. "Organization Structure: How Does It Influence Attitudes and Performance?" *Organizational Dynamics,* Autumn 1976.
1,2,3,4	Cummings, Paul W. "Occupation: Supervisor," *Personnel Journal,* August 1975.
1,3,5	Drucker, Peter F. "How to Manage Your Boss," *Management Review,* May 1977.
1,4	Fulmer, William E. "The Making of a Supervisor," *Personnel Journal,* March 1977.
1,2,3	Gellerman, Saul W. "Supervisor: Substance and Style," *Harvard Business Review,* March-April 1976.
1,3,5	Gibbons, Charles C. "Marks of a Mature Manager," *Business Horizons,* October 1975.
1,5	Leavitt, Harold J. "Beyond the Analytic Manager," *California Management Review,"* Spring 1975.

Chapter	*Articles*
2,3,4	Limerick, David C. "Authority Relations in Different Organizational Systems," *Academy of Management Review,* October 1976.
2,3	Lorsch, Jay W. "Organizational Design: A Situational Perspective," *Organizational Dynamics,* Autumn 1977.
3,4	Luke, Robert A., Jr. "Matching the Individual and the Organization," *Harvard Business Review,* May-June 1975.
1,2,3,4,5,6	Mintzberg, Henry. "The Manager's Job: Folklore and Fact," *Harvard Business Review,* July-August 1975.
6	Mintzberg, Henry. "Policy as a Field of Management Theory," *Academy of Management Review,* January 1977.
4,5	Morano, Richard A. "Managing Conflict for Problem Solving," *Personnel Journal,* August 1976.
5	Oxenfeldt, Alfred R. "Effective Decision Making for the Business Executive," *Management Review,* February 1978.
2,3,5,6	Perrow, Charles. "The Bureaucratic Paradox: The Efficient Organization Centralizes in Order to Decentralize," *Organizational Dynamics,* Spring 1977.
1	Robbins, Stephen P. "Reconciling Management Theory with Management Practice," *Business Horizons,* February 1977.
2,3	Sayles, Leonard R. "Matrix Management: Structure with a Future," *Organizational Dynamics,* Autumn 1976.
5	Shuler, Cyril O. "How Good Are Decision Makers?" *Business Horizons,* April 1975.
1,2,3,4	Smiley, L. M., and Westbrook, P. R. "The First-Line Supervisory Problem Redefined," *Personnel Journal,* December 1975.
5	Summers, I., and White, D. E. "Creativity and the Decision Process," *Academy of Management Review,* April 1976.
2,3,4	Van Fleet, D. D., and Bedeian, A. G. "A History of the Span of Management," *Academy of Management Review,* July 1977.
1,2,3	Wallach, Arthur E. "The Man in the Middle," *Personnel Journal,* December 1977.
5	Watson, Charles E. "The Problems of Problem Solving," *Business Horizons,* August 1976.

PART II

JOB MANAGEMENT

○ Planning and controlling

○ Productivity: Improving methods
   and developing performance
   standards

○ Matching individuals and jobs

Chapter 7

Learning objectives

○ To gain an understanding of the planning process and the nature of management's role in the process

○ To appreciate the value of time, its utilization in planning, and the need for effective personal time management

○ To appreciate the various types of plans, the difficulties of planning, and obstacles to effective planning

○ To understand the control process, its relationship to planning, and some of the common control methods used

Planning and controlling

Major topics

Top management's role in planning.

The supervisor's responsibility in planning.

The lack of time and supervisory job design.

Personal planning.

Time utilization.

Time management.

The need for total planning.

Evidence of poor planning.

Why planning seems difficult.

The planning formula.

Types of plans.

The obstacles to planning.

The control function.

Cost control and budgets.

Quantitative techniques for control.

Effective managers cannot afford to wait for problems to occur and then react to them. They must continuously evaluate past performance, prior decisions, and present conditions in relation to the organization's goals. In addition they must be aware of what is going on around them, trends that are becoming apparent, economic forecasts, and other predictions which may be available. The net result of this effort is to try to decide what a manager wants to happen and how to go about accomplishing it. In essence this is the planning function.

All plans are based on assumptions of what will happen in the future. The difference between forecasting and planning is this: Forecasting is predicting the most probable course of events within a range of probabilities, while planning involves deciding what to do about them. It is necessary for top management to forecast the demand for the company's products and to plan the use of all its resources in terms of these forecasts. If management does not plan or if it plans poorly, the company will suffer from wide fluctuations in productivity—waves of hiring and firing, expanding and retrenching—with the result that it loses money and no one has a secure job.

It is impossible for managers to keep their heads above water if they run a business or a department by decisions made in a crisis day after day. The objective of this chapter is to show the supervisor and manager the need for planning, how to plan the use of time, and how to plan and control the work of a department.

Planning improves with practice; the more one plans, the better one's planning becomes. The more extensively planning is practiced in an organization, the easier it becomes for everyone to plan because there is greater certainty of how others will operate.

Top management's role in planning

As is the case with all other managerial activities, top management establishes the example for the rest of the organization in planning. A chief executive committed to a comprehensive planning program will go a long way toward developing an awareness of the need for and the desirability of planning among managers on all levels. Well thought out overall organization plans establish the frame of reference for operational plans throughout the company. Consistency of planning effort, along with reasonable adherence to formulated plans, is required to convince lower level managers that planning should be a necessary part of their activity. Including their thoughts and ideas in higher level organizational planning is also a necessary requisite to an effective planning program.

As Figure 7–1 indicates, the increasing complex environment in which business organizations operate has caused them to place greater emphasis on formal planning programs. There is also a tendency to prepare more

Figure 7–1
The corporate planning cycle

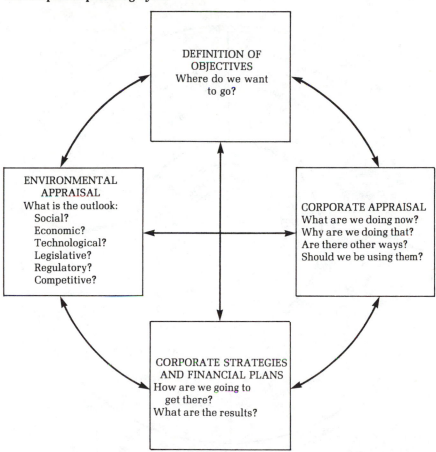

DEFINITION OF
OBJECTIVES
Where do we want
to go?

ENVIRONMENTAL
APPRAISAL
What is the outlook:
Social?
Economic?
Technological?
Legislative?
Regulatory?
Competitive?

CORPORATE APPRAISAL
What are we doing now?
Why are we doing that?
Are there other ways?
Should we be using them?

CORPORATE STRATEGIES
AND FINANCIAL PLANS
How are we going to
get there?
What are the results?

The corporate planning cycle is goal-based and results-oriented; it encompasses consideration of the external environment in which the company operates and the internal environment's capabilities to achieve desired and planned results.

detailed long-range plans and look further into the future. Corporate commitments are being developed for activities which may take place in the next century. Part of this is caused by a rapidly changing technology, but it is also a product of the more sophisticated processing of data and the development of decision-making techniques based on quantitative methods such as operations research and linear programming.

Figure 7–2 demonstrates how the corporate planning cycle is translated into action. Provision is made to accomplish eight steps from the receiving

Figure 7-2
Putting the corporate planning cycle into action

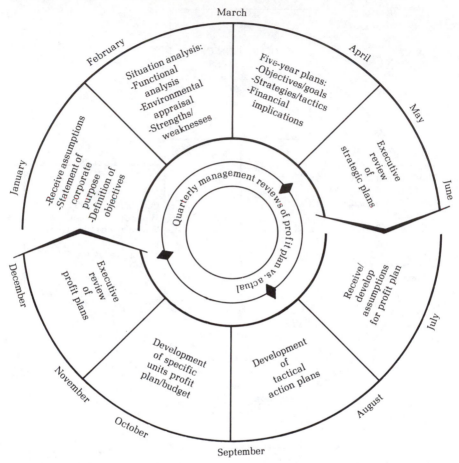

Calendars specifying exact dates are distributed by corporate planning in January and July of each year.

of assumptions in January to an executive review of profit plans during November and December.

The days of the "seat of the pants" executive, operating by intuition and hunch, are rapidly drawing to a close. This is true for all levels of management, and it would be well for middle- and first-level managers to develop their knowledge in the areas necessary for understanding more sophisticated planning. As large organizations develop more comprehensive plans, they will have an effect on the operation of all aspects of the company's activity. Lower level managers who prefer the luxury of not committing themselves to particular deadlines or who may feel too busy with daily activity to take the time necessary for the consideration of basic problems in an area of responsibility will find themselves left at the starting gate.[1]

The supervisor's responsibility in planning

Each supervisor has the responsibility and the authority for the efficient operation of a unit. A unit has a definite purpose—a mission, a definite job to do—and it is up to the supervisor to see that the job is done. In order to do this job, supervisors have at their disposal materials, people, machines, money, and methods, and they must use these factors to the greatest advantage. To do so requires planning and controlling the flow of work through the department. Planning is deciding the what, why, when, where, who, and how of the work to be done. Controlling is the checking of the progress of work against plans or standards and then taking corrective action when necessary.

As aids in planning and controlling, the supervisor may have the services of a production control department, a standards department, or other staff agencies. However, the final responsibility for getting things accomplished lies with the supervisor. If a department is not operating efficiently, it is the supervisor who gets the blame.

Of the five resources the supervisor has to work with (people, materials, money, machines, and methods) the most important factor is people, because they are the ones who will use the other four factors in a way that will either save or waste them. The actions of people, therefore, are the key point in planning, but supervisors cannot push the responsibility for planning onto subordinates. Most employees will not, of their own initiative, conserve materials to the utmost, use machines in the best manner, use the best methods, or put their time to the most productive use. However, if the supervisor takes the lead by planning the work and checking its progress, subordinates know that he or she knows what is going on, and they act accordingly.

The lack of time and supervisory job design

"No time for planning" is a frequent supervisory complaint. The claim is that the nature of the job prevents the supervisor from devoting the energy and time necessary to managerial duties such as planning with any degree of effectiveness. This problem is not always the supervisor's fault. There is no doubt that an individual's competence is one of the deciding factors in effective managerial performance, but organizational demands

---

[1] For an excellent and comprehensive analysis of the entire area of business planning, see George A. Steiner, *Top Management Planning* (New York: Macmillan Co., 1969).

beyond the control of the first-level supervisor can prevent the proper execution of some responsibilities.

Some companies that have supervisory training programs carefully exposing participants to management functions fail to recognize that this may only add to the frustration of a supervisor if the working environment does not allow the person to use newly acquired knowledge. Organizational shortcomings frequently prevent a supervisor from practicing management. Because responsibility is thought to be work-focused, a supervisor may be cast in the role of technician and problem solver. This can require the individual to perform many tasks that are not management-related. During any given work day the supervisor may be involved in work problems, technical assistance, handyman chores, and the like. To the extent that too much time is spent on such things, management activities are naturally sacrificed. In fact, a supervisor most likely does not even consider himself or herself a manager but some kind of trouble shooter-technician.

Many supervisory jobs suffer from poor design. It isn't that the supervisor has too many people to supervise; it's that there are too many *things* to look after personally. The answer does not lie in stripping a supervisor of responsibilities but rather in examining responsibilities to see which are the most important in meeting the objectives of the department, which should be performed personally, which should be delegated to subordinates, and which should be handled by other departments.

Since most companies don't think of job design as the cause of, or treatment for, problems, this chapter suggests to supervisors that they should take the initiative in improving the design of their jobs and that the way to start is through planning. Time should be apportioned to give a minimum amount to routine work, a maximum to creative work, and a comfortable cushion to emergency work.

The creative work takes in both short- and long-range planning. It takes in planning to get out the daily or weekly work load, planning for solving immediate problems, and planning for preventing future problems from arising. It takes in planning for cost improvement in specific areas—waste, labor efficiency, and equipment maintenance. It takes in planning for training or retraining subordinates so that they will be able and willing to take over new duties and adjust smoothly to new systems, new equipment, and new processes.

The supervisor's first step in planning is to analyze the way his or her own time is spent.

Personal planning

While conceding that planning, controlling, and other practices of good management are worthwhile, many supervisors say they just don't have the time for them. The purpose of the discussion on personal planning is to show supervisors how to investigate the manner in which they spend this time, and to point out how they may be able to redistribute their time in order to allocate more of it to the more important aspects of the job. In brief, the purpose is to show "how to take time to save time."

What are some indications that supervisors need to make a study of the way they are using time? If they are just keeping up with their work—that is, taking care of one emergency after another—or if they are just getting or not quite getting essential jobs done, if they need to be in three places at the same time, if they have to put in excessive overtime, if they have no time for self-improvement, if they have to do everything themselves, or, finally, if they dare not take a day off when ill: then it behooves them to make an evaluation of how they are spending time

"On my vacation I'm going to do things I've always wanted to do—get a haircut, shave everyday, wear a suit — —."

Reprinted by permission The Wall Street Journal

Sometimes personal planning interferes with one's job.

When supervisors evaluate and redistribute time, they no longer operate in a panic but are masters of the situation. They can achieve a certain self-confidence and peace of mind by recognizing that they can do just so much and if they are doing it, the job is being done. Usually by time redistribution supervisors can reduce overtime, strain, and excessive fatigue. The job becomes easier because they find they can delegate or eliminate some of the work that has been snowing them under.

An important by-product of getting better control over the job is that the supervisor becomes better prepared for promotion; a person practicing crisis management is not ready for advancement. Advancement comes to the individual who has the opportunity and takes the time to plan and organize, improve methods, cut costs, and build up the morale of his group. In other words, the higher management jobs go to the individuals who show they can perform these more important managerial activities.

The supervisor's personal log sheet.   Figure 7–3 is a sample of a log sheet on which a supervisor can keep a record of how he or she is spending time. It is recommended that the supervisor fill out the sheet at least every two hours—at coffee breaks, at lunchtime, and before going home in the evening. In the appropriate space there should be listed what was done during the previous two hours. The supervisor should be perfectly honest in making out this log, since it is for personal use and need not be shown to anyone. At the end of the day the supervisor should analyze the activities listed and classify them according to the five categories listed below the figure.

The logging should be carried on for two, three, or four weeks to give a good picture of the way the supervisor distributes time. Any duties that did not occur during that period should be taken into account. These duties might be the preparation of monthly reports, quarterly reviews,

Figure 7–3
The supervisor's personal log sheet

	Monday	Tuesday	Wednesday	Thursday	Friday
A.M. 1st half					
2d half					
P.M. 1st half					
2d half					

To find out how the supervisor is distributing time, list in the appropriate space all activities of the previous two hours. At the end of each day analyze each activity on the list and label it 1, 2, 3, 4, or 5:

  1. *Duties that only the supervisor can do.*
  2. *Responsibilities that can be partly delegated.*
  3. *Responsibilities that can be entirely delegated.*
  4. *Activities that might be eliminated as unnecessary.*
  5. *Activities that might be handled by some other department.*

budget estimates, personnel evaluations, and such items that occur infrequently but consume time.

After the supervisor has made enough log sheets to give a representative sample of what is done and how much time is spent doing it, the activities that are taking up time should be evaluated. Investigations of how supervisors spend their time have revealed that some time is consumed by work that should be done by the other departments. In some cases the supervisors assume these tasks; in other cases they have been dumped upon them. For example, keeping materials available, seeing that work is moving from one place to another, seeing that machines are set up on time—all these are activities that can be handled by the production control department. Machine breakdowns and minor repairs should be handled by the maintenance department. Some types of training can just as well be done in the training department.

When supervisors study their log sheets, they find tasks that could be delegated to subordinates. The checklist in Figure 7–4 divides a supervisor's responsibilities into those which must be done personally (duties), those which can be partly delegated to subordinates, and those which can normally be delegated in full (corresponding to 1, 2, and 3, in Figure 7–3).

Redistributing time.   The supervisor should study the present distribution of time so that it can be redistributed to make time available for more important duties. The supervisors should ask themselves, What is the purpose of my department? If my department ceased to exist, what work of the organization would remain undone? They should consult the job description, if there is one, and see how it lists duties and responsibilities.

With the job purpose and job description in mind, supervisors should study the time log to see if too much time has been spent on activities that they are not necessary to the running of the department. If they have, they should consult the organization manual, the procedures manual, and their superiors to determine if such operations could be eliminated or, if they are necessary to someone else, could be done by some other department.

While supervisors are finding out if certain activities could be done by other departments, they should examine the boundaries between their activities and the various service activities to see which tasks are duplicated or overlapped by, or belong properly to, the service departments and can therefore be eliminated.

The activities that are to be done by a supervisor's department, should be sorted out so that those that can be delegated and those that must be done alone are separated. In apportioning time to personal duties the supervisor should ask what to spend less time on and what to spend more time on, in order to accomplish the most effective job of managing. Figure 7–5 is a graphic depiction of a study of the first-line supervisor's job which the author conducted for a large clerical employer. At first the job was studied as it existed, and the diagram indicates how job responsibil-

Figure 7–4
Supervisor's responsibilities

DUTIES THE SUPERVISOR PERSONALLY MUST DO

1. Planning and controlling the work within the section.
2. Setting standards.
3. Estimating the budget.
4. Making accident investigations.
5. Cooperating and coordinating with other supervisors.
6. Keeping the boss informed.
7. Self-improvement.
8. Maintaining an adequate work force.
9. Getting the right person on the right job.
10. Getting to know employees and taking an interest in them.
11. Promoting teamwork and cooperation.
12. Evaluating subordinates.
13. Determining areas in which subordinates need training.
14. Developing and training subordinates.
15. Transferring subordinates.
16. Keeping subordinates informed; eliminating rumors.
17. Building morale and creating better attitudes.
18. Motivating subordinates.
19. Helping subordinates with their personal problems.
20. Disciplining subordinates.
21. Handling gripes and grievances.
22. Settling disputes among workers.

RESPONSIBILITIES THE SUPERVISOR MIGHT DELEGATE PARTS OF
TO SUBORDINATES

1. Maintaining quality and quantity of production.
2. Improving methods and procedures.
3. Keeping costs down (conserving time, materials, space, tools).
4. Care of equipment.
5. Training workers.
6. Explaining jobs.
7. Inducting new workers.
8. Accident prevention.
9. Attendance control (absence and tardiness).
10. Requisitioning tools, equipment, and materials.
11. Handling details or paper work relating to routing, scheduling, and dispatching.
12. Maintaining records.
13. Preparing vacation schedules.
14. Attending meetings.

RESPONSIBILITIES THE SUPERVISOR CAN NORMALLY DELEGATE
TO SUBORDINATES

1. Setting up machines.
2. Sharpening and resetting tools.
3. Keeping records and making reports.
4. Checking and inspecting raw materials.
5. Maintaining good housekeeping on the job.
6. Care of tools and other equipment.
7. Running errands (getting blueprints, supplies, and so on).
8. Answering the phone.

Figure 7–5
Study of first-level supervisor's job

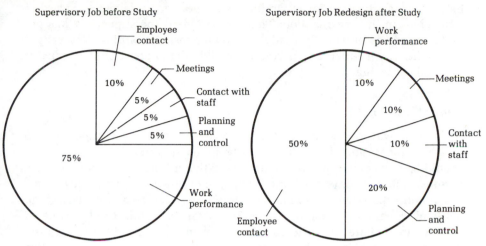

Supervisory Job before Study   Supervisory Job Redesign after Study

ities were divided at that time. The results of redesigning the job after the study are pictured in the other half of the diagram. It is interesting to note that prior to the study supervisors were really lead workers, with only 25 percent of their effort devoted to functioning as managers. In fact, many of the supervisors did not even devote this much time to management activities.

Since human relations problems were mushrooming and middle managers in this firm were overburdened with duties that should have been performed by first-level supervisors, the senior management wanted to increase first-level supervisor participation in management activities. The outstanding change in the new job was cutting down work performance from 75 to 25 percent and increasing employee contact from 10 percent to 50 percent. This study and the topic of job design will be covered more fully in Chapter 9, on matching individuals and jobs.

Actually the type of work being done has considerable influence on the way supervisors apportion their time. In some situations it may be necessary for a supervisor to spend considerable time making various informal contacts with people outside his or her immediate work group. Although the formal structure and the job description may make no provision for such contacts, both the work flow and the supervisor's perception of the job may convince the supervisor that they are necessary. In fact there are a number of supervisors who believe that such contacts help them to be more effective supervisors. They feel that it is part of their responsibility to be well known throughout the organization so that their area of responsibility can gain support and cooperation. Further, they believe that to handle work problems properly it is desirable to establish relationships horizontally with peer supervisors and diagonally with managers on various levels who are neither subordinates nor their direct superiors. It may be particularly fruitful for an ambitious supervisor to develop upward relationships in the organization. This is desirable if the supervisor has promotables and is personally ready for greater responsibilities. Naturally, if this is the way a supervisor perceives the job, time apportionment must be planned accordingly.

Time utilization

Another way of looking at time may be useful for the supervisor. In most instances time is evaluated only in its quantitative dimension. It should be recognized that there are qualitative differences in time use and minutes, hours, or days are not the only way to evaluate time utilization.

An interesting comparison can be drawn between two important things many of us value—time and money. For instance, certain funds are necessary for immediate needs while others are invested for future purposes. Some we set aside for specific obligations, such as charity and education; but even the wisest individuals waste some of their money.

All that must be done is to substitute the word "time" for the word "money" in the above sentences and the comparison becomes more clear. In a supervisor's daily work all kinds of demands are placed on available time. To overcome the time problem the supervisor may frequently resort to expedient measures such as handling only pressing matters, taking shortcuts, completing only part of the task, taking work home, and turning out work that may be lower in quality than he or she desires it to be.

Time spent for immediate results.   A certain amount of the work one does yields immediate results. These are the tasks which affect daily work. For instance, the supervisor makes work assignments to subordinates and expects them to meet the deadlines; helps an employee with a knotty problem; dictates letters and prepares reports; answers the telephone; and coordinates the efforts of a department. All of these time uses have an immediate result. The supervisor expects a payoff in direct relation to the time invested.

Time invested for future results.   This type of time expenditure is carried out with the future in mind. Weeks or months may go by before the supervisor gets a return on the investment, and an element of risk is present. The supervisor may not always get the results that are expected. Nevertheless, time must be invested if future reward and improvement are expected. The time spent training and developing subordinates may come back in the form of greater efficiency for the department. Working on the development of new methods, on improving relations, or on a program of self-development is an investment of time in the supervisor's future and the future of his or her employees. Planning for the next six months or year enables an assessment of needs and anticipation of problems. This investment returns in the form of a more smoothly functioning work group with a minimum of crises.

Time for the company as a whole.   While most of the effort of any supervisor is directed toward the improvement and effective functioning of his or her own area of responsibility, the supervisor must be concerned with the relationship of the department with others in the company and with the company as a whole. After all, any organization is no more effective than the sum total of effectiveness generated by all of the units which make up the organization. Thus when a supervisor is concerned about a policy interpretation and discusses this concern with superiors, this may return to that supervisor as greater understanding and clearer communications. Keeping staff specialists informed of the effect of installing a new procedure or program, such as work measurement, brings returns to the supervisor in the form of better cooperation with staff departments, and it gives them a better understanding of line operations. Discussing matters of mutual importance with other supervisors, preparing reports for higher management, attending meetings—all of these can result in more overall efficiency, greater understanding, and better interdepartmental coordination. Following established policies and procedures, so that the supervisor does not have to continually explain all actions to superiors gives the supervisor time for the improvement of his or her own department.

Wasted time.   No matter how hard a supervisor may try not to, some time will be wasted. Many individuals have been involved in conversations that are unnecessary, in misdirected telephone calls, and in searches for information that nobody really needed. Then there are the informal conferences on World Series games, pretty women, handsome men, politics, and other "important" topics that steal time away from busy days.

There are some supervisors who pad their efforts to make their jobs seem more important. Others take too long on coffee breaks, telephone calls, or memorandum writing. They do work that could be delegated to subordinates, or they argue needlessly with a superior and end up doing what was requested in the first place.

Not all time that is spent on matters not directly connected with a supervisor's work is wasted, however. Every supervisor should spend some time just thinking. This thinking could include an evaluation of personal performance in the discharge of responsibilities and plans for self-development. Conversations with superiors, peers, and subordinates can create bridges for better understanding. Reading periodicals and books that are job-related can prepare the supervisor for future responsibility.

Time management

Because of increased awareness of more effective time utilization as one key to greater management efficiency, many programs, seminars, movies, and books have been developed on time management. Some companies encourage managers and supervisors to take these courses while others develop their own courses for in-house training. There are several consultants in this area as well who give courses and even work with managers on an individual basis.

These programs cover much of the same material presented earlier in this chapter.

1. Analysis of time spent using a diary, log sheet, or dictating equipment to indicate clearly to the manager how time is actually spent. This is particularly valuable since few people really know how they spend their time.
2. Establish priorities for time use by analysis of log sheets and diaries and checklists. By establishing priorities, one doesn't fall into the trap of doing work which may be liked but unnecessary.
3. Avoid time wasters. Discourage too many "friendly" visitors and telephone callers. By learning how to say "no" to requests that can be done by others, considerable time can be saved. Going to unnecessary committee meetings can be another time waster. Perhaps a subordinate can represent the manager on some committees, and this may even serve to develop that subordinate. Above all, one should not procrastinate by putting off difficult, complex, or distasteful tasks which must be done.

The fundamental message of time management is more organized, planned, and knowledgeable use of time. All of the people who seem to accomplish many different things effectively carry out some form of time management.

The need for total planning

In Chapter 2 the systems approach to organization structure was discussed. This same concept is useful in planning. Proper coordination of all organizational activities is necessary if goals are to be met effectively. By recognizing the organization as a total system made up of several interdependent substructures, planning can and should consider the relationships of all parts of the structure. Consideration should also be given to the effect of one activity on other activities and whether or not the accomplishment of a subgoal distorts or makes difficult the attainment of other organizational goals.

Such a dilemma apparently exists in the airline industry. Airplanes have been designed to be comfortable, and the jet engine has revolutionized air travel. Passenger volume has increased greatly, and indications are that it will grow still further. New planes are being developed to go faster and carry more passengers than present models. In fact many airlines are using airplanes which can carry hundreds of passengers. So the goal of serving passengers in relative comfort and speeding them to their destinations seems to have been met—or has it? One of the bottlenecks that the airlines apparently did not adequately plan for is baggage handling. Baggage claim areas are crowded and confusing and frequently inefficient. Baggage is lost, stolen, mislaid, or placed on wrong flights and does not reach the same destination as the passenger who owns it. At times it catches up with the passenger on a later flight, but this may mean considerable waiting and undue inconvenience. Crowded airways, landing delays, terminal facilities that are overcrowded, poor parking for automobiles, and ticket errors are among the other factors negating goal achievement. So the objective of service to the customer-passenger has not been fully realized.

Apparently the aviation industry is the victim of poor planning and has not recognized the total dimensions involved in effective passenger service. Getting a passenger to a destination is just one part of the total system, which includes such obvious things as ticket purchase, baggage handling, parking space, terminal facilities, scheduling, pricing, advertising, personnel recruitment, customer relations, airports, airways, and many others.

Obviously there are many other industries and organizations in our society that could furnish examples of the lack of total planning. Any organization should consider its planning effort as contributing to the total system. All aspects of that system should be considered if goals are to be achieved satisfactorily. Naturally this requires an uncommonly effective management team with an appreciation for the systems approach.

Evidence of poor planning

Supervisors should suspect poor planning if they are run ragged trying to get work done; if the department is unable to meet deadlines; if it is a place of conflict and confusion; if work is held up for lack of materials, tools, or trained workers; or if employees are rushed to the point where quality suffers, housekeeping is sloppy, and accidents are high. Some of the indications of poor planning are:

Delivery dates not met.
Machines idle.
Materials wasted.
Some machines doing jobs that should be on smaller machines.
Some employees overworked, others underworked.
Some workers stalling in order not to run out of work.
Skilled workers doing unskilled work.
People fumbling on jobs for which they have not been trained.
Quarreling, bickering, buck-passing, and confusion.

When there is good planning in a department, section, or unit, the work flows through in a swift, shallow stream. People are busy but not rushed. There is good housekeeping, cooperation among the workers, and respect for the leadership of the supervisor. Some of the benefits of good planning are:

Jobs turned out on time.
Good relationships with other departments.
People using their highest skills.
Workers knowing how their jobs fit into the total pattern.
Machines doing their proper jobs.
Equipment in good shape.
Materials available.
Waste kept to a minimum.

The difference between good planning and poor planning is the difference between order and confusion, between things being done on time and not being done on time, between cooperation and conflict, and between pleasant working relationships and a workday full of discord.

Why planning seems difficult

Planning involves setting up in advance what things are to be done, when they are to be done, how they are to be done, who is to do them, and where they are to be done. Planning cannot be achieved without effort. It requires thinking, and most people like to avoid thinking. It is easier mentally to muddle through than to think one's way through. It is easier to engage in trial and error than to weigh advantages and disadvantages. It is easier to do jobs just as they occur, moving from one job to the other, keeping busy, than it is to sit down and figure out a way of getting more done and being less busy. Planning requires knowledge, foresight, judgment, and experience.

The planner—that is, the supervisor—must have *knowledge*. He or she must know the skills and capacities of employees, their strong and weak points, the jobs they can do well, and the jobs that they do poorly. The supervisor must know the equipment, the type of work it can do, the accuracy of the work it can do, and that one machine can do the same job as another machine but do it better. Materials and their relative cost should be known along with the knowledge of how to divide big jobs down into smaller operations.

A supervisor must have *foresight* and know how to anticipate difficulties, thus avoiding them. The length of time the jobs take and what margin of safety to allow in order to meet due dates must also be known. A supervisor must have *judgment,* as well as a good sense of priorities to weigh the various factors and make decisions. The supervisor must have *experience,* and must have profited by that experience so that the same mistake will not be made twice. There is a difference between 20 years' experience and 1 year's experience repeated 20 times. The more obstacles the supervisor has overcome, the more that individual will be able to anticipate. The more a supervisor plans, the better he or she will be able to plan.

Planning, then, requires work with the head instead of with the back. It requires that things be figured out before they are tried out.

The planning formula

Most jobs that are to be planned can be analyzed by applying the questions of what, why, when, who, where, and how. The answers to these questions can be set up in terms of routing, scheduling, and dispatching.

In the analysis of a job, the first question to be answered is, *What?* What are the operations to be performed on this job? What is the function of this department with regard to this job? What are the quantity and quality requirements of this job?

The next question is, *Why?* Why is it necessary to perform all the operations? Why is it necessary to follow a certain sequence in the performance? Why is it necessary to do this job at all? In answering the why questions, the supervisor may be able to detect unnecessary operations and perhaps eliminate them.

The next question to ask is, *When?* When is this job to be started in order to meet deadlines? Before the supervisor can answer this question, it is necessary to know how long the operations will take. There is a need to have accurately determined standards of performance or at least good estimates based on comparable jobs. When the supervisor knows how long the operations will take, deadlines can be established that will permit the maximum utilization of people, materials, equipment, time, and space.

Next, the supervisor asks, *Where?* It is necessary to know where the various operations should be performed in the unit. What machines can perform the operations best and what machines are available to perform the various operations is also necessary information.

After this, the supervisor asks, *Who* will do it? Who in the group has the skills necessary to perform the various operations, so that employees using their highest skills will be utilized as much as possible.

Then, finally, comes the question, *How?* There may be several methods from which the supervisor can choose for performing various operations, and there may be better methods which can be devised.

The questions need not always be asked in the above sequence, nor can one question be answered without considering the other questions; the answer to each question will influence the answers to all the other questions. As the questions are answered, the supervisor is laying out a plan for the job along the following logical steps:

1. Analyzing the job (work order) or product to be produced.
2. Determining the total number of units to be produced in a unit of time.
3. Breaking down the separate operations or tasks.

4. Arranging the operations or tasks in the sequence in which they are to be performed.
5. Determining what is needed for each operation—materials, supplies, equipment, space, blueprints, sketches—and arranging for ordering them.
6. Estimating the number of labor-hours needed for each operation.
7. Estimating the total number of each kind of worker needed.
8. Working out a time schedule for each operation—when each should begin and end.
9. Providing for any training that will be necessary to prepare employees for the work.
10. Showing at what points, and to whom, instructions and directions should be given.
11. Making provisions for checking the progress of the work and for making adjustments in the schedule if necessary.

These 11 steps incorporate the activities of routing, scheduling, dispatching, and controlling.

Types of plans

It is obvious that all levels of management should be involved in planning, but there is no doubt that higher management probably spends more time in this activity. They, however, are concerned with overall planning for the organization, while middle- and first-level managers develop specific plans for relatively narrower areas of responsibility. They can and do use the plans established at higher levels as the frame of reference for their planning.

Supervisors are largely concerned with two types of plans. These are:

1. *Standing plans.*   These are used over and over to handle situations which occur with a great deal of regularity. Included are such things as hiring personnel to fill openings and preventive maintenance.
2. *Single-use plans.*   These are designed to achieve a specific result over a short period of time, usually one year or less. Included in this category are budgets covering items such as production, sales, raw materials, and other expense items.

Another type of plan that should concern managers is frequently called the contingency or standby plan. Plans of this type are developed to cover situations which may or may not occur. If they do occur, however, a sound plan will enable a company to cope with the situation more effectively. Included here are plans for courses of action in the event of a transportation strike in the area where the company is located; disasters such as fires, floods, power blackouts, national emergencies, or strikes in supplier companies; early employee release on excessively warm workdays; and other unusual situations.

The obstacles to planning

The supervisor cannot plan 100 percent of the work of the department. Things go wrong; employees are absent; instructions are misunderstood; machines break down; material does not arrive on time or is difficult to work; other orders have to be pushed through.

Rush jobs—wasteful as they are—have to be handled. The best that the supervisor can do about them is to get rid of them by means of overtime, by asking people for extra effort, or by delaying some other jobs. Then, as soon as possible the supervisor should get onto a regular schedule again so that more emergencies won't be created. It often pays to keep emergency jobs off the main production line and treat them separately.

If emergencies are caused by conditions which are beyond the supervisor's control and which cannot be corrected, the supervisor should tell the boss about them and their cost. Because obstacles interfere with the scheduled progress of the work, the supervisor must allow a factor of safety or some cushion to take care of delays. When delays do occur, the schedule must be revised to take advantage of the cushion. Then the supervisor will be on an up-to-date basis to schedule additional jobs.

The control function

Control is essentially concerned with trying to make events conform to plans. This implies measurement of achievement and correction of deviations to assure effective goal attainment. Control is continuous and can best be described as a circular process (see Figure 7–6) involving:

1. An activity being performed.
2. Standards against which the performance of the activity can be measured.
3. Measurement of techniques designed to indicate to managers any deviation of actual performance from expected or standard performance.
4. Corrective action which should be taken to bring performance into line with desired results.

When managers plan, they must have an objective in mind. They must also decide how they are going to reach that objective. Thus a manager most likely carries on all three activities at the same time. When a goal is formulated, the determination of plans and controls occurs simultaneously. Controlling is keeping posted on progress. It is measuring certain elements such as time, quantity, quality, or cost against a yardstick of standards which have been set up for the purpose. Control that is applied to the work of the department is a matter of checking and correcting work while it is in process.

Checking is a process of measuring performance against schedules or plans to determine how the work is coming along. Not every operation has to be checked, but spot checks are necessary. Care must be taken not to

Figure 7–6
The control process

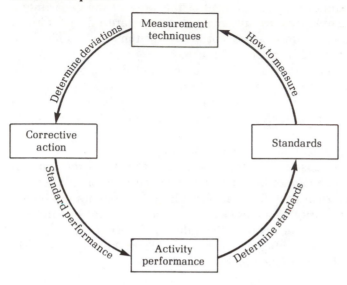

overcontrol or undercontrol. Supervisors must avoid breathing down the necks of their employees; they haven't the time to do it, and it has a bad effect on the employees. On the other hand, they can't just let things go and then be caught unaware when deadlines cannot be met.

Correcting is the making of adjustments when things are not going as planned. Some of the developments and circumstances that cause work to get behind schedule are absences, machine breakdowns, materials not arriving on time or in proper kind, and jobs being done incorrectly. When work is piling up, it becomes necessary to reschedule parts of the jobs or put some of them on a rush basis and devote overtime or extra effort or people to them in order to catch up.

To understand a control system, it must be recognized that compliance is its most vital component. This means adherence to the established goals, policies, procedures, and rules. In a sense these and such others things as work measurement, methods improvement, budgets and performance appraisal are the tools of scientific management. In using these tools, the manager must try to balance carefully the organizational necessity for adherence with individual creativity. No control system should be developed which puts a straitjacket on supervisors, requiring from them unquestioning compliance. This will only tend to stifle initiative and turn the supervisor into someone who does everything "by the book."

Cost control and budgets

The first-level of supervision is the scene of action for cost control. Supervisors have the greatest influence on the utilization of direct labor and supplies and the greatest degree of control over errors and rework. Therefore it is essential that they have an understanding of the cost structure and budget system so that they can measure their own performance and take corrective action when costs are out of line. The standard for judging whether current costs reflect satisfactory performance is the budget.

Budgets. Budgeting is a form of cost control by which the actual performance of a department may be measured against what that performance should be. Budgets are the estimated amounts of resources that should be sufficient to turn out a given amount of products or services during a definite period of time such as a year. Both the resources and the product may be expressed in dollars, or they may be expressed in labor-hours, labor-dollars, or volume.

In a production department there are direct labor budgets, direct material budgets, and a variety of indirect expense budgets such as those for indirect labor, supplies, building maintenance, machine maintenance, and utilities.

The real expenses incurred during the year are a measure of the actual performance. The difference between the actual expenses and the budgets are called *variances*. These variances measure the efficiency of the department.

In order to set up and use operating budgets effectively in an organization, it is necessary to:

1. Forecast the sales volume of the company's product for the coming year.
2. Compare this volume with the capacity of the organization.
3. Make adjustments in order to determine the probable percentage of facility utilization during the year.
4. Investigate, predetermine, integrate, and agree upon what the types and amounts of the operating expenses should be.[2]
5. Consistently check actual expenses against budget expenses.
6. Investigate the causes of variances.

Budgets are made in terms of a definite amount of output. A plan running at half capacity will have more than half the expenses of a plant running at full capacity, because some of the expenses are fixed. That is, building maintenance, management salaries, and so forth are the same for both situations; other expenses are variable. Direct labor and product materials vary directly with output, while other expenses like indirect labor, supplies, and machine maintenance are semivariable—a portion of each is fixed and a portion is variable. Thus the first step in setting up the operating budgets is to make a sales forecast for the coming year. The second step is to use this tentative forecast to determine what the approximate percentage of plant utilization will be. If this percentage is low, it may be necessary to allocate more money for extra sales effort to increase volume, or to take on an addi-

---

[2] These decisions must be in line with the objectives of the business, or the budget will misdirect managerial behavior. In order to stay within budget, a manager may put off needed expenditures and let greater costs build up in some other direction.

tional line of products, or to produce in the plant some work that is now being subcontracted. On the other hand, if the sales forecast exceeds the capacity of the plant, it may be necessary to provide for overtime or a second shift or to subcontract more work. Adjustments have to be made to balance plant utilization with forecasted sales. For example, Figure 7–7 illustrates the relationships among sales, inventory turnover, and plant use. These three factors should be balanced before budgets are set up.

When budgets are being investigated, predetermined, and integrated, the department heads who must live within the budgets should be consulted about the amount of money available, and they should help in drawing up budgets for their departments for the coming period. A manager who has some say about the budget and expenses is more inclined to make an added effort to keep down the actual expenses of the department.

Actual expenses should be checked against budgeted expenses frequently during the period that the budgets are in effect. Managers should be promptly supplied with figures of actual expenses so that they can compare them with budgeted expenses and investigate the variances.

If the actual expenses are above budget expenses, steps should be taken to reduce costs. When actual expenses are below budgeted expenses, the budget should not be cut, but people responsible for the saving should be

Figure 7–7
Interrelationships of sales, inventory, and plant utilization

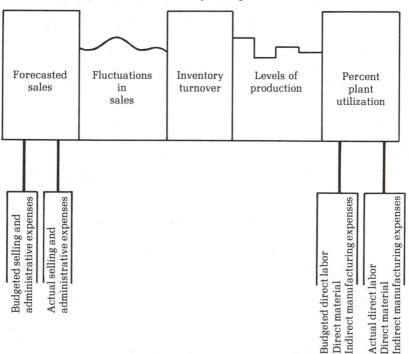

rewarded. Some companies cut the budget instead of giving a commendation. When managers fear the budget will be cut, they may be tempted to protect themselves by uneconomical spending toward the end of the budget period.

Zero-base budgets. This is an approach to budgeting which has been given a lot of publicity in recent years. Government agencies and business organizations are experimenting with this budgeting process. The term *zero-base* derives from the idea that each program or departmental budget should be prepared from the ground up or base zero. This is in contrast to the normal budgeting practice which builds on the base of a previous period. By calculating the budget from a zero base, all costs are newly developed and reviewed entirely to determine their necessity. Various programs are reviewed and costed thoroughly and then ranked in degree of importance to the organization. Managers are presumably forced to look on a program in its entirety rather than as an expense add-on to an existing budget.[3]

Quantitative techniques for control

If one traced the history of scientific management from the days of Frederick W. Taylor up to the present, the supervisor could see an ever-increasing use of quantitative methods on the various factors which relate to managerial decision making. Taylor's time studies reduced the worker's efforts to bits of time which could be measured and used as the basis for determining productivity and the rate of compensation. Present-day use of mathematics is far more sophisticated. This is partly caused by increased knowledge of the applications of quantitative analysis to management problems and partly by the increased complexity of the problems and the nature of the decisions required to solve them. Another vital contributing factor is the development of highspeed electronic data processing, which gives the manager access to far greater amounts of information than he has ever had. To use this information effectively and to apply it to problem solving and the control of operations, quantitative methods must be employed.

Operations research. Operations research was developed during World War II when the military called upon scientists for aid in solving strategic and tactical problems. Teams of various kinds of scientists, engineers, and other scientifically trained individuals use the scientific method, mathematical techniques, and other logical means to develop possible solutions to problems which confronted managers.

Accurately defining operations research seems to be somewhat difficult. There are several definitions in the literature, which has grown in amount since the end of World War II. There is, however, common usage of the

---

[3] For a more thorough description of this budgeting process see P. A. Pyhrr, "Zero-Base Budgeting," *Harvard Business Review*, vol. 48 (November–December 1970), no. 6, pp. 111–21.

terms "scientific method," "mathematical model," "quantitative analysis," "optimization," and "decision making." Churchman, Ackoff, and Arnoff have this to say:

> Each practitioner's version of O.R.'s method (if recorded) would differ in some respects. But there would also be a good deal in common. For example, most would agree that the following are the major phases of an O.R. project:
>
> 1. Formulating the problem.
> 2. Constructing a mathematical model to represent the system under study.
> 3. Deriving a solution from the model.
> 4. Testing the model and the solution derived from it.
> 5. Establishing controls over the solution.
> 6. Putting the solution to work: implementation.[4]

Miller and Starr describe operations research in this manner:

> Operations research *is applied decision theory*. There is nothing vague about this notion. But clearly, the domain it encompasses is enormous. In practice, such enormity of scope is evident.
>
> Operations research requires the use of scientific, mathematical, or logical means to structure and resolve *decision problems*. Construction of an adequate *decision model* is crucial. Questions of strategy development, recognition of states of nature, competitive considerations, outcomes and utilities, etc., are not just matters of tools and techniques. *Implementation abilities* for the decisions reached are implicit requirements for model construction. This is the decision context that enables a manager to achieve a thoroughgoing rationality in dealing with his problems.[5]

Operations research offers a systems approach to problems because it considers the way a problem (inventory size, for instance) affects problems in other areas (economic lot sizes, production costs, production planning, finance, marketing, customer service, model changes, warehousing, stability of employment, motivation, and so on). It investigates these related problems in terms of the objectives of each part of the organization and seeks a solution that is best for the organization as a whole. O.R. is a problem-solving research into the economics of operations. It uses mathematical models that are part of the technique and constructs new models, using analogies from other disciplines. There are O.R. models for such problems as production lot sizes, inventory control, allocation of resources, waiting line (queuing), replacement, and maintenance.

Although the mathematical tools and techniques could be utilized by a researcher working alone, one of the particular advantages of operations research is gained through team effort. Most business problems have many sides—physical, biological, psychological, sociological, economic, and engi-

---

[4] C. W. Churchman, R. L. Ackoff, and E. L. Arnoff, *Introduction to Operations Research* (New York: John Wiley & Sons, Inc., 1957), pp. 12–13

[5] David W. Miller and Martin K. Starr, *Executive Decisions and Operations Research*, 2d ed (Englewood Cliffs, N.J.: Prentice-Hall, Inc., 1969), pp. 132–33.

neering aspects. To see them all and grasp their interrelationships requires a team approach. The professionals on an O.R. team might be a physical scientist, an engineer, and a psychologist or social scientist. The team should also contain one or more persons thoroughly familiar with the overall operations of the company—for instance, from accounting, marketing, purchasing, or administration.

When people from a variety of disciplines are confronted with a problem, each brings to it a viewpoint and a method of attack drawn from the theories in his or her own field. This diversity of backgrounds is an advantage in recognizing, identifying, and analyzing the various aspects of problems and in adapting mathematical, statistical, and other scientific techniques to their solution. An essential arrangement in O.R. is that the team consult with managers whose operations would be affected by changes, and that the team have free access to top-level management in order to get needed information and action.

If the decision maker accepts the recommendations resulting from an O.R. study, the researchers have the responsibility for making the recommendations usable and acceptable to the people affected by them. The specialized techniques and equations employed in solving an inventory problem, for instance, would scarcely be usable on a daily basis by people

"Who says I can't argue with a computer?"

Reprinted by permission The Wall Street Journal

Computers are as useful as humans allow them to be.

without advanced mathematical training. One of the requirements of O.R. is that solutions to problems be translated into easy formulas, decision rules, and procedures for applying them.

CPM and PERT.   The planning, scheduling, and controlling of huge projects can be handled by techniques such as CPM (critical path method) and PERT (program evaluation and review technique).[6] These techniques are part of the growing assortment of mathematical tools for decision making. They evolved from a combination of mathematical theory and various scheduling and charting techniques.

PERT was devised between 1956 and 1958 for the Navy Department, to keep track of the thousands of details involved in the development of the Polaris submarine missile. It is a network flow chart with built-in uncertainty; there are three estimates of the time needed to complete each task— an optimistic estimate, a normal one, and a pessimistic one.

CPM was designed in 1957 by Remington Rand for Du Pont, for use in scheduling the construction of a chemical plant. CPM uses a single estimate of the time each task will take. Both techniques diagram the events on a network. Figure 7–8 is an illustration of such a network and the use of CPM in selecting the most economical schedule for a small hypothetical project.

The key concepts of both techniques is the *critical path*. It determines which jobs should be rushed in order to get early completion of the whole project and which jobs, if slowed down, will delay the completion of the project. Of all the activities involved in a project, only a small percentage control the schedule for the entire project. For instance, in building a house some of the tasks can be done at almost any time; but the foundation must be poured before the frame can go up and the roof go on, and the heating must go in before the plaster. These essential activities are the ones that must be done in proper sequence: Something must be completed before something else can be started. These events are the ones on the critical path: The time needed for their completion determines the total time for the project. Most jobs don't lie along the critical path; if they take a little longer than expected, they won't delay anything. They provide a certain amount of slack and even in emergencies seldom have to be put on a rush basis. Their start can be delayed, or people can be taken off them and transferred to the more critical activities.

The first step in constructing a network is to analyze all the work that must be done, break it into tasks in their technological order, estimate the time required to complete each task, and specify the immediate prerequisite task. (Supervisors may be called upon at this stage to supply time estimates and the proper order in which operations must be performed.) Each task is drawn on the graph and marked with its identifying symbol and time. In Figure 7–8 the tasks are diagramed as arrows and their completion dates as

---

[6] For a detailed discussion, see Richard I. Levin and Charles A. Kirkpatrick, *Planning and Control with PERT/CPM* (New York: McGraw-Hill Book Co., 1966).

Figure 7-8
CPM is illustrated on a tiny hypothetical project

How a Computer Decides the Cheapest Schedule for a Project

Job	Normal		Crash		Cost of crashing
	days	cost	days	cost	dollars per day
A	3	$140	2	$210	$70
B	6	215	5	275	60
C	2	160	1	240	80
D	4	130	3	180	50
E	2	170	1	250	80
F	7	165	4	285	40
G	4	210	3	290	80
H	3	110	2	160	50
Total		$1300		$1890	

Major industrial projects, such as the building of a ship or a factory or the development of a missile, involve so many activities that no human mind can keep track of all that is going on, much less schedule every detail in the most efficient way. New mathematical techniques, however, are giving project managers a clearer view of their work and a better opportunity to use their judgment effectively. The essential steps in one of these new techniques, Critical Path Method, are demonstrated on this page by the analysis of a tiny hypothetical project. The manager begins the scheduling by listing all the jobs that must be done (see chart at left) together with estimates of normal time and cost for each. Next he estimates how much it would cost to rush each job to completion by a crash program. All this information is fed into a computer. As the totals show, the manager could get each job done as fast as possible by spending an extra $590. But he may be able to shorten the time of completing the whole project without "crashing" every job. This is what the computer will investigate.

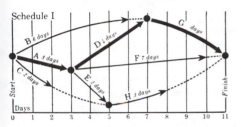

Schedule I

The manager diagrams the order in which the jobs must be done. This shows, for example, that C can be done in parallel with A but that D cannot be started until A is finished. The computer calculates the "critical path" (**ADG**) from this information. The jobs on this path determine the time (eleven days) needed to complete the whole project; the rest can be delayed somewhat (broken lines) without affecting the over-all schedule.

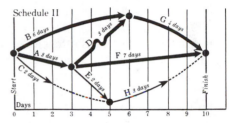

Schedule II

Next the computer calculates ways to shorten the over-all schedule by crashing some of the jobs. There may be several ways, but the computer selects the cheapest. The diagram above shows that if D is accelerated to three days instead of four, the over-all schedule can be reduced to ten days. Two more jobs, B and F, become part of a critical path, but there is still some leeway in C, E, and H. The cost of crashing D is an extra $50.

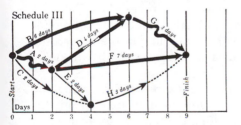

Schedule III

Again rescheduling the project so that it can be finished in nine days, the computer finds that it is best to crash both A and G by one day. Surprisingly, the extra effort put on these jobs makes it possible to relax a bit on D and allot the normal four days for its completion. Crashing A and G will cost a total of $150, but the relaxation of D saves $50, so the acceleration of the whole project from ten to nine days costs only $100 more.

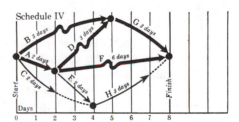

Schedule IV

If the manager wants to lop another day from the schedule, he can do so most economically by crashing three jobs: B, D, and F. Although the chart shows that F could be shortened by as much as three days, the extra hurry would have no effect on the over-all schedule, so F is shortened by only one day. The manager has now spent $300 on the crash program, compared with the $590 he might have spent to crash all the jobs.

Schedule	I	II	III	IV
Duration (days)	11	10	9	8
Direct cost	$1300	$1350	$1450	$1600
Indirect cost	$1210	$1100	$990	$880
Total cost	$2510	$2450	$2440	$2480

To decide which schedule is actually best from all viewpoints, the manager can instruct the computer to take other factors into account. There may be a penalty for failing to complete the project on schedule. Sometimes in actual practice contractors have found that they can make more profit by proceeding slowly and paying a penalty rather than paying heavy overtime. The chart on the left shows how the computer might include in its calculations indirect costs—e.g., overhead or penalties. In this example the indirect costs amount to a flat $110 per day, and the chart tells the manager that the cheapest schedule is the one that takes nine days.

Source: James E. Kelley, Jr., Mauchly Associates, Inc.; adapted from George A. W. Boehm, "Helping the Executive to Make up His Mind," *Fortune*, April 1962, pp. 128 ff.

Figure 7–9
Simplified PERT network

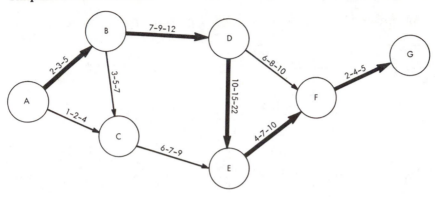

circles. (More commonly the circle represents the task and the arrow points to the next task in the sequence, as in Figure 7–9.) If the scheduler wants to hasten the completion date, he or she esimates the costs and results of speeding up tasks on the critical path. On a small project these calculations can be made manually. On big projects a computer is needed to take into account all the variables and keep track of the interrelated projects.

A simplified version of a PERT network is illustrated in Figure 7–9. Essentially this is a pictorial description of the work necessary to complete a project. All activities are identified and the activity sequence is arranged in a flow diagram. Duration times in three figures (optimistic, likely, and pessimistic) are shown for each activity. The total of the times along the most lengthy sequence of activities results in an estimated total span of time for project completion. This is the critical path (heavy line in the figure), the path that controls the project because delays along this path will delay project completion.

The control feature of these techniques is exercised by asking the questions: Did something happen that was supposed to happen on this day or did it not? If it did not, how will it affect the total performance and how much time must be regained? How shall the time be regained? Which tasks along the critical path can be speeded up (crashed) most economically?

PERT and CPM are not intended for use in repetitive operations or as production control tools; they are too expensive to use when other techniques will do as well. They are used for planning and scheduling the research and development of new products, getting new products into production, constructing buildings and highways, moving plants to new locations, handling big maintenance jobs to reduce downtime, and monitoring large contracts. The need for optimum control of time, cost, and personnel is spurring further developments in the basic critical path techniques so that a wider variety of problems can be handled.[7]

Break-even analysis. Another technique used in planning and control is called break-even analysis. Sales volume is assumed to be the key factor in planning, and by the use of various forecasting techniques such as market research, economic forecasting, and extrapolation, a reasonable prediction of sales volume can be achieved. Then a break-even chart such as Figure 7–10 is prepared. The analysis starts with the fact that every company has certain fixed expenses such as taxes, insurance, maintenance, and electricity. They go on whether the company sells 1,000 units or 10,000. They will not rise with increased sales. Other expenses, such as labor cost and material cost, rise in direct relation to sales. The cost line for the case illustrated in Figure 7–10, *AB*, starts at $200 and rises with sales to $450. The point where line XY, representing sales in thousands, crosses the cost line *AB* is known as the break-even point. This is the point at which the company's sales volume meets its costs exactly but makes no profit. It can be seen that

Figure 7–10
Break-even chart—The break-even point is reached when revenues equal expenses

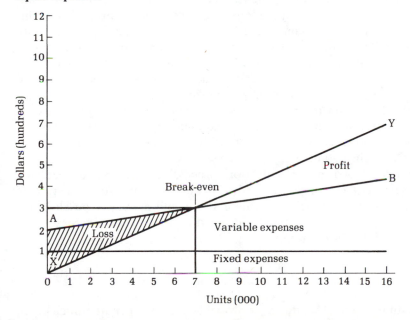

---

[7] Some of these techniques are: PERT/COST, PERT II, PERT III, PEPCO, and Super PERT. Another technique, SPAR (scheduling program for allocating resources), is an extension of the work load smoothing algorithm and is used in scheduling projects having limited resources. A technique similar to it is RAMPS (resource allocation and multiproject scheduling).

after that the profit tends to grow faster with increases in sales volume. Fixed expenses are then spread over a large number of units manufactured and are a lesser percentage of unit cost. The break-even point in Figure 7-10 comes when the company sells 7,000 units at $300 each.

Naturally this is a simplified example. Generally a company's break-even point does not remain constant. Fixed costs can rise, and if they do, the break-even point will rise. It will then take more unit sales to make the same profit. A rise in price will lower the break-even point, increasing profits it costs remain constant. If variable costs such as labor and material go up, the break-even point rises and profits lower unless a price rise per unit can be passed on to the buyer.

Companies use break-even analysis by comparing projected charts with actual charts for each product manufactured.

There are many more quantitative approaches to decision making and control.[8] These have been developed in recent years to handle many of the recurring problems which managers face. The electronic computer and its capacity for handling and processing data, coupled with mathematical techniques, have made this possible. Routine control systems and decisions are now being processed on computers in many organizations.

Management information systems. With the increased use of computers and the explosion of data in large organizations, the proper use of information for planning, control, and decision making becomes more complex. The flow of data, representing a continuous record of all pertinent factors in an organization, goes on daily. Part of management's responsibility is to determine what data is critical and then make it available to all levels of management to enable them to make better decisions.

Critical information for middle managers and first-line supervisors includes that which will assist in control and planning and operational information which relates to daily activities and enables evaluation of performance against standards.

Systems developed for the collection, processing, storage, and feedback of this information to managers are called management information systems (MIS). Computers are utilized for this activity, and managers on all levels are kept informed on a more timely basis with data that can increase their effectiveness if it is used properly.

Summary

Forecasting is predicting the most probable course of events from a given range of probabilities. Planning is deciding what to do about them. Planning

---

[8] For a more thorough discussion, see R. E. Schellenberger, *Managerial Analysis* (Homewood, Ill.: Richard D. Irwin, 1969); and R. I. Levin and C. A. Kirkpatrick, *Quantitative Approaches to Management* (New York: McGraw-Hill Book Co., 1965).

is setting up in advance the things that are to be done, when they are to be done, how they are to be done, who is to do them, and where they are to be done. As is the case with all other managerial activities, top management sets the example for the rest of the organization in planning. Because of the increasing complexity of our society, many organizations have now established formal planning programs to assure that suitable plans will be made for all organizational activities.

Each manager has a responsibility for planning. The work of a unit must be planned to make certain that the unit's plan coincides with the overall plans of the organization. The supervisor who fails to plan goes from one crisis to another and never has time to take the actions necessary to prevent problems from arising. The first step in improving planning is to analyze the way supervisors spend their own time. If the job is poorly designed, it probably has too many things which demand personal attention. Some of them are probably unnecessary, some could be done better by others in the company, some could be delegated to subordinates, and some could be eliminated. When supervisors plan a better distribution of their own time, they are taking action to improve the design of their jobs. They should try to allocate a minimum amount of time to routine work, a maximum amount to creative work (solving problems), and an adequate amount to emergencies.

Proper coordination of all organizational activities is necessary if goals are to be met effectively. Every activity has an effect on other activities, and this effect must be considered when planning takes place. There is a need for total planning on all levels and in all activities of the organization.

The control function is concerned with trying to make events conform to plans. This implies measurement of achievement and correction of deviations to assure effective goal attainment. In recent years there has been an increase in the use of quantitative techniques in the development of control systems. Operations research is one of these and is used in a great number of organizations to aid in the solving of such recurring problems as inventory control, production control, and preventive maintenance. The planning, scheduling, and controlling of huge projects calls for techniques such as PERT and CPM. They have been and are being used by many government agencies and large organizations. Break-even analysis is another quantitative technique used by managers to aid in the determination of the profitability of products manufactured and sold by a company. Many other quantitative techniques are now being utilized by managers in all types of organizations.

The use of mathematics has been made possible by the advent of electronic computers, with their capability to handle large amounts of data very rapidly. These computers are utilized in the development of management information systems to enable managers on all levels to receive accurate and timely data to assist them in the planning, control, and decision-making functions.

CASE 7-1

Jim Walton was recently promoted to a supervisory position at Case Electronics. The company produced a variety or products for use in tape recorders, tape decks, stereo receivers, and various other kinds of consumer electronic equipment. Walton was an electrical engineer, and he supervised several other engineers and their technical support people as well as the department's clerical force. One of the department's responsibilities was to work on design changes if field difficulties were encountered with any of the components produced by the company.

The engineering vice president recently spoke to Jim about a problem the company was having with the tape transport mechanism in a component produced for a large tape recorder manufacturer. It seems that the tape was sticking, moving irregularly, and sometimes breaking, and the vice president wanted Walton's group to check the problem. Jim called two engineers he knew well, told them about the problem, and asked them to look at the design as soon as they could. Two weeks went by and the engineering vice president called Walton to see if the problem was solved. Jim replied that it was being worked on and should be solved shortly. He then went to the two engineers to find out how they were doing. He was amazed when they told him they hadn't even started on the problem. They mentioned how busy they were on other projects and the fact that he had told them to get to it when they could.

1. *What was Walton's basic error?*
2. *How could it have been prevented?*
3. *How should a project of this kind be handled?*
4. *What can Jim Walton do now?*

CASE 7-2

The company started a suggestion system about a year ago. During this period of time Hal Gold, one of your clerks, has turned in over 50 suggestions. None of them has been accepted. Naturally he is disappointed; but you have seen them all and they are either impractical or poorly thought out.

Hal is spending so much time on suggestions that his work is suffering. Because of his lower productivity, others in the unit have to make up his work. You have spoken to Hal about his disruption of the unit's work flow, but he is still determined to come up with a winning suggestion.

1. *How do you handle Hal without destroying his determination?*
2. *What can you do about his low productivity and its effect on work flow?*
3. *Can you get him to plan his work more effectively?*
4. *When should an employee work on suggestions?*

CASE 7-3

The X manufacturing company has 2,000 employees, and a great deal of its work consists of special orders (jobbing shop work). Most of the employees are taking the "rest" too literally in relation to the restrooms. About 20 percent of the workers make it a practice to waste from 15 to 30 minutes in the restrooms at the beginning of each day. However, once they get started working, they do not waste much time. Midmorning and midafternoon rest periods are provided.

The big boss has passed the word down the line that too much time is being lost, that he expects everyone to start working at the beginning of the day, and that better planning by the supervisors would help to correct the problem.

1. *How can the supervisor use planning to get the people started?*
2. *What are some of the difficulties involved in getting started promptly? How can they be overcome?*
3. *What are some of the methods supervisors may use for cutting down the abuse of restroom privileges?*

CASE 7-4

In the past two years Horton Manufacturing Company had expanded very rapidly. It was producing a unique electronic device, and sales were excellent. Because of this expansion many additional employees were added in most areas of the company's operations. This increased staff required more first-level supervisors, and these people were largely promoted from the existing work force. In most instances the supervisors were chosen because they were efficient and dependable workers who knew their jobs well. The rapid growth of the company caused much overtime work, and many employees became used to the extra income this provided. Horton was a nonunion company and had a very good labor relations record.

When employees were promoted to supervisory positions, they were considered members of management, and they became salaried employees. They usually entered the salary range for the job just above the minimum but were considered for increases in six-month periods until they reached the midpoint of the range after which annual consideration took place. Thus a newly appointed supervisor who performed well could reasonably expect three or four increases in the first two years on the supervisory job. Supervisors, however, did not receive overtime pay which was restricted to the hourly paid factory staff and the nonexempt office clerical employees.

In the past six months ten people had been promoted to first-level supervisory positions. Eight of these were in manufacturing and two in the office administration area. All of these people along with eight more supervisors are now confronting the company's president with the fact that they are now earning less money as supervisors than they did as line employees when the regular overtime they worked increased their pay. They were quite adamant about their position, believing that they had more responsibility and were working harder than ever. They firmly believed that they deserved overtime pay or a higher salary.

1. *What should the president do?*
2. *Are the supervisors justified in their complaint?*
3. *Should supervisors be paid overtime?*
4. *Could the company have planned their growth and promotion process more effectively?*

CASE 7–5

A typical weekly occurrence in my company is the rush work that absolutely has to be done immediately or the world will come to an end. My boss usually arrives with a pleading look in his eyes and promises his undying appreciation if I will drop everything and do this rush job. I usualy say yes and then give my employees a pep talk that is better than a football coach at half-time when the team is losing. Even though the employees are used to this, they speed up and get the job out in record time. My boss thanks us all with his usual gratitude. The trouble is that in about half of the cases, our "rush" job was not really necessary since the work stays around for a day or more before it goes out. My employees keep needling me for not telling the boss where to go, and they keep threatening not to work on another rush job.

1. *Are the employees justified in their criticism?*
2. *What are some reasons for rush jobs?*
3. *Why should there be any rush jobs?*
4. *What can you tell your employees and your boss?*

CASE 7–6

Lou Kane is the department head of a clerical operation in the accounting division of a large firm. There are 50 people in the department, including 5 statistical typists and 8 stenographers.

During the first three months of each year, the department has to prepare a great deal of year-end work such as statements, tax forms, balance sheets, and other accounting data. The volume of work generated during this period requires considerable overtime for all of the employees. It averages 10 to 12 hours a week, including Saturdays.

The labor market in which Lou's company operates is characterized by extreme shortages of competent clerical employees and high labor turnover. Lou has been short one statistical typist and one stenographer for several months; another statistical typist has been hospitalized for several weeks, and it is not known when she will return. These shortages of help have placed increased pressure on the other employees, none of whom are enthusiastic about all of the overtime work. Lou has been somewhat successful in recruiting typists from other areas of the company to work overtime during this period.

Recently one of Lou's best statistical typists, who had been with the company five and a half years, was married. After being gone for a two-week honeymoon, she indicated on her return that her husband would not allow her to work overtime.

Lou is concerned about losing her overtime contribution, but he is more worried about the effect of her refusal to work overtime on the other workers, who already feel negative about overtime work.

1. *What can Lou do to convince the other employees to continue overtime work?*
2. *Should he transfer the newly married woman to another area of the company?*
3. *Is the woman justified in refusing to work overtime?*
4. *What other courses of action are open to Lou to alleviate his problems?*

CASE 7–7

The nontechnical people assigned to the research division complain that they are looked down upon by the research engineers and administrative staff (also engineers). The engineers insist that this attitude isn't allowed to affect personal relationships.

Purchasing is handled for (and at) the research division by a purchasing department headed by a local purchasing agent. He reports to the head of the purchasing division at another location. Purchasing department personnel are not employees of the research division. The purchasing department runs into problems in placing for bid the complex technical materials required. It must in most cases rely on the specifications of the engineering staff, who feel that engineers should have the prerogative regarding source, quantity, and price.

The engineers do not question stockroom items unless there is a short part; then they inform the research director that his activities are being interrupted by a stock shortage. He storms into the purchasing agent's office to complain that valuable engineering time is being lost because a two-cent part is not available. It is company policy to control these items on a minimum-maximum basis, using six-month usage to set the maximum. In items of low use the entire stock is often withdrawn on a single requisition.

Another difficulty arises out of the research engineers' dislike for paper work. They bring materials into the plant from vendors without getting a purchase order; they buy materials from petty cash; they "borrow" items brought into the plant in the briefcases of vendors. The purchasing agent learns of these purchases when he receives the bill from the supplier. Engineers often promise an order to a vendor before the purchasing agent receives the requisition. Sometimes thousands of dollars' worth of materials are being assembled on vendor premises without covering paper work.

The engineers take pride in this freedom and flexibility in their operations. Engineering department heads and the director of research share this feeling.

1. List the technical problems involved in this case.
2. What controls might be established to minimize them?
3. Will such controls reduce the personal problems?

CASE 7–8

You supervise a group of 15 people of various specialties who were drawn from other groups in the company and brought together six months ago to work on a project. The work requires constant interaction between the various specialists in the group. They were cooperating well until two weeks ago when, on March 1, you brought up the subject of scheduling their summer vacations.

You told them to decide among themselves when each one should take his vacation, since they knew which people could be absent at the same time without disrupting the work. You gave them sheets listing the amount of vacation each was entitled to because of length of service. The periods are one week, two weeks, three weeks, and four weeks. You reminded them that company policy forbids split vacations, off-season vacations, and vacation scheduling that disrupts production.

Although seniority governs vacation scheduling for hourly workers in the shop, it has never been established as a policy in salaried groups such as yours. The company has always stated that the requirements of the work should govern the scheduling.

Since you turned over the vacation scheduling to your group, the opportunists are buzzing around making deals that will fix themselves up with the choice schedules. People are aligning first with one faction and then with another, whichever will give them the best deal. A few are refusing to deal on the grounds that their seniority or status should entitle them to first choice. All this political maneuvering is taking up time and interfering with the cooperation that is essential to the progress of the work.

1. What should you do now?
2. How should a supervisor go about setting up policies in a newly formed group?
3. What cautions should a supervisor observe in bringing subordinates into decision making?
4. How much time should be allowed between bringing up a problem like this and forcing it to a solution?
5. How can the supervisor ward off problems of conflict between status and seniority?

CASE 7–9

Don Finley is one of those people who can't say no to any request. As a result his section is always in a state of chaos. Everything is a crisis or a crash effort, and very little is done on time. Priorities are always changing and his subordinates rarely know where they are at.

The work gets done, but everyone is usually exhausted at the end of the day. Don is a generous person and his employees like him; but they wish he was a better planner and that he wouldn't always promise more than they can deliver.

1. *How can Finley plan his work more effectively?*
2. *Can his employees help him?*
3. *Do some bosses take advantage of a person like Finley?*
4. *Why would someone consistently run a haphazard operation?*

CASE 7–10

Many people become involved in a variety of tasks and then find they do not have enough time to do them well. What usually happens is that the favorite ones are done, deadlines are changed, or some of the tasks are not even completed.

Students going to evening college or full-time day college students frequently have part-time or full-time jobs. Sometimes they find the course work more difficult than anticipated, and either their job suffers or their grades are less than desirable for the course work. Because they are so busy with these two aspects of their lives, they receive little satisfaction from either since both usually are not being done well. In addition there is little time for leisure activity without guilt feelings. One way to approach this rather common problem is to manage one's time more effectively.

1. *For a period long enough to get a representative sampling of how you use your time (at least a week), fill out a log accounting for all of your waking time. You can do this in a note book or use a small cassette recorder.*
2. *Include work time, leisure time, and all other time you use. Remember that each seven-day week has a total of 168 hours.*
3. *Study the distribution of your time among all of your activities. Evaluate your time distribution in relation to your goals.*
4. *Establish the priorities necessary to achieve your goals by reapportioning your time use.*

Chapter 8

Learning objectives

○ *To gain an understanding of methods improvement and performance standards and their relationship to employee productivity*

○ *To become aware of some of the methodology used in work improvement and the development of standards*

○ *To appreciate the role of the supervisor in work improvement and standard setting*

○ *To become aware of the need for managerial performance standards and cost reduction as a way of measuring performance*

Productivity: Improving methods and developing performance standards

Major topics

Work improvement.

Opposition to methods improvement.

The work measurement program.

Standards and the work measurement or time study department.

Standards and the supervisor.

Laying the groundwork for standards.

Gathering information for standards.

Determining the quantity or the "how much."

Determining the quality or the "how well."

Introducing standards of work performance.

Getting results from standards of work performance.

Standards of managerial performance.

Cost reduction.

Much recent publicity has been given to employee productivity. All of the media, including television, have discussed blue-collar and white-collar job performance and its impact on the economy. The economic aspects of the complex subject of productivity are beyond the scope of this book, but there are some dimensions that have importance for all managers. Simply put, productivity increases have a close relationship to the amount of money any organization can pay for work performance. Because of this, all types of organizations—in both the private and public sectors— have focused increased attention on employee performance as it relates to productivity.

Some combination of individual worker performance and technology result in a measure of productivity. As costs rise, there is considerable pressure on each organization to try to increase employee productivity. These attempts include technological improvement and work performance measurement. In recent years overall productivity increases have lagged behind wage and salary costs. This is one of the causes of the economic pressures mentioned above.

Closely related to the productivity lag is the fact that the numbers of employees in service industries and in government jobs have grown more rapidly than those in manufacturing. Technological improvement also tends to have a greater productivity impact in manufacturing. In general, office or white-collar jobs are more difficult to measure and develop performance standards for, so work measurement has been more firmly established in manufacturing industries. This has added to the productivity problem.

The pressure for greater efficiency has raised the old speed-up issue whenever a company decides to pay increased attention to work performance standards. Recent situations have demonstrated that workers will go out on strike, slow down performance deliberately, increase tardiness and absenteeism, sabotage work quality, and refuse overtime assignments when they believe management is trying to establish performance standards which are thought to be unreasonable.

One of the most troublesome questions in the employer-employee relationship is that of what constitutes a fair day's work for a fair day's pay. Problems of salaries, wages, and effort are packed with emotion, which adds to the difficulty of determining and getting agreement on what is fair. Adding to the confusion are a number of other issues which relate to the fairness of compensation in exchange for work. A combination of increasingly complex technology in both factories and offices and a shortage of skilled labor has caused many companies to lower their expectation for what is considered acceptable performance. A tight labor market tends to increase recruitment, selection, and placement costs. Added to this is the increased cost of training what is generally a lower quality labor supply. Considerable pressure is placed on the supervisor to keep labor turnover down. Under such circumstances one may tolerate poor performance rather than discipline an employee who may quit for another easily obtainable job. Large clerical employers in particular are caught in this type of situation. In many instances, they do not have accurate job descriptions nor do they really know how much each operation costs.

The situation is somewhat different in factories, where labor unions have had a greater impact. The matter of the fair day's pay is a subject for bargaining, and so is the matter of the length of the workday. But the matter of what *rate of production* constitutes a fair day's work is a matter for measurement.

For supervisors to manage effectively they must know how well their units are performing. The control process and forward planning require yardsticks so that reasonable decisions about performance can be made. If goal achievement is a basic activity of organizations, managers must be able to determine the degree of success their units demonstrate toward such goal achievement. To the extent that standards of work performance are established—standards of quantity (how much) and standards of quality (how well)—there can be common understanding of what is required.

The common understanding of what is required is essential to any control system. The very nature of control implies measurement; and if work activity is to be guided effectively toward a predetermined goal, the control system also has to indicate whether the activity is achieving desired results.

The importance of widely accepted standards of performance should be recognized by the manager. To supervise employees effectively, the manager must be able to indicate what is expected of them. They in turn have to know what kind of performance will bring them rewards along with the other ingredients of job satisfaction. The extent of tolerated deviations from the norm is also a requisite of the control system. Correction should take place promptly when the tolerance is breached.

In a sense, an effective control system is a vital communications device indicating to all concerned what is expected of them to achieve the goals of the organization. The establishment of fair standards of work performance is of significant concern to supervisors. Such standards give them one of the tools needed for supervision. Success in achieving established standards allows the superior to measure the effectiveness of supervisory performance. Cost control and budgeting also grow out of established standards; so the importance of developing standards of work performance can be readily seen.

Methods improvement is closely related to the development of performance standards. In most instances there are several ways a job can be performed. Because increasing productivity is a significant management responsibility, the effort to try and find better ways to accomplish work gets considerable managerial attention. Management is largely a diagnostic problem-solving process using a variety of procedures, methods, and programs. Some of these have been discussed in earlier chapters. This chapter will focus on methods improvement, performance standards and measurement, and management by objectives.

Work improvement

The first step in any standard setting process is to specify the conditions under which the standard should apply. This specification includes the physical and functional characteristics of the output from a job or department, the type and condition of input materials to the job, the skill of the workers, the nature of the equipment and machinery to be used, the layout of the workplace area and the department, and the way in which workers should perform the tasks that make up their jobs. All of these things are related to and constitute the work of the department.

Seldom are supervisors or middle managers given the opportunity to design the entire operation of a department from scratch. Rather, they inherit the operation from predecessors who probably worked with various kinds of analysts, industrial engineers, and other staff people who evolved the methodology over time. Nevertheless, managers and supervisors are responsible for the adequacy, appropriateness, implementation, and continued evolution of the methods and operation of the work in their departments. This requires their continued involvement in work improvement.

Work improvement is an organized approach to studying and solving work problems and reducing costs through the use of systematic analysis and focused creativity. Work improvement enables people to do better work with less effort, to do it in less time without hurrying, and to do it with greater safety and at less cost. Thus, the criteria most often applied to evaluating work improvements are human factors, safety, and cost. Some more specific objectives of work improvement are:

1. Eliminate or minimize unnecessary and nonessential activities.
2. Eliminate or minimize duplication of effort.
3. Eliminate or minimize waste of effort, time, materials, and improper equipment use.
4. Increase the effectiveness of necessary activities by making them less fatiguing and safer to perform.
5. Improve the work climate and develop a positive receptivity to desirable changes.
6. Improve product and/or service quality.
7. Reduce costs where possible without reducing quality, thereby increasing productivity.
8. Consider such socially responsible dimensions as energy conservation, environmental protection, and the quality of work life.

Work improvement and its objectives apply to a wide range of operations including not only manufacturing concerns, but also offices, stores, hospitals, government agencies, and the military.

Work improvement is inherent in the supervisory job. They need to understand the technical knowledge and skill used in analyzing and improving the work of their departments. They generally have the responsibility for the efficient operation of their departments and for obtaining smooth and successful adoption of the innovations, improvements, and cost reductions that are essential to the profitability of the enterprise.

Supervisors need to understand the principles and techniques of work improvement to recognize and correct inefficiencies in their own departments and to prevent poor methods from evolving when new work is introduced. Understanding of the required work and work methods is necessary when carrying out the management functions of directing and controlling. Workers have to be shown the proper way to do their jobs and to be told why it is the proper way. To implement the control system effectively, supervisors must improve work in order to meet department standards and help improve company performance.

The responsibility for work improvement varies from one organization to another. For some organizations it is mostly a line activity; in others it is handled by a methods department, or an industrial engineering department; and in still others it is a joint effort of several experts, including the line supervisor. This kind of joint effort becomes more important as systems and equipment become more complex and departments become more interdependent. Nevertheless, in most organizations supervisors have both the initiating and implementing responsibility for work improvement. They must define areas which could benefit substantially from work improvement and help others study it. They must also help their employees adapt to the new methods after they have been designed.

In large organizations the methods department or the work measurement or industrial engineering department is established primarily to devise better ways of accomplishing work. It can make work improvement investigations on an organizationwide scale, starting with the raw material and ending with the finished product. Not confined by departmental lines, it can develop, make, or recommend major changes involving plant or office layout, process layout, and general work improvement including the redesign of equipment and procedures.

In handling work improvement problems, a systematic approach has been found to be more productive than undisciplined ingenuity. The systematic approach described in this text is the seven-step problem-solving technique explained in Chapter 5. Other experts have designed slightly different steps in the process, but the essence of the work improvement process is the same for all of them.

People handling a work improvement problem may say they are making a "process analysis" or an "operations analysis," but they are actually doing more than analyzing. They are applying a systematic problem-solving technique. Analysis is just the step of interpreting the information about an existing problem. A person who is improving work must not only analyze the problem, it must also be defined and solved. Analysis is step three of the seven-step method. Figure 8-1 outlines the process. Going through the seven-step process thoroughly will enable the development of improved work methods. Figure 8-2 illustrates a flow process chart which is one of the descriptive aids commonly used in methods improvement. Figure 8-3 explains the symbols used on the process chart, and Figures 8-4, 8-5 and 8-6 demonstrate how an operation is charted for study and improved.

Thorough discussion of alternatives with employees, methods engineers, and other concerned individuals helps considerably in the development of effective work improvements. Supervisors should try to place themselves in the positions of those employees who will have to use the new methods to gain some insight into the application of the improvement. If possible the supervisor should try out the new method on a small group to correct any errors, oversights, or misjudgments in it. This can eliminate the need for tinkering with the new method once it is fully implemented on the job.

Opposition to methods improvement

No matter how thoroughly supervisors have paved the way for methods improvement, they have to be prepared for a certain amount of difficulty at the time of installation. Considerable help can come from the company's reputation in the handling of past work improvements. If there are policies which limit the layoff of employees by implementing reductions in staff to attrition or having no demotions or pay reductions, then methods improvement is more readily accepted. This sounds relatively easy, but remember that cost savings will only materialize if the payroll is actually reduced. The key factor is to reduce it over time rather than by a short-range wholesale layoff. Supervisors should be patient, understanding, and encourage employees. Training should be given to employees in the use of new methods, and sufficient time should be allowed to them to learn the new methods.

All of this is not as easy as it sounds. People really do not always want change. If the change will help them solve some of their problems, it may be welcome. Much about motivation will be said later in the text, but supervisors should be aware that change is not always readily accepted. A group of supervisors in a management training program compiled the following list of answers when asked how their employees felt about work improvement.

Figure 8–1
Outline of a work improvement process

Step 1.	**Select a target for work improvement.**
Clearly define the problem or problems.	A. Pick a bottleneck, a new job, a labor-hours consumer, an unsafe or unpleasant job, an inefficient procedure, a cause of error or scrap. B. Limit the extent of the study. C. List the benefits expected.
Step 2.	**Describe the current work.**
Gather the information.	A. Observe and interrogate. B. Use descriptive aids.
Step 3.	**Analyze the present work.**
Interpret the information.	A. Decide on the depth of the study. B. Ask, What? Why? Where? When? Who? How? C. Apply principles and checklists.
Step 4.	**Develop several work improvement alternatives.**
Develop solutions.	A. Eliminate. B. Minimize or maximize. C. Combine. D. Rearrange. E. Substitute. F. Simplify.
Step 5.	**Select the best practical alternative.**
Select the best practical solution.	A. Consult others: Superiors, subordinates, associates, staff specialists. B. Evaluate the solutions in terms of the human, safety, cost, and time factors. C. Get necessary approvals. D. Chart the proposed method or procedure.
Step 6.	**Try out and install the new method.**
Put the solution into operation.	A. Make a limited trial application. B. Explain to, prepare, and train those affected.
Step 7.	**Follow up the improved method.**
Evaluate the effectiveness of the solution.	A. Periodically compare actual performance with the new standard. B. Investigate variations from the new method.

Figure 8–2

FLOW PROCESS CHART						NUMBER					

PROCESS

☐ MAN OR ☐ MATERIAL

		ACTIONS		SUMMARY	
				NO.	TIME
CHART BEGINS	**CHART ENDS**	○	OPERATIONS		
		⇨	TRANSPORTATIONS		
		☐	INSPECTIONS		
CHARTED BY	**DATE**	D	DELAYS		
		▽	STORAGES		
DEPARTMENT		DISTANCE TRAVELLED (Feet)			

DETAILS OF ☐☐ PRESENT / PROPOSED METHOD	OPERATION / TRANSPORTATION / INSPECTION / DELAY / STORAGE	DISTANCE IN FEET	QUANTITY	TIME	ANALYSIS WHY? — WHAT? WHERE? WHEN? WHO? HOW?	NOTES
1	○⇨☐D▽					
2	○⇨☐D▽					
3	○⇨☐D▽					
4	○⇨☐D▽					
5	○⇨☐D▽					
6	○⇨☐D▽					
7	○⇨☐D▽					
8	○⇨☐D▽					
9	○⇨☐D▽					
10	○⇨☐D▽					
11	○⇨☐D▽					
12	○⇨☐D▽					
13	○⇨☐D▽					
14	○⇨☐D▽					
15	○⇨☐D▽					
16	○⇨☐D▽					
17	○⇨☐D▽					
18	○⇨☐D▽					
19	○⇨☐D▽					
20	○⇨☐D▽					
21	○⇨☐D▽					

Figure 8–3
Flow process chart symbols

SYMBOL (ASME)	NAME	REPRESENTS	EXAMPLES
○	OPERATION	Performance at a specific location, workplace, desk, that advances the work toward completion. Something is added, subtracted, changed, or created. An operation occurs when information is given or received or when planning or calculation takes place	Drill, burr, mill, weld, spray, assemble, clean, pack, type, read, sign, repair
⇨	TRANSPORTATION	Movement of work-in-process, or person, or form, or letter, from one location to another	To Dept. X by hand truck. To next machine by conveyor. To assembly by lift truck. To next desk by messenger. To accounting by pneumatic tube
□	INSPECTION	Examining or checking an object in relation to quality or quantity requirements	Check, count, weigh, gauge, check for damage. Verify address or amounts, proofread, read gauge
D	DELAY	Condition that prevents the next step in the process (such as operation, transportation, or inspection) from being started	Await truck, on skid, await elevator, in tote box, machine breakdown, waiting in line, out of information, supplies, or materials, in incoming or outgoing basket, waiting for signature
▽	STORAGE	Locating an object in a place where it is protected against unauthorized removal	In storeroom, in storage, in safe, in file cabinet

In charting a process, each thing that happens to the subject is either an operation, transportation, inspection, delay, or storage. The symbols above are used to portray these various steps as they are recorded on a flow process chart (see Figure 8–2).

An operation is some form of work performed by a person or machine at a specific location. When a person is performing a job at a fixed work station or desk, any or all movements within approximately a five-foot radius may be considered as one operation.

A transportation is a movement between specific locations. A distance traveled over five feet may be considered as a transportation.

An inspection occurs when something is checked, verified for quality or accuracy, or counted.

A delay is a stoppage of the work-in-process while it is waiting for an operation, inspection, or transportation.

A storage occurs when something is held in protective custody and requires authorization for its release.

Figure 8–4
Example of a flow process chart for material (stocking lumber at point of use—present method)

FLOW PROCESS CHART No. Y-4 Page 1 of 2

SUMMARY						CHART SUBJECT:	Blocking Lumber – 4" x 4" x 8'		☐ MAN ☒ MATERIAL

		PRESENT		PROPOSED		DIFFERENCE	
		NO.	TIME	NO.	TIME	NO.	TIME
OPERATIONS	O	1800					
TRANSPORTATIONS	⇨	901					
INSPECTIONS	☐						
DELAYS	D						
STORAGES	△	1					
TOTAL ELEMENTS		2702					
DISTANCE TRAVELLED		33,300Ft.			Ft.		Ft.

DETAILS OF CHART SUBJECT: This lumber is piled in an outside storage yard by the vendor. When needed it is loaded on a truck manually, moved to the 23" Mill and unloaded manually. Move from 23" Mill pile to R.R. car as needed.

COMPANY ABC PLANT " X "
DEPARTMENT Rolling Mills UNIT 23" Mill
INVESTIGATED BY John Doe DATE 5/1
REVIEWED BY Richard Roe DATE 6/1

	DETAILS OF PRESENT METHOD	OPERATION	TRANSPORT	INSPECTION	DELAY	STORAGE	DISTANCE IN FEET	QUANTITY	TIME	ACTION ELIMINATE	COMBINE	CHNGE. SEQ.	SIMPLIFY	NOTES
1	Pick up 1 piece 4" x 4" x 8'	O	⇨	·	D	△		1						300 pieces comprise
2	Carry to truck	O	⇨	·	D	△	15	1						a truck load
3	Pile on truck	O	⇨	·	D	△		1						
4	Move to 23" mill by truck	O	⇨	·	D	△	1800	300		x				Change location of storage pile
5	Pick up 1 piece 4" x 4" x 8'	O	⇨	·	D	△		1						300 pieces
6	Move to storage pile by hand	O	⇨	·	D	△	15	1						300 pieces
7	Place on pile	O	⇨	·	D	△		1						
8	Hold for usage	O	⇨	·	D	△		1						
9	Pick up 1 piece 4" x 4" x 8'	O	⇨	·	D	△		1						
10	Carry to car	O	⇨	·	D	△	75	1						300 pieces
11	Place in car	O	⇨	·	D	△								
12		O	⇨	·	D	△								
13		O	⇨	·	D	△								
14		O	⇨	·	D	△								Conclusions:
15		O	⇨	·	D	△								Original storage of
16		O	⇨	·	D	△								blocking should be at
17		O	⇨	·	D	△								the mill storage area.
18		O	⇨	·	D	△								
19		O	⇨	·	D	△								
20		O	⇨	·	D	△								
21		O	⇨	·	D	△								
22		O	⇨	·	D	△								

20

Source: United States Steel Company, *Methods Engineering Manual*, 1951. Explanation of the chart is given in the caption below Figure 8–5.

Figure 8–5

Example of a flow process chart for material (stocking lumber at point of use—proposed method)

FLOW PROCESS CHART   NO. Y-4   Page 2 of 2

SUMMARY						CHART		
	PRESENT		PROPOSED		DIFFERENCE			☐ MAN
	NO.	TIME	NO.	TIME	NO.	TIME	SUBJECT: 4" x 4" x 8'	☒ MATERIAL
OPERATIONS ○	1800		600		1200			
TRANSPORTATIONS ⇨	901		300		601			
INSPECTIONS ☐								
DELAYS D								
STORAGES △	1		0		1			
TOTAL ELEMENTS	2702		900		1802			
DISTANCE TRAVELLED	33,300ft.		22,500ft.		10,800 ft.			

CHART SUBJECT: Blocking Lumber - 4" x 4" x 8'

DETAILS OF CHART SUBJECT: Lumber is now piled in 23" Mill by vendor. Move to R.R. car as needed. Compare movement of 300 pieces with present method.

COMPANY ABC   PLANT "X"
DEPARTMENT Rolling Mills   UNIT 23" Mill
INVESTIGATED BY John Doe   DATE 5/15/
REVIEWED BY Richard Roe   DATE 6/1/

DETAILS OF PROPOSED METHOD	OPERATION / TRANSPORT / INSPECTION / DELAY / STORAGE	DISTANCE IN FEET	QUANTITY	TIME	ACTION (ELIMINATE / COMBINE / CHNGE. SEQ. / SIMPLIFY)	NOTES
1 Pick up 1 piece 4" x 4" x 8'	○⇨☐D△		1			
2 Carry to car	○⇨☐D△	75	1			300 pieces
3 Place in car	○⇨☐D△		1			
	○⇨☐D△					

Source: United States Steel Company, *Methods Engineering Manual*, 1951.

As charted in Figure 8–4, blocking lumber used by one plant for loading slabs and billets in railroad cars was delivered by outside vendor trucks to a central storage building in the mill. Here, the truck drivers unloaded the lumber by hand and piled it according to size. Whenever the mill needed more lumber for blocking, they would call the service department and order a truck and several laborers to load the blocking lumber and take it to a storage point adjacent to the shipping area, unload it, and pile it by size. As the loaders blocked the car, they would carry the lumber from the pile to the car. This method of handling the lumber was an old and established one and, as a result, was accepted as standard practice. An awareness of an existing problem was brought about by the fact that labor force schedules were frequently disrupted by urgent demands for blocking lumber at the mill.

After the material flow chart was completed, three main points stood out: (1) there was excessive handling of blocking lumber, (2) two storage areas were required although neither was generally full, (3) the frequency of occurrence was very regular and the operation never varied.

Questions were raised as follows: What can be done to eliminate excessive handling? Why not unload the material directly into the pile adjacent to the railroad tracks? This would resolve the first two factors by eliminating the labor and truck for handling and freeing the main storage area for necessary material. Final ideas were recorded on chart.

As charted in Figure 8–5 the new handling operation is obviously simplified. The vendor's truck will unload the lumber and pile it by size at the storage area adjacent to the car tracks. The service department is no longer involved, and the loaders work from a conveniently located supply of lumber.

Figure 8–6 is a flow diagram showing the layout conditions of this problem, the locations of the lumber storage areas in the old method and in the proposed method. The diagram is actually a picture of where the loading and unloading is performed. The diagram is keyed to the process chart by symbol and step numbers.

Figure 8–6
Flow diagram of the problem charted and explained in Figures 8–4 and 8–5

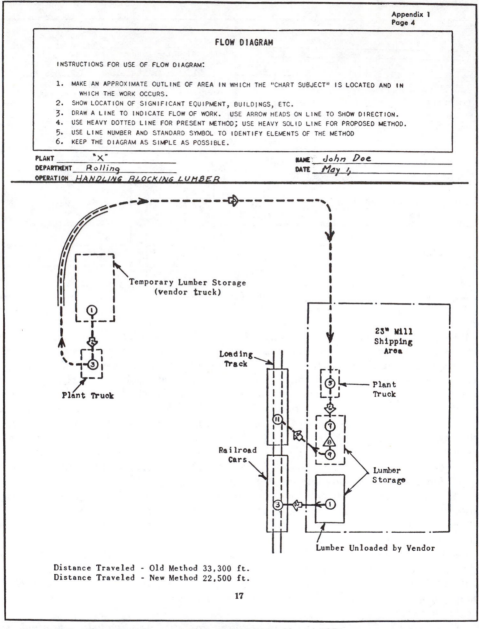

Source: United States Steel Company, *Methods Engineering Manual*, 1951.

The present method is portrayed in broken lines, the proposed method (steps 1, 2, and 3 at lower right) in solid lines; work stations are in light outline. The symbol numbers in the diagram are keyed to the step numbers in the process charts.

They don't like changes. They don't want to change their habits. They are not prepared for change. They don't see any reason to change the pres ent method.

They don't understand.

They feel they will be expected to do more work for the same money.

They fear their earnings might be reduced.

They think they might have to learn a new job.

They devised the present method and don't like other people changing it.

They think that the proposed method was already tried and found to be unsuccessful.

They fear that they will be replaced by machines.

They feel that they are being criticized.

They feel that maybe they should have thought of the change themselves.

They object to having outsiders tell them how to do their jobs.

They feel secure in the old method.

They object to not being consulted in advance.

They worry about how the new method will affect them and how they will learn to do the new jobs.

They fear they may lose a portion of their jobs.

They feel that their trade secrets are being impinged upon and their skills diluted; that they could thus be replaced more easily.

They fear that if the new method gets more work done with fewer people, they (or their friends) will be out of a job.

The supervisors didn't mention that employees fear a loss of status and dignity, a downgrading in importance, or loss of their hopes of getting ahead. When employees feel that a change in their jobs is depriving them of something they value, the change may be met by a prolonged drop in production, by hostility, grievances, absences, and quits. Resistance to change and ways to decrease it are discussed in Chapter 16. Techniques for introducing change must be combined with techniques for improving methods and applied with skill in human relations.

The work measurement program

Once improved work methods have been installed, work performance can be measured. Work measurement is one of the tools of management, designed to minimize the inevitable subjective judgments by which supervisors evaluate their subordinates. It is primarily concerned with improving productivity, and in this sense it helps a supervisor to do a more effective job. It is hoped that a work measurement program will aid the supervisor in making work assignments, training new employees, and planning and scheduling work. Forecasting personnel requirements and determining costs are obvious additional benefits.

Since a work measurement program has a wide impact on an organization, it must have a total commitment from all levels of management. Obviously the first-level supervisor's acceptance of the program is critical to its success. After all, it is at this level of supervision that the greatest involvement with the measurement and control aspects of the program take place. Supervisors should have a significant role in the development of standards, and every effort should be made to make it their program. Even where a trained staff of analysts is used, supervisors should be consulted, and they should approve the standards set for those jobs for which they are responsible. If the first-level supervisor accepts and supports the work measurement program enthusiastically, this will go a long way toward gaining general acceptance among all employees whose work is measured.

While middle managers are not as directly involved with work measurement as are the supervisors who report to them, they have their familiar "person-in-the-middle" role here. They are expected to support the top-management decision establishing the program and to indicate their approval to the lower level supervisors reporting to them. Middle managers are also expected to communicate to their superiors the problems, thoughts, and opinions of their subordinates.

As the program develops and becomes well established, middle managers will find it very useful as a yardstick for the performance of first-level supervision. By holding the first-level supervisor responsible for the utilization of standards, the middle manager has a reasonably objective measurement of the effectiveness of the first-level supervisor. Such a measurement is particularly useful when recommending pay increases and promotions for first-level supervisors.

As indicated earlier the establishment of a work measurement program is usually a top-management decision. Once the decision is made, there should be an indication of the wholehearted approval of senior management. It is particularly desirable that such a program have their backing, for they are the individuals who establish the leadership pattern for the organization. A senior executive who reports to the chief executive should be given responsibility for the program, and the chief executive should make it clear that he or she is interested in the success of the program.

Standards and the work measurement or time study department

The job of setting standards of work performance is usually a function of the time study or work measurement department, but on some jobs the supervisor has to establish the standards. In order to do so, he or she should be acquainted with the techniques used by the work measurement staff. The supervisor should get the time study people to show how they determine normal performance from observed performance and how they make allowances for personal needs. The following definitions will establish a basis for discussing measurements and work pace.

Definitions. A standard of work performance is defined as the quality and quantity of work that *should* be produced by a *normal* employee working at a *normal* pace under *normal* conditions. "Normal" does not mean average, because the average performance may be poor performance under poor conditions.

A normal employee is a trained employee with sufficient aptitude and skill plus a positive attitude and a will to work.

A normal pace is that pace which a conscientious person can maintain day in and day out without suffering any ill effects. It is a daywork pace, and it has not been hastened by a wage incentive or any other stimulus to hurry up.

Normal conditions mean: (1) that the materials, equipment, and working environment do not hinder the employee, (2) that the employee is subjected to a minimum of interruptions, (3) that the best available methods as determined by, or equivalent to, those developed by methods improvement techniques are being used.

Examples of standards of work performance are shown in Figure 8–7. They are standards for office work in Standard Oil Company of California. Some other examples of standards of work performance would be:

In a shop: 3 pieces drilled per minute; 10 percent of time devoted to safety education.

In an office; 70 to 80 invoices written per day.

In a sales department: 6 or 7 calls per day.

In a social agency: 8 to 12 cases handled per week.

In a mail-order house: 3,000 sales slips sorted per hour.

Techniques for measuring performance. The standards set up by the time study department are used for daywork standards, wage incentives, production planning, scheduling, standard costs, and similar purposes. The three major techniques used in setting the standards are stopwatch time study, standard data, and work sampling. While all of the above systems have some differences in application and approach, they have common objectives. Essentially they are used to analyze work in relation to the basic motions necessary for its performance.

Standards and the supervisor

While the work measurement or time study department ordinarily sets up standards for repetitive tasks—standards that must ordinarily by expressed in definite quantitative measurements—there are many jobs that cannot and need not be measured so rigidly. These are the jobs on which

Figure 8–7
Work performance standards—typing and filing

```
                          PERFORMANCE STANDARDS
                    STENOGRAPHER-TYPIST and FILE CLERK


                                     Hours          Minutes          %
  1.  Total Hours Paid For:  (Daily)      8            480           100
  .   Total Hours Allowance:  (Daily)     1             60           12.5
      Total Net Productive Hours:  (Daily) 7           420           87.5
```

LINES

2. 30 Lines Per Letter: Dictated and Transcribed
   30 Lines Per Letter: Straight Copy

LETTERS

3. Production (Net Production Time) - in Seven (7) Hours, or 420 Minutes:
   Dictated and Transcribed Letters (30 lines each) = 10-1/2 letters, or Straight Copy Work *
   (30 lines each) = 21 letters

TIME STUDY ANALYSIS

4. Fifteen (15) Minutes Average Dictation Time for 30-Line Letter
   Twenty-Five (25) Minutes Average Transcription Time for 30-Line Letter
   Twenty (20) Minutes Average Copy Time for 30-Line Letter

AVERAGE DAILY TIME

5. Net Production Time: Seven (7) Hours, or 420 Minutes:
   Minutes Per Dictated Letter (40) = 10-1/2 - 30-Line Letters in Seven (7) Hours
   Minutes Per Copied Letter (20) = 21 - 30-Line Letters in Seven (7) Hours

Note: *Typing time to transcribe a full page or equivalent from voicewriting*
machine cylinders or records is figured at 20 minutes per letter. The
average cylinder contains approximately 120 lines of typing. The
number of cylinders completed per day should total 7 or more.
In general, stenographers spend 65% of productive time on dictation
and transcription and 35% on typing from copy or manuscript, resulting
in a combined total production of 13 full pages per day.

FILING

6. (a) Fifty (50) Units of Mail Per Hour using a numerical file system is the average and
       includes General File upkeep.
   (b) One hundred fifty (150) Units of Mail Per Hour, filing alphabetically, is the average
       and includes General File upkeep.

These production standards are based on the results of numerous surveys of stenographic work
and represent actual production of stenographers having average ability.

CODE ARRANGEMENT:

Have steno or typist place initials on copy.
Use "T" for transcribing from longhand material or typed copy.
Use "D" for dictated letters.
Use "V" for voicewriting machine.
Make notation on working paper describing material typed if not practical to make
   copy such as contracts, complicated statements, and legal documents.
Show typing time on each letter or typed material.

* From handwritten copy

Source: Used by permission of Standard Oil Company of California. Exhibit ''L,'' part 2, page 44 of
More Profit—Less Paper, prepared by Joseph W. Lucas with the assistance of other members of the
department on organization of Standard Oil Company of California.

the supervisor must set standards in order to plan and schedule work, know personnel needs, and estimate budget needs. Another use of standards is in comparing and evaluating methods improvement suggestions one against another.

The supervisor must have standards of performance in order to evaluate the performance of subordinates and to handle disciplinary problems and grievances. If an employee is to be discharged for unacceptable performance, there must be evidence that he knew the standard and knew that his work was substantially below it over a definite period of time. A supervisor who has a set of standards of work performance can measure each subordinate's performance and know whether the person should be rewarded, encouraged, given extra training, transferred, or warned. The employee who knows the standard knows what is expected; knows whether performance is outstanding, satisfactory, or unsatisfactory and whether due for a reward or a warning.

Standards of performance serve both supervisors and middle managers in making possible the delegation of authority and responsibility. A delegator is still accountable for work turned over to a subordinate and must have some system of information (records and reports) to find out if the work is being done and some measure by which to judge how well it is being done. This, of course, is controlling—one of the major activities of management. A system of controls permits management by the exception principle: That is, managers have the exceptions to the standard brought to their attention, so that they can spot misuse of authority or failure to carry out responsibility and take corrective action. Standards are a help to the subordinate to whom responsibility and authority are delegated, because he or she knows what is expected.

Laying the groundwork for standards

When a supervisor is preparing to set up a standard, the job is analyzed from the standpoint of the tasks it contains and just what the worker is doing or supposed to be doing. It may be found that the job is not very well set up—that the tasks are not fitted together to make a well-designed job. Also, the workplace may be poorly arranged, or there may be delays and inefficiencies that can be corrected. If investigation of a job shows that a methods improvement program is needed, the job should be improved before a standard is set.

While the supervisor is still looking over the job from the standpoint of what it consists of, the job description should be consulted. At this point the supervisor may wonder why standards have to be set up at all, if the job is all written up in the job description. But if the supervisor tries to use a typical job description to evaluate performance, he or she will find that it describes what the person is to do, but not *how much*; it describes the skills and abilities necessary—but provides no means of measuring how well the job is being done. But the job description makes a good starting spot in that it furnishes information on job content and probably lists the tasks that make up the job. When the job is broken down into the different tasks of which it is composed, it becomes easier to measure.

Gathering information for standards

The supervisor who performed the job while a member of the rank and file has a very good idea of how much should be turned out. If the job has been supervised over a period of time, the supervisor has seen it performed by a number of workers and under varying conditions. The more performances that have been studied, the better the judgment will be as to what amount constitutes satisfactory performance.

The time study or work measurement department can supply valuable information about the amount of work and the pace of the normal worker. Time study analysts are always working with this problem; they have to have an accurate idea of what the normal pace of a qualified operator is in order to work out their time studies. They need to determine the difference in pace between the hourly paid employee and the worker on piece rates. They also need to know the difference between the worker they are observing and the normal worker in order to set the performance requirements to fit the normal worker. With this background they can be of great assistance to the supervisor in determining what the pace of a normal worker should be.

When setting up standards, it is often profitable to consult the workers as to what it is they do or should be doing. When supervisors investigate the *what* of a job, they should keep the purpose of the job in mind so as to list the tasks in the order of their importance, and they should describe the tasks in clear, simple, specific, and definite action words. For an example of a well-written standard, see Figure 8–7.

Determining the quantity or the "how much"

After lining up or writing down the tasks that make up a job, the supervisor next determines the quantity of work that will constitute satisfactory performance. Here both the needs of management and the capacities of competent, trained, and qualified employees will have to be considered. The standard to be established should not be an ideal goal that can be attained only by an outstanding worker under conditions that are just right. The standard must be set at a mark that the normal worker—as defined early in this chapter—can reach and an above-average employee can exceed. The preciseness with which output can be measured varies from number of pieces per hour, as determined by the time study department on repetitive jobs, to the vagueness of work that is purely creative and in which the amount is anybody's guess. The great majority of jobs in industry do not belong in the purely creative class, however, and can be measured in some manner.

The type of job under study will greatly influence the way the quantitative measure is expressed. Instead of expressing output in terms of pieces per hour or a range of pieces, it might be expressed in terms of deadlines. Payrolls, for example, must be completed by a certain deadline. Or output might be expressed in terms of getting the job done so that people will not have to wait or be held up: for example, supplying materials to machines or setting up machines. Another basis might be that the job is to be completed within a certain period of time after it is received: For example, all correspondence must be answered within one or two days of receipt. The same measure might go for different types of reports.

In measuring the quantity of output, the supervisor has to set standards that encourage workers to give their best efforts to the company. A standard that emphasizes output at the sacrifice of judgment and cooperation is demoralizing.

Some examples of quantity standards are:

Punch information at the rate of 110 to 120 cards per hour.

Sort between 900 and 1,000 pieces per hour.

Validate claims at the rate of 325 to 375 per week.

Answer all outside correspondence within 12 working hours.

Finish tabulation and send to payroll department half a day before the payroll is to be started.

Post 750 accounts per day.

Determining the quality or the "how well"

Work may be turned out in great quantity at the expense of quality; but if it is not acceptable, it is a waste of people, materials, money, and equipment.

There are two ways of getting at the problem of determining satisfactory quality. The first is the positive way, in which the supervisor asks, "What is the purpose of this work? What is the end that it has to serve?" If the work fulfills its objective, the quality is necessarily satisfactory.

The other approach—and the easier one—is the negative approach: that is, uncovering the points at which the work is unsatisfactory and asking why it is unsatisfactory. When a supervisor asks, "Why is this work being rejected?" or "Why am I rejecting this work?" the quality aspects of the job are being measured.

It is necessary for the supervisor to relate quality and quantity in their proper balance in setting up measures of performance. Generally, the higher the quality requirements of any job, the lower the volume will be. Pieces that have to be machined to close tolerances cannot be turned out as fast as those machined to loose tolerances. This theory follows through in most work. Therefore, the supervisor should not call for quality that is higher than necessary for the successful accomplishment of the job. Neither should workers be encouraged to do a piece of work beyond the requirements called for.

Quality standards can be set up on a number of bases. They can be in terms of rejects by the inspection department. Or they may be set up in terms of the amount of waste—for example, an amateur painter painting a ceiling might do an excellent job but get more paint on the surrounding areas than on the ceiling. Another basis is that of reworks. This may be not only in terms of what the worker has to do over again, but also in terms of the amount of extra work caused for somebody else in subsequent operations: Boxes piled up backward have to be turned around by someone in order to be identified. Quality may be set up in terms of errors—that is, three mistakes in a hundred. Another basis will be in terms of a worker's doing a job safely in relation to himself and others. For example, in stacking materials, a job is not satisfactory if a person does not lift properly or if the articles are piled in a manner that would allow them to fall over and injure someone or damage equipment. Quality of work should include the proper use of machines and tools.

It is necessary that the supervisor relate the quality standards to the quantity standards and give each its proper importance when setting up performance standards and explaining them to his employees.

Some examples of quality standards are:

Punching errors should not exceed 5 to 10 in 1,000 cards punched.

No more than 2 or 3 sorting errors in 10,000 pieces.

No more than 3 or 5 claims incorrectly validated in processing 1,500 claims.

On letters, margins should be even and there should be no smudges or misspellings.

Introducing standards of work performance

The critical stage in the development of a work measurement program is gaining acceptance of the program among the employees whose performance is to be measured. As is the case with any new or different program, there is bound to be some resistance and suspicion about standards of performance. It is rather difficult for an employee to understand how standards of performance will help that employee before the program starts. Thus it is vital to involve and inform employees as soon as possible. Early information will help offset the inevitable rumors about a "speedup" and "cutting payroll" that accompany the introduction of any attempt at performance measurement.

Because employees are primarily interested in their own welfare, the supervisor must emphasize the relationship of performance standards to the individual employee. It is natural for employees to fear change because of the uncertainty that it implies. Obviously it is therefore necessary for the supervisor to be as specific as possible in allaying employee fears.

The detail which goes into writing up a standard will vary with the importance of the tasks and the number of people performing them. New standards should be tried out on a temporary basis until they are found to be satisfactory. Then they should be put on a permanent basis and not changed unless there is a substantial change in the job content or in the method of doing the job. A standard, to be worthwhile, must be considered a measure that will not vary.

Reprinted by permission The Wall Street Journal

Performance standards can result in rapid and accurate feedback.

When the work group has a good attitude toward the company, the employees themselves can participate in setting the standards; people setting their own standards usually set them high and are much better motivated to work toward attaining them. Work groups that are accustomed to taking responsibility for seeing that the total job is done can participate in standard setting in group meetings. If a group agrees on a standard, it puts pressure on individual members to conform to it and gives help to individual members to achieve it. The *process* of setting standards can result in a better understanding of the objectives of the unit and a greater willingness to accept responsibilities.

Merely discussing standards of work performance with employees can be a morale builder. If workers know the standards, they can measure their performance against them and know where they stand. They will realize that the important item is work—not just pleasing the boss. When workers know that output is being checked against standards, they know that success on the job depends on performance and not on factors beyond their control. They cannot claim that performance is being evaluated according to how the boss feels that day or other subjective judgments. Nor can the workers claim that they are being overloaded or discriminated against and that other employees are getting away with murder.

Getting results from standards of work performance

Standards of work performance determine in concrete terms what constitutes the satisfactory performance of a job. When actual performance is not up to the standard, the supervisor can investigate immediately to find out the cause. The material may be at fault. If material is of the wrong kind or the supply is inadequate, the supervisor can take immediate steps to try to correct the situation. Investigation may show that there is something wrong with the equipment, and it may have to be repaired. Or the investigation may show that there is something wrong with the worker. Observing unsatisfactory performance may disclose a specific need for further training, the fact that the employee is not fitted for the job and should be transferred or has a gripe and needs to get it settled before normal production can be achieved again.

Supervisors with standards of work performance can do a much better job of planning the work of their sections; they are in a position to answer more accurately the questions: When? Where? Who? Standards of work performance help in estimating the number of worker-hours needed for future jobs. They permit the supervisor to balance the load better among the workers and avoid overloading the more willing workers. The supervisor who measures work against a standard is not likely to be charged with favoritism, inconsistency, or arbitrary action.

Measuring actual performance against a standard enables the supervisor to uncover and reward outstanding performance. At the other end of the scale, it enables the supervisor to prove that some performances are unsatisfactory and gives a basis on which to take action, As far as the average qualified worker is concerned, the performance standards are a means of letting him or her know what is expected and how well it is being done.

Of course, quality and quantity are not the only measures of employee performance. An individual may perform a job adequately and still not be a desirable employee. This person may be a troublemaker, quarreling with other employees, engaging in unsafe practices, and stirring up resentment against the supervisor or the company. In an overall evaluation, such behavior would outweigh performance in determining that employee's usefulness to the organization.

Standards of managerial performance

Performance standards for managers are more difficult to develop than those for employees in most nonsupervisory positions. That managerial performance should be measured is undeniably desirable. The question is how and with what degree of objectivity. Because it is necessary for an organization's growth and survival to identify, develop, motivate, and promote managers, some method of appraising their performance should be considered. Managers resent subjective judgments about their performance as much as nonmanagerial employees do. Equally distasteful is being subjected to the whim and fancy of a superior or being involved in political machinations without any opportunity to demonstrate ability on a rational basis.

Over the years a variety of methods for appraising the performance of managers have been used. These range from checking the supervisor against a list of predetermined desirable characteristics (tactful, loyal, dependable, and so on) to rather complicated forced distributions designed arbitrarily to separate good performers from poor ones.

Measurement implies a yardstick that is reliable and objective. Unfortunately such standards are not readily available for the measurement of managerial performance. Some research has indicated that managers who have an employee-centered, democratic leadership style are effective performers. Still other research demonstrates that a production-oriented, benevolently autocratic style achieves good results. The fact probably is that much depends on the nature of the work, the work group itself, the environment in which the work is performed, the individual manager, his superior, and a variety of other circumstances and variables.

Management by objectives. The nebulous nature of managerial performance standards has given rise to a results-oriented approach to manager performance appraisal. These systems are variously called "management by results," "accountability management," and "management by objectives."[1] They all use performance standards as their basis, and in many instances these standards are arrived at through superior-subordinate consultation and agreement. Obviously the standards reached are goal-oriented, and these goals are related to overall organizational goals. In these programs, managerial standard setting and the consequent appraisal is viewed as a continuous process very much a part of each manager's job.

Standards of performance of management people are best set up in terms

---

[1] For a thorough understanding of management by objectives, see P. F. Drucker, *Managing for Results* (New York: Harper & Row, Publishers, 1964); E. C. Schleh, *Management by Results* (New York: McGraw-Hill Book Co., 1961); D. D. McConkey, *How to Manage by Results* (New York: American Management Assn., 1976); G. S. Odiorne, *Management by Objectives* (New York: Pitman Publishing Corp., 1965); S. J. Carroll and H. L. Tosi, Jr., *Management by Objectives* (New York: Macmillan Co., 1973); Paul Mali, *Managing by Objectives* (New York: Wiley-Interscience, 1972).

of objectives which state what the supervisor's managerial unit is supposed to do toward attaining the objectives of the company.

When goals are set in terms of the total enterprise, supervisory performance is measured by what each unit contributes to the larger unit above and what the individual supervisor contributes to the company through the unit and through teamwork with people in other departments. Management by objectives stresses and rewards teamwork and seeks to prevent empire building and conflicts between the various specialties in an organization.

In order for supervisors to have goals to achieve, they and their supervisors must agree on what is expected of them and their units and what they will be measured by (what kind of data or records will furnish the information on the performance of each unit). Setting objectives is a good way to reach an understanding with the boss about what is expected from the subordinate's unit. Such an understanding may not be arrived at otherwise. Research reports indicate that in a number of cases there is little agreement between subordinates and their superiors on what each subordinate's responsibilities are, which are most important, and what problems they have in carrying them out.[2] These are the matters on which a person's performance is measured; thus it is essential that there be a meeting of the minds between supervisor and boss on what the responsibilities and objectives are. The special difficulties encountered on the job enter into the evaluation of performance also; a person deserves more credit for doing a difficult task than an easy one—provided the task is necessary and the difficulties unavoidable.

The responsibilities listed in the supervisor's job description make a starting place from which to set up statements of the results that supervisor is expected to produce. These results must be matters on which records are kept so that data will be available to measure performance. As a first step in setting up standards for individual performance, the supervisor should, with the boss, make a list of the results that are expected and the data by which they are measured or could be measured. (See list on page 251.)

After completing the listing, boss and supervisor should rate each of the items according to its importance to the company and then according to the difficulties or special problems it presents. For instance, safety may be no problem, but quality may be difficult to achieve under present circumstances. Just as questions in an exam are identified as to the amount of weight each will carry in figuring the total grade, each item on the list can be given the weight it should carry in an evaluation of the supervisor's performance.

The next step in setting up goals is to write down what has been the performance in the past on each item, then to judge what should be the performance in the coming period of six months or a year—or whatever period is covered in a performance review. As a rule the manager in a goal-setting in-

---

[2] Norman R. F. Maier, L. Richard Hoffman, John J. Hooven, and William H. Read, *Superior-Subordinate Communication in Management* (New York: American Management Assn., Reasearch Study No. 52, 1961).

Results expected	Measured by
1. Attain high direct labor productivity.	1. Accounting records available.
2. Meet quality standards.	2. Number of: errors sent back for correction; rejects; complaints; returns.
3. Keep on schedule; get work done on time.	3. Record of completion dates checked against schedules. Record of overtime.
4. Maintain good labor relations.	4. Number of grievances. Rate of turnover. Record of absences.
5. Maintain a safe operation.	5. Record of accident frequency and severity per labor-hours worked. Rating on housekeeping.

terview with the boss will set high personal goals, but it is important that they be attainable; a standard that is too high may cause the person to quit trying. It is important also that the data or information used for measuring performance be supplied to the supervisor in a form that is simple, usable, and measurable. Costs must be those he is responsible for and has control over, and they should be separated according to category. Such a flow of timely information is essential so that the supervisor can be alerted to substandard performance and so that trouble spots can be located and action taken to correct them. This is *self*-control. Information that is three weeks late in arriving can be measured, but it is of little use except to assess blame.

After the supervisor and his or her boss have worked out and agreed upon the objectives, the results expected, and the data by which they will be measured, the sheet becomes something like a charter under which the supervisor operates. In a performance review at the end of the period the boss will go over the list with the subordinate to discuss accomplishments, the problems met, and what kind of help would enable better performance. Then they will set goals for the next period. A performance appraisal such as this, which starts out with definite statements of what was expected and definite measures of achievement, provides a strong motivating force, and causes a minimum of embarrassment or resentment. It reviews past performance as a preparation for the future. It discusses results and difficulties in terms of accomplishments that lie ahead.

Some companies use group meetings for setting standards. Starting at the top of the organization and working down, managers meet with their subordinates in a group to define responsibilities and objectives, discuss results expected, and have the group set standards.[3]

---

[3] Virgil K. Rowland, *Managerial Performance Standards* (New York: American Management Asn., 1960). This is a how-to-do-it book containing transcripts of stan-

Limitations of MBO. Naturally there are limitations in a mangement by objectives program, even when it is designed with the best intentions of top management. First of all there must be wide understanding of the program. If the managers involved do not recognize it as a part of their responsibilities, and goal setting is not done within the guidelines established and with objectivity, the seeds of failure are sown. Because goals are difficult to establish where managerial performance is to be measured, every attempt should be made to develop participation by all levels of management. Further, there should be no use of coercion or manipulation to arrive at goals. The goals should not be arrived at expediently, nor should organizational politics have a role.

The superior-subordinate relationship is the key here. If a strong manager imposes personal views on subordinates and goals for performance are "accepted" by these subordinates—rather than their contributing to the formulation of these goals—the programs will suffer. Obviously the goal setting process on lower levels of management has to be within the guidelines established by senior management. If the firm's top management decides that a sales increase of 10 percent is desired and this in turn requires a production increase of 5 percent, then a first-line supervisor of a production unit can only arrive at goals for his or her area of responsibility that support the overall company goals.

The fact that an MBO program stresses the use of quantitative goals adds to the objectivity of measurements. However, there is a disadvantage to this, since such quantitative measures may encourage forcing data or even falsifying it. In fact excessive recordkeeping becomes red tape and helps destroy the MBO program. There is also a need for fully considering qualitative goals, and this may sometimes be overlooked in the process of arriving at numerical goals, which may be considered less subjective.

Cost reduction

Because productivity is such an important managerial concern, cost reduction is an ever-present consideration. The pressure for cost reduction may come from either customers or competitors. Customer resistance to price increase works in a cycle: After the selling price gets too high, customer demand for the product falls off, the volume of production has to be reduced, so there are fewer units produced over which to distribute the costs, and therefore the cost per unit has to go up. This causes further resistance and continues the undesirable cycle.

The pressure from competitors comes when they are able to improve methods, making possible a reduction in the cost of production and the price.

dard-setting sessions. See also William F. Treuhaft, "Executive Standards of Performance," in Harwood F. Merrill and Elizabeth Marting, eds., *Developing Executive Skills* (New York: American Management Assn., 1958), pp. 56–65.

Some cost reduction practices. An unfortunate type of cost reduction practice is the panic type where top management discovers that it needs to reduce costs and passes the word down the line that cost must be reduced by 10 percent, or 15 percent, or some such figure. Management does not say how this reduction is to be achieved—all it wants is results. The department heads will usually try to cut costs in the easiest way and wherever they can in order to get these results. The difficulty with this technique is that results have to be accomplished very rapidly, costs are likely to be reduced in essential work as well as in nonessential work, morale suffers, and usually when the scare is over, costs creep up again.

Another technique is to put on a cost reduction drive—like a bond drive or a Red Cross drive. Under this technique a different culprit is attacked each month. One month it might be scrap and another month it might be the utility bills—light, heat, power, and phone.

The drive technique is superior to the crash technique but is still doing the job in a piecemeal manner—trying to reduce isolated costs. What is wrong with this approach is that products are not produced by isolated activities but by a combining of activities. For example, there is little saving in reducing direct labor costs if machines are made idle, or in cutting down inventories to the extent that people run out of work.

The supervisor and costs. In each department there are three types of costs: direct labor, direct material, and overhead. Anything that isn't direct labor or direct material is classed as overhead. Some parts of the overhead—such as depreciation, taxes, and insurance—are not under the control of supervisors and they cannot be held responsible for them. But most of the costs are within their area of control—direct labor, direct material, and much of the "burden" of indirect expenses that are allocated to each department. This burden or overhead consists of indirect labor, such as that done by maintenance people, assistants, and inspectors—all the labor that is performed in the department but cannot be attributed directly to the product. Another part of the overhead consists of indirect materials, supplies, and utilities.

Some false economies in cost reduction. The supervisor should beware of those measures that give the appearance of reducing costs but do not actually do so. Here are some of them:

Maintenance costs of machines can be reduced by neglecting minor repairs and upkeep. Scrap can be reduced by reducing the quality requirements—letting everything get by. Output in production can be increased by overloading both the machines and the workers. Tardiness can be reduced by forcing the tardy employee to take the day off and turning it into an absence. The number of reported accidents can be reduced by discouraging people with minor injuries from asking for first aid. Idleness of people can be reduced by giving them more machines to attend, but the machines waiting idle for the people to feed them may cost more per hour than the employees' services.

Sources of potential cost reduction. As emphasized throughout this text, the supervisor's main responsibility is to integrate people, materials, machines, money, and methods in an effective manner; but supervisors aren't doing this if there is idleness and waste in their departments. Therefore supervisory cost reduction should center around reducing the idleness of persons, machines, materials, and money, and doing it by the techniques of methods improvement and performance measurement.

The idleness of personnel—both direct labor and indirect labor—can be reduced by planning and scheduling work in advance. The supervisor should set the example by starting each day promptly and by seeing that the work for employees is set up in advance so that they also can start promptly. Also the supervisor needs to supervise the work by directing and checking its progress. Injuries, tardiness, and absenteeism are forms of idleness and should be kept to a minimum.

Zero Defects. Another approach to cost reduction as well as quality control is known as a Zero Defects Program. Basically it is motivational in nature and is designed to instill pride in the work and craftmanship. It attempts to put quality performance on a personal basis, encouraging employees to prevent errors by doing the job correctly the first time.

ZD, as it is called, is usually launched with considerable propaganda, including many explanatory meetings of all employees and top management. Visual aids are freely used to support the program and are posted on bulletin boards. Voluntary employee pledges of support are sought, and a reward system is used for both group and individual performance.

Because of the publicity and the enthusiasm generated at the start of a ZD program, early gains in quality performance have been accomplished by organizations using this approach. To sustain this effort, however, requires constant publicity and frequent meetings, some of which resemble revival meetings. Unless a company is willing to support the cost of such a program over a prolonged period, its use has doubtful benefit. It may also cloud (1) consideration of more analytical quality control measures and (2) recognition that there are many factors contributing to quality control which are beyond the responsibility of individual employees.

Summary

Because productivity is so important to effective and cost conscious performance, managers and supervisors should be aware of techniques used to measure and improve productivity. Methods improvement is a systematic technique of studying and improving a work situation so that people are able to do better work in less time, with less effort, at less cost, and with greater safety.

When improved methods are devised, human factors must be considered. An oversimplified job may not challenge employees, and arbitrary changes can cause hostility and discipline problems. By considering employee ideas and needs along with productivity goals, effective work improvement can be achieved.

Performance standards are vital to work measurement. Standards are necessary for effective planning and control and to enable objective measurement of worker performance. One of the major difficulties involved is determining what constitutes a fair day's work. Performance standards should be clear, definitive, and fully explained to employees. When using work measurement, standards should be applied uniformly.

Measuring managerial performance is more difficult since definitive standards are hard to develop. MBO is used in some organizations and objectives are determined mutually by a superior and subordinate. Care must be taken not to arrive at performance objectives expediently nor to overemphasize quantitative measures. Strong managers should not try to force goals on subordinates. Methods improvement and performance standards can be effective tools to encourage cost reduction thus enhancing employee productivity.

CASE 8-1

Betty Kent was hired by the Oxford Supply Company just after she received her bachelor's degree in business administration. She had graduated with honors and had very favorably impressed all of the people at Oxford who had interviewed her. From her first day on the job she showed great enthusiasm and clearly demonstrated that she was a quick learner who was not afraid of responsibility. Because of this her boss gave her a variety of assignments which she completed on time and very successfully. It didn't take too long for her reputation as an outstanding performer to become a topic of conversation among other executives in the company. Some of them spoke to Betty's boss about using her on special assignments for them. After speaking to Betty Kent and gaining her approval, he allowed her to take on other assignments since he believed this would be good for her career growth with the company. He worked out a system with Betty so that she would get his permission to do other assignments if they both believed she had the time. Her boss gave his own assignments top priority.

Kent went along this way for several weeks, but she was now under considerable pressure because both she and her boss underestimated the time a couple of the assignments would take. The president of the company had heard about Betty's brilliance, and he too had a special assignment. He went to her directly and she was quite flattered by his compliments on her work. She took on the president's assignment without checking with her boss, feeling that he wouldn't want her to turn the president's request down.

Betty now started to fall behind in her work and her boss asked her what was wrong. She told him about the president's assignment, and he became angry with her for not telling him about it. Betty complained about overwork and the fact that she was given too many things to do and had too many bosses. She asked him what the company had done before they had hired her.

1.   *Was Betty Kent being treated fairly?*
2.   *How could priorities be established more effectively?*
3.   *Should a bright, willing person be utilized this way?*
4.   *What should Betty and her boss do now?*

CASE 8–2

Because of a number of new product introductions and the modification of several existing products, the company has decided to issue a new sales manual to its sales force.

The present manual is pocket-sized, about 5 by 8½ inches, and is bound in book form. To make the new manual more efficient and to allow for more product information on each page, the size is increased to 8½ by 11 inches, and the pages are in a loose-leaf binder so that they can be easily replaced without reprinting the entire manual.

When the new manuals are issued you notice Sam Jeffries, an old-timer on the sales force, carefully cutting the 8½ by 11 pages down to 5 by 8½ inches and pasting them over pages in the old manual. When you ask him why he is doing this, he tells you that the old manual fits in his pocket, and he doesn't want to carry a big loose-leaf binder around.

1.   *What went wrong here?*
2.   *Is it worth the effort to try to convince Jeffries to use the new manual?*
3.   *Should cost factors be the only criteria in methods improvement?*

CASE 8–3

Cindy Martin had been a stenographer for the United Manufacturing Company for two years. Her boss thought highly of her and suggested to the personnel department that she be promoted to the next secretarial opening for a senior executive. Cindy's boss was an easygoing person who was not very demanding and never pressured her with last-minute requests or deadlines. She established her own filing system and planned her own work day.

A secretarial opening occurred when the financial vice president's secretary left the company because her husband found a new position in another city. She left on short notice and was not able to spend any time with Cindy, who was promoted into the opening. Since she was so highly recommended by both personnel and her previous boss, the financial vice president didn't spend any time orienting her either. He assumed that she would easily fit in, since she had been with the company for two years.

When Cindy started her new job, she found a detailed schedule for her workday on her desk each morning. Her new boss was very demanding, giving her many rush assignments and demanding a lot of overtime. He was also very precise and had a carefully developed filing system. Cindy started to fall behind in her work, and the pressure caused her to make errors. The financial vice president complained to his peers about the poor quality of secretarial help but did not say anything to Cindy or the personnel department. He treated her in a businesslike manner, never attempting any friendly gestures.

1. *How can this situation be improved?*
2. *Why might a vice president expect performance from a secretary without explaining his standards?*
3. *Should the personnel department have a role?*
4. *Should there be a standard procedure to handle transferred and promoted employees?*

CASE 8–4

Delta Finance Company wanted to increase productivity in its key-punching operation. There were 300 operators of varying skills and speeds in the operation. Rather than establish individual performance standards, which management felt would be difficult to administer, they decided on group standards.

Ten groups of 30 operators each were created, and each was given a production quota. Work measurement analysts fully realized that some operators in each group were more rapid and accurate than others. They also were aware that some operators, while slow, were very accurate and that others who were rapid made more errors. They also had to contend with the relatively frequent influx of new operators who would slow group production, since the job had high labor turnover.

The ten groups were created with as equitable a mixture of talents as possible, and the incentive system was designed so that when a group reached its quota all members shared the bonus equally. Merit pay increases were continued, to allow for and reward individual performance differences.

After the system had been in use for six months, the company found that the rapid, accurate operators resented sharing the bonus equally with slower employees. They felt that they were carrying the group and deserved greater rewards. This was the case even though the rapid, accurate operators received higher pay on a merit basis.

1. *Can the company make this type of bonus system work?*
2. *How can the resentment of the more efficient operators be overcome?*
3. *How can team spirit be developed?*
4. *Should the company abandon the system and use only merit increases?*

CASE 8–5

Sam Leonard was recruited from outside the company to take over a department employing over 60 employees. Before Sam joined the company, a work measurement and methods improvement program had been initiated for all jobs which in the opinion of the methods people could be measured. Apparently the program got off to a very bad start in this department. The employees looked upon it as a way of reducing the size of the department, and they feared losing their jobs. They resented having to account for all of their actions, including telephone calls and necessary trips to other departments.

Approximately 50 percent of the department's employees were college graduates engaged in analytical and technical work, and these people in particular resented the program. One of the best analysts, who was thought to have considerable future potential, threatened to resign, so he was excused from the program by Sam Leonard's predecessor. Resentment among the other employees increased, and several resigned.

After a year of difficulty in this department, all of the analytical and technical employees were removed from the work measurement program. The department head was transferred, and Sam Leonard was hired to take over a rather demoralized group of employees. While the higher paid employees were no longer on work measurement, the clerical staff was. They still saw no value to work measurement, and Sam found that most of the results turned in by these people were nothing better than inaccurate estimates of what they actually did. Since the company was generally satisfied with the results of its work measurement program, it was definitely going to be continued. Sam had been told by his superior that one of his first jobs as department head would be to bring order to the chaotic work measurement effort in his department.

1. *Discuss the pros and cons of hiring an outsider as department head in this situation.*
2. *What can the new department head do to reestablish the integrity of the work measurement program in his department?*
3. *How can a work measurement program be sold to employees who believe it to be a method of job elimination?*
4. *Should work measurement be applied to jobs which require judgment and are technical and analytical?*
5. *Should the one employee have been excused from the work measurement program?*

CASE 8-6

Cliff Morton, a recent college graduate, was hired by the Capital Casualty Company as a trainee in the safety engineering department. After completing a six-month training program, his function would be to conduct inspections of prospective policyholders' places of business to determine whether or not safety practices and equipment were in use and to make appropriate recommendations to the Capital underwriters about the extent of the risk involved.

Morton progressed through the program effectively and was now in the last stage. He was being introduced to the territory he would take over by an experienced safety engineer who was being transferred to a larger territory. Each engineer worked out of his home, appearing at the office only on Mondays for a departmental discussion meeting. The requests for inspections were mailed to the experienced engineer's home, and rush inspections were telephoned to him.

Each engineer planned his own daily itinerary of inspections, completing the reports at home and mailing them in to the office each day. Cliff Morton found that by carefully planning his daily route in the territory, he could easily make 16 to 18 inspections and complete the reports in a normal work day. During his first week alone in the territory, he averaged 16 inspections a day.

The following Monday, at the departmental discussion meeting the engineer who had introduced him to the territory called him aside and admonished him for turning in so many inspections each day. "You'll ruin it for us; we only turn in 8 or 10 each day. If you want to do 16 or 18 a day, go ahead, but only turn in 8 and then take a day off. No one will know."

Cliff didn't know what to say or do. He was ambitious, but he also knew he had to get along with his fellow employees.

1. *How should Cliff Morton handle this situation?*
2. *Is peer pressure to slow down something that management can control?*
3. *How can such a situation arise?*
4. *Can a new employee be effective if he resists group pressure?*

CASE 8-7

Jack Salerno was the supervisor of a computer tabulating department. He had several years of experience with the equipment and in fact could operate all of it skillfully. Because of his eagerness to demonstrate his abilities to his superiors, he timed himself on all of the jobs under his jurisdiction and arrived at a productivity figure for each job. Though he prepared a memorandum detailing all this information for his superior, he never told any of his subordinates about it.

One day he noticed that a keypunch operator who had been transferred to his department recently produced considerably less work then he could. He reprimanded her, telling her that she wasn't trying, informing her that there had better be rapid improvement, and indicating that his reprimand would be written up and placed in her personnel file.

She became angry and told him that she had never been told how much work was required of her. She further mentioned that she only had six months' experience as a keypunch operator. She then said she was going to complain to Jack's superior about his treatment of her.

1. *What can Jack do to salvage the situation he has created?*
2. *Should he allow the woman to go to his superior with her story?*
3. *What is wrong with Jack's approach to setting work standards?*
4. *How should he establish work standards?*

CASE 8–8

A recent newspaper article described a U.S. Department of Defense "Should Cost" program. The program was described as nothing more than the application of a sound industrial engineering approach to cost estimating. After extensive observance of operations and employee efficiency, the Pentagon computes what a particular piece of defense work should cost. If the figure contradicts original estimates, the Pentagon may then negotiate a reduction in the contract amount.

The aim of the program is to make sure that employees of defense contractors are laboring efficiently; otherwise, contract renegotiation will cost the company money. The Pentagon sends a team of inspectors to the defense contractor, and this is usually augmented by personnel employed by the contractor.

Managements have developed many rules and regulations as a result of this program. Among the types of rules are: keep feet off desks, cut down on smiling, reduce social conversation, no luncheon drinking of alcoholic beverages, demonstrate "observable hustle," go to water fountains and rest rooms at three miles per hour, no lingering at coffee machines, no prolonged absences from the workplace, observe rules even when supervisors are absent (since you are being observed constantly), bring no books or newspapers into the plant.

1. *Comment on the value of such a program in increasing productivity.*
2. *How might employees react to such a program?*
3. *Could such a program work in a company not on a defense contract? Why, or why not?*

CASE 8–9

You are in charge of a department turning out a quality product. You have under you several supervisors and their work groups. Relations have been very cordial between you and all those under you. The workers are conscientious. The work is on an hourly basis; it would be very difficult to put the jobs on piece rates.

Recently, business has been increasing and a backlog of work is piling up. A month ago top management asked you to increase output by 10 percent. You gave the supervisors a pep talk, and they were able to get the desired increase. Last week top management came to you and again asked for another increase of 10 percent in output. You asked for more workers, but you were told that the push is just temporary.

This morning you called your assistants together and told them the situation and asked them if they would get another increase in output of 10 percent. They refused.

1. *What might be some of the reasons for their refusal?*
2. *To what extent are they justified?*
3. *Are supervisors ever justified in holding back production in order to have a cushion or factor of safety for taking care of temporary load increases?*
4. *Should you go directly to the people on the job in order to get the second increase in output? Justify your answer.*
5. *How could the situation have been avoided?*
6. *How should you handle the situation?*
7. *How can you prevent it from recurring?*

CASE 8–10

Mary is a very efficient machine operator with an extraordinary aptitude for the work she is doing. She can make "standard" in half the required time. Most of the operators have to put forth good effort to meet standard. Others have difficulty making it.

Instead of turning out as much work as she is capable of, Mary makes standard, stops her machine, and goes to the restroom for a smoke or wastes her time in some other manner. Her supervisor allows her to do this. He argues that if she did extra work she would not get more pay, because the company does not have piece rates. Management is opposed to wage incentives. Mary is not supervisory material.

1. *Evaluate Mary's point of view.*
2. *Evaluate the supervisor's point of view.*
3. *What are the advantages and disadvantages of having standards without wage incentives?*
4. *What should management do about the situation?*

Chapter 9

Learning objectives

○ *To develop awareness of the development of jobs and job design*

○ *To gain an understanding of various approaches to dealing with individuals and jobs such as rotation, enlargement, and enrichment*

○ *To show the evolvement of job design and its relationship to the effective choice of individuals for the jobs*

○ *To develop an awareness of the importance of matching people and jobs and the relationship of the trial work period, interviewing, compensation, and other factors to the process*

Matching individuals and jobs

Major topics

How jobs develop.

Specialization and simplification.

Job enlargement.

Job rotation.

Job enrichment.

Job design and the quality of work life.

Guides for job design.

Redesigning a job.

First-level supervisor job design.

Obstacles to job design.

Matching people and jobs.

The interview.

The trial work period.

Monotony and boredom.

Compensation.

The job and the individual are basic to all organized activity. The function of organizing is presumed to be the combination of jobs and individuals in such a way as to achieve the objectives of the organization. Over the years managers have sought to make their organizations more efficient by division of labor, work simplification, and specialization. Ease of training, operational economies, and more effective utilization of people and machines have often resulted.

At the same time that these relative efficiencies were being achieved, two tragic circumstances have continually presented themselves. One is the perennial "square peg in a round hole" problem. The other is the seeming lack of meaning which characterizes work when so-called efficiency and increased specialization are the primary goals of job design.

Since the supervisor's success depends to a great extent on how well subordinates do their jobs, it is an advantage that jobs be properly designed and that people be well fitted to them. Therefore, find out what the job demands of the worker and what the worker demands of the job and then try to get the best possible fit.

Sometimes a job is so badly designed that no one fits it satisfactorily. It may have been overspecialized and oversimplified to the extent that a monkey could do it. At the opposite extreme, the job may be a hodgepodge of unrelated activities calling for an assortment of abilities seldom found in job candidates. This chapter gives supervisors information to guide them in designing jobs. It gives examples of what some companies are doing in enlarging rather than deskilling jobs.

To help the supervisor carry out the responsibility of matching people and jobs this chapter offers techniques for interviewing and selecting new employees, watching their progress during the probationary period, and eliminating misfits during that time.

Fitting people and jobs is a continuous managerial activity requiring a considerable expenditure of time, effort, and money. Involved in this activity are such things as recruiting, selection, placement, training, appraisal, development, job design, job analysis, compensation and human resource planning. While many of these activities are carried out by staff specialists, supervisors are directly involved because of the human relations implications and their responsibility for effective employee performance. Any supervisor who has had to contend with a stenographer who couldn't spell, a machine operator who was all thumbs, or a salesperson who couldn't sell can appreciate the need for sound selection and placement. Being responsible for performance in a group of jobs difficult to fill because of unrealistic requirements also brings home to the supervisor the desirability for sound job analysis and design.

How jobs develop

In order to discuss jobs and their design, it is necessary to distinguish between a task, a position, and a job. The following definitions were developed in the Occupational Research Program of the United States Employment Service.

> *Task* is a unit of work or human effort exerted for a specific purpose. For example, setting up a turret lathe is a task. Tending the machine is another task. Cleaning the machine is still a third task. When enough tasks accumulate to justify the employment of a worker—one person—a position has been created.
>
> *Position* indicates the service of one worker who accomplishes a set of duties or several tasks. Thus a turret lathe operator's position may consist of the tasks of setting up the machine, tending and operating it, and cleaning it. Such duties comprise the individual's entire working obligation. There are as many positions in the plant as there are employees.
>
> *Job* is a group of similar positions within a single establishment. Several turret lathe operators all discharging the duties of setting up, tending, and cleaning similar machines, can be said to have the same job. There may be only one turret lathe operator position in a plant or there may be many, which go to make up this job. A new job is created only when job characteristics emerge—as a result of work simplification, technological change, or mere job evolution—which are different from those that are present in any existing job.[1]

While there has been a great amount of study of work processes and the methods of performing the separate elements of work, much less attention has been given to the study of the design of jobs—the combining of work elements into tasks and assembling of these tasks into jobs.

Some jobs just grow, following a traditional pattern. Jobs may be shaped to fit the requirements of the process, to fit into the setup of the organization, or to meet the existing needs of the department. Job duties evolve through changes in the volume of work. As the volume shrinks, more duties are added to jobs. As the volume expands, duties are removed from existing jobs and made into new jobs. Jobs are designed to meet the needs of the moment, the abilities of people, and the availability of skills.

The design of many jobs is the result of taking them apart for analysis in methods improvement or work simplification programs. What was intended to simplify the work and eliminate waste was used instead to simplify the job and break it down to a few simple motions.

Specialization and simplification

The "efficiency" approach to job design assumed that people—like machines—would do their best work if each performed just a few motions. It is assumed further that all planning should be removed from the performer's job and made the responsibility of someone on a higher level. Specialization limited the number of tasks in a job; simplification reduced

---

[1] The terms are discussed more fully in Carroll L. Shartle, *Occupational Information*, 3d ed. (Englewood Cliffs, N.J.: Prentice-Hall, Inc., 1959).

the skill requirements. The simple machine-paced job became the accepted pattern of efficiency, as exemplified in the assembly line.

Specialization is a management principle upon which mass production is based. Specialization of labor enables a worker to become extremely efficient through repetition of a task, but there is a point beyond which specialization loses its economic advantages. The more a job is subdivided, the more indirect labor is needed to plan and schedule, supervise, coordinate, and inspect the work of the performers. The more a job is subdivided, the more people there are handling it and the smaller becomes each person's responsibility for quality.

Simplification of work is important and necessary to improve methods, eliminate wasted effort, increase efficiency, and reduce costs. But both specialization and simplification meet a point of diminishing returns when the job uses none of the performer's human abilities, and frustration shows up in restriction of output, irresponsibility as to quality, resistance to change, absences, grievances, transfers, and quits. These costs are more prevalent in deskilled jobs than in skilled jobs. The person on the deskilled job is expendable, "as easy to replace as a light bulb." An arm or leg might have been hired; the rest of the person had to come along. But the whole person is there and just putting in time. The individual becomes frustrated, tardy, absent; often fooling around and becoming a discipline problem.

A company may cut immediate costs by simplifying a job: A lower grade of labor can be used and a minimum of training can be given. But what is saved in wages and training costs in making the employees unimportant may have to be spent in efforts to counteract the effect this has upon them. After the individuals have become apathetic, unproductive, hostile, wasteful, and destructive, expensive campaigns are carried on to tell them how important they are and how valuable is their contribution. Off-the-job projects of athletics, sociability, and benefits may be inaugurated to improve attitudes toward the company and to substitute for the lack of satisfaction on the job.

Some years ago Peter F. Drucker analyzed traditional ideas about the assembly line and efforts to simplify jobs continually. He believes that an assembly line is not perfect engineering of human work. Rather it is imperfect engineering of machine work. His concept is stated as follows:

> We know today, in other words, that wherever the one-motion one-job concept can be used effectively, we have an operation that can and should be mechanized. In such an operation the assembly-line concept may indeed be the most effective principle for human work, but human work, in such an operation, is itself an imperfection. This is work that should properly be engineered as the work of machines rather than of men.
>
> For all other work—and that means for most of the work done today in manufacturing industry and for all the work that will be created by Automation—the principle is the organization of the job so as to integrate a number of motions or operations into a whole.

We have two principles rather than one. The one for mechanical work is Mechanization. The one for human work is Integration. Both start out with the systematic analysis of the work into its constituent motions. Both lay out the work in a logical sequence of motions. In both attention has to focus on each motion, to make it easier, faster, more effortless; and improvement of the entire output depends on improvement of the constituent motions. But the one organizes the motions *mechanically* so as to utilize the special properties of the machine, that is, its ability to do one thing fast and faultlessly. The other one *integrates* operations so as to utilize the special properties of the human being, that is, his ability to make a whole out of many things, to judge, to plan, and to change.

The technological changes under way not only make possible the realization of the correct principles but force us to apply them. They give us the means to make fully mechanic those jobs in which the human being is used as an adjunct to a machine tool. But the work that is not capable of being mechanized—above all, the work that is needed to make the new technology possible and to support it—can under Automation only be organized on the principle of integration, can, in fact, not be done at all unless so organized. Productivity will therefore increasingly depend on understanding these two principles and applying them systematically.[2]

Is specialization necessary? The commonly expressed opinion that job specialization, highly fractionated division of labor, and the assembly line are inhuman has a counterview. Part of the argument is based on the ideas of Drucker expressed above, calling for a redesign of the workplace to humanize it and have all of the nonchallenging, drudgery work done by machines. More will be said on this later in the chapter.

There is, however, a view that the assembly line and specialization are part of the price we must pay for our high standard of living and our abundant society. Leavitt, Dill, and Eyring comment on this view as follows:

The concept of organizational specialization, like the hierarchy of authority, is a popular target of criticism. It prompts us immediately to think of the Chaplinesque man on the assembly line, robotized, monotonized, dehumanized.

But life is a series of trade-offs. The assembly line *is* a dehumanizing monster. It was when it was invented, it is now, and we ought to be doing our best to get rid of it. It is also an extraordinarily productive monster. So it is unlikely that we will get rid of it entirely at the sacrifice of perhaps the major source of our industrial productivity. We still value productivity. So we try compromises, hoping the higher pay or suggestion systems will make the line a bit more human; or we look forward to the time when we can replace men with real automation, thus solving the problem of dehumanization (and perhaps creating a problem of underemployment).

But if assembly-line specialization is a monster, consider its opposite. Try to build a significant number of cars, or radios, or light bulbs, or toilet seats, or body stockings without *any* specialization of human effort. To

[2] Peter F. Drucker, *The Practice of Management* (New York: Harper & Row, Publishers, 1954), pp. 292–93.

discard specialization because it is dehumanizing is like giving up salt because it makes us thirsty. Rather than asking, "Are we for specialization or against it?" we might better ask, "Under what conditions is specialization desirable? At what cost? And in what forms?"[3]

Answering those questions is more complex than a surface glance would indicate. Dehumanizing the assembly line assumes that such work can easily be done by machines. Considerable progress has been made in this direction, but most assembly lines still require people. The assembly line is given much publicity as the cause of all sorts of human woe, yet a very small percentage of the total work force is involved in assembly line work. Further, the assumption that all people who work on factory assembly lines dislike that work may not be valid. There are some people who prefer repetitive work for a variety of reasons, not the least of which is lack of opportunities at similar or better pay and fringe benefit levels.

The answer to the question, "At what cost?" may lie in the reward structure. There are some who believe that various types of incentive pay systems may be part of the answer. This won't make the work any different, but the monetary reward to the employee may increase his sense of humanness and worth. A story about incentive pay for steel mill workers that appeared in *The Wall Street Journal* seems to support this idea. No one can question the difficulty and heat of the working conditions in a steel mill, yet this company in South Carolina has a backlog of applicants for the small number of jobs that open up each year. One example of the incentive pay in this company is described, along with many others, in the article:

> The production quota in the melting and casting operation is 10 tons of billets an hour. Each ton over that brings a 4 percent bonus for crew members. So far this year, actual output has exceeded 20 tons an hour on every work turn, and so every worker in the operation has collected bonus pay for at least 40 percent every week. One crew recently turned out 31 tons an hour in a day. Had they kept up that pace for a week, it would have got them an 84 percent bonus.[4]

It must also be appreciated that specialization is a characteristic of a highly developed civilization. Few of us would know what to do if we had to provide individually for all of our needs. Baking bread may seem romantic and worthwhile for the young homemaker trying to impress the family, but the homemaker didn't grow the wheat, grind it, mill the flour, make the oven, or the baking tin. These things were all done by various specialists, some in assembly line jobs.

Maybe the Renaissance person, expert in many things and with wide

---

[3] Harold Leavitt, William Dill, and Henry Eyring, *The Organizational World* (New York: Harcourt, Brace, Jovanovich, Inc., 1973), p. 45.

[4] "Steelmaker Raises Output and Productivity with Incentives That Make Everybody Hustle," *The Wall Street Journal*, August 9, 1973, p. 26.

interests, is to be admired—but there are very few of them around. Most people are specialits of one kind or another: accountants, some of whom specialize even further on tax matters; lawyers, some of whom specialize in criminal law; carpenters, some of whom specialize in cabinetwork; and so on. It is easy to see we have specialists within areas of specialization. Such are the complexities of our society. While some people express a yearning for the simple life, few really want to return to it and its inconveniences.

While much of the criticism of the monotony of repetitive work relates to the level of education in our society and the fact that people in those jobs are not sufficiently challenged, there is another side to this problem. Many areas of this country have poor schools, and some people who attend them come from disadvantaged backgrounds. When these people enter the labor majket, they are ill-equipped for so-called challenging jobs. In fact many of them are not even qualified for simple repetitive clerical or assembly jobs. Because of shortages in some labor markets, companies spend considerable amounts of money to teach these people to read and write properly and then train them for the much-maligned repetitive jobs.

Job enlargement

The fact that repetitive jobs may be dull and monotonous has not escaped managers. Over the years various attempts have been made to try to alleviate the problem. Many of these attempts involved what could be called external measures, that is, they did not focus on the job itself. Keeping in mind the efficiency of specialization, not much was done about changing job characteristics. Rather, the work environment was changed. Such things as piped-in music, pleasant colors on walls, better lighting, and layouts which allowed more conversation became the order of the day. These attempts certainly did no harm and in some instances productivity was increased. This was temporary, however. Once the employees got used to the new surroundings, the effect wore off. The job was still the same.

Attention now turned to the job itself. Pressures of technological change and worker discontent combined to cause managers and social scientists to take a hard look at the time-honored concepts of specialization and efficiency. One of the approaches that grew out of this effort is called job enlargement, which is basically an increase in the variety of tasks done by an employee on a particular job. Schoderbek and Reif describe the purpose of job enlargement in this manner:

> The purpose of job enlargement is to eliminate the undesirable characteristics of the highly repetitive specialized job by enlarging it to include: (1) a greater variety of knowledge and skill, (2) a more complete utilization of the important cognitive and motor abilities possessed by the worker, and

(3) more freedom and responsibility in the performance of the task at hand.[5]

Essentially, job enlargement is taking those tasks that have been made efficient through methods improvement and rearranging them so that there is an increase in the number and variety of tasks in a job, and so that the combination of tasks forms a job that will meet the human needs of the kind of person who will be hired to perform that job. A low-skilled person does not ask as much from the job as a high-skilled individual. Still, if that person is going to be a satisfactory employee giving satisfactory performance, the job must be designed in terms of human dignity.

A report on job design research in 1956 had this to say about trends in job design:

> Very recently a number of organizations have begun to experiment with changing the content of jobs in the direction of specifying job content having greater complexity, containing a longer sequence of tasks, requiring greater skills, permitting rotation between tasks, and having greater responsibility for inspection, for setting up and maintaining equipment, and for controlling production rates. This development, known as job enlargement, has been received with great enthusiasm by the public, and business community.
>
> The results flowing from job enlargement programs that have been undertaken are not those that could have been anticipated when the bases of prediction are the classic methods of job specification through job fractionation. The results reported indicate apparent gains in productivity, quality, morale, job satisfaction, and so on. The gains may be explained— although this has not been done—by a resolution or lessening of conflict existing between the individual's motivational forces and his assigned work. Such a conflict has been observed to exist in many instances. When present, this conflict may have a deleterious effect upon productivity, costs, morale, and social organization.[6]

Job rotation

One way of accomplishing an increase in job satisfaction is to use job rotation. This consists of moving or rotating an employee through several related jobs in a department over a period of time. The jobs stay the same, only the person performing them changes. The principal reason for using job rotation is to attempt to enhance motivation and productivity by exposing an employee to a variety of work and social relationships with different employees. Sometimes this approach allows the sharing of un-

---

[5] Peter P. Schoderbek and William E. Reif, *Job Enlargement: Key to Improved Performance* (Ann Arbor: Bureau of Industrial Relations, University of Michigan, 1969), p. 7.

[6] Louis E. Davis and Ralph R. Canter, "Job Design Research," *Journal of Industrial Engineering*, vol. 7, no. 6 (November–December 1956), p. 275.

pleasant jobs which must be done but would prove boring if one person did it all the time.

A related benefit is the cross training it allows, enabling several employees to become familiar with the variety of jobs encompassed by the department. The obvious simplicity of this approach sometimes causes the neglect of basic job design problems. Rotation is not the answer to poor job design. The productivity gains realized will be short-lived if improperly designed jobs are not redesigned.

Job enrichment

There are some social scientists who believe that job enlargement does not in itself encourage motivation among workers. They believe that doing more than one operation is not necessarily more motivating than doing only one. Their suggestion is that the job be enriched by deliberate upgrading of responsibility. Job enrichment seeks to improve both task efficiency and human satisfaction by means of building into people's jobs, quite specifically, greater scope for personal achievement and its recognition, more challenging and responsible work, and more opportunity for individual advancement and growth. It is concerned only incidentally with matters such as pay and working conditions, organizational structure, communications, and training, important and necessary though these may be in their own right.[7] Five studies were carried out in various British companies using job enrichment as a frame of reference. The studies demonstrated that when tasks are organized to be as authentic and motivational as possible management receives a more accurate and a continuing feedback on individual strengths and weaknesses, ability, and potential. Task support becomes a flexible instrument of management, responsive to feedback.[8]

The AT&T Studies.   Perhaps the most comprehensive and widely publicized program of job enrichment has been going on in the American Telephone and Telegraph Company. The company became concerned with high labor turnover and the related excessive training expense and increased recruitment and selection costs. Starting in the company's treasury department in 1965, the program went on there and in many other parts of the Bell System. The extent of the program up to 1969 is described in Table 9–1. The savings over an 18-month period in the treasury department are described in Table 9–2. Success has not been universal. The experience in this company has ranged from no improvement through modest improvement to the most successful program (in the treasury department).[9]

---

[7] William J. Paul Jr., Keith B. Robertson and Frederick Herzberg, "Job Enrichment Pays Off," *Harvard Business Review,* vol. 47, no. 2, (March–April 1969), p. 61.

[8] *Ibid.,* p. 78.

[9] For a complete description, see Robert N. Ford, *Motivation through the Work Itself* (New York: American Management Assn., 1969).

Table 9–1
AT&T job enrichment program

Department	Jobs (9)	Location (19 trials in 10 companies)	Size of group at start of trial
Treasury	Shareholder correspondent	New York City	28
Commercial	Service representative	Bell of Canada:	
		Toronto	50
		Montreal	75
		Illinois Bell:	
		Chicago	40
		Suburban Office 1	25
		Suburban Office 2	25
		New England:	
		Northern Massachusetts	70
		Rhode Island	60
		Chesapeake & Potomac,	
		Maryland	65
Traffic	Toll operator	Michigan Bell, Saginaw	250
		AT&T Long Lines Dept.,	
		New York City	350
Plant	Installer	Pacific T&T (large urban)	45
		Illinois Bell, Chicago	30
	Frame cross-connection	AT&T Long Lines Dept., New York City	40
Comptrollers	Service order reentry clerk	Pacific T&T, Los Angeles	30
	Service order transcription clerk		
		Southern Bell, Atlanta	20
	Keypuncher	Northwestern Bell, Minnesota	
Engineering	Equipment engineer	Michigan Bell, Detroit	30
Traffic	Toll and information	Chesapeake & Potomac	*

* More than 2,000, but this trial differs in that it was open to any supervisor in the state. Therefore, no formal control is available. Judgments will be based on past performance of this group.
Source: Robert N. Ford, *Motivation through the Work Itself* (New York: American Management Assn., 1969), pp. 48–49.

As in the case with most concepts, there is disagreement with job enlargement or job enrichment as a motivator of more effective individual performance. The engineering modifications required for job enlargement may make the cost prohibitive and changes in the workplace may be impossible to achieve because of building design. In most instances it is assumed that all employees want to have enlarged jobs because their present specialized tasks are boring and not meaningful. This assumption may not be true in all instances, and it certainly does not take individual differences into consideration. Another assumption that seems to charac-

Table 9–2
Possible savings, first 18 months AT&T treasury department—stock and bond division

27% drop in turnover, nonsupervisory specialists	$245,000
Investigation and file clerks—salaries, annual	135,000
Force reduced from 46 to 24 clerks	
Three management jobs eliminated	
Correspondents' group—salaries	76,000
Five management, four verifier jobs eliminated	
Stock transfer group, salaries eliminated	40,000
Merger of employee stock-pension unit and dividends reconciliation	
unit, salaries eliminated	100,000
Improved productivity (not priced)	?
Improved service indexes (not priced)	?
Improved tone of exit interviews (not priced)	?
Personnel selection, job rearrangements (not priced)	?
Offset—half salary, six employees who work on this part-time	(38,000)
Total	$558,000

Source: Robert N. Ford, *Motivation through the Work Itself* (New York: American Management Assn., 1969), p. 44.

terize much of the discussion about job enlargement and job enrichment is that employees place a great amount of value on the work they perform, and they are generally dissatisfied with their jobs. Two researchers found that workers in an automobile plant working on assembly line operations did not demonstrate significantly different levels of job satisfaction than utility workers or supervisors in the same plant. In other words, the employees who had more routine assignments and less freedom of movement did not demonstrate any more unfavorable or favorable job attitudes than those who did.[10] Perhaps because of the ever-decreasing workweek and the concurrent increase in leisure time, work has less importance in many employees' minds, and they gain satisfaction from a variety of alternative forms of fulfilling behavior such as hobbies, community or church work, and travel.

In any event, the dominating factor in both concepts probably evolves from our rapidly changing technology. Whenever new methods, processes, equipment, and procedures are developed, the worker-machine relationship changes. This requires an analysis of the present job in light of the new factors, and in many instances the job has to be redesigned. When this takes place, job enlargement and job enrichment should be considered, since this is an ideal time to develop job changes which may benefit both the company and the employee. Of course there is always the possibility that present employees may not be able to handle a changed job, even with additional training; and there are usually several who refuse to try. In a tight labor market with many alternative job opportunities avail-

---

[10] J. E. Kennedy and H. E. O'Neill, "Job Content and Workers' Opinion," *Journal of Applied Psychology*, vol. 42 (1958), pp. 372–75.

able, there are employees who resent any manipulation of their jobs and would rather quit than take on additional tasks.

The employee participation implied in job enlargement and job enrichment means that each individual performing the job has a role in the determination of the changed job. Because individual differences cannot wholly be taken into consideration, the resulting job will inevitably be a compromise supposedly accepted by the group. It certainly is possible that there will be group members who are as dissatisfied with the new job, as there were other group members dissatisfied with the old one. Consequently, these concepts are not the only answer to better employee performance. Perhaps more scientific selection procedures, more effective placement, better job design along with proper training, and a greater amount of employee counseling should be adjuncts to any job enlargement or job enrichment program.

Job design and the quality of work life

Recently much management literature has given attention to something called the "quality of work life." This is supposed to describe the nature of the environment and human value systems that exist in an organization. The importance of increasing productivity has been discussed earlier. This discussion centered on methods improvement and work performance measurement. The concern with quality of work life adds a dimension to productivity improvement and job design. Including this aspect in job design often presents management with a dilemma. In the first place methods improvement may increase productivity in the short run, but attempts to change the nature of the workplace may not be able to be accomplished without considerable expense of time and money. So, such effort may not even be attempted. If it is, then the definition of what might improve the quality of work life can be difficult to measure. In fact there are no definitive criteria to use that would be acceptable to all employees.

Nevertheless, many attempts have been made to arrive at some group of standards that could help solve the definition problem. One of these establishes eight criteria which Richard Walton calls major conceptual categories.

1. Adequate and fair compensation.
2. Safe and healthy working conditions.
3. Immediate opportunity to use and develop human capacities.
4. Future opportunity for continued growth and security.
5. Social integration in the work organization.
6. Constitutionalism in the work organization.
7. Work and the total life space.
8. The social relevance of work life.[11]

---

[11] W. W. Suojanen, M. J. McDonald, G. L. Swallow, and W. William Suojanen, eds., *Perspectives on Job Enrichment and Productivity* (Atlanta: School of Business Administration, Georgia State University, 1975), pp. 18–23.

As can be seen, concepts by their very nature are quite broad and subject to considerable interpretation. As a result, practical application of such criteria is difficult even for an organization that might wholeheartedly support the concepts. Even the most forward-looking managers are faced with the reality of achieving established goals, and, of course, many employees are not as concerned with the issues conceptualized above as some behavioral scientists believe.

Since jobs are central to work life, most organizations focus their efforts on attempts to design jobs that can meet the needs of work performance and hopefully encompass various aspects of work life quality improvement. Job design factors are graphically illustrated in Figure 9–1. Analyzing those factors will demonstrate that at least some of the work life concepts are considered in the ultimate job structure. Additionally, good job design attempts to recognize that job importance, skill variety, a certain amount of autonomy, and frequent performance feedback are designed into the job. This will give jobs more meaning and hopefully increase the employee's sense of responsibility along with desired productivity improvement.

Guides for job design

Actually, there has not been enough study of job design to produce principles or systematic methods for determining what should go into a job in order for it to meet the needs of the process, the organization, and the employee and still fulfill its purpose at the lowest total cost.

There are social science studies of what people want from jobs; there are

Figure 9–1
Factors in job design

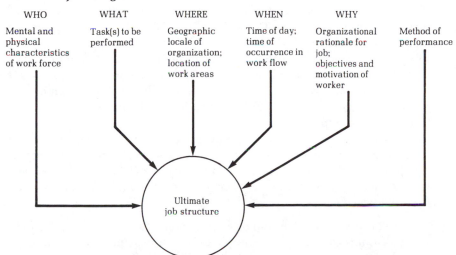

WHO	WHAT	WHERE	WHEN	WHY	
Mental and physical characteristics of work force	Task(s) to be performed	Geographic locale of organization; location of work areas	Time of day; time of occurrence in work flow	Organizational rationale for job; objectives and motivation of worker	Method of performance

Ultimate job structure

Source: Richard B. Chase and Nicholas J. Aquilano, *Production and Operations Management: A Life-Cycle Approach*, rev. ed. (Homewood, Ill.: Richard D. Irwin, 1977), p. 457. © 1977 by Richard D. Irwin, Inc.

engineering studies of what the company wants from jobs; there are industrial psychology and human engineering studies of the capabilities of people in the worker-machine system. And there are a number of studies describing changes in job design and the results achieved. From those sources are drawn the following guides:

1. Each job should have a known purpose and be meaningful to the performer. If possible, a job should consist of a series of tasks that bring to completion some recognizable portion of a product or process.
2. Each job should have skills of about the same level. If the skills are of a variety of levels, the worker capable of performing the high-skill tasks may be bored if there are many low-skill tasks. If the skills are on the same level, the performer is using his or her highest talents (the ones for which the company is paying) the greater part of the time.
3. The job should be made up of related or similar skills so that the performer can become proficient in all of them. For example, the job should not demand both clerical and mechanical skills.
4. The skills that are used in the job should be available in the existing labor market.
5. The job should engender a feeling of individual responsibility. The person should have some control over what is done—some freedom to make choices. Even on rather simple jobs, most people will put more care and effort into something for which they feel responsible. When authority and responsibility are pushed down to them, people become more involved in their jobs and more concerned about the quality of their work.
6. Each job should be a member of a family of jobs; that is, the jobs should be graded according to the various related skills, so that the person at the bottom of the pile can see opportunities for advancement to jobs of increasing difficulty—from Class C to Class B to Class A assembler or machine operator.
7. Jobs should be set up so that the performers can identify themselves with the work group as well as with the job and the process. Jobs should fit into the social organization so that people will help rather than hinder one another—so that high performance is an advantage rather than a threat to the group.
8. The job should be measurable in some way so that the performer can show accomplishment in terms of the quality and quantity of output. The job should offer a challenge to the person performing it. The performer should, if possible, be free to vary the pace rather than be machine-paced.

Figure 9–2 is the job description of a clerk in an office of the Standard Oil Company of California. It is an example of a well-designed clerical job.

Middle manager's position description.   Figure 9–3 is a middle management position description in the marketing department of a large commercial bank, the Manufacturers Hanover Trust Company. This position combines technical expertise with managerial responsibilities, and it has several first-level supervisors reporting to the position's incumbent.

Redesigning a job

In most companies supervisors have a hand in the designing of jobs. They also make or collaborate in methods improvements that result in changing

Figure 9–2
Job description of a counter clerk in a district office

```
                    J O B   D E S C R I P T I O N

         COMMITTEE APPROVAL
                              POSITION      COUNTER CLERK
  CHAIRMAN
                              NAME
  PLACEMENT
                              DEPARTMENT    DISTRICT OFFICE    LOCATION
  DATE
                              DIVISION
```

1. **NATURE AND EXTENT OF ASSIGNMENT:** Describe the position accurately and concisely under the following separate sub-headings: A. **Basic Function:** state in general terms the functions performed and the objectives. B. **Scope:** supply figures indicating the size or area of the assignment; omit if size is obvious. C. **Functions Performed:** describe the specific functions performed, indicating the percent of time.

JOB SUMMARY: Receives customer remittances and requests for service or adjustment over the counter and through the mail; follows up delinquent
open and closed accounts for collection; prepares journal memos to transfer accounts; maintains Credit History Card file; assists with routine
clerical work of office as time permits.

WORK PERFORMED:

1. Receives customer remittances over the counter in payment for service and   35%
   merchandise. Looks up bills in accounts receivable ledgers or the merchandise register as required. Gives customer a receipt and keeps stub.
   Balances money received each day against stubs, searching for errors as
   required. Completes collector's deposit tag and gives with money to
   controls clerk.

2. Receives customer requests for service or adjustment over the counter.   20%
   Completes Application for Service, Customer Service Order and Routine
   Operations Order form, as required, and files for dispatch to a Service-
   man or Salesman. Completes credit reference forms as required, and
   mails.

3. Opens mail addressed to office. Gives other than remittances or requests   15%
   for service or adjustment to Head Clerk. Balances checks received
   against stubs. When stubs are not enclosed, looks up amount of bills in
   accounts receivable ledgers or the merchandise register. Refers discrep-
   ancies back to customer. Balances amount received, completes forms, and
   routes checks as outlined in Duty 1 above. Completes forms for requests
   for service or adjustment as outlined in Duty 2 above.

4. Follows up closed accounts for collection: 10%
   a. Files customer index cards for closed accounts per follow-up
      schedule, as received;
   b. Checks accounts receivable ledgers after follow-up dates for notices of
      payment of bill; if not paid, mails form collection letter; forwards
      unpaid bills to other districts and other utility companies for
      collection as required;
   c. If not paid by collection letter series, lists delinquent accounts
      and routes to General Accounting Office;
   d. If account not paid after follow-up by General Accounting Office,
      lists accounts for collection agency and forwards to General Ac-
      counting Office for approval; forwards approved list to agency;
   e. Destroys customer index card when paid.

5. Mails "Notice of Unpaid Bill" and "Final" notices on delinquent service   3%
   accounts, and notices on delinquent merchandise accounts per established
   follow-up schedule, first checking accounts receivable ledgers or merchandise register to see if bill has been paid. Monthly prepares a
   listing of notices mailed.

Figure 9–2 (continued)

JOB DESCRIPTION

COUNTER CLERK (Cont'd)

6. Maintains (suspense) ledger for delinquent closed accounts: 4%
    a. Sets up ledger sheets from data on closing bills and journal memos;
    b. Posts data on follow-up as outlined in Duty 4;
    c. Removes sheet from ledger as account is paid and gives to File Clerk
        and Typist for filing;
    d. If account not paid in prescribed time, prepares journal memo for
        bad debt write-off and transfers ledger stub for account to bad
        debt ledger;
    e. Periodically balances ledger per procedure.
7. Prepares journal memos to transfer accounts to closed account ledger or   3%
    to another route as required, from data on customer index cards and
    closing bills received. Routes memos for posting.
8. Maintains Credit History Card file. Sets up card for each account and   3%
    posts credit rating and changes in credit rating as notified. Recom-
    mends changes in credit ratings to Head Clerk as collections indicate
    ratings should be changed.
9. Completes form if customer requests change of mailing address or for   2%
    error in name and address, and corrects meter book sheet for account.
10. Assists with routine clerical work of office as time permits. For   5%
    example: stuffs bills in envelopes preparatory to mailing, sorts remit-
    tance stubs.

Figure 9-2 (concluded)

COUNTER CLERK (Cont'd)   **JOB DESCRIPTION**

2. SPECIAL REQUIREMENTS: Specify the following under separate subheadings, where pertinent: **A. Education.** **B. Training Required:** Indicate the experience necessary to adequately perform the assignment and the name of the next lower position in which experience is required. **C. Knowledges:** list those necessary to do the assignment. **D. Other Abilities:** specify the other characteristics required for the performance of the position.

A. EDUCATION: High school graduate.

B. LEARNING PERIOD: At least six months experience in a district office. Three months' normal training time after assignment to job.

C. KNOWLEDGES: Thorough knowledge of procedures pertaining to job as outlined in District Office Manual. Type: 45 w.p.m.

D. OTHER ABILITIES: Tact in dealing with customers; neat and pleasant appearance; completeness and accuracy when taking a customer request; appraise requests; ability to follow through on multiple step procedures.

3. SUPERVISION AND FUNCTIONAL ASSISTANCE RECEIVED: List the following under separate subheadings: **A. Immediate Supervisor:** enter the position title only of the immediate supervisor to whom the employee is responsible. **B. Supervision Received:** describe the frequency and detail with which assignments are given, assistance and guidance provided, and the extent that the work of this position is reviewed, checked, and evaluated. **C. Functional Assistance:** describe the kind of functional or technical assistance available to this position, its accessibility, and its purpose.

A. IMMEDIATE SUPERVISOR: Head Clerk.

B. SUPERVISION RECEIVED: Under intermittent supervision. Work is performed according to prescribed procedures and the incumbent is expected to perform all routine in accordance therewith without reference to Head Clerk. The Head Clerk is available to answer questions on problems or work of an unusual nature.

C. FUNCTIONAL ASSISTANCE: None.

4. RESPONSIBILITY AND AUTHORITY: Describe the responsibility definitely fixed in this position under the following subheadings, and specify the authority and effect of decisions and recommendations made, i.e. the latitude delegated for making independent decisions for each: **A. Men,** including number and titles of employees supervised. **B. Materials or Products.** **C. Operations or Functions.** **D. Equipment.** **E. Money.** **F. Business Relations.** Also specify the lack of responsibility or authority when none exists under any of these categories.

A. PERSONNEL: None.

B. MATERIALS OR PRODUCTS: None.

C. OPERATIONS OR FUNCTIONS: Receives customer remittances or requests for service or adjustment over the counter or through the mail; follows up delinquent open and closed accounts for collection and prepares delinquent reports.

D. EQUIPMENT: None.

E. MONEY: Accounts for money received.

F. BUSINESS RELATIONS: Daily personal and telephone contact with district personnel and the public.

5. WORKING CONDITIONS: General Office.

COMPILED BY_____ APPROVED BY_____ DATE_____

Source: Used with permission of Standard Oil Company of California; from Joseph W. Lucas (with assistance of other members of the Department on Organization), *More Profit—Less Paper*, 1953.

Figure 9-3
Middle manager position description

MANUFACTURERS HANOVER TRUST		OFFICIAL STAFF POSITION DESCRIPTION

NAME	LAST	FIRST	MIDDLE		TITLE Director of Research & Planning
DIVISION Research & Planning	BRANCH OR DEPARTMENT Marketing - #513	SUPERVISING OFFICER Director of Marketing			TITLE V.P.

SCOPE OF POSITION
AND
NATURE OF WORK PERFORMED

FUNCTION

The incumbent is officer-in-charge of the Research & Planning unit, consisting of Research and Development and Marketing Administration units. This is a central staff department commissioned to serve senior management and all divisions and affiliates of the bank in developing and analyzing marketing plans, performing strategic and tactical market research, providing technical and administrative support services, plus originating ideas for and coordinating all product development activities. Incumbent reports directly to the Director of Marketing and works actively with senior, line affiliate, and staff managements.

SCOPE

1. Directs all marketing research studies for the bank and its affiliates, which requires mastery of professional disciplines and broad business experience. Determines what research projects are necessary to support and evaluate every phase of the organization's overall marketing effort (e.g., describe competitive market shares; profile customer and prospect characteristics and service usage; measure advertising effectiveness; analyze area dollar potential and MHT's penetration thereof, etc.).

2. Assists line division and affiliate managements to develop marketing plans. (For example, how should the institution utilize its three resources... people, plant, and funds... to best achieve market penetration). Directs staff professionals toward implementing this major component of the bank's corporate planning process in partnership with those managers responsible for carrying out such plans; also provides analysis of marketing plans submitted to senior management, relating the analysis to the bank's general policies and overall goals.

3. Coordinates the bank's product development activities, originating ideas from research studies and/or the planning process, then participating with Operations, Controllers, other staff units and line/affiliate managers involved to design and test new products or revaluate existing products and services.

4. Conducts long-range (strategic) market forecasting and planning studies, analyzing subjects such as electronic funds transfer systems (EFTS), nationwide branching, demographic and socioeconomic trends, etc., on own initiative and/or as requested by senior management... participating when necessary with Corporate Planning, Economics, or outside consultants in order to predict oncoming developments for the markets in which the bank now operates or may wish to operate in the future.

Figure 9–3 (continued)

ACCOUNTABILITY FOR

ORGANIZATION, POLICY, PLANNING, EXECUTION AND REVIEW

SCOPE (cont.)

5. Effectively manages the Research & Planning Department, accountable for some 30-35 personnel and combined administrative/marketing (project) budgets exceeding $1 million annually. Provides a high level of technical and administrative support that impacts practically all marketing activities of the organization. At all times, the incumbent must be keenly aware of the goals of the institution and balance the requests of "user" departments against these management policies.

PREPARED BY	REVIEWED BY	APPROVED BY	DATE
ERW	GR	RWK	9/77

the design of jobs. They work with job analysts when they are analyzing and classifying jobs into pay groups (job evaluation) for wage and salary administration. Supervisors will find that collaboration with staff groups and with their own subordinates is almost essential in changing the design of jobs, because the design must meet requirements in four areas:

1. It must fit the technical requirements of the process.
2. It must fit into the organization and be compatible with other jobs and with the informal organization of the work group.
3. The job must fit the people who are available to perform it. It must be realistic in its demands on a person's skills, energy, intelligence, responsibility, and judgment. The job should in turn provide opportunities that will encourage its performers to give their best efforts.
4. The job must accomplish its objectives at the lowest total cost. Besides direct and indirect labor, the other costs to be considered are work spoilage, poor quality, accidents, absences, turnover, grievances, work stoppages, and resistance to change.

How to analyze a job. The first step toward changing the design of a job is to list all the tasks it contains. If the workers are performing according to a job descriptin, it will list the total tasks. However, it won't tell what proportion of the workers' time is spent on each task. It won't tell how the tasks are apportioned among the people on the job—whether each person performs all the tasks, whether people rotate from one set of tasks to another, or whether tasks are assigned to people on the job according to skills required and possessed. For instance, the newcomer may be performing only the simplest tasks on the job.

One way to collect information about what people are doing it to use the supervisor's log sheet from Chapter 7 (Figure 7–2). The log can be filled out by each employee to show how their time is spent. They should keep track of their daily activities for the length of time it takes to get a representative cycle or else estimate the time spent on tasks that occur only occasionally.

Job analysis formula. Once the information is gathered, the supervisor must analyze it. He or she may have the help of the job analyst and may have access to information that was collected and used for job evaluation. The purpose of analyzing the job is to find out exactly what each person on the job is doing, what skills are needed to perform each task, and what responsibilities each has. The job analysis formula[12] calls for a listing of:

What the worker does (the physical and mental activities).
How it is done (the machinery, tools, formulas used and the decisions the person must make).
Why the person does it (the purpose of each task and how it relates to other tasks in this or other jobs).

---

[12] The job analysis formula and a comprehensive approach to job analysis can be found in U.S. Department of Labor, Manpower Administration, *Handbook for Analyzing Jobs* (Washington, D.C.: U.S. Government Printing Office, 1972).

The skills, responsibilities, and requirements involved include:

Responsibility for machinery, tools, equipment, product, materials, and for the work of others; honesty, initiative.

Job knowledge: amount of schooling, training, and experience needed for proficiency on the job.

Mental application: amount, degree, and frequency of mental and visual effort called for; amount of attention required (whether it is full or intermittent); judgments, decisions.

Dexterity and accuracy: precision, steady nerves, accuracy of measurement or calculation, coordination, reaction time, versatility.

It is necessary to identify the type of skill and level of skill required for the performance of each task, because the tasks assigned to a job should call for related skills and skills of about the same level. The employees who match the job will then be using their highest skills most of the time. Careful examination of all jobs in a sequence or a family should be undertaken particularly if a job is being enlarged and tasks are to be taken from one job and added to another. All of the affected jobs must be examined for the purpose of rearranging and interchanging tasks.

First-level supervisor job design

The study of the first-level supervisor's job mentioned in Chapter 7 indicated that the design of this job in some organizations needs consideration. Much is made of the importance of this job in the managerial hierarchy, but in several instances the job entails little real management responsibility.

This study pointed out that the first-level supervisor spent over 75 percent of the time in work performance. Unfortunately this is all too true of many first-line supervisory jobs. The concepts of job enrichment and job enlargement should be applied to this job as well. Interestingly, first-level supervisors often feel threatened by the idea of job enrichment being implemented for the jobs they supervise. This is usually because an enriched job for a worker means that the worker will be performing some of the planning and control functions normally done by the supervisor.

Enriching the supervisor's job usually means enlarging the span of control and requiring little or no work performance. In other words, the job design should require emphasis on managerial duties. This has become easier to accomplish in many companies, since today's first-level supervisor is frequently being recruited from the college campus rather than from among rank-and-file technicians.

In addition, this management job is becoming more complex in such areas as (1) human relations, with the introduction of more minorities into the work force; (2) data interpretation and computer use; and (3) policy implementation. If an organization is to get full value from the first-level supervisor, the job should be designed as a management job and not that of a lead worker.

The distinction between the performance of technical work of any kind and the responsibilities of first-level management must be recognized. All too frequently higher level management assumes that understanding and practice of supervisory skills is a natural outgrowth of the promotion process which moves a worker to the first level of supervision. This simply is not the case, and the first-level supervisor's job must be designed to recognize that if the incumbent is to be able to manage effectively the job design must allow for it to happen. An organization cannot expect to continue to get the same amount of work performance out of a person and then expect that person to supervise effectively as well.

Obstacles to job design

The discussion of job design has indicated that it has worked in many instances. Techniques are available which have been used in a variety of organizations. Of course, they have met with varying degrees of success; but it seems that they are worth trying where problems of high labor turnover and employee discontent are in evidence.

One might ask, "Why don't more companies attempt to redesign jobs to improve working conditions?" In a recently released report to the Secretary of Health, Education, and Welfare, the following comments attempt to answer that question:

> The reluctance of employers to move swiftly appears to stem from the following:
>
> 1. There is no end to personnel theories, administrative panaceas for revitalizing work organizations, and consultants claiming arcane knowledge of alchemical transformations. Single remedies (e.g., "job enrichment," "job rotation," "management by objectives") abound for the ills of work. Such efforts have failed because there is no single source of job dissatisfaction. In brief, the bad experiences of employers in the past have led them to ask: Whom can I trust?
>
> 2. Some employers, trusting or not, simply do not know how to proceed. They don't know how to redesign work themselves; they don't know to whom they can turn; they may not even know where to begin to look for assistance.
>
> 3. For some employers, the experimental information gained to date is in firms different from theirs, and they would prefer to have directly applicable information before making a move.
>
> 4. Some employers may be willing to make changes but lack risk capital for transitional costs. In the short run, these may not be trivial.
>
> 5. In some industries there is opposition from trade unions to the notion of job redesign.[13]

Obviously job design is not a single answer to all productivity improve-

---

[13] *Work in America,* report of a special task force to the Secretary of Health, Education, and Welfare (Cambridge, Mass.: M.I.T. Press, 1973), pp. 111–12.

ment problems. Like any other management technique, it must be used, not as a cure-all, but one of the methods available to help improve organizational effectiveness. Problems in the workplace should be analyzed systematically to determine if job design is really the heart of the problem. Other factors such as physical environment, quality of training, competence of supervision, effectiveness of planning, and policy implementation may all contribute to the possibility of less effective performance.

Matching people and jobs

Even though the job is well designed, it will not be performed effectively by an employee who is a square peg in a round hole. People differ not only in intelligence, capacity, and skill but also in temperament, ambition, outlook on life, and ability to adjust to the technical and human demands of a particular work situation. The supervisor is in daily contact with the job factors crucial to worker success or failure and knows better than anyone else what the jobs require of performers. Because of this the supervisor should develop skill in judging whether applicants have what it takes to meet these requirements.

Usually applicants are recruited and screened by the personnel department and sent to the supervisor for approval before they are hired. If the personnel department is to do a good job of selection, supervisors must furnish detailed and accurate information about the kind of people needed. They must appraise the applicants sent to them, evaluate new employees during the trial work period, and continue adjusting people to jobs all through their employment.

Supervisors have to live with the mistakes that are made in selection. Misplaced workers require more training, make more mistakes, and have more accidents. They have trouble keeping up quality and quantity of output and may become discouraged and sick at heart. They may become physically ill from having to face a job that can't be performed properly or dealing with people with whom they can't get along. They may stick it out or avoid the unpleasantness by being absent and finally by quitting if they can find another job.

Estimates of the cost of turnover on simple clerical jobs are as high as $2,500; estimates on higher level jobs range up to $10,000. Costs include induction and training of the new employees, their errors, spoilage, and breakage, their low production during learning, and the lowered production of other employees whose work is affected. The company also has to pay the expenses of recruiting, interviewing, putting people on the payroll and taking them off again. Poor selection is costly whether the misfit quits or stays.

Misplaced workers who stay on the job are faced with frustration and failure. The job may take too much out of them because they lack the native ability for it and have to put forth too much effort just to keep up. Or the job may use so little of their abilities that it holds no interest for them, and they actually despise it. To gain some outlet for emotions and energies, they may become troublemakers.

What the job demands.   The overall picture of what the job demands is expressed in the job specification sheet of the job description. In it will be found what education, experience and technical skills an employee must have. It will tell what physical and mental effort the employee must expend, what difficulties will be encountered, and what responsibilities must be assumed. The supervisor needs to know also what constitutes satisfactory performance—how much must be done and how well it must be done. This information is not usually expressed in the job description but should be in the standards of performance.

The personnel department may administer tests to measure the applicant in abilities required by the job. The supervisor may be able to get a demonstration of the applicant's proficiency by skill tests or work samples.

Employees may meet the requirements listed in the job specifications and still not work out well in the department if they don't fit into the work group. An individual's presence may stir up resentment in others, and they may refuse to cooperate with this person or help in any way. The supervisor should study the group's social structure and the characteristics of the people it accepts and likes. Group compatibility is desirable to maintain if possible.

The supervisor must also consider what opportunities exist for developing on specific jobs in his or her department—whether there are chances for advancement or whether the jobs are blind alleys. What types of people come and go? What types stay? What types give the most trouble? As the supervisor studies the characteristics which spell success or failure in the department, he or she can get a good idea of those extra things that the job demands of the new worker.

What the employee wants from the job.   The question of what people want from their jobs is discussed in Chapter 10. Social scientists have asked a great number of workers what they want from their jobs and which wants are most important to them. The resulting lists are of great value in considering the wants of a group of workers, but the studies don't tell what a particular worker wants from *his or her* job.

Some very few people value money most highly, are self-sufficient, competitive, and not "joiners." Others would sacrifice some of the money in order to enjoy the friendliness of the work group; they want the security and comfort of congenial companionship on the job. Some people go to work because they want adult companionship; they have a great need for social relationships, and they want a job on which they can talk. Many of them seek temporary assignments so they can have the benefits of employment along with the necessities of homemaking. Some people want a job on which they will get a minimum of bossing; they resent close supervision and want to be able to decide a few things for themselves. Others want a close relationship with the boss so that they can go to him or her for answers, reassurance, approval, and encouragement. Some people are content with repetitive work that lets them daydream; other people want interest, variety, challenge, and responsibility in their jobs. Some people are eager for opportunities to get ahead and are willing to make sacrifices for future gain. Others live for the moment, have lower aspirations, or have given up hope.

The particular type of work contacts required by the job may call for a certain type of personality. Is the job one in which the employee must deal with complaints, criticisms, conflicts, uncertainties, and the demands of a number of people at the same time? Is it a job in which the employee must make many demands on others—for instance, for materials, information, assistance, or just to hurry someone up? Would the applicant be able to tolerate the unpleasantness of some of these contacts, or would he or she become flustered, angered, and upset to the point where he or she couldn't do the work, would become sick, or would neglect the parts of the job that gave too much distress? A person who has a great need to be liked, to be popular, and to be approved of may not have a thick enough skin for such a job.

Supervisors know what opportunities exist on the job and whether the job is monotonous or challenging. They know their own attitude toward delegating authority and whether their best workers are the docile, the independent, or the in-between. They now must find out what kind of persons the particular applicants are, what they want from the job, and whether the two sets of wants are compatible. It is seldom possible to find the perfect fit for the job; it is a matter of compromise. The supervisor must decide whether job and person are too far apart or whether the applicant has the flexibility, the variety of experience, and the possibilities of being trained for the job. If the applicant is overqualified, he or she may be dissatisfied in a position lower than the one on which the person was previously successful. One may look upon the job as a temporary expedient or a means of getting a foot in the door. The potential employee may be unhappy with wages and working conditions that are below those to which he or she has become accustomed.

The means for finding out all this information about the applicant are the application blanks, the interview, and the trial work period.

The application blank.   If supervisors receive—and in most cases they do—the applicant's application form from the personnel department, they can get some idea from it of the applicant's educational, social, and work background.

The schooling record shows what the applicant has done in the way of education—but not what can be done or what the person might have done if an opportunity was available. High school graduates may be just as intelligent as college graduates but may have had to leave school to support themselves. Certain scores on psychological tests might be a good indication of intelligence.

Work background will show the companies worked for, the number and types of jobs held, job tenure, and how their wages compared. This information may give a pretty good indication of whether the applicant is on the way up or down and whether the person is a floater.

The interview

In the employment interview the supervisor wants to find out the answers to a number of questions: Can the person do the job? Does the person have the ability, the skill, the knowledge, the work experience, and the education necessary? Will the individual be motivated to do a good job and likely remain on the job? Personality factors also are important to assess. To seek these answers the interview will explore four areas: (1) work experience, (2) education and training, (3) work interests and goals, (4) background and outside interests. The application form provides some of this information; the interview should fill in the rest.

Most applicants in an interview are doing a selling job—putting their best foot forward. Skilled interviewers have difficulty making accurate judgments; so the supervisor must be careful not to be taken in by such things as appearance, enthusiasm, and promises. Applicants may say that they won't mind having to get up before 6 o'clock to drive 40 miles to the job every morning—that they'll get there on time. They may not mind it for several months, but it is too much to expect that such behavior can be maintained.

The interview should give the supervisor as accurate a picture as possible of the person's qualifications, either through discussion or a work sample. Getting the applicant to discuss previous jobs may indicate the amount of his or her skill; it may also throw some light on why the person left previous jobs and what the chances are of sticking to this one.

What did the candidate particularly like or dislike about each of the previous jobs? Of all the types of work that were done, which was liked best? Why? Did the person like work where there was responsibility and was there a preference for a closely supervised position? Did the person become dissatisfied or discouraged easily? How did the applicant do in jobs that required working with different kinds of people? Is the person overcritical in the way he or she comments on unpleasant situations in the previous jobs? Does the person show some strong dislikes that would give trouble in the job under consideration? Boredom and job variety are other factors to consider. Is the person's education and training suitable for the job or is it outside his or her field of preparation? Are there sound reasons for the change? What are the person's long-range goals with respect to the work? What are the person's aims for the next two or three years? Do plans fit the opportunities on the job? Will the job be a stepping-stone toward the applicant's goals?

The supervisor uses the information on the application form as the springboard to get into a discussion of the person's interests, ambitions, plans, and adjustments to past jobs. From the conversation it will be possible to tell whether this applicant is somewhat like the people who are now doing well on the job or whether the person is wholly different from them.

If the applicant is not acceptable, the supervisor should terminate the interview in a friendly manner without building up any false hopes.

If, on the other hand, as the interview progresses, the supervisor feels that the applicant should be hired, this is the time to start telling the person about the job—the qualifications necessary, the quality and quantity of output expected, the working conditions, the compensation, the type of workers with whom he or she will be associated. The applicant should be given a clear picture of the opportunities and drawbacks on the job. It is better to inform the applicant now, because he or she will find out later.

This is the time to establish a good working relationship with a new employee—to show the person that the supervisor is interested and wants the person to be successful on the job and is informing the employee what to expect and what will be expected in performance. If the supervisor oversells the job, the worker will suffer a letdown, perhaps be disgruntled, and certainly lack confidence in the boss who gave misleading information. The supervisor must ask the question: Can this job give this person what he or she is seeking? The supervisor will have to answer the question personally, because the applicant is not in a position to know.

The trial work period

No matter how carefully the supervisor analyzes the application blank and appraises the applicant, there are certain things that one cannot be sure of until one has hired the person and observed the individual on the job. The trial work period may be for one month, three months, or even up to two years.

Since a probationary employee can be terminated for the reason of unsuitability for the job, it is up to the supervisor to determine definitely in the trial period whether the person can handle the job or if it is too difficult; whether the person is a careful worker or has accidents; and whether the job is below the employee's capacity and if the employee will shortly be seeking opportunities for a better job—opportunities which may not exist in the department.

The supervisor also has to study the individual's relations with the group: What influence is the person exerting on the group? To what extent is the newcomer being accepted by the group? Is the group rejecting the person so definitely that he or she is destined to remain an outsider?

The supervisor should study the probationary worker's behavior to determine what the indications are. Is the employee cooperative, dependable, and industrious? Or are there indications of stubbornness, belligerence, or laziness that would become worse as time went on? Are there any indications of drug use or excessive use of alcohol? Do tardiness, absenteeism, and loafing indicate that the newcomer is not adjusted or is becoming dissatisfied with the job or is developing into an undesirable employee? Most voluntary quits take place in the first year of employment, but it isn't always the undesirables who quit.

Monotony and boredom

When a person complains that the job is monotonous, this is strong evidence that the individual is not fitted for the job. A job that seems monotonous to one person may not seem so to another. A young woman who was asked if her job (inspecting the same type of part all day long) was monotonous, said, "If my job looks monotonous to you, you should see my sister's job; she's a bookkeeper."

Monotony is defined as sameness or lack of variety. Boredom is defined as a state of mind involving weariness, fatigue, disinterest, and dislike. Boredom, then, exists in the mind of the worker: A job is boring if the worker finds it boring. Research studies suggest that people who suffer from boredom on the job are the young, the restless, and those who are less satisfied with things in general.

Some people take and stay on jobs that have all the earmarks of being monotonous, but they don't complain of boredom. The social life at work may keep them interested, or they may like the opportunity to daydream. They may find the job preferable to other work. They may not have a high level of aspiration, or the job may actually be somewhat of a challenge to them.

Married women have, in the past, often been apt to look on a job as temporary rather than as a career. This attitude is undergoing rapid change with a higher level of education and the trend for women to spend more of their lives in the work force. Forecasts are that the majority of young women can expect to work at least 25 years in their lives. This prospect is affecting their attitudes toward monotonous jobs.

A factor to be considered in monotony is that a job requires more attention from one person than from another. Anyone learning a job has to give it full attention. People complain about jobs that require them to be alert and watchful but provide nothing to keep them alert or hold their attention. On jobs that require little attention, people may daydream about pleasant things, or brood about unpleasant things, or grumble, or fool around.

If a whole work group considers a job monotonous, there is a need to create some variety in it—enlarge it, rotate the tasks, or change the seating or social arrangements of the group doing the job.

People sometimes accept jobs because they believe them to be opportunities for rapid advancement. These jobs may be below the capabilities of the individuals. When the opportunities don't develop as rapidly as hoped for, they become bored and dissatisfied. These people may even cause difficulties with employees who are satisfied with the job. Relationships with co-workers may also have a bearing on how well an individual is matched to a

"I know I'm overqualified, but I promise to use only half my ability."

Reprinted by permission The Wall Street Journal

Hiring someone who is overqualified may cause difficulty.

job. Pleasant social relations both on and off the job sometimes causes employees to accept and do well at work which may be less than challenging. Another reason why employees prefer certain jobs is the quality of supervision. It is easy to understand that a popular supervisor will have little difficulty with staffing.

In essence supervisors should use the probationary period to find out as much as they can about new employees and their performance. On the plus side, the supervisor can help the newcomer over the rough spots and develop the person into a qualified, effective worker. On the minus side, the supervisor can decide in a relatively short period whether or not the new employee is going to succeed and take appropriate action to either transfer or dismiss the employee.

Compensation

People are generally paid for their contributions to organizational performance. The amount of compensation for a job is one important aspect of the person-job matching process. Even though most supervisors and managers have little to do with establishing wage and salary rates, it is extremely important for them to understand how these rates are developed. In unionized organizations the wage rates are established by collective bargaining and become part of the contract between the company and the union. For nonunion employees including managers and supervisors, pay rates and job grades are determined by a number of factors. Among these are:

1. The difficulty and importance of the job.
2. The amount of education, experience, and training necessary for job performance.
3. Availability of qualified candidates.
4. The nature of the organization and its size.
5. Surveys of other organizations in the same labor market to determine what they are paying for comparable jobs.
6. The quality of employees the organization wants to attract and keep.
7. The financial condition of the organization.
8. The labor intensity of the organization.
9. The reputation the organization has in relation to its compensation practices.
10. The volatility or stability of the industry in which the company operates.
11. The relative amount of job security which work in the organization offers.

The process known as wage and salary administration is rather complicated, and even many high-level managers may have difficulty understanding it thoroughly. In general it is necessary for supervisors and managers to know enough to explain certain critical points to employees. These are some that are of interest to most employees.

1. The pay structure is uniform for all people in the same job.
2. Grades are established to recognize differences in skill, responsibility, job knowledge, and job importance.
3. The salaries paid are competitive with those of other organizations in the same labor market.
4. A range from minimum to maximum for each job is established, and the employee can move through the range based on job performance.
5. Seniority alone is not a factor in salary adjustments.

Companies may have other factors in a compensation program such as a policy on cost of living adjustments, bonuses, profit sharing, vacation pay, sick leave, holiday pay, overtime, jury duty, military service and others. Usually these policies are included in an employee handbook or other published material.

Probably the most difficulty arises for supervisors when some of their employees believe they are not being paid fairly for the work performed. Handling this type of problem may be one of the supervisor's most difficult efforts. This is particularly true if supervisors do not base their salary recommendations on job performance factors but introduce such things as personal likes and dislikes and rewarding old-timers simply because they have been around a long time. By sticking to objective evaluations, supervisors can minimize the problems encountered in the implementation of salary policies.

Summary

The supervisor has the responsibility of fitting people to jobs and jobs to people. Some jobs may be so badly designed that no one could fit them. Oversimplified and overspecialized jobs are inefficient from a technical as well as a human standpoint. A number of companies have recognized that it is easier to make technical changes than to redesign human nature, and they are enlarging and enriching jobs instead of deskilling them.

The design of jobs must meet requirements in four areas: the human, the organizational, the technical, and the economic. The chapter provides a list of guides for designing jobs and guides for job analysis. Job rotation, enlargement, and enrichment are explained along with the impact of compensation on jobs.

In fitting people to jobs, the supervisor must analyze the job and find out what it requires of the performer. The supervisor must appraise job applicants to see if they are suited to the work, to the social setup of the work group, and to the authority structure and opportunities within the organization. By means of the application form and the interview, the supervisor must judge whether an applicant has the possibilities for being successful on the job. The trial work period provides an opportunity to weed out misfits. The supervisor's responsibility for adjusting people to jobs is a continuing one, because conditions change, jobs change, and people change.

CASE 9–1

The chief inspector, Rod Russell, has a problem of choosing between Will White and Bob Black for his assistant. White has been with the company two years. The indications are that he has good leadership ability. He exercises good judgment and has the faculty of keeping his boss (Russell) and the operating people satisfied. He knows just about how much to give and take—an important trait at the present time, because the type of inspection done requires quite a bit of judgment. Because of the nature of the product, the quality standards are not set up too well as yet, nor will they be for the next couple of years.

Bob Black, the other candidate, has been with the company for three years and has a better education than either Russell or White. He has been going to night school and taking a lot of advanced work in quality control. He has been fighting hard to introduce his ideas, but Russell feels that they are premature and that the company will not be ready for them for three or maybe five years.

The company policy in promoting is to favor who have been studying on the outside; however, White seems to be better fitted for the present situation, while Black seems to be better fitted for the long-term pull.

1. *Which of the two men should Russell promote, and why?*
2. *How should he take care of the disappointed candidate?*
3. *Is Bob Black overqualified for the promotion?*
4. *Could Russell's feelings about Black's ideas be colored by envy of Black's education?*

CASE 9–2

A recent study of 100 male college graduates found that those who are six feet, two inches tall receive an average salary over 12 percent higher than those under six feet.

The men who were under six feet reported a monthly salary averaging $876. Those six feet tall reported $899. Men who were six feet, one inch reported $905. Those who were six feet, two inches received a mean monthly salary of $985. Above that height, the scale of pay headed back down.

1. *Comment on the results in the above study.*
2. *Why do you think employers might pay a premium for men six feet and two inches tall?*
3. *Are such hiring standards desirable? Why? Why not?*

CASE 9–3

Dick Talbot had started with the company as an office boy at the age of 16. Now, at age 59, he was the training director and he was in trouble.

During his career, Dick had spent time in nearly every department. While none of his service was outstanding, he was a reliable, hardworking employee. Because of his varied experience, he had been assigned to the personnel department several years ago when the company started a methods improvement program and needed a trainer. Dick was sent to school by the company to become knowledgeable in the area of methods improvement, and he became very enthusiastic about the subject. Though he had never finished high school, the company had sent him to several courses on a variety of subjects, and he had done some reading on his own. He did not, however, avail himself of the company's tuition remission plan which would have allowed him to go to school at night to improve his formal education.

He conducted several classes in methods improvement and then started a program for the preparation of procedure manuals. During this period the company grew rather rapidly and the training function expanded. Having no one else available, the personnel vice president promoted Dick to the position of training director. He also hired a young man with a master's degree as Dick's assistant. As time went on, three more bright young training analysts with master's degrees were added to the staff to meet the mounting requests for training programs from the major divisions of the company.

The company was now conducting two management development programs, one for first-line supervisors and one for middle management, a college training program for college graduates hired as executive trainees, a work measurement program, an orientation program, and several skill programs. In other words, the training department was now an important function, and Dick found that he was unable to cope with his increased responsibilities. He was afraid of the bright young men who worked for him but did not respect him. He couldn't handle the dynamic executive trainees, and he found his lack of formal education a definite handicap. He postponed decisions and continually withdrew from controversy. He exercised no leadership and his assistant assumed the responsibility. He longed for the days of the first methods improvement program he taught. The world was passing him by; to escape, he started drinking excessively. His rate of absenteeism climbed and the personnel vice president spoke to him about the problem. Dick agreed to a complete physical, as well as psychiatric help at company expense.

The personnel vice president kept Dick in his position as training director even though the department was being handled by Dick's assistant, who by now was openly critical of Dick. After a period of treatment, Dick did not show any appreciable improvement and the personnel vice president wondered what to do next.

1. *What course of action should be taken now by the personnel vice president?*
2. *What can be done with an employee whose position has outgrown his abilities and who has long service?*
3. *Is the personnel vice president at fault for promoting Dick in the first place?*
4. *Is it possible that he feels guilty about his error of judgment in Dick's case and that this is coloring his handling of the problem?*
5. *Should a company feel any sense of responsibility for promoting a man over his head?*

CASE 9-4

Since it was set up several years ago, a relatively simple job (inspecting or machine operating, for example) performed by women in a group has had a high turnover. The women complain that the pay is too low. Actually, when compared to jobs of the same difficulty, the pay is in line.

In order to raise the pay and reduce the turnover, the company plans to enlarge the job by combining it with a similar job that requires more accurate work and has a higher pay scale.

Mary Morrow, the most successful operator on the simple job, was selected to try out the combined job and was trained to perform the new tasks. She has been working on the newly designed job for three months. She continues to do the tasks of the original job very well but does the new tasks very poorly—the ones requiring greater accuracy. When asked the reason, she says she does not like the new tasks because they make her nervous. If she didn't need the extra pay, she would like to go back to her old job.

1. *What are some of the factors to be considered when enlarging jobs?*
2. *What are some of the advantages and disadvantages of combining several levels of the same type of job?*
3. *How should jobs be enlarged?*
4. *How should the above situation be handled?*

CASE 9–5

Walter Green graduated from the state university with a degree in physics. After six months of fruitless search for a job with some relationship to his education, he became desperate. He finally decided to take any job, simply to earn some money and help his ego.

He applied for a position with the Acme Insurance Company, a large clerical employer in the city where Walter lived. The interviewer was impressed with Green's background and mentioned several open clerical positions, cautioning him that these jobs were all routine ones without much challenge. Green happily replied that he would accept any of them.

The interviewer called up the supervisor of the accounts receivable section and told him about Green. At that time the section was very busy and there were three open jobs. Although the supervisor had some misgivings about a college graduate in physics in a routine clerical assignment, he was grateful for the help.

The job was routine and involved a simple checking procedure having to do with premium payments. The supervisor explained to Green that even though the job was routine, it was important, since errors could cause difficulties with policyholders.

Green promised top performance and the supervisor was pleased and explained the details of the job. Green learned the job rapidly and performed the job very well. After six months, he began losing interest in the work; his errors climbed and his attitude became negative. When the supervisor talked to him, Green said he was simply bored with the job.

1. *Should Green have been hired in the first place?*
2. *Does Green owe the company continued good performance for having been offered the opportunity when he was desperate?*
3. *What can the supervisor do about Green?*

CASE 9–6

You are in charge of a group of draftsmen, three of whom are detail draftsmen. The job description for a detail draftsman calls for a high school education or its equivalent. Of the three young people you have working on this job, one is a high school graduate, the second has had one year of college, and the third has a master's degree in foreign languages. All three were hired at the same time and at the same rate of pay.

After a few months on the job, the two people who were educated beyond the high school level show restlessness, boredom, and dissatisfaction. The quality and quantity of their work, which at first was superior to that of the high school graduate, is now inferior.

Draftsmen are scarce, and you would like to retain these two employees. You think that you could do this by changing the composition of some of the other jobs in the department and thus giving more complicated work and more pay to these two. This change would disturb the jobs of other employees, and you are afraid that the plan would be unfair to them and to the high school graduate.

1. *What are some of the advantages of modifying the content of jobs in order to have them fit more closely the capacities of the employees?*
2. *What are some of the disadvantages?*
3. *How should you handle the problem of people working substantially below their mental capacities?*
4. *How can the personnel department help you?*

CASE 9–7

Charlie Black's section had always been dominated by male employees. There were a few women hired over the years, but everyone looked on Black's section as a male preserve. In the last few years because of the impact of equal employment opportunity implementation in the company, Charlie's female work force had grown, but males still outnumbered females.

Recently Black promoted two people to supervisory positions, both of whom were excellent workers with outstanding qualifications. One was a man who was given a unit composed of ten men to supervise. The other, a woman, was assigned to a unit that employed five men and five women. This woman was the first female suprevisor in Black's area of responsibility.

Everything went along very well for about a month. Morale was high and production kept up to standards. Then Charlie began to notice a slowing of production among the five men in the unit even though the five women continued to do well. The woman supervisor told Charlie that the men were upset because several of their co-workers in other units were riding them about working for a female boss. She told Black that she didn't have any difficulty with the men but that she couldn't control the situation in other units. Black spoke to the five men in the unit, and they said they respected their new boss but that they were tired of the ribbing from the other men. It was simply getting to them and affecting their work.

1. *What can Black do about this problem?*
2. *Why are the men tolerating the kidding and allowing their work to suffer?*

3. *If Black promoted some more women to supervisory positions would the ribbing continue?*

4. *Should Black discipline the men for letting their production slip?*

CASE 9-8

In recent years the proof department of the Universal Bank and Trust Company has had considerable difficulty with labor turnover, absenteeism, lateness, and low employee productivity. The bank is located in a large midwestern city. The main function of the proof department is posting of checks and other items against customer accounts. This means that items such as deposits, withdrawals, and checks are credited or debited to the proper customer account as they are received by the bank. This work comes to the proof department from the bank's 85 branches.

The proof department is located in a large office building in the city, and there are over 1,500 employees in the department. The posting is done on a proof machine, and the working conditions are factory-like. Each operator is given work by a unit head and then—using a machine which resembles a keypunch machine—posts the items. The work is quite simple, routine, and highly repetitive.

For the last five years the operator job has attracted only female applicants, most of whom are married women and not the heads of households. They are young high school graduates ranging from 18 to 30 years of age. The new operator stays for an average of two years, although a few stay with the bank longer and these are usually made unit heads.

If they worked at full capacity, each operator could process 1,500 to 1,800 items an hour, but the average is 500 to 700 an hour. Mondays and Fridays are days when up to one third of the force may be absent.

The management is aware of the problem, knows the work is boring, and realizes that a large majority of the work force consists of minority group members who are young. The bank pays a competitive salary for this type of work, and its fringe benefits are similar to or better than most other employers in the city.

1. *What can the bank's management do about this problem?*

2. *If you were a supervisor in this department, how would you try to increase productivity?*

3. *Why do people take boring jobs?*

CASE 9-9

The job of secretary to a senior officer of the company had long been considered an honor. It was traditional to promote one of the secretaries to major department heads when such a position opened. Usually the person chosen had long tenure with the company and had demonstrated ability as an effective private secretary.

Such a person was Louise Miller. She had been with the company for 27 years and was presently serving as the secretary to the chief engineer. When the production vice president's secretary retired, everyone, including Louise, believed that she would be promoted to fill the vacancy.

A week after the vacancy occurred, it became apparent to Louise that she was not being offered the promotion. She went to see the personnel manager and was told that he was recruiting a person for the job from outside the company. He felt that the person should be a college graduate and be able to pass the battery of psychological, intelligence, and aptitude tests the company had recently started to use as part of its selection and placement procedure.

Louise Miller was quite discouraged when she left the personnel manager's office. She felt slighted and was rather bitter about the fact that her years of successful secretarial experience did not seem to qualify her for the opening. She went to her boss, the chief engineer, to ask for advice. He felt she was an excellent secretary who was eminently qualified for the promotion. He believed that her knowledge of company policy and procedures, her loyalty, and her strong motivation should result in a promotion for her.

1. *What should Louise Miller's boss do to help her?*
2. *Is the personnel manager correct in his efforts at outside recruitment to fill the open secretarial position?*
3. *Should Louise Miller's long and successful experience be considered a valid substitute for her lack of qualifications established by the personnel manager?*
4. *How should long-service experienced employees be handled when they believe they are qualified for an opening and new standards indicate they are not?*
5. *Should Louise be given the opportunity to take the test battery?*
6. *Is Louise Miller justified in her feelings of bitterness and discouragement?*

CASE 9–10

George Egan had been employed by the Link Chemical Company for three years. He was a high school graduate who came to Link with some previous business experience but none in the chemical industry. He was placed in the plant, starting in simple jobs which he quickly learned. He evidenced a desire to learn as much as he could, and this was soon noticed by Mr. Wilson, the small company's president. He encouraged Egan to acquire as many skills as possible and to familiarize himself with all jobs in the plant. Wilson then told Egan to take some technical courses at night which the company would pay for. Egan was grateful for this encouragement, and he successfully completed the courses.

Noting Egan's success with the technical courses, Mr. Wilson then informed him that he ought to study chemical engineering in the evening division of a nearby university. Egan did not feel that he could accomplish such a lofty goal; but when the president pressed him, he felt that he would have to try, since Mr. Wilson thought so mush of his ability. After a year of evening study, Egan became convinced that chemical engineering was not for him. He had enjoyed the liberal arts courses, and he was very interested in a course in personnel administration he had just started. Egan told Mr. Wilson of his lack of interest in chemical engineering and his enthusiasm for the liberal arts and personnel courses. While Mr. Wilson was disappointed and did not think liberal arts useful, he told Egan the company would continue to pay for his education.

Because of Egan's apparent change of interests, Mr. Wilson made an appointment for him to be given a battery of tests by a local firm specializing in vocational testing. The test results indicated that Egan possessed above-average intelligence and that while he could absorb engineering subjects, he could probably do much better with liberal arts and business subjects. The psychologist also pointed out that Egan did not desire to assume a leadership role, nor did he have any indicated ability, interest, or aptitude for such a role.

In the face of test results to the contrary, Mr. Wilson decided to promote Egan to the position of supervisor in the plant, where he would have direct responsibility for ten employees. He told Mr. Burton, the plant manager, of his decision, mentioning that the company had a considerable investment in Egan and that it was about time they started to get a return on the investment. Mr. Burton disagreed with the decision, pointing to Egan's interests and the test results. He further mentioned that he had observed Egan's daily work carefully and that nothing in it indicated that he would be a good supervisor. In addition, he stated that Egan had gained the reputation of being a fair-haired boy because of the president's close attention and that this would cause him trouble if he became foreman. Mr. Wilson listened to Burton's arguments, but he stressed his belief that Egan deserved the opportunity for increased compensation that being a supervisor allowed. He expressed the opinion that test results were not always conclusive evidence of a person's ability to do a job. He told Burton to assist Egan in any way possible and ended the discussion.

Grumbling among Egan's employees started about a month after he became their boss. Burton discovered that Egan was a perfectionist, and his employees could not satisfy his requirements. After two more months of smoothing ruffled waters and trying to coach Egan, Burton came to the conclusion that Egan had been given every opportunity to succeed as a supervisor and had failed.

1. *Was George Egan handled properly by the company president?*
2. *Should Egan have been promoted to "recover an investment," as the president put it?*

3. *To what extent, if any, could Egan's failure be attributed to Burton's disagreement with the president's decision?*

4. *Should an executive choose a so-called fair-haired boy, recognizing the awkward position in which this may place the person chosen?*

5. *Can the company do anything now to salvage the career of George Egan?*

SUGGESTED READINGS: PART II

Chapter	*Books*
7	Ackoff, Russell L. *A Concept of Corporate Planning.* New York: John Wiley & Sons, Inc., 1970.
8	Barnes, Ralph M. *Motion and Time Study: Design and Measurement of Work.* 6th ed. New York: John Wiley & Sons, Inc., 1968.
9	———. *Work Sampling.* New York: John Wiley & Sons, Inc., 1956.
7	Beer, Stafford. *Management Science.* Garden City, N.Y.: Doubleday & Co., Inc., 1968.
9	Belcher, David W. *Compensation Administration.* Englewood Cliffs, N.J.: Prentice-Hall, Inc., 1974.
7	Bocchino, William A. *Management Information Systems.* Englewood Cliffs, N.J.: Prentice-Hall, Inc., 1972.
7	Branch, Melville C. *The Corporate Planning Process.* New York: John Wiley & Sons, Inc., 1969.
7	Budnick, F. S.; Mojena R.; and Vollman, T. E. *Principles of Operations Research for Management.* Homewood, Ill.: Richard D. Irwin, Inc., 1977.
7, 9	Burack, Elmer H. *Strategies for Manpower Planning and Programming.* Morristown, N.J.: General Learning Press, 1972.
7	Carroll, S. J., Jr., and Tosi, H. L., Jr. *Management by Objectives Applications and Research.* New York: Macmillan Co., 1973.
7, 10	Chapanis, Alphonse. *Man-Machine Engineering.* Belmont, Calif.: Wadsworth Publishing Co., 1965.
8	Close, Guy C., Jr. *Work Improvement.* New York: John Wiley & Sons, Inc., 1960.
9	Drucker, Peter F. *Managing for Results.* New York: Harper & Row, Publishers, 1964.
10	Dunnette, Marvin D. *Personnel Selection and Placement.* Belmont, Calif.: Wadsworth Publishing Co., 1966.
7	Emery, James C. *Organization Planning and Control Systems.* New York: Macmillan Co., 1969.
7	Ewing, David W. *The Practice of Planning.* New York: Harper & Row, Publishers, 1968.

Chapter	**Books**
9	Fleishman, Edwin A., and Bass, Alan R., eds. *Studies in Personnel and Industrial Psychology.* 3d ed. Homewood, Ill.: Dorsey Press, 1974.
9	Foulkes, Fred K. *Creating More Meaningful Work.* New York: American Management Assn., 1969.
8	Heaton, Herbert. *Productivity in Service Organizations.* New York: McGraw-Hill Book Co., 1977.
7,8,9	Heyel, Carl, ed. *Handbook of Modern Office Management and Administrative Services.* New York: McGraw-Hill Book Co., 1972.
7,9	Johnson, R. A.; Kast, F. E.; and Rosenzweig, J. E. *The Theory and Management of Systems.* 3d ed. New York: McGraw-Hill Book Co., 1973.
8	Karger, D. W., and Bayha, F. H. *Engineered Work Measurement.* New York: Industrial Press, 1966.
7	King, David I., and King, William S. *Systems Analysis and Project Management.* New York: McGraw-Hill Book Co., 1968.
8,9	Lanham, Elizabeth. *Administration of Wages and Salaries.* New York: Harper & Row, Publishers, 1963.
8,9	Lehrer, Robert N. *Work Simplification.* Englewood Cliffs, N.J.: Prentice-Hall, Inc., 1957.
7	Levin, Richard I., and Kirkpatrick, Charles A. *Planning and Control with PERT/CPM.* New York: McGraw-Hill Book Co., 1966.
7	———. *Quantitative Approaches to Management.* 3d ed. New York: McGraw-Hill Book Co., 1975.
7,8	Levin, R. L.; McLaughlin, C. P.; Lamone, R. P.; and Kottas, J. F. *Production/Operations Management.* New York: McGraw-Hill Book Co., 1972.
9	Lopez, Felix M., Jr. *Personnel Interviewing, Theory and Practice.* 2d ed. New York: McGraw-Hill Book Co., 1975
7,8	McConkey, Dale D. *How to Manage by Results.* 3d ed. New York: American Management Assn., 1976.
9	Maher, John R., ed. *New Perspectives in Job Enrichment.* New York: Van Nostrand Reinhold Co., 1971.
7	Martin, E. W., Jr., and Perkins, W. C. *Computers and Information Systems: An Introduction.* Homewood, Ill.: Richard D. Irwin, Inc., 1973.
8	Maynard, H. B., ed. *Industrial Engineering Handbook.* 3d ed. New York: McGraw-Hill Book Co., 1971.
8	———; Stegemerten, G. J.; and Schwab, J. L. *Methods Time Measurement.* New York: McGraw-Hill Book Co., 1948.
8	Miller, David W., and Starr, Martin K. *Executive Decisions and Operations Research.* 2d ed. Englewood Cliffs, N.J.: Prentice-Hall, Inc., 1969.
7	Mockler, Robert J. *The Management Control Process.* New York: Appleton-Century-Crofts, 1972.
9	Myers, M. Scott. *Every Employee a Manager.* New York: McGraw-Hill Book Co., 1970.
7,9	Nadler, Gerald. *Work Systems Design: The Ideals Concept.* Homewood, Ill.: Richard D. Irwin, Inc., 1967.

Chapter	**Books**
8	Niebel, Benjamin W. *Motion and Time Study.* 6th ed. Homewood, Ill.: Richard D. Irwin, Inc. 1976.
7,9	Newman, William H., and Warren, E. K. *The Process of Management.* 4th ed. Englewood Cliffs, N.J.: Prentice-Hall, Inc., 1977.
7,8	Odiorne, George S. *Management by Objectives.* New York: Pitman Publishing Corp., 1965.
7	Prince, Thomas R. *Information Systems for Management Planning and Control.* 3d ed. Homewood, Ill.: Richard D. Irwin, Inc., 1975.
8	Payne, Bruce, and Swett, D. *Office Operations Improvement.* New York: American Management Assn., 1967.
8,9	Rathe, Alex W., and Gryna, Frank M. *Applying Industrial Engineering to Management Problems.* New York: American Management Assn., 1969.
9	Rush, Harold M. F. *Job Design for Motivation.* New York: Conference Board, Inc., 1971.
7	St. Thomas, Charles E. *Practical Business Planning.* New York: American Management Assn., 1965.
7	Schellenberger, Robert E. *Managerial Analysis.* Homewood, Ill.: Richard D. Irwin, Inc., 1969.
7,8	Schleh, E. C. *Management by Results.* New York: McGraw-Hill Book Co., 1961.
7,8	Schoderbek, Peter P., and Reif, William E. *Job Enlargement.* Ann Arbor: Bureau of Industrial Relations, University of Michigan, 1969.
8	Sibson, Robert E. *Increasing Employee Productivity.* New York: AMACOM, 1976.
7	Steiner, George A. *Top Management Planning.* New York: Macmillan Co., 1969.
9	Strauss, George, and Sayles, Leonard R. *Personnel: The Human Problems of Management.* 3d ed. Englewood Cliffs, N.J.: Prentice-Hall, Inc., 1972.
9	Suojanen, W. W., et al, eds. *Perspectives on Job Enrichment and Productivity.* Atlanta: Georgia State University, 1975.
7,8,9	Sutermeister, Robert A. *People and Productivity.* 3d ed. New York: McGraw-Hill Book Co., 1976.
9	Wolfle, Dael, ed. *The Discovery of Talent.* Cambridge, Mass.: Harvard University Press, 1969.

Articles

7	Alter, S. L. "How Effective Managers Use Information Systems," *Harvard Business Review,* November-December 1976.
7	Anderson, D. N. "Murphy's Law versus Zero-Base Budgeting," *Management Review,* October 1977.
8	Aquilano, N. J. "Multiskilled Work Teams: Productivity Benefits," *California Management Review,* Summer, 1977.
9	Austin, D. L. "A New Approach to Position Descriptions," *Personnel Journal,* July 1977.

Chapter	*Articles*

8   Bluestone, I. "Implementing Quality of Worklife Programs," *Management Review*, July 1977.

8   Clarkson, A. "Spurring Productivity in So-Called Low Interest Jobs," *Personnel Journal*, February 1977.

7   French, W. L., and Hollman, R. W. "Management by Objectives: The Team Approach," *California Management Review*, Spring 1975.

7   Goldman, H. H. "ZBB without Paperwork: An Informal Approach to Budget Planning," *Management Review*, October 1977.

9   Hackman, J. R. "Is Job Enrichment Just a Fad?" *Harvard Business Review*, September-October 1975.

9   Hackman, J. R.; Oldham, G.; Janson, R.; and Purdy, K. "A New Strategy for Job Enrichment," *California Management Review*, Summer 1975.

7   Hobbs, J. M., and Heany, D. F. "Coupling Strategy to Operating Plans," *Harvard Business Review*, May-June 1977.

8   Katzell, R. A., and Yankelovich, D. "Improving Productivity and Job Satisfaction," *Organizational Dynamics*, Summer 1975.

8   Kirby, P. G. "Productivity Increases through Feedback System," *Personnel Journal*, October 1977.

7   Koontz, H. "Making MBO Effective," *California Management Review*, Fall 1977.

8   Kostick, M. M., and Pearse, R. "The Dynamics of Productive Compatibility," *Management Review*, September 1977.

9   Lawler, E. E., III. "For a More Effective Organization—Match the Job to the Man," *Organizational Dynamics*, Summer 1974.

9   Luthans, F., and Reif, W. E. "Job Enrichment: Long on Theory, Short on Practice," *Organizational Dynamics*, Winter 1974.

7   Mason, J. G. "How Much Is an Hour of Your Time Really Worth?" *Management Review*, June 1977.

9   Mears, P. "Guidelines for the Job Enrichment Practitioner," *Personnel Journal*, May 1976.

8   Miller, D. A. "How to Improve the Performance and Productivity of the Knowledge Worker," *Organizational Dynamics*, Winter 1977.

8   Mollenhoff, D. V. "How to Measure Work by Professionals," *Management Review*, November 1977.

9   Mruk, E. S., and Giblin, E. J. "Compensation as a Management Tool," *Management Review*, May 1977.

8   Odiorne, G. S. "MBO in the 1980's: Will It Survive?" *Management Review*, July 1977.

8   Peters, E. B. "Job Security, Technical Innovation, and Productivity," *Personnel Journal*, January 1978.

7   Radius, D. "Time Conservation," *Personnel Journal*, May 1976.

8   Ronan, W. W.; Talbert, T. L.; and Carroll, K. I. "Measuring Clerical Job Performance," *Personnel Journal*, November 1976.

Chapter	*Articles*
7	Salton, G. J. "The Focused Web—Goal Setting in the MBO Process," *Management Review,* January 1978.
7	Schwartz, E. B., and MacKenzie, R. A. "Time Management Strategy for Women," *Management Review,* September 1977.
7	Steers, R. M., and Spencer, D. G. "Achievement Needs and MBO Goal Setting," *Personnel Journal,* January 1978.
7	Turney, J. R., and Cohen, S. L. "Managing Time Effectively: The Worker's Perspective," *Personnel Journal,* November 1976.
7	Villareal, M. J. "Improving Managerial Performance," *Personnel Journal,* February 1977.
9	Whitsett, D. A. "Where Are Your Unenriched Jobs?" *Harvard Business Review,* January-February 1975.
8	Zenger, J. "Increasing Productivity," *Personnel Journal,* October 1976.

PART III

DEVELOPING EMPLOYEE POTENTIAL

○ Human behavior: Motivation and morale

○ Managing human resources: Training and orientation

○ Managing human resources: Personnel planning and performance appraisal

Chapter 10

Learning objectives

- To develop an understanding of human behavior in the work place

- To become aware of some theories of motivation and their relationship to human performance

- To understand the practical implications of motivation theories to people and their jobs

- To become aware of what people might want from their jobs and how morale may be affected

Human behavior: Motivation and morale

Major topics

Early developments.

The scientific management movement.

Research in human behavior.

Individual needs and motivation.

Motivation problems.

Personal problems of employees.

What people want from their jobs.

Motivation and morale.

Determinants of morale.

Development of high morale.

A well-designed job, sound policies and procedures, an effectively structured organization, and careful planning and control all have a significant impact on employee productivity. The actuating ingredient, however, is human behavior. If people are unwilling or less than enthusiastic about the work they are doing, productivity suffers. All of us have seen one person work very hard to achieve goals while a co-worker with very similar experience and ability performs poorly and is a troublemaker. Why one person is very ambitious, continually seeking responsibility, and strongly desiring a management position and another is content just to get by doing the bare minimum of work is one of the mysteries we have yet to solve.

Supervisors and managers are constantly concerned with the "why" of human behavior. Even the least sophisticated supervisor knows that getting the work out effectively requires human behavior that is positively directed toward job accomplishment. All kinds of approaches have been tried to get improved performance and greater productivity. From the $5-day established by pioneer automobile manufacturer Henry Ford at a time when prevailing wages for factory work were half that amount, to the many motivation theories developed over the years, we have been trying to learn more about human behavior. Obviously organizations want to achieve the greatest return on their investment as possible. It doesn't take any manager very long to recognize that people are necessary for this.

Trying to determine what people want from their jobs, the intensity of their desires, the ways they react to conflict and frustration, and their differences in goal desires and perceptions are all a matter for continued study by the supervisor and manager who wants to do an effective job. While there are no sure-fire answers, it is desirable to understand something of the background of human behavior in industry and some of the prominent motivation theories. Such understanding can help supervisors handle the complexities of their jobs in a more effective manner.

Early developments

Everything accomplished by humans has a history. An individual's relationships with other human beings in the workplace are no exception. The casual observer may look upon the American economy in wonderment or take it for granted. We use the products of its factories, do business with its banks and insurance companies, avail ourselves of many offered services, and have a variety of relationships with a myriad of other organizations without giving much thought to their complexity. Rarely do we reflect on the varied knowledge, talents, and experience possessed by the individuals who are responsible for the success of these organizations. The fact that so many are successful is due in no small measure to the ability of diverse human beings to work together in organized activity toward the objectives established for the particular organization. To understand more fully the importance of effective human performance in the workplace, it is necessary to examine at least some of the important developments that have contributed to the present state of the art of human behavior in organizations.

The typical business at the beginning of this century was a relatively small operation utilizing few methods which are familiar today. Little attention was paid to management problems as we know them today. The factory and its growing need for machinery was preeminent in the minds of managers. One of the dominant characteristics of the era was the prevalence of the owner-manager. This individual was usually a self-made man who had personally started his own business and nursed its early growth. His thoughts were largely directed toward his machines and the processes they made possible. People to run these machines were necessary but incidental. Though necessary, they were relatively easy to obtain, and the wages that had to be paid were the lowest possible for the maximum hours possible. There was little or no governmental regulation or interference from other outside agencies, so that the businessman was left to make his own rules. Among other things, this led to a work orientation with an emphasis on production. The newly discovered usefulness of machines and their dependability in turning out uniform products at relatively lower prices were of prime importance and interest to the manager. The resultant division of labor made it possible to hire people who had little of the artisan skill of their predecessor journeymen. The machine did the skillful operations, and the person became merely an extension of the machine.

The transfer of skill from person to machine had been developing in other countries for some time. Now it was rapidly taking hold in the United States. As in other countries, the attendant social and moral problems of this transfer were given scant attention here. The development was looked upon as an industrial one, and the social problems were not considered to be the concern of entrepreneurs. Their efforts were directed toward production and profit. Because the community at large viewed industrial growth in this manner, these companies were left free to develop as they saw fit. Government generally felt that business should develop unhampered by regulation. The population was largely uneducated by today's standards, and there were few or no strong unions. Actually, economic and social pressures for growth were all on the side of any aspiring entrepreneur. The United States had a great potential waiting to be tapped by any diligent businessman. The Puritan philosophy of colonial times, which frowned on leisure and treated work and productive effort almost like a religion, created the framework for the industrial growth of this country.

The scientific management movement

It was in this climate of technological and social change taking place in the late 19th century that managers started to seek better ways to cope with the increasing complexities in their enterprises. Quite naturally, emphasis was placed on production efficiency, but the human's contribution to this efficiency began to be recognized.

Frederick W. Taylor, frequently called "the father of scientific management," was one of the pioneers who recognized that the worker was as important to efficiency as the machine. In his early studies he found that it was the worker and not management that set the pace for production. The foreman might give orders as to what was to be done, but he didn't say how or at what speed. As a result each worker set his own pace and did the job as he saw fit, in many cases continuing poor methods he had acquired by observation of other workers. Taylor initiated his motion studies at the Midvale Steel Company to determine the motions required for each job as well as the time required for each motion. He felt that wages paid should have some relationship to the amount of work done. In this sense, Taylor is said to have rationalized production. But he saw his efforts as going beyond that goal. Believing that scientific management was not an efficiency device, a system of cost determination, or just time and motion study, he felt that it involved a complete mental revolution on the part of both workers and management. Testifying before a congressional committee, he described this mental revolution as follows:

> The great revolution that takes place in the mental attitude of the two parties under scientific management is that both sides take their eyes off the division of the surplus as the all-important matter, and together turn their attention toward increasing the size of the surplus until this surplus become so large ... that there is ample room for a large increase in wages for the workmen and an equally large increase in profits for the manufacturer.[1]

Taylor firmly believed that scientific management was not a collection of techniques to increase efficiency, but a philosophy of management and a way of thinking. He saw a mutuality of interests for workers and managers which would result in greater productivity and a more equitable distribution of the economic results of this effort. Taylor's disciples, Henry Gantt and Frank and Lillian Gilbreth, with their search for the "one best way" of doing a job, also believed in the mutuality of interests of workers and managers. Lillian Gilbreth dealt with the applications of psychology to management in one of her early books[2] and made the following claims for scientific management:

1. Physical improvement of workers (increased health, better color and general appearance).

---

[1] Frederick W. Taylor, *Scientific Management* (New York: Harper & Row, Publishers, 1947), pp. 29–30.

[2] Lillian M. Gilbreth, *The Psychology of Management* (New York: Sturgis and Walton Co., 1914), chap. 10.

2. Mental development (wider interest, deeper interest, increased mental capabilities).
3. Moral development (personal responsibility for others, appreciation of standing, self-control, "squareness").
4. Contentment, brotherhood, and the "will to do" (the natural consequences of item three—moral development).

It can be seen that even though the pioneers of scientific management considered increased productivity as a primary goal they had the broader goals of society as a whole and its individual components—workers, employers, consumers, and business owners—in mind as well. The mutuality-of-interests idea pervaded their thinking, and they firmly believed that if scientific management was carried out properly it would result in a society with limited strife, benefiting all participants. While these pioneers were given credit for rationalizing production, they also contributed to the development of concepts of human relations.

Research in human behavior

Much of the work of scientific management's pioneers took place before World War I. Many of the techniques were expanded after the war and were refined, particularly in the areas of time and motion study, wage determination, and cost analysis. Unfortunately the "mental revolution" aspects of scientific management never truly caught on in industry. In this sense, the expectations the pioneers caught on in industry. In this sense, the expectations the pioneers had for scientific management never were achieved. A combination of factors contributed to this failure. Many employers cut the piece rate when productivity went up, thus destroying the incentive to work harder. Increasingly powerful labor unions and employees felt that increased individual productivity only meant fewer jobs. Time and motion studies frequently led to production speedups, and many companies found that scientifically determined standards did not always lead to unlimited cooperation between employees and managers.

Perhaps the principal reason for the failure of the "mental revolution" was the fact that "economic man" did not exist. Financial needs are not always paramount in the minds of workers. They may slow their pace to allow slower group members to keep up, because their need for affiliation may dominate their thinking. On the other hand, they could be reluctant to be known as "rate busters" and be derided by co-workers for exceeding the established rate for the job.

During the 1920s, attention turned away from the basically economic work motives emphasized by the developers of scientific management. Many writers of the period assumed that people did not like to perform work and, therefore, money would not motivate them. In many companies there were attempts to develop noneconomic fringe benefits to satisfy employee desires for recognition and security. Probably the most significant event of the 1920s was the start of the Hawthorne studies, since many people believe that this was the modern beginning of the human relations movement.

The Harvard studies at Hawthorne. The most famous study of people at work was directed by Elton Mayo and a group from Harvard University in the period between 1927 and 1932. The study was made at the Hawthorne (suburban Chicago) works of the Western Electric Company and yielded a vast amount of information about workers' unfavorable attitudes toward management, about informal social organization, and about the restriction of output under an incentive plan.

The publication of the research[3] drew attention to the importance of friendly supervision; to the worker's need for association, accentance, security, and stability in the work group; and to the disruptive effects of technological change upon work relationships. The studies attacked the concept that the worker was an "economic man"—a person whose cooperation could be bought or whose hand could be hired and whose only concern would be to maximize earnings. The employees interviewed at Hawthorne held down their output and earnings for reasons that involved emotion more than logic.

The Hawthorne research emphasized the group—the informal social organization—as a prime factor in motivation. Mayo theorized that people have a basic need for affiliation—a theory that has come in for questioning in later studies.

Perhaps the most significant findings were those that disrupted some of the traditional management thinking of the day and pointed the way for later study, much of which is still going on today. The formal organization structure was shown to be merely a charting of functional relationships. The organization was really a social system made up of many small groups with their own status systems, many emotional factors, rumors, grapevines, and a series of complex interrelationships. Mayo discounted the "rabble thesis," which implied that workers in an organization were a disorganized rabble of individuals all working in their own self-interest in as logical a manner as possible. Rather, he found that work was a group activity and that the employee placed a great deal of importance on his other relationship with the work group. The impact of this finding is brought forth when we consider that much of present-day human relations research centers on the work group. The findings on morale and productivity did much to change management thinking and resulted in greater attention to nonfinancial incentives as part of the reward system for employees.

---

[3] F. J. Roethlisberger and W. J. Dickson, *Management and the Worker* (Cambridge, Mass.: Harvard University Press, 1939). An evaluation of the research was made 25 years later by Henry A. Lansberger in *Hawthorne Revisited* (New York: School of Industrial and Labor Relations, Cornell University, 1958). The experiments are reported and evaluated in a number of books, including Morris S. Viteles, *Motivation and Morale in Industry* (New York: W. W. Norton & Co., Inc., 1953).

The Michigan studies. The Institute for Social Research at the University of Michigan has carried on studies on work groups since about 1947.[4] These studies focus on the attitudes and behavior of first-line supervisors and the effects these have on productivity and attitudes of subordinates. The researchers found that in many cases the high-producing supervisors: (1) spent more time in supervision than they did in doing the same work as their subordinates; (2) practiced general supervision rather than close supervision, delegated authority to subordinates, and were themselves under bosses who delegated authority; (3) were employee-centered rather than production-centered; (4) supervised a group in which people got along well together and helped one another.

An employee-centered supervisor was defined as one who established good personal relationships with his or her subordinates and put the emphasis on creating positive employee motivation. The production-centered supervisor was one who put the pressure on for production and was apt to supervise closely and be autocratic. Further studies revised the concept of employee-centeredness to show that there must be concern for production along with concern for people; just being popular isn't enough to make a supervisor effective.

A study by N. C. Morse and E. Reimer at the Prudential Insurance Company in 1956 indicated that production-centered supervision could get faster cost-cutting results. In a year's time there was a 25-percent increase in productivity in the tightly controlled, autocratically led sections and a 20-percent increase in the groups supervised through participative methods and general supervision. However, morale suffered in the autocratic sections; good employees began to leave the company, and the employees developed unfavorable attitudes toward the high producers in their group.

Rensis Likert's studies have developed a model for work groups. In his book, *New Patterns of Management,* he states it in this way:

> The following description of the ideal model defines what we mean by a *highly effective group.* The definition involves reference to several different variables. Each of them can be thought of as a continuum, i.e., as a characteristic which can vary from low to high, from unfavorable to favorable. For example, a group can vary from one in which there is hostility among the members to one in which the attitudes are warm and friendly. The ideal model is at the favorable end of each variable.
>
> The highly effective group, as we shall define it, is always conceived as being part of a larger organization. A substantial proportion of persons in a company are members of more than one work group, especially when both line and staff are considered. As a consequence, in such groups there are always linking functions to be performed and relationships to other groups to be maintained. Our highly effective group is not an isolated entity.

---

[4] The Michigan studies are summarized by the retired director of the Institute for Social Research, Rensis Likert, in *New Patterns of Management* (New York: McGraw-Hill Book Co., 1961).

All the persons in a company also belong to groups and organizations outside of the company. For most persons, membership in several groups both within and outside the company is the rule rather than the exception. This means, of course, that no single group, even the highly effective work group, dominates the life of any member. Each member of the organization feels pressures from membership in several different groups and is not influenced solely by loyalty to any one group.

Since the different groups to which a person belongs are apt to have somewhat different and often inconsistent goals and values, corresponding conflicts and pressures are created within him. To minimize these conflicts and tensions, the individual seeks to influence the values and goals of each of the different groups to which he belongs and which are important to him so as to minimize the inconsistencies and conflicts in values and goals. In striving for this reconciliation, he is likely to press for the acceptance of those values most important to him.[5]

Likert then lists and describes 24 characteristics, ending with the leader and his or her selection. Supportive relationships are given particular emphasis and the influence of the leader by virtue of his or her position in the organizational hierarchy is deemphasized. Likert feels that a leader who depends on rank for maintaining group effectiveness is acting ineffectively and that the leader should minimize status factors between self and the group in a variety of ways:

Listening well and patiently.

Not being impatient with the progress being made by the group, particularly on difficult problems.

Accepting more blame than may be warranted for any failure or mistake.

Giving the group members ample opportunity to express their thoughts without being constrained by the leader pressing his own views.

Being careful never to impose a decision on the group.

Putting his contributions often in the form of questions or stating them speculatively.

Arranging for others to help perform leadership functions which enhance their status.[6]

Remember, Likert called this an *ideal* model. Nevertheless, it would call for an unusual person to assume responsibility in the above manner and would, for that matter, call for an unusual work group. The pressures that inevitably evolve in any complex organization would make it rather difficult for the supervisor to act consistently in the manner prescribed in the above list. In some work groups, members would resent performing leadership functions, feeling it was not their responsibility. The imposition of decisions on a group is frequently out of the individual supervisor's hand. He may have a decision imposed by higher authority with no alternative but to carry it out. Obviously an entire organization would have to adhere to the ideal model, and perhaps this is too much to expect from the lead-

---

[5] Ibid., p. 165.

[6] Ibid., p. 171.

ership selection process, the availability of talented managers, and the vagaries of human nature.

Theory X and Theory Y. No discussion of human relations would be complete without consideration of the work of Douglas McGregor. Believing that any managerial act rests on some theoretical assumption, the way in which a manager implements these theoretical assumptions is the key to the development of sound human relationships in the workplace. Human relations courses may make managers aware of participative approaches to management, and they may even answer questions on human relations quizzes in the so-called correct way, but they may practice human relations on the job in quite a different manner. Essentially, McGregor was concerned with the superficiality of human relations program in the workplace, and McGregor felt that even though a manager might be aware of human relations concepts he or she more frequently was dominated by traditional autocratic concepts in the practice of management. He characterized this traditional view of direction and control as "Theory X" and described it as follows:

1. The average human being has an inherent dislike of work and will avoid it when he can.
2. Because of this human characteristic of dislike of work, most people must be coerced, controlled, directed, threatened with punishment to get them to put forth adequate effort toward the achievement of organizational objectives.
3. The average human being prefers to be directed, wishes to avoid responsibility, has relatively little ambition, wants security above all.

   ... Theory X is not a straw man for the purposes of demolition but is in fact a theory which materially influences managerial strategy in a wide sector of American industry today. Moreover, the principles of organization which comprise the bulk of the literature of management *could only have been derived from assumptions such as those of Theory X.* Other beliefs about human nature would have led inevitably to quite different organizational principles. Theory X provides an explanation of some human behavior in industry.[7]

In contrast to the Theory X approach to management, McGregor felt that many modifications in the utilization of human beings in the workplace had occurred over the years. Many managements were deeply concerned with the human equation in their organizations, and this was evidenced by the great number of personnel policies and procedures and fringe benefit programs developed and implemented by these organizations. Nevertheless, McGregor believed that many of these developments had been accomplished without changes in the traditional theory of management. Changes in society caused by increased union power and social legislation gave impetus to greater emphasis on human relations. This

---

[7] Douglas McGregor, *The Human Side of Enterprise* (New York: McGraw-Hill Book Co., 1960), pp. 33–35.

tended to change authoritarian techniques to the "keep them happy" approach to human relations, which still was quite paternalistic and certainly superficial. The work going on in the study of human behavior by social scientists gave McGregor the backdrop for a new set of assumptions about the management of human beings. He called these "Theory Y," and they are as follows:

1. *The expenditure of physical and mental effort in work is as natural as play or rest.* The average human being does not inherently dislike work. Depending upon controllable conditions, work may be a source of satisfaction (and will be voluntarily performed) or a source of punishment (and will be avoided if possible).

2. *External control and the threat of punishment are not the only means for bringing about effort toward organizational objectives. Man will exercise self-direction and self-control in the service of objectives to which he is committed.*

3. *Commitment to objectives is a function of the rewards associated with their achievement.* The most significant of such rewards, e.g., the satisfaction of ego and self-actualization needs, can be direct products of effort directed toward organizational objectives.

4. *The average human being learns, under proper conditions, not only to accept but to seek responsibility.* Avoidance of responsibility, lack of ambition, and emphasis on security are generally consequences of experience, not inherent human characteristics.

5. *The capacity to exercise a relatively high degree of imagination, ingenuity, and creativity in the solution of organizational problems is widely, not narrowly, distributed in the population.*

6. *Under the conditions of modern industrial life, the intellectual potentialities of the average human being are only partially utilized.*[8]

McGregor goes on to further analyze his Theory Y assumptions and contrasts them to the Theory X assumptions described earlier.

These assumptions involve sharply different implications for managerial strategy than do those of Theory X. They are dynamic rather than static. They indicate the possibility of human growth and development; they stress the necessity for selective adaptation rather than for a single absolute form of control. They are not framed in terms of the least common denominator of the factory hand, but in terms of a resource which has substantial potentialities.

Above all, the assumptions of Theory Y point up the fact that the limits on human collaboration in the organizational setting are not the limits of human nature but of management's ingenuity in discovering how to realize the potential represented by its human resources. Theory X offers management an easy rationalization for ineffective organizational performance: It is due to the nature of the human resources with which we must work. Theory Y, on the other hand, places the problems squarely in the lap of management. If the employees are lazy, indifferent, unwilling to

---

[8] Ibid., pp. 47–48.

take responsibility, intransigent, uncreative, uncooperative, Theory Y implies that the causes lie in management's methods of organization and control.

The assumptions of Theory Y are not finally validated. Nevertheless, they are far more consistent with existing knowledge in the social sciences than are the assumptions of Theory X. They will undoubtedly be refined, elaborated, modified as further research accumulates, but they are unlikely to be completely contradicted.

On the surface, these assumptions may not seem particularly difficult to accept. Carrying their implications into practice, however, is not easy. They challenge a number of deeply ingrained managerial habits of thought and action.[9]

McGregor's prediction for acceptance of Theory Y have been largely borne out by later research and by actual developments in industry. Considerable emphasis has been given to attempts to change managerial attitudes. This is a recognition that managerial practices that have been long-established are difficult to modify. Theory Y assumptions have been considered controversial and still are by many present-day managers. Likewise, the attempts to change traditional managerial behavior patterns are also highly controversial.

The Managerial Grid.® In an attempt to reach a compromise between scientific management and the human relations school, Robert R. Blake and J. S. Mouton have developed what they call "integrated management," based on rating managers on the Grid shown in Figure 10–1. They have shown that the most effective managers are neither "production (scientific management)-oriented" nor "people (human relations)-oriented." Grid sessions are conducted which are somewhat similar to sensitivity training, except that they are more structured and directive and there is less personal criticism of the participants. The managers are induced to move toward a 9,9 type of management, which Blake and Mouton call "team management," evidencing a maximum concern for peole and a maximum concern for production. Best results have been achieved when both peers and superiors support the behavioral changes necessary to achieve 9,9 management. Perhaps the most desirable aspect of this approach is that it provides a useful communications device and a framework for behavioral issues. The relatively intangible ideas of organizational climate are made tangible by assigning a concrete numerical evaluation on the grid scale.

Organizational climate or environment. Recent research has stressed the organization as a social system. To a certain extent, the Hawthorne studies established this approach as a frame of reference for human relations research. It is reasoned that the climate within an organization, as well as the environment in which it operates, has a considerable effect on the managerial practices in that organization. Paul R. Lawrence and Jay W. Lorsch, of the Harvard graduate business school, have been

---

[9] Ibid., pp. 48–49.

Figure 10-1
The Managerial Grid®

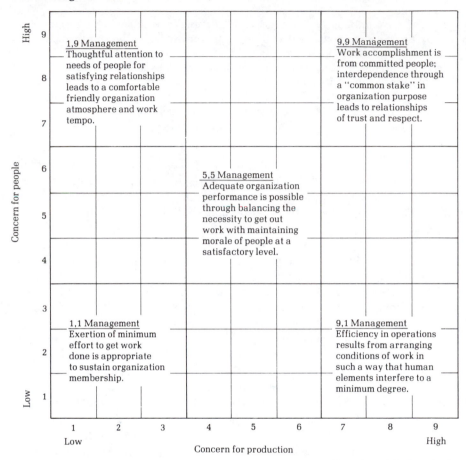

Source: R. R. Blake, J. S. Mouton, L. B. Barnes, and L. E. Greiner, "Breakthrough in Organization Development," *Harvard Business Review*, vol. 42, no. 6 (1964), p. 136. For a more thorough development of this concept, see R. R. Blake and J. S. Mouton, *The Managerial Grid* (Houston, Tex.: Gulf Publishing Co., 1964).

carrying out this type of research, trying to determine how to develop more effectively organizations in relation to their tasks and environment.[10] By studying several different types of organizations in various industries, they have attempted to answer such questions as: How can the overall tasks of an organization be more effectively subdivided? What methods for achieving integration should be suggested for a particular organization? What control systems and reward systems will aid in the

[10] Paul R. Lawrence and Jay W. Lorsch, *Organization and Environment* (Boston: Division of Research, Graduate School of Business Administration, Harvard University, 1967).

motivation of managers to achieve the integrated and differentiated performance required? Their research indicates that industrial environments characterized by uncertainty and rapid rates of technological and market change place different requirements on organizations than do stable environments. In addition, they found that the behavior patterns and managerial practices of managers in high-performance industries differed from those in more stable industries.

Individual needs and motivation

Anyone familiar with the workplace soon finds out that the equipment is usually given better care than the people working there. Preventive maintenance is carried out on computers, turret lathes, typewriters, and telephones in a careful recorded, routine manner usually periodically scheduled. Human beings are handled differently. Generally a problem must arise before any attention is given to human factors on the job. As individuals we tend to take better care of our automobiles and television sets than we do of ourselves. Only recently have we begun to turn our attention to some of the human problems caused by technology, such as air and water pollution, noise, urban blight, and ineffective utilization of scarce resources.

When a machine does not perform efficiently, we look for the cause and fix it. Similar malfunctioning in human beings is more difficult to isolate and repair. Because of this there is a tendency either to minimize or turn away from human problems. In some cases, there are attempts to seek simple solutions to the human problems. Perhaps the simplest solution for the handling of problem employees is to fire them. Effective supervisors, however, seek greater understanding of their employees.

Finding out what makes humans "tick" has occupied people for many years. Probably the most significant findings to come out of Elton Mayo's Hawthorne experiments is that human beings are unpredictable and do not always do what is expected of them. The attention given to the Hawthorne studies down to the present day is our indication of how little is known about human behavior.

Psychologists have attempted to define human needs in a variety of ways. To understand motivation and employee attitude, it is desirable to be acquainted with some of the major theories relating to human needs.

The hierarchy of human needs. Psychologist A. H. Maslow developed a theory based on the assumption that people exert effort to satisfy their needs and that, once these needs are satisfied, they no longer are motivated toward further effort.[11] The key, of course, is related to timing. When do people decide that their needs are satisfied? Maslow suggested that there is a hierarchy of human needs and that once a lower level of need is satisfied

---

[11] A. H. Maslow, *Motivation and Personality* (New York: Harper & Row, Publishers, 1954), material paraphrased from chap. 5, pp. 80–106.

the individual can only be motivated by a desire to satisfy the next level of need in the hierarchy. The need hierarchy is graphically illustrated in Figure 10–2 and described below:

Figure 10–2
Maslow's need hierarchy

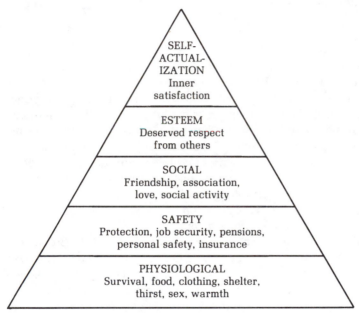

1. *Physiological needs.* Essentially these are concerned with the needs necessary for survival, such as food, clothing, and shelter. For most people in our society, these needs are relatively well satisfied. The high level of employment, with its obvious implications of reasonable material well-being, tends to minimize the motivating effect of need fulfillment on this level.
2. *Safety needs.* When physiological needs are reasonably gratified, individuals want to protect this attainment. They become concerned with such things as pension plans, job security, personal safety, workmen's compensation, and other related things which would minimize future deprivation and economic-social security. In this sense, safety needs are related to physiological needs, with the emphasis on future fulfillment of survival needs.
3. *Belonging and social activity needs.* Once the first two levels of needs are fairly well satisfied, people turn their attention to the need for friendship, association, love, and social activity. They join clubs, athletic teams, other social groups, and an affiliation with a desirable work

group within a larger acceptable organization becomes more critical. Off the job this level of need is fulfilled by marriage, family relations, and neighborhood social activity. Maslow calls this level of need one of the higher needs. The first two levels are finite and once fulfilled have little impact on the motivation of effort. The higher level needs tend to be infinite and can continue as motivators, since their level of fulfillment is hard to define in concrete terms.

4. *Esteem and status needs.* People want to have a stable firmly based high evaluation of themselves. They must feel that they are worthy and that they are doing worthy things. There is a desire for prestige and good reputation, for achievement and competence. Since the first three levels of needs are usually partly satisfied in our society, this need becomes very important as a motivator for individuals. In the workplace they want recognition, approval, and appreciation for their efforts. This relates not only to the type of work performed but also to relationships with superiors and co-workers. Satisfaction of these needs leads to feelings of self-confidence, personal worth, capability, adequacy, usefulness in the world, self-respect, and a sense of purpose. The most stable self-esteem is based on deserved respect from others.

5. *Self-actualization, self-fulfillment, and self-realization needs.* The needs on this level are the capstone to all of the other levels of needs. The needs on this level are related to the realization of the individual's potential. To fulfill such needs, the person seeks work that is challenging and difficult. He or she wants opportunities for self-development and self-expression. The desire for creativity and freedom to express this creativity are very important on this level of the need hierarchy. Inner satisfaction is the goal sought by the person as a motivator on this level. Essentially, fulfillment on this level means becoming everything that one is capable of becoming.

Some conclusions become apparent from an analysis of Maslow's need hierarchy. Needs have a priority for the individual; once needs on one level are at least partially satisfied, he seeks fulfillment on the next level. The two lower levels of needs are more or less universal, but their satisfaction may have different intensities with each person. One person may need more food than another. Shelter needs may be satisfied with a tent or a substantial private home. One could argue that the expensive home does more than satisfy shelter needs and could be classified as filling status or self-esteem needs. This is probably true of other low-level needs as well.

The lower level needs are largely fulfilled by economic efforts. The individual works for enough money to exchange for the food, clothing, and shelter he or she believes necessary. As the person becomes motivated by higher level needs, social effort and behavior become entwined with economic effort. Managers who believe that people are solely motivated by money still believe in the "economic man" concept, which is based on the notion that all human desires can be met with economic motivators. This idea only applies to the first two levels in Maslow's hierarchy. Managers who fail to recognize this will more than likely have difficulty with some of their employees. The implications of the higher levels in the need hierarchy are important to supervisors, since they can contribute significantly to the satisfaction of needs on these levels. While the listing of needs may seem to be an oversimplification of the complex behavior of human beings, there is little doubt that considerable satisfaction is derived from recognition, status, and the opportunity to develop one's capabilities to the fullest extent possible. The work environment which includes supervisory input which allows the employee to achieve fulfillment of higher level needs is usually the most satisfying to that employee.

Supportive-participative management style as a motivator. Using Maslow's basic idea of a need hierarchy and assuming that lower level needs are satisfied to a great extent, the higher level needs loom as most important. Chris Argyris and Rensis Likert are two well-known believers of this idea.[12] Essentially, they feel that the nature of the managerial and organizational environment contributes significantly to the satisfaction of higher level needs. In particular, their assumptions are built on relationships of the individual to the organization and to its management. Where the employee is part of a group which can participate in such managerial functions as goal setting and decision making, the chances for self-realization become much greater. The work takes on more meaning for employees, and they have a greater feeling of belonging and identification with the work group and the organization as a whole. By being able to participate in decisions which affect their lives, they can exercise creativity, have it recognized, and gain self-actualization. Organizations which do not practice this style of management, therefore, create an environment which minimizes the chance for self-actualization.

The motivation-hygiene theory. Frederick Herzberg and his colleagues conducted studies of 200 or so engineers and accountants to determine what factors made them feel exceptionally happy and exceptionally unhappy about their jobs.[13] Out of this study evolved the motivation-hygiene theory which, put simply, indicates that there is a duality in people's feelings about their jobs. Further, these feelings are not expressed as opposites for each other. In other words, lack of job dissatisfaction does not mean job satisfaction. Conversely, the opposite of job satisfaction is not job dissatisfaction, but rather no job satisfaction. Two essential findings came out of the studies. Factors which produced job satisfaction were separate and distinct from

---

[12] For a thorough treatment, see Chris Argyris, *Integrating the Individual and the Organization* (New York: John Wiley & Sons, Inc., 1964); and Rensis Likert, *The Human Organization* (New York: McGraw-Hill Book Co., 1967).

[13] For a complete description of the studies and the philosophy behind them, see F. Herzberg, B. Mausner, and B. B. Snyderman, *The Motivation to Work*, 2d ed. (New York: John Wiley & Sons, Inc., 1959); F. Herzberg, *Work and the Nature of Man* (Cleveland, Ohio: World Publishing Co., 1966); and F. Herzberg, *The Managerial Choice* (Homewood, Ill.: Richard D. Irwin, Inc., 1976).

the factors which led to job dissatisfaction. Employees named different types of conditions for positive and negative feelings. For example, if opportunity for advancement was given as a cause of positive feelings, the lack of such opportunity was rarely given as a cause for negative feelings about the job. Instead some other reason was given, such as poor administration or inadequate company policies.

1. Achievement.
2. Recognition.
3. Work itself.
4. Responsibility.
5. Advancement.
6. Salary.
7. Possibility of growth.
8. Interpersonal relations—subordinate.
9. Status.
10. Interpersonal relations—superior.
11. Interpersonal relations—peers.
12. Supervision—technical.
13. Company policy and administration.
14. Working conditions.
15. Personal life.
16. Job security.

It should be noted that six of these are motivational factors. They are factors 1, 2, 3, 4, 5, and 7 on the list. All of the rest are maintenance factors. Motivational factors relate directly to the job and the employee's performance and are therefore job-centered. The rest are related to environment. Herzberg found that the job-centered factors were more significant motivators than the maintenance factors. Interestingly enough, most fringe benefit programs are based on maintenance factors. The traditional approach to motivation includes environmental aspects rather than job-centered ones. This is partly based on the idea that management can better implement environmental factors than they can job-centered factors. The motivational factors require changes in leadership style on the part of supervisors, particularly if they are following autocratic-paternalistic methods. This naturally is more difficult to accomplish, and that is the principal reason for managerial emphasis on maintenance factors for motivation of employees.

Maslow's and Herzberg's theories have some similarities in that they are concerned with human needs. Maslow's approach centers on a need hierarchy that is part of human behavior in all aspects of an individual's life. Herzberg focuses on people's needs at work. Job conditions are emphasized as critical in need determination. In addition, Herzberg indicates that the essential needs are Maslow's two higher level ones, self-actualization and esteem. He assigns the term hygiene factors or maintenance factors to the three lower level needs on Maslow's hierarchy. This is graphically illustrated in Figure 10–3.

The Vroom expectancy theory. Adding to the important theories in this field, Victor Vroom developed the expectancy theory of motivation.[14] Enlarging on the concepts of Maslow and Herzberg, he interprets motivation

---

[14] For a thorough explanation, see Victor H. Vroom, *Work and Motivation* (New York: John Wiley & Sons, 1964).

Figure 10–3
A comparison of Maslow's and Herzberg's theories

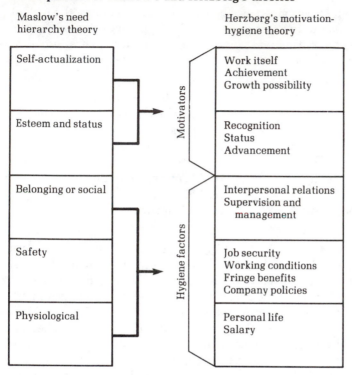

as a process in which behavior is conducive to the attainment of "outcomes." An outcome is anything an individual wants to attain. There are two parts to Vroom's theory. One part has to do with the selection pattern of an individual when faced with a series of alternatives. The strength of the individual's positive or negative orientation toward a particular outcome is called a "valence." This refers to the degree of satisfaction one might get from the achievement of a particular outcome. The individual's preferences are related to first-level outcomes and how they are related to second-level outcomes. The second part of the theory has to do with "expectancy"; that is, the force of the individual's behavior toward attainment of perceived first- and second-level outcomes.

An example might be an employee who desires a promotion to a position as a computer programmer. The conditions for achieving this outcome are excellent present job performance and voluntary evening education in computer technology. The strength of the employee's desire (valence) to achieve the goal of being a computer programmer is based on his or her behavior (expectancy) toward attaining the goal. If the person feels strongly about the ultimate outcome, he or she will perform very well on the present job and take the necessary evening courses to achieve the goal of promotion to computer programmer. The first-level outcomes (success on the job and in education) are, in a sense, means toward the end, the second-level outcome (promotion).

Vroom's expectancy theory gives some insight into motivation by its attempts to demonstrate the influence of goals and their perception on the behavior of individuals and the force of their willingness to expend efforts to achieve these goals.

McClelland's achievement need theory. Further insight into reasons why people work toward goals is given to us by David McClelland.[15] He believes that motivation is closely related to learning and individuals acquire their needs from their association with the environment and its culture. He focuses attention on three major needs: affiliation, power, and achievement. People who prefer social interaction are satisfying affiliation needs, and to these individuals task accomplishment is less important. Winning arguments and influencing the behavior of others is the hallmark of people who enjoy and seek power. By taking risks and becoming very goal-

"Thank you for this great honor. And I would like to take this occasion to apologize to all the boys I climbed over to make this dream come true."

Reprinted by permission The Wall Street Journal

One's achievement needs may affect other people.

[15] For further explanation, see David McClelland, *The Achieving Society* (Princeton, N.J.: Van Nostrand Co., 1961).

oriented, managers are filling their achievement needs. Obviously rewards for goal achievement such as participation in an MBO program are directly related to McClelland's theory.

Behavior modification. Recently much attention has been given to behavior modification or reinforcment theory. Many organizations are trying this approach to employee motivation which is based on the work of B. F. Skinner.[16] Essentially it is related to the idea that, if desired behavior is positively reinforced with suitable rewards, that behavior will be continued. Thus high performance rates an extraordinary pay increase, and it should come soon after the high performance occurs. Most incentive systems are based on reinforcement theory. There is a negative side as well. Behavior such as lateness must be immediately negatively reinforced by docking the pay of the tardy employee. Hence this theory is frequently called the reward-punishment approach to motivation. Most of the current uses of this approach, however, are based on positive reinforcement. Many managers are reluctant to use behavior modification techniques because they are similar to techniques used in animal training. Nevertheless, those companies who have used the techniques to modify behavior have found them to be successful. Lateness and absenteeism have been reduced, and work performance in some routine assignments has improved.

Motivation problems

Many of management's problems with motivation of employees are based on trying to induce the employee to be more productive by offering rewards to be enjoyed off the job rather than on it. Relatively few companies try to make actual job performance a rewarding experience. On the "pay for pain" basis, high salaries enable employees to have hobbies into which they can pour the creative energies and enthusiasm not called for on the job. The routine job offers very few of these intangible rewards. An employee comes home from the job and goes to work on some project that is personally enjoyed and on which he or she does the planning and makes the decisions. If some of this enthusiasm could be harnessed to the job, it could mean a considerable increase in productivity and job satisfaction.

There are some situations in which an employee is blocked or frustrated in all attempts to get satisfaction from the job. Frustration of needs may lead employees to aggression expressed in hostility, conflict, grievances, spoilage, slowdowns, destruction or property, insubordination, or similar undesirable behavior. Or frustrated employees, instead of striking back in hostility, may simply withdraw in spirit from the job. They may refuse to use their initiative or participate in the work situation beyond just performing what is required of them. They may become indolent, passive, unwilling

---

[16] For a thorough explanation, see B. F. Skinner, *Beyond Freedom and Dignity* (New York: Alfred Knopf, 1971); B. F. Skinner, *Science and Human Behavior* (New York: Macmillan Co., 1953); and "At Emery Air Freight: Positive Reinforcement Boosts Performance," *Organizational Dynamics* (New York: AMACOM, vol. 1, no. 3, 1973), pp. 41–50.

to accept responsibility, and unreasonable in their demands for wages and other economic benefits.

The money motive.   The money motive is not a simple one to diagnose. A few people are "economic humans," and all their lives the money motive is uppermost. For them, money seems to serve as a substitute for love or emotional security.

In other people, the money motive is something that changes with the changing of their circumstances. Young people starting out with high hopes and expectations have strong money motives because they need so many things. After they have achieved the standard of living to which they aspire, money may take on a more symbolic meaning. It may be thought of less for its purchasing power and more as a measure of personal worth. The money motive may drop in importance, but it can rise in a hurry if someone else gets a raise.

At the low end of the financial and social scale, among people who live from hand to mouth, money and savings don't represent security. Security lies in the steady job. Money is something to be enjoyed at the moment because not enough of it can be accumulated to make any real improvement. People have to see some solid possibility of bettering their situation before they are ready to respond to the incentive of money.[17]

The statement, "I would be willing to do anything for money," doesn't apply to very many people. An employee may relate such things as the amount of skill and knowledge necessary to do the job well, the time and expense of attaining that skill and knowledge, and the status or prestige of the job to the amount of money he or she receives for job performance. Another important factor is equity in pay as it relates to other jobs and to other people on the same job. This is discussed later in this chapter.

Individual differences.   Any discussion of people's motives and wants should emphasize that each person is unique. He is different from all others in his wants. She is different in her heritage of size and strength, in dexterity and muscular coordination, in the quality of sight and hearing. Each is different from others in intellectual abilities and emotional makeup. To compound the differences, each person is further changed by life with his or her parents and the influence of friends. People are changed by all their experiences, education, and training. All the things in a person's life—plus the situation at the moment—enter into shaping his or her thinking about what is wanted out of life, how it will be obtained, and how much effort will be put into it.

People differ in their work aptitudes and abilities, in the work habits they have learned, in the pace they can maintain, in their susceptibility to boredom. They differ in their emotional stability and in the strength of their needs for security, autonomy, and affiliation. They differ in the strength of their motives for achievement.

People with a high need for achievement may be more risk-oriented and

---

[17] For studies of the money motive, see William F. Whyte, et al., *Money and Motivation* (New York: Harper & Row, Publishers, 1955), chap. 14.

willing to assume greater amounts of responsibility. They tend to set challenging but realistic goals for themselves and do the planning necessary to aid in the attainment of these goals. They want relatively rapid feedback on their performance in the form of promotions, money, and status, and they search for opportunities where there is more possible.

But people change. Physical changes add to or take away from their strength and energy. New experiences affect their way of looking at things. The footloose young fellow becomes the family breadwinner, looking for opportunities and needing more money. The person who started the job with such enthusiasm becomes bored with it as interests change, or dissatisfied with it if friends distinguish themselves in other fields. The woman who looked on her job as a fill-in until marriage starts considering it as a career when her friends are married and she chooses to remain single.

Considering the differences between people and the changes within a person during a lifetime, it becomes obvious that there is no simple formula for solving all the human problems at work. Supervisors find they can't treat all people alike, because the same treatment will bring a favorable response from some and an unfavorable response from others. They must take individual differences into account in fitting people to jobs, in making assignments, in praising, rewarding, criticizing, and disciplining.

When supervisors in a conference discuss individual differences and the treatment of people as individuals, some supervisor will usually say that the way to treat people is to follow the Golden Rule "Do unto others as you would have them do unto you." Some other supervisor usually answers, "How do you know the other person wants to be treated the way you want to be treated? If I treated the workers in my department that way, they'd get mad."

Personal problems of employees

Every supervisor knows there are problem employees—irresponsibles, troublemakers, crybabies, alcoholics. Some people never mature emotionally; they find and make problems. They have difficulty adjusting to life and to the demands of the job. Other people have temporary upsets in their emotional lives. They find some combinations of difficulties and frustrations just too much to handle at one time.

The alcoholic employee is a problem calling for expert help. He or she may be shy, withdrawn, and supersensitive. Problem drinkers may be overambitious perfectionists who are seeking escape from less-than-perfect conditions at home or on the job. Employees with alcohol, drug, marital and other emotional problems need professional help and should be put in contact with a person or an agency able to help them.

When an employee's personal problems are affecting his or her behavior and interfering with performance, it is up to the supervisor to do something about it. The supervisor may find that the employee's mental distress is caused by poor placement, insecurity, fear of getting hurt, gripes, grievances, resentments, and frustrations. Sometimes the employee can be helped over a low spot by changing job assignments, injecting some new interest into the job, or moving the person into a more congenial group. The supervisor may be able to let the employee know just how far the company is willing to go along with substandard performance resulting from off-the-job problems. Bringing the matter out into the open may give the troubled person some relief. Sometimes when the supervisor hears the problem, he or she can suggest avenues of assistance—for instance, if the employee is over his or her head in debt and doesn't know where to turn.

Sometimes the employee can be helped to arrive at a more accurate evaluation of his difficulties. The supervisor should not consider the solving of employee problems a personal responsibility. One can point out solutions, but the person who has to live with the solution should make the choice.

What people want from their jobs

Surveys have been made of the wants of people on jobs, out of jobs, applying for jobs, and quitting jobs. Some surveys were made by asking people to think of the things they desired from their jobs and to list them in the order of their importance. Other surveys used this information to compile "ready-made" lists of wants which the employees or the job applicants were asked to rank in importance to them. The following list was taken from several surveys.[18] People said they wanted:

Security.	Fair wages.
Work that is meaningful.	Freedom from arbitrary action.
Opportunity for advancement.	A voice in matters affecting them.
Recognition.	Congenial associates.
Competent leadership.	Satisfactory working conditions.

The most important thing to be remembered in studying a list of wants is that it does not represent a profile of the wants of any one person. It is simply a combination of many lists. A person would not list wants in the same order this year as he or she did five years ago. Quite possibly the things listed as most important are the things that he or she lacks or is dissatisfied with at the moment. A satisfied want seems to drop in importance until something threatens the satisfaction. The fact that wages and working conditions are so far down the list could mean that people were fairly well satis-

---

[18] For an analysis and compilation of a great number of surveys, see Frederick Herzberg, Bernard Mausner, Richard O. Peterson, and Dora F. Capwell, *Job Attitudes: Review of Research and Opinion* (Pittsburgh: Psychological Service of Pittsburgh, 1957). Herzberg's compilation found that security, intrinsic aspects of the job, and opportunity for advancement were in the one, two, three positions; wages were sixth.

fied with them at the time—that they were not burning issues. The fact that security, meaningful (or interesting) work, and opportunity for advancement were one, two, and three on the list may indicate that they were the things lacking in many jobs.

Frequently supervisors and managers have different perceptions of what their employees want than do the employees themselves. Many managers believe financial factors to be more important to employees than the employees do. Managers and supervisors should not close their minds to the ideas of their employees. Many are surprised to find their stereotyped views wrong after talking to groups of employees about their job desires.

It is important to remember that not all employees desire job satisfaction as it is commonly understood. Some people work because it is a socially acceptable practice, but their lives focus on need satisfactions away from the job. Such people do not expect much from their jobs, do not look for challenges, and are not too disappointed by so-called lack of opportunity. Needs are filled by family, travel, hobbies, community effort, and other activities not related to the job. The job is just an avenue to allow time and money for outside activities.

Equally important is the fact that job satisfaction is difficult to describe simply. Measures of job satisfaction are complex, and it is difficult to generalize from any one study. John Wanous and Edward Lawler, in a recent study on the measurement and meaning of job satisfaction, conclude:

> The data suggest that there probably are several types of feelings that people have which can be called satisfaction about their job. With respect to pay, for example, people may have a feeling that stems from how much they would like to earn and a feeling that stems from what they feel they should earn. Both of these feelings may be called feelings of pay satisfaction and, indeed, both probably do influence responses to a direct satisfaction rating. At this point, it would seem to be important to develop theories that explain both how these feelings came about and how they are related to a number of independent and dependent variables since they may be differentially related.
>
> As far as the measurement of satisfaction is concerned, the data suggest that there is no one best way to measure it. The "best" measure may depend upon what independent or dependent variable the satisfaction measure is to be related. It is likely that certain measures, because of the aspect of satisfaction they tap, are better related to certain dependent and independent variables than are others. The data also suggest that it is possible to measure satisfaction validly with different job facets. Satisfaction with the different facets has been shown to have differential correlations with various dependent variables just as the different ways of measuring satisfaction do. This would argue that theory and research are needed which map in detail the relationships among the different ways of measuring satisfaction, the various kinds of facet satisfaction, and a number of independent and dependent variables.[19]

---

[19] John P. Wanous and Edward E. Lawler, III, "Measurement and Meaning of Job Satisfaction," *Journal of Applied Psychology*, vol. 56, no. 2 (April 1972), pp. 104–5.

Security.   A breadwinner's need for security is most often expressed in terms of steady work and steady wages. The lack of job security plays havoc with people. The resultant worry interferes with learning a job and performing it. People who are insecure on the job will try to protect themselves in peculiar ways: They will resist changes, play it safe, pass the buck for responsibilities, refuse to take initiative, restrict production and manufacture, and pass along rumors.

Insecurity brought on by automation or threats of automation is reflected in featherbedding, conflicts over work standards, and demands for a shorter workweek.

The security that the supervisor can provide is the assurance that as long as the employee keeps on doing the job well, the employee's position is safe except for circumstances outside the supervisor's control. An employee needs to feel that continuing tenure on the job is the normal situation. Except for the few individuals who respond only to threats, the supervisor should not use fear as a motivator. The "heads will roll" and "one mistake and you're out" relationship is not the way to develop initiative and responsibility in subordinates. People need security and approval in their relationship with the boss before they can develop their abilities and give their best performance.

Work that is meaningful.   A job that is absorbing and challenging to one person may be a frustration to another. Professionals want jobs on which they can make a significant contribution to knowledge or to their own success and that of the company. Skilled workers want jobs that use their highest skills. People want a feeling of achievement from their work. The achievement motive may be the one that is most effective in sustaining high performance. People keep on achieving long after they have provided for their financial wants.

Many jobs have no meaning to the performers because no one took the time or trouble to explain to them the purpose of what they are doing. They don't know the ultimate use of the parts they are working on, the reasons for the methods, or the difficulties that will be caused by defective work.

Wherever possible, the supervisor should find ways of making work more meaningful so that employees can get some kind of satisfaction from mastery of the job. Designing jobs, fitting people to jobs, training people for jobs, and explaining the purpose of jobs are ways in which the supervisor can help subordinates find meaning in their work.

Opportunity to advance.   Whether or not people take advantage of the opportunity to advance, they like to feel that it is there. Lack of opportunity and dissatisfaction with pay are the two reasons most frequently given for changing jobs. They may not be the true reasons, but they look good on the next application blank. People don't want to burn their bridges behind them or label themselves as troublemakers or misfits; they need references for the next job.

Ambitious, upward-striving people certainly need to see an opportunity to advance. They are willing to prepare themselves for higher level jobs and to make present sacrifices for future gains. They desire the money, the status, the challenge, or the achievement that comes with advancement. Advancement is one of the incentives that drives them to put out extra effort, and they expect to get the advancement as recognition and reward for their efforts. Advancement, when it is received, is a spur to still higher effort. If the advancement does not come, employees may lose interest in the job, reduce their efforts, becomes embittered, or look elsewhere for a job. Professional employees are highly motivated to advance. They seek status not only in the company but also in the professional society and in their group of professional friends.

On the other hand, many employees who have reached the top of their salary classification continue to give devoted service. Many people reach a spot on the advancement ladder and wish to stay there because they have attained the height of their ambitions or because they have the job under control and feel comfortable at that level. Some people are not willing to put out the effort and make the personal sacrifices entailed in advancement; other enjoyments in life are more important to them. Some people are comfortable with their friends on the job and would be uncomfortable with the people on a higher level. (The socially mobile person may be one who doesn't make deep attachments and can shuck off old teammates and adjust readily to new ones.) Some people find a job they like and just want to stay on it.

In a unionized job, seniority, with its privileges and security, may become a substitute for promotion. Through seniority a person may be able to transfer to a job that is easier, cleaner, or "higher class" even though it may not involve higher pay. A work group may push for advancement in the form of improvements or concessions that represent evidence of getting ahead of another group.

Recognition.   The desire for recognition—for praise, appreciation, importance, prestige, and esteem—is a powerful drive in some people. The desire for distinction in the group or in the community can inspire a man to undertake responsibility for a project and to put tremendous effort into making it a success. The desire for prestige—when accompanied by the ability and energy to achieve it—can motivate a person to high performance.

Even if some people do not have a high drive for achievement, they still desire recognition and appreciation as individuals. They need recognition to bolster their belief in their own worth. Their dignity is affronted when they are addressed as "Hey you" or are considered as only numbers on an IBM card. If they cannot get attention in the form of approval, they may get it by being negative or aggressive.

The supervisor should try to help people achieve something worthwhile and then see that they get the credit for it. Glad-handing isn't enough. The supervisor should help them get recognition outside the department also—in the company newspaper, social committees, safety committees, athletics, and similar activities. The supervisor's special problem in giving recognition is to do it in a way that does not arouse the jealousy or ill will of the group. One person should not get all the credit for something accomplished by group effort. Credit given to one member must somehow be made to reflect credit on everybody.

Competent leadership. Employees have a stake in the job; their futures are tied to it. They have to rely on the leadership of the company to maintain a productive and profitable business that will survive and be able to provide steady work and good wages. The company leadership sets up the environment, the policies, the leadership climate, and the spirit of the organization within which employees and their immediate supervisors must operate. The company's policies and controls shape the attitudes and actions of its supervisors.

An employee's emotional state on the job is influenced to a great extent by supervisory attitudes and ability. An employee wants a boss who has the job under control and is able to plan and schedule the work so that deadlines can be met without frenzy. A person wants a boss who doesn't blow up under pressure or take it out on subordinates—a boss who is willing and able to spare them from unnecessary anxieties, frictions, pressures, and frustrations. The employee wants a boss who is not too fearful for his or her own security and can tolerate a few mistakes.

Fair wages and equity. The burning issue with wages is *fairness.* Is the pay in line with the status of the job? Is it as much as other groups are getting for work of this class and difficulty? Is it as much as other people are getting for like amount of effort and achievement? Is it more than people are getting for lower class jobs? There are traditional relationships between jobs in status and pay, and any disturbance of the accepted arrangement will arouse bitter resentment in the person or group that feels injured.

The supervisor should be close enough to subordinates to know their attitudes about the pay they are getting. The supervisor should get the information needed to handle rumors about the good wages that are being paid "for practically no work" in other departments and in other companies. If raises are based on the employee evaluation system, he or she should see that subordinates get their share. The supervisor should know the company's job evaluation plan and should explain it to subordinates.

If wages in the department are in line and the employees are complaining about them or quitting for jobs elsewhere, the supervisor should suspect that there is something else wrong with the job. If people are getting very little satisfaction from their work, money becomes more important to them as a means of buying off-the-job satisfactions. If the job is unpleasant, they want more money for putting up with it. If they feel pushed around, they'll push back with a money demand. Money is something concrete to complain about when personal satisfactions are lacking on the job.

One of the principal gripes employees have about pay relates to equity. As mentioned above, they want fair wages for the level of job, but their concept of fairness goes beyond this. In nonunion white-collar work, most employees are annoyed when their performance is not rewarded in direct relationship to its quality. Nothing bothers an individual more than to get the same raise as another employee when the other person is clearly not as good a performer. Supervisors who think they can keep everyone happy by spreading available raise money among all employees without clearly differentiating the amount relative to performance quality are sadly deluding themselves.

In this sense the employee is looking beyond the dollar amount alone and is using the size of raise as a status and recognition factor. Closely related is the practice of many companies of paying what the labor market requires for new, inexperienced employees and not maintaining an adequate pay differential for the employee who has been on the job for a year or more and is performing adequately or better.

Freedom from arbitrary action. Freedom from arbitrary action means that there is no favoritism, no discrimination, no prejudice, no preferential treatment for the in-group; it means there are no black sheep, no insiders or outsiders.

If employees feel they are victims of discrimination, they are in a frame of mind to put an unfavorable interpretation on every management action and communication. After they mull over grievances for a while, it may become almost an obsession. Resentment may erupt suddenly in undesirable behavior or unreasonable demands. The grievance procedure provides an outlet to drain off some of the ill will of an employee who feels victimized by an injustice.

Because some employees seem to find injustices where they don't exist— or at least were not intended—the supervisor must avoid even the appearance of favoritism. Employee evaluation, transfers, raises, promotions— when within the control of the supervisor—should be based on merit and on accomplishment. They must not be made on hunches, prejudices, or because the employee is a likable person. Whenever a promotion or a transfer is made, the reason should be explained, not only to the person being moved but also to those who thought they were in the running.

A voice in matters affecting them. Not everyone has strong needs for autonomy or for having a say about how things should be done on the job. Some employees are more comfortable doing what they are told; they don't want to get involved in anything that would increase their own risk on the job. Because of their personalities, their upbringing, and their work experiences, they prefer the tight-ship, no-nonsense kind of supervision. They are willing to let the boss make the decisions, make the mistakes, and hold the responsibility.

At the other extreme are the scientific and professional employees. They want to select their own projects, go about them in their own way, and be freed from organizational regulations and controls.

In between the two extremes are the great numbers of employees who know they must trade some of their freedom for employment but who still want some say about things that concern them and their jobs. They are unable to accept the idea that a job is nothing more than doing what they are told. Much of what looks like unreasonableness or stubbornness on the part of such employees is their reaction to feeling pushed around—having to take it or leave it. They want to feel that they are offering their cooperation freely. They don't want anyone telling them what to do if they already know. On the other hand, they become upset if they don't know what they should be doing and can't get the help they want from the supervisor. Their jobs put them in a position of dependence; yet they feel that independence is essential to their self-respect.

Congenial associates. People in an office or a shop form a community. Since they have to be together on the job for so much of their lives, they don't want to be annoyed by one another all the time. They want to be with people like themselves—people with whom they can share their plans, jokes, and ideas. They want teammates who will pitch in with them when the going is rough, who will lend a helping hand, a sympathetic ear, or a pat on the shoulder. When people who must work together are able to get along well, there are fewer frictions on the job; people catch and correct mistakes for one another; they look out for one another's safety. People who are accepted into the group are happier on the job and less apt to be absent or quit. Being a member of a congenial group may make up for some of the lack of interest or challenge in a repetitive job.

There are a few people who want to work by themselves, to mind their own business, and to be let alone. Sometimes they are let alone, but at other times they may be made the butt of jokes or horseplay. Often these loners do a better-than-average job, and the supervisor might wish there were more like them if they could be placed on jobs where they would not have to work with others.

Satisfactory working conditions. An employee's satisfaction with working conditions depends to a great extent upon background, education, and expectations. And it depends a whole lot on what kind of conditions other people in the company are having to put up with. There is a certain satisfaction in job mastery, but it doesn't extend to putting up with unnecessary inconveniences and hazards. Certain types of minor annoyances and discomforts make people think that the company doesn't care what happens to them. Things like unrepaired water fountains and air conditioners or hot water and soap cut out to save expenses can become gripes of major proportions. Unfairness or lack of consideration in scheduling hours of work can distress an employee to the point of looking for another job.

The supervisor can show concern for the group by making the department clean, orderly, and safe. The supervisor can see that things are kept in repair and can go to bat for subordinates to correct conditions that bother them.

Motivation and morale

Morale is the spirit of an organization. It is the state of mind of employees—individually and as a group. It is the way they think and feel about the work itself, the working conditions, the supervisor, co-workers, the company and its management, the fairness of the pay, and the prospects of a steady job.

Morale is a measure of the satisfaction employees are getting in their attempts to satisfy their needs. It is a measure of their confidence in the job as something in which they can invest their most precious asset—their futures. It is an indicator of the degree to which they are getting what they want from the job. Or, more importantly, it is a measure of their confidence that in the future they will get what they want from the job.

If the above description of morale on the job is analyzed, it can be seen that there is some relationship between morale and motivation. The factors which, if satisfied, motivate employees also lead to the development of higher morale among these employees. High motivation does not always mean high morale, but it is reasonable to assume that employees who are highly motivated will tend to have high morale more often than not. Problems arise in discussions of morale and motivation because of the lack of concrete understanding of the term "morale." William G. Scott describes three approaches to the problem of morale definition:

1. The *"classical" approach* stems from the "needs psychology" school. Personal determinants of morale are emphasized in this approach. Needs are visualized as emanating from the ultimate problem of human survival. Thus, satisfaction of basic needs is seen as a primary morale factor.
2. The *psychological approach* stresses the hierarchical and dynamic nature of needs. When basic needs are satisfied, then higher motives, such as accomplishment, recognition, and participation, emerge to dominate an individual's behavior. High morale from this point of view results from a continual satisfaction of the so-called higher motives.
3. The *social approach* to morale is a product of the work of Elton Mayo and the Hawthorne researchers. Morale is considered as a social phenomenon caused by the strong desire of man to be associated with his fellow man. Thus morale is determined by the social situation at work.[20]

Determinants of morale

Morale must be considered as both an individual and a group attitude. On an individual basis, morale has frequent ups and downs. One's morale goes up as one sees prospects of getting ahead on the job; it goes down when the prospects grow dim. It goes up when there is an opportunity to show what the employee can do and get recognition for doing it. It goes down when the

---

[20] William G. Scott, *Organization Theory, A Behavioral Analysis for Management* (Homewood, Ill.: Richard D. Irwin, 1967), pp. 293–94. © 1967 by Richard D. Irwin, Inc.

plums go to someone else and the employee's own role and opportunities are curtailed. It goes up when the employee achieves status and prestige; it goes down when a technological development or organizational change pulls the rug from under the employee. It goes up when things are going well in the individual's personal life; it goes down when the situation fails to measure up to expectations.

Morale on a group basis is less volatile. In a company that has maintained good relations with its employees over a long period of time, there is a backlog of goodwill that supports group morale through some minor grievances and temporary dislocations. Morale has a kind of momentum that prevents it from reversing itself promptly with each company action. If it is on a steady upward trend, it can absorb some minor jolts. As long as the unfavorable conditions don't last too long, the flare-ups they cause are just temporary disturbances. When employees have confidence in the company's good intentions, morale sinks rather slowly under stress and can regain its losses if management doesn't delay too long in taking remedial action.

It is only when pressures have gone on for considerable time that employees lose their optimism and suffer a collapse of morale. Then there may be a rash of absences. Or the low morale may show up in a less spectacular way in apathy, malingering, sloppy work, waste of materials, destruction of property, disregard for the rules, hostility, and unwillingness to carry out orders or to cooperate.

Once the employees have lost faith in the company and their morale is down, even trivial events or rumors can send it plunging lower. Whatever the company does is suspect. Even significant concessions made by management get at best a grudging acceptance. Employees whose experience has taught them not to trust the company are slow to change their attitudes; so the company's job of rebuilding morale is a slow and discouraging one. The alternative to rebuilding morale is to operate on a police state basis.

Some companies make morale surveys in order to measure the state of morale and prevent a collapse. The surveys yield some enlightening statistics on employee dissatisfactions—information that would not otherwise finds its way to upper management to influence policy making. Just providing the survey as a channel through which employees can complain serves to improve morale. Some employees won't complain otherwise, because they don't want to be labeled as troublemakers. But they need a channel through which to express their grievances. The channel can be the opinion survey, a formal grievance procedure, or a boss who will listen to gripes, recognize their bearing on motivation and morale, and take action.

Development of high morale

There are several factors which promote high morale in an organization. The focal point is the job and its importance to the employee. The job must be difficult and interesting enough to challenge the individual and offer promotion opportunities. Performance must be measured objectively and the individual rewarded in direct relation to that performance.

Co-workers and supervisors also have a significant role in morale development. Since people spend so much time at work, it is obvious that the people with whom they work are important to social interaction and the creation of a climate for high morale. Competent leadership and congenial co-workers aid in the development of an employee's opinion about the job and the company. The company's reputation in the community and the manner in which it treats employees also contribute to the level of employee morale. The amount of information employees receive about company operations, their jobs, and the willingness of management to share information and encourage upward communication can go a long way toward making employees feel they are truly important contributors to company effectiveness.

Summary

Managers and supervisors find that human relations problems occupy much of their time, and the successful solution to these problems can have considerable career impact. Understanding human behavior is enhanced by consideration of the contributions of scientific management, the Hawthorne studies, and much other research. This research contributes to present thinking about organizations as social systems that require effective job design, team building, and equitable work assignment.

Motivation theories developed by Maslow, Vroom, Argyris, Likert, McClelland, Herzberg, and others all contribute to knowledge about the "why" of human behavior. An understanding of these theories should help supervisors and managers create a more effective climate for job performance.

Most of the fringe benefit programs in industry are maintenance programs designed to offer rewards which the employee can utilize off the job. Not too many organizations have turned their attention to what may be the most fruitful source of motivation and high morale—the work itself. The supervisor should recognize the limitations of money as a motivator. There are few economic people who are solely motivated by economic rewards. Individual differences, job tensions, personal problems, and group relations all contribute to how humans feel about their jobs. People want a variety of things from their jobs, and it is difficult to categorize neatly the wants of a particular individual. Among the things they want are: security, meaningful work, advancement opportunity, recognition, competent leadership, equitable compensation, congenial associates, participation in decision making, freedom from arbitrary action, and satisfactory working conditions.

A relationship has been established between motivation and morale, though morale is difficult to define. Essentially morale should be considered as both an individual and a group attitude. There are many things that contribute to individual and group morale. These are: the job itself, the level of group productivity, co-workers, the supervisor, the organization, individual pride, age, background, education, and the effectiveness of communication.

The successful development and maintenance of high morale among a group of people with varying backgrounds and aspirations and differing reasons for working is a most challenging assignment for the supervisor and manager.

CASE 10–1

Because of a recent surplus of liberal arts college graduates the company has been hiring several to work as stenographer-typists. These people have taken these positions largely because no more attractive positions have been available. During the same period a similar number of steno-typists have been hired who are high school graduates with secretarial training. Both groups have progressed to secretarial positions, but the young people with college degrees have been able to take on additional responsibilities of various kinds. Many of them have worked on special projects as research assistants, and they have written excellent reports.

These people have been made administrative assistants and are now doing what is called "professional work" in the company. These positions have more responsibility and higher pay. The people hired as steno-typists with high school diplomas have not progressed as rapidly as their college graduate counterparts, and this has caused a morale problem. Many of the high school graduates believe they have performed more effectively as secretaries than the college graduates, and they can't understand why these people were promoted to higher level jobs.

1. *What explanation can be given to the high school graduate secretaries?*
2. *Could job enrichment for them help?*
3. *Should some high school graduates be given similar opportunities?*
4. *Should they be encouraged to go to college at night to qualify for higher level positions?*
5. *Should the company restrict its hiring of steno-typists to either college graduates or high school graduates?*

CASE 10–2

A technician had been temporarily hired by the company to help with a special project that the electronic data processing section was developing. He was researching various programs and was given access to all of the equipment. The keypunch machines and printout machines, along with other related equipment, were located in a soundproof room separated from the rest of the office so that the noise level would not disturb other employees.

One day the technician was waiting for a printout of some data, and he happened to notice several speakers attached to the wall at various places just below the ceiling. He walked over to one of them, saw a volume control knob, and turned it up. Music poured forth and the technician wondered why none of the speakers were turned on, since the music was very pleasant. His answer came in very short order when one of the employees told him to turn off the speaker. The request was so vehement that the technician questioned the employee about his very negative reaction to the music. The employee replied, "We have to listen to the noise in here; we don't have to listen to the music."

1. *How can you account for the negative reaction to the piped-in music?*
2. *Should the employees have been asked if they wanted music before it was installed?*
3. *To what extent did the isolation of these employees contribute to their attitude about the music?*
4. *What can management do to offset this attitude, recognizing the fact that the noise level of the machines requires isolation from the rest of the office?*

CASE 10–3

Henry Barrett was called to the personnel vice president's office and offered the opportunity to spend two weeks at a sensitivity training session to be held at a conference center some 50 miles away from the office. The company had been involved in this program for over a year, and Henry had wondered when he would be asked. It was common knowledge that even though accepting the offer was voluntary no one had turned it down. Barrett didn't particularly care for the idea, but he didn't want to be the first manager to say no.

Barrett supervised a department of 35 people, 20 of whom were technical salesmen and the others various kinds of support personnel. Barrett reported to a vice president, and they differed in leadership style, so there was conflict from time to time. Barrett did a good job, however; his department always exceeded its quota and labor turnover was low. Although Barrett's boss was more participative, while Barrett was autocratic, the boss could not fault him on results.

Barrett accepted the offer and on the following Monday he was at the conference center for the opening session. Much to his surprise, so was his boss. The group was made up of vice presidents and department heads, all from the headquarters office. Barrett decided to go along with the effort as it was outlined. Over the two-week period he and his boss had several clashes, and at one of the sessions Barrett told off the vice president without mincing words. After all, he thought, wasn't this what a T-group was all about? You were supposed to be honest and open up to let the other person know how he affected you.

After the program was over, there was no contact between Barrett and his boss for a week and then contact was decidedly on the cool side. Barrett wondered about his career and if he should have behaved as honestly as he had in the T-group.

1. *Should a company have sensitivity training which includes superiors and subordinates in the same session?*
2. *How can Barrett reestablish an amicable working relationship with his boss?*
3. *Should he ask for a transfer?*
4. *Under the circumstances, should Barrett have behaved less openly at the sensitivity session?*

CASE 10–4

Jake Wilson has worked for the company for several years. You have supervised him for the last five years, and he has been one of your best producers. The company is a life insurance firm, and salesmen are compensated on a commission basis. As a branch manager your pay is partially determined by how well the salesmen working for you perform. You are pleased with Jake's effort, since he has beaten the quota for the last three years; this has made you look good and fattened your bonus as well.

Jake has two children and he wanted both to be professionals. The two sons have both completed college; one went to law school and the other son graduated six months ago, in June, as a dental surgeon. You are studying sales figures for your office, and you note that Jake's production has shown a steady decline since June.

You call him in to your office and in reply to your question about his performance he states, "The boys are on their own now. I don't have to work as hard, since my wife and I have simple tastes. Giving them a good education was my goal and I achieved it—now it's time to slow down."

1. *How can you solve this problem?*
2. *Can a person like Jake be persuaded to maintain his previous high level of performance?*
3. *In this kind of situation, should the employee be allowed to determine how hard he will work? Why? Why not?*

CASE 10–5

Ted Foster had just retired after 35 years of service with the company. During his last five years he served as a section head, supervising 15 employees, including Elsie Prince. Ted's last year on the job was characterized by considerable coasting on his part, and discipline in the section became very lax. Considerable freedom developed about lateness, lunch hours, coffee breaks, and quitting time.

Elsie Prince has been promoted to replace Ted Foster. She has noticed the laxity of the past year but has also noticed that, while several employees do abuse their privileges, the entire work group has high morale and its labor turnover is well below the company average.

Elsie is 28 years old and is career-oriented. She is married, has no children, and feels she has a very good future with the company. This promotion has given her further indication of her opportunities. She feels she must establish firmer control over the employees, yet she is worried about the effect her efforts will have on the group.

1. *How can Elsie enforce company rules and still maintain the same level of morale?*
2. *Should she seek help from her superior?*
3. *Should she continue the pattern of laxity established by her predecessor, in view of the low labor turnover and high morale?*
4. *What positive things can Elsie do to offset the reestablishment of company rules?*

CASE 10–6

Kay Miller was in charge of a secretarial pool in the executive offices of a large company. While each person under her supervision was assigned to one or more executives, Kay was responsible for work assignment, training, performance evaluation, selection, and general supervision of the executive secretaries. Kay had few supervisory problems, since assignment to the executive secretarial pool was considered a privilege and carried considerable status in the company.

One woman, however, was getting to be a problem. Florence was an excellent secretary who performed her work flawlessly. Because of this, Kay had assigned her to the company's financial vice president, who was very demanding and had a high level of expectation for all of her subordinates. She had been very pleased with Florence, and frequently complimented Kay on her wise assignment.

The financial vice president took frequent trips to visit company offices in other sections of the country. She also came in late several mornings a month because she attended meetings away from the company premises.

Kay began to notice that Florence also came in late on the days the executive vice president was at a meeting or out of town. She also took longer lunch hours when the financial vice president was absent. After several of the other people started grumbling, Kay called Florence into a conference room and spoke to her about her lax punctuality. Florence asked if the financial vice president had complained. Kay replied that she hadn't because she didn't even know about Florence's infractions of company rules. Florence then said that as far as she was concerned the financial vice president was her boss, and she was satisfied with her work, because she frequently told her so. Kay tried to establish the fact that she was Florence's supervisor, but Florence replied that until the financial vice president complained she would not change her behavior. Kay wondered what to do next, because she knew that the financial vice president was very pleased with Florence's work, and she didn't have another secretary as capable.

1. *Can Kay effectively discipline Florence under the circumstances?*
2. *Should she speak to the financial vice president about Florence?*
3. *Why would Florence feel justified in coming in late and breaking other rules?*
4. *How can Kay avoid similar problems in the future?*

CASE 10–7

You are the supervisor of the assembly department of a company manufacturing electronics equipment. You have 50 women doing assembly work, most of which is routine. About eight months ago the company received an order for some special and rather complicated equipment. You selected three of your best workers to handle the assembly work on this order. You explained to them that the job would be tough and that they would have to work apart from the rest of the department. The job turned out to be a nightmare; the engineers hardly waited for the solder to cool before they changed their minds. Work had to be done over, time and again. The big bosses were always dropping in to observe the progress of the work. The women worked under continuous pressure until the job was completed about two months ago. They appeared happy and took no time off.

When the workers returned to their old jobs, they were the center of attention, telling their experiences. Now things have settled down into the old routine. However, the three women seem to be listless in doing simple assembly work. You had to seat them far enough apart to put an end to their continuous chatting about things that happened on the special job.

A while back, the three women started coming in to work late together. You reprimanded them. Now they are beginning to take days off together.

1. *Why did the workers appear to be happy when working under the strain of the special job?*
2. *Why are they not adjusting to the old routine?*
3. *What steps might you have been able to take to help them make the adjustment?*
4. *How are you going to handle the absentee problem?*

CASE 10-8

Lorna Burk is a young administrative assistant in your department. She had been showing considerable promise, but recently her work effort has deteriorated and she has become quite defensive and fearful. Where before she had ambition, now she doesn't want to take any risks and seems to have lost all of her self-confidence.

Your experience over the years has led you to believe that such a radical change in behavior must have been caused by some drastic experience. You call her in to your office and start talking about her work. When confronted with your recognition of her poor performance, Lorna becomes upset and gives you the reasons. She has just separated from her husband after five years of marriage and one child. She tells you that her husband had started drinking excessively a year ago, frequently beat her and the child, and stopped giving her any money. She is now very worried about her job because of her need to support herself and her child, and the uncertainty of her future is also worrying her considerably.

1. *How can you motivate Lorna to perform up to her past ability?*
2. *Should you get involved in her personal problems?*
3. *Can you do anything to restore her self-confidence?*

CASE 10-9

Paul Nathan was president of his own company, a medium-sized concern enjoying moderate success in a very competitive industry. Quite naturally Paul was very enthusiastic about the firm's prospects, and he kept telling all of his employees how successful they would be if they stayed on his team.

Nathan was generally the first to arrive each morning, usually at 7:00 A.M. By the time the rest of the group arrived at 9 o'clock, he had frequently dictated several letters and memoranda, and his secretary was expected to transcribe these immediately. He frequently reminded her and other employees that he had done a day's work before they arrived. He also stayed late each day, frequently starting a meeting with some of the executives at 4:00 or 4:30 P.M. These meetings usually lasted well past the normal quitting time.

Because of his great interest in the company, Paul Nathan made it a practice to work on Saturdays, though that day was not a part of the normal work week. His efforts on that day also produced a large number of memoranda, and he frequently asked his secretary to come in on Saturday to transcribe his output from the dictating machine. Willingness to come in on Saturdays or the lack of it on the part of the company's executives was used by Paul Nathan as a rather significant standard to measure their degree of enthusiasm for their jobs and the welfare of the company. Because his own work habits included the devotion of so much time to the business, he felt that all senior executives should follow the same pattern. Of the ten executives concerned, three did not mind following Nathan's lead. The others grudgingly came in one or two Saturdays a month, and they resented the time spent. Their particular criticism centered on the general lack of accomplishment and the fact that much time was spent merely satisfying Paul Nathan's ego. None of the executives had any stock in the company, although they were involved in profit sharing on gross revenues in addition to their salaries.

Quite naturally, those executives who came in every Saturday received an inordinate amount of praise from Nathan, and the others were keenly aware of the need to demonstrate enthusiasm and dedication. Nevertheless they felt it was unfair to be measured by the amount of time expended on the job rather than by what was accomplished. They believed it necessary to spend time away from the firm and that their families deserved a portion of this time. Paul Nathan was aware of the feelings of most of his executives, and he claimed that no one was pressured to work on Saturdays or any evening of the week for that matter.

1. *Is Paul Nathan realistic in his desire for executive performance?*
2. *Can the chief executive and owner of a company expect the same amount of dedication and enthusiasm that he has?*
3. *What can the president of this company do to change the attitude of his immediate subordinates?*
4. *What can the executives do to change Paul Nathan's approach to performance evaluation?*

CASE 10–10

You graduated from college a year ago and were taken into a company to be trained for a supervisory position. You are a hard worker and anxious to move up in the ranks of management. After the first six months of the company's junior executive training course, your work is recognized, and you are given a supervisory job as part of your executive training.

Three assistants are under you, and it is necessary for you to work very closely with them. These assistants are much older than you and have been with the company for a number of years. From the very start you run into difficulties with your oldest assistant, John Brown. He is lazy, and he always changes your orders in carrying out his assigned tasks. When you speak to him about work in front of the other employees, he always has the comeback that he knows what is to be done and that in years past it was always done differently. To avoid his back talk, you give most of his work to the other assistants or do it yourself.

After a while you get tired of Brown's behavior. You do some discreet inquiring to find out if he was always that way, and you learn that years ago he was in the private employ of the owners of the concern and he is sti' well liked by them. The other supervisors have always stayed clear of him.

Your boss lets you know that he will have nothing to do with the situation. If you go over his head and complain, it will not look good for you, because Brown has been working in the plant for ten years with never a complaint against him. You feel that this is a test of your supervisory ability, and you want to do something about it.

1. *How might Brown be viewing the situation?*
2. *How might your boss be viewing the situation?*
3. *How do you view the situation?*
4. *What might be some of the mistakes you are making?*
5. *How should you go about disciplining Brown?*
6. *What must have been wrong with the way the previous supervisor handled Brown?*

Chapter 11

Learning objectives

○ To develop an understanding of the need for training and the desirability of it being a continuous process in an organization

○ To become aware of the orientation and induction of new employees and its importance to effective performance

○ To understand the evolving nature of the work force and the process of developing training programs to meet their needs

○ To become aware of the learning process and its relationship to training

Managing human resources: Training and orientation

Major topics

What is training?

Induction and orientation.

The new employee and the personnel department.

The new employee and the supervisor.

The new employee and the group.

The induction procedure.

The young adult's first job.

On-the-job training.

Uncovering training needs.

Principles of learning and techniques of training.

Choosing a trainer.

The four-step method of job training.

Special training programs.

Evaluating training programs.

As indicated in the previous chapter, motivated employees are more capable of performing well on their jobs. But motivation is not enough. To do the job efficiently and have the opportunity to grow, employees must have the knowledge, skills, and techniques necessary to maximize their motivation. This can be accomplished by well-planned orientation of new employees. Once these people are on the job, there must be properly designed training programs to develop employees into effective job performers and to maintain that effectiveness as jobs change and employees grow. The increasing complexity of our society and the rapid changes occurring no longer allow the luxury of long apprentice periods with employees patiently waiting years for promotion. Labor statistics indicate that about three fourths of the quits are people with less than six months of service with an organization. These are people who become discouraged or disillusioned before they take the time to put down any roots. A highly mobile work force and relative ease in obtaining skilled jobs add to the problem. When the costs of such turnover are added to the costs of having a poorly trained work force, the need for effective orientation and training becomes obvious.

The training of employees has broad implications for any organization that undertakes such a task on a wide scale. A number of large companies, as well as governmental agencies, hospitals, schools, and other organizations in our society, have found that the skills available in the labor market simply do not meet their needs. Many of these organizations have recognized that employee training has to be a continuous process. Gone are the days when the new employee could be turned over to an experienced one to be given haphazard instructions in rapid sequence, observe the job for a short time, and then do it. In short, learning by trial and error has been recognized as too costly and new employees then have to be convinced that the organization they have joined is interested enough in their future to train them properly for the job they are supposed to do.

Employee training and development has grown to be a significant factor in business organizations. Estimates of the annual cost in business and industry is in the billions of dollars. Many companies have been founded which specialize in the preparation of packaged programs of audio and visual materials, including films and video tapes, for all types of subjects. Then there are thousands of consultants who serve clients in various capacities, from the design of programs and preparation of materials to the actual instructional process. There are also many companies producing hardware for training such as projectors, audio- and videotape recorders, television cameras and other camera equipment, visual aids, and a myriad of other products to assist in the training process. In short, employee training is big business.

What is training?

Training is the continuous systematic development of all employees in an organization. This means on all levels of management, supervisory and nonsupervisory positions, in all the skills, knowledge, and attitudes necessary for the optimum performance of these positions. Training is a neverending task, because people change and jobs change and supervisors must keep people fitted to jobs and jobs fitted to people. This is necessary if they are to get high performance from them and they are to get satisfaction from their jobs.

Rationale for training.   A primary concern of professional management should be the development of employee interest in job assignments. An employee who is highly motivated and interested in the job will more than likely take pride in the work and be more productive. Of even greater importance are some hard facts which the managements of many organizations have had to face.

Rapidly changing technology in both factories and offices, coupled with an affluent society, has created shortages of skilled labor. Many young people of the type who entered the labor market as high school graduates years ago are now going to colleges, junior colleges, and universities. In many areas of the country, the failure of educational institutions to prepare people properly for the world of work has added to the problem. The pressures of labor shortages, government, and a growing awareness of many organizations of their responsibility in our society have accelerated the entrance of various underqualified members of our society into the work force. These factors, among others, have caused many organizations to undertake comprehensive programs of employee training and development. Courses in good grooming, computer programming, English, arithmetic, spelling, reading, typing, shorthand, and a myriad of other skills and techniques are common in a growing number of companies and other organizations.

Management has found that there are not enough skilled people to go around and those that are employed are given the training necessary to perform adequately on open jobs. In terms of numbers, training needs are most apparent among new employees or those just starting out on a new job. The problem is somewhat more difficult with employees already on the payroll.

Some people become unsuited to their jobs for reasons of health, accidents, aging, or change of interests. Or the jobs may change to the extent that the employee is having to struggle too hard just to keep up. People who are unsuited to their type of work may be able to perform well on some other job.

A person who has been on a job for a while may resent being told that performance is inadequate, methods slipshod, and that he or she—and nobody else—needs training. One way to get around this type of resistance to training is to have short refresher courses periodically for everybody. The instruction could combine job methods with procedures or with safety and housekeeping. Such a plan is good for the sick and not bad for the well, in that a refresher course offers the supervisor a definite time and opportunity to introduce improvements in methods and techniques.

The supervisor must provide training when production schedules expand and contract, and people are shifted around as a result. Training is called for when employees get transfers, when they are upgraded, and when they are promoted. Ambitious people want to keep developing and achieving, and they are willing to put the effort into learning new jobs. Training is called for when the supervisor decides to delegate some of the routine responsibilities to subordinates and when he or she is preparing subordinates to be able to operate under general supervision. Training is called for when jobs are enlarged or enriched and when employees rotate from job to job in order to substitute for one another during absences and vacations.

Training is called for when scientific discoveries result in innovations in products, processes, and equipment. The age of automation is accelerating change at a rate that, it is predicted, will displace a worker three times during that person's work life and make it necessary to prepare three times for some other kind of work. Training problems of these proportions should turn the supervisor's attention to the emotional impact of change upon people. The supervisor should develop an interest in the principles of learning and techniques of training to be used in preparing people to undertake new jobs.

A continuous process.   Because of the growing recognition that training must be a continuous process, many companies have made considerable investments in the training function. The comprehensive programs mentioned earlier require trainers and physical facilities. Training has moved from its status as an ancillary activity to one which has become an integral part of a well-managed organization's functioning. This has caused these organizations to give careful attention to the training function, and several new thoughts and ideas have been developed. Gordon Lippitt lists several trends in his book, *Organization Renewal:*

A trend toward a focus on improved performances rather than on increased individual knowledge.

A trend to deal with situations rather than individuals.

A trend to see training as the way management gets its job done rather than as a function of a department in the organization.

A trend toward building up in-house capabilities rather than dependence on outside experts.

A trend toward insistence on evaluation of the results of training rather than accepting rosy reports on faith.

A trend toward designing learning that will focus on learning-how-to-learn.

A trend toward training that is based on action-learning rather than on one-way communication.

A trend toward training that provides reinforcement and follow-up experience for trainees rather than "graduating" them from a training program.

A trend toward dependence more on the learning to be self-motivated by the learner rather than imposed on the learner by the trainers.

A trend for training to be goal-oriented rather than a vague assurance that it will be "good for you."

A trend toward greater homogeneity in the persons being trained.

A trend toward emphasis on the importance of organizational climate as an essential factor affecting change.[1]

The above list may not be all-inclusive, but it certainly demonstrates that the thinking about training has become far more critical. Training is now recognized as a vital factor in sound organizational growth and development and very much a part of effective human resource planning, a topic covered in Chapter 12.

Training: A systems approach. The foregoing discussion gives strong support for applying systems thinking to the training process. As mentioned in Chapter 2, if the organization is a total system, one of the ways of keeping that system functioning effectively is by having capable, well-trained employees with the updated skills and knowledge necessary for efficient job performance on all levels of the organization. Any weakness in this area will make the total system (organization) less effective. Figure 11–1 illustrates a continuous training system.

Induction and orientation

Essentially, induction and orientation programs are developed for new employees, although, as will be discussed later, there is a need for induction of transferred and promoted employees. The need for these programs arises from the management's desire that a new employee learn as much as possible about the organization in a short period of time, to enhance the employee's adjustment to the new environment. As we all know, first impressions can be quite important, and they are made wehther or not a management plans them. New employees will inevitably face disappoint-

Figure 11–1
A continuous training system

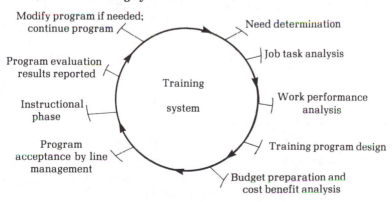

[1] Gordon L. Lippitt, *Organization Renewal* (New York: Appleton-Century-Crofts, 1969), p. 210.

ments and problems on their jobs. Some co-workers will go out of their way to convince the newcomer that a mistake was made in joining the company. The induction and orientation program should help build a reserve of positive knowledge about the organization and develop a useful frame of reference against which to judge the varied impressions employees will receive in their early days with the company. The high incidence of first-year labor turnover is another powerful reason for a well-planned orientation program. Naturally, some of the turnover cannot be prevented when employees can easily find other jobs if they are disappointed. Some turnover takes place at company request, because all new hires do not succeed in their new jobs. But many employees who leave in their first year of employment could have developed into valuable and effective staff members if more attention had been given to their orientation and initial training.

A well-planned induction and orientation program can materially assist management in the development of a uniform approach to the understanding of company policies, procedures, and rules and thereby aid the supervisor in the handling of his subordinates.

"There's always a place in our organization for a fine, compassionate human being—but he must have the killer instinct, too."

Reprinted by permission The Wall Street Journal

Inducting a new employee should be as thorough as possible.

The new employee and the personnel department

Getting employees started off right is a two-part program: first, the personnel department introduces the employee to the company, and second, the supervisor introduces the individual to the work group and to the job. The personnel department's part in induction begins at the time the applicant is accepted for employment. The personnel interviewer usually gives the person a booklet or employees' handbook, typically containing the following information:

History of the company.	Rules of conduct.
Activities of the company.	Safety rules.
Personnel policies.	Employee benefits.
Employee activities.	Education benefits.
Career opportunities.	Vacation policy.
Leaves of absence.	Holidays.
Grievance procedure.	Profit sharing.

Other pertinent company policies.

The personnel interviewer goes over this information with the new employee, explaining the various points and giving whatever other information will help the person feel better acquainted with the company as a whole. More comprehensive programs are carried out by many organizations. The personnel department usually develops and implements these programs. They frequently take a half-day or a day, although some companies have programs which take several days. A program for a comprehensive induction and orientation program is shown in Figure 11–2. Such programs are given as frequently as is necessary so that all new hires will be exposed to the program.

Some companies include a plant tour or headquarters tour as part of the induction process. Others feel that this type of tour has little meaning for a new employee and either do not have such a tour or carry it out after the employee has been with the organization for several months. The end of the probationary period is frequently considered an appropriate time because it is felt that the new employee will know enough about the company at this time and the tour will be more interesting. If the tour is carried out after the employee has some experience with the company, the flow of the work is often stressed to demonstrate to the employee how the various functions take place and what contribution the work makes to the entire process.

Several organizations use films depicting the history and accomplishments of the enterprise as part of the orientation. In some companies the films are professionally made, while in others they may be produced by the training department and consist of color slides depicting important aspects of the firm's activities. Visual aids enhance the program, and many firms include various types of audiovisual aids to cover such topics as grooming, fringe benefits, safety, and activities.

An induction program should, of course, be tailored and timed to fit the needs of the specific company. The content of the program should be evaluated periodically against the rate of turnover, the disciplinary records and accidents of new people, and any information gleaned from exit interviews.

The personnel department's portion of the induction program may take place a day or so before the new employee reports for work. From there on, induction is the responsibility of the supervisor. He or she must integrate the new person into the department and into the work group.

Figure 11–2

XYZ Corporation, Personnel Department
New Employee Orientation Outline

Time: Five hours

Topic	*Speaker*
A. Welcome to company	Personnel director
1. Purpose of orientation	
2. Each employee introduces self, indicating background and assignment	
3. Greetings	Senior manager
B. The personnel department	Assistant personnel director
1. Functions of personnel department	
2. Lateness and absenteeism	
3. Work schedule	
4. Time sheets or cards	
5. Payroll deductions	
6. Time off and leaves of absence	
C. Company benefit program	Benefits manager
1. Holidays and vacations	
2. Hospitalization insurance	
3. Major medical insurance	
4. Life insurance	
5. Disability insurance	
6. Pension plan	
7. Profit sharing	
D. Safety	Safety manager
1. Company safety record	
2. Safety equipment	
3. Importance of safety	
E. Compensation program	Compensation manager
1. Job analysis	
2. Job descriptions and specifications	
3. Wage and salary reviews	
4. Performance evaluation	
5. Overtime	
F. Education and training	Training director
1. Tuition remission plan	
2. Company training programs	
3. Employee eligibility	
4. Promotion from within policy	
G. Suggestion program	Chairperson of suggestion committee
1. Nature of awards	
2. Eligibility for awards	
3. Reasons for program	
H. Employee activities and recreation	Chairperson of employee activities committee
1. Athletic teams	
2. Hobby clubs	
3. Longevity and service awards	
4. Other activity programs	
5. Charity drives	
I. Company history	Assistant personnel director

The new employee and the supervisor

The supervisor's first contact with a new employee is usually in the application interview—a time when the applicant is exuding self-confidence and doing a selling job (selling his or her services). After the newcomer closed the deal and is told when to report for work, he or she starts to worry. Quite a change comes over the person while waiting to go on the job. The newcomer has time to think it over and ask himself a lot of questions: Was I wise to change from the old job? Will I be able to handle the new job? What kind of people will they be? What will my boss really be like? What are my chances of getting ahead of the others already established on the job? Or my chances of just getting along with them?

The more the employee thinks about these things, the less sure he or she is about the new job. As a result, the morning the new employee reports for work, instead of being a self-confident seller of services, the individual is worried about what he or she has gotten into.

The supervisor now has the selling job to do by describing the company as a good place to work. The supervisor is selling the performance standards as necessary and attainable—something that the new employee is accepting as part of the contract to work. The supervisor is selling the working conditions, the rules, the requirements for quality and safety, and the company's techniques for improving methods and keeping down costs, the opportunities offered in the job—or perhaps the security and congenial work associates.

The supervisor is also demonstrating interest as someone who will be concerned with the employee's welfare and success and will provide the guidance and training to make that success possible.

A person starting on a job is interested, receptive, and eager to cooperate. He or she welcomes attention from the supervisor, accepts suggestions and constructive criticism. The newcomer is open to ideas and in favor of improvements, because he or she has no involvement in maintaining existing conditions. This is the "learnable moment," and the supervisor should make the most of it to build up good attitudes toward the job, toward the level of effort that will be required, toward the beahvior that will be expected, toward the quality requirements, and toward safe working habits.

Particularly the supervisor wants to build up the new employee's confidence that this is a good place to work and that the training program is a well-planned means to achievement—to getting the things he or she wants from the job.

Orientation checklist.   An example of one company's approach toward developing cooperation between the personnel department and the new employee's supervisor is the Manufacturers Hanover Trust Company's orientation checklist shown as Figure 11–3. It is designed to be completed by the personnel department and various people having direct and indirect relationships with the new employee. It covers a period up to the employee's

Figure 11–3
Orientation checklist for new employees

MANUFACTURERS HANOVER TRUST COMPANY

ORIENTATION CHECKLIST & 3 MONTH PROGRESS REPORT

NAME	BR. OR DEPT.	PAYROLL NO.	DATE TRIAL PERIOD ENDS:

INTRODUCTION: THE MAJORITY OF NEW EMPLOYEES BEGIN THEIR JOBS WITH AN HONEST DESIRE TO BE SUCCESSFUL. NEW STAFF MEMBERS LOOK TO THE MANAGEMENT OF THEIR DEPARTMENT OR BRANCH FOR INFORMATION ABOUT THEIR JOBS, THE ULTIMATE VALUE OF THE WORK THEY PERFORM, AND THE REGULATIONS THAT APPLY TO THEIR WORK. THE SUCCESS OR FAILURE OF NEW MEMBERS OF THE STAFF RESTS IN LARGE PART UPON THEIR SUPERVISORS. THIS CHECKLIST HAS BEEN PREPARED AS A MINIMUM MEASURE OF THE SUPERVISORS' RESPONSIBILITY FOR ORIENTATION. QUESTIONS ABOUT THIS FORM SHOULD BE DIRECTED TO THE TRAINING SECTION OF THE PERSONNEL DEPARTMENT, 350-5729.

1. THIS FORM IS APPLICABLE TO ALL NEW STAFF MEMBERS.

2. PLEASE COMPLETE EACH POINT ON THE CHECKLIST ADHERING TO THE TIMETABLE AS CLOSELY AS POSSIBLE. WHERE SPACES ARE PROVIDED, ACKNOWLEDGE COMPLETION WITH YOUR INITIALS.

3. PAGE NUMBERS REFER TO PERSONNEL POLICIES AND PROCEDURES.

4. THE COMPLETED CHECKLIST AND PROGRESS REPORT IS TO BE SENT TO THE PERSONNEL DEPARTMENT DURING THE EMPLOYEE'S TENTH WEEK OF EMPLOYMENT. THE PROGRESS REPORT WILL BE THE BASIS ON WHICH DECISION IS MADE TO RETAIN THE NEW EMPLOYEE PAST THE THREE MONTH PERIOD.

5. PLEASE NOTE THAT BEFORE REPORTING TO THE DEPARTMENT, NEW EMPLOYEES HAVE BEEN TOLD ABOUT THE FOLLOWING:

   STARTING SALARY, SALARY REVIEW SCHEDULE, DATE OF FIRST PAY, OPTIONAL DEDUCTIONS FOR CHARITABLE ACTIVITIES AND SAVINGS PLANS, TRIAL PERIOD, WORKING HOURS AND WORK WEEK, ANY UNUSUAL OVERTIME REQUIRED BY THE JOB, ATTENDANCE, TUITION REFUND, IDENTIFICATION CARD AND BENEFIT PLANS. THE NEW EMPLOYEE HAS CHOSEN NOT TO ELECT PAYROLL DEDUCTION FOR THE FOLLOWING BENEFITS: _____

   (AN OUTLINE OF THE ABOVE INFORMATION MAY BE OBTAINED FROM THE PERSONNEL TRAINING SECTION, 350-5729.)

   EMPLOYEES HAVE BEEN PROVIDED WITH THEIR EMPLOYEE IDENTIFICATION CARD, AND A PACKET CONTAINING THE BOOKLETS, ABOUT MANUFACTURERS HANOVER, EMPLOYEE RELATIONS PROCEDURE, RETIREMENT SYSTEM, PROFIT SHARING PLAN, BLUE CROSS/BLUE SHIELD BENEFITS, GROUP MAJOR MEDICAL INSURANCE, GROUP LIFE INSURANCE, GROUP ACCIDENT INSURANCE PLAN, AS WELL AS A STATEMENT CONCERNING CONFLICTS OF INTEREST. THEY HAVE ALSO BEEN INFORMED THAT THEY WILL RECEIVE DURING THE FIRST WEEK A BOOKLET EXPLAINING THE EMPLOYEE CHECKING ACCOUNT, AND AN INITIAL SUPPLY OF CHECKS. IT HAS BEEN EXPLAINED THAT THEIR CHECKING ACCOUNT WILL NOT BE OPENED UNTIL THEY RECEIVE THEIR FIRST PAY STATEMENT AND THAT NO CHECKS CAN BE DRAWN AND NO DEPOSITS CAN BE ACCEPTED UNTIL THAT TIME.

SUPERVISOR

GENERAL

_____ A. DEVELOP OPEN COMMUNICATIONS WITH NEW EMPLOYEE. FOR THE FIRST TWO WEEKS FIND A REASON TO MAKE SOME CONTACT AS MANY AS 5 TIMES EACH DAY.

_____ B. SEE THAT THE SPONSOR, TRAINER, AND EVENING STUDY REPRESENTATIVE UNDERSTAND THEIR RESPONSIBILITY AND COMPLETE THEIR ASSIGNMENTS ACCORDING TO THE CHECKLIST.

_____ C. SEE THAT EMPLOYEE ATTENDS THE NEW EMPLOYEE ORIENTATION AND THE TRAINING CENTERS NOTED ON THE LETTER OF INTRODUCTION, FORM 5476.

_____ D. ARRANGE FOR NEW EMPLOYEE'S ATTENDANCE AT ANY DIVISIONAL ORIENTATION PROGRAM.

_____ E. LIST FOR THE TRAINER UNDER THE TRAINER SECTION OF THE CHECKLIST, THE FUNCTIONS THAT THE NEW EMPLOYEE SHOULD BE ABLE TO PERFORM AFTER 3 MONTHS OF SERVICE.

II   FIRST DAY

_____ A. WELCOME NEW EMPLOYEE TO DEPARTMENT AND ACQUAINT YOURSELF WITH HIS/HER BACKGROUND AS IT RELATES TO THE JOB.

   INQUIRE ABOUT TRANSPORTATION TO WORK, SCHOOLS ATTENDED, PREVIOUS EXPERIENCE AND AMBITIONS; ENCOURAGE QUESTIONS.

_____ B. INTRODUCE NEW EMPLOYEE TO THE BRANCH/DEPARTMENT OFFICERS.

_____ C. GIVE EMPLOYEE THE OPERATIONS MANUAL OR ITS EQUIVALENT FOR THE JOB AND EXPLAIN THE FOLLOWING:

   1. NATURE OF TRAINING
   2. TRAINING PERIOD
   3. NAME OF TRAINER

5483
10M 1/76

Figure 11–3 (continued)

_____ D. EXPLAIN THE WORK OF THE DEPARTMENT/BRANCH.

    1. PURPOSE
    2. ORGANIZATION AND WORKFLOW CHART
    3. RELATIONSHIP TO THE DIVISION/REGION

_____ E. EXPLAIN THE JOB.

    1. DUTIES
    2. WORKFLOW CHART AND WHERE HIS/HER JOB FITS IN
    3. IMPORTANCE OF THIS JOB
    4. ANTICIPATED OVERTIME
    5. NEED TO HELP OTHERS WHEN NECESSARY
    6. SUPERVISORY CHAIN OF COMMAND

_____ F. DISCUSS THE FOLLOWING EMPLOYEE RESPONSIBILITIES:

    1. PUNCTUALITY
    2. REGULAR ATTENDANCE, REPORTING ABSENCES TO SUPERVISOR WITHIN ONE HALF HOUR OF STARTING TIME
    3. NO PAID ABSENCES IN FIRST THREE MONTHS
    4. TIME SHEET PROCEDURE
    5. COFFEE BREAK POLICY, LUNCH SCHEDULE
    6. SOUND FINANCES
    7. LEAVING DEPARTMENT
    8. HOUSEKEEPING
    9. CONFIDENTIAL NATURE OF WORK
    10. IMPORTANCE OF ACCURACY, LOSSES DUE TO ERRORS, WASTE PREVENTION
    11. PROPER GROOMING, SMOKING REGULATIONS

_____ G. EXPLAIN:

    1. HOW TO REPORT CHANGE OF ADDRESS AND STATUS
    2. LOCATION OF DESK AND LOCKER
    3. EMERGENCY PROCEDURES

_____ H. SUPPLY NEW EMPLOYEE WITH YOUR NAME AND PHONE NUMBER.

_____ I. REMIND EMPLOYEE THAT HE/SHE CANNOT DRAW A CHECK UNTIL HIS/HER FIRST PAY HAS BEEN CREDITED TO HIS/HER ACCOUNT.

III. SECOND DAY

_____ A. DISCUSS SALARY ADMINISTRATION.

    1. PAY PERIOD (WED. THROUGH TUES.)
    2. MERIT SALARY REVIEW SCHEDULE (PP. 111-D AND 111-E)
    3. SALARY RANGE
    4. CONFIDENTIAL NATURE OF SALARY
    5. AUTHORIZED OVERTIME PAY POLICIES (PP. 113-114)
    6. NAMES OF PERSONS AUTHORIZED TO APPROVE OVERTIME WORK
    7. FACTORS ON WHICH PERFORMANCE IS JUDGED (SHOW SAMPLE REVIEW FORM)

_____ B. DISCUSS:

    1. CAREER PATH (PP. 100-101-A)
      A. MENTION POLICY OF PROMOTION FROM WITHIN (P. 100)
      B. MENTION BANK'S USE OF SKILL FILE (P. 102)
      C. DISCUSS IMPORTANCE OF EDUCATION, DESCRIBE SCHOOLS AND COURSES AVAILABLE, AND EXPLAIN BANK'S TUITION REFUND PLAN.
    2. TELEPHONE USE:
      A. PROCEDURE FOR ANSWERING AND TRANSFERRING CALLS
      B. LIMITATIONS ON PERSONAL CALLS
    3. SECURITY AND PROTECTION PROCEDURES APPLICABLE TO THE BRANCH/DEPARTMENT TO WHICH HE/SHE IS ASSIGNED
    4. VACATIONS (PP. 218-223), HOLIDAYS (P. 216), SPECIAL DAYS (P. 215-D)

IV FIRST PAY DAY

_____ A. GIVE EMPLOYEE HIS/HER PAY STATEMENT AND SUPPLY OF PERSONALIZED CHECKS.

_____ B. DISCUSS EMPLOYEE CHECKING ACCOUNT (P. 111-H):

    1. PROPER HANDLING
    2. PLACE AND TIME TO CASH CHECKS
    3. WARN AGAINST ANTICIPATING DEPOSITS
    4. MENTION OVERDRAFT POLICY (P. 111-I)
    5. CAUTION AGAINST BORROWING AND LENDING OF BLANK CHECKS

V SECOND WEEK

_____ A. DISCUSS PROGRESS IN TRAINING AND OBTAIN REACTIONS TO THE JOB.

_____ B. INVITE DISCUSSION OF SUBJECTS WHICH MIGHT NEED CLARIFICATION OR ADVICE.

_____ C. MENTION:

    1. TOPICS
    2. SUGGESTION SYSTEM (P. 519)
    3. EMPLOYEE ACTIVITIES

Figure 11–3 (continued)

AREA SUPERVISOR

I   FIRST DAY (OR SOMETIME IN FIRST WEEK)
_____ A.   WELCOME TO THE DIVISION/REGION.

_____ B.   DISCUSS BRIEFLY THE DIVISION:
             1.   THE WORK OF THE DIVISION AND ITS IMPORTANCE
             2.   RELATIONSHIP TO THE BANK AS A WHOLE

_____ C.   DISCUSS THE IMPORTANCE OF CUSTOMER SERVICE AND PUBLIC RELATIONS.

_____ D.   DESCRIBE BRIEFLY THE DEPARTMENT TO WHICH THE EMPLOYEE WILL BE ASSIGNED.

_____ E.   EMPHASIZE THE ROLE AND COMPETENCE OF THE SUPERVISOR:
             1.   IN TRAINING AND COUNSELING
             2.   AVAILABILITY AT ALL TIMES FOR QUESTIONS

II   DIVISIONAL/BRANCH ORIENTATION (IF THERE IS AN ORGANIZED PROGRAM IN THE DIRECT AREA):

        DATE OF ATTENDANCE _____

             1.   WORK AND ORGANIZATION OF THE DIVISION/BRANCH
             2.   TERMINOLOGY USED IN DIVISION
             3.   REMINDER OF TELEPHONE ETIQUETTE AND REGULATIONS

EVENING STUDY REPRESENTATIVE

        SECOND WEEK

             DISCUSS:
             1.   EMPLOYEE'S EDUCATIONAL PLANS
             2.   TYPES OF STUDY QUALIFYING UNDER THE PLAN
             3.   APPROPRIATE SCHOOLS AND COURSES
             4.   TUITION REFUND PLAN

             PLEASE ACKNOWLEDGE THAT THE ABOVE HAS BEEN COMPLETED:

             SIGNATURE_____   DATE_____

THREE MONTH PROGRESS REPORT (TO BE COMPLETED DURING THE EMPLOYEE'S TENTH WEEK OF EMPLOYMENT.)

1.   DO YOU FEEL THAT IT IS IN THE BEST INTERESTS OF THE BANK AND OF THE STAFF MEMBER TO CONTINUE EMPLOYMENT
     HERE?   _____YES   _____NO

     IF NO, WHY? _____

2.   ARE THERE ANY PROBLEMS THAT MAY INHIBIT THIS EMPLOYEE'S PROGRESS IN THIS JOB, DEPARTMENT OR BEYOND?
     _____YES   _____NO

     IF SO, WHAT ARE THEY? _____

3.   WHAT ARE THIS EMPLOYEE'S EDUCATIONAL PLANS?_____

4.   IS THE PRESENT ASSIGNMENT THE BEST SUITED TO THE EMPLOYEE'S ABILITIES AND INTERESTS?   _____YES   _____NO

     WHY?_____

5.   PLEASE RECORD:

     NUMBER OF DAYS ABSENT SINCE DATE OF EMPLOYMENT   _____
     NUMBER OF OCCASIONS OF ABSENCE   _____
     NUMBER OF DAYS OF LATENESS SINCE EMPLOYMENT   _____

6.   ADDITIONAL COMMENTS: _____
     _____
     _____

7.   RECOMMENDATIONS MADE TO STAFF MEMBER TO FULFILL POTENTIAL AND IMPROVE PERFORMANCE:

     1. _____
     _____
     2. _____
     _____
     3. _____
     _____
     4. _____
     _____

8.   EMPLOYEE ACKNOWLEDGEMENT _____
                                        (SIGNATURE)

     SUPERVISING OFFICER _____   DATE_____
                                   (SIGNATURE)

Figure 11–3 (concluded)

VI   FOURTH WEEK

_____ A. BENEFIT PROGRAMS:
        1. RETIREMENT SYSTEM (P. 313), IF APPROPRIATE
        2. PROFIT SHARING (P. 117)
        3. GROUP LIFE INSURANCE (P. 120)
        4. BLUE CROSS/BLUE SHIELD (P. 121)
        5. GROUP MAJOR MEDICAL (P. 122)
        6. GROUP ACCIDENT INSURANCE (P. 128)

_____ B. EXPLAIN MEDICAL DEPARTMENT SERVICES (PP. 506 – 508.)

_____ C. COUNSEL NEW EMPLOYEE ABOUT HIS/HER PROGRESS.

VII   FIFTH WEEK

_____ RE-CAP:
        1. VACATIONS (PP. 218 - 223)
        2. HOLIDAYS (P. 216)
        3. MILITARY LEAVE (PP. 320 - 323)
        4. LEAVE WITH PAY FOR MARRIAGE (P. 215-F)
        5. MATERNITY LEAVE (P. 213)
        6. SPECIAL DAYS (P. 215 - D)

VIII   TENTH WEEK

       COMPLETE PROGRESS REPORT

SPONSOR (A FRIENDLY AND EXPERIENCED CO - WORKER)

FIRST DAY

_____ A. INTRODUCE NEW EMPLOYEE TO CO - WORKERS:
        1. GIVE BRIEF DESCRIPTION OF THEIR WORK
        2. GIVE NEW EMPLOYEE CHART OF OFFICE OR DEPARTMENT LAY - OUT WITH NAMES OF CO - WORKERS LISTED

_____ B. SHOW LOCATION OF:
        1. LOCKERS
        2. WASHROOM
        3. BULLETIN BOARDS
        4. DINING FACILITIES

_____ C. EXPLAIN SUPPLY PROCEDURE.

_____ D. ARRANGE FOR THE NEW EMPLOYEE TO HAVE LUNCH WITH YOU AND CO - WORKERS FOR HIS/HER FIRST FEW DAYS.

TRAINER

I _____ INTRODUCE EMPLOYEE TO ANY FORMALIZED DEPARTMENTAL TRAINING.

II _____ TELL THE EMPLOYEE ABOUT THE FOLLOWING FUNCTIONS THAT ARE TO BE MASTERED IN THE FIRST 3 MONTHS OF
        SERVICE (TO BE LISTED BY SUPERVISOR.):

                                                              WEEK MASTERED

_____

_____

_____

_____

III _____ MAKE A PLAN TO TEACH THE WORK.
        A. ENTER THE WEEK IN WHICH EACH FUNCTION IS MASTERED (IE. FIRST, SECOND, THIRD, ETC..)

        B. IF THERE IS NOT A FORMALIZED DEPARTMENTAL TRAINING PLAN, USE THESE TRAINING TECHNIQUES AS A GUIDE:
            1. PREPARATION
                A. HAVE JOB PROCEDURE MANUAL OR OTHER WRITTEN MATERIAL READY FOR EACH FUNCTION
                B. BE SURE EMPLOYEE HAS DESK AND MATERIALS NECESSARY FOR PERFORMANCE OF JOB

            2. MOTIVATION
                A. IMPRESS UPON EMPLOYEE THE SIGNIFICANCE OF THE JOB
                B. MENTION THE REWARDS, MATERIAL AND OTHERWISE, OF GOOD PERFORMANCE

            3. PRESENTATION OF MATERIAL ACCORDING TO YOUR TRAINING PLAN. INCLUDE YOUR OWN DEMONSTRATION OF
                THE OPERATION TO BE PERFORMED.

            4. PERFORMANCE OF EACH OPERATION BY EMPLOYEE AND REVIEW TO ASSURE UNDERSTANDING

            5. APPLICATION BY EMPLOYEE INDEPENDENTLY. (ENCOURAGE HIM/HER TO ASK QUESTIONS OF THE APPROPRIATE
                PERSON - YOU, A CO - WORKER OR SUPERVISOR - WHENEVER NECESSARY.)

            6. FOLLOW UP BY CHECKING TO SEE IF EMPLOYEE KNOWS AND UNDERSTANDS THE PROCEDURES OF THE JOB ONE
                MONTH AFTER TRAINING PERIOD.

Source: Reproduced by permission of the Manufacturers Hanover Trust Co., New York, N.Y.

first salary review, and its basic purpose is to ensure that the employee is given all of the information necessary for an understanding of the various policies that have an effect on the individual's performance on the job and his or her overall well-being as an employee of the bank.

This company found that there was no uniformity in the amount of time spent on orientation and induction by supervisors. Some were diligent and gave as much time as necessary while others spent no time at all, expecting the employee to pick up the information as time went by. The checklist attempts to assure that each supervisor does in fact take the time. Obviously, the quality of the effort is not assured by the checklist; but since it does become part of the employee's permanent record, the bank has found that the effort is being made and fewer information requests come to the personnel department.

While such a checklist may seem to be added paper work, the need for effective information flow to the new employee is critical. Anything which enhances this flow and tends to minimize insecurities among new hires can help in lowering first-year turnover and employment costs.

The new employee and the group

Dropping new employees into a department and letting them fend for themselves is like playing a pinball game. If the ball doesn't happen to connect in the scoring area, there will be no payoff. Instead of playing a game of chance in introducing new people into the department, the supervisor should set up provisions to keep them from losing momentum or dropping out before mastering the job and making a place for themselves. During the trying days of learning the job and getting adjusted to its demands, newcomers must somehow be made to feel wanted and needed. They must be protected from the embarrassment and discouragement of ignorance and isolation in front of people who all seem to know what to do and where they fit.

Even the most self-sufficient people feel lost in their first days on a new job. They might not mind isolation if they were absorbed in some project and confident of their ability to handle it. But they are insecure in the job and need help with the work, and they are worried about how they will fit in with the people around them. At lunchtime and at breaks they don't know what to do with themselves. Everybody else seems to be comfortably established.

Most people have vivid memories of the way they felt in getting started on a new job. They can recall the strangeness and tension and tiredness. They can remember how often they felt like quitting.

The group can't be blamed for being inhospitable to the newcomer. People have their own jobs to protect, and their own social relations to preserve and cultivate. Once people have achieved a kind of stability and predictability in their work lives, they find a certain joy in the routines and don't want to risk being crowded out.

Newcomers to a group are a threat to the stability of the group as a whole and to each member of it. Strangers may insinuate themselves into the social life and edge others out of position. They may break up some nice little arrangement on the job or may get in the way of some plans for the future. They may be overambitious to get somebody else's job.

It just takes time for some of these barriers to break down, but the supervisor can do a lot to prevent the original formation of much of the hostility and suspicion. If the group feels competent and confident, it doesn't have so much to fear from a newcomer. A group that is let in on the news that a new person is to be hired will feel less threatened than if one is just sprung on them without warning or explanation. The supervisor should make it a point to prepare the group for the coming of a new employee. The word should be passed along about what work the newcomer is to do and where he or she fits into the pattern as far as they and their plans are concerned. When the new employee arrives, the supervisor should make sure that introductions are pleasant and establish some kind of bridge of interest between individuals. The supervisor should draw people into conversations with the new person to discuss job problems.

The newcomer must be started off on the right foot with the people who will be most closely associated with him or her on the job. Introductions should make clear the status arrangements if one is expected to give directions to the other. Introductions should also make clear whether the new employee should ask for, and expect to receive, help from the other.

The newcomer should be provided with a sponsor—an employee who will eat lunch with him or her the first day or so and after that will look after the person for a while so that he or she will not be standing around alone.

The induction procedure

It is not only the newly hired who need inducting; anyone who is changing jobs within the company needs some kind of induction. People who are being transferred are strangers to the job and to the work group. They will have questions in mind about how this job ties in with other jobs held and how the future is being affected by the transfer. In order to be prepared, the supervisor should get whatever information is available from the personnel department or from the individual's previous supervisors.

If an inductee is a college graduate trainee, the supervisor should find out from the personnel department what kind of program the trainee is on and what part the department is expected to play in it.

Special care must be used in inducting supervisors into new jobs, particularly if they are being moved from the rank and file into a first supervisory job. They may have received coaching for the new job but are now entering into a new set of relationships and moving into a position of more authority. These relationships must be clarified and established so that there is no doubt about the scope of authority, and responsibilities, and recognition by new associates and new subordinates.

If an inductee has just come to the company as a new hire, the application form will give information about past work experience, education, and previous training. This background serves as a guide to the kind of induction needed, the kind of things already known, and the kind of information to be given. The employee on a first job needs many more things explained than does the experienced person. For one thing, there are so many things the beginner is uncertain about that he or she may be afraid to ask any questions and expose ignorance. The following six steps can be the basis for a suitable induction procedure.

1. Welcome the new employees and learn more about them.
2. Explain the work of the section and the part they are to perform.
3. Let them know what is expected.
4. Show them around and introduce them to co-workers.
5. Turn the newcomers over to a sponsor or competent instructor.
6. Follow up on each new employee's progress.

The young adult's first job

Business needs youth, with its optimism, its enthusiasm, its daring, its willingness to try anything once, and its frequently ingenious ideas. For many young people, employment is a new world, and they don't know what kind of behavior is expected of them on the job. While they are familiar with school and the teacher-student relationship (which has become increasingly democratic in recent years), they may take some time in making the adjustment to the usually more autocratic boss-subordinate relationship in business and industry.

At home and in school they generally maintained close relationships with people of their own age, while on many jobs their co-workers may be older and less tolerant than school friends. Breaking into the cliques existing in every work group may be difficult when the new hire has little in common with established and older employees. The workplace is usually more confining, and a first job is frequently a routine assignment. At school the young person could move around more freely, and each new class period meant discussion of something different. While many of them may have held part-time jobs, the workday is longer in a full-time position and tardiness is frowned upon, usually causing disciplinary action. Frequent vacations and holidays characterize the school year, while few fringe benefit programs in industry include more than one or two weeks of vacation in the early years of employment. Each week at school there would be examinations or quizzes, and the young people would know how they are doing. Performance measurement in business is not as frequent nor as easily understood. At the end of the semester or school year, promotion or progress to the next level took place. Promotions in business do not come with the same ordered frequency, nor are they as automatic as those in many schools. Guidance counselors, faculty advisers, and teachers abound in the world of education. Usually these people take considerable interest in the young people coming to them for help. Such is often not the case with supervisors in business, whose principal concern may be meeting deadlines and coping with the pressures of management activity.

"Do you have any other qualifications other than good vibes?"

Reprinted by permission The Wall Street Journal

Young people frequently need training on the first job.

In short the work world is very different than the one from which the young adults came. In most cases the onus is placed on them for making the necessary adjustments and changes in behavior required for success in business. Not enough supervisors have the time, talent, or inclination to spend large amounts of time with young employees, helping them to make the transition from school to business by smoothing out some of the rough spots. More frequently there will be complaints from these supervisors about the poor quality of the new hires and their lack of appreciation for the golden opportunity afforded them in the company.

One difficulty that some companies have when hiring college trained people is the method of introducing them to their first jobs. Often these jobs are not sufficiently challenging, nor do they make use of the knowledge the recent students have acquired. At times the new graduates are placed in so-called traditional entrant jobs where they are supposed to learn the work from the ground up. This can be costly both by having overqualified people do work too easy for them and by causing them to quit in disappointment. Another problem that occurs is caused by assigning new graduates to supervisors who do not relate well to young people. With this type of introduction to the work world some young people become disillusioned and unproductive.[2]

Minorities. The above difficulties have been compounded in recent years in many areas of the country by a much greater influx of young minority group members into the work force. Many of these youngsters have all of the problems of their more affluent counterparts coupled with the added problems of coming from inadequate backgrounds, a different culture, and a different value system. Many have levels of aspiration beyond their education or their ability. They resent the way minority groups have been treated and are inevitably suspicious of more of the same. Some may seek refuge in the fact that they are members of a minority group. An orderly existence and routine work are very unusual for some. Discipline for work habits and rule infractions that a supervisor considers normal may be interpreted as discrimination by the minority group employee.

Some companies, recognizing the special problems involved in the successful induction and early job training of minority group employees, have established special training programs for them which include a considerable emphasis on the behavior required for effective performance in the work environment. Very often they are assigned a "buddy" who may be a member of the same minority and who has made a successful transition on the job. In addition, companies that hire relatively large numbers of minority group members have developed special orientation programs for supervisors so that greater understanding of the special problems of these young minority group members can be enhanced. It may be quite difficult for supervisors who think they have come up the hard way to understand that others may have had it much harder. Their reaction may be quite negative, and they may take out their negativism on the employees. A program which tries to develop awareness of real problems and considers some of the hard facts of the labor supply and the civil rights of minorities can assist in a more successful introduction of minorities into productive job performance.

The federal government has recognized problems in the area of minority employment. In 1968 a JOBS program was started to support efforts by private industry in the training and employment of hard-core unemployed people, most of whom were members of minorities. The private sector formed the National Alliance of Businessmen, headed by prominent busi-

---

[2] For a broader discussion of young people in business, see John S. Morgan, *Managing the Young Adults* (New York: American Management Assn., 1967).

ness executives, to implement the JOBS program. Hundreds of thousands of full-time and summer jobs for hard-core unemployed people from all over the country have resulted from this industry-government cooperation.

On-the-job training

The most widely used method of training new employees or those promoted or transferred to new jobs is called on-the-job training or OJT. It is training at the workplace by either the supervisor or someone he or she has chosen as a trainer. At its worst it is a trial-and-error approach where new employees observe the experienced performer for a short period and then are left to their own devices. At its best it is a formal program conducted by someone versed in training techniques as well as job knowledge. Many employee complaints and some labor turnover can be traced to poor training. The pressure to get a new employee up to reasonable productivity in a short time may cause neglect of critical steps in the learning process and not enough emphasis on safety.

When done properly, on-the-job training has many advantages for the company as well as the employees. The employees learn the job correctly and gain greater satisfaction, since performance will meet requirements and they will usually be rewarded for effective performance. They gain experience in the environment of the job, thereby lessening the adjustment period. The company gets productive workers who perform the job correctly and may feel more favorably disposed toward the company for the effective and positive training experience to which they have been exposed. F. A. DePhillips, W. M. Berliner, and J. J. Cribbin list the following practices as necessary requisites for satisfactory accomplishment of on-the-job training:

1. The person selected to do the training should be a good teacher.
2. He should know the job he is to teach thoroughly.
3. He should prepare an organized training plan or have it prepared for him by the training division.
4. He should be given sufficient time to carry out the training effort and, if possible, be removed from his responsibility for work production.
5. He should have access to information about the person he is to train, so that he is able to gauge the trainee's needs as accurately as possible.
6. He must be able to perform the job at a normal pace in the proper manner. He does not have to be an outstanding performer. In fact outstanding performers frequently lose patience if the trainee does not learn the job rapidly.
7. A timetable should be developed so that the trainer can assess the trainee's progress and report on it to both the trainee and the supervisor.
8. If the supervisor does the training, then he must be able to devote the time necessary without neglecting his other supervisory and work duties.
9. Try to assign the trainee to the work station he will ultimately be employed in, in order to maximize the advantage of working in the job environment.

10. After the trainee has developed sufficient skill to be left on his own, let him know that he can call on the trainer for further guidance.

11. The trainer should follow up on the trainee as often as is necessary to ascertain the results of the training and the amount of job knowledge retained by the trainee.[3]

Organizations of all sizes use this type of training, and it is the backbone of the training effort in small companies. Where hiring frequency and job requirements make it feasible, it may be desirable to establish "vestibule" training for larger groups. Here the workplace is simulated and employees are usually trained by more professional methods. A vestibule school may be less expensive than the one-on-one requirement of on-the-job training. Many firms use vestibule training for entrant jobs that have a relatively large population in the company.

Whether or not they do the actual training of new employees, supervisors need to know training techniques. Every time they explain a process or a procedure, they are training. Every time they demonstrate a technique, they are training. Every time they explain an assignment to a subordinate, they are training. Training is the means by which they build work teams. Training enables new employees to perform their jobs properly and to meet the standards of performance. Training makes it possible for present employees to acquire more skill, to be more versatile, to be ready for promotion. Training reduces errors, accidents, spoiled work, and damage to equipment. Training reduces frictions, tensions, fears, frustrations, dissatisfactions, behavior problems, absences, and quits.

With a well-trained and flexible work group, the supervisor doesn't have to spend the day putting out fires—correcting errors, repairing damage, reprimanding the makers of mistakes—or making routine decisions that subordinates should be making. He or she can turn over the work to them with confidence that it will be done and done correctly.

Uncovering training needs

Many work difficulties have their origin in lack of training, but training is not a cure-all. When things go wrong, supervisors should suspect other causes before they decide that training is the answer: Is selection poor? Is the wrong person on the job? Are wages low? Is equipment run-down? Are working conditions unfavorable? Is supervision lax? Are jobs poorly designed? Are attitudes bad? If the trouble cannot be charged to any of these causes, then supervisors should suspect that a need for training is indicated by the following conditions:

Standards of work performance not being met.
Accidents.
Excessive scrap.

---

[3] F. A. DePhillips, W. M. Berliner, and J. J. Cribbin, *Management of Training Programs* (Homewood, Ill.: Richard D. Irwin, 1960), p. 300. © 1960 by Richard D. Irwin, Inc.

Frequent need for equipment repairs.

High rate of transfer and turnover, absenteeism and lateness.

Too many low ratings on employee evaluation reports.

Many people using different methods to do the same job.

Excessive fatigue, fumbling, discouragement, struggling with the job.

Bottlenecks.

Deadlines not being met.

The supervisor and the training analyst should investigate the job or jobs involved in any of these conditions and observe the performance to determine what training is necessary. If close observation does not uncover the difficulty, the supervisor or the training analyst should make an analysis along the following steps:

1. List the duties and responsibilities or the tasks of the job under consideration, using the job description as a guide.
2. List the standards of work performance for the job.
3. Compare actual performance against the standards.
4. Determine what parts of the job are giving employees trouble—where are they falling down in performance?
5. Determine what kind of training is needed to overcome the specific difficulty or difficulties.

After the training has been given, its effectiveness should be judged by whether or not it improved the conditions it was intended to correct. Are standards of performance now being met? Are employees using better methods and getting higher ratings? Is the work going more smoothly? Has there been a reduction in accidents, damage, waste, turnover, transfers, bottlenecks? If the training has accomplished these goals, it has been successful and should be continued.

Principles of learning and techniques of training

On-the-job training will be much more efficent if trainers will keep in mind some principles of learning and use them when they are instructing.

Motivation to learn. Employees will not learn very much unless they are motivated to learn. Research by industrial psychologists[4] indicates that rewards are much more effective than punishments in stimulating learning—that priase is superior to blame. Harsh criticism may interfere with learning, and so may fear, anxiety, tension, and emotional disturbances.

Motives for learning may be both financial and nonfinancial. People may want higher earnings, advancement, more security, more competence, or more prestige. However, they need immediate rewards for progress in learning as they go along. One such reward is the feeling of achievement in

---

[4] For a deeper study of learning as a process see Bernard M. Bass and J. A. Vaughn, *Training in Industry: The Management of Learning* (Belmont, Calif.: Wadsworth Publishing Co. 1966); Harold Leavitt, *Managerial Psychology*, 3d ed. (Chicago: University of Chicago Press, 1972).

making progress. In order to get this reward, they must be able to find out how they are doing by receiving *feedback of results.* The army found that feedback was necessary in teaching marksmanship. Target shooting can't be learned unless the shooter has some way of knowing whether the target has been hit. If it was missed, the soldier needs to know by how much and in which direction. Programmed instruction (the "teaching machine") is based upon this principle of immediate feedback. The learner studies a small segment of a subject, answers a question about it, and finds out immediately if the answer was right or wrong.

Learning by doing. Learning is accomplished through the senses. Learning a job skill is accomplished through seeing, hearing, and doing.

Learners see the demonstration of skill, hear the instruction and explanation, and perform the action themselves. They repeat the performance until they build up a habit pattern.

When a training need surfaces, an opportunity arises for an effective line-staff relationship. The line supervisor discovers the need but must have the expert help of the training department. In a staff role, the training analyst can help the line supervisor develop a program, furnish teaching aids, evaluate the results, and assist in the instruction by training a person chosen by the supervisor to do the teaching. The job of trainer is a good one on which to try out rank-and-file employees who may be potential supervisors. Rank-and-file employees do not get many opportunities to demonstrate managerial abilities, but when acting as trainers, they have to plan, organize, direct, coordinate, and control. People who are successful as trainers demonstrate that they have the ability to do these things.

Choosing a trainer

Supervisors as a rule know the jobs and the people in their department better than anyone else, but they are not necessarily the best people to do the training. Because of the nature of the supervisory job, supervisors are usually under pressure to get things done. They lack the time and the patience to do the painstaking work that teaching requires. Also, it is difficult to break down the barrier between superior and subordinate to the point where the learner can relax. In the presence of the boss, learners are often tense, afraid to make mistakes, afraid to be informal, afraid they are being judged, afraid to expose their ignorance, and afraid to ask "stupid" questions that they would feel free to ask of someone else.

In many cases it is better that someone other than the supervisor act as the instructor. In most departments there are employees who with some instruction could be made into good trainers. These are people who really know all the angles of the job, who have good attitudes, who have an interest in people, and who may have gained patience through teaching their own children. A trainer must be able to take everything calmly and to improvise when unusual situations occur.

The quality of training depends to a great extent upon the effectiveness of the trainer. The main qualifications for success in the art of training are skill, knowledge, and good attitudes, and the ability to transmit them; patience, high morale, and the ability to build confidence in the trainee.

Much of the success of teaching comes from the attitude of trainers. They must have a strong liking for teaching and have a deep interest in having the learner succeed. They must have a good attitude toward the company, the department, the work, and the workers, and be patient enough to correct the same mistakes over and over again. They must repeat instructions time and again, changing the approach and the emphasis to fit the learner, and encourage the learner when progress is slow.

Trainers must be able to diagnose training needs and develop programs to fit them and be able to:

1. Tell the learner *what* needs to be done.
2. Have the trainee learn *how* to do it.
3. Explain why it should be done in the prescribed manner.

Goals and subgoals. People learn faster if they are working toward a goal. First of all they must have a reason for wanting to learn. Then they need a definite target—some level of accomplishment they intend to achieve. Then they should have subgoals—a definite amount of progress they expect to make that week. Goals should have been set by studying previous learners on the same job, charting their progess, and constructing a learning curve. If learners can see where other people had difficulty, were slowed in their progress, and then picked up again and forged ahead, they are more confident that they can do it too.

Goals mustn't be set too high. People have some successes to fortify them through periods of little progress. In learning, nothing succeeds like success, and a learner's success is knowledge that progress is being made. On the other hand, goals shouldn't be too easy or they will be no challenge to achievement.

People who are trying to master a skill like to have their goals and subgoals set up in a timetable so they can see where they are and how they are progressing. Like the target shooters, they want definite reports of just exactly when and where they are making hits, and just how far off they are on the misses. Telling learners they are doing fine isn't definite enough; they want to know which part of the work is fine.

Plateaus. People sometimes hit plateaus in their learning—periods in which they seem to be making no progesss. These are the times in which they become discouraged. They may quit trying, quit the job, or be absent just to escape the frustration. The trainer needs to encourage them and to assure them that trying harder will pay off. Sometimes employees think they have reached the limit of their learning, when actually they are on a plateau and could enter another period of improvement.

Individual differences. Not everyone learns at the same rate or achieves the same high degree of skill. Some people have to try a lot harder than others. If a learner is making nowhere near the standard rate of progress, he or she may lack the native ability or the motive, or the instruction may be poor.

Blocks to learning.   Resistance to change is one of the blocks to learning. The causes of resistance to change are discussed in Chapter 16. Research on resistance to change has demonstrated that employees ordinarily object so strongly to changes in their jobs that they have difficulty learning their new tasks and getting their speed up to the performance standards. But groups that participate in designing the changes in their jobs learn their changed jobs quickly and get their speed up to the standard. Resistance to learning a changed job seems to be reduced if employees have a lot of opportunity to air their ideas about the changes.

The supervisor and the trainer should remember that employees have no urge to learn a job that displeases them or seems to be a threat.

A person may have difficulty relearning a job that was changed by sudden, arbitrary, or unexplained action of management. Sometimes resistance to a new method takes the form of an attempt to show that it won't work. attitudes toward the supervisor may affect the speed with which an employee learns a changed job. Sometimes employees hold down their rate of output so they won't show up the slower members of their group.

Learning by parts.   People learn in small doses; they cannot, even if they want to, attend to many details at the same time. Breaking the task into small, digestible portions expedites learning. It also creates a number of subgoals which the learner gets the satisfaction of achieving.

The learning curve.   This is a way of measuring the progress of a trainee through the various stages of learning. It is illustrated in simple form in Figure 11-4. A brief explanation of the stages follows:

1.   Novice stage.   The employee may be clumsy and easily discouraged, needing considerable support from the trainer.
2.   As understanding grows, learning is rapid. Employee self-confidence grows and job satisfaction emerges.
3.   Overconfidence may cause some regression to poor performance. At this stage more training does not result in significant increases in performance.
4.   As the employee practices, job performance becomes effective, and at this stage the trainee reaches peak performance based on learning and experience.
5.   Continued training may only cause boredom since the trainee already knows the job and has reached standard performance.

It must be remembered that each employee has an individual learning curve. Not all people progress in the same manner. Some are more motivated and have innate abilities enabling them to learn faster and reach peak

Figure 11–4
A simplified learning curve

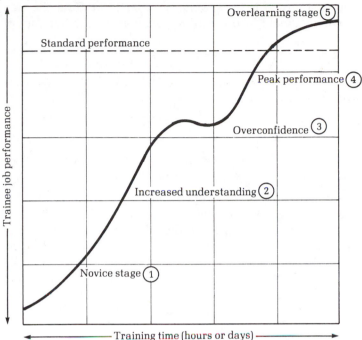

The four-step method of job training

performance sooner. Others may end up doing the job just as well, but they need more help and time to reach standard performance.

The four-step method of job training

Many supervisors and trainers are familiar with Job Instruction Training (JIT) sometimes called Train the Trainer—a very effective method of transmitting a well-defined but not too complex skill from one person who possesses it to another who does not. It is founded on the principles of good teaching and is used as the basis for the following discussion.

Before instructors start to instruct, they must have the whole program worked out in advance. They have to determine which people need instruction, what kind, how much, and when they can be fitted into the schedule. This calls for making up a training timetable.

After determining what training is necessary, the trainer must set up the instruction in a teachable form. This can be accomplished by using a job breakdown sheet. On the left-hand side of the sheet, the instructor should list the *steps* and on the right-hand side of the sheet, the corresponding *key* points should be listed. The steps constitute what is to be done, and they are set up in the sequence in which they are to be performed. Opposte each step is listed its key points—how it is to be done in order to perform the step successfully, and why it should be done in this manner. Some examples of key points are:

Do not touch leads until motor stops . . . .   to avoid possible shock.

Finish piece within certain limits . . . .   so that it will fit mating part.

Use a stick to push work past the saw . . .   to avoid cutting hand.

Measure with micrometer . . . .   to get accurate reading.

Line up sheets against guidelines . . . .   so that lines will be straight.

Press down pencil or pen . . . .   so the last carbon is readable.

Boil in water 20 minutes . . . .   to sterilize.

By planning the instruction procedure in advance, the trainer will be able to move from step to step. The trainer will foresee many of the difficulties the worker will run into and be prepared to guide the learner through them. It is also necessary to have all the equipment ready, so there will be no delays when the actual training begins. The work place should be carefully prepared—everything clean and orderly—to set the correct example from the start and let the trainees know how they are expected to keep it.

The trainer is now ready to start instructing according to the four-step method:

Step 1. Preparation of the learners

1. Put learners at ease—relieve the tension.
2. Explain why they are being taught.
3. Create interest—encourage questions—find out what the learners already know about the job or other jobs.
4. Explain the why of the whole job, and relate it to some job the workers already know.
5. Place the learners as close to the normal working position as possible.
6. Familiarize the employees with the equipment, materials, tools, and trade terms.

Step 2. Presentation of the operation

1. Explain quality and quantity requirements.
2. Go through the job at the normal work pace.
3. Go through the job at a slow pace several times, explaining each step. Between operations, explain the difficult parts or ones in which errors are likely to be made.
4. Go through the job at a slow pace several times, explaining the key points.
5. Have the learners explain the steps as you go through the job at a slow pace.

6. Have the learners explain the key points as you go through the job at a slow pace.

Step 3. Performance tryout

1. Have the learners go through the job several times, slowly, explaining to you each step. Correct mistakes and, if necessary, do some of the complicated steps for the trainees the first few times.
2. You, the trainer, run the job at the normal pace.
3. Have the learners do the job, gradually building up skill and speed.
4. As soon as the trainees demonstrate that they can do the job, put them on their own but don't abandon them.

Step 4. Follow-up

1. Designate to whom the learners should go for help if they need it or if they need to ask questions.
2. Decrease supervision gradually, checking the work from time to time against quality and quantity standards.
3. Correct faulty work patterns that begin to creep into the work, and do it before they become habits. Show them why the learned method is superior.
4. Compliment good work; encourage the trainees and keep them encouraged until they are able to meet the quality and quantity standards.

The use of the term steps implies a strict progression from Step 1 to Step 4. In effective instruction this progression is not rigid; rather there may be a blending of the steps throughout the process. Preparing, motivating, presenting, and explaining are as necessary near the end of the lesson as they are in the beginning.

Special training programs

Because of the rapidly changing nature of organizations and the training needs indicated as a result, many companies offer their employees a wide variety of special training programs. In some instances the company training department designs or buys an off-the-shelf program while in others employees will be sent off-premises to be trained. What decides this is the frequency of need and the numbers of potential trainees involved.

A public speaking course is an example. A few employees may be sent to one, and upon their return they demonstrate enthusiasm and considerable improvement. A decision may then be made to develop an in-house program and offer it to all employees whose jobs call for such skills. Similar approaches can occur with report writing, listening, reading improvement, counseling, and other skill subjects. In addition there may be telephone training, training in the use of dictation equipment, personal finance, and retirement counseling.

All of these programs are supposed to help develop employees into more effective performers thus enhancing their growth along with that of the company.

Evaluating training programs

Any training program, no matter how elaborate, well-prepared, and effectively presented is only as good as the results it achieves. The value of a training program can be best demonstrated by its evaluation against some standards, preferably quantitative. In effect what should be measured is whether the training has successfully altered trainee behavior to perform the job. This depends on how effectively the trainee can transfer the knowledge, skills, and attitudes learned in the training program to actual job performance. This is relatively easy to accomplish in skill training, where rates of performance before and after training can be obtained with minimum trouble. On the other hand, human relations and supervisory and management training are not so easy to measure.

It is necessary, however, to go beyond faith or belief in the desirability of such programs. They are expensive and should more than pay for themselves. Arriving at some desired behavioral objectives before the program and then carefully monitoring job performance by observation for a period after the program is a way to evaluate a management training program. The supervisor's boss and sometimes his other subordinates can be involved in this process.

Some companies have made the training department a profit center in the sense that it sells its services to using departments throughout the company on a cost basis. The using department's budget is charged for the training services it "buys" from the training department. If the training department produces a "profit" for its efforts over the budget period, it is presumed to be performing effectively.

Summary

The personnel department introduces employees to the company. The supervisor introduces them to the job and to the work group. Induction by the supervisor serves to let employees know what will be required if they are to be successful on the job. They are also told how the job will serve their needs. Induction and orientation are designed to assure new employees that this is a good place to work. They help build confidence in the training program and give encouragement while they are learning their new jobs. Induction speeds an employee's integration into the work group.

The induction and orientation procedure must be adapted to fit the type of job and the needs of the person; teenagers and inexperienced people need more help and attention. Special problems and circumstances are involved in the induction and orientation of young adults. This is particularly true of minority group members. Supervisors should give extra care to the orientation of young people because of the high labor turnover among this group.

On-the-job training should probably be done by someone other than the supervisor. An employee skilled in the work might be developed into a trainer. The person should have patience and a liking for teaching and should become acquainted with the principles of learning: motivation, goals, subgoals, feedback of results, individual differences in ability and learning speed, plateaus in learning, and the importance of encouragement and confidence.

On-the-job training serves to speed up the learning of a new job and the time needed to reach performance standards. Continued training is needed to adapt to change—changes in employees and changes in jobs. Training increases employees' versatility for transfers and qualifications for promotion. It increases their skills and abilities to perform their present jobs. It reduces frustrations, frictions, errors, waste, and struggles with the job. Supervisors who have a well-trained work group can delegate responsibilities and devote time to the important parts of their jobs.

The four-step method of job training (JIT) provides an effective instruction plan. Standards should be established to measure the effectiveness of training programs to determine their usefulness to actual job performance.

CASE 11–1

Laura King, the vice president in charge of development, had a reputation as an excellent manager. This was particularly true in relation to the number of promotables who had come out of her area of responsibility. Many other departments in the company were grateful for the bright, young, and well-trained people they had received from King's department.

King had made it a practice to hire young people who were former school teachers and place them in the training section of her department. Here they became training analysts who were assigned to various areas of the company to help determine training needs. They then helped design training programs to fill these needs and frequently taught portions of the programs they developed. After about a year of this work, the young people became quite knowledgeable about other areas of the company and they also became good analysts. By teaching in some of the training programs, they gained self-confidence, presence, and communication ability. In addition they came to the attention of several managers who attended some of the programs.

As a result it was not unusual for these young trainers to be offered promotions to other areas of the company after about a year of this work. Laura King had congratulated herself several times for the success of her efforts on behalf of these people. One person who did not join in the congratulations was Paul Garth, the training director. Laura King was his boss and while he admired her overall competence, he believed her rapid promotion policy for training analysts was making his job very difficult. It seemed that each time he was successful in developing a first-class trainer he lost this person to another part of the company. He certainly didn't want to stand in the way of anyone's progress, but he felt the loss of so many experienced trainers was impeding his own progress. After all, if he spent all of his time developing new people, he certainly couldn't do some of the more creative things in training that he had long wanted to implement. The recent promotion of one of his best trainers had been the last straw. He decided to confront Laura King to get her to change her policy.

1. *What can Paul Garth tell his boss?*
2. *Is Laura King's policy a desirable one?*
3. *Should a company's training department be used as a source of promotables?*
4. *Given the widespread acceptance of Laura King's promotion policy, can anything be done to modify it?*

CASE 11-2

The shift operation managers are from the ranks and have grown up with automation. The nature of their responsibilities prohibited them from being able properly to analyze and forecast production except through "seat of the pants" planning. Putting out fires and dealing with ever-present personnel problems occupied a large portion of their time. A new quality control group was established to assist the shift managers by teaching them new techniques to help improve production and cut down on errors. This group was headed by a young, aggressive MBA fully qualified in statistics for quality control and systems analysis. He did not have any background in the operations of a 24-hour shift check processing department in a commercial bank. The shift managers looked forward to learning the new techniques that were supposed to help them. They fully recognized that statistical analysis would be useful, and they did want to cut their error ratio and improve productivity.

The shift managers were surprised when they first met the new quality control manager. He was so young, and when he told them he really didn't know anything about check processing, they started to worry. After all, even though they were only high school graudates, they had from 15 to 30 years of experience in check processing. How could this young kid help them? A serious morale and learning problem developed when the MBA started his instructional process by "talking down" to the shift managers. He seemed to enjoy their lack of understanding of his explanations and their attempts to justify their lack of knowledge by talking about their long experience on the job.

Even though the managers were perfectly willing to be helped, they simply would not listen to this "dumb college kid" as they called him.

1. *What can be done to salvage this situation?*
2. *Can the generation and education gap be overcome?*

3. *Why do some bright young people "talk down" to experienced employees?*
4. *Should the young person be replaced by an older person with similar technical background?*

CASE 11-3

The industrial relations department is in charge of the program set up to train recent college graduates for supervisory positions. Part of the training consists of job rotation. Each person spends about a month in a department, then moves to another department. The purpose of rotation is to acquaint the new trainees with the functions of the various departments and help them find the type of work that is in line with their interests and thus find a niche in the organization. When a trainee finishes his time in each department, he writes a report outlining the functions of the department head also submits a report giving his impressions of the trainee who has been working for him.

One of the trainees, Richard Rice, has had conflicts with most of the supervisors. He is supercharged with bright ideas, energy, ambition, enthusiasm, self-confidence, and tenacity. But he is tactless, abrupt, positive he is right, ruthless and outspoken in his criticism, has as his motto "survival of the fittest," and thinks that "easy does it" is a cover-up for laziness or cowardice. What he calls "speaking factually," the supervisors term "a young know-it-all shooting his mouth off." In dealing with him, the supervisors seem to figure that the best defense is a good offense. Their reports about Richard Rice, and Rice's reports about the departments, are extremely critical—much more so than reports on or by other trainees.

You, the industrial relations director, are responsible for this training program. Your subordinate, Tom Thomas, the training supervisor, has kept you informed of Rice's conflicts and has now brought in the pack of reports on Rice. You see from the reports that all he got in some departments was "busy work."

1. *How should the problem of Rice be handled? Justify your answer.*
2. *Outline a plan for developing greater cooperation between supervisors and trainees in terms of the objectives of the program.*

CASE 11-4

A few days ago you hired Harold White to replace the resigning head of the toolroom. The day White reported for work, you were out sick, and he was put to work by your assistant, Jim Jones. You had neglected to inform Jim about the new man and the job he was to fill.

As soon as you get back on the job, you ask Jim about White. He replies: "White says he is going to quit at the end of the week because he is tired of being pushed around."

You ask Jim how he started the new man on the job. He reports that since he didn't know what White was hired for he asked him, and White said he was hired to work in the toolroom. Since Jim didn't know that the present head of the toolroom planned to resign, he couldn't see where the new man was to fit into the picture; so he kept him busy for a few hours studying the employees' handbook. Then he introduced White to the 20 people in the section; next he told him to look at the various jobs being performed and then go home. The next day Jim thought White should start earning his keep, so he gave him a job on the conveyor line. After a day of it, White complained that he couldn't stand that type of work; so in the afternoon, Jim took White to the head of the toolroom and told him to put White to work helping his assistant. The assistant put him to work cleaning some equipment.

1. *What were some of the mistakes that Jim Jones made in inducting White?*
2. *What would be the normal reaction of White after the first day? After the second day?*
3. *How are you going to correct the situation?*
4. *How would you have inducted White?*
5. *Outline the steps of a procedure for inducting a new employee.*

CASE 11–5

You are in charge of a large section doing office work. All your new workers come to you through the training department. They are turned over to you as being completely trained to do their jobs. However, you receive numerous complaints about the errors these new employees are making. When you approach the training supervisor with a list of recurring errors, she becomes indignant. She tells you that she is a trained teacher—that she is teaching the trainees what they need to know and that she is not taking orders from you on what should be taught.

1. *What are the advantages of training workers away from the job in a training department?*
2. *What are the disadvantages?*
3. *What are the advantages of training workers on the job?*
4. *What are the disadvantages?*
5. *How valid is the saying: "Forget all you learned in school and learn the way we do it on the job"?*
6. *How can the work of the training department and the operating departments be better coordinated?*

CASE 11–6

In a company manufacturing electronics equipment, the training section of the personnel department handles the induction and training of new production workers. The induction or orientation program lasts for a week.

Lectures and tours take two hours each day; the rest of the time is spent taking a battery of tests, receiving skill training, and doing wiring and soldering exercises. The misfits are weeded out during this week. The people who are retained are ready to produce at the shop pace when they are turned over to the shop at the beginning of the second week.

The production department contends that because operators quit without notice a call for replacements means that they need them immediately and not a week later. They argue that a half-day's specialized training is all that is necessary—that all the rest of it is fancywork to justify the existence of the training department.

1. *What are the advantages and disadvantages of induction programs?*
2. *What are the advantages and disadvantages of a training department?*
3. *What are advantages and disadvantages of training on the job?*
4. *How should induction be divided between the personnel and the operating departments?*
5. *How should training be divided?*
6. *Evaluate your own company's training program.*
7. *Evaluate your own company's induction program.*
8. *How can each be strengthened?*

CASE 11-7

Each supervisor has full responsibility for the training of all production employees on the job. The supervisor selects an experienced operator to do the training. All workers are on a piece rate, and the learners are guaranteed a minimum wage plus a 10-percent bonus if the supervisor considers their progress to be satisfactory. The operator who does the training is compensated to make up for the production he loses while giving advice to the new employee.

The personnel department recommends that workers be trained in a training department where they will have the guidance of a skilled trainer. The training period will be eight weeks, during which time speed and output will be measured against a learning curve developed by observing on-the-job trainees. Whenever the learner's performance falls behind that shown on the learning curve, the 10-percent bonus will be stopped.

The production supervisors oppose this plan. They think that new employees are better off if they are put into the regular job environment at once. The supervisors claim that on-the-job training is more satisfactory and is usually completed in less than eight weeks; thus quick learners can be taken off the bonus and costs reduced.

The personnel department advocates uniformity in teaching the best work methods. It claims that supervisors are too busy to devote the time required for constant checking on learners. Consequently, inefficient learners are not weeded out soon enough, and the company loses money through low production.

1. *What are some of the advantages of vestibule training?*
2. *What are some of the disadvantages?*
3. *What are some of the advantages of on-the-job training?*
4. *What are some of the disadvantages of having an operator do the training?*
5. *Is there a way to combine the advantages of the two types?*
6. *Is this learners' bonus plan a good one?*

CASE 11–8

Steve Lyons, a young Ph.D. in psychology, was recently hired by a large commercial bank to do human relations research. During the interview he said that research was his principal interest and that he had turned down several teaching offers. His first project was to conduct a test validation study to meet requirements of the recent U.S. Supreme Court decision on test use by employers.

He was given some other assignments by the personnel vice president. All of these were completed rapidly and efficiently. However, Steve looked upon these and the other short assignments as interruptions of his work on test validation. He had become fascinated with the study so far, and he devoted as much time as possible to it. He had plans for several articles, and he outlined these. Anyone whose attention he could get was subjected to long discourses on test validation. Little by little people began to shun Steve. He chalked this up to their lack of knowledge about the subject and did nothing about it.

Other assignments kept coming to him from the vice president, and Steve began to let these slide to continue work on the validation study. Finally, the vice president called him to his office and asked what was the matter. Steve enthusiastically reported on his progress on test validation. The vice president then told him that he wanted the other studies completed first; test validation could be put on the back burner for the time being. Steve became angry and said that the research was important and that the vice president just didn't understand how to utilize a person of his talents properly, wasting his time on work that could be done by clerks.

1. *What should the vice president do now?*
2. *How can Steve be made to understand organizational priorities?*
3. *Should he have been hired on a full-time basis?*
4. *Could the vice president have oriented Steve more effectively?*

CASE 11–9

Harry Carson accepted a position as a management trainee with Acme Stores, a large national chain of department stores. Harry was very interested in retailing and had majored in marketing at college. He looked forward to the training program since Acme had an excellent reputation and getting a job with them was a real plus.

The first six months of Carson's work involved him in a comprehensive formal program at company headquarters. All phases of store operation were included, and each aspect was taught by excellent trainers who were very knowledgeable in their respective fields. In addition several members of top management talked to the trainees about their work and the desirable future at Acme. Harry also got some line experience since each trainee worked in several departments in the large store located at company headquarters.

Carson was very pleased with his choice of a career and with Acme as a company in which to pursue it. He felt he couldn't have made a better choice. Considerable enthusiasm characterized his outlook as he prepared for his first field assignment. He was sent to the Boston store and reported to the general manager on the first day. Greeting Harry in a perfunctory manner, the manager said. "Another college hotshot—oh well, we'll now teach you the retail business! You wasted four years in college and six months on that nonsense at headquarters. It's about time you got around to earning your pay!"

1. Why would a high-level manager induct a new employee in this way?
2. What might happen to Carson's enthusiasm about the company?
3. Why are experienced managers so often critical of formal training programs?
4. To what extent has the company failed in its training program?

CASE 11–10

People in the financial management training program go through two stages of training. The first lasts for three months of formal classroom work, and then the trainees are assigned to a line manager for on-the-job training. Six months in this type assignment allows them to apply the knowledge received in the classroom. They then go back for three more months of formal training which is more sophisticated, and it builds on what they have already learned.

Some of the early classroom instruction is given by advanced trainees who have demonstrated outstanding competence. An instructional assignment is considered a high honor by the trainees. The teaching assignment also includes supervisory responsibility since the instructor-trainee is responsible for performance evaluation of those trainees reporting to him.

On several occasions the close peer relationship among trainees has caused the instructor-trainees to be less than entirely candid when evaluating a poor performer and when discussing poor performance with the trainee. Because of this the training program manager has not detected problems as early as possible, and corrective action was not instituted when it could have been most helpful. Some trainees have completed the program and have been assigned to jobs where their bosses found they could not function effectively.

1. *Is it a good idea to use advanced trainees as instructors?*
2. *How can these people be convinced to be more accurate and thorough in performance evaluations of their peers?*
3. *Why would they consider the assignment a high honor and then not discharge their responsibility effectively?*

Chapter 12

Learning objectives

○ To develop an understanding of performance appraisal, its complexities and its relationship to more effective human resource utilization

○ To understand the nature of employee promotion and various policies and procedures related to promotion

○ To become aware of personnel planning for organizations and career planning for individuals and their relationship to organizational growth

○ To understand employee mobility, internal transfers, and employee development as part of effective personnel planning

Managing human resources: Personnel planning and performance appraisal

Major topics

Organizational growth and development.

Personnel planning.

Performance appraisal.

Appraisal is systematic rather than haphazard.

Difficulties in rating.

Some common types of rating errors.

Suiting the plan to the purpose.

The appraisal interview as a means of improving performance on the job.

Rating the probationary employee.

Interview problems.

Promotions and the people who want them.

Advantages and disadvantages of promoting from within.

Evaluating and developing supervisors and managers.

Career planning.

The fast-track manager.

Internal mobility.

Remedial transfers.

Other reasons for transfers.

Transfer policy.

The environment for career development.

Other factors in personnel planning.

Most texts on management theory create the impression that the growth and development of an organization is an orderly process. Discussion centers around objectives, policies, structure, control, direction, planning, staffing, and several other management functions. Once goals are identified, a suitable formal structure is designed and the enterprise is off and running.

That this rather simplistic approach to organizational development rarely, if ever takes place, is both one of the most perplexing problems and one of the most significant challenges presented to managers. To understand the impact of the problems and challenges and the various factors involved in them is a necessary part of the manager's responsibility.

The purpose of this chapter is to show managers and supervisors what organizational development and personnel planning mean to them from a career as well as a managerial viewpoint.

Organizational growth and development

Managers make several decisions over a period of time which have a variety of consequences for their organizations. Increased demand for the products or services a firm offers may require decisions to hire more people. More people could require more space and, therefore, a decision to enlarge a plant or an office. Pressure on managers to increase production could cause them to ask for more help. A positive response from superiors would enlarge a supervisor's span of control, causing a decision to promote someone to be an assistant. Thus a new supervisory position is created, changing the nature of the formal organization structure and the established reporting relationships. An opportunity to acquire a company in a related field results in a decision which may take the firm into a different set of circumstances and problems than those with which its managers are familiar. Increased size usually means greater complexity, and this could result in more levels of management as well as requirements for additional supervisors and other employees.

While the growth of some organizations may appear to be "Topsy-like," in actuality it is usually not spontaneous. It is the result of management decisions made by individuals who try to move the organization toward its goals as they perceive them. This does not imply that some of the decisions are not haphazard. In fact the decisions that may have the most effect on an organization are frequently made without full consideration of their total impact. What results in some cases is an organization resembling a patchwork quilt that becomes very difficult to manage.

It is relatively easy for individual managers to plan for their own area of responsibility. Understanding the relationship of their plans to the rest of the organization is a more difficult task. It is precisely this difficulty that causes many of the problems in dynamic organizations.

Growth and development are frequently thought of a synonymous. That they are not is pointed out by Hicks and Gullet in *The Management of Organizations*. They state:

Consider organizational growth to be any increase in the size of the organization or any movement toward a given objective. And consider organizational development, on the other hand, to be formation of new combinations of resources or the formulation of new attainable and visionary objectives. Development involves policy decisions that change organizational objectives. Growth, on the other hand, involves technical or administrative improvement (originating either within or outside the organization) by which it is possible to more effectively accomplish old objectives.

Development is the broader of the two concepts; it occurs through innovation and it provides the framework within which growth can occur. Growth, being narrower, occurs within a given stage of development. Reaching or attaining the maximum output with a given stage of development is a process of attaining maximum growth. Growth asks: How does the organization get more out of what it now has? Development asks: How can the organization achieve something different?[1]

Longevity is not necessarily characteristic of an organization. The number of business failures of both large and small companies each year attests to this. Likewise the large number of mergers and acquisitions of recent years also indicates that a particular organization can disappear as a separate entity by being taken over. To a very great extent, the length of time that an organization exists has a direct relationship to the effectiveness of its managers. Their ability to handle growth and development while establishing and achieving objectives and encouraging efficient operation has a good bit to do with organizational longevity.

Earlier mention was made of recent research indicating that organizational climate had a definite effect on the requirements of that organization. The philosophy of its management in relation to present situations and future considerations is also a dominant factor. The effective utilization of resources, especially human resources, contributes much to organizational longevity. Assuring a constant and adequate supply of cabable managers and other employees is vital to sound organization development. This means the creation of a development environment which will demonstrate that senior management is serious about growth and development and that it will encourage employees on all levels to take advantage of the internal climate to optimize their individual careers.

In the early 1950s, Peter Drucker, in discussing the development of managers, described his thinking—which is still very timely:

The prosperity if not the survival of any business depends on the performance of its managers of tomorrow. This is particularly true today when basic business decisions require for their fruition an increasingly long time-span. Since no one can foresee the future, management cannot make rational and responsible decisions unless it selects, develops, and tests the men who will have to follow them through—the managers of tomorrow.

. . . Manager development cannot be just "promotion planning," confined

---

[1] Herbert G. Hicks and C. Ray Gullet, *The Management of Organizations,* 3d ed. (New York: McGraw-Hill Book Co., 1976), p. 89.

to "promotable people" and aimed at finding "back-up men" for top-management vacancies. The very term "back-up man" implies that the job of a manager as well as the organization structure of a company will remain unchanged so that one simply has to find people to step into the shoes of today's executives. Yet, if one thing is certain, it is that both job requirements and organization structure will change in the future as they have always done in the past. What is needed is the development of managers equal to the tasks of tomorrow, not the taks of yesterday.

    ... The concept of the back-up man for top-management jobs also overlooks the fact that the most important decisions regarding tomorrow's management are made long before a man is promoted to a senior position. Tomorrow's senior positions will be filled by men who today occupy junior positions. By the time we have to find a man to take over the managership of a big plant or sales organization, our choice will already be limited to three or four people. It is in appointing people to positions as general foreman or department superintendent, as district sales manager, as auditor, and so on, that we make the decisions that are crucial. And in making these decisions the typical back-up planning helps us little, if at all.[2]

These rather prophetic remarks form a suitable frame of reference for what we today call organization development. In addition to managers, staffing of the entire organization, the climate created, and the seriousness of management's purpose are the totality of organizational growth and development. This includes several factors, among them:

1. Effective recruitment, selection, training, and placement of new employees.
2. The creation of a climate that will encourage self-development and upward mobility.
3. An effective compensation and reward program.
4. Performance appraisal carried on systematically and as objectively as possible.
5. An effective program of internal mobility, including promotion and transfer of employees, that is mutually acceptable.
6. Early identification of promotables.
7. Supervisor and management development programs (both on-the-job and structured programs) which recognize the inevitability or organizational change.
8. Career planning for employees in which they, as well as their superiors and the personnel department, have a role.

Personnel planning

The above list certainly will not appear as anything particularly new to the reader. Many organizations have been carrying out such practices in one form or another for several years. The point is that in many instances there

---

[2] Peter F. Drucker, *The Practice of Management* (New York: Harper & Row, Publishers, 1954), pp. 182–84.

is no attempt at any coordination of all of the factors. By carrying them out in a fragmented and haphazard manner, the organization cannot reap the total benefit of such programs.

In recent years the combination of rapid technological change and a growing shortage of capable people to fill open jobs of all kinds has caused forward-looking organizations to develop comprehensive personnel planning programs. Such coordinated and systematic effort is therefore new for most of these organizations. Accurately anticipating staffing needs is both complex and obscure. Making a rather definite commitment to employees about their careers may be difficult for a management that has preferred to carry on discussions about employee promotability without including them in the discussion.

Two factors which are basic have encouraged the development of sound and comprehensive personnel planning. In the first, promotion from within policies have become very common among all types of organizations in our society. A variety of reasons have caused such wide acceptance of this policy. Probably most critical is the ever-increasing cost of recruiting and training an effective work force in a rapidly changing and relatively prosperous economy. Retention of employees becomes critical when the labor market does not have a plentiful supply of potentially capable employees and supervisors.

Closely related to the first factor is the wide choice of job opportunities available to the capable (and frequently the not so capable) individual. The full employment policies followed by the federal government have had a considerable impact on the type of unemployment existing in our economy. Frank H. Cassell of the Inland Steel Company quoted the following statistics in a speech published by the Industrial Relations Center of the University of Minnesota:[3]

> A full employment policy, however, has varying degrees of impact upon employment, depending on the level of skill, knowledge, and experience needed, and the availability of those qualities in the work force by geographical area. For example, at a 4.1% overall employment rate, unemployment [rates] for people with varying skills are as follows:
>
> | | |
> |---|---|
> | Managers and officials | 0.9 |
> | Professional, technical, and kindred workers | 1.5 |
> | Craftsmen, foremen, and kindred workers | 2.2 |
> | Clerical and kindred workers | 3.7 |
> | Service workers, ex. private workers | 5.1 |
> | Operatives and kindred workers | 5.4 |
> | Laborers (nonfarm) | 8.1 |

When geographical differences, specific occupations, and the age of employables are all taken into consideration, the problems confronting an organization's personnel department become more apparent. It is easy to see why effective personnel planning is an absolute necessity.

When people are already employed, it is quite natural for them to look to

---

[3] Frank H. Cassell, *Corporate Manpower Planning* (Industrial Relations Center, University of Minnesota, Special Release 6, February 1968), p. 3.

"Some day, son, you'll probably try to take
this all away from me."

Reprinted by permission The Wall Street Journal

*Effective personnel planning aids in manage-
ment succession.*

their own companies for career opportunities. This is certainly true if they
are satisfied with their present jobs. Part of job satisfaction should come
from knowledge of the quality of employee performance as indicated to that
employee by the supervisor.

Performance appraisal

Most organizations have some formal or informal way of evaluating employees—for judging their performance, behavior, abilities, and potentialities. Formal evaluating is done by filling out an appraisal form. The second
step is usually an interview with the appraised employee and a discussion
of the evaluation. In most cases the immediate supervisor does the evaluating—or is one of the evaluators and handles the interview.

The program may be called employee evaluation, merit rating, employee rating, efficiency rating, service rating, performance review, performance appraisal, progress report, personnel review, employee appraisal, or some such name. It may be tied to pay raises or it may be separate from salary adjustment. It may be part of a program of identifying promotable people, or it may concentrate on improving effectiveness of performance on the present job. It may be a perfunctory "handing out of report cards," or it may be a constructive session reviewing performance for the purpose of planning for future performance. It may be an embarassing or hostile session probing into personality flaws, or it may be a means of increasing the effectiveness of performance. Of course, some people do not want to hear about their performance—particularly if the report is negative and too critical. Such an appraisal may destroy an employee's self-image and personal attitudes about ability. Nevertheless, feedback on employee performance is vital to an effective supervisor-employee relationship, and the majority of employees find it to be a useful and frequently a rewarding experience.

Evaluating and developing employees is a continuation of the supervisor-subordinate relationship begun in induction and carried on in training. Evaluation is a means by which the supervisor lets the employee know how he or she is doing. It is part of the feedback of results and can be used to stimulate the employee's continued learning and continued improvement on the job. It is a way to direct efforts into channels that will enable the employee to become more valuable to the company.

Evaluation is of particular importance to new employees. It gives them an opportunity to find out whether they and the boss agree on what is expected and how well they are doing it. It gives them guidance to help prepare for a future with the company. If they want to advance, they are concerned about the opportunities and what should be done to prepare for them. If they are not doing well, they are entitled to a warning and to counseling on what's wrong and what can be done to correct it. If they aren't suited to the work, they should find out before too much time is invested.

On some jobs employees can measure the quality and quantity of their own performance against standards of work performance and know where they stand on production. But there are other factors that enter into job performance and value to the company. Does the employee get along well with others in the performance of the work? Is the employee steady, interested, and willing? Is job knowledge adequate or is constant help needed? Are instructions, rules, and regulations complied with and understood? Does the employee work safely and influence others to work safely? Is prodding necessary or is the employee a self-starter? Can the person work without close supervision? Is the employee punctual and regular in attendance? Can he or she be relied on to carry through a job properly? Does the person use initiative, contribute good ideas, and cooperate in improving methods? Is the employee flexible and adaptable in adjusting to changed conditions? Does he or she have knowledge of related jobs that could be handled in emergencies? Is there willingness to learn new duties? Is there promotion potential for the employee? How soon?

The performance appraisal process is graphically described in Figure 12-1. Of particular importance is feedback to employees on the results of their appraisals.

Figure 12-1
The performance appraisal process

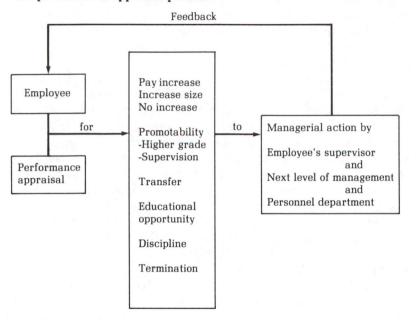

Appraisal is systematic rather than haphazard

The supervisor makes infomal evaluations of employees in everyday decisions about them. Judgments are made about them when special jobs are assigned, when training is given, and when raises and promotions are recommended. The supervisor is making judgments when recommending transfer, demotion, or dismissal. Some of the decisions may be impulsive ones, made to fit the needs of the moment. A planned system of employee evaluation should make the decisions more deliberate, factual, and fair, because it will be based on systematic comparison of person against person and person against standard.

Having to write an evaluation periodically forces supervisors to be more analytical about their people and their performance. When they have to back up some of their opinions, they may realize that they were unfounded and unfair. Since they have to have evidence for evaluation, they have to measure the amount of work people are doing and the quality of it. They have to compare it to the standards of work performance to see if people are measuring up to requirements and if they are improving or slipping. Attendance records must be studied to see which employees are getting to work on time every day and which ones are taking a lot of time off.

If an employee's work and behavior record are so unsatisfactory that the person should be discharged or if the work is so poor that the individual should be demoted, the evidence collected and recorded on the rating form is support for the action. It is difficult to discharge or demote an employee who has been getting good ratings on the job; so the supervisor must collect objective evidence over the whole rating period and be as factual as possible in the evaluations.

Evaluation of people involves subjective judgment as well as performance records, and it is subject to error. But if supervisors are given training, they can improve their rating abilities. The act of gathering, studying, and comparing information on all the employees improves the quality of decisions concerning each one of them and reduces the danger of being unfair.

Difficulties in rating

Figure 12–2 reproduces a form for rating hourly employees, listing factors of quality, quantity, dependability, job knowledge, and adaptability. In a later section, a form for rating supervisors is shown and discussed; it lists a greater number of factors. The discussion in this section is concerned mainly with the supervisor who must rate subordinates on the kinds of factors shown in Figure 12–2.

Ratings on these factors may be used to compare performances on a companywide basis rather than just within a department. It is important therefore that supervisors be trained to rate on a uniform basis. If some rate tightly and others loosely, an injustice will be done to the employees who are being appraised for promotion, training, discharge, merit increases, salary changes, or bonus payments. Some of the criticism of employee evaluation stems from the lack of uniformity among raters.

Forced choice.   In order to get away from supervisors' leniency or bias in rating, some companies use forms that don't list factors or degrees (such as unsatisfactory, fair, good, excellent, outstanding—or their numerical or alphabetical equivalents). Instead, a "forced choice" form is used, presenting groups of statements describing behavior. In each group of statements the supervisor is required to check the one most applicable to the person being rated. On some forms he must also check the statement that least resembles the person being rated.[4]

Examples of such behavioral statements follow. They usually include a measurement scale ranging from one indicating least applicable to six indicating most applicable.

---

[4] For more about rating methods, see L. L. Cummings and Donald P. Schwab, *Performance in Organizations* (Glenview, Ill.: Scott, Foresman and Co., 1973).

Figure 12–2
Form for rating hourly employees

LOCKHEED AIRCRAFT CORPORATION - MISSILE SYSTEMS DIVISION

EMPLOYEE PERIODIC HOURLY REVIEW

DEPT.	PLANT	S	NAME		OCCUPATION	SENIORITY DATE MO. DAY YEAR	EMPLOYEE NO.

EFFECTIVE DATE OF THIS REVIEW	PRESENT RATE	WAS EFFECTIVE MO. DAY YEAR	SENT TO DEPT. MO. DAY YEAR	THIS REPORT MUST REACH INDUSTRIAL RELATIONS BEFORE	MO. DAY YEAR

Describe specific work employee has been performing during this review period

State approximate length of time on this type of work in your department.

THIS FORM WILL ACT AS A CHANGE-OF-STATUS IF A MERIT INCREASE IS RECOMMENDED AT THIS TIME.

NOTICE PREPARED BY	DATE	KARDEX POSTED	(IF NO CHANGE, ENTER 'SAME') NEW PAY RATE→	CHANGE CODE 1	GRADE	DIFFERENCE

APPROVALS

LAST RATE CHANGE

IMMEDIATE SUPERVISION	PERSONNEL REPRESENTATIVE
DEPARTMENT HEAD	EXECUTIVE

The following factors are to be rated. The order in which these factors are listed in no way reflects their respective value.

DEPENDABILITY
Your Confidence in Employee's Ability to Accept Responsibility

Refuses to or not able to carry much responsibility; needs constant follow-up.

Usually follows instructions; needs some follow-up

Willing and able to accept responsibility; requires little follow-up.

Outstanding ability to follow through on all assignments with no detail supervision.

QUANTITY
Output - Speed

Exceptionally fast; unusual output.

Does more work than expected; is fast; exceeds requirements

Output meets acceptable standards; is satisfactory

Output below normal requirements; definitely slow.

ADAPTABILITY
Versatility; Adjustment to Job or Changed Conditions; Ease with which New Duties are Learned.

Meets changed conditions with little effort; has outstanding ability to pick up new jobs.

Learns well with minimum amount of instruction; adjusts himself well in a short time.

Learns fairly well but needs detailed instruction for each new job.

Is slow to learn; has trouble adjusting himself to changed conditions; needs constant instruction.

JOB KNOWLEDGE
Technical Knowledge of Job and Related Work.

Has limited knowledge of his job; knows nothing of related work.

Knows his job fairly well; has little knowledge of related work.

Seldom needs help; has good knowledge of his job and related work; is well-informed.

Has excellent knowledge of his job and related work; is very well-informed.

QUALITY
Accuracy in Work; Freedom from Errors

Makes practically no mistakes; highest accuracy.

Makes very few errors; is accurate; does high grade work.

Makes some errors but does passable work.

Makes mistakes frequently.

COMMENTS:

RATED BY

Source: Reproduced by permission of Lockheed Aircraft Corporation, Missile Systems Division.

1. High capability for technical work.
2. Suited for staff assignments.
3. Willing to make decisions.
4. Very helpful in regular assignments.
5. Capable in work related discussions.

A complete rating form would have 25 or more such statements. Some are favorable and some are not, and some depend on interpretation. For instance, "High capability for technical work" is favorable if the employee is being considered for a higher level technical assignment, but unfavorable if a supervisory position is under consideration.

The essential problem with this approach to rating is that supervisors do not know how it will be used or which statements are favorable. The grading of the statements and the totaling of the scores is done by the personnel department. The supervisor can only guess how the statements will be scored and whether the employee is being given a favorable or unfavorable rating. This makes the form somewhat useless for couseling the employee and explaining how and why a particular rating was determined. The development of this type of appraisal system is very difficult since a great deal of effort and research is necessary to define a valid, job-related group of behavioral statements to use.

Defining factors. Where forced choice is not used, raters must have a common understanding of the definition of the factors they are rating. *Dependability, for example, could mean a number of things: Does it* mean that the employee shows up for work every day and gets there on time and in condition to work? Does it mean that he or she can be trusted to carry the money to the bank? Does it mean that the person can be relied upon to get the work done properly? This third meaning is the one given in the Lockheed rating form (Figure 12–2). If it were not defined, then under *dependability* one supervisor would be rating attendance, another would be rating honesty, and the third would be rating work performance.

Defining the degrees. When the rating form lists factors and degrees of factors, there is a problem of getting agreement between the raters as to what is meant by the various degrees. The degrees (such as excellent, superior, average, fair, or poor) constitute the measuring stick, and it is essential that all raters use the same stick. What is "excellent" to one rater should not be "superior" to another, and what is "fair" to one rater should not be "poor" to another. The rating system must set up some kind of bench mark for what is average, and some kind of guide for judging the degrees above and below it.

Forced distribution. This method is similar to what students call "grading on the curve." The supervisor is supposed to rank subordinates in categories such as superior, above average, satisfactory, and inadequate. Typically, the top 20 percent would be rated as superior, the next 30 percent as above average, the next 30 percent as satisfactory, and the bottom 20 percent as inadequate. This system is designed to minimize overlenient ratings by supervisors. It assumes that all work groups have a distribution of performance quality which can be neatly "curved," and this is the principal objection to this approach by supervisors who use it.

Fairness in rating.   In judging people against a bench mark, the fairest way to do it is to take one factor at a time and rank all of the people on that one factor (rather than take one person at a time and rank him on all of the factors). In rating people on job knowledge, for instance, it is not too difficult to identify the highest and the lowest people in the group. It is the in-between people who are difficult to place. They can be compared one to another and then ranked in order of best to worst on that one factor.

Supervisors must base their ratings on evidence that is as objective as possible and that is gathered over the whole rating period. They should not rely on impressions or base judgments on a few outstanding successes or failures. Daily observations over the entire rating period help to put any "off-day" difficulties or unusual performances into their true perspective. Incidents that are going into the record to be used against employees must be discussed with them at the time of their occurrence, so that they have an opportunity to explain what happened.

In order to protect against prejudice and errors in judgment, some companies have more than one person work on the rating of an employee. A number of people who are acquainted with an employee's work may act as a committee in making an appraisal. Or a personnel representative may act as a counselor to assist the supervisor in making out the ratings. Or the rater's boss may go over the ratings to judge their accuracy. The employees may be able to appeal the ratings if they consider them unfair.

Some common types of rating errors

Some supervisors have a tendency to rate their groups too high. They don't want to cause hard feelings, and they think that low ratings reflect on their own abilities as trainers and leaders. Some groups will be out of the ordinary in one direction or the other, but the supervisor should be able to produce evidence to prove it.

Some supervisors who have not gathered evidence about all of the factors they must rate will rate the ones they are in doubt about as "average," which is an injustice. This error is called the "central tendency." Other supervisors make a worse mistake in handling factors on which they have too little evidence. They rate the unknowns the same as some other factor they do know about. That error is called the "halo effect." For example, a supervisor has evidence that an employee's quality and quantity are poor but doesn't know the person well enough to know his or her attitude. The supervisor just assumes that the attitude must be poor also and rates it that way.

Supervisors must not let their ratings be influenced by conscious or unconscious prejudice against a race, nationality, or religion or by partiality to friends, relatives, and social acquaintances. When supervisors are rating employees, they must guard against softness—a tendency to be good to everybody; spinelessness—and unwillingness to take the risk of unfavorable decisions; hurry—failure to take the time to do a good job; and harshness—a tendency to underrate everybody, particulary new employees.

Suiting the plan to the purpose

There are a number of types of evaluation plans and a number of purposes which they are designed to serve. *Merit rating* plans are designed to stimulate people to high performance in order to get pay increases and upgrading. Merit rating is based on the belief that people who perform better on the job should be paid more, and it provides a system for judging their performance and rewarding it. Rewards of pay increases follow a pattern upward on a range set by job evaluation. On the same job a person of outstanding ability might be paid quite a bit more than a person who was just adequate. The factors on the rating sheet get a numerical rating, and the score determines whether the employee gets an increase for that period. In unionized companies, seniority may be more of a factor in advancement than merit, and the prevailing sentiment may favor raises for everybody rather than just for the high performers.

Measuring potential for advancement.   Some types of employee evaluation plans are heavily slanted toward management development. The rating forms emphasize personality, appearance, enthusiasm, mentality, sociability, and other traits considered desirable for a higher job. The assortment of traits may be designed to identify people who are outstanding in the qualities necessary for particular jobs. A person's score on the appraisal may be compared to the scores of employees in all parts of the company in order to determine which ones should be groomed for promotion.

When employee evaluation is used primarily for appraising advancement potential, raises, promotions, and preparations for higher jobs become the central theme. But the future just doesn't hold quick promotions for everybody. Overemphasis on promotion frustrates and demoralizes employees who are passed over time after time. For this reason some companies have two types of evaluation: one (just discussed) for appraising potential for advancement, and the other (discussed below) for evaluating current job performance.

The appraisal interview as a means of improving performance on the job

Accurate information about employees' performance on their present jobs is a very necessary aspect of effective personnel planning. Not only can the appraisal interview aid in helping employees toward better performance on their present jobs, but it also may give some idea of their transferability to other work of a similar nature. In other words, this kind of information increases the options of both the employer and the supervisor. Figure 12–3 shows one company's suggestions for appraisal interviews.

If the employee evaluation is to result in improved performance on the job, the appraisal interview should be centered on performance and not on innate abilities or personality traits. In order to discuss performance, the supervisor should have evidence of the quality and quantity of work and whether it meets the standards. In telling the subordinate what parts of the work are satisfactory and what parts unsatisfactory, the supervisor should talk in terms of results rather than faults. The supervisor should try to get the subordinate to fill in the information about the circumstances that led to the results. The subordinate should be encouraged to discuss his or her own performance and anything in the situation which made it hard to do the job. If job difficulties are matters of personality, the employee should be asked to evaluate and discuss them in terms of job performance and suggest what could be done about them. Employees seem to be able to accept correction that relates to their performance and behavior but not to their personalities. Subordinates may criticize themselves on their own lacks and weaknesses, but if the supervisor has to do the criticizing, it had better be confined to observed behavior rather than to the flaws in the personality that caused the behavior.

If subordinates have weaknesses that can't be changed or if they are working right up to the limit of their capacity, nothing is to be gained by deflating egos.

Subordinates who are doing a passable but uninspired job and could do much better should be asked to appraise their own performance and abilities. They should be pressed to work out a plan for improving performance and to set up a schedule for it. People seem to need definite plans, with deadlines built in, in order to get started and keep going until they achieve the goals they set. The supervisor should follow up at specified times to see if the employee is improving.

Interviewing the unsatisfactory performer. If an employee's performance is unacceptable, the supervisor should find out—before the interview—whether to talk in terms of transfer, demotion, or discharge. The appraisal sheet should show cause to support the action. The appraisal interview should give warning of what the employee is to expect.

If employees are capable of satisfactory work but are not trying, they should be told what is unsatisfactory about their performance and what must be done to correct it. A date should be set by which the required amount of improvement should be demonstrated. The plan and the timetable should be put in writing as evidence that employees were given a warning and an offer of help. Then if they do not improve, the supervisor will be in a position to take action.

If people are making an effort but failing on the job, and training can't solve the problem, the supervisor must find out if it is possible to transfer or

Figure 12–3
Suggestions for appraisal interviews

REMEMBER TO ....

Select a good time and place to talk.
Begin discussion on mutually familiar ground.
Be relaxed, natural, and a good listener.
Can you lead into your points indirectly?
Keep the discussion out of irrelevant or emotional areas.
In a direct approach, let the person "save face."
Make the person sure your primary interest is in him or her.
Don't "talk down" to the employee.
Make the employee want to come back.

PRINCIPLES
OF
GOOD MERIT RATING
INTERVIEWING

Industrial Relations Division
Bell & Howell Co.

CHECKLIST FOR INTERVIEW

OUTSTANDING ABILITIES OR QUALIFICATIONS

AREAS REQUIRING IMPROVEMENT

SPECIFIC TRAINING RECOMMENDATIONS

ANALYZE DISCUSSION RESULTS:

What does the employee hope to achieve within the Company?

What is the person doing to improve?

What immediate plans for improvement did you agree upon?

PURPOSES OF COUNSELING INTERVIEW FOLLOWING MERIT RATING

A.   Getting the employee to do a better job through making clear your standards of performance. You, too, have peculiar traits. Here is a chance for the employee to learn your preferences in quality, quantity, and methods of work and to understand your reasons for these standards.

B.   Giving the employee a clear picture of how he or she is doing with emphasis upon strengths as well as weaknesses. Much trouble can result in business and industry from employees whose self-rating is sharply at variance with their supervisor's evaluation.

C.   Discussing plans for improvement, and projects to better use employee's abilities.

D.   Building strong personal relationships between supervisor and employee in which both are willing to talk frankly about the job, how it is being done, what improvement is possible, and how it can be obtained. Improving person-to-person understanding so that closer, stronger relationships exist.

Source: Reproduced by permission of the Industrial Relations Division, Bell & Howell Co.

To help their supervisors handle merit rating interviews, the Industrial Relations Division of the Bell & Howell Company gives each supervisor a folded card outlining the purposes of the interview and giving suggestions and a checklist for conducting it.

demote them to a job for which they are better fitted. Often separation from the company is really a kindness to such people. Too often supervisors procrastinate and allow the unsuited employee to struggle on year after year while the problem becomes worse rather than better. The supervisor would do well to consult the personnel department before interviewing the employee who can't make the grade.

Rating the probationary employee

Many of the problems of the unfit employee could be avoided through a more careful rating of performance during the probationary period. This is the time to study ability, performance, and behavior and to decide whether the employee should be permitted to become permanent. The decision has long-range significance, since dismissal will never again be this easy and the employee may stay on in the company for 30 years. Many an unsatisfactory, disgruntled employee is the result of the supervisor's failure to take decisive action.

The trial work period is the most reliable test for determining whether the new person is going to become a desirable employee. It is superior to any of the techniques of selection developed thus far. If the trial period is long enough, new employees will show their true colors during it. If they are undependable or have a tendency toward tardiness, absenteeism, drunkenness, troublemaking, or other undesirable behavior, some symptoms will show up. If they fail to make satisfactory progress toward proficiency in the work, they are probably not suited to it and never will become good producers. If it is doubtful whether they have the minimum qualifications necessary to become successful employees, they should be terminated.

On the other hand, when trial employees have the qualifications, and the evaluation sheets show that they have reached the standards of performance for the tasks they are performing, the supervisor should make sure to tell them so. At the end of the trial work period, the supervisor should call the person in, offer congratulations for making the grade, the rating should be discussed, and praise given for the progress that has been made. Then the supervisor should spend the greater portion of the interview working out a program for the employee's future development.

Some companies provide for a follow-up evaluation three months later. Frequent evaluations of new employees provide an opportunity to counsel them, guide them, help them become more effective on their present jobs, and show them that it is worth their while to be ambitious and cooperative.

Interview problems

Supervisors have to use the type of interview that suits their personalities, the personalities of the subordinates, and the circumstances and problems involved.

One of the problems that turns up in an appraisal interview is that subordinates object strongly to the evaluation put on their performance; they simply don't see it that way. Some supervisors meet this one by narrowing the area of disagreement. They ask subordinates to fill out a sheet the way they believe it should be. Then they find the points on which the two sheets do agree. They ask the subordinate to tell them why they rate the remaining factors as high as they do. If the explanation isn't convincing, they go back and review the points of agreement. Then they return to a discussion of the disputed items and try to get agreement on some of them. If subordinates won't change their stands, they ask them to take a few days to think it over.

When a subordinate is not getting an expected raise or promotion, and loses his or her temper, the individual should be allowed to blow off steam. If the employee accuses the supervisor of unfairness, he or she should be encouraged to discuss it thoroughly. If old gripes are brought up that are still bothering the employee, this is a good time to let the person get them out in the open. Whatever the subordinate's reaction, the supervisor should avoid being dragged into an argument. Arguing with an angry person doesn't lead to a plan for future development.

It is not the supervisor's purpose to tell employees how to run their lives, but to help them see realistically the qualities of their performance, their problems, abilities, skills, strong and weak points, and the areas for possible development and self-improvement. Employees have to look at themselves realistically and see where they stand before they are ready to think about self-improvement.

When the supervisor starts to discuss an employee's work performance, the employee is naturally apprehensive and defensive. The more the person is on the defensive, the less advice he or she will take. If lack of effort is the reason for inadequate performance, the supervisor should make it clear that it does not imply a lack of ability.

Evaluations of ability and personality may strike at the employee's ego. To imply that a person has a serious lack is to risk wounding the person to the point of barring any further communication. When it is necessary to call attention to weaknesses, the supervisor should try to get the employee to do it. Much of the hostility in an appraisal interview comes from the employee's feeling that his or her personal worth is being attacked.[5] If the supervisor will keep this in mind, the discussion will be about performance rather than about traits. When the supervisor is talking about strong points and weak points, he or she will do it from the standpoint of their application to the performance of a particular job and as they look from the evidence at hand. The supervisor will put the emphasis on the job and its objectives and

[5] For suggestions on handling the appraisal interview, see Marion S. Kellog, *What to Do about Performance Appraisal,* rev. ed (New York: AMACOM, 1975); Alan Locher and Kenneth Teel, "Performance Appraisal—A Survey of Current Practices," *Personnel Journal,* vol. 56, no. 5 (May 1977), p. 245; Douglas McGregor, "An Uneasy Look at Performance Appraisal," *Harvard Business Review,* vol. 35, no. 3 (May 1957), p. 90.

responsibilities, and on the problems encountered in carrying out the job. The focus will be on what the subordinate does and not what the subordinate is. The supervisor will talk about the problems the subordinate runs into but not about the problems of the individual's personality.[6]

Generally, most employees will react favorably to constructive criticism. If it is presented in a positive manner, employees can be made to recognize that their own welfare will benefit from a positive reaction. On the other hand, an employee who does not have the talent or desire to do the job well may react negatively and try to blame environmental conditions such as the workplace, fellow employees, tools, and even the supervisor.

Promotions and the people who want them

Not everyone in the organization is eager to become a high-level manager. Some want to stay put; some want to advance part way; some want to get to the top. Many employees don't want the risks that go with advancement and with the assumption of authority and responsibility. They may be top-notch performers right where they are, and that is where they feel comfortable. They will take their advancement in the form of wage increases and service pins.

People who are capable of becoming supervisors have more belief in their own competence and their ability to control circumstances and shape results. They have more of what is called "tolerance for ambiguity." They are willing to take some risks and get a certain enjoyment out of carrying responsibility and exercising authority. They are willing to trade some of their comfort for accomplishment. They will keep pushing until they find themselves at a level at which they like to operate. They may stop at the first, second, or some higher level of management where they have fulfilled their ambitions or are near capacity. At the proper level such a person usually has a good team, has everything under control, is stable, and can always be depended upon. He or she handles the group with skill and has people working efficiently and they are happy working together. Such a person is valuable right where he or she is and should get recognition for the good job being done. The person should be made to feel secure in that job and not be pushed to advance to a higher one. He or she is a carry-the-load individual who has found the spot at which he is happiest and can operate the best.

Some other person may have his or her sights set on the top job. This person takes a special joy in the competition and excitement of fighting his or her way up. The idea of achieving steady advancement is primary, and the person is discontent if he or she has to stay in one spot too long.

---

[6] For excellent suggestions on an interview of this type, see Mortimer R. Feinberg, "Is the Performance Review a Threat or a Promise?" in Elizabeth Marting, Robert E. Finley, and Ann Ward, eds., *Effective Communication on the Job*, rev. ed. (New York: American Management Assn., Inc., 1963), pp. 233–42; and Robert Hoppock, "Seventeen Principles of Appraisal Interviews," ibid., pp. 242–45.

The successful organization needs a good mixture of these three types of people. The system of rewards should be designed so that each one can work toward his or her own level of satisfaction. For the people who want to get ahead, there should be definite paths of promotion and guidance in preparing for them.

Advantages and disadvantages of promoting from within

Promotion stimulates individuals to greater effort, enables them to develop to capacity, and keeps them from leaving the company to seek opportunities elsewhere. A policy of promotion from within builds high morale because employees can see that extra effort is rewarded.

When people move up the line, they bring with them knowledge and experience gained in the jobs handled in the company on the way up. They know the way the company operates, the way its people operate, the policies and problems of the organization, and what has and has not worked in the past. Their closeness to the organization is a mixed blessing, though; they are not new brooms or new blood and are not bringing in the fresh viewpoint or the new ideas that come with executives recruited from another company. Disadvantages of inbreeding can be overcome to some extent by getting new ideas from outside sources—evening-school courses, books in the management field, trade publications, professional meetings, and business clubs.

Promotions must be made with great care because mistakes are hard to rectify. Whenever a person is promoted, someone else may be disappointed or jealous. If the wrong individual is chosen for the job, there are charges of favoritism. If the person chosen does not have the ability to fill the job, the efficiency of everyone under his or her supervision is impaired. If the person has to be replaced, there is the problem of what to do with the individual. It may be impossible to put that person back on his or her old job. If the person leaves the company, an employee who was at least good enough to be considered for promotion is lost.

Evaluating and developing supervisors and managers

Probably one of the best indicators of potential for higher management positions is the quality of performance as a first-level supervisor. Many experts believe there will be a shortage of managers in future years.[7] Because of this, well-run organizations have a variety of programs to evaluate and develop future managers. Many of these programs are based on

---

[7] For one such viewpoint see John B. Miner, *The Human Constraint: The Coming Shortage of Managerial Talent* (Washington, D.C.: The Bureau of National Affairs, 1974).

performance evaluations of the present assignment and an evaluation of potential using such factors as the following:

1. Outstanding abilities and weaknesses.
2. Individual ambition and progress made toward achieving the goal.
3. How close the person is to the top of job performance capacity.
4. Personality factors including attitudes.
5. Effectiveness of judgment, planning, and organizing.
6. Nature of initiative and innovative behavior.
7. Effectiveness of cost control in present assignment.
8. Individual's demonstrated leadership style.
9. State of morale in present area of responsibility measured by such things as the amount of lateness, absenteeism, turnover, discipline problems, complaints, accidents, grievances, and the number of promotables coming from the work group.
10. Ability of individual to train and develop others.
11. Amount of self-development undertaken.
12. Quality of peer, superior, and subordinate relationships.
13. Ability of self-expression in speech and writing.
14. Willingness to assume greater responsibility and take on extra assignments.
15. Degree of objectivity in relation to ethnic, racial, religious, educational, sex, and economic status of other people.
16. Individual's flexibility in both job and people relationships.
17. Ability to handle job pressures.
18. Attitudes about achievement and the need to succeed.

There are others that could be included, but those listed should demonstrate the type of factors considered to be important to managerial success. Obviously the person must want to be a higher level manager by clearly indicating the desire to superiors in everything he or she does on the job.

Figure 12–4 is an example of a form used to evaluate supervisory performance and potential. Included on this form is space for identifying specific accountabilities and the results achieved, a series of behavioral factors, traits, counseling recommendations, and comments by the reviewer and the supervisor being evaluated. Senior management also adds comments. This form is completed annually for each supervisor thereby building a detailed performance and potential record to enable more effective promotion choices.

Career planning

The evaluation of factors such as those above frequently constitute one of the first steps in career planning for an individual. When the supervisor's boss rates the person high on performance and the forecast for promotability is favorable, higher management becomes interested in his or her devel-

Figure 12–4
Rating supervisory performance and potential

Performance Planning and Evaluation   **Supervisory Format**

Supervisor's Name		Title		Sal. Class	Cost Ctr.	Evaluation Date	Last Eval. Date
Number of Employees Supervised in Each Salary Class				Total No. Supervised		Time in Position	Time under Reviewer
						Yrs. Mo.	Yrs. Mo.

Instructions: Read Performance Planning and Evaluation Manual Supervisory Format (No. 04 0068) in entirety. Refer back to the Manual for any phase of this evaluation form which may need further clarification.

Part I: Goals/Accountabilities *Total Weight Factors =50*

Instructions: Record and weight specific goals/accountabilities. Record Target Date. At the review, record the specific performance results and comments in the appropriate space. Evaluate these results on each goal/accountability and indicate the weight factor in the column which most accurately describes the performance. Total the figures in each column and multiply by the appropriate multiple *(see below)*. Add these figures together for Part I Total and transfer this Total Figure to Page 4 *(where indicated)*.

Weight	Specific Goal/Accountability	Target Date	Results and Comments	U	A	C	F

Total	**Definition of Terms:**						
	0=Unsatisfactory (U): Goal/Accountability was not achieved; progress and/or results below an acceptable level.	X		0	.5	1.0	1.5
	.5=Acceptable (A): Goal/Accountability was not fully achieved but progress considered sufficient and/or results justified.						
50	**1.0=Accomplished (C):** Goal/Accountability was achieved as agreed upon and within target date.						
	1.5=Far Exceeded (F): Denotes a superior level of achievement, well beyond the stated goal/accountability and within target date.				**Total**		

Transfer to Page 4

Figure 12–4 (continued)

Part II: Required Performance Factors *Total Weight Factors Part II and Part III=50*				
Instructions: Assign weight factors to each category at the start of the performance period. When evaluating the supervisor, consider every phrase in each statement in relation to the supervisor's performance. Indicate the weight factor in the column which best describes the supervisor's performance. Total the figures *(see below for definitions of terms)* in each column and multiply by the appropriate multiple. Add these figures together for Part II Total and transfer this Total Figure to Page 4 *(where indicated).*				

Weight	Communications	L	D	B	F
	With Management: keeps in contact with superiors, reporting both favorable and unfavorable situations; generally able to orally express situations clearly and directly. Comments:				
Weight	**With Staff:** keeps in contact with supervised employees; is accessible to them; willing and available to listen, answer questions and help with problems; keeps supervised employees informed on important departmental and company policies. Comments:	L	D	B	F
Weight	**With Reports and Documentation:** Submits thorough reports when necessary; maintains adequate written records on personnel and workflow; meets deadlines on reports. Comments:	L	D	B	F
Weight	**Staff Development** Teaches and assists supervised employees; develops and encourages most to progress; able to retain adequate staff; trains replacements; willing to promote top performers into other areas. Comments:	L	D	B	F
Weight	**Planning and Organization** Usually attacks workload systematically; sets priorities; generally works from predesigned plans; creates realistic schedules; structures most tasks for smooth workflow without constant supervision. Comments:	L	D	B	F
Weight	**Performance Evaluation** Uses performance evaluations as a method to motivate and encourage employees to better performance; evaluates fairly and consistently in most cases; documents performance; identifies means and counsels employees on how to improve their performance; identifies and rewards top achievers and takes necessary measures with unsatisfactory performers. Comments:	L	D	B	F

Total	Definition of Terms:

0=Less than Statement (L): Performance generally less than that described by statement. Must be documented in Comments.
.5=Described by Statement (D): Performance generally described by statement. Comments encouraged.
1.0=Better than Statement (B): Performance generally better than statement. Comments encouraged.
1.5=Far Exceeds Statement (F): Performance consistently far exceeds the statement. Must be documented.

X | 0 | .5 | 1.0 | 1.5

Total
Transfer to Page 4

Total II & III = 50

Figure 12–4 (continued)

Part III: Optional Performance Factors	*Total Weight Factors Part II and Part III=50*

Instructions: Determine the areas to be evaluated and the weight factors to be assigned at the start of the performance period. At the review, evaluate only those areas already agreed upon. Then proceed exactly as instructed in Part II. Transfer the total to Page 4 *(where indicated).*

Weight		L	D	B	F
	Use of Authority: exercises leadership when necessary; has earned the respect of most superiors and subordinates; uses discipline and rewards appropriately, in most instances. Comments:				
	Delegation: assigns responsibilities and tasks appropriate both to function and to individual's knowledge; follows up to be sure the task is understood and progressing. Comments:				
	Decision-Making: recognizes when a decision should be made; makes most decisions only within scope of authority; gathers pertinent and adequate information; decisions are usually sound and timely; accepts responsibility for most decisions made. Comments:				
	Motivation: generally aware of what motivates own staff to maximize their performance. Comments:				
	Technical Job Knowledge: sufficient knowledge of own function, that of the area and its place in the overall operation; makes adequate use of staff's technical expertise; keeps informed on innovation and changes in the field which might affect the unit. Comments:				
	Customer and User Feedback: recognizes customers' needs; deals effectively with other areas; courteous in dealings with users; thorough and reliable on follow-through. Comments:				
	Innovation and Creativity: offers some practical new ideas within the scope of the area; generally creative in supervision; sees job as more than nine to five routine; accepts innovative suggestions from staff. Comments:				
	Initiative: readily accepts new projects and direction; sometimes seeks additional responsibilities Comments:				
	Personnel Policies: has adequate knowledge of Personnel policies and is able to apply them equitably, in most cases, to resolve staff problems; uses Personnel Manual when uncertain of proper procedure; seeks advice from local personnel unit when in doubt on written policy. Comments:				
	Optional Factor (Personnel Representative must be notified at the start of evaluation period) Comments:				
	Optional Factor: Comments:				

Total	**Definition of Terms:** X	0	.5	1.0	1.5
	0=Less than Statement (L): Performance generally less than that described by statement. Must be documented in Comments. **.5=Described by Statement (D):** Performance generally described by statement. Comments encouraged. **1.0=Better than Statement (B):** Performance generally better than statement. Comments encouraged. **1.5=Far Exceeds Statement (F):** Performance consistently far exceeds the statement. Must be documented.		**Total**		

Total II & III = 50   Transfer to Page 4

Figure 12–4 (concluded)

Scoring

Total Points	Rating Ranges	Use This Box When Making Salary Adjustments
Part I *(from Page 1)*	**Outstanding** (131 - 150)	Scores 1st Review
Part II *(from Page 2)*	**Commendable** (86 - 130)	2nd Review
Part III *(from Page 3)*	**Fully Satisfactory** (41 - 85)	3rd Review
		4th Review
Total Points *(Transfer to next column)*	**Must Improve** (21 - 40)	(Sum of Scores) — (No. of Perf. Evaluations)
	Unsatisfactory (0 - 20)	

See Rating Ranges to Determine Overall Rating for Salary Adjustment

Transfer to Page 2 Line 8 Box 145 of PL 906A

Counselling

Specific Plans for Improvement:

Additional Comments and Signature of Reviewer:

Signature   Date

Comments and Signature of Supervisor Being Evaluated:

I have reviewed this document and discussed the contents with my immediate supervisor. My signature means that I have been advised of my performance status and does not necessarily imply that I agree with this evaluation.

Signature   Date

Comments and Signature of Senior Management:

Signature   Date

03 0211 (12-74)
167 066

opment. Some companies set up *appraisal panels* to watch over the development of managerial talent. A panel may consist of three or four higher managers who (1) evaluate present and potential abilities of the management person, and (2) plans the individual's future development for advancement in management. The findings of the panel are reviewed by top management. This review permits top management to become acquainted with the sources of executive replenishment over the next five or ten years. The appraisal panel, meeting as a committee, inaugurates and maintains a program of planned future development for each supervisor by means of coaching, committee work, job rotation, special assignments, and, often, more formal education.

From an organization's viewpoint, career planning must take place for individuals both as individuals and as an assurance that a pool of capable persons will be available for promotion as the need arises. In fact, there is some current thinking that opportunities should be created for high-talent employees so they can be given responsibility as soon as possible.

An organization must conduct a constant search for managerial talent and lay plans for systematically developing its orderly progress up the ladder. If a company is to be able to promote from within, it must plan its personnel needs, discover suitable candidates, provide training for them, and constantly evaluate the progress that people are making toward preparing themselves for higher responsibilities. A large corporation may keep track of its talent pool by using the computer to store up-to-date information on the skills, experience, and job desires of its managerial, scientific, and technical personnel.

Another important dimension to career planning is the participation of individuals whose careers are being planned. In recent years companies have recognized that personnel planning could not be wholly successful without consideration of the desires of individual employees and their ideas about career goals and opportunities. In a number of situations, people were chosen for advancement or transfer who then turned down these offers. It is important to remember that in such instances the person receiving the offer, only to turn it down, is informed after the decision to make the offer is made without consulting the individual concerned. As a result many companies have included personal career planning as an integral part of overall personnel planning. Individuals are encouraged to develop their own career plans in consultation with supervisors and staff assistance from the personnel department. In some cases a complete program of self-development, off-premises education, and job rotation becomes a part of the employee's career plan. While no guarantees are given to the employee, the existence of career plans for many individuals in the organization contributes significantly to more effective overall personnel planning.

Assessment centers.   As noted earlier, if a mistake is made in the promotion of a manager, it can be costly in human as well as in monetary terms.

Because of this, many organizations try a variety of ways to minimize error in the identification of managerial talent. One of these methods used by several large organizations is called the assessment center.

A typical pattern of such a program might be:

1. An accurate and objective as possible identification of behavioral characteristics desirable for managerial performance in that organization.
2. Use of a professionally developed and validated test battery to be given to each candidate.
3. Candidates are chosen by their supervisors, and in some cases they may self-select if they meet certain criteria.
4. Exposure to several simulations such as cases, in-basket exercises, business games, role plays, and situational exercises all designed to simulate the reality of a manager's job.
5. Careful observation and critiquing carried on by higher level managers specially trained and chosen to do this work. In some organizations an outside consultant is also used.
6. Evaluation and analysis of the performance of the candidate on the test battery and simulations by the team of managers.

This effort usually takes five days or longer and is based on the idea that present behavior is a useful predictor for future performance. Companies such as IBM and American Telephone have used this approach successfully.[8] It is expensive to establish and carry on, but the indications are that it is well-received by candidates who believe it to be more objective than traditional evaluation and identification methods.

Career tracks.   In those large organizations that have devoted effort to career planning, a necessary supplement has been developed called a career track. The purpose of the career track is to present a lovical promotion ladder through which an employee may go to reach a particular goal over a time period. They are usually designed to show the entrant job (in Figure 12–5, a check clearance clerk) in which a new hire will start. In Figure 12–5, the entrant job is for a high school graduate at age 18 with no previous experience. The time in each job and the length of time employed represent averages. Progress can be accelerated by outstanding performance, evening education, and unanticipated openings because of expansion or labor turnover.

The career track or ladder gives an employee some reasonably firm ideas of what his or her progress might be without any guarantee. It also gives supervisors and the personnel department a promotion timetable, so that capable employees will not be left in a given job too long. Career tracks are

---

[8] For a thorough explanation of the AT&T experience, see Douglas W. Bray, Richard J. Campbell, and Donald L. Grant, *Formative Years in Business: A Long-Term AT&T Study of Managerial Lives* (New York: John Wiley & Sons, 1974).

Figure 12–5
Career path in a large branch-system commercial bank

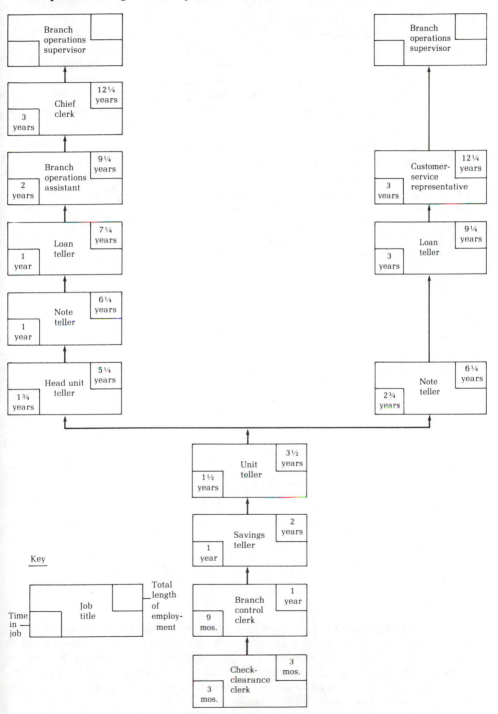

also useful to assess staffing and training needs. They are usually prepared for high-population jobs in large companies.

Personnel replacement chart.   The personnel inventory maintained on the organization's computer is often supplemented by personnel replacement charts. These charts enable management appraisal committees and the personnel department to know at a glance the status of employees in a given department. For instance, in the simplified example shown in Figure 12–6, it is readily apparent that the department head will retire in two years when he reaches age 65. It is also apparent that the assistant department head will probably not be his replacement because of the quality of his present performance and his promotability rating. Further, it can be seen that the supervisors of sections C and E have outstanding ratings in both categories. If these ratings continue for the next two years, one solution could be to promote one of them to department head and move the other to another higher opening in the company. Of course there are other possibilities, but the point is that such a chart prepared and reviewed annually is a very useful managerial tool.

Figure 12–6
Personnel replacement chart

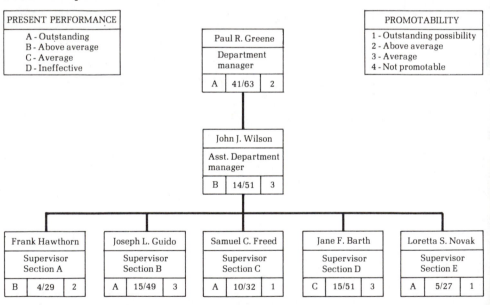

This is a simplified version of a replacement chart. Normally an entire organization's formal structure would be included. The qualitative measures are self-explanatory and are derived from the results of performance appraisals. The first number in the center of each box is the employee's tenure with the organization. The second number is his or her age at the time the chart is prepared. Such charts are usually prepared annually after the performance appraisal takes place.

Benefits to individuals. When a company carries out systematic personnel planning using a personnel inventory and replacement charts which are updated annually, it also makes forecasts five or six years in advance each time the inventory and charts are updated. Retirement, illness, and other reasons create openings. Expansion and organization changes are also anticipated. Naturally when one promotion takes place it sets off a chain reaction, if the company follows a promotion from within policy. Such an approach to personnel planning tends to minimize the chance that a talented individual will be missed when considering candidates for promotion. It also makes it difficult for a manager to hoard capable individuals.

Probably the most important benefit of this approach is the career opportunities it makes apparent to individuals in the company. The personnel department, the employee's supervisor, and the management appraisal committee can meet with the employee and design suitable career tracks or paths for the individual. He or she can express interests and desires also. By taking the usual mystery out of promotion decisions, the company can help assure that talented individuals will not seek opportunities elsewhere.

Staff assistance in supervisory development. While the development of supervisors is primarily a line responsibility, sound personnel planning helps create an atmosphere of cooperation between line managers and the personnel department. Since line managers may tend to be somewhat parochial in their approach to staffing and promotions, the personnel department can assist them in developing a companywide viewpoint. Over a period of time it can be demonstrated that even though a particular department may lose a talented individual to another part of the company, it will also receive talented people from other departments. Planning also reinforces the idea that one of the manager's prime responsibilities is to develop promotables. Among other ways that the personnel department can assist line departments in the development of supervisors for the entire organization are:

1. In the selection of candidates, it can bring to their attention people from other sections and departments and even those within an individual's own department that may have been missed. It can furnish the results of tests administered to applicants. Working together, the line and personnel departments can uncover hidden talents, and the line superior can escape charges of favoritism.

2. The personnel department can design and conduct supervisory training courses and orientation courses whereby actual and potential supervisors are trained in seeing the relationships between production, marketing, engineering, personnel, and other departments—trained to consider the broader picture in their thinking and their decision making.

3. The personnel department can handle job rotation whereby candidates for higher positions spend time working in various departments, partic-

ularly switching from line to staff jobs so that they can work more co-operatively later on when they are promoted.

4. The personnel department can suggest education and other self-improvement programs for people being groomed for supervisory positions.

Taking the time and effort to train supervisors pays off for both the line department and the personnel department because it cuts down on the work of handling grievances, turnover, and absenteeism; and on the positive side, it builds up morale and production.

The fast-track manager

In recent years, another approach to career planning has been receiving attention in business periodicals and in some texts. Earlier in this chapter it was pointed out that many people in a company do not desire the responsibilities that accompany promotions to higher levels of management. Some reach a level at which they feel comfortable and desire no further advancement. On the other hand, many organizations have found that there are people who have both the desire and the capability to reach senior management positions. It is estimated that approximately 10 to 15 percent of an organization's managerial personnel is in this category.

Obviously the identification and careful nurturing of these managers is a critical necessity. The business pages of any large city newspaper carry daily news of managers who change jobs. Executive search firms are constantly looking for high-talent managers to serve the needs of their clients. Some companies find out about their talented people the hard way. Losing a bright young manager to another firm can be a sobering experience to a company that already has a shortage of such people.

There seems to be a high degree of mobility among managers of this type.[9] They are highly competent, young, ambitious middle managers who are strongly motivated by responsibility and challenge. To keep them, many companies have placed them on a "fast track" of increasingly greater responsibility. When a manager of this type is identified, usually by a combination of testing, performance, and recommendations by superiors, he or she is rapidly promoted, often with significant increases in salary. In some organizations, the "sink or swim" approach is used by giving the manager a position which may be too difficult for him. Naturally it is hoped that the individual will succeed, and in many instances companies have found that the person chosen does succeed. In fact notions about long years of seasoning in a variety of so-called understudy jobs have been dispelled. In several companies the fast track has come about out of necessity. There simply are not

---

[9] For a more thorough analysis, see E. E. Jennings, *The Mobile Manager* (Ann Arbor: Bureau of Industrial Relations, University of Michigan, 1967).

enough managers to fill open positions, and they are not readily available in the open market.

When managers are placed on a fast track, they are carefully watched by superiors, and their career plans are given considerable attention. Jobs are chosen for them which will continually broaden their knowledge and responsibility. Rotational assignments are quite common. So are geographical moves if the company has several locations. Companies which follow the fast-track approach are openly developing a cadre of young managers who will succeed to top-management positions relatively early in their careers.

Internal mobility

A combination of labor market realities and equal employment opportunity legislation and compliance has caused many an organization to look to its internal labor market for more effective placement of employees. Rather than waiting for emergencies, management has encouraged and developed systems enabling transfers of employees with greater ease and efficiency. Companies have found that most transfers take place within a department or division. While this is desirable, they also want to encourage transfers on an interdepartmental basis. In this manner there can be more effective utilization of the present work force and possibly lower labor turnover. This is usually true where an employee is unhappy with his or her present position and is able to find a new one in the company, rather than quitting and seeking employment elsewhere.

A transfer serves to move an employee to another job in the same company. The move may be made to rotate jobs for training purposes, to accommodate organizational changes, to satisfy a disgruntled employee or the supervisor, or to protect an employee from a layoff. While most transfers are lateral in nature (to jobs usually paying the same amount), some transfers result in demotion of the employee.

Even though moving people around in a company can be costly and in some cases complicated, it is usually beneficial to both the company and the employee. The costs involved in recruiting new employees are generally greater than those incured by transfers. Most important of all is the effective use of the internal labor market and the greater flexibility this gives the management of the company.

Remedial transfers

There are many reasons why people may need to be transferred out of their present jobs. Initial placement may have been poor, or the job may have changed to the extent that the person is no longer suited to it. The employee may have changed in physical condition or in knowledge, skill, interests, or attitude. He or she may have run into problems of social adjustment to the work group or to the supervisor.

If the supervisor made a mistake in fitting a person to a job, it may be possible to correct it by moving the person to another job in the department and training the individual for it. If the right job doesn't exist within the department—or if the problem is one of relationships between people—the supervisor should ask help from the personnel department in getting the person placed in another department.

Health and safety.   Physical disabilities can incapacitate people for their present jobs. They may be partially disabled by an accident, by poor health, or by age. The job may make too heavy physical demands upon them or be too hazardous. They may be a hazard to other people if they are having accidents or near-accidents. Their physical or emotional state may make them fear that they are going to be injured on the job. Their sight, hearing, or coordination may be impaired. Their condition may make them unable to learn new skills called for by changes in the job.

Sometimes the job can be redesigned to accommodate the physical disabilities, but more often the employee is given a transfer or demotion to some position that can be handled.

Change of interest or skill.   Sometimes people's interests change from their present assignments. They may be going to school at night, preparing for a type of work entirely different from the present job. The field in which they are studying may require several years of preparation, during which time they are being upgraded and receiving raises on the present job. Then when they want to change over to the type of work they have been preparing for, they find that they have to start at the bottom at a low salary. Rather than make the financial sacrifice, they may remain on the present job, discontented and discouraged. The supervisor can prevent misfits of this kind by keeping in close touch with subordinates and keeping informed of their ambitions and their outside training. Before it is too late for them to make the change, the supervisor can arrange transfers into jobs related to their fields of training.

Personality problems.   Often, transferring employees to another department is a means of solving human relations problems. In any group of people working together, there are bound to be personality clashes. If they are minor, people learn to adjust to one another, but occasionally a situation arises in which two people cannot get along with each other, no matter how they try; then their work suffers, and they should be separated. Such a separation is especially desirable when there is conflict between a superior and his subordinate. No superior should be expected to keep under his or her jurisdiction a subordinate who is a constant irritation or whose actions are continually causing problems. The supervisor should first look upon the person as a challenge to his or her skill as a leader and try to win the employee over. If the supervisor cannot do this, then the employee should be transferred. The subordinate who is a headache to one supervisor and a misfit in one group may turn out to be a star performer somewhere else.

The failing employee.   Occasionally an employee who is a failure in one department and should be fired can be saved to the organization by a transfer to another department. Under such circumstances, the supervisor should tell the personnel department the whole story about the employee and ask to have that person placed elsewhere in the organization. Such an employee should be told the truth about the transfer—that this is a chance to make good and that this is an opportunity to prove that he or she has been misjudged. Sometimes such people change; but if they do not improve after one or two such transfers, serious consideration should be given to terminating them.

Whenever a person is transferred, the reason should be known and the person should have the opportunity to protest a transfer. Knowing the why of a transfer, no matter what it is, is better than not knowing. A person transferred without knowing the cause suffers quite a shock to personal security. A person transferred to a new department should receive an induction that will enable an easy adjustment and the achievement of satisfactory performance rapidly. The new group should be given preparation to receive this person.

Requests for transfer.   Employees often initiate requests for transfers, either requesting them of their supervisor or bypassing the supervisor and going directly to the personnel department. When supervisors are bypassed on such requests, they should ask themselves whether they have been showing employees that they have their interests at heart, or if they have been holding onto people when they should have been taking the initiative in helping them transfer to jobs better suited to them. When a number of people request transfer out of a department, the supervisor should suspect something wrong in the department and take action to correct it.

Some companies have instituted a system of open transfer. Employees desiring a transfer can request it and, if there is an opening in the job of their choice and they are qualified for it, they may be transferred. This system is based on the idea that some employees have multiple skills and interests, and if the company has openings that can utilize such an employee, it is more desirable than going outside.

Another related approach is called job posting. When an opening occurs, the job is posted on company bulletin boards, and any employee who is qualified may request an interview and a chance at filling the position.

The Manufacturers Hanover Trust Company, a large commercial bank, has a total system for the internal mobility of its employees. They have open transfer requests (see Figure 12–7 and 12–8), supervisory initiated transfers, personnel department initiated transfers, and job posting of open jobs (see Figure 12–9). Such a program attempts to utilize fully the internal labor market, and it also plays a significant role in the identification of promotables. In addition to the benefits to employees, the program allows for more effective affirmative action in compliance with equal employment opportunity legislation.

Figure 12–7
An open internal employee transfer system

INTERNAL TRANSFER APPLICATION

Bank policies provide that vacancies are filled by the promotion of staff members whenever possible, that promotions are based on merit and that staff members will be assigned to work of the greatest interest to them when this is consistent with individual qualifications and the best interests of the Bank.

To be considered for a transfer, you may (1) record your interests in the computer skill file, (2) talk with your supervisor, (3) talk with a Personnel Officer or (4) submit this transfer application to the Mobility Section of the Personnel Department. Please read the additional information about transfer applications on the back of this form.

Address Envelope To: Mobility and Recruitment Section, Personnel Department, 25/320

From: _____
          Name   Department

I would like to be considered for a transfer to the following assignment:

I believe that I am qualified because:

_____
     Signature   Date

You are asked to give the carbon copy of this application to your supervisor to keep your department informed but are not required to do so.

6099
10M 10-75   **(PERSONNEL COPY)**

INTERNAL TRANSFER SYSTEM

THESE PROVISIONS APPLY TO INTERNAL TRANSFER APPLICATIONS:

1. To use this procedure, a staff member should have at least one year of employment. (Three years to apply for the Management Program).

2. Staff members using this procedure will in no way adversely affect their standing in the Bank.

3. There shall be no discrimination with respect to race, creed, color, age, sex or national origin in all matters applying to employment with the Bank.

4. This application should be used to apply for a new job assignment rather than to present a problem (Use the Employee Relations Procedure Form) or to submit a suggestion (Use the Suggestion Form).

Upon receiving this application, the Mobility and Recruitment Section will arrange, through your supervisor, for you to be interviewed by a staff member of the Personnel Department. The subsequent steps will result in one of these conclusions:

1. You are better off in your present department as a result of personnel changes that have not yet been announced.

2. You are qualified, based on further interviews, for the assignment you have requested and a vacancy is available. You will be transferred at the earliest possible time and, if at all possible, without the availability of a replacement as a factor.

3. You are qualified, but an opening is not now available. In this case, the Mobility Section will record your interest so that for the next year you will be considered when the particular vacancy cannot be filled by a staff member from within that division. You may renew your request after one year.

4. You do not have the necessary qualifications for the job for which you have applied in the view of the personnel interviewer or the supervisor with the vacancy (who has the final decision). However, you will be told the reasons so you will know how you might ultimately qualify.

5. Your work record is not satisfactory as a consequence of attendance, punctuality, attitude or performance. You will be told the circumstances by the personnel interviewer and encouraged to re-apply in six months, so that your record may be evaluated again.

Source: Used with permission of the Manufacturers Hanover Trust Co., New York, N.Y.

Other reasons for transfers

Training.   Rotational assignments of increased responsibility and diversity are useful for people being developed for higher level positions. Many organizations use this approach with success. Intradepartmental transfers can also be used to cross-train people to increase staff flexibility. Emergen-

Figure 12–8
Program to supplement internal mobility

```
                    "DIAL-a-JOB PROGRAM
                        (350-4575)
                    _____


  The "Dial-a-Job Program has been devised as an additional means
  of informing staff members of career opportunities available within
  the Bank.

  We are utilizing four telephone-recording machines in order to
  insure immediate availability of recorded messages.  Additionally,
  the phones are in service 24 hours a day to insure access to
  employees on all shifts.

  Our recordings, to be updated each Wednesday, will list 2 to 3
  vacancies and the required qualifications.  The choice of positions
  and the content of the messages will be taken from our weekly Job
  Postings.  (See Procedure for Internal Posting System for details.)
  All inquiries and responses will be directed to the Mobility Section
  which is responsible for the maintenance of the program and the
  processing of all transfer requests.  (It should be noted that the
  positions recorded are open only to present staff members, not to
  outside job applicants.)
```

Source: Used with permission of the Manufacturers Hanover Trust Co., New York, N.Y.

cies can be handled more easily, and jobs can be enlarged and enriched allowing increased pay.

People who have some flexibility have less to fear from changes in technology, method, or procedure, although most people resist being shunted around from job to job. The amount of transferring done for training pur-

Figure 12–9
Job posting program

Bank policy provides that vacancies are filled by the promotion of staff members whenever possible. One means of implementing this policy is periodically informing the staff of promotional opportunities.

STAFF MEMBERS ARE INVITED TO APPLY FOR TRANSFER AS:

<u>Reviewer</u> (Grade 09) - consults with Investment Officer to determine amount of funds available for investment; places orders for reinvestment of funds; insures that money involved is accurate and required approvals have been received; initiates correspondence regarding purchase and sale programs; participates in raising funds for commissions, taxes, etc.; prepares common Trust Funds intentions and insures funds are available or reinvested. Applicants must have a four year degree and excellent communications skills. (Opening in Personal Trust).

<u>Insurance Analyst</u> (Grade 08) - obtains renewals of insurance policies; maintains expiration control records; notifies the Mortgage Department of any changes in types and amounts of insurance coverage; maintains all liability suit files; checks status and reports to Legal Department every three months and assists in preparing monthly mortgage expiration list. Property, casualty or fidelity insurance experience is required. (Opening in Insurance Department).

<u>Fiduciary Administrator</u> (Grade 09) - assists in administration and settlement of estates and trusts; prepares material for transmittal to attorneys and/or their accountants and confers with them in connection with problems arising on preparation of accounts; makes cash adjustments; pays bills and expenses incurred; arranges for distribution of securities to beneficiaries; evaluates estate assets; prepares inventory for use of co-executor, counsel and Bank and assists in preparation of estate tax returns. Applicants must have a four year degree and excellent communications skills. Acoounting knowledge, business administration courses and personal trust experience are highly desirable (Opening in Personal Trust Division).

<u>Computer Financial Systems Specialist</u> (Grade 16) - selects and samples daily transactions to insure accuracy of general ledger balances; analzes control techniques and procedures and recommends changes where necessary; compiles and evaluates quality control statistics; interfaces with user departments to control deficiencies; participates in planning for periodic audit reviews; assists in researching and resolving items under review; verifies and reconciles accuracy of basic account balances and performs special analytical assignments at the request of the manager. A minimum of five to eight years experience in computerized financial operations, control and review procedures, knowledge of computer input - output devices, familiarity with current computer systems design, logic and control procedures and excellent communications skills are required. A four year degree in accounting or equivalent work experience is highly desirable. (Opening in Loan Accounting Control).

<u>Project Analyst</u> (Grade 12) - Experience in practical applications of work measurement, in an industrial or financial organization. Experience in using predetermined time systems (MODAPTS, MTM, WORK FACTOR, or MCD) and standard unit costing. College graduate preferred or equivalent work experience. (Opening in Financial Planning & Control).

(Continued on reverse side)

You may apply by completing an Internal Transfer Request Form (# 6099) and forwarding it to:
Personnel Department, Recruitment and Mobility Section, 25/320

Figure 12-9 (continued)

Project Analyst (Grade 12) - Experience in operational analysis, work measurement, documentation of procedures, work flow analysis, cost analysis. College graduate with major in accounting management, industrial engineering preferred. (Opening in Financial Planning & Control).

Legal Secretary (Grade 10) - responsible for light dictation, heavy typing (accuracy is essential), operating call director, making reservations and other general clerical duties. Two years of secretarial experience, including a working knowledge of Mag card II, is required. Candidates must be willing to work overtime. (Opening in M.H. Leasing Corporation).

Project Manager (Grade 18) - Experience in manual systems analysis, including - product line profitability; corporate systems; policies and plan; operating procedures; methods and forms analysis; equipment evaluation, and feasibility studies in a banking or related financial environment. Exposure to computer systems, specifically input/output design. College graduate preferred or equivalent work experience. (Opening in Financial Planning & Control).

Systems Analyst (Grade 16) - Experience in systems analysis. Programming a plus. Experience in financial application and user liaison. Knowledge of financial reporting systems, and automated general ledger systems. College graduate or equivalent work experience. (Opening in Financial Planning & Control).

Accounting Analyst (Grade 16-18) - Diversified accounting experience preferable in banking with some public experience. E.D.P. exposure (audit or user) required. College graduate or equivalent work experience. (Opening in Financial Planning & Control).

You may now call Dial-a-Job on 350-4575 to hear a recording of current openings in the Bank. If you wish to apply for a job that is listed on a Staff Opportunities Bulletin or one that you heard on Dial-a-Job, please forward an Internal Transfer Request Form to the Mobility Section, 25/320.

Please Remove: July 29, 1977

Source: Manufacturers Hanover Trust Co., New York, N.Y.

poses will depend upon the union contract, the needs of the company, and the costs of training. Supervisors who understand the social arrangements in work groups can do much to smooth the way for short-run transfers that are in the company interest. They may be able to show employees that in times of rapid technological change employees are in a more favorable position if they know how to perform several jobs.

Change. Employees may be routed out of their jobs by changes in the volume of work or by changes in technology, product, equipment, procedure, or method. The company has an investment in these employees, and in most cases it wants to protect the investment by transferring them to other jobs and retraining them. If employees are laid off frequently, the best of them will find other jobs that are more stable. The others, when they are called back, become wary of implementing changes and find ways to make their work stretch over longer periods.

A company that has a good reputation for taking care of its people will have less turmoil in introducing new methods and improvements.

Seniority. Union contracts usually have provisions for retaining senior people. The process known as "bumping" occurs when there is a layoff and the more senior workers bump those with less seniority from their jobs. Senior employees may also request better assignments under some union contracts. Even if there is no union contract, there may be a desire for some supervisors to retain more senior employees if a reduction in force is necessary. In recent years there has been considerable pressure from young people, minorities, and women, all of whom tend to have little seniority, to remove seniority clauses from union contracts and to minimize the use of seniority as a transfer or promotion determinant in nonunion organizations.

Transfer policy

An organization obviously must have transfer policies which protect it against possible abuse of the transfer privileges. An attempt should be made to prevent transfers from becoming a method of unloading problem employees from one department on to another. Policies should discourage supervisors from trying to pirate workers and should deter employees from seeking easier jobs in other departments. If reasonable equity is maintained between employee requests, supervisory requests, and company needs, transfer policies can aid the company in establishing optimum use of its internal labor market. This should be the overriding force in the handling of transfers.

The environment for career development

There is no doubt that the policies a company has concerning organizational development and personnel planning play a considerable part in creating an atmosphere of encouragement for employees who are willing to assume responsibility and have the capabilities for advancement. Nothing is so frustrating as working for a boss who stifles initiative and discourages individual growth. Supervisory and managerial attitudes have considerable impact on the climate for employee growth and development. In the final analysis, it is each individual supervisor who really creates the growth climate for capable subordinates. Daily relationships with subordinates can really aid young, ambitious employees to grow, or they can stifle these employees if the supervisor is negative.

Not every company can offer rapid promotion, and some supervisors may spend several years under the same boss. The influence the boss has on subordinates in such situations can be very important in the development of their abilities.

In capsule form, there are some suggestions for providing an environment that will foster supervisory development.

1. Delegate authority and responsibility. There is no use in just telling subordinate supervisors that they need to assume more responsibility: Put it on their shoulders.
2. Expect a lot from subordinate supervisors. Most assistants can do and are willing to do more than they are now doing. Make each supervisor's job a challenge.
3. Make accomplishment the basis of security and advancement.
4. View mistakes by subordinates as a necessity for their growth. Convert these mistakes into opportunities to learn.
5. Recognize that success breeds success.
6. Develop a spirit of mutual concern, trust, and confidence between you and your subordinates.
7. Reduce the social distance between you and your assistants.
8. Provide your subordinates with experience so that they can grow.
9. Have a development program in process for each of your subordinates. Tailor it to fit each of their needs.

Of course, the basic factor in career development is the individual. Each person must want to get ahead and must also willingly want to perform the work necessary to achieve goals. Most companies want to promote from within. Superiors look for talent in their subordinates. They often give special assignments to test the attitudes and ability of those people seeking promotions. When a vacancy occurs, they are certainly going to consider the person who has demonstrated some evidence of self-development by keeping up with the managerial and technical developments in the field and who continues to improve performance on the present job while fully cooperating in the acceptance of special assignments and greater responsibility.

Other factors in personnel planning

There are several dimensions to personnel planning beyond the very important ones of career development and employee performance appraisal.

Brief mention of some of these will demonstrate the scope of personnel planning.

Flexible staffing. In many companies, the nature of the work is such that there are peaks (when a greater number of employees are needed or excessive overtime occurs) and valleys (when there is not enough work to go around). The unionized company partially solves this problem by the layoff. But a large number of companies in service and white-collar businesses practice flexible staffing. They use temporary employees, either developing a list of their own or hiring them from a temporary help contractor.

Early retirement. With the relative affluence of our society and better pension plans, many employees desire to retire before the usual age of 65. Some companies have instituted early retirement programs to enable them to offer early retirement to those individuals who desire it and who are qualified. Many of these plans allow for retirement at age 60 with no loss or a slight reduction in benefits. This then allows the company to promote younger and better qualified people into jobs occupied by people who may be coasting and who may have "retired" while still holding the job.

Minority training. Many companies have developed various skill and attitude training programs designed to upgrade minority employees. Large numbers of people need such training because of lack of education and different cultural values which may make it difficult for them to adjust to the workplace and learn how to perform a particular job effectively. For the rapidly increasing numbers of middle-class, upwardly mobile nonwhite employees, the emphasis is on promotion and advancement.

Second careers. There seems to be an increasing frequency in the number of people who leave responsible, well-paying positions when they are in their 40s or 50s to seek a second career. In many instances this second career has no relationship to the individual's prior experience. The personnel planning implications are obvious. A company cannot afford to lose too many people who are in responsible positions. If the second-career idea becomes very popular, organizations will have to assess employee potential carefully and handle career planning accordingly.

Women in business. With women constituting 40 percent of the workforce and increasing numbers interested in employment, the emphasis now is on the promotability and upward mobility of women employees. Company personnel departments now give considerable attention to the identification of female promotables and their rapid advancement. Other impacts include part-time work, flexible work hours, training and retraining programs for older women, and adjustments of transfer policies when both husband and wife work.

Outplacement. Because of the dynamic nature of business, such things as company relocation, closing unprofitable plants, mergers, loss of business, and early retirement programs can occur. All of these can result in the loss of jobs for several people. An increasing number of companies have created an outplacement service to attempt to find jobs for employees they are terminating. Contacts are made with other employers, newspaper ads are placed, and often interviewing space is made available on the terminating company's premises. This effort is looked upon as a social responsibility, and it often creates considerable goodwill.

Summary

Organizational growth and development is rarely spontaneous. It comes about as a result of managerial decisions which result in change. Though some of these decisions may be haphazard, they have an impact on the company and its managers. If an organization is going to continue to achieve its objectives over the long term, it must develop an effective personnel planning program to assure an adequate supply of capable managers for the future.

Most companies have promotion from within policies developed largely because of tight labor markets and high recruitment and training costs. To carry out its personnel planning effectively, an organization should systematically appraise the performance of its employees. Performance appraisal permits a company to try to improve present job performance and to identify promotables. Several methods are available, and the one that suits the company's purpose should be chosen.

Not everyone wants to be promoted to higher level jobs for a variety of reasons. Those who do, however, if they are capable, should be given every opportunity to grow in the organization. Once promotable employees have been identified, the company should develop career plans for them. They, their supervisors, and other interested managerial personnel should be involved in the development of the career plan. Job assignments, education, increased responsibility, and other special assignments should be carefully planned to optimize the growth of these employees.

Companies should plan for replacement of managerial personnel years in advance of need. Career plans and replacement charts will assist in this effort. These are particularly desirable because they tend to minimize labor turnover among capable candidates for higher management positions. Some of these capable individuals may be young and highly mobile and have given evidence of potential for top-management responsibility. In such cases some companies have developed "fast-track" career paths, where promotions and salary increases come rather rapidly and responsibility increases as fast as the employee can absorb it.

The internal labor market is more effectively utilized by having an enlightened transfer policy. Transfers should be made with the employee's welfare as well as the company's in mind. While transfers may be costly, they generally are less costly than recruiting and training new employees.

Each company should try to create an environment which encourages career development for its employees. But in the final analysis, it is the individual who must want to grow, and he or she can demonstrate this to superiors by undertaking a program of self-development.

Personnel planning has several dimensions beyond career development and employee performance appraisal. Among these are flexible staffing, early retirement programs, minority training and development, understanding of second careers, identification of management potential among female employees, and outplacement of employees terminated because of business dynamics.

CASE 12-1

As a part of an overall corporate planning process, a large company conducted a thorough analysis of its possible future personnel needs. A formal human resource planning program was developed based on a five-year projection with an annual update. Each department head was to designate a possible successor, and this person was to be chosen to attend the company's middle management development program. Any person chosen as a possible successor was not guaranteed the position since choices were subject to change based on employee performance, technology, the market for the company's products, and services.

The new program caused C. R. Smith to assess carefully his three immediate subordinates. After all, he was 59 years old and 65 was the retirement age. In fact he was thinking about retiring early to take advantage of the company's plan which allowed retirement at 62 with no reduction in pension.

The department had 95 employees almost equally divided among the three subordinates. Smith had always looked upon the three as equals even though he knew their performance differed. All three were good friends and worked together harmoniously. Nevertheless, he had to make a choice so he looked at their last performance appraisals, and he noted the following information:

R. L. Dixon—52 years old, 25 years with the company, 18 years in the department, broad technical experience, excellent customer relations, problems as a supervisor, particularly with young people, weak in interpersonal skills except with customers.

G. D. Swift—55 years old, 25 years with the company, five years in the department, broad experience but lacking in technical expertise in the department, promoted to present supervisory position 1 year ago and seems to be working out well.

H. K. Barnes—44 years old, 11 years with the company, all in this department, very competent, effective performer, considered good manager by peers and subordinates.

It was obvious that Barnes should be chosen, and Smith sent his name to the personnel department. He then discussed his choice with Barnes, telling him that it was not carved in stone but that if he kept up his high performance level he had an excellent chance for the department head's position. He did not discuss the matter with the other two subordinates, and he asked Barnes to keep the information confidential.

Barnes was chosen to attend the middle manager's program, and this was obviously noticed by Swift and Dixon. When Barnes returned from the program, Smith took him along to an important divisional planning meeting. This also was noticed by his two peers. Dixon accepted the choice of Barnes. He liked him and believed the choice was deserved. On the other hand, Swift was upset and resentful since he had wanted to attend the important meeting and felt left out.

1. *How should Smith handle the situation?*
2. *How might Swift react in the future?*
3. *Should Barnes do anything about the problem?*
4. *Will the harmonious relationship change and if so what can Smith do about it?*
5. *Is it wise to designate a successor three to five years before the incumbent retires? Why? Why not?*

CASE 12–2

Jeff Roberts has worked for the company for 18 months—all of it as a test technician on the production test line of one of the company's products. He is fast and accurate and takes pride in the quality and quantity of his work. He has been testing this particular instrument longer than anyone else on the line. The company has a policy of moving production test line personnel around in its various test lines but didn't move Roberts because the product he tests is a rather complicated device and it takes two or three weeks to train a person to test it. Several other technicians have been moved from the line after they requested a transfer to another instrument.

Several new employees have been added to the test line recently, and the number of instruments required for shipment has decreased. The test line therefore is overstaffed. Twice during the past month Jeff has been approached by management about transferring to another test line. Both times he said he would rather stay where he is. The section manager feels that a transfer would benefit both the employee and the company; but it is not really necessary, since two other technicians on the test line have requested a transfer to other product lines.

Jeff is about 38 years old, unmarried, and has some income from investments. His salary is comparable to other technicians at the same experience level.

1. *Should employees be required to move around to get wider experience?*
2. *If an employee doesn't want to move around, does that make him of less value to the company?*

CASE 12-3

Each year the company recruited 50 to 75 college graduates for its management training program. This program lasted 18 months, and successful trainees usually were placed in a lower level managerial responsibility at the completion of their exposure to the training. The program was highly competitive and, though selection was careful, approximately 25 percent of the participants were released by the company before they completed the program.

It was decided to expand the company's promotion from within policy and allow present company employees to apply for the management training program along with those recruited from the outside. While a bachelor's degree was necessary for the outside applicant, the company decided to waive that requirement for present staff provided they had at least five years' experience within the company and had availed themselves of the company's tuition remission program and were presently enrolled in an evening bachelor's degree program at one of the colleges in the area. In addition, they would be required to take the same personality, aptitude, intelligence, and skill tests that outside candidates took. They would also be subjected to the same multiple and depth interviewing process that the outside applicant was given.

Lou Swanson met all of the requirements, having worked for the company six years since his high school graduation. After a variety of clerical jobs he had been promoted to a group leader's job. After receiving the promotion, he enrolled at an evening college and was presently one third of the way through the bachelor's degree program. His job as a group leader was not really a management position, since he had no real responsibility other than as a pacesetter in one of the large clerical departments.

Lou decided to apply for the management training program and made an appointment to see the personnel director. He impressed the personnel director with his enthusiasm, apparent ambition, and interest in the company. Everything was going along very well until Lou stated that he could see no reason to take any of the tests that the department used in the screening process. He felt he had already proven himself in the company and the tests were not necessary. He also felt they were an invasion of his privacy. Because of Lou's adamant refusal to take the test battery, his application for the management training program was denied.

1. *Was the personnel director correct in refusing Lou Swanson's application?*
2. *Should an employee who has a successful record in a company be subjected to testing for a job whose requirements are different than the one in which he is presently engaged?*
3. *Should Lou have applied for the training program feeling the way he did about the testing requirement?*
4. *Based on the information available, do you think Lou would have been a good risk for the training program?*

CASE 12–4

Tom Merrill started with the company when he was discharged from the service at the end of World War II. He had been a combat pilot and had risen to the rank of captain. The company, a major petroleum firm, placed Tom in its aviation marketing division to take advantage of the knowledge he had acquired in the service. Tom was successful and progressed through various positions, receiving raises and promotions as time went on. Tom was sent to several company training programs to develop his managerial ability and was given continually increased responsibility. After several years in the aviation division, Tom was given a variety of rotational assignments in other divisions to broaden his knowledge of company operations. Clearly Tom was a young man with a great future. During this period the company prided itself on its promotion from within policy, placing great emphasis on experience in company operations. Little emphasis was placed on education; several executives had not gone to college. There were many success stories in the company of people who had started in minor jobs and risen to high managerial posts. Tom, who had not gone to college, apparently was emulating this type of company success story. After serving in a variety of posts, Tom was assigned to the sales staff of the marine division. He continued his pattern of success, receiving merit increases and promotions until he was placed in charge of marine sales, reporting directly to the divisional vice president. Tom had participated in more company-sponsored executive development programs, and these, along with his experience, had apparently developed him into a very capable, articulate administrator.

During the period of Tom's service in the marine division, the company effected a change in policy. While it still basically adhered to a promotion from within policy, more emphasis was placed on education. College graduates were hired for executive training, thus bypassing the time-honored clerk-to-president approach of the past. Master's degree holders were recruited for several understudy positions and, in fact, Tom had a few working for him.

Tom's boss, the divisional vice president, was pleased with Tom's performance and frequently told him so. Each year it was his responsibility to conduct a formal performance evaluation of those managers reporting to him. Part of the evaluation program provided for the ranking of peer group managers in the order of their worth to the company. This ranking reflected the opinion of the evaluator as well as his superior. For four years Tom was told that he had received a high ranking each year, and his raises reflected the esteem in which he was held. Tom questioned his superior about promotional opportunities and each time was told not to worry and to be patient. Tom did not press the issue; he was reasonably satisfied with his progress and was flattered by the high ratings he received. He began to reflect on his career, however, and wondered when he would be promoted. He had been with the company almost 25 years and was now 45 years old. He felt he could assume major management responsibility and his ratings seemed to prove this. He also believed that a promotion must come in the near future or he would be bypassed by younger people in the company. He felt he was still marketable as an executive for another company but that if he waited much longer, he would be too old. After considerable thought in this vein, he decided to have a heart-to-heart talk with his superior.

He opened the discussion by questioning his boss on the meaning and value of the peer-ranking aspect of the performance evaluation program. His boss told him it had considerable importance in determining a person's promotability and the size of the annual increase. Tom then pressed for more specific information regarding his evaluation. While reluctant to do so, his superior then told him that he had been ranked number one for the past four years by both the executive vice president and himself. His boss went on to say that the size of pay increases Tom had received reflected this thinking and that he was now being paid a salary over the top of the range for his position. Tom then asked the logical question, "Why have I not been promoted?" His boss then replied, "It's because of your lack of formal education. The company has decided that only college graduates will be considered for promotion to senior management positions."

1. *Do you feel the company is justified in the position they have taken with regard to the promotability of Tom Merrill?*
2. *Should Tom's superior have told him about his rating and the decision about his promotability? Should he have been told sooner?*
3. *What should Tom do now?*
4. *Does a company's management have any responsibility to communicate how a policy change may affect an employee's career?*
5. *To what extent did Tom contribute to his predicament by not getting a degree by going to evening college during his career with the company?*
6. *Is the company placing too much emphasis on the value of a college education and by so doing, discriminating against employees like Tom Merrill?*
7. *Is there a possibility that there may be another reason for not promoting Tom, and his superior may have used his lack of education as a convenient excuse? If so, to what extent should a superior be frank with a subordinate when discussing his career?*
8. *Can the company justify paying Tom a salary higher than the top of the range for his position and still not promoting him?*

CASE 12–5

For a long period, the company was behind in its orders, and the labor market was tight. Since workers were hard to get, you and the other supervisors had a tendency to overrate your employees on the evaluation sheets; and, in discussing the rating with them, you emphasized their good points in order to keep them happy. As a result, practically every employee was rated "superior."

Now business is falling off, and it is necessary for a number of employees to be demoted or laid off. Top management tells all the supervisors to use their employee-evaluation sheets as the basis for such actions and to discuss these ratings with the employees when they are being demoted or laid off.

1. *How should the supervisors handle the situation?*
2. *What should they say to the workers?*
3. *What are some of the cautions to be considered in evaluating employees?*

CASE 12-6

During the course of an attitude survey which involved depth interviews of a cross-section of employees in each department, the consultant retained by the company had a long talk with Carol Barton. She was a black employee in a large clerical department and worked on the 4:00 P.M. to midnight shift. Having started as an inexperienced high school graduate ten years earlier, she now was in charge of training the new clerks for that shift. She had one assistant.

The shift had an overwhelming majority of female employees, and the common wisdom was that they chose that shift because of home responsibilities which did not allow them to work in the daytime. One of the things the consultant questioned Carol about was her thoughts on shift work. While she believed that most of the women preferred that shift, such was not her case. In fact, she said, she had requested a transfer to day work several times and had been turned down for a variety of reasons such as no openings at her pay level, no replacement for her, not qualified, and no requests for her experience.

Carol was not bitter and seemed resigned to her fate. She didn't want to leave her job because of her ten years' seniority and the benefits that accrued, including a longer vacation. She did, however, state that she believed her growth to be limited in the department. She had taken several courses at a nearby college over the years and wanted to continue her education toward a degree. The evening shift received a 10 percent pay differential, and she was asked if she was prepared to give that up for day work. Her reply was firmly positive if she could get a job that promised growth.

The consultant spoke to her immediate supervisor, who was very enthusiastic about Carol's performance. He was asked if he was willing to lose her to day work. While he didn't want to lose her, he was willing to recommend transfer if a good opportunity was available. He also believed Carol's assistant was qualified to take over. He mentioned that he had agreed with and passed on to higher management her earlier transfer requests.

The next day the consultant mentioned this situation to the company's personnel director, who became quite interested. It seemed there was an opening for a training assistant in the central training department, and Carol could fill that position. It was a lateral transfer as far as pay was concerned, but it represented a significant opportunity for her growth, since she would be exposed to a much wider variety of training activities than were possible in her present assignment.

After checking with her and getting her enthusiastic approval, the personnel director told her to request a transfer once again, naming the specific job he had offered. He was quite pleased with this turn of events, since it enabled the company to promote a black woman to a desirable position. Carol put her request in, her supervisor approved—and it was then turned down by the person in charge of the entire department, both day and evening shifts. His excuse was that they couldn't afford to lose her.

1. *Why do you think Carol's transfer was turned down again?*
2. *What can the personnel director do about it, and should he?*
3. *Should the consultant have gotten involved as he did?*
4. *What can Carol do?*

CASE 12–7

The following display advertisement appeared in the newspaper of a suburban town located about 40 miles from the central city. It covered about one quarter of a standard size newspaper page and had enough white space and a type size large enough to be easily seen by even a casual reader of that particular issue of the paper. It represents a somewhat novel approach to management development:

ARE YOU A RECENTLY RETIRED TOP CALIBER
VICE PRESIDENT—FINANCE AND ADMINISTRATION?

We are an exciting, active, consumer goods company located in ———, with annual sales over $50,000,000 and an excellent growth record, that needs you for not more than three years to give seasoning and training in broad-gauge responsibilities to a brilliant 28-year-oldster who will then take over. If you're looking for the enjoyment of being active and seeing a potential vice president "bloom and develop," please write in confidence to Box XYZ, —— — News.

1. *Comment on the desirability of this approach for the development of a young executive.*
2. *What can the company do to help ensure the success of such an approach?*
3. *What disadvantages may be encountered by the company?*
4. *As an executive taking this job offer, what would you expect the company to do to utilize your abilities effectively?*

CASE 12–8

Tom Jones has been with his company for over 45 years. For the past 15 years he has been supervising a small section in one of the departments located at the company's headquarters. His job requires a great amount of detail work, and over the years Tom has developed his own methods and systems to assure that everything that leaves his desk is without mistakes. Some of his methods are duplications and could be simplified, but Tom is completely satisfied with his own procedures. Tom is scheduled to retire within two years under the company's mandatory retirement program, and he has been frequently absent in the past year due to illness.

Because Tom's work involves a great deal of detail and because of his frequent absences, Bob Stevens, who is over 20 years younger than Tom, was assigned to Tom's section to learn the job and to take over in Tom's absence.

They have been working together for three months, and Bob is already quite familiar with the procedures and methods established by Tom. He feels, however, that some of the duplications of effort can be eliminated and the job simplified. Tom, however, insists that everything should be done the same way he has done it for the past 15 years. These arguments have caused a good deal of friction between the two. Of particular annoyance to Bob is Tom's practice of answering any question with an explanation of the entire procedure, along with case histories and several repetitions. He will not listen to reason, insisting on completing the entire explanation each time.

Tom has been asked by his superior to give special assignments to Bob and to let him employ his own methods as long as the end result is the same. He promises to do this, but before long he will again insist that Bob should follow his established procedures. Bob has indicated that if this keeps going on he will ask for a transfer, because he cannot work under such conditions for two years. On the other hand, Tom's knowledge of the job is valuable, and he is needed to train Bob fully. Bob is the only person who is qualified to be trained for Tom's job, and the department does not want to lose him.

1. *Can the two men be convinced to work together more effectively? How?*
2. *Is it a good idea to place Bob in an understudy position two years in advance of Tom's retirement?*
3. *Why do you think Tom is reacting to the training of Bob in the manner described in the case?*
4. *Is Tom the only one at fault, as the case implies?*
5. *Assume that Tom continues his present behavior pattern. How would you then handle the situation?*

CASE 12–9

Ed Davis had been assistant department head of the accounting department for eight years. During this period he had assumed he was doing a good job, since he had heard nothing to the contrary. He had been receiving periodic salary increases, and his boss seemed satisfied with the way things were going. Ed was 42 years of age and was looking forward to taking over as department head in one year when his superior was to retire.

The financial vice president had decided, however, to promote Ken Forest, a 28-year-old supervisor of the accounts payable section. Ken had been a supervisor for three years, and he reported to Ed Davis. During this period Ken had considerably impressed the vice president as a knowledgeable and effective manager. The vice president felt that Ed Davis did not have the ability to be department head but that he was a competent number two person. None of the vice president's thinking had been communicated to either individual, nor to the department head slated for retirement.

Ken had been attending a management development program conducted for the company by an outside consultant. He had impressed the consultant, and when he asked for advice, the consultant listened with interest. It seems that Ken Forest had analyzed his situation and felt that his opportunities in the company were limited. He mentioned that Ed Davis would probably be department head and, since Ed was 42, this meant 23 years of waiting for Ken. Ken did not want to wait until he was 51 to become head of the accounting department. The consultant told him that though the outlook appeared somewhat dark, many things could happen in a large company and Ken should not be discouraged. Ken replied that he probably would seek other employment so that he could advance more rapidly.

The consultant thought about Ken's dilemma and his indicated potential. He felt that the personnel director should be aware of Ken's thinking, because he felt the company should not lose a person of Ken's caliber if it could be avoided. When the consultant spoke to the personnel director about Ken, he was told of the financial vice president's plans for Ken. The consultant then asked why Ken had not been told, and the answer was that management was not yet prepared to make a firm commitment.

1. *Was the financial vice president handling his personnel planning properly?*
2. *How can a company keep a bright young executive satisfied without clearly delineating the future for the individual?*
3. *Is it wise to allow the assistant department head to assume that he will be promoted when his superior retires?*
4. *Can the company do anything to resolve the problem it is facing?*
5. *Will it be able to keep both Ed Davis and Ken Forest?*

CASE 12-10

John Shelly planned to retire at the end of the year. He had been in charge of the staff research unit for several years. The unit consisted of 4 supervisors, 27 people doing economic and personnel research, and 7 clerk-typists. The purpose of the unit was to prepare support information for senior management to aid in more effective policy formulation and resource allocation.

During the past year, Shelly had been grooming one of the first-level supervisors, Betty Cole, as his possible replacement. Shelly had mentioned this to his superior, and he had also strongly assured Betty Cole that she would get the job when he retired. Shelly's superior, Ray Morgan, a senior vice president, was not sure about this course of action since he believed that Shelly was not as effective as he might be and that any person chosen by him could be similarly ineffective.

Three months before Shelly's retirement, the senior vice president transferred Carol Brown to staff research from another division of the company. She was a very bright person with excellent educational background and an outstanding performance record in the other division. He told Brown that she should work with Shelly and absorb as much as possible in the three-month period so a smooth transition could be made when she assumed Shelly's responsibility. Morgan also informed Shelly about the transfer and told him to give her a complete exposure to the unit's activities.

John Shelly questioned his boss on the need for the transfer of Carol Brown since he believed his choice was fully qualified. Morgan told him that a choice of successor was not his decision and that he, Morgan, believed that Carol Brown was more qualified and had greater potential. Shelly persisted in his arguments, but Morgan cut him off by saying, "Sorry, John, but Carol Brown is my choice, and that's how it's going to be!"

Carol Brown arrived to take on her new job in the staff research unit. She was greeted very coolly by Shelly. He introduced her to Betty Cole, asking Betty to explain the unit's activities to Carol. Cole refused, saying it was not her responsibility. John Shelly awkwardly dismissed her and then gave Carol some material to read, saying he would get back to her. For the next two weeks the situation went down hill. Carol Brown received little or no cooperation from John Shelly. He even criticized her frequently in front of other staff members, and Carol felt she was in a no-win situation. Believing that it would be difficult to take over the unit after Shelly retired and finding that Betty Cole was openly hostile to her, she went to the senior vice president and told him what was going on.

1. *What can Morgan do now?*
2. *Should Carol Brown continue in the staff research unit?*
3. *Should a retiring manager pick his successor?*
4. *What should be done about Betty Cole?*

SUGGESTED READINGS: PART III

Chapter	**Books**
11	Bass, Bernard M., and Bass, Vaughan. *Training in Industry: The Management of Learning.* Belmont, Calif.: Wadsworth Publishing Co., 1966.
10	Bassett, Glen A. *Management Styles in Transition.* New York: American Management Assn., 1966.
10	Bennis, Warren G. *Changing Organizations.* New York: McGraw-Hill Book Co., 1966.
11	Bienvenu, Bernard J. *New Priorities in Training.* New York: American Management Assn., 1969.
10	Blake, R. R., and Mouton, J. S. *The Managerial Grid.* Houston: Gulf Publishing Co., 1964.
12	Bray, D. W.; Campbell, R. J.; and Grant, D. L. *Formative Years in Business.* New York: Wiley-Interscience, 1974.
12	Burack, Elmer H. *Strategies for Manpower Planning and Programming.* Morristown, N.J.: General Learning Press, 1972.
12	Buskirk, R. H. *Your Career.* Boston: Cahners Books, Inc., 1976.
12	Cummings, L. L., and Schwab, D. P. *Performance in Organizations.* Glenview, Ill.: Scott, Foresman and Co., 1973.
10,11,12	Davis, Keith. *Human Behavior at Work.* 5th ed. New York: McGraw-Hill Book Co., 1977.
11	DePhillips, Frank A.; Berliner, William M.; and Cribbin, James J. *Management of Training Programs.* Homewood, Ill.: Richard D. Irwin, Inc., 1960.
11,12	Diamond, D. E., and Bedrosian, H. *The Impact of Manpower Placement and Training Programs on Low Wage Industries and Occupations.* New York: New York University, College of Business and Public Administration, 1971.
10	Dowling, W. F., and Sayles, L. R. *How Managers Motivate: The Imperatives of Supervision.* 2d ed. New York: McGraw-Hill Book Co., 1978.
12	Doeringer, Peter B., and Piore, Michael J. *Internal Labor Markets and Manpower Analysis.* Lexington, Mass.: D. C. Heath & Co., 1971.
12	Drucker, Peter F. *Management: Tasks, Responsibilities, Practices.* New York: Harper & Row, Publishers, 1974.
12	Finkle, Robert B., and Jones, William S. *Assessing Corporate Talent.* New York: John Wiley & Sons, Inc., 1970.

Chapter	**Books**
10,11,12	Fleishman, Edwin A., and Bass, Alan R., eds. *Studies in Personnel and Industrial Psychology.* 3d ed. Homewood, Ill.: Dorsey Press, Inc., 1974.
10	Gellerman, Saul W. *Motivation and Productivity.* New York: American Management Assn., 1963. (A review and appraisal of 40 years of motivational research. Studies included are Harvard, Michigan, Pittsburgh, Whyte, Argyris, McGregor, McClelland, Schacter.)
11	Goldstein, Irwin L. *Training: Program Development and Evaluation.* Monterey, Calif., Brooks/Cole Publishing Co., 1974.
10	Golembiewski, Robert T., and Blumberg, Arthur, eds. *Sensitivity Training and the Laboratory Approach.* Itasca, Ill.: F. E. Peacock Publishers, Inc., 1970.
10,11,12	Gooding, Judson. *The Job Revolution.* New York: Walker & Co., 1972.
12	Haas, Frederick C. *Executive Obsolescence.* New York: American Management Assn., 1968.
11,12	Habbe, Stephen. *Company Experience with Negro Employment,* vols. 1 and 2. New York: Conference Board, Inc., 1966.
10	Hackman, Ray C. *The Motivated Working Adult.* New York: AMACOM, 1969.
11,12	Hall, Douglas T. *Careers in Organizations.* Pacific Palisades, Calif., 1976.
10	Herzberg, Frederick; Mausner, B.; and Snyderman, B. B. *The Motivation to Work.* New York: John Wiley & Sons, Inc., 1959. (Study of engineers and accountants, and the relationship of job satisfaction to motivation.)
10,11,12	Jenkins, David. *Job Power.* Garden City, N.Y.: Doubleday & Co., Inc., 1973.
10,12	Jennings, Eugene E. *The Mobile Manager.* Ann Arbor: Bureau of Industrial Relations, University of Michigan, 1967.
11,12	Johnson, Lawrence A. *Employing the Hard-Core Unemployed.* New York: American Management Assn., 1969.
12	Kellog, Marion S. *What to Do about Performance Appraisal.* Rev. ed. New York: American Management Assn., 1975.
10	Lawler, Edward E., III. *Motivation in Work Organizations.* Monterey, Calif., Brooks/Cole Publishing Co., 1973.
10	Lawrence, Paul R., and Seiler, John A. *Organizational Behavior and Administration: Cases, Concepts, and Research Findings.* Rev. ed. Homewood, Ill.: Richard D. Irwin, Inc., 1965.
10,12	——, and Lorsch, Jay W. *Organization and Environment.* Boston: Division of Research, Graduate School of Business Administration, Harvard University, 1967.
10,11	Leavitt, Harold. *Managerial Psychology.* 4th ed. Chicago: University of Chicago Press, 1977.
11,12	Levitan, Sar A.; Mangum, G. L.; and Marshall, Ray. *Human Resources and Labor Markets.* New York: Harper & Row, Publishers, 1972.
10,11,12	Lefton, R. E.; Buzzolla, V. R.; Sherberg, M.; and Karraker, D. L. *Effective Motivation through Performance Appraisal.* New York: Wiley-Interscience, 1977.

Chapter	**Books**
10,11	Likert, Rensis. *New Patterns in Management.* New York: McGraw-Hill Book Co., 1961. (Summarizes social research at University of Michigan Institute for Social Research.)
10,12	———. *The Human Organization.* New York: McGraw-Hill Book Co., 1967.
10,11,12	Lippit, Gordon L. *Organizational Renewal.* New York: Appleton-Century-Crofts, 1969.
11	Lynton, Rolf P., and Pareek, Udai. *Training for Development.* Homewood, Ill.: Richard D. Irwin, Inc., 1967.
10	Maslow, A. H. *Motivation and Personality.* New York: Harper and Row, Publishers, 1954.
11	McGehee, William, and Thayer, Paul W. *Training in Business and Industry.* New York: John Wiley & Sons, Inc., 1961.
10	McGregor, Douglas. *The Human Side of Enterprise.* New York: McGraw-Hill Book Co., 1960.
10,11,12	———. *The Professional Manager.* New York: McGraw-Hill Book Co., 1967.
11,12	Miner, John B. *The Human Constraint: The Coming Shortage of Managerial Talent.* Washington, D.C.: BNA Books, Inc., 1974.
10	Morgan, John S. *Managing the Young Adults.* New York: American Management Assn., 1967.
12	Patten, Thomas H., Jr. *Manpower Planning and the Development of Human Resources.* New York: John Wiley & Sons, Inc., 1971.
10,12	Pigors, Paul, and Myers, Charles A. *Personnel Administration.* 8th ed. New York: McGraw-Hill Book Co., 1977.
10	Roethlisberger, F. J., and Dickson, W. J. *Management and the Worker.* Cambridge, Mass.: Harvard University Press, 1939.
11,12	Roseman, Edward. *Confronting Nonpromotability.* New York: AMACOM, 1977.
10,11	Sayles, Leonard B. *Managerial Behavior.* New York: McGraw-Hill Book Co., 1964.
11,12	Schneider, Benjamin. *Staffing Organizations.* Pacific Palisades, Calif., 1976.
12	Shaeffer, Ruth G. *Staffing Systems Managerial and Professional Jobs.* New York: Conference Board, Inc., 1972.
10,12	Smith, H. P., and Brouwer, P. J. *Performance Appraisal and Human Development.* Reading, Mass.: Addison-Wesley Publishing Co., 1977.
10,11,12	Special Task Force Report to Secretary of Health, Education, and Welfare. *Work in America.* Cambridge, Mass.: M.I.T. Press, 1973.
10	Steers, R. M., and Porter, L. W. *Motivation and Work Behavior.* New York: McGraw-Hill Book Co., 1975.
10,12	Tagiuri, Renato, and Litwin, George H., eds. *Organizational Climate.* Boston: Division of Research, Graduate School of Business Administration, Harvard University, 1968.

Chapter	**Books**
10,12	Tannenbaum, Arnold S. *Social Psychology of the Work Organization.* Belmont, Calif.: Wadsworth Publishing Co., 1966.
10	Taylor, Frederick W. *Scientific Management.* New York: Harper & Row, Publishers, 1947.
11	Tracey, William R. *Evaluating Training and Development Systems.* New York: American Management Assn., 1968.
11	———. *Managing Training and Development Systems.* New York: AMACOM, 1974.
10	Vroom, Victor H. *Work and Motivation.* New York: John Wiley and Sons, Inc., 1964.

Articles

Chapter	
11	Antil, F. H. "Meeting the Training Challenge," *Personnel Journal*, October 1975.
10	Bekirouglu, H., and Gonen, T. "Motivation—The State of the Art," *Personnel Journal*, November 1977.
10	Carrell, M. R., and Dittrich, J. E. "Employee Perceptions of Fair Treatment," *Personnel Journal*, October 1976.
12	Dahl, D. R., and Pinto, P. R. "Job Posting—An Industry Survey," *Personnel Journal*, January 1977.
10	Dodd, W. E., and Pesci, M. L. "Managing Morale through Survey Feedback," *Business Horizons*, June 1977.
11	Elkins, A. "Some Views on Management Training," *Personnel Journal*, June 1977.
11,12	English, J., and Marchione, A. R. "Nine Steps in Management Development," *Business Horizons*, June 1977.
11	Fisher, D. W. "Educational Psychology Involved in On-the-Job Training," *Personnel Journal*, October 1977.
12	Fottler, M. D. "Management Commitment and Manpower Program Success," *California Management Review*, Spring 1977.
11,12	Hanson, M. C. "Career Development Responsibilities of Managers," *Personnel Journal*, September 1977.
12	Harley, J. P. "The Transferee's Physical Move—Does It Have to Be a Headache?" *Personnel Journal*, August 1975.
12	Haynes, M. G. "Developing an Appraisal Program," *Personnel Journal*, January 1978.
11	Hollman, R. W. "Let's Not Forget about New Employee Orientation," *Personnel Journal*, May 1976.
12	Johnson, G. R. "Flexible Performance Evaluation," *Personnel Journal*, December 1977.
11,12	Kearney, W. J. "Management Development Programs Can Pay Off," *Business Horizons*, April 1975.
11	Kolb, D. A. "Management and the Learning Process," *California Management Review*, Spring 1976.

Chapter	Articles
10,11,12	Kothari, V. "Promotional Criteria: Three Views," *Personnel Journal*, August 1976.
10	Lawler, E. E., III. "Developing a Motivating Work Climate," *Management Review*, July 1977.
12	Levinson, Harry. "Appraisal of *What* Performance?" *Harvard Business Review*, July–August 1976.
12	Massey, D. J. "Narrowing the Gap between Intended and Existing Results of Appraisal Systems," *Personnel Journal*, October 1975.
12	Millard, C. W.; Luthans, F.; and Ottemann, R. L. "A New Breakthrough for Performance Appraisal," *Business Horizons*, August 1976.
11	Newell, G. E. "How to Plan a Training Program," *Personnel Journal*, May 1976.
12	Patz, A. L. "Performance Appraisal: Useful But Still Resisted," *Harvard Business Review*, May–June 1975.
11	Pinder, C. C. "Concerning the Application of Human Motivation Theories in Organizational Settings," *Academy of Management Review*, July 1977.
10,11,12	Reeser, C. "Managerial Obsolescence—An Organizational Dilemma," *Personnel Journal*, January 1977.
10	Schein, E. H. "In Defense of Theory Y," *Organizational Dynamics*, Summer 1975.
10	Wadsworth, M. D. "How to Evaluate the Job Satisfaction of Critical Employees," *Personnel Journal*, September 1976.
12	Walker, J. J. "Human Resource Planning: Managerial Concerns and Practices," *Business Horizons*, June 1976.
12	Zawacki, R. A., and Taylor, R. L. "A View of Performance Appraisal from Organizations Using It," *Personnel Journal*, June 1976.

PART IV

MANAGING HUMAN BEHAVIOR

○ Leadership

○ Communication

○ The legal and social environment for supervision

○ Managing change

Chapter 13

Learning objectives

○ *To become aware of leadership theory and its complexity*

○ *To understand leadership styles, their variety and their relationship to supervisory and managerial performance*

○ *To become aware of the various limitations of leadership and to recognize their limitations on the manager and supervisor*

○ *To understand how a new supervisor is introduced to leadership responsibilities and how they evolve*

Leadership

Major topics

To paraphrase the well-known television commercial, "Leadership is the secret ingredient." The quality and type of leadership will very often mean the difference between successful and inadequate performance by a work group. A quite common occurrence in business is a change in supervision which results in much higher quality performance of employees in the same environment, using the same resources. "The crux of leadership is the acceptance of responsibility—the idea or fantasy that one can make a difference in the course of events. This sense of personal involvement in life is not simply a passive experience. It is an impelling urge to make a difference and use oneself in effecting outcomes."[1]

A frequent error is made by describing manager, supervisor, and leader as the same term. Managers and supervisors are supposed to exercise leadership as one of their activities, but they also do many other things such as planning and organizing, neither of which necessarily require leadership skills. People who are not managers and supervisors also can be effective leaders. Witness the person who is the leader of an informal group. Such a person has no formal managerial responsibilities; yet he or she can have considerable influence over members of the group. On the other hand, being in a formal supervisory or managerial position does not guarantee leadership effectiveness.

This chapter considers the supervisor's job of leadership as one of carrying out company objectives with and through people and making the best possible use of the company's most valuable asset—its people. Since people tend to follow leaders who can help them get what they want, supervisory leadership is based on demonstrating to subordinates that they will get some of the things they want if they provide the organization with what it wants—and that they will fare better by following the supervisor's leadership than by working against it.

Supervisors want their leadership of employees to achieve:

1. Willing, sustained, and high-level job performance.
2. Readiness to accept change.
3. Acceptance of responsibility.
4. Involvement of people so they will use their brains, abilities, initiative, and ideas.
5. Improvement in problem solving, cooperation, and morale.
6. Development of people to be self-starting and self-controlling.
7. Reduction of turnover, absences, grievances, tardiness, and waste.

The talents, skills, and interests of subordinates—be they scientists, clerks, salespeople, production workers—and their attitudes and expectations may determine the kind of leadership that will be appropriate. Other factors that influence the supervisor's leadership and the freedom with which one can exercise it are: the kind of organization one is in, the kind of

---

[1] Abraham Zaleznik, *Human Dilemmas of Leadership* (New York: Harper & Row, Publishers, 1966), p.1

boss one has, the conditions surrounding the job and the labor market, the kind of peer supervisors one has, and the kind of person one is.

This chapter will consider the ways in which these factors limit supervisors, how they can best operate within these limitations, and how they can overcome some of them through increasing their own effectiveness.

Leadership

Leadership has been a popular discussion topic for centuries. Even today it ranks high in the research efforts of behavioral scientists. Some idea of the broad area of study may aid in understanding the elusive nature of this very important ingredient of organizational performance. Many individuals pattern their efforts after those of successful leaders by studying their actions. Studies of leadership patterns have resulted in the many "how to" books and articles written on the subject.

The trait or personality characteristic approach. Leaders are observed for their personality characteristics. Lists of many qualities result. Such characteristics as integrity, perception, sense of humor, tact, honesty, drive, enthusiasm, and initiative, among others, are usually found. Of course, the writer's bias may be reflected in the list, leaving the reader to decide which list is best and how many qualities are necessary for successful leadership. These studies have shown that all leaders do not possess the same characteristics and vastly different personalities are successful as leaders. Nevertheless, they are useful because they do indicate that personality factors are important in leadership and that people can be effective leaders despite considerable individual differences.

We have all known of situations that have required leadership in an unusual degree. Studies of these situations have given rise to the following approach.

The situation or circumstance approach. A situation arises which requires leadership and a leader emerges from the group. Group behavior is studied to determine the nature of its behavior and what occurs to produce leadership. The informal leadership theories are based on this approach. Many groups have informal leaders even though there is a formal leader designated by higher management. Usually a combination of situational and environmental factors contribute to the emergence of the informal leader. In fact, there is a management development technique which attempts to create leadership opportunities in various situations so that group members can exercise leadership and develop themselves for greater responsibility. Research in this area has demonstrated that job differences and environmental factors require different types of leadership.

In the final analysis, the success of any leader depends upon the acceptance or rejection of their leadership by those under their jurisdiction. Studies in this area are described as the follower approach.

The follower approach. In any group situation the reaction of followers reflects on the effectiveness of the leader. Additionally, the personality of the follower determines the kind of leader for whom he or she will perform effectively. The type of work performed and the age, sex, status, and background of the followers have a definite relationship to the effectiveness of the leader. Results of studies in this area indicate that any leader has to pay close attention to the individual differences that exist among the people supervised. The leader must treat each person as a unique individual in order to maximize performance on the job.

The following approach to the study of leadership is often called the opposite of the trait approach.

The leadership structure approach.   This approach is based on the idea that there is no such thing as a "one-person show" in the leadership of a group and that each individual in the group has some influence over the behavior of the group. Such an approach hopefully results in cohesiveness of group behavior. While there is no doubt that multiple influences affect any group, someone has to assume responsibility, make decisions, set examples, and communicate with the group. Of course it is possible that more than one person in a group may perform these functions, but a group usually looks to one individual for its direction.

The charismatic leader.   An offshoot of the trait approach is the association of charisma with a leader. The idea here is that a person has magnetism, excitement, and an ability to inspire others, even to the extent of blind devotion. Charisma is most frequently associated with religious, political, and military leaders, usually for or against some emotional cause. There are some business and labor leaders who possess the nebulous quality of charisma also.

Employee-centered leadership.   Another approach to democratic leadership places the employee in the focal point of leadership effort. Likert's studies mentioned earlier in the text indicated that effective supervisors and managers placed primary emphasis on human relations and employee problems. Developing effective work groups with high performance goals required the development of a cohesive group that was mutually supportive. Likert found that long-term gains in productivity were possible this way although he did admit that autocratic methods could produce impressive short-run gains.

Contingency theory.   Anyone who has any leadership experience knows that no one approach suits all situations. One behavioral scientist, Fred E. Fiedler, has devoted considerable research to the development of a contingency theory of leadership.[2] His research focused on three situational factors:

1. *Leader-member relations.*   This is the degree of acceptance or confidence the employees have in the leader. The attractiveness of the leader is pertinent as well as loyalty expressed by the leader's subordinates.

---

[2] For a complete discussion of this theory, see Fred E. Fiedler, *A Theory of Leadership Effectiveness* (New York: McGraw-Hill Book Co., Inc., 1967), and Fred E. Fiedler, and Martin M. Chemers, *Leadership and Effective Management* (Glenview, Ill.: Scott, Foresman & Co., 1974).

2. *Task structure.* The clarity and detail of subordinates' job descriptions is the key. The leader is held responsible for task accomplishment and must get subordinates to achieve these tasks. Whether the jobs are routine and easily measured or unstructured is also important. The leader will require differing approaches in relation to the nature of the jobs supervised.

3. *Position power.* Position power is the amount of formal authority possessed by the leader by virtue of the person's position in the organization. The support the leader has from superiors and his or her ranking in the managerial hierarchy of the organization are key factors.

Fiedler found that task-oriented leadership was effective in extreme situations of certainty or uncertainty. Disasters and routine work assignments would represent these extremes. A considerate leadership style works well when leader-member relations are good and there is moderate certainty in the work. Where good relations are paramount such as in a research laboratory, this style of leadership can be effective. Using a measurement to determine variables, which he called the LPC (least preferred co-worker), Fiedler argues that it is difficult to change personal attitudes and behavior of a leader. As a result he feels that it is easier to change the work situation to fit the leader's style. Thus his efforts are commonly known as "job engineering" or designing task structure to suit the leader.

Path-goal leadership theory. Utilizing Vroom's expectancy theory of motivation, Robert House and Terence Mitchell developed the path-goal leadership theory.[3] This designation is used because the focus is on how the leader can influence the employee's work goal perceptions, self-development, and the paths to the attainment of these goals. They claim that leaders are effective if they have a positive impact on the follower's satisfaction, ability to perform the job, and motivation to work. The relationship to Vroom's expectancy theory of motivation is that an individual's attitudes, job satisfaction, and behavior are highly related to the degree in which job performance is seen as leading to various outcomes and the preferences for these outcomes. The extent to which the leader can affect these outcomes by using a particular style influences employee expectancies or goal paths and the desirability of these goals.

All of the studies agree that leadership is a complex subject and that no single approach can give all the answers. One idea, however, becomes apparent; leadership is a continuing process for any supervisor. We all know that a particular managerial position includes certain leadership prerogatives and that the amount of influence and power an individual possesses affects the person's ability to lead. Command, which is the power granted by the formal organization structure, continues with the job, regardless of the incumbent. There is no doubt that knowledge and skills, along with personal characteristics, contribute to the effectiveness of the leader. A supervisor

---

[3] For a thorough description, see Robert J. House, "A Path-Goal Theory of Leadership Effectiveness," *Administrative Science Quarterly* (September 1971), pp. 321–39. Also see Robert J. House and Terence R. Mitchell, "Path-Goal Theory of Leadership," *Journal of Contemporary Business* (Autumn 1974), pp. 81–98.

should remember that, most importantly, leadership means continuing to learn from experience and understanding that each individual reacts differently to a given set of circumstances.

Styles of leadership

For most people, leadership is highly personal. The way it is carried out is usually a summary of past experience and personal convictions. A particular approach to a problem is tried; if it works, the individual will use that approach whenever a similar situation arises. These situational and environmental approaches, combined with the individual's inherited characteristics and collected learning experiences, contribute to his or her leadership style. Generally environmental factors play the dominant role in the development of a leadership style. Education, work experience, people an individual admires, and the nature of his or her behavior loom large in the development of the manner in which a person leads others. The type of leadership that an individual exercises is frequently the kind which is most admired and respected in the person's own life experience.

Power and influence. If one had to describe employee feelings about the power and authority of their bosses, they could best be summed up by the word "ambivalence." In other words, employees have mixed emotions about their personal independence and their job dependence. This attitude was recently demonstrated during a television interview when a worker in one of the large automobile companies was asked about compulsory overtime, presently a management prerogative. He replied, "The high overtime pay helps my family live better, but I don't want the company to force me to work overtime—I want to decide!" If some independence is not allowed on the job, employee resentment will manifest itself in lateness, absenteeism, work spoilage, pilferage, and other negative activity.

As was mentioned earlier in the text, the working relationship implies mutuality. The employee trades a certain amount of independence for a job and a paycheck. The terms of this "contract" and how well they are carried out constitute one of the leadership challenges for the manager.

There is no doubt, however, that a supervisor does influence the behavior of subordinates and that this influence is characteristic of superior–subordinate relationships throughout the organizational hierarchy. An individual's leadership style will influence acceptance of that person's leadership by members of the work group.

An insight into the relationship between influence and power and its effect on employees was developed by French and Raven.[4] They proposed that there are five bases of power:

1. *Coercive power.* This is based on fear. An employee performs and conforms to the wishes of the superior because failure to comply could be

---

[4] This approach was developed by John R. P. French and Bertram Raven, "The Bases of Social Power," in Darwin Cartwright and A. F. Zander, eds., *Group Dynamics,* 3d ed. (New York: Harper and Row, Publishers, 1968), pp. 259–69.

very negative. Losing one's job, getting poor work assignments or excessive reprimands are all characteristic of coercive power.

2. *Reward power.* This approach to power is the opposite of coercive power. It is based on the idea that compliance with the desires of the supervisor will lead to higher pay, better job assignments, and compliments.

3. *Legitimate power.* This is power derived from the position of the individual in the hierarchy. The president of a company has more legitimate power than a vice president and so on down the line to the first-level supervisor who has legitimate power over the operating employees.

4. *Expert power.* This is power based on expertise, knowledge, special skills, and know-how. Possession of these attributes allows the person to influence others. Such influence, however, does not have to be a superior-subordinate relationship. Peers may also respect expert power and react favorably to it.

5. *Referent power.* The charismatic leader mentioned earlier has referent power. Followers are attracted to such leaders because of personality traits, philosophical ideas, and physical appearance which are admired and consequently can influence some people. Examples of individuals who have been called charismatic leaders are John Kennedy, Martin Luther King, Jr., Winston Churchill, and Douglas MacArthur.

Another theoretical approach to leadership style that has been popular over the years is that three basic power styles are adopted by persons in leadership positions. This theory supports the idea that the way a manager uses power determines the style of leadership. The popularity of this approach is probably based on the notion that we can easily categorize leaders as using one of the three styles most often discussed: autocratic, democratic, or laissez-faire leadership.

Autocratic leadership. Persons in this category are usually characterized as "hard-boiled autocrats" or "benevolent autocrats." In both cases leaders center decision making in themselves and completely dominate the work situation for their employees by paternalistically structuring everything they do. They assume full responsibility and demand unquestioning acceptance of their orders. There is no encouragement of individual initiative among subordinates. In fact such initiative would be considered a threat by the authoritarian supervisor. There is little or no free flow of communication and the subordinates are insecure in their relationships with the supervisor. He or she maintains control and exercises power by keeping them insecure and fearful.

While both types of autocrat are very similar in their style, the "hard-boiled" autocrat's leadership is more negative in nature. This person's employees are more resentful, and turnover is likely to be higher. On the other hand, the "benevolent" autocrat is often popular with the work group. The person becomes the dispenser of all rewards and takes credit for all the good things that happen to the work group. Many people respond quite positively to this style of leadership. This is probably due to their having grown up in a

"You can march to the beat of whatever
drummer you choose. Just remember that
I'm the metronome."

Reprinted by permission The Wall Street Journal

*An individual's leadership style affects em-
ployee behavior.*

culture of benevolent autocracy, with this style of leadership exercised by
parents, teachers, clergymen, scout leaders, military superiors, and other
leaders to whom they were exposed. Another reason given for the relatively
wide acceptance of benevolent autocracy[5] is that most people prefer to work
in a strongly structured climate, knowing what is expected of them and not
having to make any decisions about their work. They expect the boss to be a
strong person and prefer not to assume any responsibility themselves.

Nevertheless, frustration, conflict, and poor morale tend to develop more
readily when the boss is an autocrat. When leadership is negative, it tends to
destroy any attempt at self-development; very few promotables evolve from
such a work group. People do not try to give their best because they are not
really encouraged to do so. One of the prime ways the autocrat exercises
power is by keeping aspirations low.

Democratic leadership.   In contrast to the autocratic supervisor, the supervisor who practices a democratic style of leadership rarely makes unilateral decisions. The individual tries to develop subordinates by having them
participate in decisions which affect their work. This approach is often
called consultative management. Attempts are made to develop group problem solving by keeping all group members informed about all of the factors
that may have an effect on their jobs and the work unit's relationships with
the rest of the organization. Initiative and self-development are encouraged
and ideas and suggestions for improvement frequently result. Promotables
are far more likely to come from this type of work group than from the

---

[5] For an interesting discussion of this style, see R. N. McMurray, "The Case for Benevolent Autocracy," *Harvard Business Review*, vol. 36, no. 1 (January–February 1958),
pp. 82–90.

groups supervised by autocratic supervisors. There are some people, however, who do not respond to this kind of leadership. They may even interpret supervisory attempts at group problem solving and consultative management as signs of managerial weakness. They believe that the manager is paid to assume responsibility and they are paid to do the work, and they want no part of activities they believe are the province of the manager.

Free-rein or laissez-faire leadership. In this style the supervisor really does not exercise any leadership at all. There is a tendency to avoid power and the responsibilities of management. The person may be an authority symbol because of the position, and he or she usually does serve as a contact between the work group and the rest of the organization, but that is about as far as leadership goes. Employees in this kind of situation set their own goals and must provide their own impetus for achievement. What can happen in such a work group is a chaotic approach to the job. There is little or no attempt at coordination, and people frequently work at cross-purposes. Obviously this is not a desirable leadership style, but it does occur when a person who is an outstanding work performer is promoted to a supervisory position he or she really does not want. The person merely continues to perform the job as it has been done before, without any regard for the managerial implication sof the new position.

Other approaches to leadership style were mentioned in Chapter 9. They are the Theory X (authoritarian) and Theory Y (democratic-consultative) styles of Douglas McGregor and the Managerial Grid,® which establishes managerial styles based on the manager's position on a grid designed to measure style.

One outstanding fact becomes apparent in the study of leadership. There is no one best method which, once learned, will solve all leadership problems. The very nature of leadership is based on a fluid superior-subordinate relationship. To be effective, supervisors must recognize this fluidity and the fact that it exists on all levels of an organization. Most satisfactory performers of the art of leadership use the various approaches as they are called for by the confronting situation. If autocracy is called for, they will use it. In a situation that indicates a democratic approach, this will be the approach; and so on. Of course the style a person develops more than likely polarizes around one of the approaches because of individual personality and experience.

In any event, leadership is always judged by what others do rather than by what the leader does; therefore, it can be concluded that a successful leader is one who influences others to respond in the direction intended. Simply stated, the possession of certain personality characteristics, a position of authority, and the desire to influence others are not enough. People can be called leaders only when they obtain a positive reaction to their direction more often than not and the groups accept them as their leaders.

Figure 13-1 helps in the understanding of the interrelationship of the several factors blended together in the person functioning in a leadership role. Figure 13-2 demonstrates the implementation of leadership style, and that

Figure 13–1
An integrative perspective of leadership

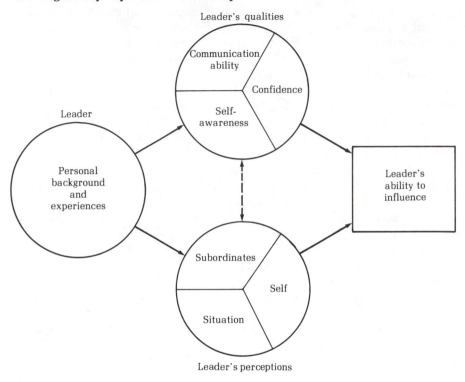

Source: J. H. Donnelly, Jr.; J. L. Gibson; and J. M. Ivancevich, *Fundamentals of Management*, rev. ed. (Dallas: Business Publications, Inc., 1975), p. 229.

experience usually results in a pattern of behavior encompassing several styles of leadership.

How to choose a leadership pattern

The leader who involves subordinates in decision making and the leader who makes all the decisions represent the two extremes of leadership behavior (loose versus tight control, democratic versus autocratic, permissive versus strong or directive). In between is a whole range of leadership behavior measured by the amount of authority exercised by the leader and the amount of freedom given to subordinates to make decisions. The following classification of leadership behavior and the discussion of it is based on a study by Tannenbaum and Schmidt.[6]

---

[6] Robert Tannenbaum and Warren H. Schmidt, "How to Choose a Leadership Pattern," *Harvard Business Review*, vol. 36, no. 2 (March–April 1958), pp. 95–101. An updated version of the same article appears in *Harvard Business Review*, vol. 51, no. 3 (May–June 1973), pp. 162–80.

Figure 13-2
The implementation of leadership style

Part A

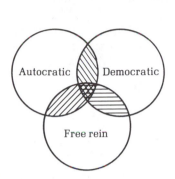

Part B

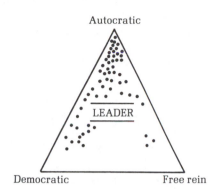

The figure shows that the practice of leadership is not a process of extremes. The effective leader will usually combine or blend various leadership styles, as indicated in Part A. The Part B diagram demonstrates that even a basically autocratic leader uses other styles as the occasion demands. Each dot in the triangle represents an incident of leadership behavior.

1. The manager who exercises tight control makes all the decisions himself, announces them, and expects them to be accepted and obeyed on the power of his authority.
2. Next in line is the manager who makes all the decisions but tries to "sell" the decisions by showing employees that they have something to gain by going along with them.
3. The manager makes the decisions but gives his subordinates an opportunity to discuss them, to ask questions about them, and to get an explanation of his thinking and his intentions.
4. The manager makes a tentative decision which he presents to his subordinates and asks for their reactions to it. He may change the decision if there are serious objections to it.
5. The manager defines the problem, presents it to the group, and asks for suggestions as to what would be good decisions. Then he selects the decision that seems best to him.
6. The manager defines the problem, sets the limits within which the decision must be made, and asks the group to make the decision. (He is responsible and accountable to his superior even though the group and not he makes the decision.)
7. The manager lets the group define the problem and make the decision within the prescribed limits. This type of decision making might be done by scientists in a research organization.

It is important that the manager be honest in letting the group know how much authority is being kept and how much is given to the subordinates. If managers intend to make decisions themselves, they should not try to fool subordinates into thinking it was their idea in the first place. Using participation as a technique to manipulate employees is a shortsighted policy that is apt to backfire.

From Tannenbaum and Schmidt comes the following list of forces or factors which play a part in determining what types of leadership are practical and desirable:

Forces in the manager:
　　His attitude toward sharing the decision making.
　　His confidence in his subordinates' ability.
　　His own leadership inclinations.
　　His feelings of security in an uncertain situation (his "tolerance for
　　　　ambiguity").

Forces in the situation:
　　The type of organization.
　　The way the manager is expected to behave.
　　The size and geographical distribution of the work unit.
　　The need for keeping plans confidential.
　　The effectiveness of the group in working together.
　　The difficulty of the problem itself.
　　The pressure of time.

Forces in the subordinate: Each subordinate has a set of expectations about how the boss should act in relation to him. . . . Generally speaking, the manager can permit his subordinates greater freedom if the following essential conditions exist:

1. If the subordinates have relatively high needs for independence. (As we all know, people differ greatly in the amount of direction that they desire.)
2. If the subordinates have a readiness to assume responsibility for decision making. (Some see additional responsibility as a tribute to their ability; others see it as "passing the buck.")
3. If they have a relatively high tolerance for ambiguity. (Some employees prefer to have clear-cut directives given to them; others prefer a wider area of freedom.)
4. If they are interested in the problem and feel that it is important.
5. If they understand and identify with the goals of the organization.
6. If they have the necessary knowledge and experience to deal with the problem.
7. If they have learned to expect to share in decision making. (Persons who have come to expect strong leadership and are then suddenly confronted with the request to share more fully in decision making are often upset by this new experience. On the other hand, persons who have enjoyed a considerable amount of freedom resent the boss who begins to make all the decisions himself.)

The manager will probably tend to make fuller use of his own authority if the above conditions do *not* exist; at times there may be no realistic alternative to running a "one-man show."

The restrictive effect of many of the forces will, of course, be greatly modified by the general feeling of confidence which subordinates have in the boss. Where they have learned to respect and trust him, he is free to vary his behavior.

... Thus the successful manager of men can be primarily characterized neither as a strong leader nor a permissive one. Rather, he is one who maintains a high batting average in accurately assessing the forces that determine what his most appropriate behavior at any given time should be and in actually being able to behave accordingly. Being both insightful and flexible, he is less likely to see the problems of leadership as a dilemma.[7]

Leadership, human relations, and attitudes

The Michigan studies by Likert indicate that a great many groups perform well under a supervisor who is friendly, approachable, available, and helpful—one whose supportive relationship builds the employees' sense of personal worth and importance. In getting high performance from the group, such a supervisor builds good attitudes through personal attitude—which enables one to practice good technical management without arousing hostility. Rather than putting pressure on from the top, one acts as a yeast, generating confidence, responsibility, and cooperation in working toward goals. One trusts subordinates and gives them leeway to do their work without close supervision. This type of supervisory behavior is classified as general supervision and the type of leadership is described as democratic or participative.

The Michigan research team found much to support their premise that this was the most effective pattern of supervisory behavior. The researchers also discovered many situations in which these findings did not fit.

Other research groups have sought to identify the conditions that influence the effectiveness of the supervisor's behavior.[8] Supervisors may find democratic methods unprofitable if their superiors are autocratic, the company climate unfavorable, or the subordinates hostile. Some types of work may be unsuited to democratic human relations. Some subordinates may be overdependent and may expect and prefer autocratic behavior from the boss. Perhaps the supervisor should be selected to fit the existing human relations climate if the company has no intention of changing it. On the other hand, adaptable supervisors can accommodate themselves to the existing situation and make gradual improvements designed to raise the level of motivation and morale.

---

[7] *Ibid.*

[8] For a comprehensive summary of research, see James G. March, ed., *Handbook of Organizations* (Chicago: Rand McNally & Co., 1965) and Marvin D. Dunnette, ed., *Handbook of Industrial and Organizational Psychology* (Chicago: Rand McNally & Co., 1976).

There is evidence to demonstrate that each organization has different requirements because of environmental considerations. Because of this, it is
necessary to treat each organization individually and try to design a human
relations approach designed to fit the situation. Recognizing the organization as a social system is of considerable importance. The formal structure
may establish the formal relationships and the levels of the hierarchy; but
people in the organization have their own motives, abilities, likes, and dislikes, and they develop many informal relationships within the formal
structure. In daily contacts they form ways of working together that are different from the ways provided by the formal organization. They establish
shortcuts and do favors for one another. They work more closely with some
people than with others, and they build up loyalties toward some and antagonisms and hostilities toward others. People who give and receive help become bound together by shared work experiences and attitudes. They build
detours around people they dislike and around inadequate bosses. They step
up to fill weak spots in the management structure of procedures and are accorded respect for their unofficial positions.

These complex relationships that form between people and groups
around the job are known as the informal social organization or, more simply, as the informal organization. Some groups are large and some are small.
Some follow the lines of the organization structure, and some groups are
within others or overlapping others. There are the friendship groups—tight
little cliques of people who chum together off the job and on. The people in
them are attracted to one another by some common ground of religion or nationality, education or culture, age or marital status. The friendship clique
forms a strong bond that holds the worker to the job and forms a tight little
circle from which others can be excluded.

There are interest groups—occupational groups maneuvering for advantages and jockeying for power against other occupational groups in the total
organization. The interest group puts pressure on the union and on management to get adjustment of its grievances and action on its demands.

The most essential factor when considering human relationships in organizations is the avoidance of superficiality. Any executive who believes that
a short course on human relations or the reading of a few books will have a
lasting effect on behavior is practicing self-delusion. Companies that expect
miracles from human relations training programs or send to them people
who should be fired are not really coping with the deeper meaning of human
relations. In an article on human relations and the nature of man, H. P.
Knowles and B. O. Saxberg conclude:

> The quality of human relations in any organization, from the political state
> to the business enterprise, reflects first of all its members', and particularly
> its leaders', view of the essential character of humanity itself. It makes a
> great deal of difference in systems of social control whether those involved
> tend to view man, in general, as good or evil. If we assume that man is good,
> we can believe that misbehavior is a reactive response rather than a mani-

festation of character. This will lead to a search for causes in his experience rather than in his nature. If we are to find a cause for behavioral failure, we are more apt to look outside the offender than inside and thus consider a whole new range of variables and contributory circumstances.

If, on the other hand, we assume that man himself is bad, a priori, then we are prone to assume that misbehavior is caused by something within him which we cannot alter directly. Accordingly, our attention will focus on limiting his freedom to choose and to act through external curbs and controls. In limiting the causes of behavior, we exclude ourselves from powerful internal sources of control.

Thus the underlying human value which predominates is readily perceived in (a) the way social relationships are structured, (b) the kinds of rewards and penalties that are used, (c) the character of the communication process which links people together, and (d) the other elements of social control that characterize a relationships or an organization.[9]

Attitudes.   No discussion of human relations should exclude the important factor of employee attitude. When an organization hires an individual, it gets someone who has a background shaped by past environment, experience, education, knowledge, and the multitude of other things, including attitudes and opinions, that shape a personality. This gives individuals a frame of reference from which they react to situations that occur on the new job. Their attitudes about events will be distorted if past experience represents gaps in information and knowledge as well as experience. The opinions they have may be firmly established, tending to solidify attitudes about certain topics. Such things as reaction to supervision and attitudes about religion, politics, ethnic groups, racial groups, and members of the opposite sex all are usually shaped before a company hires an employee. A simple example might be demonstrated by this chain.

1.   Past experience and inadequate information that women are not interested in careers forms the individual's frame of reference.
2.   His opinion then is that women are not promotable to management positions.
3.   His attitude about women employees, growing out of his limited frame of reference and his already formed opinion, manifests itself in such ways as not recruiting women college graduates, not considering women for jobs beyond low-level clerical-typing work, and treating them in a patronizing manner.

It can be seen that attitude has a considerable relationship to human behavior. One of management's responsibilities is, then, to try to develop positive attitudes among employees, thereby encouraging goal-oriented behavior and high productivity. This is no small task and it occupies a significant portion of an effective manager's time.

---

[9] H. P. Knowles and B. O. Saxberg, "Human Relations and the Nature of Man," *Harvard Business Review,* vol. 45, no. 2 (March–April 1967), p. 178.

Too much human relations?

There are management people who say that human relations in business and industry has been carried too far—that it is a softness toward employees which stands in the way of getting the job done, that it gets in the way of changes and improvements which might upset people. Human relations is said to let employees shuck off their responsibilities and find excuses for failure. It is accused of being a cult that would keep the inefficient on the payroll rather than support them on the tax roll.

Some complain because the practice of human relations has limited itself to being a matter of communications—getting employees to see things or maybe even manipulating them to make decisions. Some concede that human relations in the form of participation in decision making is necessary in the motivation of managers and of professional personnel but scarcely applicable to people in routine jobs, where it would call for a redistribution of power in an organization.

One of the most critical articles on human relations was written by Malcolm McNair for the *Harvard Business Review*.[10] He believed that far too much emphasis was being given to human relations courses in both business schools and industry. He felt that too much preoccupation with people caused executives to lose sight of their jobs and the results they were supposed to achieve. He did not believe that human relations concepts were wrong, but that they were treated too superficially, and that a cynical view could be developed which could lead to the belief that the study of human relations is designed to develop skill in the manipulation of people to achieve goals.

More recently several writers have taken a critical approach to participative and democratic styles of management. Emphasis has been placed on the fact that participation does not work in all circumstances. It is entirely possible that autocratic methods may be necessary in certain situations and that some supervisors and some groups cannot function effectively under democratic management. It is difficult to generalize about all managers and all organizations, and therefore it may be necessary to take a highly individualized approach toward the determination of what makes for successful human relationships in a particular organization.

Any consideration of the problems of human relations must take into account the fact that a business does not solely exist for the purpose of providing jobs and job satisfaction. The problem of using people most effectively is one of finding ways to make them most productive in the long run. The present ways of utilizing people may be getting the most output per hour but not the most per year—or per 30 years of a person's employment. Prevailing theories and practices of management have grown up around the

---

[10] Malcolm P. McNair, "Thinking Ahead: What Price Human Relations?" *Harvard Business Review*, vol. 35, no. 2 (March–April 1957), pp. 15–23.

concept that the machine and the system must be the constant factors in production and the person the variable one. People have been expected to change their nature and adjust themselves—and be adjusted to—the system. If they do not fit very well, they have to be influenced to be cooperative and productive.

The answer to the problem may be discovered in the kind of studies that put astronauts on the moon. In such studies, a person's abilities and limitations are determined and then become the constant factor around which the machine and the system are designed. There is no question of throwing out scientific methods or abandoning a quest for utmost efficiency. The human factor is simply recognized and incorporated in to the design in the way that will yield the highest efficiency. The ingenuity of these designs gives reason for belief that research and experiment will find better ways of fitting the organization of work to the human qualities of workers. The insights gained in studies of people can be put to use in the study of the organization of their work and the design of their jobs.

To the question: Is there too much human relations? the answer may be that there has been too little of it in the vital area of the relation of individuals to their work.

Effective leadership within the limitations

Employee-centered behavior, general rather than close supervision, willingness to delegate authority to subordinates and to let them share in decision making—all these things have their roots in supervisory attitude toward subordinates. This attitude is a belief in their value, their capacity to grow, their ability and willingness to handle responsibility and to do a good job.

Sometimes supervisors' attitudes have to be based on faith, because they must make the first move even though subordinates seem to be suspicious and resentful. One has to establish a climate of approval before people will be willing to take the risk of assuming responsibility. One has to train subordinates, help them, encourage them, forgive their mistakes, and make them less dependent. Giving employees any amount of freedom to regulate themselves and to participate in decision making is not something that can be done overnight. Rather it calls for a period of careful preparation, particularly if subordinates are accustomed to and expect tight control.

The effectiveness of supervisory leadership rests mainly on recognizing and understanding the various factors that limit the supervisor and adjusting operations to cope with them. Some of the limiting factors can be changed and improved. Others are beyond personal control; but rather than be hamstrung by them, one should accept them as challenges to build up one's effectiveness in whatever directions are open.

Personality factors. The supervisor's own personality plays a big part in determining what type of leadership role fits most comfortably. Perhaps one doesn't have a warm and outgoing nature that enables the establishment of friendly and informal relationships with one's subordinates. The supervisor may not be interested in their home lives, but some subordinates will be just as glad that he or she isn't. One does not have to be a backslapper in order to be employee-centered. Employee-centeredness is essentially a sincere concern for the welfare of subordinates and a willingness to listen to them, help them, and stand up for them. If a supervisor is scrupulously fair in dealings with subordinates, they will respect the supervisor and have confidence that they will get a fair break from this person. Some of the supervisor's own personal limitations can't be changed so he or she should take a realistic attitude toward them, quit worrying about them, and build on strong points. If energy has been dissipated in needless conflicts and prolonged hostilities, the supervisor may find it helpful to analyze personal attitudes. Developing empathy can enable the supervisor to achieve more understanding of the behavior of others. If the supervisor can remember that a whole lifetime of experiences and ingrained beliefs go into shaping an individual's personality and the way the employee will react to a situation, the behavior of others and his or her own behavior will be less upsetting. Bitterness and chagrin over disappointments, mistakes, and criticisms sap a supervisor's energy and make it difficult for the person to get along with people. Maybe the supervisor can write them off as sunk costs or look at them from an angle of "win a few, lose a few—and some are rained out."

Another approach to leadership behavior relates to the types of skills necessary for leadership performance. There is general agreement that any management job is difficult. All levels of management require some combination of technical, conceptual, and human relations skills. Personal development efforts should include recognition of this requirement. Self-confidence which is a requisite to effective leader performance should be based on professional competence.

The combination of the three skill areas mentioned above varies with the level of managerial responsibility and position. Presuming human relations skills to be a constant on all levels, the two variable skills are technical and conceptual. First-level supervisors need more technical skill than do their colleagues on higher levels of management. Because this level of management is concerned directly with work performance, an individual at this level needs competence in work methods, procedures, processes, and techniques. On higher levels managers must view their jobs in more overall terms with greater emphasis on relationships, ideas, and concepts. At the top of the organization, strategy and planning become more important and require considerable conceptual ability.

As people move through the levels of management, they must develop more conceptual skill. Those that do not begin to see the holistic nature of broader management responsibility often fail in managerial assignments beyond the first level. Figure 13–3 graphically describes the relationship of skills to levels of management.

Figure 13-3
Relationship of skills to level of management

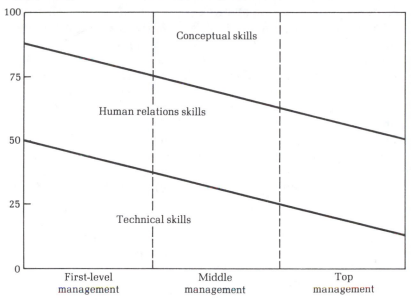

The boss as a limiting factor

Some bosses want to make all the decisions and are simply unable—as well as unwilling—to turn over any authority to subordinates. By their very nature they want tight control over everything for which they are responsible. They want to give strict and definite orders and to be obeyed in every detail. Some subordinates, even those in supervisory positions, are happy with this type of leadership. They like to have what they are to do spelled out for them exactly, so that they in turn can give detailed orders to their subordinates. They don't want to use their own judgment or make decisions, and they don't want their subordinates doing it either. They don't want to take any risks or be blamed if things don't turn out well; they have to be covered at all times. They like to follow clear-cut rigid orders, to obey and be obeyed. When boss and subordinate are both of this type, they work very well together. They understand each other and get satisfaction out of operating in this manner.

But supervisory subordinates who want to be free to use their ideas and abilities on the job just want to be told the goals and allowed to choose their own way of reaching them. They want a minimum of bossing and are willing to take the risks involved in making their own decisions. They are the ones who operate well under general supervision. Luckily, there are bosses who have this philosophy of management. These bosses just naturally tend to exercise loose control. They give their subordinates as much freedom as possible to choose their own leadership pattern, to work out their own problems, and to use their own judgment. They set up goals and let their subordinates choose the means to attain them. In a relationship such as this, ambitious and capable subordinates have an opportunity to learn by their own mistakes and prepare themselves for positions of greater responsibility.

It is the exceptional boss (or subordinate) who is an extreme example of either tight control or free rein. As we saw in Figure 13–2, most people can be classified as somewhere in between. The way most bosses operate depends on circumstances—the kind of training they have had, the nature of the work that is being done, the kind of boss *they* have, and the kind of people they are supervising. Most superiors believe in the principle that authority and responsibility should be delegated as far down the line as possible, but many of them have trouble in carrying this out. Managers may hold back authority and responsibility for a number of reasons; for instance:

1. They may simply like to exercise a great deal of authority.
2. There may be certain types of jobs that they enjoy doing themselves.
3. They may not have a system of controls worked out to enable them to keep track of delegated jobs to be sure they are being performed properly.
4. The amount they can delegate may be restricted by established job descriptions.
5. They may feel that the subordinates are not capable of carrying out certain responsibilities.
6. They may have no policies for subordinates to use as guides in making decisions.
7. They may be unable to communicate ideas to the subordinates.
8. Their subordinates may be unwilling to accept responsibility.
9. They may be unable to train subordinates or unwilling to take the time to do it.

The supervisor who is frustrated by a boss who won't delegate enough authority can do a number of things to improve the situation. First of all he or she should make a real attempt to find out if the present responsibilities are being handled in the way the boss wants them handled. The performance review may present an opportunity to come to a better understanding with the boss about the amount of authority the boss is willing to delegate, the problems met in doing the job, and the projects he or she would like to undertake. Communicating skill will help the supervisor present ideas in terms of the boss's viewpoint and get a better hearing for them. A subordinate who wants to sell the boss a plan of action must have it well thought out, intelligently organized, carefully worded, and presented from the boss's point of view.

If a supervisor insists on maintaining tight controls, maybe it is because this person lacks confidence in the subordinate's ability to handle the job. The way to earn the boss's confidence is to build a high degree of efficiency in the work group so that the boss can depend on effective goal accomplishment.

In order to avoid conflicts with a superior, the subordinate should study the superior's personality, work methods, decision making, strong and weak points, and opinions. A subordinate should realize that the boss faces problems and difficulties on the job, carries the responsibility for the department, and is accountable for everything that happens in it. Being mindful of the superior's welfare includes keeping that person informed of the things he or she needs to know and will have to answer for, being loyal, and never short-circuiting the superior.

The structure and climate of the organization as a limiting factor

The structure of the organization may limit a supervisor either by directly defining and curtailing authority or by putting pressures on the supervisor to conform to the accepted pattern of behavior. If the company is a large one, the need for uniform action leaves little room for making a special case out of every problem and settling it on its merits. The supervisor must learn to operate within the framwork of the organization, and it can be done more effectively if the supervisor will learn the history and the why of the policies, procedures, and rules that must be observed.

In the small plant or branch, personal leadership is the general rule, and personalities have a much greater impact on the organization. Everyone knows everyone. The personality of the individual in charge strongly influences the operations of everyone down the line. Quick decisions can be made; mistakes show up rapidly. Policies, procedures, and rules are often not set forth clearly. Problems are handled according to their individual merits, and decisions are often arbitrary. Authority and responsibility tend to gravitate toward those who grasp most vigorously. In the small concern, the leader must have a keen understanding of personalities and the relationships between people.

The reputation of the company, its policies on salary, and the steadiness or seasonality of employment all combine to influence the style of leadership. People may be hired and laid off in great waves as production schedules change or contracts are completed or canceled. The leader under such circumstances can scarcely do anything about developing people on a long-term basis. This person must do the best he or she can with people who are more concerned about prolonging their jobs than about giving their best to the company. If the organization is in a constant state of crisis or crash programming, leaders are inclined to exercise a high degree of authority. They don't take time to consult with subordinates on decisions; but these periods of organizational upset are the very ones in which subordinates need to discuss managerial plans, air their fears, objections, and resentments, and ask questions about things which are bothering them.

The line-staff relationships within the organization may reduce first-level supervisory authority and influence. Supervisors may be smothered by staff experts giving them information and advice, performing services for their departments, checking up on performance, and insisting that they adhere to prescribed policies, procedures, or methods. Effective supervisors learn as much as possible about the various staff specialties and the services they can provide and avail themselves of everything they can use. Their attitudes toward staff experts promotes employee acceptance of staff innovations.

Peer supervisors as a limiting factor

Peer supervisors influence the supervisor in the exercise of leadership. The departments preceding and following in the work flow can either hamper or help an individual supervisor. Cliques, jealousies, and unbridled competition can interfere with operations. The old gang may resent the eager beaver, the newcomer or the very bright young person. But no matter what a person has to put up with from peer supervisors, he or she can feel sure that personal actions can improve the situation.

Competence, dependability, and good work are essential to building a good relationship, because peer supervisors resent being hampered by a weak person who can't get the work done properly or on time. The supervisor can show concern for their success and welfare by doing his or her own job properly, not passing the buck, and not building personal prestige at their expense. Good use should be made of every occasion on which supervisors get together. By comparing notes, an individual can clear up misunderstandings and conflicts over who is responsible for what, and he or she can find out if any personal actions are putting the other supervisors on the spot.

Tact and good humor will go a long way toward gaining goodwill. It may take time, but meeting peer supervisors halfway and cooperating with them more than competing against them will help the supervisor become an influential member of the supervisory team.

The union as a limiting factor

The existence and the status of the union in the plant will have an influence upon the exercise of leadership by the supervisor. The shop steward may usurp or be permitted to usurp some of the supervisor's authority. Union members may look to the steward instead of to the supervisor for leadership. The steward's operations may make it difficult to build up a spirit of teamwork. Contract provisions must be followed in rewarding and punishing employees. Promotions, discharges, transfers, and layoffs must be handled according to contract. Enforcement of rules and standards may be appealed through the grievance procedure and have to be defended before an arbitrator. Mistakes become more serious in that they set a precedent (past practice) that may give away management rights. The need for prudence and uniformity of action may cause decision making to be transferred from the supervisor to the labor relations department.

In order to operate effectively under a union contract, supervisors must understand and abide by contract provisions. They should study the types of grievances that go through the grievance machinery and the settlements that come out of it. They should study the decisions and opinions of arbitrators and should forestall the occurrence of grievances by observing the provisions of the contract. They must guard against even the appearance of discrimination or arbitrary action, and handling of grievances must be correct as well as perceptive. Handling of discipline must measure up to the requirements of just cause and due process.

Since the union limits supervisory authority, they must develop compensating skills in dealing with people. By avoiding threats, displays of anger, head-on collisions of wills, and mistakes in handling personnel matters, they can minimize the chances of having his decisions reversed or of having to back down. By knowing more about people and the needs and wants they seek to satisfy, he can build positive motivation. By knowing the shop steward's rights and obligations, the supervisor can build better relations all around.

The work group as a limiting factor

Supervisors must adapt their pattern of leadership to the employees being supervised. The work group may be young people on a routine clerical job with relatively low pay and little chance of advancement. Here it is important to help the workers find satisfaction in their association with the group. It may be possible to design the job so that there is a feeling of group responsibility for getting out the work and seeing that each one carries a fair share of it. It may be possible to let the employees divide up the work themselves or rotate. It may be possible to stimulate interest by setting up competition with another group.

The leader's job here is to teach, train, guide, and encourage young people who have little experience in settling down to a full day's work and are not considering it as a career. The role is one of friendliness and firmness, showing what is expected and demanded in good work habits, responsible behavior, and emotional maturity.

A work group may be made up of relatively uneducated and unskilled production workers performing simple repetitive tasks paced by a conveyor. The nature of the work may limit the contacts between people. A supervisor on an assembly line may not be able to do anything about redesigning the jobs, but he or she can teach people how to handle several different jobs so they can at least get some variety by rotating. The supervisor can take some of the pressures off them by being friendly and understanding, by listening to them and explaining why the job has to be done just that way and can be there to help them when they get into trouble.

The supervisor may be confronted by a group of workers who are restricting production and sabotaging changes and improvements. Coming into such a situation, a supervisor should set about building up trust and confidence in his or her leadership. The supervisor can show people by personal actions that he or she has their interests at heart. Treating them with absolute fairness, helping them with job problems, clearing up points of friction, removing unnecessary unpleasantness, and respecting the customs that are important to them are useful approaches. The supervisor should study the informal organization to see if it is possible to work through its leaders.

The job as a motivating factor

Some jobs are so badly designed that no one can fit them or get satisfaction from their performance. In order to lead people to high performance, it may be necessary to redesign these jobs. Factors that must be considered in the design of a job are discussed in Chapter 9.

Fitting people to jobs. If people are to perform well, they must be fitted to their jobs. Placement is a supervisory skill calling for technical knowledge to analyze the tasks that make up a job and determine the amount of skill, knowledge, judgment, and exertion demanded of the performer. In order to choose a person who can do the job and will do it and get satisfaction from it, the supervisor must know the individuals and their abilities, ambitions, and limitations. How much variety is needed to hold their interest? How much responsibility do they seek? How much judgment are they able to exercise? Some people are stimulated by challenging jobs and should have responsibility thrust upon them. Others become upset and discouraged by anything unusual. People who have to struggle to keep up in one job may distinguish themselves in another. Placement is a continuing activity, because jobs change and people change.

Putting meaning into jobs. A leader is expected to create job enthusiasm—to show employees the significance of what they are doing and to make them want to do it better. On many jobs people just don't know the meaning of what they are doing unless they are told. They don't know what uses will be made of the hole they are digging or the figures they are handling. They don't know what failures or losses will result if their work is not done properly. Dramatic improvements in quality and in job interest have resulted from showing employees what happens to the product or process if their work is defective.

The supervisor can add meaning to the job by the way assignments are matched to the performer, by the way the purpose of the work is explained, by the amount of confidence shown in the subordinate's ability and judgment, by the way suggestions and criticisms are given, and by the way the performance is evaluated and recognition is given for good work.

Maintaining high standards on the job. Supervisory leadership is not a matter of being popular and keeping people happy no matter what they do or don't do. The leader who lets people get by with poor performance and undesirable behavior is then annoyed and dissatisfied with subordinates, but disapproval does nothing to improve their performance; actually it tends to make it worse. People are insecure and resentful when the boss disapproves of them. Lax discipline leads to misunderstanding, antagonisms, and blowups when rule-breaking or poor performance gets out of hand. Conscientious employees are uneasy under a leadership that lets people get by with sloppy work and disregard for rules. They don't like to carry the load while others fool around, and they are afraid they will be hurt in the crackdown when it comes.

People have respect for, and confidence in, leaders who insist on high standards. They let them know what is expected of them and how they are doing. They give them constructive criticism and make it possible for them to accomplish something worthwhile. By insisting on high performance and the kind of behavior that merits approval, the supervisor is able to approve of subordinates and give them recognition for the good work they do.

Fortunately most employees are not allergic to work. When management sets up a climate favorable for it, they accept responsibility and direct their own efforts toward objectives which they understand and support. Many employees can practice a high degree of self-control and do their best work under a leadership pattern using management by objectives. Such leadership gives people high goals to shoot for and sets up definite measures by which to review performance. It sets agreed-upon quantitative standards and provides the information by which people can measure their own performance. If conditions permit a supervisor to use this type of leadership, he or she does not have to breathe down the necks of subordinates to get work out of them. The supervisor can give them the freedom that fits their self-respect and stimulates them to excel.

The newly promoted supervisor

In any dynamic organization people are promoted to supervisory positions frequently. Such people are usually inexperienced in supervision, and they can face difficulty on their new jobs. When a person is promoted through the ranks to a supervisory job, the individual brings along job knowledge and technical skills and a pretty good idea of the way the work of the section is handled. Now the person has to learn management principles, practices, techniques, and skills, and to make the best use of the professional assistance available. Through association with the work group, the new supervisor can learn what is behind its attitudes, opinions, habits, and behavior. The person knows how the group interprets management's actions and what influences inside and outside of the group cause it to give or hold back cooperation with the supervisor.

An individual promoted from the ranks shares some of these attitudes, and the problem now is to make a shift of viewpoint so that the new supervisor can look at job problems from the point of view of management as well as from that of the subordinates and obtain the cooperation of employees by helping them derive satisfaction from their jobs.

Getting started on a supervisory job. The coming of a new supervisor may bring on behavior problems in a work group. Employees are apprehensive of changes that may be made. Many of them feel that the new supervisor will not understand them and shut them off from opportunities to advance through the ranks. Some are resentful because they wanted or expected to be chosen for the job themselves. A disappointed candidate has had a blow to personal pride, and if the person is going to be a satisfactory employee from this point on, he or she must be shown that the selection was made on some basis other than favoritism. Such people need to know why they were passed over and what their chances are for the future. They must be helped to gain a realistic attitude about opportunities and about the value of improving performance on the present job. Too often the people who also ran (or at least thought they were in the running) lose interest in the work or refuse to cooperate with the new boss and thereby disqualify themselves for future chances at promotion. The job of explaining should be done by the previous supervisor or by the supervisor's boss.

Coaching the new supervisor

The new supervisor's on-the-job training from the middle manager should consist of both coaching and counseling. Counseling was discussed in the previous chapter as part of the employee evaluation and development program. A manager counsels subordinate supervisors by telling them how they are doing and how they can do better. A person just starting in management is receptive to criticism of his or her performance. The more achievement-minded one is, the more one wants to be told precisely what is wrong and what is right about the way one is working. If there are things about behavior, speech, dress, or attitude that stand in the way of getting ahead, this is the time to tell the person about them.

Coaching, on the other hand, relates to the daily how-to-do-it part of the job of supervising. The following coaching suggestions are presented for the middle manager who is training a subordinate for a supervisory position. (They are for subordinates too, so that they can recognize the value of coaching and can make the best use of it.)

1. Start the person on some of your more routine activities.
2. As soon as possible, give the individual complete authority and respon-

sibility for some phase of the work and some task that can be personally accomplished.

3. Show the person how you analyze and solve some of your management problems.
4. Show the new supervisor how to plan the work to be done.
5. Indicate the *present* extent of his or her authority and responsibility.
6. Let the person know what the full extent of his or her authority and responsibility *will* be.
7. Increase the person's authority and responsibility gradually.
8. Keep others informed of the new supervisor's authority and responsibility.
9. Correct mistakes as they occur and show how you would handle the situation.
10. Keep the supervisor advised of your problems.
11. Get the person acquainted with your associates and your boss.
12. Teach the person to come with decisions instead of for decisions.
13. Protect the individual from short-circuiting.
14. Support the new supervisor.

And, depending upon circumstances, you might give informal training by means of:

1. Special projects, in which a procedure or method can be improved (often in cooperation with a staff person), thereby increasing the person's ability to solve problems.
2. Work rotation, whereby the person works on various types of jobs in the department in order to become more familiar with them and, later on, better able to supervise them.
3. Training assignments, whereby the individual develops and conducts on-the-job training and thus improves human relations techniques.
4. Committee work, in which he or she attends or substitutes for you on interdepartment committees.
5. Participation in technical or professional societies, with attendance at local meetings to keep abreast of the field.
6. Acting as an "assistant to"—being in the same office with you, taking over details of your job, listening in, and learning how you operate.
7. Sending the person to the boss's office to represent you. This is good practice for the employee, and it also gives your boss the opportunity of becoming acquainted with the new supervisor.

Successful leadership on the job—an application

Leadership should be judged from the results it accomplishes in performance and in building an effective work group. As a practical example of leadership judged by results, Figure 13–4 shows a supervisory leader's performance as viewed by the boss, peer supervisors, subordinates, and per-

Figure 13–4
The performance of a successful leader named Jones

The boss says that Jones:	Peer supervisors say that Jones:	Subordinates say that Jones:	Jones says:
Keeps production up	Does top-notch work	Explains jobs well	My boss consults me,
Keeps costs down	Does it on time	Sees all angles of jobs	likes my ideas,
Makes good decisions	Has good ideas	Has things thought	gives me freedom,
Has good ideas	Cooperates	out	gives me more
Has initiative	Delivers what is	Gives a square deal	authority and
Is dependable,	promised	Is not taken in	responsibility
loyal, and well	Speaks well of us,	Has job under	My department runs
liked	the company, the	control	smoothly
Takes responsibility	boss	Has group under	There is a minimum
Has few grievances	Handles problems	control	of conflict
Has few accidents	well	Plays no favorites	My people work
Has low turnover	Handles people well	Protects us	well, are loyal,
Turns out good work	Has the loyalty of	Helps us get ahead	don't ask for
Carries out orders	subordinates	Lets us know where	transfers out
Doesn't short-circuit	Does not pass buck	we stand	
	Can be trusted	Praises good work	
		Reprimands properly	

These four reports can be summarized into six essential things a leader does:

1. Makes good decisions.
2. Motivates people.
3. Has control of the situation.

4. Assumes responsibility.
5. Gives everyone a square deal.
6. Inspires confidence.

sonally. Their judgments are recorded on the chart and from them can be extracted six essential elements of the leader's job. These elements have been discussed throughout the chapter.

The leader personally

All that has been said in this chapter and in other chapters relative to the leadership role gives clear indication of the importance of the personal interactions involved. Obviously, there must be followers if there is to be a leader.

There are some uniquely personal aspects of leadership which also should be given attention. The role of leader involves a considerable responsibility which should not be taken lightly. On any level of management, the individual manager can and does have a great deal of influence over the lives of not only subordinates but all those other people in the company and outside it with whom he or she comes in contact. When dealing with a supplier, a customer, or the general public, the person *is* the company. When working with peers and superiors in the company, personal attitudes, ideas, and behavior shape opinion about all of the people who work for and with the individual.

Self-understanding. Self-understanding is most vital to effective leadership. The leader should be aware, for example, that he or she has a short temper, does not bear grudges, is too demanding at times, works well under pressure, and has various prejudices. In short, one should try to see himself as others do. The personal impact one has on other people can affect their morale, motivation, and group cohesiveness.

Empathy. Self-understanding should help the manager begin to appreciate the other person's viewpoint. When dealing with subordinates, supervisors can accomplish much more if they try to see their request as the subordinates see it. Getting a letter out when quitting time is five minutes away may mean meeting a deadline for the manager, but it means breaking a date for the secretary. This ability to view things from the other person's vantage point is known as empathy. How many times have we done something we thought best for a family member, friend, or employee, only to find it resented?

Empathy doesn't mean that managers should not do things which may not be desired by subordinates if they firmly believe it is correct. All it means is that managers ask themselves how subordinates may feel about this course of action. By putting themselves in their shoes, they should be better able to cope with possible objections and create more understanding for their views.

Objectivity and maturity. Perhaps one of the greatest compliments an individual's peers can give is to consider the person a true professional in the performance of the job. This means handling the various situations which occur with maturity and objectivity. It is difficult not to get emotional about some happenings or people whose actions may be perplexing, but the really effective manager cannot afford the luxury of excessive temper too frequently. At least the supervisor shouldn't do so in front of employees or the boss.

Most employees prefer fair, detached evaluations of their performance rather than those based on emotion or the supervisor's personal values. By keeping results in mind, as well as the employee's ability to achieve desired goals, the supervisor goes a long way toward making judgments objectively.

Summary

This chapter's discussion covered various approaches to the study of leadership and leadership style because of their importance in developing an understanding of the entire subject. Emphasis was given to the idea that there is no one general-purpose type of leadership which will suit all situations or all individuals. In reality, supervisors and managers usually develop a style based on their personalities, knowledge, experience, and the styles which they have responded to over the years. While inherited characteristics play a role in an individual's leadership style, environmental factors are more important.

Effective leaders recognize that different approaches are required for each situation and each individual. They will, however, tend to adopt a style which suits them and practice it most of the time. Supervisors do have restrictions on their freedom to make decisions, and these restrictions may limit the style they can use. The amount of decision making that can be turned over to subordinates and the kind of leadership that will be appropriate and effective depend on the structure and climate of the organization; the presence or absence of a union; the abilities, attitudes, and expectations of subordinates and the work they are doing; the supervisor's own personality and ability; the operations of peer supervisors—all these things plus the boss's attitude toward delegation of authority. The supervisor, through increasing personal effectiveness, can overcome some of these factors that limit him or her. The supervisor can learn to operate within the ones that can't be changed.

Employees are motivated in greater or less degree to satisfy their wants for status, recognition, approval, and accomplishment, as well as their basic needs for security. Leaders must know their people as individuals and understand their wants and abilities in order to fit them to jobs that enlist their interests and stimulate them to high performance. Some employees are stimulated by general supervision. Almost all employees will respond well to participation in some of its many forms and degrees.

In order to get people to follow their leadership, supervisors must show them by attitude and behavior that they value them as people, that they can be trusted, and are able and willing to help them get some of the things they want from the job. Effective supervisory leadership calls for character and courage as well as managerial, technical, and human relations skills and good practices. In order to establish and maintain leadership, supervisors must—among other things—make good decisions, motivate people to work with them, have control of the situation, assume responsibility, give everyone a square deal, and inspire confidence. Self-understanding, empathy, and objectivity will help supervisors make more mature judgments and create a better relationship between them and their employees.

CASE 13-1

Vince Peters was recently promoted to a middle management position in charge of a department of 100 people, including 5 first-line supervisors. The department was under constant pressure, particularly late in the afternoon when stringent deadlines had to be met.

He found that the leadership quality of the five supervisors left something to be desired and that the department was heavily staffed with junior employees who had been with the company less than two years. There were 20 senior clerks, with varying amounts of tenure up to 20 years.

Peters found his major problem to be the oldest of the five supervisors. He was 53 years old and had worked in the department for 30 years, the last 10 as a supervisor of 20 clerks. This man constantly lived in the past and kept commenting about the good old days when they were a happy family and all of the clerks were dedicated. On a number of occasions he openly criticized the lack of quality among the employees in his section, thus alienating them.

The younger members of the group were particularly upset. Several of them were members of minority groups who thought he was particularly directing his criticism at them. The senior clerks understood him and tolerated his criticism, since many of them had worked with him for several years.

Peters had found the quality of work lacking; but with so many newer employees and high turnover, little could be done. In addition, the entire community where the company was located had similar problems with low-level clerical employees. The high schools didn't do a particularly good educational job, and several of the young people looking for jobs came from low rungs on the socioeconomic ladder.

Every few months the supervisor would lose his temper about the poor quality of help. On one occasion he publicly berated Vince Peters because he believed him to be responsible for the poor quality of help and unwilling or unable to do anything about it.

Vince decided the time had come to read the riot act to the supervisor, though he had no replacement for him and didn't want to fire a long-service employee.

1. *How should Peters handle the supervisor?*
2. *What positive measures, if any, might be taken?*
3. *What can a company do about a generally poor quality of new employees?*

CASE 13–2

Recently you were appointed as the supervisor of a unit of machine operators in which you were formerly one of the rank and file. When you were selected for the job, the big boss told you that the former supervisor was being transferred because he could not get work out of the gang. He said also that the reason you were selected was because you appeared to be a natural leader, you were close to the gang, and you knew the tricks they were practicing in order to hold back production. He told you that he believed you could lick the problem and that he would stand behind you.

He was right about your knowing the tricks. When you were one of the gang, not only did you try to hamper the supervisor, but you were the ringleader in trying to make his life miserable. None of you had anything against him personally, but all of you considered it a game to pit your wits against his. There was a set of signals to inform the group that the boss was coming so that everyone would appear to be working hard. As soon as he left the immediate vicinity, everyone would take it easy. Also, the operators would act dumb to get the boss to go into lengthy explanations and demonstrations while they stood around. They complained constantly and without justification about the materials and the equipment.

At lunchtime the operators would ridicule the company, tell the latest fast one they pulled on the supervisor, and plan new ways to harass him. All this seemed to be a great joke. You and the rest of the gang had a lot of fun at the expense of the supervisor and the company.

Now that you have joined the ranks of management, it's not so funny. You are determined to use your leadership position and your knowledge to win the group over to working for the company instead of against it. You know that, if this can be done, you will have a top-notch unit. The operators know their stuff, have a very good team spirit, and, if they would use their brains and efforts constructively, they could turn out much greater production and get greater satisfaction out of their jobs.

Your former buddies are rather cool to you now, but this seems to be quite natural, and you believe you can overcome it in a short time. What has you worried is that Joe Jones is taking over your old post as ringleader of the gang, and the gang is trying to give you the business just as they did to the former supervisor.

1.   Was management wise in selecting you for the job? Justify your answer.
2.   What advantages do you have over an outsider?
3.   What disadvantages do you have? How are you going to overcome them?
4.   How would you develop cooperation between yourself and the gang?
5.   How would you handle Joe Jones?
6.   Plan a program for changing the group's attitude toward the company.

CASE 13–3

Harold Connors had been an informal leader in his department for several years. The other men came to him with their gripes and problems and the discussions which took place usually were fruitful. The department head was an autocratic boss and did not encourage upward communication among the employees.

Among the topics Harold discussed with the group in several conversations was leadership style. Quite naturally, autocratic supervision was much criticized, and the men constantly pointed out the virtues of democratic or participative management to each other. In fact, there was general agreement among the group that participative management was the best approach for a supervisor to follow.

In general, the group was self-motivated and most took considerable pride in their work, which was analytical and technical. They were all engineers and they were quite interested in the maintenance of their professional competence. The fact that they could not effectively communicate with their superior rankled them, but their animosity was partially offset by the frequent discussions during which Harold Conners acted as informal leader.

The department head retired and Harold Connors was offered the post. He welcomed the opportunity to get credit for what he had been doing informally for several years. The rest of the work group was very pleased with the choice, and they pledged their support and cooperation. Harold assumed his position and proceeded to implement his democratic approach to the leadership of the department. He continued the same type of discussion he had with the group before and willingly shared responsibility with his subordinates. Group goals were discussed freely and then assignments were made by voluntary acceptance by various individuals. While the previous department head had done all recruiting, Harold shared this effort and any group member was able to make recommendations. This same kind of participation characterized the setting of departmental priorities and goals as well as the utilization of manpower and other resources.

After six months, Harold began to notice that group participation was not working. The theory discussed favorably many times with the group was not successful in practice. He found that he had to use autocratic measures to meet departmental deadlines. Some group members who had accepted responsibility for the accomplishment of a particular goal were not achieving the goal. The discussions that were formerly friendly now became gripe sessions. Individual members sought Harold out to curry favor for their own pet projects and requested special treatment without considering its impact on the group. Harold learned from several of his employees that the formerly popular group meetings were now considered a waste of time—that while some were necessary, they should be infrequent. Harold was quite disillusioned, but he vowed to himself to continue to try participative management.

1. *Why did the efforts to achieve a participative work group apparently fail?*
2. *Could they have succeeded if an outside manager had been placed in charge of the group?*
3. *Was Harold hoping for too much in his desire to continue the same kind of relationship he had with the group when he was its informal leader? Why?*
4. *Should Harold continue to try to develop a participative atmosphere or should he revert to more traditional autocratic methods?*

CASE 13–4

George Francis walked into the personnel manager's office late one afternoon and told him he had a petition signed by 250 employees and that he had been chosen as a spokesman for the group. George Francis was a black man who had been employed by the company one year before as a computer trainee. He had since progressed to full status as a computer operator.

The company's data processing division employed approximately 2,000 people, of whom 30 percent were black.

The personnel manager quickly read the petition and saw that the central theme had to do with cafeteria food. It seemed that the petitioners were asking for better quality food in the company cafeteria, and they wanted "soul food" one day each week.

The personnel manager told Francis that he would need time to consider the request and that he would have to take it up with senior management. Francis replied that the company should not stall on this issue since it was considered important by all employees, and he left the office.

The following day George Francis was called to the data processing manager's office and fired for insubordination, excessive absence from his work station, general trouble making, and poor attitude.

1. *Was this problem handled properly?*
2. *What attention should be given to the petition?*
3. *Could it have been developed into a positive situation?*
4. *What might be employee reaction to the firing of George Francis?*

CASE 13–5

One of your assistants, Joe Blue, graduated from a small midwestern college several years ago. In his school days he was a leader in campus activities, president of his fraternity, manager of the track team, and so on. He has a superabundance of enthusiasm, initiative, and aggressiveness. These qualities, while necessary for leadership, seem to be overdeveloped in his case. You recently put him into a minor supervisory position with the hope of developing him into an executive.

His group turns out a satisfactory amount of work. He is well liked by his subordinates because he has a lot of bounce and he helps them with the details of their jobs. However, he does not get along well with the other supervisors of equal rank. He competes actively against them, grasping any of their authority and responsibility that comes his way. Occasionally he makes decisions that should be reserved for you. In fact, you have been informed that he is telling his subordinates how he would run the whole section if he were in your position.

He seems to have no interest in life other than getting ahead rapidly. He is unmarried and lives alone in a room. He spends practically all his waking hours on the job—the first one to get to the office and the last one to leave. Thus he gets quite a bit of extra work done. The other supervisors do not care for this behavior either.

1. *How do the other supervisors see the facts?*
2. *How does Joe Blue see the facts?*
3. *How do his subordinates see the facts?*

4. *How do you see the facts?*

5. *What are some of the leadership qualities Joe lacks?*

6. *How can you develop Joe without destroying the good qualities he now has?*

CASE 13–6

Ray Foster has been with the company for 35 years. He has worked in your department as a senior clerk for as long as you have been there. You have found him to be a loyal, efficient employee. Although he has limited ability, he has done his job well, and his attendance and punctuality record has been excellent.

He comes to you with a personal problem. His wife has become chronically ill and the woman who cares for her during the day must go home before Ray gets home from work. Ray has asked to leave a half-hour early each day so that his wife will not be alone. He cannot come in early in the morning because the practical nurse does not get there early enough, having her own family to care for. Ray mentions the difficulty in securing such help and the fact that he is lucky to have a dependable woman to care for his wife during the day. Ray even offers to take a cut in pay if you will grant his request.

You listen to his problem with considerable sympathy. His long, loyal service to the company weighs considerably in your decision. Although there is no company policy to cover such a situation, you decide to allow him to leave early each day. You turn down his offer to accept a pay reduction. Ray is very grateful and you feel very good about your decision.

Two weeks go by and three employees come to you to ask for similar privileges. All have been with the company less than five years, and they are average performers. None of their reasons are as compelling as Ray's in your judgment.

1. *Should you grant the requests of the three employees?*

2. *Should you have granted Ray's request in the first place?*

3. *How can you explain special treatment for a long-service employee to other employees in the department?*

4. *Should a company have special-privilege policies for long-service employees?*

5. *Should you go to higher management with your problem and suggest a company policy to cover such problems?*

CASE 13–7

John Benson had been head of the department for about eight years. Over this period the department had high labor turnover and a considerable current of discontent among its 25 employees. John was an autocratic supervisor. Because he seemed to have the support of the division manager, the people in the department did little outward complaining about his leadership.

Nevertheless it was common knowledge in other departments in the division that the majority of the people in John's department were very dissatisfied, to say the least. These people were career employees performing technical work, and they received personal feelings of accomplishment from their work. Few compliments were forthcoming from their boss; while they resented this, their personal pride and possible fear of retribution kept them from saying anything to John. One of the things they resented most was John's frequent practice of taking credit for ideas and efforts of subordinates so that he could enhance his own reputation with his superior, the division manager.

One of his subordinates, Will Michaels, had become the informal leader of the department, although he did not seek the role. Other employees sought him out for advice and guidance, and he became the focal point of the gripe sessions which had become more frequent as time passed. These gripe sessions were quasi-social occasions such as lunch, and they usually ended with Will telling his fellow employees to complain openly about their grievances to both John and his superior. Will had done this several times and, while he gained no positive results, he at least had the satisfaction of having a clearly stated position. This may have been one of the reasons why the other employees turned to him for advice. In any event, Will evidenced no fear of his boss, and he was generally recognized as a superior employee by his peers.

The division manager retired and was replaced by a member of one of the departments in the division. He had not had prior administrative experience in the company, although he had had managerial responsibility at prior places of employment. Because he was familiar with the problems in John Benson's area of responsibility, he recognized it as a trouble spot; and after some consultation with the assistant division manager, he decided to replace John Benson as department head. John was quite surprised, since he had assumed that he could continue under the new division manager as well as he had under the one who had recently retired. When the new division manager demoted John, he said he could stay with the company as a technician in the department he had previously managed. This was done because of John's long tenure with the company and the fact that he was only eight years from retirement. John accepted the demotion with considerable dejection and malice, but he felt he had no choice under the circumstances.

Will Michaels was called in by the new division manager and asked to assume the department head position. He was informed of his former superior's demotion and the fact that John would now be working for him. The division manager told Will that he was chosen because it was believed that he could weld the department into a cohesive operating unit of the division. Will accepted the responsibility with what could be called confident apprehension.

1. *In making the transition from informal leader to formal leader, can Will maintain the same relationship with his fellow employees?*
2. *What problems do you feel he will have with his former superior in the changed relationship which now exists?*
3. *Did the new division manager handle the situation properly?*
4. *Should Will have accepted the position as department head?*
5. *What kinds of problems does an informal leader face when he becomes the formal leader?*
6. *Is it wise for management to promote a generally recognized informal leader to a managerial responsibility?*

CASE 13-8

The Jordan Consulting Group had been located in New York City for over 30 years. During the last several years, it had found that the majority of its business came from the New England states, and the senior management decided to relocate to Boston, Massachusetts. All employees were offered jobs at the new location; they and their families would be relocated at company expense.

About 50 percent of the clerical, stenographic, and support employees accepted transfers, and over 80 percent of the consultants and managerial personnel also elected to go to Boston. The company retained real estate consultants to aid in the search for houses and apartments in the Boston area.

Ralph Fredericks, the office manager, elected to go to Boston. He had been with the company for 25 years and enjoyed his job. However, he decided to keep his house in a New York suburb and go there on weekends to be with his family. The house was fully paid for; he and his wife had lived there all their married life; his children were in college nearby; and his elderly parents lived with him as well.

He found a room near the office in Boston and lived there during the week. He would leave the office at 3:45 P.M. on Fridays to take a train to New York and come in about 10:30 A.M. on Mondays after taking a train to Boston from New York. During the week he worked late most nights, since he was alone and preferred to stay in the office rather than go to his one-room apartment.

Ralph had been carrying on this regimen for over a year when the firm's president called him into his office and told him he could no longer leave early on Fridays and come in late on Mondays. Fredericks was flabbergasted but decided to comply, though this meant less time with his family. He was 58 years old; he began to think about early retirement.

1. *Why would the firm's president take such action?*
2. *Was he justified in doing so?*
3. *Was Fredericks taking advantage of the firm?*
4. *Could this problem have been solved differently?*

CASE 13-9

Len Olsen, at age 55, had been with Douglas Manufacturing for 33 years. He had come to them as a young engineer right out of college. For the past five years he had been senior vice president in charge of plant operations in the main plant, which employed over 7,000 people. Len had come up the hard way, progressing slowly but steadily over the years. He was not brilliant, but he was a dependable, capable employee.

His dependability had caught the eye of Henry Steele when he was in Len's present position. Steele liked dependable, steady subordinates, and he took Len under his wing. He and Len got along fine: Steele made all the decisions and Len carried them out without question. Three years before Steele retired, the company made him executive vice president in charge of manufacturing. It was at that time that he promoted Len Olsen to senior vice president. Nothing really changed in the relationship except the titles of the two men.

Though Steele had wanted Olsen to succeed him when he retired, he was not able to convince the company president. Instead, a 39-year-old senior vice president from another division of the company was promoted to the manufacturing executive vice presidency. Everett Jackson was the classic bright young executive with a great deal of drive and energy, well educated in managerial practice, with a superb reputation in the company. He liked subordinates who could make decisions, run with the ball, and accept responsibility.

Olsen, who was used to going to Steele with everything, just couldn't figure out Ev Jackson. Every time he went to him for a decision, he was told to do it himself or present alternatives. He had never had to do this before, and he began to feel like a fish out of water. Jackson wasn't very happy, either. He found Len a roadblock and promoted a bright young man to assist Len. Then he found himself working with the young man and around Olsen.

After one year, Jackson decided he had to get rid of Olsen; and since no job could be found for him in the company, he was asked to take early retirement.

1. *How can a manager who is used to one type of superior change his behavior?*
2. *Could Jackson have done anything to change Olsen?*
3. *To what extent was Olsen's fate decided by Henry Steele?*
4. *How can managerial obsolescence be avoided?*

CASE 13-10

Sally Minton has just been asked to take over a small but important department in the company which has several problems. After nine years with the company and the last five in managerial assignments, Minton has been identified by several bosses as an excellent manager with effective human relations skills and a mature sense of responsibility. In her early 30s, she looks upon this new assignment as a real challenge and an opportunity to continue to demonstrate her capabilities. She feels success here will mean a much bigger position. Her superiors agree since they feel she has the ability to achieve a senior management position with more experience.

One of her problems in the new assignment is Murray Barber who has been with the company 27 years, 6 of which have been in this department. Murray is 48 years old, and at first Sally thought her age and the fact that she was a woman might be contributing to the problem. But she soon found out that Murray's weaknesses predated her arrival. Murray is simply one of those people who will not exercise any leadership. A number of individuals report to him, but he refuses to recognize his managerial responsibility. By checking Barber's personnel file, Sally has determined that his apparent lack of management skill was noted by prior supervisors, all of whom admired his technical competence.

Minton read further in the file and discovered that Murray had started in the company at a low-level job and went to school at night. After several years he received a B.S. degree, married, had a family, and rose slowly but steadily to his present supervisory position. Sally wondered if his early ambition and promise could have been discouraged in some way. She planned to discuss this with Murray, but before she could get around to it one of Murray's subordinates who had a history of instability became unable to handle his job. This person had demonstrated erratic performance in the past ranging from competent to inept. When Murray came to her with the problem, Sally told him to handle it. Murray believed it wasn't his responsibility, wanting to refer the matter to the personnel department. Sally refused to listen and literally badgered Murray into facing the responsibility until he finally did. Barber contacted the man's wife and his family doctor who agreed to place the person under psychiatric care.

With this limited success, Sally Minton decided to try further in the development of Murray Barber. When she received authorization to add three employees to the staff, she asked Murray to work with the personnel department on the recruiting and interviewing. He reluctantly accepted the assignment, but his choices for the open positions have been superior.

1. *Why has Sally Minton been apparently successful in moving Murray Barber to accept some managerial responsibility?*
2. *What may have caused his past reluctance?*
3. *What should Sally do if Murray reverts to past behavior?*
4. *If Sally had failed in her approach, what should she have done?*

Chapter 14

Learning objectives

○ To develop an understanding of the communication process and its importance to managers and supervisors

○ To consider several dimensions of communication with others and the value of understanding them

○ To become aware of the barriers to effective communication and how to cope with them

○ To identify and be able to understand guidelines to effective superior-subordinate communication in an organization

Communication

Major topics

The supervisor's area of communicating.

Communicating is an art.

Perception.

Words are tricky.

Learning to listen.

Jargon.

Symbols and symbolism.

Behavioral factors in communication.

Distractions muddle orders.

Putting across a new idea.

Difficulties in discussion.

Unfavorable attitudes build up listener resistance.

Good attitudes facilitate understanding.

How to give orders.

Getting orders from the middle manager.

Keeping the middle manager informed.

Lack of understanding between subordinate and superior.

How managers can promote more effective communicating.

Communications systems, networks, and the flow of management information.

The last chapter, on leadership, showed that if managers are to be effective leaders they must relate well to subordinates, peers, and superiors. Coupled with this is the rationale for organization, which is to develop a cohesive unit which can achieve a common purpose. The initial step toward the accomplishment of this common purpose is communication. In fact, all functions that a manager must preform require communication. Any analysis of the daily efforts of superiors will indicate that they spend the majority of their time communicating in one form or another. Conversely, many of the human relations problems that occur can be traced to some kind of communications failure.

The field of communicating takes in all the ways in which people try to impart their ideas to others—spoken words, written words, pictures, gestures, even silence or a raised eyebrow. Communicating in business may be face to face or by phone, memos, letters, bulletins, reports, house organs, notices in pay envelopes, and so on. The emphasis on the importance of communications in business raises the questions: What are these messages that are being sent? Why is it so important that they be understood and accepted? What are the hindrances to the giving and getting information?

To understand more fully the relationship of communication to managerial practice, it should be considered as another process which like decision making, planning, goal setting, and organizing is available for use by managers and supervisors. As is the case with all management functions, communication is not carried out separately but in the context of an organization and in relation to other functions performed by supervisors and managers.

Scott and Mitchell have developed an approach to conceptualizing the process of communication in an organization. Figure 14–1 demonstrates the interdependence of the organizational communication process.

The supervisor's area of communicating

Supervisors have to get things done through and with people; thus their effectiveness depends on getting ideas across so that people understand what to do and are willing to do it. Face-to-face communication, talking and listening are the areas of principal concern for line managers.[1]

In order to gain skill in communicating, they must have an understanding of those things that get in the way when one person tries to impart ideas to another. Why is it that people don't get what is said to them and do get meanings that were never intended? Some of the trouble arises because

---

[1] This chapter emphasizes talking and listening aspects of communication since verbal effort characterizes so much of managerial work. The reader will be alerted to some causes of misunderstanding, and if one desires to improve overall communication, then a study of written communication must also be undertaken. There are many texts on business writing. Among these are: Raymond V. Lesikar, *Business Communication: Theory and Application* (Homewood, Ill.: Richard D. Irwin, 1976); and George T. Vardaman and Patricia B. Vardaman, *Communication in Modern Organizations* (New York: John Wiley & Sons, Inc., 1973).

Figure 14-1
Functions of organizational communication process

Function	Orientation	Objectives sought	Theoretical and research focus
1. Emotive	Feeling	Increasing *acceptance* of organizational tasks.	Personal and inter-personal satisfaction; resolution of tension; definition of role; expression of attitudes.
2. Motivation	Influence	Seeking commitment to organization objectives.	Power, authority, compliance; behavioral modification; reenforcement and expectancy theories.
3. Information	Technological	Providing data necessary to rational decisions.	Decision making; assessment of data; organizational intelligence.
4. Control	Structure	Clarifying duties, authority, accountability.	Organizational design and redesign.

Source: William G. Scott and Terence R. Mitchell, *Organization Theory: A Structural and Behavioral Analysis*, 3d ed. (Homewood, Ill.: Richard D. Irwin, Inc., 1976), p. 193. © 1976 by Richard D. Irwin, Inc.

people attach their own meanings to words. Some comes from the way the words are arranged in the sentence, and the sentences arranged in relation to one another. Some of the difficulties can be charged to the interference of distractions; some have their roots in feelings, attitudes, backgrounds, and experiences. For example, a worker complains:

> He told me: "Now hear this. That number has to go on every job you handle and don't ever forget it." So I copied the number down and I've put it on every job just like he said. I didn't know I was supposed to put a different number down every time. I didn't know those numbers on the sheet were contract numbers. I thought I was supposed to use my special number on everything I handled.

It's up to supervisors to make themselves understood and to find out what the other person has in mind. Poor communication results in stupid mistakes and costly failures. The subject, therefore, is a profitable one to investigate.

Supervisors communicate all day long. They are communicating when interviewing applicants and trying to find out if they can and will do the work and if their personalities, backgrounds, interests, ambitions, and goals fit them for the job. Their manner of talking gives the applicants a picture of the company, of the job, and of the kind of boss their supervisors might be. Can they be relied on for a square deal? Are they approachable, considerate, friendly? Do they describe the job in an understandable way?

Supervisors are communicating when they introduce new employees to the department and to the job, teach them, train them, find out their job interests, encourage them to develop their talents, let them know they are interested in them as individuals, and indicate that they want to help them get ahead on the job.

They are communicating when they delegate authority and responsibility to them, direct their efforts, praise their work, point out mistakes, let them know how they are measuring up to the standards, listen to their gripes, answer their questions, counsel them in merit rating interviews, discipline them, settle grievances, ask for their suggestions, and get them to participate in improving job methods and in putting changes into effect.

They are communicating when they make assignments; give orders; explain standards of quality and quantity; check the progress of the work; give assistance, suggestions, or encouragement; sell management's ideas and interpret policies; explain and enforce rules; give training in safety; assign overtime; or ask for extra effort.

Almost everything the supervisor does involves communciation. And the communicating may be done in a way that antagonizes subordinates and causes them to be suspicious, resistant, and resentful; to do a minimum and to pass the buck. Or the communicating may be done in a way that makes their subordinates feel pride in their work, responsibility for their part in it, and willingness to do their best.

Supervisors should suspect that their communicating is at fault whenever jobs are not carried out according to instructions; when people are working at cross-purposes; when they work grudgingly, refuse to accept changes, duck their responsibilities; and when misunderstandings, gripes, and grievances interfere with production.

There is no doubt about the importance of effective communication. Many writers in the field believe that it is basic to the practice of management. It certainly is easy to understand this belief just by reflecting on what is mentioned above about the supervisor's area of communicating and the amount that is done. Strong, silent types may be desirable characters in a romantic novel, but they would have considerable difficulty functioning as supervisors in a modern complex organization.

Inadequate and ineffective communication can impair the practice of management. Keith Davis calls communication a possible bottleneck to worker productivity, and he graphically describes it thusly (see Figure 14-2).

Communicating is an art

Communicating is an art by which a person finds a way to reach the mind of another and share an idea or create an understanding. The sender of a message may write it or speak it, or may draw a picture of the idea. Whatever art form is used to carry the message, the person must learn the principles and techniques of the art and the rules governing the structure and arrangement of its parts. In writing the person must depend on words and the way they are organized to convey the message intended. In speaking,

Figure 14–2
The communications bottleneck

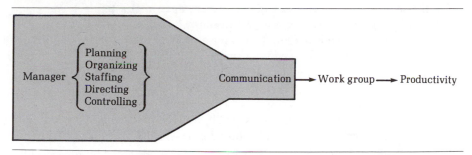

Source: Keith Davis, *Human Behavior at Work*, 5th ed. (New York: McGraw-Hill Book Co., 1977), p. 374.

one can reinforce his or her meaning with tone of voice, motions, and facial expression and can see how the message is being received and make adjustments to fit the receiver.

For supervisors communicating is an art to be studied and practiced. When they communciate a message, it is for the purpose of getting a response from the receivers—getting them to do something, know something, or accept something. Whether the communication will be successful depends in great measure on the meaning which the receiver attaches to it. Dictionary meanings of words don't tell what meanings the receiver has in mind. The words themselves are merely symbols to which each person attaches meanings of his or her own.

Study of communication includes a study of the characteristics of human behavior and the factors that influence a person's reaction to the messages received. Figure 1–2 in Chapter 1 illustrates why one person will never perceive anything exactly as someone else would or exactly as that person would perceive it at some other time or place, in some other state of mind, or under other circumstances.

Predicting the reaction of a person to a message is the basis of persuasion. The TV commercial is pitched to a particular type of customer and designed with the expectation of getting a favorable response. The supervisor has an advantage when it comes to predicting the responses of subordinates to a message: He or she is close to them and to the group that influences them. If the supervisor was once a member of that group, he or she knows its system of values—the things that are important to its members. The supervisor can choose words, examples, and approaches that fit their experience and can shape his or her communication in terms of their attitudes.

Perception

For communication to achieve even a reasonable success, there must be some sense of common purpose and values among the parties involved. If this commonality does not exist, understanding will not result, and there may even be resistance and hostility among the individuals.

When confronted with a particular event, each of us tends to perceive that event against our own frame of reference. Inevitably it will have a different meaning for each person. Consider a power failure during a summer thunderstorm and its possible effect on several people and how they might perceive it. The repair crew sees it as a dreary job of finding and repairing the break in the wire in the pouring rain. The person who has just loaded his or her freezer with expensive steaks begins to worry about spoilage and a loss of money or a huge steak dinner. The power plant manager wonders how long the storm will last and about the possibility of more power failures, because he is short of repair crews due to vacations. The power company president worries about the impact of several recent power failures on the request for a rate increase the company has placed before the state's public utilities commission. All of these people are confronted with the same event, but all of them perceive it differently and it has varying degrees of importance for them.

All people have values which distort and filter what they hear and see. Any attorney who has handled accident cases can attest to the varied impressions of several witnesses to the same accident. It certainly would help if the communicator could know what filters and distortions the audience is using so the sender could attempt to overcome them. Translated into managerial practice, this means that the supervisor should try to know the employees, peer supervisors, and superiors as well as possible.

Figure 14–3 is an interesting exercise in visual perception. The two examples demonstrate that what we see may not be what really is.

Figure 14–3

**Are the circles in the
center the same size?**

**Is the hat's height longer
than its brim?**

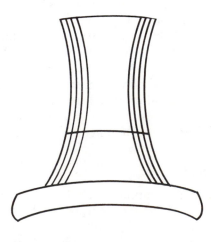

Words are tricky

When a speaker uses a word, there is an inclination to assume that the listeners would use that word just the way the speaker is using it. Few people take into account that the 500 most used words in the English language have more than 14,000 meanings listed in the dictionary. There is a real risk that a word used one way by the speaker will be interpreted another way by the listener.

The word "job" for instance is a simple one. What trouble could there be with it? The job analyst considers a job as a group of tasks or duties which are performed by a person. The employment interviewer normally takes the word job to mean a vacant position that some applicant will be hired to fill. To the supervisor of a production department a job may mean order No. 402 for 500 pieces to be fabricated by Wednesday.

A worker says, "I'll be glad to get off this job; it's driving me nuts." What does the employee mean? What is the supervisor going to think the person means? What happens if the supervisor is thinking of job No. 402 (which has really been a tough one) and replies, "Tomorrow's your last day on it, and I hope it's a long time before you get another one like it"? The worker wasn't thinking of No. 402; he or she was just talking about knocking off work at 4:30 and getting a chance to relax after a hard day. So here's the supervisor trying to fire him.

How can the supervisor prevent things like this from happening? Once a misunderstanding has occurred, how is the supervisor going to spot the trouble, get it out into the open, and clear it up before it gets any worse?

He or she can't go around all day defining terms and asking employees to define theirs, but the supervisor can detect misunderstandings by improving listening and keeping in mind the questions: Do I really know what the employee is talking about? Does the employee know what I am talking about?

Word use.   Then there is the seeming deliberate effort by some people to use words that are confusing, obliterate meaning, and make the intended message difficult to understand. These people believe that the use of multisyllable words impresses others. In everyday life all of us have been confronted with such confusing words as "fatuous" when "foolish" would be better; "affable" instead of "agreeable"; "erudite" instead of "learned"; "abated" instead of "lessened"; "maudlin" instead of "sentimental," and so on. Of course the idea of creating an impression with words is not without merit. The airlines have both "first class" and "tourist" seats. Somehow "tourist" sounds better than "second class." "Simulated leather" sounds better than "imitation leather" and "decade" may convey to some a longer period than the ten years it means. In fact, some years ago a faculty colleague at New York University posed the question of the meaning of "decade" to 480 college freshman and while 364 gave the correct answer, 116 responded in a range of 1 year to over 1,000 years.

At times government agencies and business organizations go out of their way to use words which may confuse. In a recent press release announcing a new job appointment for an executive, the company issued the following statement, "Mr. Blank has been named director of the division manufacturing man-operated residential refuse collection and compaction vehicles." Presumably they meant garbage trucks.

Learning to listen

Supervisors are lucky that most communicating is the face-to-face kind because of the opportunity to detect and correct misunderstandings before they become serious. Communicating in writing enjoys no such advantage; the words stand there to be read over and over, to be interpreted one way or another according to the background, experience, mood of the reader. It is no accident that delicate negotiations are carried on in face-to-face contacts so that each participant can sound out and observe the reactions of the other, make adjustments, ask questions, and tailor the presentation to fit the person receiving it.

The supervisor who misunderstood the worker's statement, "I'll be glad to get off this job," needs only to be an observant listener in order to catch the mistake. The worker's face may register surprise, anger, consternation, or some other emotion that seems unwarranted. Whatever the employee says or does at this time just won't make good sense in the situation as the supervisor sees it. Here is where the supervisor has to assume that there has been a misunderstanding, and he or she can ease some of the tension by taking the blame for it. The other person is probably upset, and it won't help any to insinuate that the employee is stupid and can't understand plain English. "Did I say something that didn't sound right? I didn't intend to," will spread oil on the waters while the rescue boat is operating. It is much easier to straighten out a mistake in an atmosphere of friendliness than in one of bitterness.

The supervisor has to ask questions in a manner that inspires trust and draws out information. He or she has to resist the inclination to think that if what was said before (and what caused all the confusion) is just repeated in a louder voice, everything will be straightened out.

Jargon

Another interesting dimension of words and communication is the special or technical language used by work groups and social groups. It is also called jargon, argot, or shop talk. Group members may forget their use of special language when speaking to outsiders and become surprised when there is poor understanding. This aspect of word usage was brought home to the author when he was to deliver a talk on the use of staff assistants to a group of top-level Japanese business executives, none of whom could understand English. The talk was to be simultaneously translated into Japanese, and the author was told to be careful not to use any slang or peculiarly American idiomatic expressions.

All of us have been exposed to the jargon of the astronauts, and such expressions as "A–OK" and "All systems are go" have become part of the general language. Another example is the patois of teenagers, with a variety of words and expressions that give them an identity and tend to change as frequently as young people become teenagers and communicate to each other. Then there is the patois of various ethnic and racial groups, which also gives them an identity and a certain exclusivity. Here again many expressions have found their way into everyday speech. Examples are the young people's use of "together," meaning integrated, and "cool" as a noun ("don't blow your cool"); "right on," the black's expression of agreement or encouragement; "chutzpah," the Yiddish word meaning supreme self-confidence or gall; and "blitz," a contraction of the German word "blitzkrieg" meaning an attack in war conducted with great speed and force (now used to describe such things as the rush of defensive linebackers on the passer in a football game). These are only a few examples of the many lodes from which new words are constantly being mined and added to everyday "English."

"If you want layman's terms,
go to a layman!"

Reprinted by permission The Wall Street Journal

Professional jargon is frequently difficult to understand.

It becomes obvious that new employees with no previous experience must be introduced to the jargon or slang of their new work group. Until they fully understand it, they will feel like outsiders and their performance will suffer. Some companies and even entire industries have prepared terminology glossaries giving the meaning of words and expressions peculiar to that particular industry.

Symbols and symbolism

Closely related to word usage is symbolic meaning. The word "management" has one type of meaning when used in the title "professor of management" and quite another when used by a militant labor union negotiator to describe his adversary in the bargaining process. Many words in our language are quite symbolic, all conjuring various shades of meaning to the particular person: liberal, conservative, strong, weak, love, hate, rich, poor, and so on. Many expressions can convey social status, recognition or the lack of it, and a feeling of belonging or ostracism.

The expression, "We hired him because he's our kind of people," can mean just that the individual is a pleasant, capable, cooperative person who will get along well; or it can be a statement of discriminatory practice. Words are used in employment advertisements which appear innocent but may be designed to convey a particular meaning to get around fair employment practice laws. Such expressions as "recent high school or college grad" may be used to indicate age level and discriminate against older people who may be qualified for the job. "Out-of-town college grad" may be used in a large city newspaper advertisement where local colleges have a large percentage of minority students and the firm placing the advertisement does not want to hire them. In an advertisement for a typist, the expression "front-office-type person" is meant to convey that the job is for a good-looking female, thus discriminating against male typists and females who may not be considered beautiful.

One other type of symbolism is worth mentioning because it has considerable importance both in conveying meaning and in supervisory judgments. These are the appearance symbols, such as long or short hair, beards, Afro haircuts, excessive makeup, types of clothing, American flag decals, peace symbol decals, and religious crosses and stars, among many others. All of these are communicators, and frequently the message conveyed is not what the user intended. Many people develop firm opinions about individuals based on such symbols, and objective analysis of their performance on a job may be impossible.

Behavioral factors in communication

The discussion on symbols gives some indication that all interpersonal communication is not verbal or in writing. In addition to the symbols mentioned above there are several others that have a significant role in communication.

1. Facial expression. A frown can indicate discontent without any words being spoken. Similarly, a raised eyebrow may signal skepticism, amazement, or disbelief. Antagonism can be demonstrated by a tightening of the jaw and squinting one's eyes. In fact the eyes play a considerable role in communicating. Direct eye contact may denote sincerity, while a downcast look may show disappointment. Lack of eye contact can demonstrate fear or shyness.

2. Body movement. Some writers in the communication field call this body language. The way one walks, sits, or stands can send signals of varying kinds. Slouching can mean disappointment; a springing step shows enthusiasm; a tensed stance may indicate anger; and sitting on the edge of a chair with one's shoulders hunched forward may demonstrate rapt attention. Tapping one's fingers or feet can indicate boredom or nervousness. Very often we measure a person's sincerity by the type of handshake given in a greeting. Putting an arm around the shoulder of an employee while instructing the employee may show warmth and interest in the discussion.

3. Status symbols. Such things as the size and location of one's office and the size of the desk and type of decoration all communicate individual status. The very fact that we call factory workers "blue collar" and office workers "white collar" is also a way of communication. All of us know that the type of automobile one drives, the size of house or apartment one lives in as well as the neighborhood communicate things to the person viewing them.

It is apparent that humans communicate in many ways. The perceptive manager should be aware of the variety of media used and deal with each effectively. In many instances the social and psychological dimensions of communication play a significant role in communication effectiveness and the creation of understanding.

Distractions muddle orders

In management training conferences, role playing serves as an excellent means of awakening supervisors to the realization of how their words and meanings are misinterpreted. In a role-playing interview as part of a training conference, two supervisors discuss and try to solve a problem when each knows only his or her own side of it. (The audience of supervisors knows both sides.) When tape recordings are made of interviews, the two supervisors are always surprised by the playbacks ("Did I say that?"). Before the playback, the whole group discusses the way the two supervisors handled the interview: How did they define the problem? What solution did they work out? What course of action did they agree on? The listeners are never in complete agreement ("He said. . . ." "That wasn't what I thought she said." "You promised him a raise." "No, I only said that. . . ." "You were threatening him." "I only told her. . . ."). The two who did the talking are positive that they didn't say the things being attributed to them. Each wonders how everybody missed the point. When the tape is played back, they want to borrow it in order to find out for sure what happened to the things they intended to say and how they could have missed the import of the other fellow's words. They are surprised to learn that a part of the time they were just talking *past* one another rather than *to* one another.

If it were possible for a supervisor to make a tape recording of the orders given, it would be discovered on the playback that there are gaps in the information: Things the supervisor thought were said just aren't there; ideas that had all been worked out on the supervisors mind and ready to pass along were lost somewhere. Some of the gaps could be charged to having his or her attention distracted by phone calls or something interesting going on across the room. Some thoughts were lost because words were drowned out by noises or weren't spoken clearly and sounded like something else.

As the supervisor studied the recorded instructions, he or she could see where there was failure to pass along some important pieces of information, and the person could understand why subordinates would run into trouble on these points. But how about instructions that are complete? Why are they misunderstood?

Putting across a new idea

A person who teaches for a living knows the amount of effort it takes to put across a new idea. The teacher must first set the stage for it, tell what is the need for it, distinguish it from things that it resembles and might be confused with; then express it one way, give examples, ask questions, express it another way for those who might be confused by word meanings; hit the high points again; and then summarize the whole business.

An idea that the supervisor has been working on for weeks becomes so familiar that the person may assume that the listener should be able to keep right up with the explanation. Actually the poor individual may not even be able to figure out what this new idea relates to. Veteran public speakers have a three-step formula for putting across a message.

1. Tell them what you're going to tell them.
2. Tell them.
3. Tell them what you told them.

People are not able to grasp many ideas at a time; a motorist getting ravel directions has trouble remembering more than three turns in the road. If information is given in big doses, some of it spills over and is lost. The order giver needs to observe the listener's reactions to see if the person is getting the order. If the subordinate has lost the thread of the story, the speaker can summarize, tell the relationship of the new idea to familiar ideas, give examples, and repeat the key points in different words than were used before.

The listener's mind may be occupied with problems he or she is going to have in carrying out the order. The order giver needs to observe the attitude of the listener to see whether the person is accepting the idea of building up objections to it. If the worries or objections can be brought out into the open, the explanation can be presented in a way that will take them into account.

Here is where it is important for the boss to be a good listener, to be approachable and friendly so that people will ask questions about what ais puzzling them. The boss can't fill in gaps in the information until he or she learns where the gaps are; the supervisor needs to ask questions and to be alert to the meaning and feeling of the answers, and then in terms of these answers to modify what is said and how it is said. This is *feedback*—the principle by which a machine checks on its own performance and corrects it; this is the way the thermostat on the wall regulates the amount of heat from the furnace according to the information (the temperature of the air) fed to it. Accuracy and speed of comprehension increase with the amount of feedback in conversation. Experiments indicate that certain types of information cannot be communicated accurately without feedback—that is, without permitting the receiver to ask questions and get answers to them.

When people like and trust each other and know some of the difficulties involved in communicating ideas, they can question and listen in a way that will result in understanding.

Difficulties in discussion

The supervisor has to deal with many complaints, requests, and excuses that sound unreasonable to everyone but the person making them. When the supervisor is listening to a complaint that sounds foolish or unfounded, she asks, "What's wrong with this person or situation to make him say such a thing?" Maybe there isn't much wrong with the person except the way he is expressing himself. It could be that his statement is true from the angle from which he is looking at it. Each person sees a situation with himself at the center; so his point of view is going to be different from that of the next person.

If an employee complains, "This is an unfriendly company," the supervisor might wonder what quirk in her personality keeps her from making friends among so many congenial people. Rather than contradict her and point out all the instances of friendliness he is thinking of, he should ask himself, "Is she making a sweeping statement to express a couple of instances of unfriendliness?" He might ask her, "Are we talking about everybody in the company or just a few people who give us a lot of trouble?" Expressing the question so that *we* (not *you*) are having trouble will make it unnecessary for her to build up her story; she will probably feel free to admit that it's the two workers next to her who are making her life miserable. The essence of this type of questioning is to avoid any display of superiority, criticism, amusement, or disbelief. The purpose is to get information and avoid any contest in which employees feel obligated to defend their stands.

Most supervisors can recall occasions on which people have argued over sweeping statements, contradicting one another, stirring up illfeeling, and wasting a lot of time. In many of these cases, a simple question asked in a helpful way would have exposed the fact that the sweeping statement was intended simply to express a particular instance, and the speaker hadn't considered the matter any further than that. A question instead of a contradiction will often bring to light that there is no real difference of opinion—the seeming difference is simply a matter of stating the problem.[2]

Facts or conclusions?   It makes a person angry to have someone dispute a fact—something that can be verified, weighed, measured, or attested to by records or by unimpeachable witnesses. Some of the ill-feeling that enters into discussions arises because people think their facts are being contradicted. Actually, many of the statements that people offer as facts are really opinions, interferences, conclusions, or judgments.

If a supervisor says to the boss, "I need more employees to get job No. 402 out on time," the supervisor regards this statement as a fact. If the boss replies, "I don't think you do," it sounds like a contradiction of a fact. If they will move the discussion over to facts, they might set it up this way: job No. 402 is half finished; production records show that it took 100 man-hours to do that half; continuing at this rate, it will be only three fourths completed by the deadline.

It may still turn out that the only way to finish on time is to use more people, but if the problem can be handled by considering facts rather than arguing about conclusions, at least the door hasn't been shut on other possibilities and less emotion will be involved in the exchange of ideas. When people's conclusions or opinions are attacked, they are inclined to feel they are being attacked personally, and they concentrate attention on defending themselves and their positions.

Unfavorable attitudes build up listener resistance

The discussion thus far has dealt with the communication of ideas which were fairly logical to start with but became distorted either at the sending or at the receiving end. Supervisors who are communicating will encounter thinking on the part of subordinates that isn't logical—thinking in which feelings, attitudes, and prejudices strongly influence the selection and weighing of facts as well as the inferences and judgments that are made from them.

---

[2] For an excellent discussion of sweeping statements and talking past one another, see Irving J. Lee, *How to Talk with People: A Program for Preventing Troubles That Come When People Talk Together* (New York: Harper & Row, Publishers, 1952). For an insight into the emotional impact of words, see S. I. Hayakawa, *Language in Thought and Action* (New York: Harcourt, Brace & World, Inc., 1949).

Employees may feel that the supervisor is discriminating against them and is the cause of all their troubles on the job. They may build up hostility and resentment about changes made in their jobs. They become so stirred up emotionally that they simply do not hear explanations or arguments that run counter to their beliefs. People hear what they expect to hear, because their emotions and additudes filter out evidence that contradicts their stand. Figure 14–4 illustrates the barriers between the sender and the receiver of a message.

Figure 14–4
Communicating

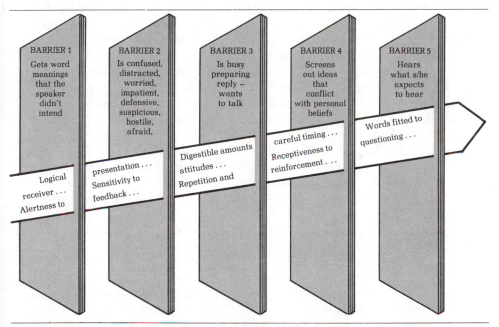

BARRIER 1
Gets word meanings that the speaker didn't intend

BARRIER 2
Is confused, distracted, worried, impatient, defensive, suspicious, hostile, afraid,

BARRIER 3
Is busy preparing reply – wants to talk

BARRIER 4
Screens out ideas that conflict with personal beliefs

BARRIER 5
Hears what s/he expects to hear

Logical receiver ... Alertness to

presentation ... Sensitivity to feedback ...

Digestible amounts attitudes ... Repetition and

careful timing ... Receptiveness to reinforcement ...

Words fitted to questioning ...

Barriers to understanding and how to penetrate them. Supervisors need to recognize these barriers in themselves as well as in others and to cultivate the attitudes and techniques that will enable them to understand and be understood.

A subordinate who dislikes and distrusts the boss will build up a resistance to understanding the person. Such an employee will be so intent on getting the most unfavorable interpretation of every communication that he or she won't hear what the boss is actually saying. A person's problem may be based more on feelings than on facts; but those feelings look like facts to that person and the individual will go to some lengths, often unconsciously, to make them look like facts to others. Subordinates don't feel they are being unreasonable; they feel the boss is being unreasonable. It takes wise and sympathetic listening and questioning on the part of the supervisor to find out what is actually on the person's mind, overcome the resistance, clear the channels of communication, and arrive at a better understanding of the person's point of view.

Good attitudes facilitate understanding

The supervisor can't spend the day playing psychiatrist; he or she has work to get out. Luckily, many of the day's work assignments are routine and require only a few words to get them rolling. Subordinates are so accustomed to the asignments and the words that go with them that they are listening only to find out the supervisors mood and assure themselves that everything is going along all right. The supervisor's manner when handing out assignments communicates some kind of emotion to workers, and it will have an effect—good or bad——on their willingness to do the work.

If the supervisor is grumpy, surly, threatening, or sarcastic, subordinates will feel imposed upon, angry, resentful, uncertain, afraid to ask questions, and unwilling to use their initiative, stick their necks out, or do anything to please the boss. If, on the other hand, the supervisor knows the people as individuals with their good points and their shortcomings and their needs for reassurance, friendliness, human warmth, and importance, the supervisor can at least let them know he's not mad at them. In the few seconds that it takes to make an ordinary assignment, the supervisor may be able to convey the feeling that the employees can do the work well and the expectation is that they will want to do it well. And most people tend to do what they feel is expected of them.

Subordinates who feel secure in their relationships with the boss—who respect and trust the individual—are not out to misunderstand his or her words and misinterpret intentions. They will overlook occasional slips on the boss' part—things that wouldn't have been said (or said that way) had the boss taken time to think them over. They know the supervisor under pressure and that everybody has to let off steam once in a while.

If they have good attitudes toward the supervisor, they will work with that person to achieve understanding. The supervisor builds up this attitude of receptiveness in subordinates by demonstrating to them by words and actions that he or she is interested in their welfare, understands their problems, and appreciates them as people. The better the supervisor's relationships with subordinates, the more they will help in his or her job of communicating with them.

How to give orders

Ask some supervisors how they give orders, and they say they don't—or at least seldom—find it necessary to "order" anyone to do anything. They have the work set up so that people know what they're expected to do and take the responsibility for getting it done. When work has to be assigned piece by piece, these supervisors say they issue their orders in the form of requests. But the directing of subordinates is an essential part of supervising, and authority is the right to give orders and have them obeyed; so the word "orders" is used here to include all the ways of assigning work and instructing subordinates how to do it.

Whether the supervisor says "I'd like you to take care of this when you have time" or "I want this finished by four o'clock" depends on the circumstances and the kind of person receiving the order. Fitting the order to the receiver means knowing the extent of the employee's competence, remembering strong and weak points in previous situations, and knowing individual attitudes and how the person is motivated. Fitting an order to the receiver requires that words be used in the sense that the employee uses them. ("Hit it hard" means one thing to the dentist and something quite different to the stakedriver.) Examples and explanations used to put across the meaning of words must refer to something within the experience of the listener. The amount of instruction and attention to detail must be suited to the receiver and the situation. For example, in a candy factory the workers took turns working a late shift to clean the sticky residue out of the machines. The supervisor assigned a new person to take a turn and left that person with the same three words of instruction that had been used very successfully on the others: "It's all yours." The candy hardened in the machines overnight into an expensive mess.

Order givers must organize their presentation of ideas into a logical pattern based on knowledge of *what* is to be done and *why* it is to be done, and how much leeway the subordinate has in choosing a method and making decisions. In delivering this information, supervisors may have to divide it into digestible portions, making them clear one at a time by asking and answering questions. If supervisors invite questions as they go along, they can modify the presentation in terms of the difficulties revealed in the answers. Repetition helps to clear up misunderstandings, particularly if different words and examples are used; but it is well to let listeners know that what they are learning *is* a repetition—a reinforcement of what was said before and not a presentation of an additional new idea.

Supervisors must be reconciled to the fact that, no matter how careful the presentation, a certain amount of the information won't get through, and another portion of it will be forgotten. They should spot-check while the order is being carried out. Then if the job is going wrong because of a misunderstanding, they can find and repair the weak spot in the communicating. An order will be carried out more intelligently and willingly if subordinates know why they were chosen to do it, how important it is, and what it will be used for. People want to know that what they are doing is important. They have a basic need to feel that what they are doing is worthwhile; it is one of the factors that motivates them to do a good job. They also want to know the why of quality requirements: What does the part have to fit to? What are these figures going to be used for? How legible does this reproduction have to be?

If safety instructions go along with the job, supervisors can give them in a manner that shows they are interested in the well-being of their subordinates.

Getting orders from the middle manager

When supervisors taking a management training course discuss the topic of communicating, the discussion always seems to focus on what they find wrong with the oral orders they get from their superiors. The faults they find with their bosses' order giving will cover a range such as: too vague, not thought out clearly, too hurried, too detailed, not complete enough, too much how and not enough why, too much in one package, not practical, mixed up, indistinct, interrupted by phone calls. Some supervisor will say, "I go out of his or her office not knowing what is wanted and just hoping I can make a lucky guess." But supervisors who can't find out what the boss wants undoubtedly have under them workers mumbling, "Why didn't the boss say what he or she meant? How was I to know? I'm no mind reader."

Each person is inclined to think what he or she is saying is crystal clear, just like taking a detailed picture out of his or her own mind and setting it up on an easel in the listener's mind. It's natural for a supervisor to say of the boss, "I can't find out what the boss wants; he or she doesn't make it clear," and then of his or her own workers: "They're either stupid or inattentive or stubborn, or they couldn't make the mistakes they do after I've told them exactly what I have in mind."

Keeping the middle manager informed

The supervisor should supply the next management level with complete and accurate information to use in making decisions, issuing orders, and reporting in turn up the line. A subordinate has an obligation to the boss (accountability) to report on the way responsibilities are being carried out and authority is being used. One of the difficulties in carrying out this obligation is the unexpected demands that a boss may make for information that is wanted right away because upper management has called upon the boss to account for some item or condition brought to light in a control report.

A person has to protect the boss from being caught unaware of, and uninformed about, things for which the boss is responsible. But the supervisor should not be called upon to produce instantaneous information, 100 percent correct, on matters that do not in themselves require such recordkeeping. If the boss should need to ask for such figures, the supervisor should be able to tell the superior that he or she doesn't have them and that it will take a certain length of time to gather them and prepare the information. Keeping the boss informed should not obligate the supervisor to have on tap all kinds of assorted information just as a precaution in case the boss should suddenly ask for it. Collecting and compiling information unnecessarily is a waste that can be avoided if the boss will give the supervisor time to prepare special reports.

But there is a great deal of regular day-to-day information that the supervisor is expected to supply to the next management level. The boss needs to know, for instance, how work is progressing, what difficulties are being encountered, what improvements are needed, how orders are being carried out, if any actions of management are getting unfavorable reactions at the work level, and if there is any trouble brewing.

It can be seen from this discussion of communication between a person and his or her superior that the channels of the chain of command exist not only to send orders down from the top to the bottom of an organization, but also to pipe information back up the same line—each individual to his or her superior.

Coloring the information. If upward communications are to fulfill their purpose, everyone in the chain of command must recognize those human traits that tend to distort information. There is a natural tendency to keep the boss happy by overemphasizing the good aspects and playing down the unfavorable aspects of a situation. It is human nature to distort information so as to escape blame—to color reports so that the boss will think you're on the ball, to filter out anything that might make you look careless, stupid, or unfit for the job.

The amount of censoring, filtering, and coloring of information hinges upon the kind of relationship a person has with the boss. If the relationship is one of mutual helpfulness, the subordinate can admit that a mistake was made, that things aren't going too well at the moment, that it looks like trouble ahead, and that something needs to be done about it. If a supervisor doesn't have to phrase reports in terms of self-protection, he or she can send up the channel the kind of information that upper management needs to make its decisions and to formulate its communications in terms of the people who will receive them.

Lack of understanding between subordinate and superior

Research reports indicate that there is a sad lack of understanding between superiors and subordinates. One survey of high-middle managers and their bosses revealed that they had not reached a good understanding of the duties of the subordinate's job and that they had even less agreement about the qualifications required to fill the subordinate's job, the future changes that would affect that job, and the difficulties that the subordinate was encountering in doing the job.[3]

Without such an understanding, managers don't really know what their superiors expect of them, don't know how performance is going to be mea-

---

[3] Norman R. F. Maier, L. Richard Hoffman, John J. Hooven, and William H. Read, *Superior-Subordinate Communication in Management*, American Management Association Research Study No. 52 (New York: AMA, 1961).

sured, and don't have any way of knowing how well they are doing or what they should be doing differently.

Another survey—this one of supervisors and their superiors—revealed that they didn't agree on the extent of supervisory authority.[4] The supervisor in most cases thought that his or her authority was more limited than the boss said it was. On some matters the supervisors thought that they had more authority than the superiors said they had.

A survey of what the superiors think their subordinates want from the job showed little agreement with what the subordinates themselves said they wanted.[5] The bosses overestimated the importance subordinates attached to economic factors and underestimated the importance they attached to human factors: such things as getting along well with boss and co-workers and having a chance to do interesting and good quality work. If managers are misinformed about what subordinates consider important on the job, they don't know what motivates them to high performance.

Barriers to understanding.   In addition to the ordinary hindrances in the way of getting information, there are a number of other barriers that make it difficult for supervisors to achieve understanding with their superiors. Supervisors worry about the existence of these barriers, and they bring them up for discussion in management training conferences. It is from such conferences that the material for this discussion was derived.

Fear seems to be a very important barrier to the free flow of information. The relationship of employees to their supervisors is not a free and easy one. Individuals are dependent on their bosses for security, status, recognition, and success on the job. They wonder if they are pleasing the boss, and they worry about what the boss thinks of them.

Supervisors admit that they are afraid to ask questions of the boss—afraid of appearing dumb or insubordinate. They are afraid to doubt the infallibility of information coming down the line through the boss and afraid to raise objections to the boss's ideas, even when the objections are valid. Many of these fears seem to come from lack of security.

Supervisors tend to feel that the boss looks with favor on the bearer of good news and with disfavor on the bearer of bad news; and nobody wants to look bad in the eyes of the boss. Nobody wants to tell the boss about failures or mistakes. People look like blunderers if they tell their own mistakes, and are informers if they tell someone else's.

Some supervisors say their superiors' attitudes tend to shut off communi-

---

[4] Chester E. Evans, *Supervisory Responsibility and Authority,* American Management Association Research Report No. 30 (New York: AMA, 1957). Based on this report is an article by Lee E. Stern, "The Foreman's Job: What Are the Boundaries?" *Supervisory Management,* vol. 3, no. 7 (July 1958).

[5] Robert L. Kahn, "Human Relations on the Shop Floor," in E. M. Hugh-Jones, ed., *Human Relations and Modern Management* (Amsterdam: North Holland Publishing Co., 1958). This survey is summarized in Rensis Likert, *New Patterns of Management* (New York: McGraw-Hill Book Co., 1961), pp. 49–51.

cation. The bosses have a "just-do-as-you're-told" attitude, or they act bored, or they seem to be too busy to listen ("Can't spend all day sifting through a lot of chaff and chatter just to get a few grains of useful information").

Or the bosses insinuate that the subordinates can't see the whole picture or aren't intelligent enough to understand it. Some bosses think they don't need to be told because they already know what subordinates think. Some bosses are not receptive to information because they lack open-mindedness. Some resent having their decisions questioned by subordinates. Some bosses like to avoid reality—no news is good news; what they don't know won't hurt them; and they don't want to get involved in the personal problems of their subordinates.

On the other hand, some supervisors are not interested in communicating; others do not see the importance of passing along information either up or down the line. Some supervisors stop communicating up the line because no action was taken on previous communications they sent up. Some supervisors won't communicate because they are suspicious of upper management.

How managers can promote more effective communicating

In order to promote more effective communicating, managers must realize the value of the free flow of information and establish a climate in which truthfulness and openness can prosper. A relationship of helpfulness and trust between superior and subordinate is needed throughout the organization if people are going to overcome those human failings that cause them to doctor up information as they pass it along.

Managers must realize that their own attitudes determine to a great extent the kind of information they will get from their subordinates. It takes courage for subordinates to tell their superiors the whole truth and nothing but the truth; if the superior has a bad reaction to it or shows displeasure toward the bearer of the news, the diet of information is apt to be cut down and flavored to suit the boss's taste. Information can be selected that will please the boss, doubtful situations can be colored with optimism, and bad news can be withheld until the superior seeks it out personally.

A good way for a boss to build up a relationship of openness and trust with subordinates is to reduce to a minimum his or her social distance from them. Managers must have subordinates work closely with them so that the subordinates can know how the managers operate and will feel free to confide in them. Managers should let them know that an occasional error won't be held against them. A boss can set up the framework for an easier exchange of information by showing interest in subordinates' ideas, seeking their suggestions, and providing opportunities for them to take part in the discussion and solution of departmental problems.

Communications systems, networks, and the flow of management information

One of the maxims of traditional organization theory is that information in the form of orders flows down the chain of command, and acceptance of these orders in the form of accountability flows up. Because most complex organizations have managements which are essentially autocratic in nature, this concept has some validity. There is, however, a filtering process on each level of the organization as managers interpret and explain what they believe has to be accomplished, based on their understanding of the orders and direction of higher management.

Classical theory further assumes that upward communication takes place in much the same way, with each level of management passing information upward so that higher levels of management can know what is happening in the entire organization. While this view is basically correct, incisive study of any organization and its communications flow will indicate that management information systems are more complex.

Another way to understand communication patterns in an organization is to view these patterns as networks with certain definitive characteristics. In addition to the traditional hierarchical model there are several types of communication networks in most organizations. Four of these are:

1. The chain.   Here there is a group of peers who communicate with each other. Communication is relatively accurate, effective, and considerable interchange is possible. This type of network tends to be less effective at higher management levels since there are fewer peers to develop a chain. The chain may also encourage the emergence of an informal leader who may be perceived as having greater access to higher level communication.

2. The modified chain or Y.   This network is also characterized by peer communication, but it can also be hierarchical. Here there is a chain but an outsider will communicate with one member of the chain. This outsider can be a higher level manager, a manager from another department, a staff expert, or a lower level employee. The one member receiving communication from the outsider may be the informal leader of the chain.

3. The circle.   In this network communication can originate with anyone in the circle, and there usually is no informal leader. In such a network communication is slow and frequently inaccurate since none of the members have particular access to outside sources of information.

4. The wheel.   This network has a designated formal leader who communicates with each member of the network. The wheel characterizes many formal superior-subordinate communication patterns. Communication is rapid, accurate, and leader directed. Interchange, however, is quite limited.

See Figure 14–5 for a graphic portrayal of the four networks.

Since communication involves transactions between people, it is vital to the understanding of organizations. When all of the channels of communi-

Figure 14–5
Basic network communications patterns

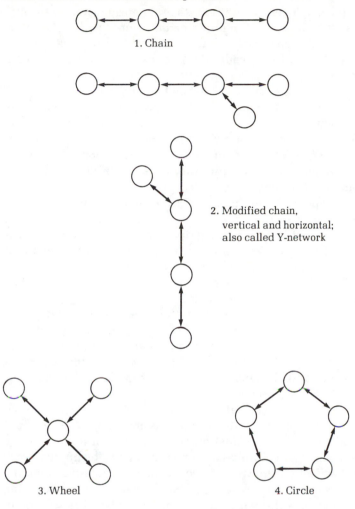

1. Chain

2. Modified chain,
   vertical and horizontal;
   also called Y-network

3. Wheel

4. Circle

cation in an organization are studied and identified, the organization becomes recognizable as a network of information centers. Coordination becomes possible with a flow of this information, and the persons who receive
and send information tend to gain status and power in the organization.
Communication can be the stimulus to perform, and this performance can
be measured; hence communication is also vital to any control system.

The manager can transmit information as an order or a command. This is
a "chain of command" communication, and as such it has an effect on those
subordinates reporting to the particular executive. They will tend to react to
such an order quite differently than they would to an order coming from

someone else in the organization. For instance, an employee may receive an order from a staff executive (such as the personnel manager) and though it may be followed, the employee is not under the same responsibility to comply as he or she is with an order from an immediate line superior. An informal group leader may also give orders, but no one in the group need follow these orders because the informal leader does not have a chain of command position. Nevertheless, even the communications of the informal leader contribute to the network of organizational information and in this sense have a bearing on group behavior. The staff executive may be trying to usurp line authority and, by giving orders, may confuse the work group, but here, too, there is an information flow which contributes to the total network. Each organization is made up of several senders and receivers of communications on all levels. Some senders have the authority of position while others are just senders in the informal sense.

Rumors and the grapevine.   Perhaps the best example of informal sending and receiving is the grapevine. It is the unofficial carrier of information in an organization. In most instances the grapevine is speedy, and it serves to spread the news of management's plans whether or not management intends them for publication. Some employees are more active news passers than others, possibly because of their personalities, possibly because they have more opportunities and more contacts with people. Almost everyone becomes more active on the grapevine when they are confused and apprehensive about what is going on. When people feel helpless and threatened, spreading rumors is one way of expressing and alleviating anxiety. Rumors tend to become most rampant in those departments where managers deliberately withhold information because they believe this allows them to exercise power and control subordinates.

While some managers believe that the grapevine is a useful device because it is considered by them to be the normal passing along of news about what is going on in the company, most other managers call it a necessary evil. In fact, it is usually an unreliable communications technique, very often harmful in its effect on the work force. A rumor about an impending change could distress employees, who may believe that the change is going to cause firings or increase the work load. When the official news finally comes through, the proposed change may not be at all bad, but the employees have been conditioned against it and their response is hostile. There also seems to be a relationship between the grapevine and the level of management in an organization. The tendency among employees to tell their superiors what they think they want to hear may effectively insulate them from the rumors that are being spread among employees. J. W. Keener, a former president of the B. F. Goodrich Company, comments on the grapevine:

> Every company has an executive suite or its equivalent. Once you get up there people will not talk to you the way they used to, and certainly you get off the grapevine. The higher up in the organizational structure I went, the

further off the grapevine I got. I don't think that is unusual. There are people still on the grapevine who are supposed to keep me informed of what I can't find out for myself. I am sure that I don't get the full flavor, but I get enough of it to be able to see that any problems that develop receive the attention or support they deserve.[6]

It is evident that the grapevine is an important part of an organization's informal communication system. Even though the information that travels the grapevine may be lacking in accuracy, few managers can afford not to pay attention to the nature of the information. For further insight into the nature of the grapevine, Trewatha and Newport offer the following characteristics:[7]

1.   A significant percentage of employees consider it to be their primary source of information about organizational affairs. Thus, since the grapevine is perceived by employees as a personal type of communication, it frequently has a stronger impact on them than is true of formalized channels of communication.

2.   The grapevine is much more flexible than formal channels. As a result, it embellishes information and supplies inferences that are otherwise unavailable.

3.   The grapevine transmits information rapidly. After a "newsy" event occurs in an organization, the grapevine makes information available almost immediately. In fact, the speed of transmission appears directly related to each situation and to the perceived importance of the information. Generally, then, identical information travels more quickly through the grapevine than through formal channels.

4.   Although the grapevine can be accurate in many cases, it is still more likely to produce a low level of understanding among recipients. This is especially true where rumors are concerned. Many times, rumors are fragmented with missing parts being filled in by individuals in the communication channel. The result is a distortion of the original message as it passes from person to person. Of course, since there are no formal authority relationships involved in the grapevine, none of the people participating in the rumor are accountable for its truthfulness. And, although most rumors do not start with the intent of being pervasive or destructive, they often end up that way.

5.   In the grapevine, information is usually transmitted through oral channels. However, written channels are also utilized when word of mouth is not convenient, or may be too obvious.

6.   A person in the grapevine who passes on information usually communicates with several individuals, rather than with only one. Of the people receiving a message, however, only a limited number will be involved in passing it on to others.

7.   The grapevine is a convenient way for individuals to pass on infor-

---

[6] "The President Looks at His Job," *management Record*, national Industrial conference Board, May 1962, pp. 2–11.

[7] Robert L. Trewatha and M. Gene Newport, *Management: Functions and Behavior*, rev. ed. (Dallas, Tex.: Business Publications, 1979). © 1979 by Business Publications, Inc.

mation that they may not wish to transmit formally. For example, when the boss looks around the office with a scowl, the word spreads quickly that this is not a day when he will tolerate mistakes. Likewise, the grapevine can be valuable in assessing the reaction of employees to an announcement before it is made through formal channels.

It is apparent that the grapevine is not efficient as either a sending or receiving communications device. Perhaps management's best efforts should be applied to an analysis of the frequency, number, and type of rumors circulating on the grapevine. This would indicate where the formal communications networks are not functioning and would show areas of employee interest, poor morale, misinformation, and other communications difficulties. It would seem that if the employees were given accurate, timely, and optimal information in areas of their major interest, the effect of the grapevine would be minimized.

Figure 14–6 demonstrates the relationship of formal communication in an organization to informal channels.

Figure 14–6
Informal communication system within the formal organization

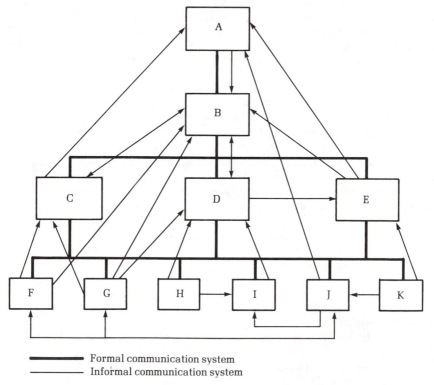

━━━━━━━━━ Formal communication system
────────── Informal communication system

Source: Robert L. Trewatha and M. Gene Newport, *Management: Functions and Behavior*, rev. ed. (Dallas, Tex.: Business Publications, 1979). © 1979 by Business Publications, Inc.

Communication systems. There is little doubt that the success of any organization is directly related to the efficiency of its communication system. All of the management functions such as goal definition, policy formulation, planning, direction, control, coordination, and staffing require an accurate and consistent flow of communications. Since human organizations are imperfect, it becomes necessary for management to develop a system of internal communication which minimizes these imperfections.

Data or information must be acquired, processed, analyzed, distributed, and displayed to and from all levels of the organization. Feedback is as essential as the distribution of information. To control effectively as well as to develop awareness, management must know what is going on. Feedback and peer communication should be an integral part of the communication system.[8]

Above all, communication must be timely. People who should know have to receive the information before the grapevine distorts it. Nothing is as frustrating or disappointing to supervisors than to hear about a promotion, raise, or transfer of one of the employees or personally through the grapevine before they get an official notification of the event. Everything management can do to encourage a free and open flow of the information necessary for the effective functioning of the organization will be more than worth the effort involved.

In complex organizations, each part of the total system depends on and bases its activities on the communication process. In fact, if the theory of organizations as total systems is accepted, communication is the mortar that binds the bricks of the system together. Information inputs from both the internal system and the external environment in which it exists are vital to the effective functioning of the organization.

Every system must have interaction and feedback. Since communication is an interactive process, the methods of gathering, sending, receiving, and acting on information represent that organization's communication system. In recent years very detailed management information systems (MIS) utilizing computers have been designed for complex organizations (see Chapter 7 for the relationship of MIS to planning). Actually a management information system is one kind of communication system, developed to utilize the quantitative data gathered, processed, and stored in computers.

Summary

There is hardly any part of management's job that does not involve communication. All of the managerial functions require effective communication if they are to be carried out successfully. Poor communication can

---

[8] For a thorough analysis and discussion of the entire subject of communication, see Lee Thayer, *Communication and Communication Systems* (Homewood, Ill.: Richard D. Irwin, 1968).

develop fear, anxiety, distrust, and dislike among the people in an organization. Serious mistakes can be made because orders are misunderstood, and casual kidding can cause unnecessary anger. Off-hand remarks by senior management can lead to rumors which cause considerable unrest among employees.

Since the supervisor's job is to get things done through and with others, effectiveness depends on the ability to reach an understanding with employees. The supervisor's attitude toward subordinates is the basis on which understanding is built.

For communication to achieve reasonable success, there must be some sense of common purpose among the parties involved. Individuals perceive events differently based on individual frames of reference.

Misunderstandings can be caused by the use of jargon by various work groups and social groups when communicating with people new to the group or outside the group.

Misunderstandings between supervisor and superior have their roots in attitudes. Fear of the boss deters the supervisor from questioning him and causes the supervisor to color and filter information.

Misunderstandings between supervisors and between line and staff arise when each is protecting his own area from the other and there is no shared purpose.

Misunderstandings arise about management's intentions in making changes and about the effects these changes will have on jobs. Employees oppose changes for a number of reasons: fear of losing the job or the "advantage" of the job; feeling that the change criticizes or belittles them; resentment about not being consulted; pressure from the group to oppose it. Fear and resentment stand in the way of becoming proficient on the changed job. If status relationships are reversed and people have to take orders from their inferiors, they may be unable to work together. Job security, changes that take care of human needs, and good two-way communication will prevent some of the disturbance caused by change. If employees participate in planning the change, they are less apt to resist it.

The grapevine, while a necessary evil, is not an effective transmitter of internal communications in an organization. It is best countered by a free and open flow of accurate and timely communications on a "need to know" basis. The flow of information in an organization evolves into a series of networks which enable a greater understanding of the organization. Because human organizations are imperfect, it is necessary for management to develop internal communications systems which minimize these imperfections.

CASE 14–1

The president of the company discovered that confidential management plans were being discussed throughout the organization within hours after middle-management conferences, so at the next conference he emphasized the need for protecting the company by not betraying its confidences. The leaks continued, and the president questioned the ten middle managers about the amount of information they were giving out.

Since there had been no problems of this type in previous years, the president wondered if perhaps the newest man, Ames, might be the culprit. To test a hunch, he called Ames in and talked to him about being prepared in a general way for possible expansion of his department that could come about if some company plans worked out well, told him that it was all uncertain, and cautioned him against discussing the matter with anyone. Within three days the organization was buzzing with a rumor that a big expansion was on the way.

Ames admitted that he had divulged the information, but his defense was "I tell my subordinates what I feel they are entitled to know." A check with Ames's previous boss revealed no trouble of this type but indicated that he was well liked, cooperative, and a high producer.

Ames had been hired as a first-level supervisor by his present company four years earlier, and after three successful years on that job was promoted to his present position. The president didn't want to lose the man, so talked to him at length about the seriousness of the breach and told him his job depended upon respecting confidences. Two months later Ames leaked an important piece of information to his subordinates.

1. *What are a manager's obligations for protecting company secrets?*
2. *Why would a middle manager give out confidential information to his subordinate supervisors?*
3. *Was there a better way to handle this problem?*
4. *What should be done with Ames now?*

CASE 14–2

Here is an exercise in perception. You can try it on a friend or fellow student. I am going to describe a person and as the description unfolds, I want you to envision this person in your mind's eye. The person:

1. Is 37 years old.
2. Is married and has two children.
3. Lives in suburban Cleveland, Ohio.
4. Is a graduate of the University of Michigan and has a law degree from Notre Dame University.
5. Is a practicing attorney and a partner in a Cleveland law firm.

Envision a person whose appearance would fit this description. Fix this perception in your mind, and then describe your mental picture.

See if you, or your friend, would be disconcerted to find that the next point on the list is: (a) he is black; (b) he has long hair and rides a motorcycle, (c) is a woman. Do you stereotype certain professions, kinds of people, and "proper" appearance or customs?

CASE 14–3

You are the head of a large department and several supervisors report to you. Recently you were confronted with a knotty problem. It seems that one of the supervisors had gotten into a loud and disagreeable argument with an employee. You called the supervisor to your office to hear his story.

The supervisor admitted losing his temper and shouting at the employee, but he believed it was justified. He had been observing the employee over the year the man had been with the company. During this period the employee had been frequently late, and his absentee rate was above average. In addition, the supervisor went on to say that the employee was a socializer on the job, frequently leaving his work to talk to other employees and to use the telephone for personal calls. The supervisor then said that the proverbial last straw caused his outburst. The employee had come in late, and after about an hour of work he made a telephone call which the supervisor had timed as lasting 14 minutes. The supervisor then started his tirade. The employee denied being on the telephone that long, the supervisor called him a liar, and they continued the vituperative exchange which ended when you called the supervisor to your office.

After listening to the supervisor, you asked him if he had disciplined the employee before, since apparently he had a poor record. You also asked if the employee had been placed on probation or had been warned. The supervisor looked at you sheepishly and seemed reluctant to answer. You pressed him for an answer, and he finally blurted out that he was afraid to discipline the employee because he was a black. He stated that the impression he had from you and higher management was that black employees should be given special treatment so that they would feel welcome and not discriminated against. He felt the company wanted to impress the public with its forward-looking employment practices and didn't want any trouble with the black community. As a result, he was lax in discipline and had kept a hands-off approach with all black employees until his outburst. He said he couldn't stand it any more, and the 14-minute telephone call caused him to lose his temper.

1. *Why would a supervisor find it difficult to communicate with a black employee?*

2. *Could the company have done anything to offset the misunderstanding the supervisor apparently had about the treatment of black employees?*

3. *To what extent did the supervisor's lack of communication encourage the employee to think his behavior was satisfactory?*

4. *What would you now tell the supervisor?*

CASE 14–4

Lillian Martin, one of Art Henderson's best employees, was known to be an habitual gossip. By the end of each day, Art was filled in on everything that went on in the department. Usually she stopped him as he went by her desk during the course of the workday to give him the latest details of events. At times she would come to his office on a pretext so that a particularly interesting item could be communicated immediately.

Art Henderson had been giving considerable thought to the situation. At lunch one day he discussed Lillian and her gossip with one of his friends who had been a department head in the company for many years. The old-timer advised him to continue the relationship. He said that every department had such a person, who seemed to enjoy telling the boss everything that went on. He went on to say that Art might as well be realistic and make use of the gossip; even though most of it wouldn't amount to anything, there would be some that he could use to his advantage in running his department.

As a result of his conversation with his fellow department head, Art allowed Lillian Martin to continue feeding him information. Some of it proved useful to him in his job, and from time to time he checked the validity of her stories and found them to be true. Lillian apparently was an accurate reporter of departmental happenings.

1. *Should Art have continued to use Lillian as a communications vehicle?*

2. *Are there any disadvantages to such a relationship?*

3. *What effect could it have on departmental morale?*

4. *Could the employees be using Lillian to communicate with their boss?*

5. *What can a supervisor do to discourage an employee like Lillian Martin?*

CASE 14–5

John Royal was brought in from the outside about six months ago and made general manager of a major department of a large company. The president was active in recruiting him, and he believes that Royal is doing an outstanding job. Before coming to the company, Royal had been the general manager of a small company in a similar industry.

Since arriving, John Royal has been very aloof and unapproachable to his subordinates. They don't know what he thinks of them or anybody else for that matter. When they ask him questions, he responds with questions for them and they feel foolish. In effect, John Royal has cut off upward communication. If he formulates a policy, he tells them about it but there is no discussion. He then tries to convince them they should accept it as a joint decision.

A few of his more effective subordinates have resigned because they resented the high-handed treatment. These have been replaced by people who agree with Royal, some of whom worked for him in the other company. Royal frequently makes snap judgments without consulting his subordinates, and they often have to do extra work to rectify his errors in judgment. When his subordinates raise objections, he tells them he is not interested in objections—only results.

1. *Why would a new general manager be so unapproachable?*
2. *Why would the president think Royal is doing an effective job?*
3. *Should his subordinates communicate directly with the president?*
4. *To what extent has Royal's hiring of agreeable former subordinates insulated him further?*
5. *Could Royal be afraid of his larger responsibility in the new position?*

CASE 14–6

The president of a medium-sized company had long been dissatisfied with the performance of the controller. He decided to have the entire matter of corporate financial management discussed at a board of directors' meeting. After much discussion the board authorized the hiring of a treasurer who would be the chief financial officer of the firm. The question of the controller was not completely settled, since it was decided to allow the new treasurer to make a judgment as to his competence after a period of time, and it was felt that the controller would be helpful in assisting the treasurer until he became familiar with the financial aspects of the company.

The company's public accounting firm was enlisted to help in the search for the new treasurer. The accounting firm was one of the largest in the country and had numerous contacts. They offered executive search as a service for their clients. All interviewing was to be done on the premises of the public accounting firm and the effort was to be carried out by the board chairman, the president, and two board members. The company's personnel department was bypassed, since the board chairman wanted the selection of a new treasurer to remain secret so that there would be no upsetting influence on the present controller and the accounting department.

One afternoon about two weeks after the secret recruiting effort had begun and several applicants had been interviewed at the public accounting firm's offices, the manager of the data processing section sought out the personnel manager. He said he was bursting with curiosity and had to speak to someone. A friend of his had been interviewed for the treasurer's position and had called him to find out more about the company. The data processing manager now confronted the personnel manager with this information and demanded to know what the story was.

The personnel manager, not being privy to the secret recruiting program, could only claim ignorance and, of course, the data processing manager did not believe him. Although the data processing manager asked the personnel man to keep the information in confidence because he did not want to jeopardize his position or the chances of his friend, the personnel manager told the story to the board chairman. He was then informed by the chairman about the recruiting effort and the apparent need for secrecy.

1. *Should the personnel manager have been made aware of the recruiting effort before it was undertaken?*
2. *Why would a company attempt secret recruiting for a managerial postiion?*
3. *Is it desirable and a sound practice?*
4. *How should the data processing manager be handled?*

CASE 14-7

Doug Lewis prepared a monthly sales analysis which was sent to the sales vice president about the middle of each month. Lewis had been preparing these reports for five years, ever since the previous sales vice president asked for a sales analysis before considering some territory changes.

The previous sales vice president had only wanted one such analysis, but Doug Lewis continued to furnish him with the analysis monthly and since there were no orders to the contrary, Lewis thought his effort was appreciated. In fact, the analysis had become the central focus of Doug's job, and he had a clerk-typist help him prepare it each month.

When the present sales vice president took over, Lewis continued to send him the monthly report. Recently the company started a cost control program and retained an outside consultant to aid in the effort. One of the projects studied was that of internal communications. The consultant traced all reports from preparer to user to determine whether or not they should be continued.

He spoke to Doug Lewis and got a thorough explanation of the scope and desirability of the monthly sales analysis. He then spoke to the sales vice president and was surprised to find out that he had never seen the monthly report. The consultant investigated further and found that the sales vice president's secretary, who had also served his predecessor, had a complete file of these reports. When questioned she replied, "My prior boss only wanted one analysis, but when Mr. Lewis kept sending them monthly I filed them in case there was another request. I was never asked for the report, but I thought Mr. Lewis must have been preparing them for a reason."

1. *How could this have happened?*
2. *Who was at fault?*
3. *Should a company frequently analyze the usefulness of written reports?*
4. *Why would Lewis continue to prepare such a report?*

CASE 14–8

Mr. Smith is the plant superintendent. It is his custom to take frequent tours of the plant. During these tours he stops and engages the workers in conversation. It is his theory that this boosts the morale of the rank and file. He asks them questions about the equipment, production, materials, and so on. Often the information he receives from the workers is incomplete or inaccurate; sometimes it is absolutely false.

At his weekly conference meetings with his section chiefs, he demands explanations of pieces of information received during his tours. His subordinates would have to spend hours making investigations and collecting data to account for and explain away the erroneous impressions he picks up on these tours.

His subordinates have asked him if they might accompany him on his tours and thus be able to answer his questions on the spot. He states that when he is talking to the rank and file he is getting the truth; when he is talking to his assistants all he gets is a bunch of statistics. He also states that the workers will not talk when their immediate superiors are around.

1. *What might be some of the reasons for the superintendent's actions?*
2. *To what extent might his subordinates have contributed to this condition? Explain.*
3. *Develop a plan that the section chiefs could work out which would provide a good channel of communications up and down.*

CASE 14–9

There were six major banks in the city. All of them were affected in various degrees by a cost squeeze prevalent in the banking industry. Two of the banks laid off several hundred employees. Ajax Trust released 250 people, including 60 officers. Benson Bank released 600 employees, including 90 officers. Rumors permeated the industry and many employees were worried about their jobs. The Cortlandt Trust, the fourth largest bank in the city, announced the release of 700 employees, 200 of whom were officers.

Now the rumors became really heavy. The Hawthorne Trust Company, second largest in the city, had no intention of releasing any employees. Even in the deep depression of the 1930s, no employee had ever been released because of poor business. The senior management of Hawthorne simply planned to let a no-hiring rule and normal attrition handle the problem. They were a conservative group and felt that any announcement of their decision might appear to be flamboyant in the banking community, so no mention was made to the press or to the employees of the bank. It was felt that the employees would understand the bank's tradition of no releases due to business conditions, which wasn't a stated policy but had a long history.

Over the next several weeks, many supervisors reported poor morale, jittery employees, and a drop in productivity. All of this was traced to the releases in competitor banks and the ever-present worry that Hawthorne would be next.

1. *Comment on management's decision not to announce their decision to either employees or the press.*
2. *Should they have told employees?*
3. *Was too much emphasis placed on traditional behavior?*
4. *If you were employed as a supervisor at Hawthorne Trust, what would you do to cope with the problem?*

CASE 14–10

A personnel service company had been undergoing several cost control programs along with a moratorium on the hiring of new employees as replacements for unfilled jobs. These economies had caused considerable unrest among the employees. A rumor began to circulate that the company was in poor financial condition and had to borrow money to meet its payroll. In fact, it had just negotiated new banking arrangements which allowed borrowing at a more favorable rate than from its previous bank. The normal practice of borrowing by a business had probably given rise to the rumor about the company's financial condition.

To stop the rumor, the chairman of the board held a meeting with all executives, informed them of the new banking arrangements, and assured them that the company was solvent. He instructed them to pass this information along to their subordinates so that the entire staff could be made aware of the incorrect impression the rumor was creating among the staff.

Quite independently of the above circumstances, the company had a disagreement with the landlord in the building in which it was located. The disagreement was based on the amount of service to be rendered by the landlord. One evening after the building had closed, the landlord, in a fit of resentment, removed all of the company's listings from the building directory in the lobby. The next morning one of the employees noticed the missing listings when he came in to work. He started the going-out-of-business rumor all over again, citing the removed listings as evidence.

1. *Did the board chairman handle the rumor effectively?*
2. *What should be his course of action in view of the rekindled rumor?*
3. *Should the employee who started the rumor again be disciplined?*
4. *How can a company offset the occurrence of rumors such as those in this case?*

Chapter 15

Learning objectives

○ To understand the legal and social environment in the United States and its relationship to management and supervisory practice

○ To become aware of pertinent legislation and the role of government intervention on supervisory and management responsibilities

○ To determine the nature of various employee problems in union and nonunion organizations and how supervisors cope with them

○ To understand disciplinary procedures and practices and their use in effective employee relations

The legal and social environment for supervision

Major topics

Each person has some notion about and longing for the "good old days." Such wishful thinking usually paints the past in rosy hues and decorates the present in much darker tones. Generally the desire for a better period in the past confronts supervisors and managers when problems arise to which solutions are difficult.

There is no doubt that present-day managers and supervisors are working and living in a different environment than their predecessors. Changing values, life-styles, increased education, and more government regulation all affect the way employees are managed. Many of the employee problems that supervisors must face are similar to those of the past. Employees still come in late, are absent, have poor attitudes, have inadequate skills, and use alcohol excessively. But the basic nature of the work force is changing, and how these problems are dealt with may be quite different today than in the past. Of course there are some new problems such as drug abuse, discrimination, and some older problems receiving greater attention such as unionism, safety, and working conditions. How these problems, both old and new, are handled along with increased governmental intervention present today's supervisors and managers with some of their greatest challenges.

Supervisors, managers, and value systems

What some people call the generation gap really represents a conflict in value systems. Everyone is a product of personal environmental inputs over a lifetime. Each individual is affected by the culture to which that person is exposed. These cultural values provide individuals with guidelines to behavior. Thus a person's reactions to a given situation can be shaped by the values that person brings to the situation.

Many people in their middle years have the work ethic as the foundation of their value system. Because of a change in values among many younger people, they do not respect the work ethic in the same way. As a result this generation gap can cause differing viewpoints on the value of work and the need to achieve material rewards. Another cause for differing values is the increase in the female work force. In some cases this may diminish notions about the male as the sole provider and further contrast the values of people.

Still another issue gaining in importance relates to individual privacy and due process. Many employees want to be included in the decisions affecting their lives and the various managerial judgments made about their performance. This topic is explored further in Chapter 16.

Actually culture and values are rather complex forces finding their roots in education, religion, ethnic and racial background, geographical location of an individual's early life, and chronological age. Supervisors and managers need to recognize differing cultural values as a very necessary part of the climate in which they manage. Not doing so can only cause problems to which solutions are exceedingly difficult. Everyone is familiar with the ar-

Figure 15–1
Example of bipolar values

Column A	Column B
1. Conservative, traditional, against innovation.	1. Liberal, progressive, revolutionary.
2. Repression and restraint.	2. Spontaneity and exhibition stressed.
3. Law and justice emphasized.	3. Mercy and compassion stressed.
4. Emphasis on duty, discipline, conscience.	4. Emphasis on zest for life, not guilt, stressed.
5. Sacrifice, fear of pleasure.	5. Leisure welcomed.
6. Distrust of research and inquiry.	6. Encourage creativity and inquiry.
7. Build, produce, save.	7. Enjoy, appreciate, consume.
8. Competition stressed.	8. Cooperation stressed.
9. Sex differences maximized, especially in dress.	9. Sex differences minimized, especially in dress.
10. Rational, abstract, cause and effect relationships.	10. Emotion, intuition, and instinct.

Source: George R. Terry, *Principles of Management,* 7th ed. (Homewood, Ill.: Richard D. Irwin, 1977), p. 53. © by Richard D. Irwin, Inc.

guments between parents and their children about such things as length of hair, clothing styles, eating habits, and political viewpoints. The bipolar values of individuals is demonstrated in Figure 15–1. If one could imagine two people working together, each possessing the differing values on the two lists, the possibilities for differences of opinion and arguments become huge.

Environmental considerations

Against the backdrop of differing value systems which require managerial concern are many changes in our society. These have been brought about by increasing governmental intervention and greater individual concern with a variety of things which affect our daily lives. One example of this concern is in the area of environmental pollution. Not too many years ago a network of interstate highways was built both for easy automobile and truck travel and as a stimulant to our economy. Now building a highway is exceedingly difficult due to negative social pressure and increasing regulations impact on the automobile industry to produce energy efficient and pollution free vehicles. Of course there are many other examples, but the one stated above gives an indication of part of the growing complexity of organizational life. Such complexity makes the work of supervising and managing more difficult. The ability of any organization to attract and retain capable employees and managers has great significance for that organiza-

"Well, that does it for this week's work ethic
. . . now for two glorious days of loaf ethic."

**Some people's changing values are placing
less emphasis on work.**

tion's survival. The nature of people available in the labor market, their
concerns and value systems, and governmental sanctions imposed on organizations are all part of the environment in which these organizations exist.

The changing nature of family life with an ever-increasing divorce rate
and larger numbers of people deciding against marriage also relates to work
performance. With smaller families and less responsibilities people may
look upon work differently than their predecessors. Families where the husband and wife both have successful careers increases their collective independence as well as their income. One outcome has been increasing
reluctance to accept transfers to other locations.

The increase of working women has had an impact on men who still may
look upon males as dominant. If a man with these cultural beliefs finds
himself reporting to a woman boss, he may become a discipline problem.
The clash of cultures in the workplace tends to cause more informal organizations based on ethnic, racial, and religious factors where a deviant of any

kind may be ostracized. These are just some of the environmental and cultural factors which increase the number of problems supervisors and managers can have with employees.

Legal considerations

Any modern supervisor and manager soon recognizes that there are few decisions that can be made involving employee relations without regard for some law. The increasing legal costs to business organizations attest to the growing complexity in this area. Federal, state, and municipal statutes all may restrict management's behavior toward employees. In fact there may be two or more laws with conflicting provisions which apply to the same situation. Some things may be legal under one statute and illegal under another. Just a listing of some of the federal laws relating to terms and conditions of employment demonstrate the breadth of legal impact on managerial decisions involving employees.

1. Fair Labor Standards Act.
2. Public Contracts Act.
3. Immigration and Naturalization Act.
4. Civil Rights Act.
5. National Labor Relations Act.
6. Labor Management Relations Act.
7. Social Security Act.
8. Occupational Safety and Health Act.
9. Employee Retirement Insurance Security Act.

It is beyond the scope of this text to go into detail on all of the above mentioned legislation. As a practical matter most supervisors and managers have the guidance of staff experts in their company's personnel and industrial relations departments to help them. Nevertheless, it is the line manager who is responsible for implementing some of the legislation in the workplace. Employers must observe laws when establishing hours of work, wages, physical working conditions, safety, hiring and promotion practices, occupational disease, unemployment, accidental injury, retirement, and the right of employees to organize and join a union.

The supervisor's and the manager's role

While it is true that first-level supervisors and middle managers do require staff advice on many of the legal issues which may arise, they do play a critical role in the day to day implementation of company policies and procedures developed by higher management and staff experts. Even though many supervisors and managers would like to shift the burden of responsibility upward, they must face the reality that such things as salary and promotion recommendations, employee transfers, on-the-job training, discipline, and productivity among others are their direct responsibility. They must deal with the opportunities and problems presented by increasing numbers of young people, older people, minorities, women, and white males possessing an educational level that ranges from nonhigh school to advanced university degrees.

Affirmative action programs.   Facing the realities of equal employment opportunity legislation is one of the supervisor's most difficult tasks. No matter how well-developed the organization's affirmative action program is and that it is accepted by the various governmental agencies charged with monitoring compliance, the line managers must make that compliance work effectively. They must train and develop minorities and women and recommend them for promotion while maintaining that delicate balance with white male employees that will demonstrate no reverse discrimination. They must also conduct fair, unbiased performance appraisals of all employees and be prepared to justify all of their disciplinary actions by accurate, uniform records.

Interestingly, some minorities and women resent special treatment such as training programs designed especially for them while others demand such programs. Here again, supervisors must recognize those that need and want help and those that don't while maintaining a viable relationship with their entire work force.

The combination of social pressures, cultural differences, and legislation have all changed the environment for supervisors and managers. They must be far more attentive to employee needs and rights than they have in the past. Developing a high degree of professionalism in dealing with subordinates and superiors is critically necessary. This means increased awareness of the environment both inside the organization as well as in the society at large. It also means increased knowledge of the subject matter we call management practice. Hence the increase in training and development programs for supervisors and managers in private sector organizations, semipublic ones such as hospitals, religious organizations and social agencies, and government groups of all kinds. Many of these organizations have never before felt the need for such programs. Of course, many people are now studying management in our colleges and universities as well. Perhaps all of this effort will result in greater managerial professionalism.

Minorities and the manager.   Supervisors and managers are increasingly confronted with the need for showing increased concern for the rights of all people in their employ. Although the population of the United States consists of a variety of minority groups, only one, white males, have been dominant over the years. With the passage of the Civil Rights Act of 1964 our society was compelled to deal with the problems and desires of less dominant minority groups. For managers and supervisors who are responsible for quality of performance and productivity, the increased concern for nonwhite minorities and women presents more complexity.

In recent years, increasing emphasis has been placed on hiring and train-

"Hi there! I understand you're an equal opportunity employer!"

Reprinted by permission The Wall Street Journal

Equal employment practice is increasingly important.

ing various nonwhite minorities. Some of these people come from economically and socially disadvantaged circumstances. Many do not have white middle-class values and therefore may not place the same importance on such things as coming in on time, grooming, hard work, and ambition as do others in the work group. Some may be very impatient with what they perceive as the red tape of the organization and may demand jobs for which they are not qualified. Others may be difficult to discipline since they are not qualified. Others may be difficult to discipline since they may feel attempts in this direction are really discrimination. Where minority groups are treated as outcasts by the dominant white work group, morale can rapidly deteriorate. The supervisor will have to take additional time and give special attention to these problems. Productive assimilation of minorities into the work group is a top supervisory priority. As more members of minorities enter organizations and are productively employed, the problem will diminish. In those companies that have had significant percentages of minority employees on the payroll for prolonged periods of time, the problems are not as great. However, the workplace is one part of our society; and until the society at large fully recognizes these problems and positively responds to them, the workplace will merely reflect the total society's reactions.

The fact that women have been employed by business firms in considerable numbers over the years gives their status special significance now. Women have constituted a considerable percentage of the work force in the past, but the emphasis now is on their promotability into managerial, technical, and professional jobs beyond the relatively low-level clerical and factory jobs that have been traditional. Women tend to resent being restricted in opportunity, even though all may not desire it. Those who want careers do not want second-class ones or token assignments that are not in the mainstream of corporate life. They want equal consideration with men for management and professional jobs, desiring to be measured on their qualifications and not their sex. They particularly resent the type casting that keeps them in clerical and secretarial jobs when they possess college degrees and are qualified for higher level opportunities. Another source of consternation is doing the same job as a man, sometimes with greater skill, and having a lesser title and lower pay.[1]

As the impact of affirmative action programs grows, the inevitability of controversy increases. In some organizations men complain about women in jobs that require heavy work such as lifting or moving heavy equipment or other kinds of considerable physical requirements. The complaints center on the equal pay for equal work dimension since in some instances women are unable to perform some of the physical tasks required. One possible solution to problems of this kind is job redesign and repricing. Another area of increased concern relates to so-called reverse discrimination promotions where the aggrieved party believes that the person promoted was unqualified but promoted because of minority status. There are several cases pending in both areas and the ultimate solution to such problems lies in the courts.

Whether employees are young, old, male, or female, and whatever their color or ethnic background, supervisors who understand the expectations which today's employees bring to the job can help them adjust to the realities. While looking for recognition and promotion, ambitious employees of all kinds have to be provided with opportunities to develop abilities and to receive even-handed treatment both for those opportunities and when reprimands and discipline are necessary.

Unions and employee problems

From a supervisory and managerial viewpoint, unions change the relationship with those employees covered by a collective bargaining agreement. A contract usually restricts management's decision making with regard to many aspects of employee behavior. Union contracts specify such things as pay rates for particular jobs, seniority rules in relation to job transfers and layoff, and the specific acts that are regarded as discipline possibilities along with the degree of severity of that discipline. The contract also includes the nature of discipline handling, a grievance procedure with the steps necessary for implementation and the use of arbitration. In short, a union contract is restrictive and definitely changes the role of first-level supervisors. Even though they are charged with the responsibility for the implementation and maintenance of the bargaining agreement, they frequently are frustrated in their attempts to do so. In fact, the collective bargaining

---

[1] For a thorough and somewhat controversial study of work, see "Report of a Special Task Force to the Secretary of Health, Education, and Welfare," *Work in America* (Cambridge, Mass.: M.I.T. Press, 1973).

agreement gives union members access to higher levels of management by use of the grievance procedure. In many instances this results in bypassing the first-level supervisor in disciplinary matters.

Disciplinary policy

Good management seeks to make the most effective use of employees; so the aim of a disciplinary policy should be to prevent misbehavior and to catch backsliding before it becomes serious. A good disciplinary policy is designed to warn, correct, and reform offenders rather than just give them what is coming to them. Such a policy of *corrective* or *progressive* discipline provides for:

1. Rules that are reasonable, necessary, definite, known, and understood.
2. Enforcement that is certain, reasonable, uniform, consistent, and fair.
3. Penalties that are appropriate and corrective. Immediate discharge must be reserved for gross offenses only. For other rule-breaking, lighter penalties are appropriate for the first offense and harsher penalties for repetitions, then discharge when other methods of correction fail. There should be flexibility in the penalty schedule to take into account the degree of guilt, the contributing causes on the job or at home, the employee's length of service, and his or her record.
4. A procedure specifying the steps of the discipline process from the time of the rule violation to the closing of the record. The procedure should be designed to achieve line and staff cooperation in handling discipline. It should protect the rights of employees, provide for informing them of the charges against them, give them an opportunity to explain and to defend themselves before a penalty is assessed, and provide a channel through which they can appeal a penalty considered to be unjust.
5. Provision for furnishing supervisors with the information, training, and help they need to handle discipline problems and maintain their leadership. They must know the extent of their authority and what kinds of decisions will be supported by upper management.

Rules

The purpose of company rules is to tell people how they should act as members of a specific group. Without the rules they would have no way of knowing what time they were expected to be at their desks or workplaces, what time they could leave, whether they must get permission to leave their own area, and when and where they could smoke. Rules tell employees that they can't use company time for their own personal phone calls, visitors, and mail or for reading magazines, chatting, overstaying coffee breaks and rest periods, loafing, taking long lunch hours, and leaving early. Punching the time clock for another employee looks like a friendly act rather than a serious offense. People could scarcely be discharged for it unless it was established as a rule and specifically brought to their attention. Ignorance of the law is a perfectly good excuse within a business organization.

Rules must be clear and definite in order to avoid being misinterpreted. They should be direct and specific so that people can't get around them. And in order to be effective they must be known and enforced. They should be published in employee handbooks, in memos, letters to employees, and on bulletin boards in work areas and restrooms. They should be explained to new employees in the induction procedure and reviewed periodically. Some companies require the supervisor to review the rules with subordinates every six months.

Normally people are willing to abide by rules of conduct if these rules make sense to them, if practically everyone is obeying the rules, and if the few who do violate them are penalized. On the other hand, rules set up arbitrarily and without explanation are looked upon as encroachments on personal liberty rather than protection of the general good. People are slow to figure out the reasons for rules. They will grumble about a no-smoking rule with never a thought of the fire hazards it protects them against. They complain about the inconvenience of using safety equipment. Safety rule enforcement entails constant reminders, campaigns, slogans, displays, gimmicks, cautions, warnings, and penalties. Safety is emphasized in induction and training. Some employees still don't become safety-conscious until they have served a turn on the safety committee and had the responsibility of enforcing the rules and investigating accidents and hazards.

If there is general violation of a rule, something may be wrong with the rule itself or the way it is presented or explained. Even though supervisors do not have the power to change the rules, they do have the job of enforcing them, and they should make strong recommendations for revisions of rules that do not work well. Too many rules or rules that seem petty, arbitrary, or unreasonable defeat their own purpose. Giving highly motivated people as much freedom as possible and treating them as responsible adults pays off in cooperation, team spirit, and high morale.

Having few rules and depending on the spirit rather than the letter of the law works better in small groups than in large, however, and may run into penalty reversals in a unionized company. An arbitrator may ask for evidence that the rule really existed and that the employees were aware of it—particularly if the prohibited act is something that is permitted in other companies.

Penalties

This discussion of penalties and the discussion on rule enforcement that follows it take into account that a union contract places definite restrictions on the type of penalty that can be assessed. Extremely serious offenses—sabotage, for example—usually call for immediate dismissal: no need for a warning, no need for a notice, and no obligation to try to reform the offender. Offenses that are less serious call for some milder penalty aimed at correction. Corrective (progressive) discipline calls for lighter penalties for the first offense and harsher penalties for repetition. After a certain number of offenses—regardless of whether they are identical—the company resorts to discharge. The schedule of penalties under a union contract is essentially as follows:

1. Oral warning of which no record is made in the employee's folder.
2. Oral warning with a record of it put into the employee's folder. This warning notice is proof that the employee was advised of management's intention to discipline him or her for repetition or continuation of his or her behavior. Such a record is needed to justify a discharge for repetition of the offense or a discharge for a series of offenses. It is needed to justify a discharge for repeated failure to meet production standards.
3. Written reprimand. This form may carry one or more signatures—that of the immediate supervisor, the department head, superintendent, or labor relations officer.
4. Suspension (disciplinary layoff) for a definite period of time, which might be a few hours, a day, a number of days, or months. During a suspension an employee does not report for work and does not get paid. Some companies don't use suspension as a penalty because they find it creates too many operating difficulties. While the suspended employee is gone, his or her work has to be done by someone else, which creates a hardship for the other employees. Or else a replacement must be brought in temporarily and trained to do the work. A company that does not suspend employees would add one or more warnings to the sequence of penalties leading up to discharge.

    Some people use the word "layoff" only for a reduction in force. They feel that the use of the word "layoff" in connection with discipline may give the idea that disciplinary layoff is a way to get rid of undesirables without having to go through the discharge procedure and without having to answer for violating seniority rights. A disciplinary layoff is a penalty whose length is in proportion to the seriousness of the offense it punishes. The exception to this definition is the practice of sending an employee home while the offense is being investigated. Such a suspension enables supervisors to handle offenses that require immediate action but may warrant a penalty more serious than they have the authority to assess.
5. Discharge—the capital punishment of industry. A discharge cuts off the rights and benefits an employee had in the job. The employee may even be unable to collect unemployment benefits if the law of the state provides that no benefits will be paid to a person found to be discharged through his or her own fault.

Several other types of penalties are used in some organizations. Demotion or downgrading to a lower paying job is a rather special type of penalty that in unionized companies is usually restricted to cases of unsatisfactory performance caused by incompetence. Withholding of benefits is another penalty whose use is usually restricted by the union contract. Benefits that might be withheld are merit increases, promotions, overtime work, holiday pay, or vacation pay. At one time the trend was to incorporate into the contract a schedule of all possible offenses with the exact penalty that would be assessed for the first offense, the second, and the third (and the fourth and fifth if there were that many) before discharge. In recent years the "price list" approach to penalties has fallen into disfavor, and most contracts have a broad "just cause" provision which is less rigid than a list and allows for the exercise of more judgment.

Incompetence and negligence

The supervisor's disciplinary problems include the job performance of subordinates as well as their behavior. Unsatisfactory job performance may be due to incompetence or to negligence, and, because one calls for different treatment than the other, a distinction should be made between them.

Incompetence.   Incompetence is defined in various ways: (1) being substantially deficient in the work, (2) being incapable of performing the work safely, (3) being unable to turn out work in proper quality or quantity, (4) being unable to keep up with the standard of performance of others on the job. Employees may be incompetent because they never had the required ability. Or their performance may have been satisfactory at one time but deteriorated because of illness, aging, or lack of motivation. The job itself may have been changed and made more difficult. Production standards may have been raised. The employee may have been promoted to, or transferred to, a job that he or she was unable to handle.

Negligence.   Negligence (as distinguished from incompetence) indicates that the employees are able to do the job but are careless, thoughtless, or do not follow instructions. They botch up the job and cause loss of materials, customers, or money. They do not pay attention to what they are doing, have accidents, damage machinery, or wreck vehicles. They neglect to lock up valuables and use inflammables carelessly.

Employee failure to use reasonable care may cause heavy property damage and may endanger life as well. The incidents may be so costly, dangerous, and frequent that they cannot be trusted on the job. (Deliberate and malicious destruction of company property is counted as sabotage rather than negligence and—if it can be proved—is punished by discharge.) Negligence is considered to be more a matter of attitude than of ability, and the standard penalties are warning, suspension, and discharge. Demoting an employee to punish that person for carelessness is considered an improper penalty unless specifically provided for in the contract. There are exceptions, however, and the dividing line between negligence and incompetence becomes very thin at times. There are cases in which repeated accidents indicate that an employee is unable to perform a job safely. In such cases arbitrators may rule that demotion or transfer to less hazardous work is the proper treatment.

Gripes and grievances

The term *grievance* has come to mean an employee's formal complaint about the job—usually a written complaint—presented to management. A company's contract with the union may narrow the definition by specifying that the complaint must concern matters covered in the contract. Then a grievance is considered to be a dispute between the employee and the company concerning the violation or interpretation of the terms of the contract. This definition is important in that it labels certain complaints as illegitimate and not subject to arbitration.

Complaints that don't fit the definition of a grievance may be labeled as *gripes*. These definitions obviously are management definitions. From the standpoint of employees, they have a grievance if they feel they have suffered an injustice. They have a gripe if something is annoying or irritating.

Supervisors have to deal with every type of complaint—real or imagined, oral or written—covered by a contract or not covered by a contract. They also have to deal with dissatisfactions that haven't been put into words but are having a bad effect on performance or morale. In any job there are irritants, annoyances, vexations, disappointments, conflicts of interest, and real or imagined injustices that give rise to gripes and grievances. An accumulation of these dissatisfactions creates a contagious kind of unrest that interferes with performance of the job.

Employees may be griped by the people they work with, by the way the boss orders them around, by last-minute requests to work overtime. They may be griped by discomforts and inconveniences—warm water in the drinking fountain and restrictions on the use of the telephone.

A sense of injury from a long-standing gripe has a way of transforming itself into a complaint that fits the company's definition of a grievance. This substitution of one complaint for another complicates the handling of grievances. The supervisor has to dig beneath the surface explanation to find the real basis of the trouble.

Typical grievances are claims by employees that the job was improperly classified, wages improperly figured, seniority violated in a layoff, transfer, or promotion; that they were disciplined unjustly or too severely or discriminated against for union activities; that the supervisor discriminates against them, gives them the dirty jobs, or doesn't give them a fair share of overtime.

Handling grievances

First-level supervisors are responsible for the implementation of the union contract. They deal daily with employees and their elected representatives, the union stewards. The type of relationship that the supervisor has with the steward probably reflects the relationships at the top between the company and the union.

Stewards have a unique position. On the one hand they are employees of the company, doing regular jobs under the jurisdiction of first-level supervisors; on the other, they are elected officers of the union with certain rights and freedoms that other employees don't have. In their official capacity they are protected by contract provisions and labor laws. They have an obligation to their constituents to hear and investigate their grievances and argue them vigorously with the supervisor. The vigor they may use in their official capacity is beyond that permitted to them as regular employees. They have the job of policing the contract and seeing that its provisions are lived up to. They can question the supervisor's decisions and advise employees of their rights under the contract.

Contract and plant practice govern the amount of time and the conditions under which they may be away from the workplace to handle union matters. The contract also regulates the type of union business they can handle on company time. It is customary for the company to pay them for the time spent handling grievances.

Understanding the steward's position calls for understanding a little of the internal politics of the union. Political rivalries within the union may influence the attitude of its leaders toward supporting and settling grievances. Grievance rates may rise around the time for electing local officials. Certain types of grievances may be pushed just before contract negotiating time. Under some circumstances grievances may be cooked up to embarrass the company. A union must decide whose cause to support when a grievance by one group of members asks for something at the expense of another group. An adjustment of seniority, for instance, or a promotion, is always made at the expense of another employee.

A good working relationship between supervisors and steward can facilitate the settlement of grievances at the first level. The supervisor should take the initiative in establishing courteous and businesslike relationships with the steward. The supervisor can be agreeable rather than grudging in regard to the time the steward is entitled to spend on union duties. The supervisor can make it a point to introduce each new employee to the steward and can set a pattern of courtesy in the way the steward is informed of production schedule changes, overtime expected, layoffs proposed, and disciplinary actions pending. The steward can't be expected to cooperate in meting out punishments to constituents but can reinforce warnings to members whose misbehavior is endangering their jobs.

The handling of gripes

The discussion of grievances concentrated on an environment in order to show the operation of union grievance machinery. The handling of gripes is informal, and supervisors everywhere must handle them as they come or have them build up to the point of interfering with the job.

A gripe is something more than just being unsatisfied with the job. Few people are completely satisfied with their jobs, and few people consider work as a joy and a blessing, although they would be lost without it. To most people work is a necessary chore that requires sacrifice either to a small or to a great degree. Complaints about the job may be the employee's way of letting off steam about a situation that he or she realizes cannot be corrected. Or complaints may indicate that the employee has a gripe.

Gripes may be real or imaginary. They may have their origins in something that is actually wrong in the work situation or in something that the employee only thinks is wrong in it. Having someone bang the window shut every time it is opened for a breath of fresh air may be one of the most irritating things in a person's life. The hot-blooded and the cold-blooded people may have a running feud about temperature, drafts, windows, and air conditioning. The discomfort involved can assume the proportions of a persecution.

Minor unsatisfactory conditions cause undue annoyance to an employee whose actual gripe is something else. A poorly lighted work area may send a typist into a frenzy of errors and complaints when actually he or she is burning up because a good typewriter was taken away without explanation and given to another typist.

Gripes may manifest themselves by some sort of change in the behavior of the aggrieved employee: The happy-go-lucky one becomes sullen; the center of the crowd becomes a loner; the enthusiastic worker becomes a daydreamer; the safe worker becomes careless; the good housekeeper becomes sloppy; the good attender starts taking time off. Sometimes there will be a flare-up and the employee will refuse to follow orders. Occasionally someone will "boil over" and "tell the boss off."

When a group of employees has a gripe, it may show itself in quarreling, gossiping, faultfinding or stalling on the job, mistakes and waste, a drop in quality and quantity of work done, or an increase in absences.

The supervisor can't afford to ignore gripes and leave their handling to upper management or to the personnel department. And the supervisor certainly shouldn't leave them undiscussed and unsettled to be turned into grievances to be handled by the union if there is one.

Supervisors are the logical people to handle gripes since they are close to the scene and can detect a gripe in its early stages. They should know what employees are thinking about and what is important to them. However, some supervisors lack sensitivity or turn away from gripes hoping they will disappear. They fail to realize the impact of the emotional time bomb ticking away in the workplace until it explodes into a major problem. Other supervisors try to pass the gripe along to the next level of management or the personnel department. In still other situations the gripes may directly involve the supervisor.

To remedy such situations and to offer employees an avenue of appeal, some companies without union contracts have developed procedures which allow for the airing of gripes to levels of management beyond the first level of supervision. One such procedure is shown in Figure 15–2 and 15–3. This form is placed in containers attached to bulletin boards located in every work area of the organization. The employee can send the problem to the next level of management or directly to the company's personnel policy committee which is made up of members of top management. The employee may even request confidentiality, and this request will be honored.

Such a procedure acts as a safety valve to defuse the emotional content of gripes. Other companies have used "speak-outs" in the same manner. These are open meetings where gripes are aired to senior managers and immediate answers are given where possible. If the gripe is complex, then the employee will receive an answer as soon as possible. Still other companies have gripe hot lines enabling an employee to call a number manned by a personnel specialist who will make every attempt to expedite solutions. Several companies have used their company newspapers as vehicles for exposing employee gripes. Employees are encouraged to write their gripes for publication and suggested solutions.

It is clear that many organizations recognize the importance of employee gripes and the need for giving employees a chance to communicate these gripes to people who may be able to do something about them. By dealing with gripes openly and fairly, these organizations have less difficulty and higher morale.

The managerial impact of OSHA

In 1970 the Occupational Safety and Health Act was passed by Congress and signed into law by the President. The law was an outgrowth of increased concern in our society for the welfare of workers on-the-job. Even though many organizations had a long time concern for the safety and health of employees, it now became a legal requirement for all firms which do business in interstate commerce. This includes industry, offices, service organizations, farming, nonprofit organizations, transit companies, and all other commercial organizations. The law is administered by the U.S. Department of Labor.

The intent of the law is to set uniform standards nationally and enforce them so that safe and healthy conditions exist in those organizations covered by the law. The standards are enforced by on-site inspections, and advance notice need not be given by OSHA inspectors. As is the case with most new regulatory legislation, the standards are not fully developed or uniformly applied. There is some confusion and varied interpretation resulting in misunderstandings by both OSHA inspectors and company managers. One certain outcome is that compliance will increase costs not only by changes needed in the work environment but also by the increased record-

Figure 15–2
Employee relations procedure

Is something about your job worrying you?

Tell us about it...*CONFIDENTIALLY.*

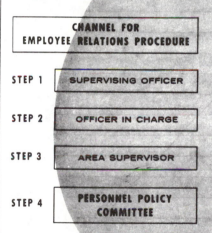

CHANNEL FOR EMPLOYEE RELATIONS PROCEDURE		ALTERNATE CHANNELS
STEP 1	SUPERVISING OFFICER	When a problem personally involves an officer who functions at any step in the Procedure, you may omit this step and proceed to the next step.
STEP 2	OFFICER IN CHARGE	You may write directly to the Personnel Policy Committee if the matter is of such a nature that you do not wish to discuss it orally at any step.
STEP 3	AREA SUPERVISOR	You may consult officers and counselors of the Personnel Department, at any time, if the subject is of a personal or embarrassing nature, or if advice on use of the Procedure is desired.
STEP 4	PERSONNEL POLICY COMMITTEE	

If you indicate that you wish your name to remain undisclosed, it will not be divulged without your permission.

— fill out this form, submit as follows: —

Figure 15–3
Employee relations procedure—employee form

MANUFACTURERS HANOVER TRUST COMPANY

EMPLOYEE RELATIONS PROCEDURE

NAME	DATE
HOME ADDRESS	BRANCH/DEPARTMENT
	OFFICE TELEPHONE

STATEMENT OF PROBLEM

_____

SIGNATURE

MAIL THIS FORM TO THE PERSONNEL POLICY COMMITTEE IN THE ENVELOPE PROVIDED. IF YOU DO NOT RECEIVE AN ACKNOWLEDGEMENT AT YOUR HOME WITHIN THREE DAYS, TELEPHONE AN OFFICER OF THE PERSONNEL DEPART-MENT.
AVAILING YOURSELF OF THIS PROCEDURE WILL IN NO WAY ADVERSELY AFFECT YOUR STANDING IN THE BANK, YOUR OPPORTUNITY FOR ADVANCEMENT OR YOUR SALARY PROGRESS.

4889 6M 7-65

keeping necessary for compliance. All accidents, injuries, and illnesses which require medical treatment, or loss of time from the job, or which result in unconsciousness, death, handicap, transfer to another job, or termination, must be recorded and the records must be up to date and then kept for five years.

Many companies, of course, will increase their staffs of experts in health and safety, and these experts will be available to line managers and supervisors for guidance and assistance. But the major responsibility for implementation on-the-job lies with these line managers. Enforcing workplace cleanliness, keeping aisles free, and seeing to employee adherence to safe procedures and practices become a major supervisory responsibility. Supervisors are the major monitors of compliance with the law, and this becomes another added burden to a complex job.

Absenteeism and tardiness

Absenteeism and tardiness are considered together because they cause the same kinds of problems for the supervisor and because penalty systems treat them as related offenses. If employees are several minutes or hours late in getting on the job, they are tardy. If the time stretches out beyond a half day, they are considered absent. In measuring absences, some companies don't count as an absence the time lost by employees who are away from their jobs because of sickness, injury from accidents, death in the family, or a legitimate excuse of that type. Other companies count as an absence *any* failure of employees to report on the job on a day they are scheduled to work.[2]

Effects of tardiness and absenteeism

Absences and lateness upset the supervisor's planning. Jobs have to be shifted; the relationship of each job to others has to be revamped. Employees have to be put on work they are not familiar with. They have to be given additional instructions and directions. Their work has to be inspected more frequently. An employee who is unfamiliar with the work makes more mistakes, turns out less work, and reduces the efficiency of others. If a number

---

[2] Absence statistics and costs, therefore, don't compare very readily from one company to another. The following formula is one of many in use for figuring the percentage rate of absence:

$$\text{Absence rate} = \frac{\text{No. of worker days lost through absence during month}}{\text{Average no. of employees} \times \text{no. of working days}} \times 100$$

Count all worker-days lost except vacations and unpaid leaves of absence. To compute the average number of employees, add the total work force figures for each pay period within the month being measured and divide by the number of pay periods. An absence rate of 2 percent is considered excellent.

of employees are absent, their work may have to be done by scheduling overtime.

Other costs that may be charged against absences are salaries paid to the absentees, benefit payments, salaries of replacements, and salaries of people who must check up on absentees, interview them, and keep records. Overhead costs go on even though equipment stands idle and the work is not done while people are absent. Estimates of the cost of absenteeism range from 4 percent of the payroll up to 40 percent.

The absences of professional people are costly. One study[3] in 1963 reported that the total direct and indirect cost of a one-day absence of an engineer amounted to $273.10. This included eight hours of overtime to catch up on the engineer's work. Consider what inflation has added to this cost.

In some companies the tardiness of professional people becomes a problem. Some of these people like to work irregular hours—start an hour or so late in the morning and work until midnight. Even though they as individuals may be making great contributions to the company, some of their value is lost because their activities are not coordinated with the activities of other people in the organization. The work of dozens of people might be held up pending information to be obtained from the professionals who have not shown up for work on time. Sometimes resentment is built up against them; "Who do they think they are anyway?" and "If they can come in late, why can't I?" Some companies have found it necessary to insist that everybody in the organization *with no exceptions* start the work day at the regular time.

Finding and treating the causes

In order to study the attendance problems in their own departments, supervisors should be supplied with company figures on absences and their costs. Rates and costs should be broken down by departments so that they can see how their units compare to others. They should get regular reports showing who in the group was absent or tardy, how many times, how many days in a row, what days they were, what excuse was given.

A certain amount of tardiness and absence is to be expected for causes of illness, accidents, family emergencies, deaths, and funerals. Sudden increases in the rates might indicate excessive overtime, job-caused fatigue, gripes, or unsettled grievances. Low morale may manifest itself in absences as well as in turnover. People may be disturbed to the point of taking time off to go job hunting. When a job becomes too disagreeable, employees may

---

[3] Made at Stevens Institute of Technology and reported by Frederick J. Gaudet, *Solving Problems of Employee Absence,* American Management Association Research Study 57 (New York: AMA, 1963). This thorough study of absences doesn't claim to solve the problems, but it does describe them and report what a number of companies are doing about them. It also gives a survey and evaluation of research studies of absences and absentees. It presents 41 formulas for measuring the absence rate.

develop such headaches or stomachaches that they feel justified in staying home.

Employees' personal troubles.   One school of thought lays the blame for excessive absences on the personality of high-absence employees; they are typed as *absence-prone.* In a good many instances a small number of employees account for a majority of the absences. These employees usually don't get along well with people, don't like their supervisors, have trouble at home, or are generally dissatisfied with their jobs.

Some studies show a correlation between the employee's attendance and his or her opinion of the supervisor. In a University of Michigan study the high attenders felt free to discuss their personal and job problems with the supervisor.[4] In a study by William Noland, the poor attenders thought their boss was difficult to get along with, unfair, and never showed appreciation of good work.[5]

Keith Davis comments on the relationship of organization size and employee absenteeism. "Increasing size of operations introduces what might be called a *behemoth syndrome,* by which increasing size develops a series of interrelated symptoms and problems. For example, larger size is associated with lower employee satisfactions, which tends to increase absenteeism."[6] Employees can feel overwhelmed in a large organization, believing that they are insignificant and unimportant. Such feelings of insecurity can cause them to feel sorry for themselves, develop imaginary illnesses, and take days off to get even.

Women tend to have higher absence rates than men. This is particularly true of younger women who are not career-oriented and look upon their jobs as way stations on the route to marriage.

Programs for the "hard-core unemployable" have special problems with absenteeism and tardiness. Habits of punctuality, responsibility, and the desire to advance are learned through a lifetime of training, work opportunities, family pressure, and encouragement and reward on the job. People who grow up surrounded by these attitudes will have their behavior shaped by them. Unfortunately, some people have not been exposed to this type of environment. Many have living conditions that are not conducive to getting up and being on the job every day. They may sleep four or more in a bed, lack medical care, or have such bad home conditions that they stay out all

---

[4] Floyd Mann and Howard Baumgartel, *Absences and Employee Attitudes in an Electric Power Company* (Ann Arbor: Survey Research Center, University of Michigan, 1952). This study was made in the Detroit Edison Company. The findings were supported in studies made in insurance, railroading, and manufacturing groups also. The high attenders also had better feelings toward their fellow employees.

[5] William E. Noland, "Foreman and Absenteeism," *Personnel Journal,* June 1945, pp. 73–77. In this study of 500 workers in New York, the good attenders were satisfied with the treatment they got from the supervisor.

[6] Keith Davis, *Human Relations at Work, The Dynamics of Organizational Behavior,* 5th ed. (New York: McGraw-Hill Book Co., 1977), p. 207.

night. Supervisors may have special problems in trying to discipline such people, because the same techniques that have worked for other employees may not work for them. A good deal more attention and patience may be necessary before the supervisor is able to convince people who have been severely underprivileged and out of society's mainsteam that their values and those of the company should be similar.

Studies of people who are frequently absent serve to emphasize the effect that attitudes have on attendance. In looking for causes of absences, the supervisor should keep in mind that an absence seems to be the result of a number of factors working together to influence an employee to take time off.

Talking with employees about their absences will often bring to light personality clashes, fears of being hurt on the job, suspicions of discrimination, feelings of not getting a square deal, and a host of other causes of low morale—including problems at home. All of these complaints must be listened to. Talking with offenders and helping them find ways to solve their problems is discussed later in this chapter.

Social relations on the job affect attendance. A tightly knit group with high loyalty seems to have fewer absences than a group that is beset by conflicts. People who are absent excessively may be separating themselves from the group for some reason; or the group may be rejecting them. Supervisors need to know their people and understand where and how they fit into the group. Then they will be in a better position to avoid setting up conflicts within the group.

Job factors.   Causes and remedies for absenteeism are not all in the field of human relations. The design of jobs, the way a person fits the job, and the adequacy of training can influence attendance. The opportunity to make decisions and to feel useful and necessary keeps people from taking time off. Absences tend to be high where the skill level of the job is low. If certain jobs have high absences, the supervisor should consider redesigning them to make them more interesting, challenging, responsible, or agreeable. This might be accomplished through job enlargement, job rotation, partnership work, or even just an improvement in the seating arrangement.

The supervisor's ability to plan may affect attendance. If employees stand around waiting for work, they get the idea that they won't be missed.

Accidents causing injuries on the job result in absences and may indicate the need for a better management of safety. Other causes of absence are poorly maintained equipment, poor light, fumes, noise, and inadequate ventilation. People try to escape from unpleasant situations, job irritations, and frustrations.

Suggestions for the supervisor in handling tardiness.   The supervisor's own attitude toward tardiness will shape the employee's attitude toward it and will determine the amount of effort the employee will make to be on time. If the supervisor just gets in under the wire, is late, or doesn't take any action when people come in late, conscientious, well-organized employees come to feel that nobody appreciates their effort—and it is an effort—to be on the job on time every day.

The employees who would be late to their own weddings go on thinking that punctuality just isn't very important. It takes a great deal of effort on their part to regulate their lives so that they can be punctual. And it takes a certain amount of constant pressure to keep them reminded of the need to sustain that effort. Young people need to be helped to value time and to build good work habits. People under 20 have the worst attendance records.

Counseling the absentee

Almost any company plan for reducing absences will work for a while, not because of the method used but because the employees become fully aware that the company is deeply concerned about their absences. But gimmicks for improving attendance don't take the place of direct personal contact between supervisor and employee. When employees return to work after an absence, the supervisor must talk to them about the reasons for their absences. Points to be put across are that the company is extremely concerned about absences, that the employees were missed and needed, and that the lack of their services caused difficulties for others.

If the employee's absences are chronic, the supervisor should go on from this point to try to find out the reasons. This is an opportunity to clear up misunderstandings and to show an interest in the employee's welfare.

Employees should be shown their attendance records and asked to set up a plan of correction. In many cases, employees simply don't realize how bad their records are. They don't understand the purpose of the company's policy for sick leave benefits. They have no idea of the cost of absences or of all the trouble caused by poor attendance. Some employees, when they get the total picture, will see that their poor attendance is a violation of fair play.

Employees should be shown that their absences are hurting their chances of getting ahead in the company. The important assignments are given to people who can be depended upon to show up for work. The chronic absentee will be passed over in promotions. Unreliability will show up in merit rating and prevent getting a merit increase. They should be warned of the penalties awaiting a continuation of this behavior.

In tight labor markets employers sometimes find it difficult to control absenteeism and tardiness. Even though such poor practices may be costly, the companies find that recruiting new hires may be very difficult, and they may tolerate more absences and lateness than they would if replacements were easily obtained. Large white-collar employers in big cities who employ mainly young clerical help tend to have more problems with lateness and absence. Attempts to control it by passing over employees for merit increases may work, but more often than not the employee will quit and seek employment elsewhere. In some critical skill areas such as typing, stenography, keypunch, computer programming, and proof machine operation, there is a strong likelihood that employers will overstaff to diminish the effect of absenteeism on the work pace.

Another reality that employers have had to face is the deterioration of public transportation in the big cities and the increased traffic on highways feeding into these cities. Tardiness is often caused by poor transportation, and it is very difficult to convince an employee to get up an hour earlier to get to work on time, particularly when large numbers of employees are late and the poor transportation gets considerable news coverage.

Problems with alcoholics

Heavy drinkers who are actually alcoholics are usually an attendance problem. They are a problem in other ways too—putting off work because they are too foggy to handle it, delaying decisions, being evasive, elusive, and undependable, and being hard to get along with until they have a drink. It is difficult to confront a subordinate with specific instances of this type of behavior, but an attendance record is something concrete on which to base a discussion of performance and drinking.

The U.S. Federal Labor Department estimates that alcoholics lose about 28 man-days per year. A few studies of alcoholics' attendance indicate that their days off may be scattered through the week and not just concentrated on Mondays and Fridays. These same studies indicate that tardiness does not seem to be a problem typical of the alcoholic employee but that he or she may disappear and leave before the day is over. Supervisors should realize that alcoholism is an illness and not a moral problem and that it does not improve by itself. In fact it is apt to get worse; so they are not doing employees a kindness by protecting them and covering up for them. Nothing is to be gained by getting angry with alcoholics for their failures to handle the work. There is no point in lecturing about the dangers to their health or suggesting that they drink beer or save their drinking for weekends. They would if they could.

A distinction must be made between heavy drinkers who don't let their drinking interfere with the job and the alcoholic who seems to let nothing interfere with his or her drinking. Since very few people will admit to being alcoholic, the supervisor should seek some expert help in identifying the alcoholic employee. It is important to find out if the company has any policy or program for treating alcoholics. Some companies have recognized that the alcoholic is worth treating and that the company is repaid many times over for its part in restoring this person to health and to a useful life. Companies with alcoholism programs report that over half the employees who have *sought* treatment have been helped. In fact, some companies boast that many of their restored alcoholics have moved up to higher jobs.

The supervisor's difficulty is to get the alcoholic to seek treatment, because treatment cannot be forced upon the employee. Alcoholics must take the action and probably won't do it unless they are made to realize that they have to do it in order to keep the job. They seem to be unable to recognize that they have a problem on which they must take action.

If the company has no program for taking care of alcoholic employees, supervisors would be doing a great kindness if they made a contact with Alcoholics Anonymous to have someone take the employee to a meeting. They could go with the employee since meetings are attended by nonalcoholics—wives, husbands, friends, doctors, and sociologists, as well as bosses. The professional person may be there because he or she is an alcoholic or because he or she is concerned about someone else who is one.

Drug use and abuse problems

Another social problem appearing with increasing frequency in business and industry is the use of illegal drugs by employees. Companies have found employees using all the well-known hard and soft drugs, including heroin, cocaine, LSD, amphetamines, barbiturates, hashish, and marijuana. For many companies and their supervisors this is a new problem, and they don't know how to cope with it. In many organizations, no policy, procedure, or rule exists to guide the supervisor. When drug use by an employee is detected, the usual solution is quick termination of that employee. However, in some companies the use of certain drugs is so common that other approaches must be used. It is not unusual to find marijuana use prevalent in some organizations. Newspaper stories in recent years have indicated the use of this drug, and of amphetamines and barbiturates, is quite common in factories, particularly in large cities.

A difficult part of the problem for a business organization is that drug use is often not easy to detect. Managers must be trained to be able to identify the common illegal drugs and the symptoms displayed by a user. Many companies have such programs in existence. In addition, part of the preemployment physical examination in some companies include a urine analysis test to determine drug use. Further, a supervisor who suspects drug use by an employee may require that employee to go to the company medical department for this test.

As far as treatment is concerned, the methodology is quite similar to that used for alcoholism. While some companies solve their drugs problems by firing the discovered offenders, others are trying rehabilitation of their known users or are referring them to appropriate agencies in the community for help.

The tragedy of drug abuse is its commonness among young employees who could have a good future with a particular company. In any event, the supervisory job is becoming even more complex, and one wonders how many more things other than job knowledge one must be familiar with to function effectively.

Preventing disciplinary problems

It is clear that there is both a legalistic approach and a human relations approach to the handling of employee problems. While a union contract or narrow interpretations of rules in a nonunion organization may reinforce the supervisor in many problem situations, it is not the only answer. Building a case is not as important as building a person's will to work and willingness to live up to the rules and standards. Studying penalties and the problems attached to assessing them serves to emphasize the need for preventing violations. Preventing fututure problems beings with analyzing the present ones to see what caused them.

Studies indicate that the majority of discharges are not for inability to do the work but rather for some undesirable personal trait in the employee—dishonesty, laziness, carelessness, unreliability, or lack of initiative. The best way to avoid problems with such people is to avoid hiring them. If they slip through the selection procedure, it may be possible to catch them in the probationary period. Most companies have such a period of from 30 to 90 days (or even up to two years) during which the new employee is on trial and can be dismissed for any reason except union activity. This is the time to find out if the employee is willing to put out the effort to produce in a satisfactory fashion, has good work habits, gets to work every day and on time, has a good attitude toward the job, and gets along well with the other employees. This is the time to get acquainted with the employee and find out if the job suits the person's abilities, interests, ambitions, and plans.

At times employee performance is good during the trial period and then deteriorates. Finding out the cause for this is a supervisory responsibility. The problem may be personal, caused by illness, finances, or difficulties at home. Talking with and listening to the employee may help solve the problem. Frequently all an employee wants is an understanding person to discuss the problem with. If there are company policies that allow assistance in such situations such as an employee loan fund, the supervisor should recommend their use.

Perhaps the problem is caused by recent job changes and more training may be necessary. The employee may not fully understand the job and the responsibilities it includes. The person could be overqualified or underqualified for the job. Here job rotation, job redesign, or job enrichment might work. Personality problems among co-workers may be solved by changing work partners or locating the employee at a different work station.

Negative supervisory attitudes, unfair work assignments, abrupt order-giving, tactless treatment, and belittling can cause job insecurities and erupt into a discipline problem. Obviously developing greater understanding of employee needs and capabilities can go a long way toward preventing discipline problems.

Dealing with offenders

When an employee's behavior or performance is unsatisfactory, the supervisor must talk to the offender. The interview might be simply a friendly inquiry about a slump in performance or a minor rule infraction. For something more serious the interview would be for a reprimand or a penalty. Supervisors must know their people and suit techniques to the person and the situation. A mild reproof or reminder may make more of an impression on one person than a suspension would on another.

Reprimands should be given in private and as soon after the need for it occurs. Since the experience could be a blow to the employee's self-esteem, the offender should be made aware of the unsatisfactory performance in a calm, dignified manner. Punishment should flow directly from the employee's own action, just as a burn comes from touching a hot stove. There should be minimal delay so that the employee won't begin to believe that no punishment is coming. There is no need to be apologetic about assessing a deserved penalty or to say, "I hate doing this to you, but it is a rule and I can't get around it." Shifting the blame from the offender to the company indicates the offense wasn't really serious enough to warrant the penalty. It may also cause the employee to lose respect for the supervisor and make future discipline more difficult.

The supervisor should plan and carry through a reprimand so that offenders have no doubts about:

1. What was unsatisfactory about behavior or performance—what one did that was wrong.
2. Why it was wrong; what rule it violated; what damage it caused; what bad effects it had.
3. What punishment (if any) is being meted out for this offense and why the penalty is a just one.
4. What will happen if one does it again.
5. How one is going to avoid recurrence of the offense, or how one is going to improve performance.

Criticizing performance. It is important to discourage employees or dwell on how poorly they have done and what future mistakes they might make. Supervisors should be sure that when they criticize they are referring only to the particular behavior that is under discussion and not belittling the person by dragging up old mistakes and implying that the offender does everything wrong. Employees need to know that the supervisor has confidence in their ability and intentions to do a good job.

If employees have mishandled an assignment because they made a mistake in judgment, it may be better to let them criticize their own performance and suggest the improvement needed. If they were doing what they thought was right, a severe reprimand may cause them to refuse to accept responsibility or use initiative in the future.

If the shortcoming is poor quality work, carelessness, low production, or lack of effort, the supervisor should try to get employees to analyze job difficulties. It may be that the employee does not understand the purpose of the job, the reasons for the quality requirements, and the cost and trouble caused by errors. The positive side of the requirements should be emphasized so that the employee can see that he or she was at fault; otherwise he or she will consider the reprimand undeserved.

Getting results.   The purpose of the disciplinary interview is to get an improvement in behavior or performance. In order to get employees to make up their minds to do better, the supervisor must appeal to their self-interest. Employees must see the several advantages in changing and accepting the responsibility for making the change. People can change their attitudes and habits for the better if they see the need to do it and if there is sufficient incentive to make it worth their while. When an employee leaves a disciplinary interview, it should be with a plan to do better because it is to his advantage to do so.

Discharge

Discharge is the capital punishment of the industrial world. Employees who are discharged lose the income their families depend on and the benefits they have accumulated.

Because of its seriousness, discharge should be a last resort; and it should be a matter of justice, not a spur-of-the-moment consequence of anger, personality clash, or misunderstanding. Personalities, differences in viewpoint, and honest differences of opinion figure largely in discipline cases. Therefore a proposed discharge should be investigated and approved by authority higher than the immediate supervisor. Because of the possibilities of injustice, there should be provision for appeal. Employees under collective bargaining have a channel of appeal through the grievance machinery. Employees in civil service have an appeal board or commission. People in private business or industry who are not union members may or may not have a formal appeal channel. In the small company they may appeal at the open door of the owner or top manager. In larger companies the personnel department may act as an appeal channel. Employees get a chance to state their case if the personnel department gives every person leaving the company an exit interview before they receive the final paycheck.

Some companies have a policy that a supervisor can discharge a person from the department but not from the company. The personnel department then makes the decision as to whether the individual should be separated from the company or given an opportunity to transfer to a job in another department.

In some cases an employee is given an opportunity to resign rather than have the discharge on record. (The supervisor can mark the record that he or she would not want the individual to work for him or her again.) In a unionized company people who quit under such circumstances may be reinstated. The quit can be processed through the grievance machinery as a discharge if there is evidence that the employee's rights were violated or that the person didn't intend to quit. In matters of work assignments and transfers, for example, if the employee is given only the alternatives of taking it or leaving it—accepting the aissignment or quitting—an arbitrator may call such a quit an unjust discharge.

Whoever is responsible for the behavior of discharged employees during their final hours with the company must see that they are escorted off the property and that they have no opportunity to give vent to their resentment by damaging anything before they leave.

Summary

The rapidly changing environment in which we live and work creates a backdrop of complexity for managers and supervisors. The conflict of value systems among the varied backgrounds of people in an organization can cause problems in the supervision of these people. This is particularly true if the differences exist between superior and subordinate. Differing views about the value of the work ethic and materialistic considerations can cause conflict and discipline problems.

Increasing governmental intervention based on more legislation and compliance requirements add to the complexity of supervisory and managerial assignments. Changes in the work force including more young people, minorities, and career-oriented women have impacted on the role of the manager. Managers and supervisors must recognize the need for even-handed treatment of all employees along with the fact that there are few decisions they can make regarding employees without the involvement of some legislation that relates to those decisions.

Line managers and supervisors are directly concerned with the implementation of such legal requirements as union contracts, affirmative action programs, and occupational safety and health. A considerable part of managerial time is spent in the handling of employee problems. Managerial effectiveness requires the fair implementation of company discipline policies and the adherence to rules and procedures. Even fair policies and rules will be broken by some employees and penalties will have to be imposed. Such penalties should be uniformly applied even though each case should be handled on an individual basis. Any hint of favoritism will only cause unnecessary trouble. Union contracts usually restrict supervisory flexibility in discipline cases. The union steward must be considered and the union contract must be adhered to in these instances. It is therefore necessary that each supervisor fully understand the union contract.

While grievances are often considered formally and established grievance procedure is applied, many employees have informal problems commonly called gripes. These should get supervisory attention before they grow into more complex problems.

Among the common problems are absenteeism, tardiness, alcoholism, drug abuse, and a variety of personal problems. Naturally there are work related problems as well. Pay, promotions, working conditions, and co-workers are numbered among these. Absenteeism and lateness are costly and require close attention. In many cases it will be found that relatively few employees account for the majority of absenteeism and lateness. Many things cause absenteeism and tradiness such as trouble at home, job dissatisfaction, poor transportation, and inadequate supervision.

Even though a union contract and other legal requirements for compliance may require a narrow, legalistic approach to discipline, supervisors should not lose sight of the human relations aspects of handling employee problems. It is generally better to develop understanding and effective work habits than to become a strict disciplinarian. Discharging an employee is a last resort problem solver and should get very careful consideration because of its impact on the employee and the rest of the work group.

CASE 15–1

Ed Donner had worked for the Porter Soap Company for several years. During this period he had become very friendly with Sam Lewis. The men had started together in the management training program, and though Sam progressed more rapidly, the friendship remained strong. When Sam was made department head and became Ed Donner's boss, they went to lunch ot celebrate Sam's promotion, and this was the first time that Lewis became aware of Donner's apparently excessive drinking. Ed had three martinis before lunch, three more drinks with the meal, and one afterward. When Sam remarked about this, Ed replied, "How often does my best friend get to be my boss? Just a little celebration, that's all."

Sam filed away the experience in his memory. Over the next several months, he noticed that Ed was coming in late, frequently took long lunch hours, and sometimes disappeared for an hour or more in the afternoon. He meant to speak to him about it but kept putting it off because he felt awkward about admonishing a friend. The social relationship continued, and Sam noticed that Ed seemed to need the drinks he had on these occasions. He wondered if Ed was becoming a full-blown alcoholic.

Sam was not the only one who noticed Ed Donner's drinking habits. They were a general topic of conversation in the department. The item of particular interest was the fact that Lewis seemed to be protecting his friend, since no disciplinary action occurred. Finally, a couple of people in the department went to Sam's boss, the division manager, and told him about the problem.

The division manager was interested for two reasons. One had to do with the apparent protection of Ed Donner and the other with the relatively poor performance of Sam Lewis's department during the last year. He conducted a careful investigation to determine what action he would take. After careful consideration, he decided to transfer Sam Lewis to head a similar department in another plant and to fire Ed Donner.

1. *Did Sam Lewis help his friend by not facing up to the problem?*
2. *What should he have done?*
3. *Comment on the division manager's approach to the problem.*

CASE 15–2

The Arden Chemical Corporation had its headquarters in New York City. About 1,000 people worked there. All of the senior management and major divisional executives were located at headquarters. In addition, there were several young, bright middle managers who were at headquarters on rotational assignment as part of their development as managers. They were usually assigned to one of the senior executives as staff assistants to learn about that particular area of responsibility.

These assignments were highly sought after, since success on one meant promotion and a good chance at a senior management post.

Dick Farnon was one of the company's bright young men. In his five years with the company he had climbed from management trainee to plant superintendent in the extrusion plant in Boise, Idaho. As vice president of manufacturing, you believed Dick would benefit from a headquarters assignment to your staff, since you are considering him for a post as head of a much larger plant in Pennsylvania.

On a trip to several of the plants, one of your stops is the Boise plant. You take Dick Farnon to lunch and tell him of your desire to move him to headquarters. Dick thanks you but turns down the offer. He goes on to say that he doesn't want to move his family to the New York area. He believes his children will be better off in Idaho, and he and his wife prefer a smaller city where they find life more pleasant. He tells you that he enjoys his job and is still very ambitious, but he draws the line on working in New York.

1. *Should you try to convince Dick to move?*
2. *What can a company do about young, bright managers who won't move to what they consider an undesirable location?*
3. *Should Dick be considered for further promotion if he doesn't accept the New York assignment?*
4. *To what extent should a company make arbitrary assignments of an employee without considering his personal values?*

CASE 15-3

You are the supervisor of a group of clerical workers in a large company. Your department consists of 75 employees, including five first-level supervisors. There are 30 black employees, including one supervisor. Relations have been reasonably good and you haven't experienced any unusual problems.

On the day after returning from the New Year's holiday all 30 black employees, including the black supervisor, crowd into your office, overflowing into the hall. A spokesman for the group (not the supervisor) informs you that they want a paid holiday on Martin Luther King's birthday and that their demand is not negotiable. Either they get the holiday or they will walk off the job. There is no union for employees in your company. After the request and the noisy murmurs subsequent to it have died down, you tell them to return to work and you will speak to the personnel vice president about their request.

1. *What will you suggest to the personnel manager?*
2. *Do the black employees have a justifiable request?*
3. *Should a company that employs large numbers of black employees consider a racial holiday?*
4. *What will you do if the request is denied and the blacks walk off the job?*

CASE 15-4

The following story recently appeared in the newspaper:

Washington, D.C. Triangle Industries has agreed to pay $748,202 in back wages to 1,600 underpaid women employees, the Labor Department said.

  The maker of electrical equipment agreed to begin processing the payments after the Supreme Court upheld a government lawsuit in the case, the department reported. The suit, filed in 1970, had charged the company with paying female workers less than men employees in violation of the Equal Pay Act of 1963.

You are the personnel director of a similar company. Your work force is 40 percent female. You read the article over twice. You have had no trouble to date.

1. *What will you do now?*
2. *Should you wait for a Labor Department investigation?*
3. *Should you check on other companies in your area?*
4. *Should you bring the matter to the attention of higher management?*

CASE 15-5

When Charlie Adams was made the manager of the computer programming section, he made company history. He was the first black supervisor they ever had. It was a great day for Charlie, but several of his new subordinates were very unhappy, and some were heard to remark that they just wouldn't take orders from a black.

Adams was faced with several cases of insubordination during his first two weeks on the job. Although he was a first-rate programmer and had worked with many of his new subordinates during the six years he had been with the company, he was the only black in the section. He had never socialized with his co-workers, either.

After experiencing insubordination several times, he went to his boss and was told to be patient. "After all, you are our Jackie Robinson, and it will take the employees some time to get used to you as their boss," his superior said.

One morning he asked one of the programmers to work on a rush job and was told to "go to hell." He went to his boss again and was told to invite the employee for a cup of coffee in the cafeteria and try to iron out the differences. Charlie Adams now stopped being a nice guy and become an arbitrary disciplinarian. He felt management was not backing him up at all. Morale went from bad to worse in the section and Adams didn't know where to turn.

1. *What can Charlie Adams do?*
2. *How should management have helped him?*
3. *Should he have been promoted in the first place? Why? Why not?*
4. *Can he stay with the company?*

CASE 15–6

Ross, White, and Benjamin is a large advertising agency located in a central city. It employs about 350 people, about two thirds of them classified as creative employees. These include copywriters and artists. Ross, White, and Benjamin has built its reputation on being a very creative agency. Its ads have won several prizes; it has had little difficulty in keeping clients satisfied. In fact, it has become an "in" agency, and clients are seeking it out rather than the other way around. The key to the agency's success has been its distinctive copy, which has won awards and sold clients' products with equal success.

One day recently the agency's administrative vice president received a memorandum signed by ten of the most successful copywriters on the payroll. The essence of the memo was that they no longer wanted to work the regular 9 to 5 workday, five days a week. What they wanted was to come in as they pleased, to work at home, and to spend no more than two days a week physically on the premises of the agency. Their argument was based on the idea that creative work should not be on a time schedule. In fact, they said, much of their best work to date had been done at home. They also felt that their success record entitled them to this request and that they preferred to be measured by results rather than adherence to fixed working hours which suited the company's convenience.

1. *What should the vice president do?*
2. *Is the request a legitimate one?*
3. *What would granting of the request of the ten best writers do to the rest of the staff?*
4. *Should highly successful employees of this kind be allowed such flexibility?*

CASE 15–7

The company employs a number of female employees to perform the intricate wiring and soldering tasks necessary in the assembly of complex control panels. It was found that women could generally perform this type of work better than men. Beverly was one of the first women hired by the company, and she came with considerable work experience in similar jobs at other companies in the area. According to the production manager she proved to be an excellent worker, performing her assigned tasks with speed and efficiency. He felt she set an excellent work example for the others who were hired to perform the same kind of work.

Difficulty started when the general manager noticed that Beverly wore particularly tight, form-fitting slacks. He mentioned this to the production manager, since he believed this type of apparel was not proper and would cause distraction among the male employees. The production manager replied that he hadn't noticed any distraction taking place but that he would speak to Beverly about her apparel. When he did, she became quite adamant, stating that she felt she could wear anything she desired unless the company furnished a uniform. She also mentioned that she could get a similar position in a variety of other plants in the vicinity and that none of her previous employers found any fault with her clothing. The production manager let the matter drop because she was an excellent worker and she would be difficult to replace in the tight labor market which existed. He did wonder however, what he was going to tell the general manager.

1. *Does a company have any right to specify what an employee will wear on the job?*
2. *Should the general manager have gotten involved in this matter?*
3. *Did the production manager handle the problem effectively?*
4. *What can he tell the general manager in view of the result of his conversation with the girl and his own opinions?*
5. *Whatever would you do if confronted with Beverly's reaction?*

CASE 15–8

Bob Ford was a management trainee in a large casualty insurance company. He had been hired 18 months previously and was now in the latter stages of the program. His present assignment was in one of the large branches the company had in an urban center. Most of his work involved experience analysis of the many large policyholders serviced by this branch.

John Crane, the branch manager, had mentioned the possibility of a permanent assignment to the branch when the training period was completed. Bob reacted favorably, since he admired Crane and they got along well. During a recent review Crane told him that he was the best trainee assigned to the branch since Crane had been manager. Naturally Bob was pleased with this compliment and looked forward to the promised permanent assignment.

An opening developed at the branch when one of the senior analysts was transferred to company headquarters. Though Bob had not fully completed the training program, Crane offered him the position, thinking him fully qualified for the opening. Bob accepted and was told by his boss that the formal request was going in to the headquarters personnel department that day and he should be ready to move into the job in two weeks, when the incumbent's transfer was to take place.

Crane went to the company's headquarters the next day for a meeting with his superior. In the course of the discussion Crane was told about the company's affirmative action plan, which they were required to file under fair employment practices legislation. Crane's boss went on to say that the company had to promote more women to responsible positions, and since there was an opening in Crane's branch they were going to promote a young woman in the management training program to fill the opening. This woman had only been with the company 11 months and still had a considerable learning period to face.

Crane was flabbergasted and told his boss of the offer to Bob Ford and its acceptance. The boss refused to listen and said that adherence to the affirmative action plan was paramount, since the company's record was less than desirable in the area of equal employment opportunity. Crane asked what he was going to tell young Ford, and the boss replied, "Tell him not to worry; he'll get the next opening."

"Why, all we are doing is practicing reverse discrimination and not paying much attention to qualifications either," said Crane. "That's about it," the boss replied.

1. *Should a company practice reverse discrimination to comply with civil rights legislation?*
2. *What can Mr. Crane tell Bob Ford?*
3. *What should Ford do?*
4. *What are the moral arguments pro and con for affirmative action programs to reverse discrimination?*

CASE 15–9

Bob Jensen is the chief engineer of State Electric and Power, a large utility company in the midwest. State, a progressive company, had been conducting research for several years in a search for more effective ways to produce electricity. Most of the plants used either oil or natural gas to develop energy, and it was obvious that other sources had to be explored.

Jensen had been with State Electric for 30 years, and he was considered an excellent, innovative engineer who was very conservative in his relationships with peers, superiors, and subordinates. During the last three years he served on the company's research committee which monitored both the research efforts and the budget needed to support them.

Among the projects being studied were solar energy, methane gas derived from garbage and other vegetable waste such as corn stalks and nuclear energy. The most promising possibility seemed to be nuclear fuel. Many other utilities were using it and they appeared to have few problems with its use. Records of other plants around the country were checked, and after considerable deliberation top management decided to go ahead and file for a permit with the public utility commission in the state.

Jensen was asked to assemble an engineering team to work on the project, and he turned to his brightest people, all of whom he believed would jump at the chance to work on the project. He was right about the first four he spoke to. When he asked Don Henry, a brilliant young engineer, he was met with a cold stare. "If this company wants to go nuclear, I'm not going to help it!" "What's more, I'll testify against the permit at the PUC hearing."

1. *What should Jensen do about Don Henry?*
2. *If an employee is unhappy with his company's plans should he do more than quit?*
3. *To what extent is Don Henry being unreasonable?*
4. *What might his future be?*

CASE 15–10

About two years ago I became the company's controller, replacing my close friend, Lou Schmitt, who is a few years older than I am. Lou started with the company 14 years ago when he finished college as an honors graduate in accounting. He worked as an internal auditor and then a tax accountant. Lou got along very well with other accountants who respected him for his knowledge and confidence when discussing technical matters. Even though he was shy and somewhat withdrawn with other people, he was promoted six years ago to the tax division head. He continued to get along well with his subordinates, who admired his professional competence. In his new job, however, he had to deal with other division heads in the company and with various government agencies. Here he got into difficulty with his rather narrow, scholarly, and accounting based approach to all problems.

Complaints about his relationships began to mount, finally causing the company president to take some action. Not wanting to lose Lou's accounting knowledge, but recognizing his apparent lack of interpersonal skills, the president made him controller since this position was largely involved with the development of and presentation of financial data to top executives and working with the company's financial vice president. Six months in the new position indicated that Lou was not able to handle this responsibility either. The president demoted him to a job as a staff assistant with less important responsibilities. Lou's demotion was probably further saddening since I was named as his replacement.

After this our relationship became quite strained, and Lou began to drink excessively, causing increased absenteeism and more interpersonal problems. I finally confronted him with his growing alcoholism, and he finally sought professional help. He has not been drinking for six months, but our relationship is still strained to say the least. The other day the president told me that Lou's salary would have to be reduced to reflect more accurately his present level of responsibility.

1. *How can Lou's boss and rather close friend handle the salary reduction?*
2. *Does a company have any responsibility when one of its executives fails in a job and seeks escape with alcohol?*
3. *Should Lou be retained by the company?*
4. *Would Lou do better if he left voluntarily to try a new position elsewhere?*
5. *Did the president treat Lou fairly?*

Chapter 16

Learning objectives

○ To understand the complexity and universal nature of change and its relationship to managing people

○ To analyze the change process in perspective and develop an understanding of its impact on organizations

○ To identify factors causing resistance to change and how managers and supervisors may effectively deal with such resistance

○ To become aware of processes that can assist in the implementation of needed change in an organization

Managing change

Major topics

The nature of change.

Change in perspective.

Employee problems and change.

Managing change.

The supervisor and change.

Higher management and change.

Resistance to change.

Organizational development.

Change has become the big story of the 1970s. Books, magazines, newspapers, and television all give us varied views of this story and how change is influencing all segments of our society. Some of the stories predict doom for our way of life and attribute many of society's ills to the rapid pace of change. Others look upon change as a challenge and opportunity and see a better world with increased leisure time, a healthier population, and better working conditions. As the old saying goes, "You pays your money and you takes your choice."

No doubt there is evidence to support both viewpoints and any individual can find negative and positive factors in any change. In fact, that is part of the fascination of managing change from an organizational viewpoint and coping with change from an individual viewpoint. The current emphasis on environmental issues is a case in point. Emission control on automobiles represents a cost, pricing, and production problem for the car manufacturer, but it means increased business to the producer of control devices. Getting rid of waste in factories and homes causes increased costs and a variety of other problems, but it is creating new jobs, new companies, and new technology to produce recycling equipment and other types of waste-processing equipment. Jet aircraft may pollute the environment with both noise and noxious fumes, but the young couple going on a low-cost charter flight to Hawaii do not think about pollution, nor does the travel agency whose increased business is based on the rapidity of the jet plane. Increased crime is a significant problem to police agencies and a cause of considerable worry to company managers and individuals in and around large cities, but it means more jobs for security guards and more business for the companies producing locks, alarms, and other security devices. Change has a variety of dimensions—some good, some bad, and some not at either extreme but nevertheless a source of problems and opportunities.

From the individual manger's viewpoint, change must be recognized as a way of organizational life. In the management of change, the manager should see change as a constant that permeates life. Being a constant, change has been with us since the dawn of time and human beings have coped with and adapted to change throughout history. The present problem confronting the supervisor, however, is the rapid acceleration of change that has occurred in recent years and that gives every promise of continuing at an increased rate in the immediate future. Although the supervisor is principally concerned with work changes, this does not diminish the impact of change, because every alteration of the environment can lead to a work change.

The nature of change

If the tempo of change has increased, so has the complexity of its nature. In a recent book, Peter Drucker visualizes us as entering into an age of discontinuity, and he believes his book to be an "early warning system." He describes major discontinuities as existing in four areas:

1. Genuinely new technologies are upon us. They are almost certain to create new major industries and brand-new major businesses and to render obsolete at the same time existing major industries and big businesses. . . . The coming decades in technology are more likely to resemble the closing decades of the last century, in which a major industry based on new technology surfaced every few years, than they will resemble the technological and industrial continuity of the past 50 years.

2. We face major changes in the world's economy. In economic policies and theories, we still act as if we lived in an "international" economy, in which separate nations are the units, dealing with one another primarily through international trade and fundamentally as different from one another in their economy as they are different in language or laws or cultural tradition. But imperceptibly there has emerged a world economy in which common information generates the same economic appetites, aspirations, and demands—cutting across national boundaries and languages and largely disregarding political ideologies as well. The world has become, in other words, *one market,* one global shopping center. . . . It is not yet a viable economy. . . . Either we learn how to restore the capacity for development that the nineteenth century possessed in such ample measure—under conditions for development that are quite different—or the twentieth century will make true, as Mao and Castro expect, the prophecy of class war, the sidetracking of which was the proudest achievement of the generation before World War I. Only the war now would be between races rather than classes.

3. The political matrix of social and economic life is changing fast. Today's society and polity are pluralistic. Every single social task of importance today is entrusted to a large institution organized for perpetuity and run by managers. Where the assumptions that govern what we expect and see are still those of the individualistic society of eighteenth-century liberal theory, the reality that governs our behavior is that of organized, indeed overorganized, power concentrations.

Yet we are also approaching a turning point in this trend. Everywhere there is rapid disenchantment with the biggest and fastest growing of these institutions, modern government, as well as cynicism regarding its ability to perform. We are becoming equally critical of the other organized institutions; revolt is occurring simultaneously in the Catholic Church and the big university. The young everywhere are indeed, rejecting *all* institutions with equal hostility. . . .

4. But the most important of the changes is the last one. Knowledge, during the last few decades, has become the central capital, the cost center, and the crucial resource of the economy. This changes labor forces and work, teaching and learning, and the meaning of knowledge and its politics. But it also raises the problem of the responsibilities of the new men of power, the men of knowledge.[1]

Drucker has a reputation for controversy, and we may not agree with his prophecies, but his observations are based on realities which already exist. The years ahead may not produce the results Drucker predicts, but there is

---

[1] Peter F. Drucker, *The Age of Discontinuity* (New York: Harper & Row, Publishers, 1969), pp. ix–xi.

no doubt that basic changes will take place in many areas that will affect the organizations in our society and the chain reaction will certainly cause supervisors to cope with problems undreamed of today.

You will note that Drucker's predictions have several implications for managers and supervisors. The nature of these changes seem to be external in the sense that no one organization can or is causing them. Yet the supervisor will be directly affected by such things as economic and political changes, the knowledge explosion, and the development of new technologies, all of these occurring at a more rapid pace than in the past.

Change may be considered as a constant, yet resistance to change remains as a complex supervisory problem. The supervisor must bear the brunt of change implementation with employees who may pride themselves on the possession of modern gadgets, air conditioners, color television, and automobiles as symbols of welcome change but who tend to fiercely resist changes in their jobs which upset traditional behavior patterns and perceptions of security. Managers must be able to cope with this ambivalent feeling about change among employees if they are to be fully effective.

Change in perspective

Predicting the future has been a favorite pastime through the ages. From the soothsayers of old who read the entrails of goats to their modern counterparts, the econometricians, operations research technicians, and corporate planners who develop elaborate and complex computer models for forecasting tomorrow's events, human beings remain fascinated with the future. Witness the popularity of astrology with practically every newspaper having a column which allows one to see what tomorrow will bring by checking his or her birth date against the appropriate astrology sign. This is even true of those individuals who firmly resist change and prefer the status quo.

While change is a certainty, its shape and dimensions are difficult to determine. None of the predictors or forecasters has been very effective at the task. It is interesting to note that even though some knowledge of principles was available in the 1930s nobody predicted such widely accepted present things as atomic energy, jet propulsion, antibiotics, and computers. While space travel was dreamed about for hundreds of years and the "Buck Rogers" comic strip was placed in the 25th century, the Russian Sputnik shook us out of our dream, and real technology was developed for our successful moon landings.

Perhaps a more useful way of dealing with change is not to try and divine the future but to look at the past. At least there we have some concrete facts about change which may increase our understanding of the process. To gain some grasp of the relative speed of change, a short look at human history proves enlightening. Starting with the premise that human beings populated our planet about 50,000 years ago, it was only in the last 10,000 years that they moved out of caves into other types of shelter. Of all the energy consumed by the human race over its history, half of it has been consumed in the last 100 years. Transportation, which we look upon as a necessity, has had a fascinating development. Around 5,000 B.C. camel caravans covered six to eight miles an hour. Three thousand five hundred years later the chariot appeared and could cover 20 miles an hour. This speed was not improved upon until the late 1880s when steam locomotives were developed with a speed that approached 100 miles an hour if the track was carefully laid. Time for change now started to condense since it was only 50 years later that some military aircraft could fly over 200 miles an hour. By the end of World War II in 1945, jet aircraft had been developed which approached speeds of 600 miles an hour. In the last 30 years supersonic aircraft fly at over 2,000 miles an hour, and space vehicles approach 25,000 miles an hour.

Product development from concept to commercial use presents another perspective. The following list demonstrates this.

Typewriter	150 years
Canning food	100 years
Telephone	56 years
Radio	35 years
Radar	15 years
Television	12 years

At present we can see the rapidity of product development since many examples exist. The electronic calculator, video games, and teflon-coated cookware are a few examples of the space age miracles we are presently using. People are working on jobs in companies producing such things as computers, silicon chips, microcircuits, petrochemicals, and plastics which did not exist a short 30 years ago.

So a brief look at the history of change demonstrates its increasing rapidity as well as its constancy. We can only assume that this acceleration will increase and that the magnitude of change will have an even greater impact on our lives. Certainly those managers who prefer the status quo will find it extremely difficult to function.

Employee problems and change

Each workday supervisors are faced with a variety of tasks. Among those which occupy most of their time are problems generated by the employees reporting to them and the changes caused by improved technology, new knowledge, organizational dynamics, and our society in general. In some instances, they can do little about either employee problems or change because they are beyond their areas of responsibility and control. But an awareness of problems and change around them will help supervisors understand its impact on the group and the company as a whole.

Several writers believe that the rapid pace of change has a great deal of influence on individual behavior and that many problems we encounter are associated with this influence. A good case can be made to support this contention, at least in part. Just by looking at current newspaper and magazine article titles, supervisors can become better informed on the nature of change and its possible relationship to employee problems they face on the job. A recent sampling will demonstrate the point:

HAS THE UNITED STATES GIVEN UP FIGHTING INFLATION?

GASOLINE DEALERS PLAN TWO-DAY SHUTDOWN

BREAKDOWNS INCREASE ON COMMUTER LINE

SUBWAY EMPLOYEES PLAN SLOWDOWN

FOOD AND FUEL PRICES CONTINUE TO RISE

RAILROAD CONDUCTORS PLAN STRIKE

HIGH COST OF ALCOHOLISM SPURS NEW COMPANY PROGRAMS

DISSIDENTS' OCCUPATION OF PLANT ENDS FOLLOWING ARREST OF TWO LEADERS

TWO MANUFACTURING COMPANIES PLAN MERGER

COMPANY WILL EXPAND LOCAL FACILITIES

MANUFACTURER WILL CLOSE PLANT BY NOVEMBER 1

LATEST COMPUTERS SEE, HEAR, SPEAK, SING, AND MAY OUTTHINK MAN

WOMEN INCREASINGLY SUE UNDER EQUAL PAY ACT

MANAGERIAL WASTE AND INEFFICIENCY TURNS OFF MORE WORKERS THAN JOB BOREDOM

CORPORATE SOCIAL AUDIT BECOMES MORE COMMON

FOUR-DAY WEEK ON STREAM IN MANY CONCERNS

COMPANY LETS EMPLOYEES CHOOSE WORKING HOURS

MIDDLE MANAGERS REVOLTING AGAINST CORPORATE LIFE

EARLY RETIREMENTS INCREASING

GOVERNMENT TO PROBE COMPANY'S PRODUCTS

These 20 headlines all have one thing in common: None was caused by a particular manager or supervisor. Yet they all impact on managers' and supervisors' job performance in one way or another. All of the transportation problems can cause lateness and absenteeism. Rising prices and inflation cause salary and wage problems. Emotional problems such as alcoholism and drug abuse cause discipline and morale problems. Pressures from women and minorities cause job matching, promotion, and selection problems. Innovations such as flexible time and the four-day work week can cause pressures from employees for similar treatment or support their arguments that lateness is no big deal. Technology changes can cause insecurities among employees who may wonder if they will be next. Merger and plant closing news can worry supervisors and employees alike about the possibilities in their own company.

The implication of the headlines above is that managing change and related employee problems is complex; supervisors need a high degree of skill and extensive knowledge to be able to cope with their jobs. They also need the support of all levels of management in the organization. They need sound, modern policies, rules, and procedures to back up their decisions.

Managing change

Before one can do anything about an activity that has an effect on the managerial process, one must develop an understanding of that activity. Understanding change is no exception. Perhaps one way of approaching this understanding is to recognize that change has both an external and an internal dimension as it relates to a particular organization. Changes can occur in society at large which may have little effect on an individual organization. Many companies and other organizations in the country continue to use time-honored methods and procedures in the face of advancing technology. Of course this approach may lead to difficulties—witness the problems of many stock brokerage firms with their back-office or clerical operations. Nevertheless, some companies seem insulated from the changes occurring in society. As mentioned in Chapter 12, they may be those which are less growth- and development-minded and are in relatively stable industries.

On the other hand, many organizations are directly affected by change in the society. In many large cities changes in the ethnic and racial population, educational changes, social and political pressures, and a changing labor market have caused many employers to hire large numbers of minority group members for clerical work. For some of these employers, this has meant a considerable increase in training cost not only for the new employees but for supervisors who have responsibility for these new employees. Among the nonbusiness organizations which are going through similar experiences are the colleges and universities, which are now actively recruiting minority groups and have experienced a variety of problems for which they were not prepared.

The quotation from Peter Drucker's book earlier in this chapter indicates several factors which are present realities and which he believes will have a direct bearing on the future of this society. There are several other present realities which give every indication of having a future effect on organizations in this country. The ever-increasing level of education of our population, with more young people going on to college, and the great increase in adult education will certainly have wide impact on such things as the quality of the labor supply, the level of aspiration of individuals, demand for various products and other marketing implications, and a host of other possibilities.

The change in our population mix as far as its age is concerned is another factor having a direct bearing on the way organizations operate. In 1960, more than half of our population was over 33 years of age. In 1970, more than half was under 25 years old. In one decade, we have seen a change from people who had their formative years during the Depression dominating our society to a majority who were born after World War II. Any business organization that employs large numbers of young people and has many supervisors who are in their forties and fifties is already experiencing the impact of the generation gap in the number and type of problems and the ways they are handled.

Anyone marveling at the magnificent effort which placed our astronauts on the moon should recognize the complex organizations required for the accomplishment of this feat. Organizations are getting more complex, and it is entirely possible that private corporations will be unable to meet all of the needs of the society. We may see more private-public corporations such as Comsat and Amtrak developed to fill needs with which private industry may be reluctant or unable to cope.

The internal view.   The point of the above discussion is to demonstrate that there is a societal frame of reference for each organization in our society. Some may be more directly and more rapidly affected by general changes in the society than others, but each will have to reckon with the external developments which take place if they are to continue their existence.

In a sense, given the above societal frame of reference, most of the chapters in this book deal with aspects of internal change. Planning, work measurement, methods improvement, organization development, personnel planning, and training all imply change and what the supervisor can do to cope with it. In other words, individual supervisors are both agents of change and implementers of change. An individual supervisor may not be aware of certain broad changes in the society, but he or she must train ten minority group members assigned to the department. The supervisor may also have to learn how to deal with a larger influx or college graduates, though he or she is only a high school graduate. Advancing technology may mean nothing more to supervisors than a changed method or procedure which they have to introduce to the work force and then help them understand it and overcome their resistance to the changes it implies. The changes that have most meaning for them are those that affect their jobs and the jobs for which they are responsible. Of particular significance will be those changes which diminish or increase their importance in the organization.

One such possibility may result from the current emphasis on organizational change based on changes in the entire approach to supervision. Organizational climate, sensitivity training, Theory Y assumptions and other nonauthoritarian approaches mentioned in this book may have a very direct bearing on the nature of the organization itself. It is possible that the formal organization structure, with its traditional bureaucratic processes, may be supplanted by more democratic approaches to supervision. Warren Bennis, a well-known behavioral scientist, has put it this way:

> It seems to me that we have seen over the past decade a fundamental change in the basic philosophy which underlies managerial behavior, reflected most of all in the following three areas:
>
> 1.   A new concept of *man*, based on increased knowledge of his complex and shifting needs, which replaces the oversimplified, innocent push-button idea of man.

2. A new concept of *power*, based on collaboration and reason, which replaces a model of power based on coercion and fear.

3. A new concept of *organizational values*, based on humanistic-democratic ideals, which replaces the depersonalized mechanistic value system of bureaucracy.[2]

Jay Forester of the Massachusetts Institute of Technology proposes a new corporate design which will include the 11 following characteristics:

1. Elimination of the superior-subordinate relationship.
2. Individual profit centers.
3. Objective determination of compensation.
4. Policy making separated from decision making.
5. Restructuring through electronic data processing.
6. Freedom of access to information.
7. Elimination of internal monopolies.
8. Balancing reward and risk.
9. Mobility of the individual.
10. Enhanced rights of the individual.
11. Education within the corporation.[3]

The proposals made by Bennis and Forrester may seem radical, but anyone with a sense of perspective and a recognition of what has happened in the last 30 years in our organizations would have to say that they have at least a chance of being adopted in the future.

In fact there are many things happening at present which give indication of the dynamics of change. Various approaches to participative processes in European companies have created an interest in this country. One example is co-determination in private sector companies in West Germany. There, labor unions are represented on the boards of directors by union members, and at least one union in this country, the United Auto Workers, has become interested in this approach.

Many young people, now in their early 30s, who graduated from college in the turbulent 1960s, are in staff and lower level managerial positions in many organizations. They bring a different value system to the workplace along with greater impatience for traditional approaches and an independence and mobility that is quite different from their predecessors. Greater emphasis on the quality of life in organizations is another growing area of interest. Unions are making this an issue in collective bargaining, and the legal dimensions mentioned in the prior chapter demonstrate government pressures in this area.

Job security is another issue appearing in more and more union negotiations, and if this idea grows, it will curtail such things as layoffs, arbitrary

[2] Warren G. Bennis, "The Idea of Change," in William G. Scott, *Organization Concepts and Analysis* (Belmont, Calif.: Dickenson Publishing Co., 1969), p. 148.

[3] Jay W. Forrester, "A New Corporate Design," in Paul Pigors, Charles A. Myers, and F. T. Main, *Management of Human Resources* (New York: McGraw-Hill Book Co., 1969), pp. 229–43.

firing, and job mobility. Some European countries require as much as three years severance pay for a fired employee. If this catches on in America, it will cut down on firings in union and nonunion organizations as well as increase costs and impinge on supervisory and managerial prerogatives.

The concepts of due process and personal privacy are also getting increasing publicity. Both of these concepts are part of American jurisprudence, but they have had little workplace application. The exception is formal grievance procedure written into several union contracts and also practiced by many nonunion employers. However, there is growing pressure for other applications. Employees are beginning to question the methodology used for determining promotions and the job relatedness of performance appraisals. Some want to participate in the decision process leading to a promotion. In the area of privacy there is some discussion on the handling of confidential personnel files. Employees want to see these, and they also want negative items removed after a period of time has passed. Where these ideas will lead is anyone's guess. There is no doubt, however, that our society will produce other ideas and concepts which, if implemented, will mean drastic change for managers and supervisors.

The supervisor and change

Since management is responsible for the internal changes in an organization, it is necessary for them to consider the impact of these changes on employees. The employee can react positively or negatively to changes, and how supervisors implement change has a direct bearing on this reaction.

Let us look at a typical change which occurs with some frequency in all organizations. This is the promotion of one individual in the hierarchy and the chain of events it sets off. A vice president is promoted to executive vice president because of a retirement, thereby creating an opening in the prior position. This is filled by promoting a department head to the vice presidency and another opening is created. The department head's position is filled by someone heading a smaller department, and this job is filled by an assistant department head. A first-level supervisor is now moved to a middle manager's job, thus creating an opening on the first level of management for an employee as well as an open job in the work force. This example is a simple chain which could be complicated by geographical location of each job, functional differences, and the availability of promotable people in the company.

When the above type of change takes place it means new bosses for many people and the insecurities this usually creates. Clear, concise, and rapid communications of promotions is a partial way of minimizing insecurity. Some companies make the error of using a conditional title such as "acting department head" for a number of reasons, one of which usually is lack of confidence in the person given the title. This is a poor way to introduce a new boss to the job and employees. If people are worth putting in the job, they shouldn't be given conditional titles.

Information and change. All levels of management should be kept informed of pending changes on a need-to-know basis. Communication is vital to change implementation, as it stops rumors and aids supervisors to support the change by making them the most knowledgeable people in their areas of responsibility. Whenever possible, group participation in the change process is desirable. It can help in overall understanding, and it gives the participants an incentive to support and implement the change. Group acceptance of change can even help bring some skeptics into line, since peer pressure may convince them of the error of their ways.

The supervisor who can firmly promise that no one will lose a job because of a contemplated change in technology or jobs has a strong argument for employee cooperation. Company offers of retraining at its expense can also help diminish the insecurities of job changes caused by new techniques or equipment.

Obviously first-level supervisors must believe in the change for effective implementation to take place. It will be difficult for them to fool subordinates if they do not support the change. Because of their importance to the change process, first-level supervisors should be brought into the decision making relative to the change as early as possible. They must really be treated as managers if they are to be successful change agents.

Supervisors are frequently the key in recognizing the need for change. Their assessment of group morale and reporting of reasons for absenteeism, labor turnover, and grievance frequency can serve as an excellent source for possible job or procedure changes. Fully utilizing the first-level supervisor as both a change initiator and change implementer is a worthwhile practice for higher levels of management.

The supervisor usually deals with the bulk of discipline problems, some caused by internal changes and others by various external forces such as those indicated in the 20 headlines, listed earlier. Of course many discipline problems may be difficult to trace to change unless we accept the idea that increased pressures in our society, changing values, and the decreased importance of work in the minds of some people constitute major reasons for negative employee behavior.

Higher management and change

While communication of contemplated changes is vital to its successful implementation, there are other dimensions to consider. Human judgments have their frailty and senior management must be particularly careful in this area. The goal-setting process for change should be handled thoroughly. In the first place the goals must be realistic. There is a natural human failure in the impatience which occurs once a complex change is decided upon. It is similar to the individual who takes over a year to decide on buying an expensive color televison set and then wants it delivered and installed within an hour of purchase.

At times top management may not understand why there is a considerable time lag between their decision and organizationwide implementation. Underestimating the time necessary for the change process can cause undue pressure on middle managers and first-level supervisors. It can also cause error, expense, and lack of confidence in the change itself. Even relatively simple changes cause some upset so one can imagine the difficulty involved when a complex computer system is introduced. Organization structure changes also take considerable time to implement fully. Because they deal with changes in reporting relationships and status changes, they can be quite traumatic to the people directly affected. The author was involved in the redesign of the first-level supervisor's job in a large, complex organization. It took five years for the new job to be established fully throughout the organization. Even though there was support for this change on all levels of management and wide participation in the process of development, there was resistance from many middle managers who believed they were being downgraded in authority. Some first-level supervisors who were functioning as technicians also resisted since they really didn't want any managerial responsibility.

It is easy to see the desirability of broad participation in the change process. The top management that recognizes this will gain easier acceptance of the change and it will be introduced more effectively. Once the goals are established realistically, cooperation on every organizational level is necessary. Cooperation is easier to obtain when people have been a part of the change process from its beginning and they understand the reasons for it.

Resistance to change

Among the many problems managers face, none is more difficult to handle than resistance to change perhaps because of the frequency of occurrence and the increasingly rapid pace of change mentioned earlier.

The success of an enterprise depends upon making changes that will enable it to keep up or get ahead in its field. Companies race to be the first on the market with a new product. They buy new equipment that will do the job faster and better. They devise new systems to handle the increase in paper work. They reorganize part or all of the company to meet problems of growth and change. They introduce new procedures, methods, techniques, work rules, and standards. They rearrange desks and equipment to fit changes in the work flow.

All of these changes must be introduced and accepted at the work level if they are to be put into successful operation. But some changes provoke hostility, restriction of output, grievances, sabotage, refusal to cooperate, errors, tears, work stoppages, absences, and quits. New equipment designed to increase output may instead result in a drop in production. For example, an engineer says of the reaction to a newly installed incentive wage system: "You'd think that people would jump at the chance to make just as much money as they're willing to work for. But no. The morning the rate goes into effect, there're more people in the nurse's office than at the machines."

"I don't want to maintain the status quo—I want to return to the status was."

Reprinted by permission The Wall Street Journal

Resistance to change is a common characteristic of human behavior.

It's up to the supervisor to introduce and get compliance with changes that are originated by others and to make improvements and changes on his own. The supervisor is the one who must somehow adapt changes to fit the needs of employees and help them adapt to fit the demands of the change.

Motives for resisting change. Not every change is resisted. People ask for changes that they feel will be an improvement. Some people actively seek new experiences—promotions, more interesting work, more responsibility.

Whatever people do, they are seeking the things they feel will be to their advantage. And conversely, they oppose things (and that includes changes) that they feel will be to their disadvantage. "Advantage" in this sense is psychological, since it is the person's private notion of what constitutes self-interest. One's idea of what is to one's advantage is based upon what one thinks is possible to accomplish and what is thought desirable. And this may be something quite different from what management expects it to be. The theory of economic man was based on the idea that everyone is motivated to make the maximum amount of money. Some people are, but probably not too many. People restrict their output—and thereby their earnings—when they feel that it is in their own self-interest to do so.

Actually, everyone has a great many motives, and no two people have quite the same assortment. Each individual therefore has personal and particular concerns over what a proposed change in the job is going to mean. Furthermore, the individual's attitude is affected by the attitude of the group. People on the job fit themselves into social groups to get a feeling of belonging in an environment of uncertainties. These groups, known as informal organizations, are described in Chapter Three. The group takes on a character of its own and dictates the behavior of its members. It puts pressure on members to resist changes that might upset group stability. If the group is hostile to the company, its members look upon change as just another management trick to get something more out of them.

Fear and insecurity are at the roots of much of the hostility toward changes originated by management. People fear the loss of the job itself or the loss of some of their psychological advantages—status, for instance. The prospect of unemployment is a frightening one that makes people take strange measures—restricton of output, for example—to protect their jobs. When a person behaves badly on a job one is trying to protect, one seems to be cutting off one's nose to spite one's face. Changes in technology carry a threat that the job will be abolished or changed so that a person's particular skills will no longer be needed.

If major changes are introduced in a time of business expansion, a company may be able to guarantee that employees will be reassigned or retrained rather than cut off the payroll. But job security encompasses more than money. People come to feel that they *own* their particular jobs and the status attached to them. This is all to the good under stable conditions; it is the basis of their taking responsibility for getting out the work and taking pride in the company, using initiative, and cooperating with others. But pride and personal involvement in the job make an employee vulnerable to the threat of loss of power or prestige. People who have influence in the present setup may be afraid of losing it in a change, and they have a real stake in proving that the change can't possibly work. Some people feel that a change in their job implies a criticism of the way they were performing it; they too are eager to prove that the new arrangement is no better.

Status problems of change.   Status anxiety exists on all levels of the organization, and people are angered, frustrated, and humiliated by changes that curtail their authority. The introduction of a computer may spread resentment throughout a company when the change of system deprives people of authority to use their own discretion in handling accounts.

A person's job and status in the work group become part of that person's self-image. Revising it downward is painful, and the prospect of being "told" by some newcomer is galling. Older employees suffer in a change because they see themselves in danger of losing the advantage they won by getting there first. In an office this advantage might be knowledge of the company's paper work-handling procedures. If these are changed, they will lose status as experts. Furthermore, they may be shifted to jobs in which they may not be so adequate. Skilled employees suffer much the same kind of severe blow to their egos if they must move to a less-skilled job.

Changes in relationships between people on the job are loaded with conflicts. A group at work has its status system: Some jobs have higher status (are "higher class") than others. People within the system develop ways of working together, adjusting to the system, and helping each other. If a change of duties reverses the relationship and has the low-status person giving orders to the high-status person, the two people may be unable to work together. Such problems can be avoided if the supervisor protects the status system when changes are introduced to the department.

Preparing people for changes. Sometimes people's only objection to a change is that it was sprung as a surprise or forced on them. Independent, energetic, provident people want to feel that they have some control over their destinies, and they want some say about their jobs. What's more, they feel that they are in a better position than anyone else to know the things that need changing. They resent the implication that they are workhorses but not bright enough or important enough to be consulted. If they are left out of the planning, the company is the loser.

Changes should be discussed in advance with the people who will be affected by them. Their questions should be solicited, their fears, problems, and objections drawn out and discussed. Companies installing computers have found it necessary to develop long-range plans for giving employees detailed information about the changeover—just what each one's job will be at each stage of the change and what it will be when the installation is completed. One company admitted an oversight: It forgot to prepare employees in unaffected departments that would be receiving employees transferred from clerical jobs taken over by the computer. The people in these uninformed departments were the ones who had trouble adjusting.

Any kind of change in people's jobs makes it necessary to break old habits and learn new ways of doing things and new ways of looking at things. If they can't adjust, they become a problem to the supervisor. It is essential that employees find something in a change that is to their advantage, and the designers of change must learn how to design jobs that satisfy human needs along with the technical needs. As a rule, the benefits that management is seeking can be attained in a number of ways, and the way that is most acceptable to employees is the one most likely to succeed. Sounding out employee ideas and attitudes and taking them into account in the plans for change calls for good two-way communication, in which the supervisor must be willing to lend a sympathetic ear.

Some research studies indicate that group participation in the planning of changes can take care of many of the problems. In group discussions, employees can let management know their objections—and can do it without being labeled as malcontents or troublemakers. A certain amount of beefing to management seems to relieve employees of pent-up resentment and helps them to settle down and adjust.

The model for change management illustrated in Figure 16–1 demonstrates how change originates in an organization and how it is implemented. Full understanding of this process can help the manager when confronted with employee resistance to change.

Management attitude about change. An appreciation by management of changing life-styles and values among employees is also necessary. The fact that many supervisors now have a greater tolerance for errors and a lower level of expectation for the quality of employee performance seems to

Figure 16–1
A model for the management of change

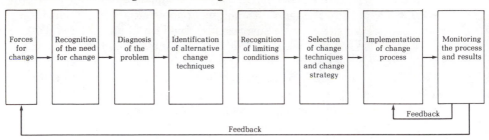

Source: J. H. Donnelly, Jr., J. L. Gibson, and J. M. Ivancevich, *Fundamentals of Management* (Dallas: Business Publications, 1971), p. 231. © 1971 by Business Publications, Inc.

indicate acceptance of the inevitable. Nearly everyone has experienced poorer service of one kind or another. Quality control in offices and factories is becoming a critical problem. No one supervisor can solve this employee problem, since it may require complete redesign of many jobs and massive attitude changes.

Perhaps a significant part of the problem is the change in values on the part of managers and supervisors. Many first-level supervisors and middle managers believe they are alienated by the organizations they work for. In a 1973 article, Dale Tarnowieski of the American Management Association describes the results of a nationwide survey of 2,800 managers in this country. Among the findings are the following:

1. 55% of middle managers believed their companies provided adequate opportunity for personal and professional growth.
2. 44% saw their companies as generally interested in overall goals and aspirations of employees.
3. 27% felt their organizations made no attempt to make themselves aware of employee goals.
4. 29% believed that while their companies were aware of employee goals they had no interest in assisting individual employees in the attainment of these goals.
5. Among middle managers, 44% envisioned an alternate career for themselves.
6. 70% expected to search for a way to make a career change in the near future.
7. More than one third gave enhanced status and authority as their most compelling reason for seeking a new employer.[4]

If this study accurately reflects management attitudes in some companies, it is apparent that problem handling and solving may not be too effective.

---

[4] Dale Tarnowieski, "Middle Managers' New Values," *Personnel,* January–February 1973, pp. 50–53.

"Some day, daughter, all this will be yours."

Reprinted by permission The Wall Street Journal

The managerial woman is part of the dynamic change process.

The changes occurring in our society have considerable impact on organizations and individuals. More employees are resisting change, change is more complex and rapid, and the manager's role in this area is a very difficult one. It certainly requires the diligent attention of all levels of management, although most importantly that of top management. In the final analysis, they establish the organizational climate and are responsible for what takes place in the organization.

Organizational development

Because of the rapidity and complexity of change in recent years several different approaches have been tried to deal more effectively with the change process. The organization is considered the unit of study to determine the impact of change and the ability of an organization to cope with it. Looking upon the organization as a total system which is subjected to both external and internal pressures for change, behavioral scientists have been attempting to develop techniques and approaches to facilitate change.

This organizational development activity commonly called OD includes all of the processes used to act on change in an organization. The objectives of OD effort are not only to react to changes but actively to seek ways to modify the organization so it is more able to cope with external and internal change. To accomplish this, an organization must have goals which are clearly defined, effective communications so that the goals are widely understood and accepted along with the feedback necessary to assess the level of acceptance, and an effective decision-making process to support the organization's ability to adapt to change.

To reinforce the change process in an organization, there are several behavioral concepts widely accepted as the basis for OD. Among these are:

1. Lewin's unfreeze-move-refreeze model. This model considers an individual's work patterns, attitudes, and behaviors are an integral part of the person's approach to life. Dealing with change without acknowledging this only encourages resistance. To deal with this, the individual must be encouraged to want to change. This "unfreezing" process might include environmental changes, removal of the threat of change, removing reinforcement for present behavior and possibly creating anxiety about present behavior. Once the person's present behavior is unfrozen, new behavior must be learned. This is known as "moving" toward change acceptance. It can be accomplished by formal training and development, on-the-job coaching, and changes in reinforcement such as amount of pay. "Refreezing" then attempts to establish and stabilize the newly learned skills and behavior by providing rapid feedback and rewards for the new behavior.

2. Learning is most effective when it occurs within the natural work group and is related to existing conditions and requirements.

3. Change must consider the interdependence of the environment, thus going beyond the individual.

4. OD consultants should help the whole organization to learn and adapt.

5. As process-learning occurs, work groups become more capable of adjusting to changing requirements and working out relationships with the rest of the organization and the external environment.

6. Organizational development is not merely one program but a continuous process of monitoring the entire organization.[5]

Organizations may be changed by changing structure, technology, and people. By redesigning structure, status and reporting relationships are changed. This results in an environmental change for individuals. Introducing new technology very frequently requires structure change. New computer systems may eliminate some jobs and create others. Individuals can cope with such change if retraining is made available. On the other hand, recruitment and selection processes may have to be modified to obtain em-

---

[5] Adapted from R. E. Miles, *Theories of Management: Implications for Organizational Behavior and Development* (New York: McGraw-Hill Book Co., 1975), pp. 191–93.

ployees who have the skills and knowledge necessary to work with the new technology. Even supervisors and managers may have to be developed differently for the newly created skill jobs.

It can be seen that the change process relates to the total organization and that change cannot be introduced and implemented without considering the totality of its impact. People resist change when they are left out of the process or not given the opportunity to become a part of the changed organization. By utilizing participatory methods in goal setting, communicating reasons for the change, appealing to employee self-interest, and providing rapid feedback on equality of change acceptance, an organization can cope with change more efficiently. In the final analysis developing organizations means developing people so retraining, continuous training, and management development are all part of an integrated approach to the management of change.

Summary

Managing change has become one of the most significant managerial responsibilities. It is a way of organizational life and should be approached by managers and supervisors as both an external and internal phenomenon. The rapidity and complexity of changes in the society at large have varying degrees of effect on the internal organizational system. Managers and supervisors should make an effort to become aware of and understand the many external changes and assess their possible impact on their jobs in the organization. Understanding the nature of change can be enhanced by studying the history of past changes. This will help develop a sense of perspective for adapting to present change. Internally managers and supervisors should act as change agents and implementers of change. Among the most difficult tasks is dealing with resistance to change. Most humans prefer the comfort of the status quo, and supervisors must encourage change acceptance if organizational goals are to be achieved. To aid this effort, behavioral scientists have evolved organizational development methods which try to consider the many factors related to the change process including changing values and priorities in our society. By using some of these OD methods, organizations may be able to cope with change more effectively.

CASE 16–1

Stu Brian was the best computer technician in the data processing department. In that group of varied individuals with many different opinions, there was total agreement that Brian was indeed the best. He could handle the most complex programming problems, and he was a wizard at debugging a program to make it work effectively. If there was such a thing as an indispensable person, Stu Brian certainly was.

The vice president in charge of the data center was under considerable pressure to promote more females to managerial positions, and he had resisted this in the past since he believed there were no qualified women ready for promotion. But in the past year Joyce Rogers had been consistently demonstrating that she not only was technically competent, but that she was that relatively rare computer technician who had clearly indicated considerable management potential. The vice president was very happy to recommend her promotion, and the opportunity was readily accepted by Joyce Rogers.

The next day Stu Brian walked into the vice president's office and said flatly that he would not work for a woman. He went on to state that he had nothing personal against Joyce Rogers—he simply would not work for any woman boss.

1. *What should the vice president do now?*
2. *How can he overcome Stu Brian's resistance? Should he try?*
3. *Why would Stu be so adamant about this?*
4. *What effect might Stu's attitude have on his career?*

CASE 16–2

"Once you know how to take him, he's not so bad." That's the standard opinion about Russ Gordon. Russ has been with the company for 14 years, having progressed through several accounting positions. He is now in charge of designing financial systems for the company. Gordon is recognized in his community as a church-going family man with well-behaved children who are active in church work. Russ believes that he and his wife have been able to raise the children with few of the problems common to young people because of strict discipline and a strong family relationship.

Russ carries this attitude over to his job where he is usually tough on his subordinates, critical of peers and superiors, and he tends to remember all mistakes, bringing them up frequently and in a negative manner. He is particularly critical of young people with long hair, modern dress, or other types of nonconformity with his standards. While most of the people who work with him complain from time to time, they seem resigned to his characteristics, and they do respect his considerable knowledge of finance.

Lately his boss has become more impatient with Russ Gordon's constant critical view of other employees and his lack of recognition of changing lifestyles. He has begun to resent the time taken to listen to Gordon, and he has tried to put an end to these conversations by cutting Russ off sharply.

Their relationship which has been reasonably good now has begun to deteriorate.

1. *Can Russ Gordon continue as a supervisor? Why? Why not?*
2. *Can his boss do anything about modifying Gordon's behavior?*
3. *How does one handle a technically competent, very knowledgeable employee who is a perfectionist?*
4. *Can and should an organization tolerate an individual with Russ Gordon's personality type?*
5. *Can Gordon's resistance to change in relation to employee behavior be dealt with by his boss?*

CASE 16–3

Jane Carlson came back from a meeting with the budget committee and proudly announced to her secretary that she was able to obtain for her one of the new electric typewriters the company was buying. It took much haggling but the fact that Ginny's typewriter was over 20 years old clinched the argument.

Ginny Morton had been with the company somewhat longer than her typewriter, and she had worked for Jane Carlson for the past ten years. They had an easy-going relationship, so Jane was quite taken aback by Ginny's frosty behavior after her announcement. "It was no easy job getting you that new electric," Jane said. "Don't you like my typing?" Ginny replied. "But it's got nothing to do with your typing—of course, you're an excellent typist," Jane said. "In fact the new typewriter will make your job easier and you'll be able to make more carbons." "I happen to prefer my typewriter to any of those new machines—they only break down frequently," Ginny said. Jane was amazed at Ginny's reaction, particularly since she was proud of the effort and argument which had enabled her to obtain the new typewriter for her secretary. She ended the discussion by telling Ginny that the electric typewriter was coming and she might as well get used to it.

1. *Indicate the reasons for Ginny's reaction to the new electric typewriter.*
2. *Did Jane handle the situation properly?*
3. *What can be done to create understanding when new equipment is introduced?*

CASE 16–4

You are the manager of a branch of a large commercial bank. Your assistant manager is a 53-year-old woman who has been with the bank 30 years, all of them in this branch. She is familiar with every job, having done each one in her rise to assistant manager. Over the years her performance has been excellent.

In the last few years changes in the operating patterns of the branch have been necessitated by ethnic, racial, and economic changes in the neighborhood in which the branch is located. Because of these changes you now feel that this woman is no longer appropriately assigned. There have been several recent touchy situations where you have had to take over customer interviews that had been started by the assistant manager. These developed mainly because of lack of understanding between the assistant manager and the customers. She has considerable difficulty communicating with customers and seems to treat them in a patronizing, disdainful manner. This is not the case, however, with those old customers whom she knows very well and with whom she has been doing business for years.

You have mixed feelings about the situation as it has developed. In one sense, you would prefer not to lose her because she is an excellent worker, knows many customers personally, and has served in the branch for her entire career. On the other hand, she cannot get along with the newer customers, and these are increasing in number, while those she can get along with are decreasing.

You have made no formal transfer request for her, but in several informal conversations with your superior you have gotten the impression that he would prefer to maintain the status quo. The assistant manager has told you that she too has informally sounded out your superior about a transfer to no avail.

1. *Should you make a formal request for transfer for this employee?*
2. *If you do, what reasons will you give?*
3. *Why do you think your superior has not acted on your informal discussions with him?*
4. *If this employee cannot adjust to the new customers in your branch, can she adjust to a different branch after having been in yours for 30 years?*
5. *If the employee stays at your branch, what can you do about her apparent inability to relate to the newer customers?*

CASE 16–5

Over the years any supervisor at the headquarters building could go to the personnel department and obtain the personnel file on any employee who reported to him. Such requests were frequently made to aid in performance appraisal, discipline, and other superior-subordinate relationships. The supervisors believed that the more they knew about an employee, the better their relationships would be.

These files contained all past employee appraisals, personal information, employment history, education, test scores, a credit report on the employee at the time of hire and more recent ones if the employee borrowed from the company's employee loan fund, and any other information about the employee that was job-related.

While some supervisors abused the privilege by discussing confidential information among themselves, company management allowed the practice to continue because of the benefits they saw in better performance appraisals. The supervisors also looked upon this privilege as a status symbol.

The company retained a consulting firm to develop an employee data bank which could be computerized. After about nine months of effort, all of the data in the personnel files was on tape stored for computer use. No longer were supervisors able to get files, since none existed in the usual sense. Requests for information about an employee now had to be approved by the personnel department. The form to be filled out required that the information was to be specific and that a suitable reason be given for its use. The supervisors could not get personal information any longer nor could they receive a complete printout of an employee's record. The new performance appraisal form, which is prepared by the computer, contains all pertinent job-related material to assist in performance evaluation.

Many of the supervisors resent this change in procedure. They look upon it as demeaning and feel that the company doesn't trust them as it did in the past. Even though they receive all necessary job-related data on the new appraisal form and it makes this task simpler, they do not like having to request information from the personnel department. They feel a staff department shouldn't have this power. Higher management has adopted a rigid posture on the issue, backing the personnel department.

1. *Why would supervisors resent this change even though it made performance appraisal a less difficult task?*
2. *Has depersonalization of the employee personnel file process caused the resentment?*
3. *Why are the supervisors venting all their resentment on the personnel department?*
4. *How can this problem be handled?*

CASE 16–6

Recently the personnel vice president received a petition signed by over 200 female employees in the headquarters office of the Clinton Power Company. This electric utility employed over 5,000 people in the headquarters office. About 40 percent were female employees, so the 200 signers of the petition represented only 10 percent of the female staff and 4 percent of the entire staff. The petition requested the company to establish a free day-care center so young preschool children of the mothers who worked for the company could be taken care of during working hours.

The problem was further complicated by the vociferous support given to the petition by a female member of the city council, who was receiving considerable newspaper and television publicity on what she called a crusade for working mothers. The female politician was threatening the organization of all working mothers in the city for a series of strikes.

1. *What should the personnel vice president do?*
2. *Are day-care centers for children an employer's responsibility?*
3. *How can business organizations react to the type of political pressure described in the case?*
4. *Should a company have a policy on dealing with employee petitions?*

CASE 16–7

Jack Detler graduated from the state university with a business degree and was hired by the Cornwall Investment Company. He was trained as a business development specialist; and his responsibilities included securing customers for the company's investment portfolio management services. The types of customers he contacted were bankers, corporate treasurers, financial vice presidents, board members, and the like.

After one year with the company, Detler was performing very well and his superiors were well satisfied. In July he took his first vacation and was gone for two weeks. When he returned, his hair was over his ears and he had grown a full beard.

When his boss saw him, he was quite surprised. Cornwall was a conservative firm, as were its customers, and no one in the company had a beard or dressed flamboyantly. "That beard and hair will have to go, Jack," his boss said. Detler did not like the arbitrary tone of the order and replied, "Why, I can't see that it makes any difference." "If you don't see that, then maybe we were wrong about you," his boss responded. Detler said, "Wrong about me—why, I'm the best new salesman you have!" The argument went on, getting louder and more belligerent. Finally Detler's boss asked for his resignation and got it.

1. *Could this have been handled differently?*
2. *Comment on Detler's judgment in growing a beard.*
3. *Can a company establish and maintain grooming standards that are somewhat different from those accepted by society at large?*

CASE 16–8

Ann Lawton has been on your line repair crew for three months. She is the first female you have had to supervise in your 20 years with the telephone company. You cursed the company for giving in to those "women's libbers," and then they had to assign a woman line repair technician to you. You had always been a fair but very direct person. As a supervisor, your subordinates always knew where they stood, since you told them in no uncertain terms. They had grudging admiration for you because you were fair, but you didn't have any friends among your crew.

When Ann joined the crew, you didn't give her any special treatment because she was a woman. If she wanted a man's job, she would be treated like a man—colorful language and all. Growling your orders to her each workday didn't build any great relationships, but you didn't care.

After a three-month period, you have noticed that Ann's work has not improved. She is passable, but that's all. She makes mistakes but seems afraid to ask questions. You have caught a couple of men on your crew trying to cover up for her by fixing her errors. You decide to give her a piece of your mind about female telephone line repair technicians.

After unloading in typical fashion, you notice she is upset. She loses her temper and blurts out, "You're horrible to work for! I've been afraid of you since the day I joined the crew. Now I don't care anymore. Go ahead and fire me—that's what you wanted all along." You are surprised at her outburst. In fact, you admire her for it. She's the first subordinate to tell you off since you've been a supervisor. You certainly don't want to fire her, and you don't want her to quit.

1. *What can you do to establish a better working relationship with Ann Lawton?*
2. *Should a woman who works in a traditional male job be treated differently?*
3. *If you change your management style in dealing with Ann, how will you treat your male subordinates?*
4   *What is equal treatment?*

CASE 16–9

Janet McCarthy started as a training analyst with Richards Finance Corporation when she completed college. The company was growing rapidly, and the training and development activity played an important role in this growth. Janet was able to demonstrate an extraordinary ability for achievement and accomplishment in a short period of time. When the training director was promoted to head personnel planning, Janet was promoted to fill the opening. In the three years she had been with Richards she had developed some excellent training programs which were highly successful. Within two years of her appointment as training director she became widely known as an innovative expert in training and development. She was in charge of all skill training, supervisory training, and management development. She took an active role in various training and development associations and delivered papers at several meetings around the country.

During this same period she met Walter Nelson, who was eight years older and a successful executive in a large chemical company. They became very friendly and began to discuss marriage. Janet informed Walter that she was committed to her career and wanted to continue to work. Nelson then brought up the desirability of having children. Janet said she was perfectly willing to have children but that she would return to work and hire a suitable person to take care of each child. Nelson was a little upset about it but didn't force the issue since he believed Janet's mind would change if she had a baby. They were married and for two years they were very happy with both of them working, earning excellent incomes, and pursuing an active social life with considerable vacation travel. They both enjoyed the so-called finer things, and they certainly could afford them.

In the third year of their marriage Janet became pregnant. She worked into her ninth month of pregnancy and, in fact, left her place of employment on a Wednesday evening, and her baby girl was born on Thursday. Both Janet and Walter were very happy with their new daughter, and Walter now started to try and convince his wife to stay at home. She adamantly refused, saying that it was her intention all along to return to her position with Richards Finance. In fact she had found a nurse to care for the baby, and she planned to return to work in six weeks. Walter tried to convince her of the need for a mother to care for her child, and Janet told him it was his child also. She returned to work six weeks after the baby was born.

When she returned, her boss congratulated her and then told her she was being promoted to a vice presidency in the company with increased responsibilities for the development of an internal mobility program and its implementation. Janet was very pleased and this promotion further reinforced her strong desire to continue her career. That evening she told her husband about the promotion, and while he was pleased and proud of his wife's new position, he knew that his desire for her to stay at home was now not even a remote possibility.

1. *Can a career and a family be compatible?*
2. *What factors should be considered to keep this marriage successful?*
3. *Should Walter Nelson pursue his efforts to have Janet stay at home? Should he stay at home?*
4. *What might happen if one of the parents is offered a promotion that would require moving to another location?*

CASE 16–10

Cliff Rezor is a supervisory geologist for Blackstone Petroleum Company. Over the years his efforts have been largely devoted to survey and exploratory work in many remote areas of the world in the search for oil deposits. He became a supervisor some years ago, and this meant he frequently headed a team of geologists and petroleum engineers out in the field. At times he would be working with only one or two other people at a site that looked promising.

This work kept him out in the field for several weeks at a time in places so remote that he couldn't call his wife and family. They had gotten used to it, and he did get home often enough to maintain a happy family relationship.

On occasion he would be assigned a trainee for on-the-job training so the new employee could get field experience. Recently Blackstone hired its first female geologist, and after an initial training period of several months at company headquarters, she was given a field assignment at a potential drilling location in a remote area of a western state. Cliff Rezor was asked to train her, and while he was somewhat anxious about training a woman, he assumed she was competent and that the assignment was nothing unusual. They were to be on location for about a month and then return to headquarters with their report.

On the other hand, Cliff's wife was very upset. She hadn't said anything about it to Cliff before he left, but after one week she became more and more upset. She was a traditional homemaker who had not been employed since their marriage. All of her efforts were devoted to home and family. Nor was she interested in a career, and, in fact, she believed the women's liberation movement was a lot of nonsense. The thought of her husband all alone with a young woman for a month in a remote location caused her considerable anxiety. She felt it was wrong for the company to allow such a situation to occur, and she was particularly angry that they chose her husband for the assignment.

After imagining all kinds of possibilities, she decided to call Cliff's boss, the vice president in charge of exploration. Getting him on the telephone, she told him how angry she was about Cliff's assignment and the stupidity of placing him in a position of temptation. The vice president tried to calm her down and told her that the company was an equal opportunity employer and could not discriminate against young women who happened to be geologists. He went on to say that the young woman was very competent, a cum laude graduate from a major university and a promising candidate for career growth with the company. He tried to assure Mrs. Rezor that both the young woman and Cliff were professionals and that her anxieties were unwarranted. Nothing he could say seemed to satisfy Mrs. Rezor.

1. *What should the vice president do now?*
2. *Is Mrs. Rezor justified in her anxiety? Why? Why not?*
3. *How might a company cope with this type of problem?*
4. *What impact could Mrs. Rezor's attitude have on her husband's career?*
5. *What can Mr. Rezor do to lessen his wife's anxiety?*

SUGGESTED READINGS: PART IV

Chapter	**Books**
13,14,15,16	Argyris, Chris. *Integrating the Individual and the Organization.* New York: John Wiley & Sons, Inc., 1964.
16	Basil, D. C., and Cook, C. W. *The Management of Change.* New York: McGraw-Hill Book Co., 1974.
16	Bennis, Warren G. *Changing Organizations.* New York: McGraw-Hill Book Co., 1966.
15,16	————; Benne, K. D.; and Chin, R. *The Planning of Change.* 2d ed. New York: Holt, Rinehart and Winston, Inc., 1969.
14	Cribbin, James J. *Effective Managerial Leadership.* New York: American Management Assn., 1972.
13,14,15,16	Davis, Keith. *Human Relations at Work, The Dynamics of Organizational Behavior.* 5th ed. New York: McGraw-Hill Book Co., 1977.
15,16	————, and Blomstrom, R. L. *Business and Society: Environment and Responsibility.* 3d ed. New York: McGraw-Hill Book Co., 1975.
13,14,15,16	Dowling, William F., Jr., and Sayles, Leonard R. *How Managers Motivate: The Imperatives of Supervision.* 2d ed. New York: McGraw-Hill Book Co., 1978.
15,16	Drucker, Peter F. *The Age of Discontinuity.* New York: Harper & Row, Publishers, 1969.
13,15,16	————. *Management Tasks Responsibilities, Practices.* New York: Harper & Row, Publishers, 1974.
13	Dubin, R.; Homans, G. C.; Mann, F. C.; and Miller, D. C. *Leadership and Productivity.* San Francisco: Chandler Publishing Co., 1965.
16	Fendrock, J. J. *Managing in Times of Radical Change.* New York, AMACOM, 1971.
15	Fernandez, J. P. *Black Managers in White Corporations.* New York: John Wiley and Sons, Inc., 1975.
13	Fiedler, F. E., and Chemers, M. M. *Leadership and Effective Management.* Glenview, Ill.: Scott, Foresman and Co., 1974.
15	Gaudet, Frederick J. *Solving Problems of Employee Absence.* New York: American Management Association, Research Study No. 57, 1963.

Chapter	**Books**
15,16	Glazer, Nathan. *Affirmative Discrimination.* New York: Basic Books, Inc., 1975.
14	Haney, William V. *Communication and Interpersonal Relations: Text and Cases.* 4th ed. Homewood, Ill.: Richard D. Irwin, Inc., 1979.
15,16	Hennig, Margaret, and Jardim, Anne. *The Managerial Woman.* Garden City, N.Y.: Anchor Press/Doubleday, 1976.
15,16	Kreps, Juanita M. *Women and the American Economy: A Look to the 1980s.* Englewood Cliffs, N.J.: Prentice-Hall, Inc. 1976.
13	Likert, Rensis. *The Human Organization.* New York: McGraw-Hill Book Co., 1967.
13,14,16	Margulies, N., and Wallace, J. *Organizational Change: Techniques and Applications.* Glenview, Ill., Scott, Foresman and Co., 1973.
15,16	McFeely, W. M. *Organization Change: Perceptions and Realities.* New York: Conference Board, Inc., 1972.
13,14,15,16	Roach, John M. *Worker Participation: New Voices in Management.* New York: Conference Board, Inc., 1973.
14	Rogers, E. M., and Rogers, R. A. *Communication in Organizations.* New York: Free Press, 1976.
16	Schneider, K. R. *Destiny of Change.* New York: Holt, Rinehart and Winston, Inc., 1968.
13,14,15,16	Scott, William G., and Mitchell, Terence R. *Organization Theory: A Structural and Behavioral Analysis.* 3d ed. Homewood, Ill., Richard D. Irwin, Inc., 1976.
13	Stogdill, Ralph M. *Handbook of Leadership.* New York: Free Press, 1974.
15,16	Sturdivant, Frederick D. *Business and Society: A Managerial Approach.* Homewood, Ill.: Richard D. Irwin, Inc., 1977.
16	Toffler, Alvin. *Future Shock.* New York: Random House, 1970.
14	Vardaman, G. T., and Vardaman, P. B. *Communication in Modern Organizations.* New York: John Wiley and Sons, Inc., 1973.

Articles

13	Adizes, I. "Mismanagement Styles," *California Management Review,* Winter 1976.
13	Argyris, C. "Leadership, Learning, and the Changing Status Quo," *Organizational Dynamics,* Winter 1976.
13	Bennis, W. "Leadership: A Beleaguered Species?" *Organizational Dynamics,* Summer 1976.
13,15	Bowman, J. S. "The Meaning of Work and the Middle Manager," *California Management Review,* Spring 1977.
15	Cherrington, D. "The Values of Younger Workers," *Business Horizons,* December 1977.
15	Cunningham, J. "Avoiding Common Pitfalls in Affirmative Action Programs," *Personnel Journal,* March 1976.

Chapter	*Articles*

15,16   Davis, K.   "Social Responsibility Is Inevitable," *California Management Review*, Fall 1976.

15   Edmunds, S.   "Environmental Impacts: Conflicts and Trade-Offs," *California Management Review*, Spring 1977.

13   Fiedler, F. E.   "The Leadership Game: Matching the Man to the Situation," *Organizational Dynamics*, Winter 1976.

15   Flast, R. H.   "Taking the Guesswork Out of Affirmative Action Planning," *Personnel Journal*, February 1977.

13   Flowers, V. S., and Hughes, C. L.   "Choosing a Leadership Style," *Personnel*, January–February 1978.

13   Frew, D. R.   "Leadership and Followership," *Personnel Journal*, February 1977.

15,16   Gery, G. J.   "Equal Opportunity-Planning and Managing the Change Process," *Personnel Journal*, April 1977.

15   Hall, F. S.   "Gaining EEO Compliance with a Stable Work Force," *Personnel Journal*, September 1977.

13,15   Hall, J.   "To Achieve or Not: The Manager's Choice," *California Management Review*, Summer 1976.

15   Hawk, D. L.   "Absenteeism and Turnover," *Personnel Journal*, June 1976.

15   Higgins, J. M.   "A Manager's Guide to the Equal Employment Opportunity Laws," *Personnel Journal*, August 1976.

14,16   Huseman, R. C.; Alexander, E. R., III; Henry, C. L., Jr.; and Denson, F. A.   "Managing Change through Communication," *Personnel Journal*, January 1978.

15   Jennings, K.   "The Problem of Employee Drug Use and Remedial Alternatives," *Personnel Journal*, November 1977.

15   ———.   "Arbitrators and Drugs," *Personnel Journal*, October 1976.

15   Johnson, R. D., and Peterson, T. O.   "Absenteeism or Attendance: Which Is Industry's Problem?" *Personnel Journal*, November 1975.

15   Kaden, S. E.   "Compassion or Cover-Up: The Alcoholic Employee," *Personnel Journal*, July 1977.

14   King, C. P.   "Keep Your Communication Climate Healthy," *Personnel Journal*, April 1978.

16   Levinson, R. E.   "How to Conquer the Panic of Change," *Management Review*, July 1977.

13   Likert, R.   "Management Styles and the Human Component," *Management Review*, October 1977.

15,16   McGuire, J. W.   "The New Egalitarianism and Managerial Practice," *California Management Review*, Spring 1977.

14,15   McSweeney, J. P.   "Rumors—Enemy of Company Morale and Community Relations," *Personnel Journal*, September 1976.

Chapter	Articles

16   Mandt, E. "Managing the Knowledge Worker of the Future," *Personnel Journal*, March 1978.

14   Mann, J. "Is Your House Organ a Vital Organ?" *Personnel Journal*, September 1977.

16   Martin, G. L. "A View of Work toward the Year 2,000," *Personnel Journal*, October 1977.

15   Mason, J. B. "OSHA: Problems and Prospects," *California Management Review*, Fall 1976.

15   Maxwell, S. R. "Corporate Values and the Business School Curriculum," *California Management Review*, Fall 1975.

16   Meyer, M. C. "Managing Organizational Change," *Personnel Journal*, November 1976.

13,15   Morano, R. A. "How to Manage Change to Reduce Stress," *Management Review*, November 1977.

15,16   Myers, M. S., and Myers, S. S. "Toward Understanding the Changing Work Ethic," *California Management Review*, Spring 1974.

16   Nord, W. R., and Durand, D. E. "Beyond Resistance to Change: Behavioral Science on the Firing Line," *Organizational Dynamics*, Autumn 1975.

15   Oberle, R. L. "Administering Disciplinary Actions," *Personnel Journal*, January 1978.

15   Ornati, O., and Giblin, E. "The High Cost of Discrimination," *Business Horizons*, February 1975.

15   Ostlund, L. E. "Attitudes of Managers toward Corporate Social Responsibility," *California Management Review*, Summer 1977.

15   Pati, G. C. "Countdown on Hiring the Handicapped," *Personnel Journal*, March 1978.

15   ———. "Reverse Discrimination: What Can Managers Do?" *Personnel Journal*, July 1977.

13   Pilla, B. "Two Perspectives on Leadership," *Personnel Journal*, June 1976.

15,16   Post, J. E. "The Challenge of Managing under Social Uncertainty," *Business Horizons*, August 1977.

15,16   Reif, W. E.; Newstrom, J. W.; and Monczka, R. M. "Exploding Some Myths about Women Managers," *California Management Review*, Summer 1975.

13,15   Singer, H. A. "Human Values and Leadership," *Business Horizons*, August 1975.

13,15   Stead, B. A. "Educating Women for Administration," *Business Horizons*, April 1975.

16   Steiner, G. "Invent Your Own Future," *California Management Review*, Fall 1976.

14   Stevens, B. E. "Improving Communications with Clerical Workers: The Nonsexist Directive," *Personnel Journal*, April 1977.

15,16   Sturdivant, F. D., and Ginter, J. L. "Corporate Social Responsiveness: Management Attitudes and Economic Performance," *California Management Review*, Spring 1977.

Chapter	*Articles*
15	Veglahn, P. A. "Making the Grievance Procedure Work," *Personnel Journal,* March 1977.
13	Vroom, V. "Can Leaders Learn to Lead?" *Organizational Dynamics,* Winter 1976.
15	Wohlking, W. "Effective Discipline in Employee Relations," *Personnel Journal,* September 1975.
13	Zaleznik, A. "Managers and Leaders: Are They Different?" *Harvard Business Review,* May–June 1977.

INDEX

A